GW01085753

AMIABLE WARRIORS – VOLUME ONE

Plays and musicals by Peter Scott-Presland

Tea Trolley (1981)
Dorothy's Travels (2001)
Leather (1989)
Wednesday Matinee (1994)
Somebody Bin Usin' That Thing: Gay Life 1870–1930 (2000)
Desire (2010)
Strip Search (2010)
La Ronde (2011)
Locked In: The Life of Keith Vaughan (2012)

AMIABLE WARRIORS

A history of the
Campaign for Homosexual Equality
and its times

VOLUME ONE: A SPACE TO BREATHE

Peter Scott-Presland

Paradise Press

Amiable Warriors
a history of the Campaign for Homosexual Equality and its times
Volume One: A Space to Breathe
by Peter Scott-Presland

First published in Great Britain in 2015 by
Paradise Press, BM Box 5700, London WC1N 3XX.
www.paradisepress.org.uk www.amiable-warriors.uk

A CIP catalogue record for this book is available from the British Library.

ISBN 978-1-904585-75-6

10 9 8 7 6 5

Printed and bound in Great Britain by Print2Demand Ltd, Hastings.

Cover design by David Tilbury.

Set in Garamond, with headings and title page in Gill Sans.

It seems likely that the condition of anti-homosexuality is somewhat more remediable than that of homosexuality. … There is some reason for thinking that, of the two opposed types, the anti-homosexual is socially the more undesirable, on account of the greater aggressive component overtly present in his personality. It is moreover pleasant to think that in this new struggle it would not be the hideous weapons of punishment and persecution that were called for, but the amiable ones of education and argument. The foundations of intolerance may be deep but its buttresses stand on the surface: and the most important of these is ignorance.

—Richard Wollheim, *The Spectator*, 4 April 1958

Without a place of its own an animal will struggle to survive.

—*Life Story*, episode 3, broadcast BBC1, 6 November 2014

To the man who got me back to work – he knows who he is.

Contents

Illustrations

Images from *Wikimedia Commons* (https://commons.wikimedia.org) may in general be freely re-used, subject to the terms of the particular licence used. Iillustrations from the *English Wikipedia* (https://en.wikipedia.org/) or the *UK LGBT Archive* (www.lgbtarchive.uk, formerly the LGBT UK History Project) may be subject to further restrictions.

In some cases it has not been possible to trace the copyright owner of illustrations. If by chance we have infringed anyone's copyright and it is brought to our notice we undertake to provide appropriate attribution in the next printing of this book, and on the website (www.amiable-warriors.uk).

Sources for illustrations

1 *UK LGBT Archive* (File: AllanHorsfall1960s.jpg).

2 *Wikipedia* (File:Mattxmas.jpg – photograph by Jim Gruber).

3 *Faetopia* (http://faetopia.com/2012-faetopia/edward-carpenter).

4 *Wikimedia Commons* (File:Havelock Ellis cph.3b08675.jpg – from US Library of Congress).

5 *A Window Somewhere* blog (http://awindowsomewhere.blogspot.co.uk/2011/01/dud-avocado.html).

6 *Circa-Club Icons Gallery* (www.circa-club.com/gallery/gay_history_icons_rupert_croft_cooke_leo_bruce.php).

7 *Polari Magazine* (www.polarimagazine.com/features/timeline-of-lgbt-anniversaries-2009-2/attachment/08-3).

8 *Report of the Committee on Homosexual Offences and Prostitution* (London: HMSO, 1957. Cmnd. 247).

9 King's College Taunton Historical Collections.

10 *UK LGBT Archive* (File:A_E_Dyson.jpg).

11 *Wikimedia Commons* (File:Michael Ramsey 1974b.jpg – Dutch National Archives; File:Julian Huxley 1964.jpg – Dutch National Archives; File:Clement Attlee.png – University of Michigan).

12 *Wikimedia Commons* (File:Emmot-Arms-in-Laneshawbridge-1.JPG – photograph by Immanuel Giel).

13 Allan Horsfall personal collection.

14 Allan Horsfall personal collection.

15 Photograph by author.

16 Photograph by author.

17 *LGBT UK History Project* (File:AEGW 60s medium.jpg).

18 Photograph by author.

19 University of Salford Library. USP/21/1139/A.

20 *Wikimedia Commons*: (File:NHWLRC plaque.jpg – photograph by Ross Burgess).

21 *UK LGBT Archive* (File:Allan Horsfall with paper.jpg – photograph by Ross Burgess).

22 Allison & Busby.

23 CHE archive.

24 HMSO.

25 Northampton Chronicle (www.northamptonchron.co.uk/news/local/bbc-presenter-from-northampton-dies-1-5693862).

26 *Ipernity* (www.ipernity.com/doc/57114/2796569, 'Albanian men dancing together'; photograph by Miss Magnolia Thunderpussy).

27 CHE archive.

28 Photograph by author.

29 Burnley Council Archive.

30 Photograph by author.

31 *Burnley Express and News*.

32 Martin Stafford personal collection.

33 CHE archive.

34 Paul Temperton personal collection.

35 Nottinghamshire's Rainbow Heritage (www.nottsrh.webeden.co.uk/#/ike-cowen/4541004696).

36 Photograph by author.

37 Martin Hallett archive.

38 Photograph by author.

39 Photograph by author.

40 Robin Bloxsidge Collection.

41 Ibid.

42 Roy Saich and George Broadhead personal collection.

43 *After Lunch* (drawing by David Baker).

44 Photograph by author.

45 Photograph by author.

46 *Lunch*, 4 (December 1971).

47 *Lunch*, 1 (September 1971).

48 CHE archive.

49 London Weekend Television, *Speak for Yourself*, 1974.

[50] Ibid.

[51] Photo by Robert Workman.

[52] CHE archive.

[53] CHE archive.

[54] *Lunch*, 17 (February 1973).

Foreword by Paul O'Grady

Paul O'Grady MBE is a comedian, television presenter, actor, and writer. He grew up in Merseyside, and has described his early experiences with Liverpool CHE in the first volume of his autobiography, *At My Mother's Knee ... and Other Low Joints.* He moved to London in 1978 and began appearing in a drag act as Lily Savage at the Royal Vauxhall Tavern and other venues, and in several popular TV shows. He retired Lily Savage around 2004, and has since been appearing regularly on television as himself.

AS A SEXUALLY PRECOCIOUS YOUNG TEENAGER in the early 70s running rampant and experimenting with both sexes of my own age, I finally came to the conclusion one afternoon as I eyed up the extremely handsome young man who came to read the gas meter that I was a most definitely, dyed in the wool, 100 per cent homosexual. I certainly wasn't traumatised by this realisation, quite the opposite in fact, even though if I was to believe my Mother who considered Homosexuality to be an abomination, I was probably doomed to a life of debauchery and eternal damnation. I couldn't wait.

But where did one find other gay men? My Mother claimed that there were two in Birkenhead and the rest were all lurking somewhere in Wallasey and the back alleys of Liverpool.

I'd seen the Birkenhead Two coming out of The Crown and Cushion pub in Market Street one afternoon, they called each other Josie and Audrey and for a neophyte like me I found them terrifying. They were caked in make-up, had ridiculously plucked eyebrows and dyed yellow hair and as I watched them ricochet down the street screeching like a pair of drunken parakeets I vowed to myself that I'd never be seen dead wearing make-up or being called by a woman's name. I got that wrong didn't I?

No, I reasoned there has to be other Gay men around who were not at all like Josie and Audrey, but where the bloody hell did I find them? The answer came in the form of a personal ad in the back of the *New Musical Express* with the phone number of an organisation called The Gay Liberation Front It burned in my wallet like a hot coal until finally I summoned up the courage and got in touch and after speaking to someone I was given the phone number of a young man called Robin who ran the Liverpool branch of the Campaign for Homosexual Equality.

I didn't know what to expect of the CHE as I nervously got off the bus on Upper Parliament Street to attend my first meeting in Robin's flat – a Bacchanalian Orgy perhaps? Or maybe I'd be chloroformed, crated up and shipped off to South East Asia to entertain sailors in a waterfront brothel. Either one of these sounded like a welcome alternative to working in a plastics factory but what I actually found was a warm welcome, a cup of tea and a chance to be with other gay men.

Until I discovered Sailors I attended quite a few meetings after that and although I didn't say much at first I did a hell of a lot of listening. It wasn't all talk: I made good friends, both platonic and romantic, was introduced to Liverpool's Gay Scene, went on a memorable gin-fuelled barge trip to Lymm* and attended the very first Gay Rights rally in 1973 that, for some unfathomable reason, was held in Morecambe.

What really inspired me at Morecambe was the constant use of the word Equality, for even at the tender age of 17 I was determined that I wasn't going to play second fiddle to anybody because of my sexuality. I was fully aware that prejudice was still rife, as the Sexual Offences Act, decriminalising Homosexuality, had only been passed in 1967, even so I was determined not to live a lie, nor was I going to hide away.

Forty-two years later I remember that day in Morecambe well, in particular sitting in the afternoon sun on the steps of a soon-to-be-demolished cinema listening to a very intense young man, not much older than myself, talking passionately about a German doctor named Hirschfeld, a man considered by many to be the father of Gay Liberation, who had famously said that 'the liberation of Homosexuals can only be the work of Homosexuals themselves.'

In other words, if you want something doing then get off your arse and deal with it.

We've certainly come a long way since then, although there's still quite a way to go but it's thanks to organisations like CHE that Gay, Lesbian, Bisexual and Transgender folk today can live their lives as they choose with confidence, and hopefully without prejudice.

This wonderful book celebrates those early days of CHE and honours those brave pioneers who weren't afraid to speak out in the fight for Equality in what were unenlightened times. I'm proud to have been there.

Enjoy.

Paul O'Grady

---

* See photograph on page 303.

Preface

MOST PREFACES ARE APOLOGETIC, SELF-JUSTIFYING WHINGES. This one is no exception. I write out of the insecurity of not being a 'proper' historian, queer theorist, or indeed any kind of academic. Instead, I bring to this project the skills of a journalist and playwright, and inevitably wonder if this is enough. That is of course for the reader to decide, but I feel the need to explain certain aspects of what I have done and why. (I won't dignify it with so august a word as methodology.)

I was commissioned to write the 'official' history of the Campaign for Homosexual Equality in 2010. Out of the blue, CHE had inherited a sizeable sum of money from Derek Oyston, a schoolteacher from Gateshead, and an appreciative if not prominent member of Tyneside CHE. CHE decided to use the money to sponsor worthy causes. Other beneficiaries included the BFI Lesbian and Gay Film Festival (the Derek Oyston Film Awards) and LGBT History Month. But, at the instigation mainly of the late Griffith Vaughan Williams, CHE's Executive Committee decided that a large part of the legacy should be spent on recording the story of CHE itself, its hundred and more local groups, its 5,000 members, its innumerable campaigns, its occasional cock-ups, and its off-shoots and heritage. After Jeffrey Weeks turned the assignment down, I put myself forward with some trepidation, and was accepted. If I'd known what I was taking on I'd have asked for more money.

As it is an 'official' history, it is very, very detailed. I had in my mind those regimental histories which line the walls of the Imperial War Museum Library. Each has several volumes, and not only records every campaign, but what every platoon in every company was doing in every campaign. So the CHE history had to be similarly inclusive, I decided. Only when I got stuck in to looking at the available material, and drawing up a list of interviewees, did I realise just how much there was; one volume quickly turned into two, and then three. For all I know, by the time we get to the end, it may be four.

There were several other reasons for treating the subject at such length. Firstly, the neglect of CHE in the annals of LGBT history so far is nothing short of scandalous. Work on the period 1950–1990 has concentrated on the Gay Liberation Front, on the Homosexual Law Reform Society, AIDS activists, and Outrage; CHE is at best only mentioned in passing or at worst ignored. The result is that it has acquired a reputation for being 'middle aged and middle class'; closeted white men with a cautious, even reactionary approach to societal change, who wouldn't have been seen dead on a demonstration. And so the only democratic lesbian and gay rights organisation which has ever existed in England and Wales (Scotland had the Scottish Minorities Group); the only group whose membership ran into several thousands; the group which had branches in little towns from St Austell in Cornwall to Boston, Lincolnshire, and in places where homosexuality was still illegal (Guernsey, Belfast); that group might never have existed if you believe those histories.

Instead the 'glamorous' GLF and its offshoots, with its street theatre and flair for publicity, has made all the running. To be fair, much of the history of GLF is vastly entertaining, the characters larger than life; its intellectual 'clout' was such that it created the most essential tools for analysing our oppression; but the upshot in popular gay mythology is that if GLF is a rainbow, CHE is beige. When the BBC produced its three-hour, three-part LGBT history of the UK in 1994, CHE did not get a single mention. In Julian Jackson's recent history of Arcadie, the French equivalent of CHE, the Homosexual Law Reform Society is namechecked, the Mattachine Society and other countries' organisations of the 50s and 60s, but not CHE. So in devoting so much time and attention to CHE I feel I am doing no more than compensating for two decades of neglect.

What also emerged as I was writing this was the significance of small things. CHE largely worked through its local groups, often in areas where there was no other LGBT life at all. In the 1970s to try to get an advertisement into a local paper, even, was a political campaign. A three-line display ad ('HOMOSEXUAL men and women join the campaign for Homosexual Equality. Local groups across the country. Send s.a.e. to CHE (Dept 23), 28 Kennedy Street, Manchester M2 4BG') was a major victory.

So the history of CHE on one level is the history of small things; and the courage of its members is the courage of small things. It serves no purpose to try to create a hierarchy of bravery, but forms of courage should be acknowledged wherever they occur. In 1972 I went on my first Pride March, a student away from home among a large group of friends in the comparative anonymity of a six-abreast column; in 1973 I went with one other person to give a talk on homosexuality to a church discussion group of 30, whose members varied from the liberally tolerant to the evangelically hostile; ten years later I was on a soapbox at Speakers' Corner with Hyde Park Gays and Sapphics, a CHE offshoot, preaching gay rights to a baying crowd. On that occasion I lasted about fifteen minutes, and there is no doubt that it was far and away the most terrifying experience of the three. But the point is that each required its own fortitude. Each felt exposed and personal in a different way.

All through the 1970s and 1980s, hundreds, even thousands, of individual members of CHE all over the country were demonstrating bravery in small things. In small communities they were writing letters to local papers, signed with their own name; teachers were telling their Headmasters they were gay; lesbians and gay men were sharing their experiences in discussion groups and giving each other strength and a sense of identity; they were telling their families (or maybe just Mum); they were in dialogue with their MPs, talking to their local doctors and priests, and each time it was laying something of themselves on the line. If CHE achieved little in the way of legislative change, this constant grassroots exposure of those people who formed opinion in their communities, to living and breathing, unstereotyped homosexuals brought about a sea-change in attitudes over twenty years. Put together enough small things, and you end up with an accumulation which can be massive, a rolling stone which has gathered a helluva lot of moss – and momentum.

Attention to detail chimes with my own predilections. When I was about nine years old, I was given for Christmas a book called something like 'The Bumper Book of Facts', and a lifetime of trivia and pub quizzes beckoned. As an activist, I also have an interest in how things are put together. I know the kind of work which goes into organising conferences, I have experienced rejection when trying to find somewhere to hold a gay disco. So when some gay historian casually says that a group held a conference in the 1950s, I want to know more. Where? Who gave permission? Was it a battle to find somewhere? How was it advertised? More, more.

I would also defend the history of small things in that the tiniest detail can either shift a conventional perspective, or fill out a picture. To take an example not directly relevant to this book, the Gay Liberation Front moved its general Wednesday meetings in mid-1971 to All Saints Church Hall in Notting Hill, and much has been written about the exhilarating, chaotic, noisy intellectual and political stew which was brewed up there. However, I started comparing GLF's success here with the many difficulties even comparatively 'respectable' CHE met when they were trying to get the use of church premises, and wondering how the 'cross-dressing, dope-smoking, communal-living' GLF persuaded an Anglican vicar to let his hall to three hundred screamers. It turns out that Fr Peter Hall had an 'open door' policy which included Irish republican groups and a Galician independence group: 'the church congregation were supportive of our "open" policy, especially towards minority groups, since they were largely West Indians who well appreciated what it meant to be marginalised by the rest of society.' Immediately the conventional view of a 'homophobic' black community is blown out of the water. And a rainbow alliance made concrete.

During the day the same hall was used by a children's playgroup, and in some way it modifies one's mental picture of GLF members to imagine the ideological arguments in a setting where they have to be careful not to tread on children's toys left lying around; and, whatever the disagreements, all had to meekly clear up after themselves to make the hall ready for the kids next day.

As part of the attention to detail, I have quoted more extensively than is customary from letters, articles, and interviews. Where it is possible to tell a story in the words of those who were there at the time, I have done so. Not only is it likely to be more accurate, it conveys far more vividly what it felt like to be part of a group, a movement, a moment. One of the most valuable insights which LGBT History can offer is the opportunity to enter into the experience of other people in other times, and to see the world, its travails and its possibilities, through their eyes. In this I am bringing my journalistic and even my dramatic skills to bear on the events and characters described in these pages.

This habit of quotation extends to a deliberate and extensive use of local newspapers; for there is no better litmus of the relationship between gay groups and the rest of society. The battleground for hearts and minds in the 1970s was to a great extent the Letters Page. Here is writ large the small incremental progress which marks the advance of the gay rights agenda. Often LGBT history seems to be written as if queers and their story exist in a kind of vacuum, whereas that story only makes sense in a social context. The very words are social/political constructs; 'gay' defines itself in relation to 'straight'.

When I submitted a sample chapter to an academic publisher, one of the comments from the publisher's reader was, 'Were the "gay clubs" discussed in Chapter Three "gay space" or "queer space" (there is a large body of academic literature exploring the differences between these two concepts built up since the early 1990s)?' My reaction was unprintable. Those who were battling to create a small enclave in which they could 'be themselves' – the phrase recurs constantly – would have viewed these finicky academic distinctions as pure self-indulgence, and so do I. How many angels can dance on the point of a pin would be more interesting. I don't want to get sucked into a tiny incestuous world of gay academics feeding off each other's work and addressing no-one else. I hope this will appeal to a more general reader, and especially those young LGBT people who are now discovering a reawakened interest in their own history and roots.

Amiable Warriors is emphatically not a work of Queer Studies. This is partly a matter of personal taste, as a writer and journalist, and as a person. I prefer work which is full of felt life to work which fits into more of a conceptual straightjacket – Jean Renoir to Hitchcock, Truffaut to Godard. It is also a matter of priorities. Working so much with primary sources, in a field which has not even been scratched with a hoe, the priority has to be to tell the reader what actually happened. There will be plenty of time in the future for others to impose what order and orthodoxies they think fit.

Speaking as a reader, and an amateur of gay history rather than a professional historian, I have had to read around queer theory to some extent. It has been hard going. I know I'm treading on corns here, but I've come to the reluctant conclusion that for me 'queer studies' is a concept which encourages an arid, self-regarding exchange between academics that gets further and further away from primary sources and what actually happened, in an attempt to impose contemporary patterns of thought on people whose experiences and life choices were profoundly different. We should not read history in an attempt to find ourselves and our beliefs reflected back at us, but rather in an attempt to enter into something which is profoundly Other. In this connection, I have freely used 'homosexual', 'homophile', 'gay' and 'gay women' where this would have been the language of the time, reserving the more acceptable 'LGBT' combinations for my contemporary commentary. It also makes for greater variety and readability.

It seems to me that as soon as theory enters into the picture, there is a danger that the weight of constructs can squeeze the life and individuality out of it. It imposes a rigidity which is profoundly at odds with life as it is lived and felt. It ignores the most important aspect of history and its forces, which is its dynamism. CHE is part of the great Amazon of effort which flows down to the Sea of Equality. It is part of the LGBT movement, and the operative word is movement. Nothing is static as we interact, grow and change, influence and are influenced. This is true of individuals and of organisations. The clichéd oppositional pitting of CHE against GLF, for example, implies two monolithic structures at daggers drawn. As Volume Two of *Amiable Warriors* (provisionally entitled *Fifty Grades of CHE*) will show, nothing could be further from the truth.

The Amazon ebbs and flows, it swirls and eddies, crosses rapids and other obstacles, gathers tributaries rising from other sources, which combine to increase the force of the current. Within it there are counter-currents. We humans are a mass of contradictions. The man who preaches that CHE needs to have an ultra-respectable image to gain acceptance of straight society is the man who works as a masseur and runs an escort agency; the feminist who denounces the way in which men ignore lesbian issues and advocates separatism is the woman who asks a male conference organiser to help her when a hotel refuses to give her and her partner a double bed. This is not to make a cheap point about hypocrisy, but to point to the necessary contradictions we all resort to in order to get through life as best we can, and to achieve our goals.

I have consciously avoided analysis as much as possible, partly because I don't think I have adequate analytical tools, but also to preserve the sense of creative flux, even chaos, in which CHE operated for much of the time. Having a shared sexual preference for a particular gender is in truth a comparatively small characteristic to hold in common. As an organisation CHE contained a spectrum of political beliefs from those who wanted to keep an age of consent of 21 to those who wanted to abolish it altogether, from those who wanted to stick to Standing Orders to those who wanted free collective exchanges of consciousness-raising. Sexuality is naturally anarchic, and it has always been far easier to unite the mass of LGBT people against a perceived threat than in favour of an agreed goal. For nearly every generalisation I could put forward about CHE characteristics and beliefs, I could also find enough exceptions to suggest that the generalisation does not hold true, or indeed that the contrary is the case.

I hope that *Amiable Warriors* will itself become an important source book for future LGBT historians, even queer theoreticians, but I also hope that it will attract a more general readership. This raises questions about how much background to include to make sense of the main narrative when much of that background has been covered in numerous other works. I have assumed in the first place that my ideal general reader will have read little or nothing in the way of gay history before, and therefore crave the patience of those who have; Chapter One in particular walks a comparatively well-trodden path.

The history of CHE poses particular challenges when it comes to giving some sort of order and coherence to the narrative. In the early years, up until 1970, it is a linear narrative, of a small group of individuals lending their weight to the campaign to implement the Wolfenden Report, and then, after the partial decriminalisation, to start Esquire Clubs to provide social centres. From that point onwards it becomes more complex, as local CHE groups start to proliferate. Several strands unravel simultaneously. As each group establishes itself, it has its particular story to tell, its characters to portray and its achievements to celebrate. Simultaneously there is the creation between 1970 and 1973 of a national structure which can harness the energies of all these different groups, establish the lines of communication which enable them to share information and learn from each other, and focus attention on particular campaign objectives. This structure also has to provide an effective democracy for members to elect representatives equitably and make choices as to where they want the national organisation to put its energies.

Further than that, there is the history of the campaigns themselves – education of the public, further sexual law reform, ending discrimination in the fields of employment, housing, or taxation. Allied with this is the gradual development, almost on the hoof, of ideas about what LGBT Equality might mean, what legal and social shapes it might take in practice, and who it might apply to. There are many steps to take from implementing an age of consent for male homosexual acts to enabling gay marriage, and none of these steps was immediately self-evident to all those campaigning at the time. It took years to forge that charter or manifesto, years of argument not just with the rest of heterosexual society but also with other homosexuals. And dotted throughout that history are the individual cases of injustice, the Tony Whiteheads and Veronica Pickleses; cases which, whether they were resolved positively or not, served to articulate the need for particular reforms, and to drive home the extent to which prejudice was still alive and well.

To do justice to all these strands coherently, I have tried to work thematically as well as chronologically. Volumes One and Two are particularly closely intertwined, as the earliest years of CHE laid down the ground plan on which so much later activity was based, particularly with regard to local CHE groups. Inasmuch as groups tended to have the same kinds of social activities, talk about the same issues in discussions, and work on the same small-scale local campaigns (e.g. getting *Gay News* into libraries), much can be assumed about local groups following a conventional pattern after a time.

This volume concentrates on the micro level of the local groups. It is above all concerned with the process of creating elbow room for homosexuals – space in which we can discover who we are, develop personal confidence, form friendships and relationships, and acquire the ability to go out into the world as ourselves, and not as ersatz heterosexuals. Hence the title, *A Space to Breathe*.

Volume Two deals with the creation of the national organisation and the forging of a national identity. It covers the first national campaigns – especially education – as well as responses to particular evils (David Reuben's *Everything You Wanted to Know About Sex but were Afraid to Ask*, the House of Lords judgement on *International Times*). It deals with the role of women in the organisation, as CHE women carved out their own space, and both men and women wrestled the sometimes virulent sexism in certain sections of the organisation. With the emergence of identity and particular ways of doing things, there were also fallings-out, as people who wanted different objectives left; this in itself created a kind of dialectic which further defined what CHE was and what it believed in. The title *Fifty Grades of CHE* may be a cheap joke, but it's also an accurate reflection of the main theme of Volume Two, how to make the many into one.

Having made this distinction between micro and macro, I have to acknowledge it is to some extent artificial, and each bleeds into the other. So there are references in Volume One to CHE institutions and processes which are only fully explained in Volume Two. I hope this will not inhibit understanding, and there is a list of abbreviations to help. Similarly, relations between CHE and the Gay Liberation Front (GLF) are covered fully in Volume Two, but GLF's hennaed head has a habit of popping up from time to time in Volume One. Throughout the period covered by the second half of this volume, GLF was a constant offstage presence whose very existence helped to shape CHE's own attitudes.

If repetition is one danger of a history of CHE, another is dryness. Much of the political action and ideology is expressed through minutes, pamphlets, press releases, conference papers and resolutions. It could be deadly dull. I have tried to avoid this by using masses of personal details, character portraits and anecdotes which I've pieced together largely from interviews. I make no apology for including details of who slept with whom, because I regard sex as a great Elephant in the Corner as far as much gay history is concerned. Gay men are, above all, men, and wherever two or three are gathered together, nookie is going to occur. It is almost a reflex reaction for gay men to check out the talent, even when going into the most exalted philosophical symposium or political conference. If we follow the battles of ideas and the marshalling of political forces, we are in danger of conjuring a series of bloodless talking heads, where the people who made the campaigns and argued the ideas were full of pride, passion and piss in equal measure.

Moreover, if people got sex as a result of going to a CHE meeting, it was far more likely that they would go back to CHE again. There was nothing like an orgasm for generating goodwill towards a CHE group. Sometimes people would form relationships, which would create formidable teams for campaigning or organising; and sometimes, conversely, they would split up, which brought groups to a halt and sent everyone close to them running for cover. No doubt a significant amount of socialising time was spent speculating on who had got off with whom. The role of gossip in binding a gay community together should never be underestimated. I hope the result is an entertaining as well as informative read; the personal and the political were always entwined.

The most valuable resource I have had to draw on is my interviewees. I am profoundly grateful to all of them, not just for the time they gave me and my microphone, but for their patience in answering all my follow-up questions. Only three people refused to be interviewed, Maureen Colqhoun, Babs Todd and David Starkey. Several people have sadly died since I interviewed them, but I am so happy that I managed to record their memories and contributions before they did. These are Allan Horsfall, Ray Gosling, Ian Buist, Michael Brown, Meg Elizabeth Atkins and Michael Schofield. Others I would dearly love to have talked to, but they slipped away before I could reach them; it is a matter of great regret that I never got to talk to Griffith Vaughan Williams, Tony Grey or Jackie Forster.

For the rest, I must record my thanks (in no particular order) to Alan Wakeman, Andrew Lumsden, Nettie Pollard, Guy Thornton, Michael Moor, Peter Norman, Robin Bloxsidge, Alan Swerdlow, George Broadhead, Roy Saitch, Glenys Parry, Liz Stanley, Sue Wise, Martin Stafford, Paul Temperton, Donald West, Michael Steed, Ken Plummer, Roger Hollier, Tony Ryde, Peter Katin, Brian Sewell, Peter Robins and Mike Harth. Several of these endured follow-up questions or second interviews, and some were kind enough to supply photos of the period, which are in remarkably short supply. 'If we'd known we were making history, we'd have taken more notice at the time.' Their partners also chipped in, providing tea and biscuits or even meals, and enduring the household disruption while the microphone was on. Thanks especially to Martin Stafford, whose memory is elephantine and who was often the authority of last resort; in addition he painstakingly read the proofs (and now any errors which you see in the text are entirely my own).

Throughout the three years' research I became something of a permanent fixture at the invaluable Hall Carpenter Archives. The staff there have always cheerfully provided the materials and catered to my sometimes erratic schedule, consistently helpful despite the cuts in funding, staffing levels and opening hours. Over the years the personnel has changed. Sue Donnelly, the *fons et origo* of the Archive, has moved to higher things and now hovers like St Teresa of Avila over the whole operation. The Archives and Special Collections Manager Anna Towlson has been endlessly patient. Then there are Silvia Gallotti, Bryony Hooper, Kate Higgins, Ben Martill, Catherine McIntyre, Gillian Murphy, Elinor Robinson, Sinead Wheeler, and Nick White, toilers at the dusty face of mounds of brown cardboard boxes. There is something of a move today to disperse LGBT material through local archives, so I can only be grateful that so much is stored in the one place, and so well cared for.

Other archives have been helpful too: David Govier at the Greater Manchester County Records Office, and Professor John Goodridge at Nottingham Trent University for access to the Ray Gosling Collection. Nor can I leave out the incredible resources at the British Library, and give especial thanks to the staff in the Newsroom, happily decamped from the cold Stalinist reaches of the Colindale Newspaper Archive.

Others have been very encouraging, particularly key members of the academic community: Matt Cook, Senior Lecturer in History and Gender Studies at Birkbeck College, Jeff Evans of LGBT History Month, Charles Smith, David Paternotte, Leila Rupp … I apologise for any omissions.

Paradise Press has been entirely supportive, and offered extremely useful advice about the production side of the book. For this I have to thank Michael Harth, John Dixon and Rod Shelton in particular. While we're on the subject of production, David Tilbury allowed us to go through a dozen modifications and variations of his cover design without complaint. I have been particularly delighted to have W. Stephen Gilbert exercising the under-appreciated craft of indexing. Steve was a pioneering gay playwright and BBC Producer in the 1970s, and responsible for getting the greatest ever gay play for TV to the screen – BBC2's *Only Connect*, by Gay Sweatshop alumni Drew Griffiths and Noel Greig. He still cherishes his CHE badge. Nice to keep it all in the family.

I benefited greatly from Brian Lymbery's generous loan of his delightful art deco flat in St Leonards-on-Sea, where I retreated to do some uninterrupted writing. The sound of the waves and the sight of the sun going down over the sea soothed many a moment of writer's block.

It is of course traditional to thank one's editor, but in this case it is much, much more than tokenism. This project would never have come to fruition without the passionate commitment and dogged determination of Ross Burgess, who has put in untold hours and ferocious concentration to bring the book to the printer. His unflagging and meticulous attention to detail has sometimes driven me up the wall and had me muttering 'Pedant' under my breath. However, for the record, you were entirely correct, Ross. His achievement is all the more remarkable for the great personal strain he has sometimes experienced. We both owe a debt to Ross's partner (now husband), Roger, for the numerous lunches he has unobtrusively served up while we were engrossed in the book, and were probably too preoccupied to appreciate properly at the time.

As the work has been commissioned by CHE, it finally behoves me to remember Griffith Vaughan Williams, whose vision kicked off this project. Nick Billingham has been equally helpful and unselfish in his unstinting devotion to getting *Amiable Warriors* to see the light of day. I'd also like to thank the current members of the Executive Committee, who have patiently listened to 'progess reports' for the last three years, no doubt secretly wondering if it was ever going to see the light of day: George Tregaskis, Nettie Pollard, Seán McGouran and Mark Delacour.

It has been a long hard slog. Thanks for sharing it with me. Now – on to *Fifty Grades of CHE*. Excelsior!

Peter Scott-Presland
Nunhead, London
10 January 2015

Abbreviations

Abbreviations used in the text

AT: Albany Trust.

CHE: Committee for Homosexual Equality (until March 1971); Campaign for Homosexual Equality (April 1971 onwards).

COC: Cultuur en Ontspanningscentrum (Dutch: 'Centre for Culture and Leisure').

EC: Executive Committee.

CHELIC: CHE London Information Centre.

FRIEND: Fellowship for the Relief of the Isolated and Emotionally in Need and Distress (later treated as an ordinary word and written as 'Friend').

GLF: Gay Liberation Front.

HLRS: Homosexual Law Reform Society.

ICSE: International Committee for Sexual Equality.

IGA: International Gay Association (later ILGA).

IHWO: International Homosexual World Organisation.

ILGA: International Lesbian and Gay Association, later the International Lesbian, Gay, Bisexual, Trans and Intersex Association.

LCC: London Coordinating Committee

LGBT: Lesbian, gay, bisexual, transgender.

LMC: London Management Committee

NC: National Council (quarterly meeting of local CHE group representatives).

NCC: National Cleansing Crusade.

NCCL: National Council for Civil Liberties (later Liberty).

NFHO: National Federation of Homophile Organisations.

NWHLRC: North Western Homosexual Law Reform Committee.

SIG: Special Interest Group

SMG: Scottish Minorities Group.

Abbreviations used in references

BSA: British Sound Archive.

HCA: Hall-Carpenter Archives.

HC Deb: Hansard: House of Commons Debates.

HL Deb: Hansard: House of Lords Debates.

MCA: Manchester City Archive.

NTU: University of Trent, Nottingham Trent University archive.

RHA: Royal Holloway Archive.

Chapter One: The Age of the Homophile

Contents

The Frozen Wastes

If, as L. P. Hartley suggests, 'the past is another country', for British gay men the 1950s is Siberia. Or maybe Outer Mongolia. Siberia for cold, Outer Mongolia for strangeness. This was an era in which the local newspapers covered trials of homosexual 'sex crimes' in terms so vague* that it was impossible to know what had actually transpired, or who had done what to whom. If, as a homosexual, you wanted to find out more about your 'condition', as it was usually called, any book which might enlighten you in the public library, such as Havelock Ellis's *Sexual Inversion*, would be in a special section reserved for 'dirty books', and you would have to read it under the beady eye of a (usually female) librarian. In doing so you risked the stigma of being publicly identified as 'queer' yourself; 'queer' being the commonest term in use, even among homosexuals. This assumes that you could find anything at all in the library. You might not even find the word to describe yourself in the dictionary.

There would of course, be nothing about you on television or radio, and when identified homosexuals did start to appear on the screen in the early 1960s, it was always in silhouette, unless they were foreign, or female. If you wanted to discuss the subject with friends or colleagues, they might well object to doing so in the presence of women. Women were also routinely excused jury service for trials for gross indecency, and when such cases were coming up, the judge or magistrate would ask any women in the public gallery to leave. When Sir John Wolfenden was discussing the procedure for the upcoming enquiry with the Wolfenden Committee Secretary, they agreed that homosexuals and prostitutes, the joint subjects, should be referred to as Huntleys and Palmers† respectively, so as not to offend the women on the committee, and, more importantly, the secretaries who would have to type up the proceedings. And this from a highly educated man, a former senior public school headmaster and Vice-Chancellor of Reading University.

Suppression and repression were everywhere. No wonder, then, that self-oppression, the homosexual belief that he is actually as inferior as society tells him he is, was almost universal. It required huge strength of mind to resist it.

The leap that has occurred within less than sixty years from the frozen wastes of the 1950s to a society where gay marriage is rapidly becoming unremarkable, where openly lesbian, gay and bisexual personalities are common on television, where heterosexuals now challenge homophobic actions and

---

* 'Improper conduct' and 'serious offences', for example.

† Huntley & Palmers was a major UK biscuit manufacturer in the 1950s, based in Reading, where Wolfenden was Vice-Chancellor.

statements, would have been almost unimaginable to homosexuals of the 1950s or 60s. If you had told Allan Horsfall and Antony Grey when they were starting on their reforming campaigns that in fifty years' time Christian hoteliers would be heavily fined for refusing double beds to lesbians and gay men, or that a pot entitled 'The Modern Family',* featuring a gay couple and their adopted mixed-race son, would be on display in the National Portrait Gallery, they would probably have dismissed the very notion as pure fantasy.

That a psychological journey so long could have been made in a period of time so short is down to what Andrew Lumsden† has described as a 'vast river of effort', involving many strands, currents and people, many of whose contributions have so far been absent from the written history. Some of those people and their organisations have also been misrepresented and misinterpreted into rigid patterns of opposition – radical versus reformist, transgressive versus conformist. If we are to recover them, to think ourselves into their heads, to understand their beliefs and their priorities, to see the world as they saw it, and to appreciate their strategies for living as homosexual in a hostile world, we need to avoid imposing current assumptions and values on the past. We must avoid being 'retrosexual'.

Relative values

For example, the debate on the importance of 'coming out' has been going on at least since the early 1950s, but the reasons for doing so have changed. In the first instance, the image used was of a mask, and of the longing to stop wearing one. An English medic wrote of going to the COC Club in Amsterdam in 1953 that he found the experience of 'hanging up his mask together with his hat and coat in the cloakroom a revelation.'[1] But in the first instance it seemed that the mask could only ever be dropped to other homosexuals. By 1960 it was part of a strategy for acceptance and integration into mainstream society: to condense the argument, 'Prejudice is caused by ignorance, and ignorance occurs because the public don't know any homosexuals. They don't know any homosexuals because homosexuals are just like everyone else. Therefore the only way to educate people is to declare yourself.' By the 1970s, homosexuals were urged to come out because it was good for them, never mind other people. 'If you don't come out, you are accepting society's estimation of you as inferior; you are not telling people you are gay because you are ashamed. Therefore the only way to purge your shame and assert your integrity and value as a gay person is to come out.'

---

* By Grayson Perry.

† GLF member and co-founder of *Gay News*.

The former position carried with it an acceptance that not everyone would be in a position to be open. It was a political strategy, and therefore hedged in by the realpolitik of the day. The second, more fundamentalist, approach implicitly criticised those people who didn't come out. It was a transmutation of the old distinction between the 'invert', who was born that way and couldn't help it, and the 'pervert', who chose to have gay sex because he was wicked. It wasn't that they couldn't come out, they wouldn't.

In his 1976 book *A Lasting Relationship*. Jeremy Seabrook picked up on this element, and the parallel between religion and some kinds of Gay Liberation. This was one of the first attempts to relate the spectrum of social arrangements and beliefs of gay men to the wider changes which had happened in society in the previous twenty years. He describes going to a GLF meeting:

> The enthusiasm of Gay Lib is often evangelical in tone; passionate, intense, impatient and sometimes intolerant. The doctrine is sexual freedom, personal liberation and fulfilment. ... The uninitiated are looked on with mildly irritated pity. ... It is a state of grace. ... it is like some profane divine comedy; quest, pilgrimage; all the imagery of transcendent mystical experience are brought to bear.[2]
>
> It is a bit like a revivalist meeting, where people expect to be called upon to testify, and they are silently rehearsing their testimony. ... Most individual accounts of coming out are like confessions of faith. 'I doubted until I declared myself, and now I am free.' Some are heroic.[3]

There is remarkable similarity between some of the language of Gay Liberation and that of born-again Christianity. Self-oppression as original sin, to be washed away by the coming out process.

The assertion that 'open = happy = good' as opposed to 'closeted = unhappy = bad' is undermined by the testimony of many British gay men who have insisted that they were perfectly capable of living full and active gay lives before the partial decriminalisation of homosexuality in 1967. For many years it was received wisdom that they were deceiving themselves, as a result of self-oppression. However that view has to be qualified. 'Coming out' is not a single, unitary act, a wave of a magic wand, but a set of gradual steps, and one can develop a contented way of being which involves acknowledgement of being gay to some people but not to others.

It also depends on having a particular view of the place of sexuality within one's life, and of its importance in creating an identity. When homosexual campaigners set off on the road to equality, they did so having made a decision that their sexuality was sufficiently important as a component of personality for them to devote large amounts of energy and time to maintaining its truth and integrity. However this is not the only possible view; sex with men can be seen almost as a hobby, like metal detecting or amateur dramatics. Or it can be seen as something which is unimportant in one's life, something which should not be a major driver at all.

Further, one person can at different stages of life hold all these views. With apologies to Shakespeare, we can construct a possible Three Ages of Queer.

First the teenager, all testosterone and spunk, getting a hard-on at everything and nothing, having wet dreams, masturbating in break times – sexuality out of focus, something to enjoy for itself, no questions, this is almost a hobby.

Then adults who have come to full awareness of who they are and what they want, still sexually active, now having relationships which are emotionally important and needing to be recognised for what they are – gay.

Lastly the pensioner, the fires of lust now dead, who is happier at the prospect of a good meal than a good lay, who looks at the whole panoply of gay life and gay culture with unutterable weariness. Identity is not fixed; many psychologists these days reject the concept of personality altogether.

Seabrook again picked up on the way that the energy and attention demanded by the process of identifying as gay and eliminating self-oppression can stunt other areas of life:

> Being gay, and becoming aware of being gay, may become a strong determinant on all future development; indeed, the only determinant, pervasive, exclusive and all-enveloping. In this way it is possible that many other potential areas of discovery may remain hidden, other talents smothered, and the whole evolution of a gay lifestyle subserves one permanent truth established at the centre of the individual consciousness: I am gay. It becomes an expanding awareness, opening out like a great tree in the shadow of which nothing else can survive; … all other points of identity can be subordinated to it: economic, social, occupational, intellectual.[4]

One of the constant refrains from many members of CHE was that they did not wish to be defined *purely* by their homosexuality. For some, certainly, this was a figleaf for timidity; for others a valid critique. Much time was spent negotiating between the extremes of total discretion and total disclosure.

However sceptically we view what were once received truths about the supposedly cautious pioneers of the gay equality movement, if we are to enter into their mindset, to appreciate their challenges and strategies, we must first examine the world that made them.

Influences come in many guises and on many levels, some conscious and some unconscious, some immediate and some going back into remotest history. In the conventional narrative, following Foucault, modern gay history starts with the nineteenth-century categorisation of sexual activities and their practitioners into sexual 'types': the principles of taxonomy being applied equally to humans as to the rest of the natural world. This view of history would imply that before Karl Ulrichs invented 'urnings'* (1867), before the novelist Karl-Maria Kertbeny's conceptualised 'homosexual'† and 'heterosexual' (1869), before the Italian Arrigo Tamassia invented 'inversion' (1878), before the busy pigeonholing of Baron von Kraft-Ebbing and his *Psychopathia Sexualis*, or Havelock Ellis with *Sexual Inversion*, there was no such thing as a homosexual, only homosexual acts.

It is true that in the later nineteenth century, following the romantics and the philosophers in the rise of individualism, science turned to the study of the individual human psyche, through the development of experimental psychology as an academic discipline. However, the start of a scientific discipline does not mean that the subject of that study did not exist previously. It is difficult to maintain that there was no such thing as a homosexual identity in the face of the evidence of the eighteenth century molly houses, with their special slang and their elaborate 'marriage' rituals, which suggest that a 'molly' had a clear and distinct social identity, separate from the rest of society. Going back even further, the court of William the Conqueror's son, William Rufus, seems to be another convincing example of a group of homosexuals collectively establishing a gay lifestyle.‡ All that changed in the classification was the context, from religious to medical. When someone was labelled a 'sodomite' or a 'catamite', it carried implications for the identity of that person (as outcast, transgressor etc.) beyond the mere description of what he might have done with his penis or anus.

Nevertheless in gay mythology the introduction of the Labouchère Amendment in 1885, and its famous use in the Oscar Wilde trials of 1895, mark the first watershed of modern gay history, as the Stonewall Riots of 1969 in New York mark the second. And it is during the period between the two that the circumstances came together to create the Campaign for Homosexual Equality (CHE), its predecessor the North Western Homosexual Law Reform Committee (NWHLRC) and its London 'midwife', the Homosexual Law Reform Society (HLRS). Inasmuch as the second Secretary of the HLRS, Antony Grey, created the circumstances in which the NWHLRC could come

* Ulrichs categorised homosexuals as a 'third sex' and gave members of this sex the name 'urning'; the English equivalent was 'Uranian'.

† Havelock Ellis, who introduced the word into English, hated 'homosexual' – ' a barbarously hybrid word' – on the grounds of its mongrel combination of Greek and Latin, and Edward Carpenter preferred 'homogenic' as a linguistically pure derivative from Greek.

‡ See John Boswell, Christianity, Social Tolerance and Homosexuality, 229–230; D. S. Bailey, Homosexuality and the Western Christian Tradition,109–125. For a fuller discussion of William Rufus' sexuality see the UK LGBT Archive wiki: www.lgbtarchive.uk/wiki/William_II.

together, and guided its earliest years through advice and through putting people in touch with each other, Grey and the HLRS need to be considered as an integral part of this history.

CHE's Northern Roots

The North Western Committee in turn was the result of the persistence of one man, Allan Horsfall, a disenchanted Labour ex-councillor who still adhered to the ideology of the left wing of the party throughout his life.

1. Allan Horsfall in the 1960s

This small self-contained committee in Manchester, with the very limited aim of supporting the London campaign to implement the Wolfenden Report, morphed into the multi-branched, fully-fledged national pressure group CHE, with an equalities agenda which would affect civil society legally and socially across the board. It became by far the largest LGBT organisation the UK has ever known – a democratic gay organisation, with five thousand members and an elective mechanism for adopting policies and for choosing representatives on an Executive Committee. It was the promoter of, at different times, over 150 local groups from Cornwall to Tyneside, from Swansea to Norwich; and it had a reach that in different ways touched many more homosexuals beyond its membership. It was a major player in helping to change the climate of opinion that made legislative change possible in the 1990s and beyond.

That transition resulted mainly from the work of a handful of people – Paul Temperton and Martin Stafford who created the national membership system and the office systems; Michael Steed and Ike Cowen who devised the constitution; Peter Norman and Roger Baker who created the template for how local groups would function; Glenys Parry and Liz Stanley who between them ensured that women continued to make a significant input when most of their sisters had fled the Gay Liberation Front. In addition, there were those who ensured that the local groups functioned and prospered, becoming the backbone of the movement and the site of the growth of individual pride and self-consciousness as lesbian and gay people.

Nearly all the CHE people so far mentioned were Northerners, and one aspect of CHE's success arose from a specifically Northern tradition of self-help and self-improvement. Although there were unions earlier in London, the Trade Union movement grew most rapidly out of the industrialisation of the North, where it had not only fought for improved conditions at work but started to foster institutions such as the Co-operative movement, a kind of DIY social security. The Rochdale Pioneers laid down the rules for running co-operatives; credit unions, friendly societies and mutuals helped people save, borrow and organise finance; mechanics' institutes furthered workers' education and provided libraries, before the expansion of literacy in the late nineteenth century. Many of these movements were also fostered by religious institutions, especially non-conformist ones – the Methodists, the Quakers, Baptists and Congregationalists. Leisure was provided by Working Men's Clubs, bars which could also provide singing, dancing, entertainment, lectures and libraries, and were owned and run by their members. These also organised Christmas Clubs as a way of making sure there was enough money saved for some celebrations at the end of the year. Although aspects of these institutions are to be found migrated to Southern England, in the North they are embedded in the culture.

The crucial difference between CHE and the London-based HLRS was that the HLRS was much more hierarchical; it helped homosexuals to improve themselves, but from the top down. By contrast, CHE (or its predecessor the NWHLRC) was a grassroots movement, drawing its membership from ordinary homosexuals in Manchester's clubs and bars. This fact gave CHE the strength to continue where others folded; it also determined its first major enterprise, Esquire Clubs. The very use of the word 'convenor' rather than 'chairman' in CHE, for someone who brings together members of a local group, has echoes of trade unions and shop stewards.

There was no inevitability about the advance of CHE. Alongside the major organisations there were myriad small ones of varying degrees of altruism which flickered and then died. MANDFHAB in Wolverhampton, run by 19-year-old John Holland, his best friend Elizabeth and their miniature poodle called Britt; the businessmen who wanted to set up a gay centre in London; Challenge, with its hundred members and three branches dedicated to proving that homosexuals were worthwhile people by doing good works in the heterosexual community; the Elmwood Association in Belfast with its 'priests and social workers and do-gooders': any one of these, and many more, might have survived and thrived under different circumstances to contribute to the emancipation of homosexuals. That they did not, and CHE did, testifies to the solidity of the CHE structure, the general appeal of the CHE mixture of sociability and campaigning, and the individual abilities of the people involved.

None of these people sprang fully armed as campaigners from the forehead of Zeus. They had attitudes, beliefs and views about what gay people were and what they were entitled to before they became involved in the struggle for lesbian and gay rights, and they developed them further as a result of their involvement. These were shaped both by their own experiences and by what they read. They were conditioned by the general temper of the times, and its intellectual climate, in the UK and worldwide.

Global Movements

Much gay history in the United Kingdom has been written as if it took place in isolation, the only acknowledgement of what was happening in the rest of the world being a salute to the Stonewall Riots and the Gay Liberation Front which spilled over into the UK version of GLF. In truth, all over the Western world, in Europe and America, parallel movements took place in many countries at the same time, and were shaped by world events and goaded by ideas which in an era of mass communications were increasingly easily transmitted round the world.

For example, the 1885 Labouchère amendment, which criminalised 'gross indecency'* between males and offered punishments of up to two years, was paralleled by Paragraph 175 (1871) in the newly unified German Empire which penalised 'unnatural fornication between persons of the male sex' and stipulated similar sentences. Again, the vagueness of wording indicates disgust, leaving it to the courts to interpret. In 1889 Finland and Sweden† both passed a new penal code which also laid down sentences of imprisonment for up two years for homosexual acts. Uniquely, the Finnish and Swedish laws applied to both lesbians and gay men.

* What constituted 'gross indecency' was not defined in the text; legislators in the UK as in other countries were probably inhibited by their revulsion from talking in any detail about what they were actually banning.

† Finland then being a semi-independent Duchy within the Russian Empire, but culturally entwined with Sweden.

These parallel clamp-downs occurred in Northern Europe. France and Southern Europe were inhibited from enacting similar legislation at the time by the influence of the Code Napoléon,* but this did not prevent increased cultural repression. In France there was increasing police surveillance, and although there were no laws against gay sex specifically, there were more general laws governing offences against public decency or immorality, which could be used increasingly and disproportionately against homosexuals, along with social sanctions such as dismissal from a job.

In the USA, with its vast size and its separate state legislatures, legal repression came sporadically and at different times, often tied in with particular election campaigns: legislation against oral sex in California in 1914 following a mass round-up of a hundred men in Los Angeles; and a clampdown on cross-dressing in New York in the late 1920s.

All this repression can be seen as part of a general crisis in masculinity; defeat in war might give rise to a need to assert a national virility, and fears about depopulation provoke a national demand for larger families; the growth of a women's suffrage movement and a demand for greater female autonomy might lead to increased insecurity on the part of men as to their proper role in society; the very awareness of the possibilities of homosexuality and the existence of homosexuals, brought to a general public attention by mass market newspapers catering for a newly-literate public, might provoke its own backlash.

On one level the ultimate assertions of masculinity can be seen in movements towards militarism and nationalism, and militarism imploded spectacularly in the clash of empires in 1914. The primary events which shaped the movement towards liberalisation across the Western world were the two world wars, which created large-scale single-sex gatherings as armies mobilised and men were billeted together; while on the domestic front the experience of women now doing men's work led them to find new friendships and freedoms with other women in the factories and offices. In particular the experience of country folks seeing the wicked city for the first time, and Americans savouring European sophistication, accelerated the drift away from the country in the inter-war period, and the further concentration in towns of people who related sexually to their own sex: 'How ya gonna keep 'em down on the farm after they've seen Pa-ree?'[5]

As a result there was a relative liberalisation in the 1920s across all Western cultures. In Russia the Bolsheviks abolished the Tsarist legal code in 1917 and

* Enacted in France in 1804 and subsequently adopted by many other countries. The Code Napoléon is a civil code, and as such did not affect criminal homosexual offences. The crime of 'sodomy' was abolished by the French National Assembly in 1791, and when the French penal code was revised in 1810, there was no discussion of reintroducing it.

a brief period of comparative freedom for the 'light blues', as homosexual men were called, followed, until Stalin recriminalised homosexual behaviour in 1934. The 'pansy craze' of the early 1930s in the US resulted, according to in Vito Russo,[6] more representations of gay characters on film in 1933 than in any other year until the mid-1960s. There were parallel gay rights groups, small and tentative, in New York and Chicago. In Berlin there were an estimated 300 lesbian and gay establishments plus Magnus Hirschfeld's Scientific and Humanitarian Committee;* in England the British Society for the Study of Sex Psychology, founded on the brink of the First World War, and a burgeoning bar scene; in France the *pissoirs* were buzzing, with minimal police interference, the bars of Montmartre and Pigalle heaved, the magazine *Inversions* appeared briefly, and in 1924 André Gide published *Corydon*, his coming-out manifesto.

This liberalisation stalled in the wake of the Great Depression of the 1930s in all countries, most spectacularly and tragically in Nazi Germany, where the Hirschfeld Institute was destroyed and its library burned. And with the German invasion of the rest of Europe a kind of universal darkness set in. In Holland the Netherlands Branch of the WhK was smashed, and the new, more radical, group 'Levensrecht' strangled at birth. European homosexuals were transported to work camps in Germany, a pink triangle stitched on their jackets. This process was only hindered where, as in Holland, the police refused to collaborate with the Nazis and hand over lists of known queers. In France the Vichy government, a Nazi puppet administration, introduced Article 334 of the Penal Code which set a discriminatory homosexual age of consent of 21, where the heterosexual age was 13.† For the first time since the Revolution, French homosexuals had to contend with legal as well as social sanctions.

Just as in 1914–18, Western society was profoundly shaken during the 1939–45 War, with the additional cross-fertilisation caused by large numbers of Americans billeted in the UK and, post-war, Germany. The GIs available in the darkness of the wartime blackout seem to have created what many gay men later regarded as the happiest days of their lives. They also introduced the word 'gay' into the vocabulary of the British homosexual.

The origins of 'gay'

The traditional derivation of 'gay' in the sense of 'homosexual' given in most dictionaries is from the 1890s, meaning 'immoral' or 'promiscuous', a 'gay

---

* Wissenschaftlich-humanitäres Komitee, WhK.

† In fact this was a watering down of a measure, which many in government supported, to criminalise all adult homosexual relationships as well.

house' being a brothel and a 'gay woman' a prostitute. By extension this came to refer to a male prostitute and then to all those who had male-on-male sex. The only problem with this is that it is not borne out by the evidence. There is little evidence for its use in the modern sense, about gays by gays, much before the 1940s. In the 1920s, the words male homosexuals used to describe themselves would have been euphemisms – 'sophisticated', 'bohemian', 'musical', 'artistic'.

In truth, the slippery world of words encompasses not only many different words for the same thing but also many possible derivations for the same word, all of which may be true and reinforce a particular usage. And to complicate things, one word may have multiple meanings.

Just as the Inuit supposedly have fifty different words for snow, because they need to, it seems that homosexuals have an endless variety of epithets to describe themselves. In the UK you might be 'sophisticated', 'bohemian'. 'musical', 'artistic' or even simply 'so'. In the US there were 'fairies' and 'queers'; George Chauncey* postulates that 'gay' acquired its modern meaning in the US during the 1920s because its ability to bear multiple meanings, and because it fulfilled a need. 'Gay' means 'brightly coloured' ('Don we now our gay apparel', as the carol goes). 'Fairies' were colourful, 'flaunting', faggots 'flamed', and hence an association between meanings started, a fruitful ambiguity. Novels of the 1930s have obviously gay characters using the word, but not entirely in its modern sense:

> 'I say, you look positively gay in the new clothes,' said Osbert.
>
> Oh, said Harold, you're lovely too, dear, and gave him a big kiss on the forehead, much to Osbert's dismay.[7]

Clancy posits a situation where 'gay' becomes a code word, used between men who were comfortable neither with being 'queer' or 'pansy/fairy', a way when meeting strangers of finding out 'who's who' and 'what's what':

> Supposing one met a stranger on a train… and wanted to find out … One might ask, 'Are there any gay spots in Boston? And by slight accent put on the word 'gay', the stranger, if wise, would understand … The uninitiated stranger would never suspect, inasmuch as 'gay' is also a perfectly normal and natural word to apply to places where one has a good time.[8]

This is far from being the triumphant march to a 'liberated' meaning.

In the UK, much has been made of the use of 'gay' in the 1920s, and especially Noël Coward's 'Green Carnations' in *Bitter Sweet* (1929):

> Haughty boys, naughty boys
> Dear, dear, dear

* *Gay New York* (New York: Basic Books, 1994), 14–21.

Swooning with affectation…
And as we are the reason
For the Nineties being gay
We all wear a green carnation.

It is just possible that Coward meant 'gay' to signal a modern meaning – he visited New York throughout the 1920s. The Gay Nineties was an American coinage – the UK term was the Naughty Nineties – made popular by a series of drawings in *Life* magazine in 1925, and had nothing to do with homosexuality. An audience at Drury Lane would not draw the inference of homosexuality from the phrase, although, allied to 'affectation' it might signal effeminacy and weediness, a recurring theme taken up again in 'The Stately Homes of England'. It remains a tentative and unproven case.

However, while on the subject of 'gay', it is worth noting that the meanings all seem to originate in the New York subculture, and since origins can feed into each other and reinforce one particular meaning, there is another possible connection to be postulated, which is that the modern sense of gay derived in part from the Harlem black/drugs slang where 'gay' meant 'high' on 'reefers'. As the song goes, 'Hey, hey, let's all get gay | The stuff is here.'[9] In the 1920s Harlem was not only the centre of the Harlem renaissance and the jazz scene, but also a burgeoning gay bar culture. It was one of the few places where white and black could mix to some extent on equal terms, and where transgression was permitted on a variety of levels.* As a linguistic transition node it was ideal, and publications like Cab Calloway's *Hepsters' Dictionary* (c.1940) facilitated the process. It is not difficult to imagine a young man out on the town in Harlem, jiving to the Duke, drinking and smoking a little weed, going off with a similarly inclined boy, and waking up with headache the next morning, groaning, 'My God, I was Gay last night.' It wouldn't have taken many years to catch on.

In 1938, in *Bringing Up Baby*, Cary Grant appears at the front door to Katherine Hepburn's aunt (May Robson) in a woman's marabou-trimmed negligee. When she asks what he thinks he's doing, he says, 'Because I just went gay all of a sudden.' Leaping and flapping his hands on the word 'gay'. Given that Grant was gay, and spent nearly the whole of the 1920s based in New York, appearing in musicals under his own name, Archie Leach, and the line was an ad lib, it could be seen as an in-joke between gay men which they have managed to slip past the Hays code. And so it entered the mainstream in time for the GIs to bring it to the UK. Even so, it didn't have widespread currency outside a small circle in London, and would not have been used in

* The crossover between cultures is personified in the figure of the black gay poet Langston Hughes. Similar 'place of transgression' were found in Saint Germain-des-Près in Paris in the 1940s, and in Soho.

Lancashire where Allan Horsfall lived until much later.

Even then 'gay' did not catch on entirely. It seemed that every homosexual had their own preferred word. Edward Carpenter's was 'homogenic', which never became current. Later, 'gay' would be rejected as being too 'militant'; some objected to it as being too American, or a euphemism – even people who belonged to GLF objected:

> The name GLF came from America, the badge we wear came from America, this is just not good enough, do we constantly have to ape the Americans in everything we do? Surely we are capable of moulding our own identity, and we must do it! ... We must choose our own name... How can we consider ourselves revolutionary and liberating when we choose to hide our identity behind a safe word.[10]

In the 1950s and 60s, 'homophile' was the preferred international term in the language of rights. When Antony Grey tried to set up a national federation of groups in 1970, they were 'homophile' organisations.* Some who clung to a culture developed out of illegality resisted 'gay' for many years and preferred 'queer'. And now 'queer' is preferred again by people who want to identify with a more inclusive 'culture of transgression'; 'gay' has *never* ruled the roost completely as a preferred self-definition. This is one reason why it is so hard to pin the meanings of 'gay' down precisely.

If the war brought men together, it also made the classes mingle, and many people found out with a jolt 'how the other half lived' in a way which would have been impossible in peace time. Reports of the acceptance of gays and lesbians within the armed forces seem to vary from regiment to regiment and service to service. Ike Cowen reported in interview that in the Air Force there was an acceptance of relationships and sympathy with a survivor when his partner was killed. In a service with a very high mortality rate, men would grab any sexual experience which presented itself, knowing it might be their last. Allan Horsfall came across something similar:

> There were some obvious gays who were fairly ostentatious who got away with it. One in my billet – we didn't have lockers, just shelves over the beds, and his was full of male cosmetics, and he was as camp as they come. And another lad I knew was very, very camp. And everybody accepted it. Nobody took the piss out of them. I remember one lad from Southampton did a mock ballet dance down the length of the billet. And it was 'Come on, do that dance again.' Just for fun.[11]

In contrast, of the two men Allan actually had relationships with in the RAF, one hanged himself after demob, and the other became a Catholic priest and

---

* See Volume Two.

had a nervous breakdown. This contrast illustrates dramatically the two tectonic plates of social forces grinding against each other, out of which tension arose the whole re-invigorated homosexual rights movement. On the one hand the relaxation of social mores in the upheaval of war; on the other the attempt to go back to the way things were before – women in the home again and not driving tractors, family units running on gender-divided roles, and all sex geared to having children after the loss of 500,000 people in the war.

In addition to bringing gay people into contact with each other, the war also brought many more heterosexuals into contact with identifiable homosexuals. Gay sex was an accepted part of service life in many regiments and squadrons, on a 'don't ask, don't tell' basis, and no-one could dispute the bravery or resource of many an obvious queen. Witness Arthur Marshall on the beach at Dunkirk with a bullet through his ankle, urging on his men to brave enemy fire to reach the little ships waiting to evacuate them: 'Come on, girls, who's on for the Botany Walk?' In the army, Marshall was known as Cynthia.[12]

This contact undoubtedly softened a significant section of public opinion regarding the draconian laws against male homosexual sex. Of course, it was illegal, but so were many other things people did after the war; such as conducting a roaring trade in clothing coupons, raising pigs outside the rationing system, or buying eggs on the black market. The war had been fought, ostensibly, for President Roosevelt's Four Freedoms.* These were widely discussed as war aims, and with this discussion the inevitable question arose, 'Freedom for Whom?'

The idea that homosexual behaviour was the preserve of effete members of the upper classes and theatrical types in silk dressing gowns was blown out of the water by the Kinsey Report. As the new Welfare State came into being piece by piece after 1945, it was even being suggested in liberal circles that British laws on sexual offences might benefit from coming into line with most of the rest of Europe.

If the growing wartime awareness of 'real' homosexuals was to engender a post-war protest movement in the UK, it was a longer time coming here than elsewhere. The point it had to grow from was one of total illegality and a conspiracy of silence. Not until the 1950s did newspapers start to give serious media attention to the 'issue' of homosexuality.

In mainland Europe, as a consequence of Nazi occupation, the break between pre-war and post-war was almost absolute, with a couple of exceptions. In Switzerland, which had remained neutral, there had been a gay

* Freedom of speech, freedom of worship, freedom from want, freedom from fear. Proposed in Roosevelt's State of the Union address, 6 January 1941.

magazine since 1933, *Der Kreis*.* This was perforce resolutely apolitical, and advocated keeping your head down to avoid attracting attention. Thus it was able to continue during the war, edited by a German-Swiss actor, Karl Meier, who had worked with Hirschfeld and constituted a link back to Weimar Berlin.

Another link was 'Bob Angelo', who had been a pre-war assistant to the founder of the Dutch branch of Hirschfeld's WhK. He started the gay magazine *Levensrecht*,† immediately after the war, from which the COC in Amsterdam emerged in 1946. Det Danske Forbundet av 1948, as the name implies, appeared in Denmark two years later, although Denmark had decriminalised homosexuality in 1933. This was followed by the Norwegian National Association, Norske Forbundet av 1948,‡ in 1953, RFSL§ appeared in Sweden in 1950, although homosexual acts themselves were legalised in 1944.**

Where homosexuality was already legal, the nature of gay organisations was different from the nature of groups in countries where homosexuality was criminalised. They were much more akin to voluntary social work organisations, acceptable social policy lobbyists able to access government funding. However, they might still feel the same pressures towards 'respectability' for acceptance's sake, as homosexuals were persecuted under different guises. In Denmark the founder of the Danske Forbundet av 1948 also ran a publishing company which produced and distributed pictures of male nudes. He and his partner were arrested in 1955 and charged with distributing material which 'may be deemed a commercial speculation with a sensual interest'. They suffered two years' imprisonment, and their mailing lists were used to locate and arrest many hundreds of gay men. Instead of rallying to the defence of their founder, the Association expelled him, concerned to distance themselves in the interests of retaining their own funding and political credibility.

1950 was also the year of the appearance of the Mattachine Society in San Francisco, the brainchild of Harry Hay. The clash between cultural openness and government repression was particularly strong here. Since the mid nineteenth century California had acted for over a century as a magnet for all

---

* *Der Kreis* also ran a gay club of the same name in Zurich. GLF and CHE member Michael Brown visited Zurich in the early 1950s because the club was the only gay place he had heard of.

† Using the same name as the pre-war organisation.

‡ There is a suggestion that these two organisations were named for the date of the UN Declaration of Universal Human Rights.

§ Riksförbundet för sexuellt likaberättigande.

** The Nazis did not recriminalize homosexuality in Denmark, as they did in Holland.

kinds of cultural and social misfits, including homosexuals, and there were established gay networks and a bar culture in several cities.* On the other hand, Californian state law for thirty years had empowered the state to regulate 'any act which openly outrages public decency'; there was a specific statute which prohibited fellatio and cunnilingus, which attracted a penalty of a maximum of fifteen years. The maximum penalty for sodomy was increased to twenty years in 1950. Further, if in prison a convicted 'pervert' showed signs of recidivism, the state was entitled to sterilise her or him. This happened to about 10,000 people up to the mid-1930s.

2. An early meeting of the Mattachine Society; Harry Hay at top left

No wonder then that the Mattachine Society met in conditions of the strictest secrecy. The names on the letterhead were respectable middle-aged women, the mothers of the founders. The only photograph of the earliest members which exists does so because the photographer lied that there was no film in the camera.

Finally, *Arcadie* in France was founded in 1953-54, in the form of a magazine with a high theoretical intellectual content, and monthly meetings in Paris where the founder, André Baudry, who rigidly controlled the organisation and its ideology, lectured the rank-and-file subscribers about the importance of

* The post-war years gave San Francisco further impetus as a gay Mecca because of its large naval base and the number of sailors who were discharged there after the war.

dignity and morality. France itself was slowly tightening its control of homosexuality through the 1949 regulation of publications 'directed' at minors – a remit extended to include anything which might fall into the hands of impressionable youngsters, whatever the publishers intended. This catch-all led not only to the fining of Baudry and destruction of an issue of *Arcadie* in 1955, but also the banning of American comics and Micky Spillane-style French novels such as Boris Vian's *I Will Spit on your Graves.*

These organisations came together under the umbrella of the International Committee for Sexual Equality (ICSE), initiated in 1951 by COC. Its founding conference a year later defined its goals as 'the improvement of public opinion and the law regarding homosexuality'.

It is hard to estimate how important the ICSE was to the English homosexual rights movement, or in the dissemination of ideas about sexuality. It was founded at a time when there were no UK organisations, and later, when the HLRS was formed in 1958, it rejected the idea of joining ICSE on the grounds that it did not want to be identified as an organisation of homosexuals. This was not necessarily a result of closetedness, more of a genuine belief that homosexuals could not be authoritative experts on their own situation. As one member, Geoffrey Whittal, complained of the first congress, there were 'no experts not directly personally mixed up with the subject under discussion', and as a result the group would become 'a crowd of fanatics fighting for their own ends.'[13]

Despite this, there were English members who participated in the annual ICSE conference, and Marc Dufour, an expatriate Englishman living in France, helped to set up its first Congress by contacting individuals about it, on a personal basis, all over Europe. He was a live wire, and set to become one of its key figures, until he blotted his copybook by asking the local organisers in Amsterdam to find him a couple of unattached pretty boys for the duration of the Congress.

This Congress, and the subsequent conferences which took place in France, Germany and Holland throughout the 1950s, attracted well over a hundred delegates, and at one point the print run for their newsletter was 14,000. Delegates came from as far away as Australia, New Zealand and Indonesia. It ran out of steam in the early 1960s, in much the same way as other gay organisations were to fold, because not enough people were prepared to organise, and too few paid their subscriptions.

The ideology of 'homophile'

If remarkably similar organisations emerged in various countries at roughly the same time, their rhetoric and ideology also sang from the same hymn sheet – a hymn sheet CHE was to pick up ten to fifteen years later. It is best summed up by the word 'homophile'. This represented both a belief and a strategy.

'Homophile' was the preferred self-description of those who wished to emphasise that lesbians and gay men were more than the sum of their sex acts. It emphasised the whole package involved in loving and relating to members of the same sex, preferably in monogamous long-term relationships. It encompassed friendship and companionship, as well as sexual pleasure. In this it was saying that what homosexuals wanted was the same as what heterosexuals wanted, and therefore the only difference between the two was the gender of the object of affection.

But not only was it a belief, it was a realistic strategy in the attempt even to get a hearing in a profoundly hostile society, where those who might be converted to a liberal humanitarian concept of civil rights for homosexuals were better wooed by reassurance than by confrontation. Mrs Patrick Campbell may have said of homosexuals, 'Does it *really* matter what these affectionate people do – so long as they don't do it in the street and *frighten the horses*!' [14] In many ways early gay rights campaigners behaved as if the public were very skittish and nervous horses who needed constant stroking and soothing. Perhaps the most extreme example of this kind of soothing was the open invitation which Baudry gave to the Paris Prefecture to attend any Arcadie meetings or dances. This was intended as an assurance of respectability, but also gave rise to the rumours that Baudry was a police informer and handed over his subscribers' address lists; many closeted homosexuals were too scared to visit.

Allied to this was the need to behave with 'dignity'. Homosexuals were all, whether they liked it or not, 24-hour PR agents for homosexuality, with all that this implied. All their interactions with society were part of the process of education which would chip away ignorance and prejudice as heterosexuals came to know that deviants were reassuringly similar to themselves.

In order to define this similarity it was necessary to repudiate the dissimilar, which meant largely the effeminate. A hundred years previously effeminacy had been a signifier of dandyism and of ineffectuality, rather than of homosexuality. Cross-dressing likewise was strictly for entertainment, a playful juggling with gender. Vesta Tilley ('Burlington Bertie') or Julian Eltinge could equally be described, as Eltinge was, as 'wholesome amusement, particularly suitable to women and children'. At some time in the later 1920s cross-dressing became synonymous with homosexuality in the popular mind, with the accompanying effeminacy. This has persisted, to the extent that if you enter 'Female Impersonation' into Wikipedia, you get redirected to 'Drag Queen'.

This association was reinforced by theories of homosexuality which placed homosexuals as women trapped in men's bodies, or alternatively as men who existed at the 'more feminine' end of some masculine-feminine spectrum.

Some gay men are undoubtedly naturally 'effeminate',* as are some straight men.† Some more 'butch' gay men, who were indistinguishable from most heterosexual men, actively played up to the 'queenly' image, as a way of indicating their identity and/or availability. It was a way of aligning their interior life, secretly desiring what only women were meant to desire, with their exterior appearance. Over time, this became self-perpetuating, as young men, newly discovering their homosexuality, took other homosexuals as a role model, assuming that in order to become a 'real' homosexual it was necessary to join the conspiracy of Camp. One of the most common descriptions of overtly gay behaviour is 'affected'.

The triangle of dignity/similarity/virility as a means of educating the general public can be seen in random quotes which might have come from any of the organisations mentioned:

> The public will never accept us while we have a total disregard for their feelings. After all, it is us who are doing the asking and demanding. One feels that demonstrating and holding grand Balls in Kensington Town Hall will not free us either – in fact will only get us laughed at. One feels that being Gay must be dealt with in a manner the public will accept. Let's show them that we don't all walk around wearing tons of jewellery.[15]

> Try to observe the generally accented social rules of dignity and propriety at all times … in conduct, speech and attire.[16]

> The worst thing in this book‡ is the intentionally frivolous tone, the wholly feminine preciousness that is really the most nauseating thing among men. This tends to give the public the impression that the homosexual world is made up of frivolous and feminine creatures.[17]

> We have duties, and perhaps … it is necessary to caution certain among us. *Watch the way you dress*, watch how you behave. This does not mean bourgeois conformism … but it does mean self-respect and respect for others and above all it means a terrible responsibility towards all other homophiles.[18]

If the duty of the homosexual is to be 'presentable', this extends, as the last quote intimates, to dress. Photos of dinners of Arcadie members, and of HLRS helpers, show the ubiquitous dark suit and tie. The international ICSE,

---

* 'Effeminate' is an unfortunate word because of the negative baggage it carries, but will have to suffice as short-hand for 'having characteristics and mannerisms stereotypically thought to belong to women'.

† The TV actor and writer David Walliams springs to mind.

‡ Michael Nelson's *A Room in Chelsea Square* (1958).

more radical and relaxed in some ways than its constituent members, leavened its Congresses with cabaret acts such as 'Lola Florès', 'Mae West', and 'Marlene and her boys', but many delegates stayed away from these shows in disgust.

One literary marker had a huge impact on all homophile movements at their inception. *Sexual Behaviour in the Human Male*, by Alfred Kinsey, Wardell Pomery et. al., appeared in 1948, and its sister volume on the human female in 1953.* Kinsey himself was no absolutist as far as orientation was concerned, and disliked defining people as heterosexual or homosexual. Nevertheless 'One in Ten', derived from Kinsey, became a kind of slogan in gay campaigning.† What Kinsey actually said was more nuanced: that 11.6 per cent of white males aged 20 to 35 had an equal attraction to males and females in their adult lives; that 10 per cent of those surveyed between ages 16 and 55 had been 'more or less' exclusively homosexual for three years at a period in their lives. It also said that 37 per cent of adult males had had at least one homosexual experience in their lives.‡ We were not alone – and how!

The first Kinsey Report sold over a million copies in sixteen different languages and influenced both homosexuals' pictures of themselves as a minority, and lawmakers' and opinion-formers' attitudes to the justice of law reform where homosexuality was illegal. To stigmatise, even criminalise, such a large portion of the population made many deeply uncomfortable.

The other significant marker laid down in these years was the United Nations Universal Declaration of Human Rights, adopted by the UN General Assembly in Paris in December 1948. Influenced by President Roosevelt's Four Freedoms and the Code Napoléon,§ it laid out rights for all, regardless of all kinds of status. The following articles were the most relevant sections which campaigners were to draw on in the battle for equal rights:

3 – Life, liberty and security of the person;
7 – Equality before the law and protection against discrimination;
11 – Presumption of innocence;

---

* Lesbian activists more rarely drew on Kinsey's figures about female sexual behaviour, perhaps because their view of female sexuality was less attuned to Kinsey's statistical, orgasm-defined, approach.

† There was a 'One in Ten' Theatre group in Birmingham, which played at the CHE Conference in Coventry in 1978. Bryan Magee's 1966 book *One in Twenty* (see page 145) reflects a more common interpretation of the statistics.

‡ There were criticisms of Kinsey's sampling technique because of his large recourse to prisoners and male prostitutes. A later adjustment which stripped those populations from the samples found that it made no change to the results.

§ The final draft was largely the work of a Frenchman, René Cassin.

12 – Protection from arbitrary interference with privacy, family, home or correspondence;
18 – Freedom of thought, conscience and religion;
19 – Freedom of opinion and expression;
20 – Freedom of assembly;
23 – Right to work and free choice of employment;
24 – Right to education 'directed to the full development of the human personality and to the strengthening of respect for human rights and fundamental freedoms. It shall promote understanding, tolerance and friendship among all nations, racial or religious groups.'[19]

The idea of applying the concept of Human Rights to homosexuals as a group occurred almost immediately after the UN adoption. Harry Hay in Los Angeles had already allied the 'homosexual cause' to that of Mexicans, Native Americans and black people by virtue of his involvement with the American Communist Party. It was part of the rhetoric of the tiny, secretive first incarnation of the Mattachine Society.

In addition it was taken up almost immediately by the American sociologist, Donald Webster Cory,* later to join the Mattachine Society, but far more right-wing than Hay (he quit because he believed that homosexuality should remain classified as a disease). Cory's book *The Homosexual in America: A subjective approach* (1951) was pioneering both because, as its title delicately hints, Cory was writing it as an open homosexual, and because it began to develop the concept that homosexuals were a definable minority. This definable group could be mobilised to political action by a decisive leadership with the confidence to be open. He elaborated this over several books:

> It is today generally recognised that homosexuals constitute a sociological minority, a factor most important in America, a land in which the minority problem, particularly as concerning the rights and the integration of ethnic groups, has admittedly become the most important domestic situation facing this country. Although many [ethnic] leaders would be the first to denounce the homosexual, … their propaganda … coincides with the aspirations of all minorities, not excluding the sexual.[20]

The concept of a minority depends on both inclusion and exclusion. A minority has to possess a trait in common which is important enough to bind the members together, and differentiates them from the rest of society, resulting in a difference of status within that society. Cory's homosexual in these terms is one of a homogeneous group; 'homosexual desire' is a unitary force, unmediated by qualifying social and psychological factors. It was only later, as 'I' was added to 'T' was added to 'B' was added to 'L' was added to

---

* Real name Edward Sagarin.

'G', that the boundaries of inclusion in LGBTI were contested.

Cory's arguments are augmented with a frankness about his personal feelings which contrasts strongly with British writing of the 1950s, and includes an engaging admission of perplexity:

> To my heterosexual friends and readers, who find outside the realm of their comprehension the desires I always carry within me, I can only state that I find their own sexual personality just as much an enigma, just as foreign to myself and beyond my powers of imagination. To be transformed suddenly and as if by magic into the body and consciousness of a heterosexual – what would I think, know, desire? My failure to be able to reply is more than an inability to imagine; it is a frightening fantasy from which I recoil.
>
> I know that I cling to my entire personality, and that sexuality is basic in this personality and can never be relinquished. But sometimes I would wish to be normal … just for a brief period. I would like to know the freedom from anxiety. … But although I should like to experience such a freedom, it would be only to return to a gay world which I can never surrender.[21]

Cory, in asserting inalienable difference, is also rejecting a kind of integration which presupposes that sexuality does not disturb a fundamental equivalence of personality, behaviour and interest.

Not only was he the first to propound the idea that the homosexual group was equivalent to an ethnic minority, he was also widely travelled, twice addressing the ICSE conference. COC's large presence in ICSE ensured that the internationalist perspective was heartfelt and thorough. One of the first resolutions of the first Congress was to send a telegram to the United Nations appealing for recognition of homosexuals as a valid minority. The telegram appealed to 'the principles of the United Nations laid down in the Rights of Man', and demanded that, in the light of the 'findings of modern psychological, biological and medical research and mankind's awareness of social injustice'* the UN should 'initiate steps towards granting the status of human, social and legal equality to homosexual minorities throughout the world.'[22] The resolution was backed by Kinsey and by Jean Cocteau. As a minority, the members of ICSE also recognised similarities with other minority movements, and its publications make reference to similarities with feminism, black rights and combating anti-Semitism. British organisations would not make the same connections for twenty years. Cory's speech and ideas fell on eager ears. His work was also available in England, and was to influence Antony Grey after he came down from university:

* Heightened by the comparatively recent revelations of the concentration camps.

> The first helpfully enlightening information I came across was … an abbreviated paperback version of Havelock Ellis' *Psychology of Sex*. Its humane and surprisingly modern broadmindedness reassured me. Later, soon after I had started living in London, I nervously bought a copy of [Cory's] *The Homosexual Outlook* – a pioneering work for its time which, with its forthright call for self-acceptance by homosexuals and an end to … discrimination gave me a constructive new perspective on my own situation.[23]

Most of the active members CHE attracted to its ranks had a history of involvement with political parties, voluntary groups or pressure groups. Amnesty International and the NCCL were the most popular. These publicised the UN Declaration of Human Rights, and in doing so described the framework within which demands for equality could be made. It was now possible to couch those demands in terms of universal entitlement and general Human Rights, rather than special pleading for a minority group. To do so turned the campaigner from being a supplicant into something much more intellectually and politically aggressive – if society was denying homosexuals their rights, the onus was on society to defend itself, not on the homosexuals to prove themselves worthy. Many campaigners took this stance, in the belief that its terms of reference would carry more conviction. It also made it possible to make such demands without necessarily identifying as lesbian or gay. It was precisely this argument of the universality of rights, turning homosexual law reform (in the first instance) into a human right, which underpinned the NWHLRC's first public meeting in 1966, and justified its title, 'Society and *its* homosexuals' (my italics).

English influences

The influences on, and motivations of, those campaigners depended on particular circumstances in Britain as well as the wider Western cultural context. Everything was conditioned by the figure of Oscar Wilde and the spectre of his trial. It is hard, now that he is surrounded for many with the halo of martyrdom, to remember how much Wilde was reviled for the forty years after his death, a fire of hatred assiduously stoked by the newly Catholic Lord Alfred Douglas, fervently repudiating his past. Beverley Nichols was caught by his father reading a copy of *The Picture of Dorian Gray*:

> Then he seemed to choke. The purple deepened on his fat cheeks. He turned to me with an expression of such murderous hate that I stepped towards the wall.
>
> 'You filthy little bastard!' he screamed … 'Don't you dare to speak to me … you scum!' He hurled the book at my head. It crashed against the

> mantelpiece bringing down two little ornaments of which I was very proud. The noise of their breaking seemed to sober him for a moment.
>
> 'Pick that book up!'
>
> I handed it to him. As I did so, he struck me across the mouth.
>
> 'Now … you pretty little bastard … you *pretty* little boy … (and as he said the word 'pretty' he sent his voice high and shrill, in a parody of typical homosexual intonation) … watch me.'
>
> I watched. My father opened the book, very slowly, cleared his throat, and spat on the title page. Having spat once, he spat again. The action appeared to stimulate him. Soon his chin was covered with saliva. Then, with a swift animal gesture, he lifted the book to his mouth, closed his teeth over some of the pages, and began tearing them to shreds.
>
> Suddenly he threw the book from him, and ground his heel into it.[24]

Wilde's contemporary, Edward Carpenter, is often hailed as a pioneer of gay rights and liberation, but we need to draw a distinction between a pioneer as seen with hindsight as part of a historical pattern, and a pioneer who had a real influence on the thinking of campaigners at the time, or serves as a role model and inspiration. Carpenter belongs in the former group. The example of his life with George Merrill at Millthorpe on the outskirts of Sheffield was a defiance of the hysteria surrounding the Wilde trial, yet also an escape from it, being out of the orbit of metropolitan gossip and comparatively secluded. His writings and his thought developed from *The Intermediate Sex* (1908) onwards.

Carpenter took Ulrichs' concept of the 'third sex', or 'urning', as the foundation of gayness. Urnings were more intuitive, empathetic and artistic, they were the natural mediators and negotiators in a society. They were also in the vanguard of a universal brotherhood, which was similar to 'the dear love of Comrades' of Walt Whitman, whom he greatly admired:

> The homogenic affection is a valuable social force and in some cases a necessary element of noble human character … the instinctive artistic nature of the male of this class, his sensitive spirit, his wave-like emotional temperament, combined with hardihood of intellect and body; and the frank, free nature of the female, her masculine independence and strength wedded so thoroughly to feminine grace of form and manner; may be said to give them both through their double nature, command of life in all its phases.[25]

Carpenter's gay writings had tiny circulations, being virtually privately printed. According to his original entry in the *Dictionary of National Biography*, they 'had more vogue on the continent than in England.'[26]

However, Carpenter in his day was hugely influential on the subject of women's rights, pacifism and trades unions. As a co-founder of the Independent Labour Party he was a great hero of the Labour movement, so much so that the members of the first Labour Cabinet in 1924 marked his eightieth birthday by each signing a collective greetings card. However, there was never any sign that this government was going to take his views on 'Uranians' seriously. It was Edward's private hobby, an eccentricity kept well out of sight, and it only affected a tiny group of people, didn't it?

3. Edward Carpenter and George Merrill

He was forgotten extraordinarily quickly. Socialism became more butch in the 1930s, the crisis of unemployment elbowing out all other considerations. Orwell denounced 'every fruit-juice drinker, nudist, sandal wearer and sex maniac'[27] bringing opprobrium onto the movement. Increasingly marginalised, Carpenter's books went out of print by the 1940s, his Uranian ideas as quaint as his vegetarianism and his sandal-making to a generation focussed on post-war reconstruction and nationalisation.

Carpenter's Wikipedia entry makes much of his status as a pioneer in the second sense, claiming that even when the books were out of print they were still stored in the 'dirty books' section of many libraries where 'they became inspirational to many gay people looking for solace'. This is not borne out by experience, at least in the UK. When the author asked a dozen of his interviewees, both in CHE and GLF, whether they had encountered Carpenter's work and whether it had influenced their thought and action, hardly anybody had heard of him until 1970 at the earliest, and nobody had read him, not even Martin Stafford who was at University in Sheffield, close to where Carpenter lived, and might be considered among the more intellectual members of CHE.

The depths to which Carpenter's reputation sank by the 1950s can be seen in Donald Webster Cory's anthology of writings on homosexuality, *Homosexuality: A Cross Cultural Approach* (1956). He reproduces Carpenter's *The Intermediate Sex*, but his editorial comment is that he is 'completely self-defeating':

> The homosexual today who reads Carpenter, if he does not ridicule the man entirely, will only feel that he is the roué he so severely condemned. The values he set … were based on distortions, contradiction and misunderstanding … they were a mirror image of a world whose values have been discarded.[28]

The only gay activist who acknowledged a debt to Carpenter was Mattachine founder Harry Hay, who sneaked a look at a copy of *The Intermediate Sex* in the library when he was eleven.

> As soon as I saw it, I knew it was me. So I wasn't the only one of my kind in the whole world after all, and we weren't necessarily weird or perverted. There were others, the book said so, and even named some who believed in comradeship and being everything to each other. Maybe, someday, I could cross the sea and meet another one.[29]

Hay, born in 1914, was a decade older than the English activists who created CHE and pushed for Wolfenden to be implemented. Antony Grey and Allan Horsfall were both born in 1927, and Tony Dyson a year later. You needed to have been that bit older to be aware of Carpenter in the prime of his influence. However he did influence some of the Great and Good who lent their names to the 100-strong Honorary Committee of the HLRS,* several of whom knew him personally: Bertrand Russell, Compton Mackenzie, Ralph Vaughan Williams. Clement Attlee, E. M. Forster.†

Carpenter first re-emerged from obscurity when claimed as a forebear by H. Montgomery Hyde‡ in *The Other Love* (1970, Penguin Paperback 1973). This was the first coherent survey of the history of homosexuality§ in English. It was the first book to give the lesbian or gay reader a sense of roots, and enable them to see themselves as part of an ongoing historical continuity, in which the contemporary struggles of the HLRS and the counselling services of the Albany Trust were but the latest manifestations of gay effort. When it

---

* See page 71.

† Forster records in his diary that Merrill touched him on the backside when they met, which made a profound impression on him.

‡ A Northern Ireland MP who managed to combine politics with a career as an intensely prolific author of forty books. Though heterosexual, he was drawn to write about gay figures – Wilde, Roger Casement, Lord Castlereagh.

§ Male homosexuality, that is. It is mainly silent on lesbians.

came out in paperback, it became essential reading for building a gay identity, and featured in the gay libraries of most CHE groups. In it Carpenter is allotted a mere three pages, fewer than J. R. Ackerley and less than half the pages devoted to John Addington Symonds. According to Hyde, Carpenter was:

> Generally regarded as a socialist crank on account of his complete disregard of social and class distinctions – engine drivers, coal miners and farm lads sitting down to meals in his cottage with parsons, dons, suffragettes and sprigs of the aristocracy.[30]

Hyde includes a touching picture of Carpenter and Merrill's life together as a couple, taken from Carpenter's autobiography *My Days and Dreams*. But he says nothing about the stuff of Carpenter's ideas, nor of his considerable body of homoerotic poetry. It was indeed as a poet that Carpenter was remembered, if at all: the 'English Walt Whitman', as Michael Davidson called him when describing Carpenter's fondling of his buttocks.

Carpenter's reputation as a radical and pioneering gay activist, a founding father of gay liberation, rests on his rediscovery by members of the Gay Liberation Front in the 1970s, almost after GLF itself had imploded. In 1973 Graeme Wollaston wrote a paper for the Cultural Studies Group on Carpenter's life and writing, which praised Carpenter's lifestyle and open defence of homosexuality, while severely critiquing some of his ideas about Uranians, about lower and higher forms of 'homogenic' love. Later Jeffrey Weeks and Sheila Rowbotham wrote more extensive biographical and political studies.*

In exploring these tenuous continuities, one other bridge is worthy of mention. In 1932 the Progressive League, an association of freethinker and humanist groups numbering Bertrand Russell, H. G. Wells, Julian Huxley and Professor C. E. M. Joad† among its members, included decriminalisation of homosexuality in its 12-point manifesto. Its agenda was in part derived from Carpenter, and also included radical reform of the divorce laws, legalising abortion and making birth control available; it would have abolished censorship, repealed licensing laws and prohibited exhibitions of performing animals.‡ It advocated complete and immediate disarmament, and much of the current Green agenda. It never got to the point of fighting any elections, and collapsed because of internal schism. However, it did include in its membership two people who were to be influential in the HLRS and the fight

---

* His name lives on in the Edward Carpenter Community of Gay Men (ECC, founded 1985), a British collective that organises consciousness-raising retreats for gay men.

† Later to find national fame on the BBC *Brains Trust*.

‡ More uncomfortably, it advocated forced sterilisation of 'the feeble-minded'.

for decriminalisation: J. B. Priestley and his wife Jacquetta Hawkes. Priestley had a gay son, and occasionally wrote articles in the popular press advocating homosexual law reform, but otherwise merely lent his name. Hawkes, bisexual, was more personally involved, attending many committee meetings. The Albany Trust is so-called because early meetings were held at the Priestleys' flat in the historic Albany apartment block in Piccadilly.

Far more significant than Carpenter in shaping the opinion of the law-makers were Sigmund Freud and Havelock Ellis. Freud's theory of human development phases* encompassed a basic six stages – the polymorphous perverse infant, the oral (up to one year old), anal (1–3), phallic (3–6), latent (till puberty) and finally genital. Freud characterised homosexuality as a form of arrested development, for which a variety of social causes could be found. His followers elaborated these so that almost anyone's background could be trawled after the event for convincing explanations of homosexuality. Thanks to Freud, homosexuals could be categorised as 'immature', a word capable of multiple meanings and thus laden with cultural baggage able to encompass a variety of deficiencies. Any gay man growing up within the period 1930 to 1970, if they were referred for, or sought, psychiatric treatment, would most probably receive it within a Freudian framework. The vast majority of psychiatric writings would also expound Freud's theories, so anyone reading up on the subject in order to find out about themselves would learn that they suffered from an over-possessive mother, a weak father, etc.

It took some strength of mind to resist this ubiquitous theory, but the mind is also capable of selective confirmation, drawing out nuggets from the most unpromising sludge to offer affirmation of one's position and behaviour. One curious paradox lies in the way that writers on homosexuality of the early 1950s who were themselves gay could continue writing in the same Freudian way. Michael Schofield† did so in the very influential *Society and the Homosexual*, and Donald West in *Homosexuality*, yet both led entirely fulfilling gay lives, Schofield with his partner of sixty years and West cheerfully promiscuous.

However, Freudian theory proved one thing: most homosexuals could not help being what they were or doing what they did. One did not punish people who were ill. Freud himself wavered as to whether homosexuality was pathological, and also as to whether it was treatable. Later he gave up trying to cure homosexuals, and famously wrote a letter to a mother about her homosexual son:

> Homosexuality is assuredly no advantage, but it is nothing to be ashamed of, no vice, no degradation, it cannot be classified as an illness; we consider

---

* In its later formulations; it went through many developments.

† Under the name Gordon Westwood.

> it to be a variation of the sexual function produced by a certain arrest of sexual development. Many highly respectable individuals of ancient and modern times have been homosexuals, several of the greatest men among them (Plato, Michelangelo, Leonardo da Vinci, etc.) It is a great injustice to persecute homosexuality as a crime and cruelty too. If you do not believe me, read the books of Havelock Ellis.[31]

Many a campaigner was to quote this when advocating law reform, and many homosexuals believed it of themselves. Though Freud was himself extremely pessimistic about the possibility of 'cure', this did not deter Freudian psychiatrists from claiming they could turn gay people straight, and practising a variety of techniques, including electric shock treatment and chemical castration, to do so.

4. Havelock Ellis in 1913

Freud in his letter mentions Havelock Ellis, to whom he owed a great debt in the development of his ideas about homosexuality. Havelock Ellis disagreed with Freud about the origin of homosexuality. He defined it as a turning of sexual feeling towards a person of the same sex as a result of 'inborn constitutional abnormality', rather than a developmental abnormality. He associated it with fear of failure, fear of women, and strong feelings of inadequacy. Equally with Freud, he argued that you should not punish someone for something which was not their fault, which they had no control over.

Ellis had much less direct impact than Freud on the view of homosexuals as objects of treatment, and on homosexual self-regard. His primary work on the subject was *Sexual Inversion.* Almost as soon as it appeared, a bookseller was prosecuted for selling it, and it was always seen in some ways as a 'dirty book', to be asked for in hushed tones at libraries and read under controlled circumstances. This was largely because of the explicitness of his twenty 'case histories', several of which concern what we would now define as paedophiles. So Ellis was widely known, but little read.

His main contribution to the development of the philosophy and aetiology of homosexuality and its social discourse was to popularise the word 'invert'. It was taken up in literature as well as textbooks. Radclyffe Hall gave it a boost as she used it of her heroine Stephen Gordon in *The Well of Loneliness*. With 'invert' developed the parallel concept of 'pervert'; an 'invert' couldn't help him or herself, but a 'pervert' did it on purpose – for thrills, because he was a jaded old roué who needed new kicks, because he enjoyed corrupting others, or because he had no access to women. It was a distinction which Edward Carpenter recognised as well:

> Too much emphasis cannot be laid on the distinction between these born lovers of their own kind, and that class of person, with whom they are so often confused, who out of mere carnal curiosity or extravagance of desire, or from the dearth of opportunities for a more normal satisfaction (as in schools, barracks, etc.) adopt homosexual practices. It is the latter class … who excite, naturally enough, public reprobation. In their case the attraction is felt by themselves and all concerned, to be merely sensual and morbid.[32]

Because he was incapable of escaping a certain high-minded Victorian puritanism,* in Carpenter's version the invert rarely had sex at all, and then only as a kind of inadvertent emission, an overspill of his pure comradely love; whereas the pervert did nothing but have sex.

This distinction, like that between the deserving and undeserving poor, was used by campaigners to wrest a modicum of compassion from those disinclined to offer any. It is taken on board wholesale by Peter Wildeblood both at his trial and in his apologia, *Against the Law*, which has brought down on his head the wrath of historians steeped in later doctrines of gay liberation. However in doing so he is couching his defence and his plea for 'tolerance' in the language his opponents will understand. Whether he really believed it or whether it was a calculated strategy is open to debate. It is in part a reaction to a popular culture in which *all* homosexuals are labelled 'perverts'. If he can begin to wrest *some* from the general opprobrium, it is a start to neutralising the opprobrium itself.

A strategy is not necessarily a belief. In the terms of the time, the average homosexual-on-the-Clapham-omnibus would, if pressed, have insisted that he

---

* Complete with stern warnings about masturbation as something which would stunt a youth's growth.

was an 'invert'. 'Perverts' were 'the rest', who 'gave homosexuals a bad name'. But most homosexuals would have not *felt* that they had female minds trapped in a man's body, nor indeed that that they were 'abnormal', except inasmuch as they were made to feel abnormal by those around them.

Campaigners like Dyson, Horsfall and Grey, hitting puberty during World War II, would have had to argue their case within the terms laid down by Freud and Ellis. Hence the ubiquity of the phrase 'homosexual condition' in the pamphlets of the period. It was only in the later 1960s that homosexual campaigners could begin to locate the problem, not in homosexuals themselves, but in society's reaction to them.

Post-war influences in England

There were other forces at work, which acted on all social groups, but on homosexuals in particular ways. There was a large post-war increase in social and physical mobility linked to the decline of traditional industry sectors such as cotton and docks, later of iron and steel; the retreat from the countryside in the wake of the industrialisation of agriculture also meant the ongoing decline of smaller market towns. The lesbian or gay man moving to the big city in search of homosocial contact was only part of a larger pattern of movement.

This mobility has always affected homosexuals comparatively more than those encumbered with families, in that companies see single people as more flexible and easier to move around the country from site to site; they may also be more able to pursue upward career paths on their own account. This had a significant effect on the pattern of development of CHE groups, in that someone who had been active in one town might start a new group in a new area which they moved to. Conversely, a group might fold if a key figure moved out of the area.

Changes in education fed into this as well, for the generation which was the first to benefit from a relaxation of the law relating to homosexual 'offences'.

The Robbins Report of 1963 recommended a huge increase in the number of university places available, enough to accommodate anyone who had the ability to benefit from it, reflecting changes that were already occurring in higher education. This meant that throughout the 1960s large numbers of people in their late teens were experiencing independence and living away from home for the first time. The geographical separation from family meant that it became easier to explore one's sexuality and to come out to friends in the university.

In addition, the Education Act 1962 laid on local authorities a statutory duty to pay for tuition fees and to provide a maintenance grant, depending on levels of parental income; this applied to vocational colleges as well as universities. As a result, not only were more people able to afford to go to college, the social range of students was far wider than previously.

In the first place this was to benefit the Gay Liberation Front more than CHE, since GLF was far more driven by student activism. Initially based at the London School of Economics,* some of its most active branches were in plate-glass universities – Sussex, Essex, Kent, Lancaster. However, there was also a considerable CHE presence in student unions and other university bodies, with Trevor Locke at Bristol having a particularly strong influence on the creation of Gaysocs.

Even for those single people who were not privileged to go to university, there was a new freedom. Before the war and for some time after, the standard pattern for young adults would be to live at home until they were married. If they didn't marry, they were expected to stay in the family home and become the carers when parents became frail. Living away from home was confined to a few selected professions – travelling salesmen, actors – and those people lived in 'digs'. Post-war, as mobility increased, digs remained the main option, and more people let out rooms in their houses to accommodate the increased demand. The essence of digs was that the landlord/lady lived on the premises (with or without their own family) and usually provided some food, and did the laundry. Antony Grey recalls that he had digs when he first moved to London from university. He went to a few gay bars, but the fact that he was in digs prevented him taking anyone home.[33] One may speculate that for many people, this constraint helped to instil a habit of cottaging which persisted long after decriminalisation.

It wasn't until the 1960s that flats became more common.† There had been 'mansion flats' from the 1870s onwards, in London and Brighton, built as accommodation became more expensive in fashionable areas, and houses were increasingly expensive to maintain. The build-up of urban population meant increase pressure on space, and for well-to-do families who formerly would have had a town house and a country house, the mansion flat was the answer. Single people living in flats in the 1920s or 30s were typically rich and regarded as somewhat eccentric outsiders.‡ Affordable flats became increasingly available towards the end of the 1950s, in conversions of large Victorian houses and in the newly-built blocks replacing those bombed out during the war. It also became more common for people, usually of the same sex, to share them. Separate entrance, own key. Suddenly greater degrees of privacy

* Noted for the radicalism of its students, although not necessarily of its staff.

† This of course does not include the social housing provided by councils and by organisations such as the Peabody Trust. These were exclusively aimed at providing affordable housing to the deserving poor, and as such are not relevant to this argument.

‡ Hercule Poirot lived in Whitehaven Mansions, Peter Wimsey in a flat in Piccadilly.

were possible, allowing greater opportunity to exercise sexual choice.* This shift is illustrated by the British films of the 1950s and 60s. In *This Sporting Life* and *The L-Shaped Room* both main characters have digs; in other iconographic films of the period – *Saturday Night and Sunday Morning*, *A Taste of Honey* – they live with parents. All are characterised by sexual frustration and a sense of pinched lives. By contrast, Michael Caine in *Alfie* and *The Ipcress File* has a flat, a 'bachelor pad' where he can bring back 'birds'. Place a homosexual in the same two sets of surroundings, and you can see a step change in gay lifestyle.†

Allan Horsfall was unusual in that he lost both his parents early and entered adulthood with a degree of freedom not available to many. He had the freedom to buy his own house quite early. His attitudes to himself would have been conditioned by Freud. Allan was not an intellectual,‡ though he did seek out books which would tell him about himself. But above all his image of homosexuals and homosexuality would have been conditioned by the popular press, which increasingly in the 1950s covered court cases in more detail, and also began 'exposés' of gay meeting-places and carried articles about the 'problem' of homosexuality.

Altrincham and the Press

One court case in particular was to haunt Allan's imagination throughout his life. Although it occurred before he was 10, he still wrote about it when he was in his sixties, and talked about it in interviews to the end of his life. 'The Altrincham case' was one of the largest, most vicious and patently unjust set of trials in gay history, and occurred only a few miles from where he grew up.

In 1936, twenty-nine men were brought to Chester Crown Court charged with offences which were variously described as 'serious offences', 'indecent conduct' and 'improper conduct'. When the case came up, even the prosecutor couldn't find the words to describe the buggery that was alleged:

> He did not suppose that in the criminal history of the country had a batch of prisoners been brought before a court on such serious charges. … Certain of the charges were about the most serious of a criminal nature which could be brought against any man. It was something just less than murder, and so seriously did the legislature look upon the acts of which the prisoners were accused that in 1861 they were punishable by penal servitude for life, or not less than 10 years' penal servitude. That, however, had been modified by more recent legislation, but the punishment in the

---

* In a 1957 BBC documentary on loneliness, presenter Gilchrist Calder reported that there were twice as many single men living alone as 25 years previously.

† According to the 2011 census, 52 per cent of homes in London are now flats.

‡ The intellectuals, with a couple of exceptions, were in GLF.

> particular cases to which he had referred was at least two years' imprisonment and five years penal servitude.[34]

The case was a public sensation:

> Crowds of people surrounded the Altrincham Police Building on Tuesday morning in the hope of catching a glimpse of the men who have been charged and remanded in custody following allegations of improper conduct. …
>
> A large section of the crowd remained outside the Police Station for more than two hours, probably anticipating the departure of the prisoners for Strangeways Gaol.[35]

The local newspaper's most recent previous headlines had been about the state of the local cheese industry and a fight on an allotment between rival cabbage growers. No wonder everyone was now agog.

These men had met each other in a few bars and cafés in Manchester. Even before the case came to trial they were treated as if they were already criminals. There was an argument about whether they should be remanded to Manchester Assizes or Chester. All the defence lawyers and defendants were agreed that they wanted to go to trial in Manchester. It was a chaotic scene in the tiny local court house where all 29 defendants were put up simultaneously and all thirteen of their defence lawyers plus their clerks tried to cram into the courtroom together. In this confusion barrister T. M. Blackhouse told the magistrates:

> It would be a gross injustice to the defence if the prisoners were sent to Chester Assizes, because all the solicitors instructed in the case, and certainly all the counsel with the exception of one, were not in the Chester circuit. It would be beyond the means of their clients to support their own defence if the case went to Chester.[36]

This was before the days of legal aid. One of the reasons so many pleaded guilty to sexual offences was the sheer cost of representation if you pleaded not guilty. And these were not rich people. Another barrister said that his client was:

> a youth of 20 years of age, and his widowed mother had raised the money for his defence. It would be a great hardship if they were to be put to more expense than was necessary. Manchester Assize Court was only a 2d car ride from [their] home.[37]

In defiance of compassion or convenience, the magistrates sent them all to Chester.

None of these offences was committed in public in any sense; they all occurred in private, and were consensual. There was hardly any evidence, except twenty-nine confessions in which each accused implicated others. The best the prosecution could produce was a tube of lipstick belonging to one defendant with an interest in amateur dramatics, and a book, *Twilight Men* by André Tellier.* True, there was a Welsh hotel register showing two of the men registering at the hotel together. But joint registration, even sharing a bed, was not evidence of crime, and anyway, the entry was from three years previously.

The heart of the defence case was that the confessions had been improperly obtained, either made up or given under pressure. Was it likely, the defence asked, that twenty-nine men would voluntarily incriminate themselves, one after the other, since that was what they had had to do in order to incriminate others:

DEFENCE: I am going to suggest that the conduct of the Darwen police renders the evidence inadmissible. I suggest that in the Darwen police station he was cross-questioned about this offence and he was told that it would be better if he made a clean breast of things. ... Unless you got a statement from him you had no evidence against him.

HARRIS: On this charge, no.

BACKHOUSE: That is the case in most of these cases?

– Yes.

– I am suggesting that you knew perfectly well that you must get a statement from this man?

– No, sir.

– When he had written what he wrote, you asked him about other men?

– No, sir.

(To magistrates) However much you may admire the Cheshire police, it is impossible for your worships to believe that one after the other these men, against whom the police had no evidence, immediately volunteered statements which convicted themselves.[38]

At this point the prisoners all cheered and gave the barrister a round of

* Tellier's lurid and ludicrous tale tells of an invert, Armand: 'He ... found a bottle of cologne, and tilting the bottle let the fragrance drop on his hair. He selected a pair of blue pyjamas and put them on with care, smoothing the white collar and sticking a dainty blue silk handkerchief in the little patch pocket over the left breast. He ... put on a pair of embroidered satin slippers.' (p. 71) He falls successively for two men, both of whom commit suicide, then goes to New York where he becomes an alcoholic drug addict and kills his father under the influence of 'hop', before committing suicide. Despite its entirely negative storyline, a selective reader would have drawn comfort from passages like, 'Yet – this was love. He could have cried aloud in his sudden, hot rebellion against society and its prohibitions. What right had they to dictate, "This is love but that isn't."? How could men be so stupid as wilfully to persecute this strange, ungovernable thing that had existed as long as the race, dateless, primeval?' (p. 111) The book ran to several pulp paperback editions, into the 1960s. Tellier too uses the word 'gay' in the ambiguous sense.

applause. This sudden outburst of gay solidarity in the face of adversity must have caused the three magistrates and the prosecution great consternation. The barrister continued:

> I suggest it is perfectly plain, and has been to anyone who has no prejudice, that at 7.00 pm yesterday it was becoming farcical; that everyone in court who had any experience of evidence was laughing at the proceedings; that person after person, after being charged, had immediately done just the thing that the police wanted. In some ways you can't blame the police … but you have to say … whether you really believe that man after man has convicted himself. Without any inducement being held out. … Did you ever know a more accommodating crowd of defendants? … They have an extraordinary urge to write statements,[39]

The magistrates admitted all the confessions and committed everyone to trial in an unprecedented sixteen-hour session. When the cases came before the judge at the actual trial, women were excused serving on the jury, because, as the Clerk of the Court said, 'the cases are … of an extremely filthy nature.' The judge upheld the reliability of the 'evidence', and the defendants, all of whom had initially pleaded not guilty, had no alternative but to change their pleas. Of the twenty-nine, five were acquitted and seven were only bound over. However, five men were sentenced to between three and seven years imprisonment, with up to eighteen months hard labour. The vast discrepancies between sentences reflected the men's ages, the relative age difference between two partners, education (one got a reduced sentence because he'd been to Manchester Grammar School), and whether in the court's opinion the offender was an invert or a pervert:

> Dr W. H. Grace, pathologist at the Chester Royal Infirmary, said that there were two types who committed the kind of offence of which Cross was accused. They were the vicious and the neurotic. Dr Grace said that Cross was in his view of the latter type, and he would recommend medical treatment for this condition.[40]

According to the hysterical papers, this 'gang' – they were always 'gangs' in these cases of mass arrest – was only the tip of an iceberg, and many other, wealthier homosexuals who were involved had fled to the South of France. The *Sunday Empire News* applauded the Irish Free State for having kept one man in prison for twenty-three years for sodomy, and suggested that Britain should follow the example of 'Herr Hitler', who two years previously 'started a campaign to eradicate this brand of vice in Germany. His method was drastic, and sentences against those convicted ranged from the death penalty to a lifetime in prison.'[41]

Years later Allan wrote of the effect the case had on the town, and how it lingered in his memory:

> Because of this, Altrincham became identified among a large section of the population as being synonymous with everything perverted. … The vision was of a town populated entirely by predatory sodomites. 'If you should happen to drop a half-crown in Altrincham,' people were solemnly warned, 'don't ever pick it up.' I have heard this warning repeated when the half-crown had given way to the fifty pence piece, and there may be areas where it lives on still.[42]

The Altrincham case and its resonance in collective gay memory were not unique. Anywhere there had been a police round-up, the story lingered on as an awful warning. Photographer Angus McBean was caught up in just such a 'vice ring' case in Bath in 1942.* It resonated with local gay men to the extent that Ken Little recalled it spontaneously 65 years later when being interviewed for Robert Howes' West Country history, *Gay West*. Robert Reid's outraged reaction to just such a case in Somerset in 1958 prompted him to write to the *Spectator*, a letter which started the chain leading to the formation of the HLRS and ultimately to law reform.

No wonder, then, that when the NWHLRC came into existence, Horsfall, like Grey in London, advised gay men not to keep diaries, letters, address books, never to plead guilty, never to make statements, and never to talk to the police if they could avoid it, unless they had a solicitor present. Here too was motive enough for starting or joining a campaign – who would want to live with the prospect of such misery in store, simply for doing what came naturally? Who would not be outraged to hear what they did with their partner in the privacy of their own home referred to as 'something just less than murder'? And if they were by nature law-abiding and orderly, they would have had a desperate need to bring the law and their personal life into alignment.

Church of England

Allan Horsfall was not a religious man, but he would have sniffed in the air a change in the political climate which was being driven largely by the Anglican Church. He regularly read several newspapers – most people did – and in the *Daily Telegraph* he would have come across this letter in 1953. Maybe he read it over breakfast to his partner of six years, Harold Pollard:

> All bodies appointed to consider the problem of homosexuals, including a Joint Committee of the Magistrates Association and the BMA, have recommended reform on the lines of the Code Napoléon. It would surely be more responsible to make this reform and then enforce a new and humane law, rather than fall back upon instruments which are as cruel as they are unjust and a potent cause of the immorality we all deplore.[43]

---

* See discussion of Bath Gay Awareness Group in Volume Two.

This was from Robert Reid, a solitary campaigner who had tried to raise the subject ten years before in the *Daily Telegraph*, and got nothing but abuse from other readers for his pains. This time however there was support, and from the clergy. 'A parish priest' wrote:

> The fact must be faced that the genuine homosexual, as distinct from the pervert, is born not made. He does not 'perversely' withhold himself from the opposite sex, but would dearly like to be normal in his affections. He is cut off through no fault of his own from the deepest happiness of domestic life. … Do we really believe that to condemn the weaker ones to terms of imprisonment does anything but aggravate the problem?[44]

Again we have the invert/pervert split, something the Church of England subscribed to when it took up the cause with a 1953 report for its Moral Welfare Council. Written by clergy and doctors, this report laid down much of the framework for subsequent discussion of the 'Problem of Homosexuality' (as the report was called). However it sub-divided perverts into 'casual perverts', who were fundamentally heterosexual but had gay sex because they couldn't access women, as in the armed services or prison, or out of curiosity, and 'hardened' perverts who did it for kicks, for money, or for blackmail. The report concluded that 'homosexual physical expression is as natural to the invert as heterosexual expression to the normal person; in both cases a means of expressing love.'[45] Further, 'In no other department of life does the State hold itself competent to interfere with the private (i.e. not anti-social – incest is biologically and domestically anti-social) actions of consenting adults.'[46]

While still buying into the myth that it was possible for people to be 'turned' homosexual, in the sense that what might stay latent could be brought out by a sexual encounter with another man, the report came out in favour of a male homosexual age of consent of 21. The report was hotly debated in Synod, and though it never became an official Anglican policy, the awareness it raised in liberal clergy was important.

One person who initially was violently opposed to any reform was the Archbishop of Canterbury, Geoffrey Fisher. When the indefatigable Robert Reid wrote to urge him to change the Church of England's line, Geoffrey Cantuar replied:

> I think you must be perfectly clear about the matter. Homosexuality is against the Christian law of morals and is rightly regarded as a social menace if it becomes in any sense widespread. There is an accumulation of evidence that homosexuality is becoming a real social evil, and I know cases where homosexuals are enticing men and persuading men who are not by nature homosexual at all into this practice. You will have seen what the magistrates have said. Quite obviously society must protect itself against this as against any other anti-social moral perversion.[47]

The role of the Church of England in the development of a gay rights movement, in the days when its liberal wing was ascendant, is insufficiently recognised at present. Support from the clerics in the later House of Lords debates, which was echoed by similar support from Methodists, Roman Catholics and Jews, was to sway much opinion, inside and outside Parliament. The offer of church premises enabled gay reform groups like the NWHLRC in Manchester, and social groups like St Katherine's in London, to meet. It even found space for the mass meetings of GLF in Notting Hill.

In the wake of the publication of the Church report, the *New Statesman* ran a special feature on the state of the law, written by the editor Kingsley Martin and by E. M. Forster. Though ostensibly on opposite sides about the timing of reform, both agreed that decriminalisation was necessary. Forster was savagely satiric about the present but pessimistic about the prospect of reform:

> Prison is a place, it is part of society, and people who are pushed into it exist, just as much as if they had been pushed into the next parish … They can of course be pushed right out of the world. That would certainly clean them up, and that has in the past been tried. It is however unlikely that the death penalty for homosexuality will be re-established. … However, change in the law is unlikely until there is a change in public opinion; and this must happen very slowly, for the great majority of people are naturally repelled by the subject and do not want to have to think about it. … Less social stigma under the existing law – that is all that can be hoped for at present.[48]

It is ironic that it should be the homosexual who was arguing against the possibility of law reform at this time.

Allan Horsfall, as a socialist, was a regular subscriber to the *New Statesman*. As the correspondence in the *NS* letters columns continued, the issue of police *agents provocateurs*, attractive young constables acting as lures and effectively inciting crime, came to the fore. Gerald Gardiner QC, later Lord Chancellor at the time of the passing of the 1967 Sexual Offences Act, wrote:

> I have been told by counsel of great experience in criminal cases that they would not, in any circumstances whatever, enter a public lavatory in central London, so great do they feel is the risk of a wholly innocent man being convicted. … The decision of a Divisional Court that police evidence of conduct consisting only of smiling, once only, at a man, repeated in respect of several men and looking 'in the direction' of their persons, is not only sufficient to sustain a conviction of 'persistently importuning' the men in question for immoral purposes, but is so clear a case as to make it 'lamentable' that the man should appeal, has not lessened the risk.[49]

Horsfall was seeing not only the argument of his life (in a literal sense) unfolding, but recognition of the problems he was discussing in gay bars in Manchester with friends on a Saturday night.

Several homosexuals, male and female, came forward in the *New Statesman*, following Martin and Forster's pieces, to give moving personal testimony, albeit anonymously. 'SCIENTIST' wrote:

> In a recent case the defendant was advised to go and see his doctor. Some years ago I was faced with a similar situation, and I discovered that I was quite unable to find anyone who would undertake to treat me for the affliction of homosexuality. The psychiatrist in whose care I have been placed said he would not attempt it.
>
> Some may be tempted to ask why the homosexual does not forever renounce all hopes of satisfaction. The answer is clear: to live in the world without affection is insupportable. If we suppress our emotional life we wither, and I for one long ago decided to be bold and take the risk. … I do not like promiscuity; I do not like soliciting; but perhaps those who condemn these actions have not imagined the desolation which has preceded them.[50]

> A LESBIAN: Fourteen years ago I met a girl. I was married at the time, but my husband was killed in 1941. With this girl I set up a home. Since then, we have lived what is to us a most normal married life, except that we are denied the joy of having children. Our lives are so normal that we forget the abnormality. Perhaps only homosexuals can know what we suffered at the hands of society in our younger years and the intensity of the secret we must keep if we wish to live on good terms with the world. But at least we are not persecuted by the law as two men would be in our position.
>
> There is morality and immorality in homosexual life just as in all love life. What is wrong is immoral homosexuality, the ceaseless and insincere drift, and the enticement of youth.[51]

ONE OF THE ANONYMOUS raised for the first time the bleak prospects offered by 'treatment':

> It has been discovered that chemically synthesised female hormones in the form of Stilboestrol, taken regularly in tablet form, will reduce all sexual desire in the male to an absolute minimum. I have availed myself of this treatment; what might be termed a mechanical celibacy has been achieved. At 40 I am physically and nervously better than for over 20 years, energies have been released for intellectual and social constructive purposes and very acute mental conflict has been reduced to manageable proportions. In short, the price of celibacy has been brought down, although this method no more 'cures' homosexuality than insulin cures diabetes. It amounts to a sort of temporary glandular castration, which can, however, be suspended by leaving off the tablets.[52]

Many readers must have wondered if the price was worth paying.

The court cases added to the sense that 'something had to be done'. Like the Altrincham case twenty years previously, the worst cases came from outside London. In March 1956 a 42-two-year old barman gassed himself and a 46-year-old carpenter who was caught with him threw himself under a train, leaving a widow and three children. The method of choice for most homosexuals committing suicide was gas. In December 1958 two lovers took this way out in the Midlands. They left a note asking to be buried together.[53]

More judicial sympathy

Despite these tragic cases. there was the beginning of openness, a change of climate, and the general public was beginning to meet some genuine and avowed homosexuals, even if only through the Letters Pages of their papers and magazines. Even supposedly impartial judges pitched in. Mr Justice Hallett:

> It will be a great joy to me and to other judges when some humane method for dealing with homosexual cases is devised, and when something more can be done than simply locking up the offenders.[54]

In Appleby in January 1959 Mr Justice Elwes discharged thirteen men, criticising the police tactics aimed at getting a chain reaction of 'voluntary statements'. He expressed sympathy for those who had lost their jobs and hoped they would be reinstated:

> If anyone thinks that punishment is due to you for what you have brought on your own head by these lapses of personal morality, they are welcome to their opinion; but I do not share it. [55]

The advocates of homosexual law reform of the early twentieth century had never succeeded in creating a coherent group of homosexuals prepared to argue on their own behalf for anything resembling a platform of gay rights. The climate was too hostile, gays were too dispersed as a minority, there were no channels of communication and few points of contact. But now the moment was right for a spark to be struck; for channels to appear through which gays could talk to each other; for concepts such as 'rights' and 'equality' to develop and take root; for 'spaces to breathe' to open up, in which lesbians and gay men could 'be themselves'.

One route of transmission of the ideas of homosexual rights, as of all intellectual causes, is through personal contact, as well as through books. If, as we have seen, the influence of gay figures from the nineteenth and early twentieth century has been overstated, there are others from the post-war period who were profoundly important; perhaps the most influential was Peter Wildeblood. Almost every member of CHE interviewed for this book described a reaction both to his trial and to his subsequent book, *Against the Law*, which was nothing less than life-changing. Antony Grey describes how reading it had this kind of effect on him, and motivated him to become a gay rights campaigner. In addition to his book, Wildeblood also had, in one intervention at least, an important influence on the will to found the NWHLRC.

There will be many another important crossing of paths. Wildeblood to Horsfall; Horsfall to Martin Stafford; Stafford to CHE General Secretary Paul Temperton. London organiser George Mortimer to Liverpool's Peter Norman; journalist Roger Baker to Tony Ryde and Michael Launder, founder of the counselling organisation FRIEND. Each contact provided energy, inspiration and ideas; there were to be many others to come.

Wildeblood, his trial and his manifesto

But in the beginning, according to this particular post-war timeline, was Wildeblood, and he had to have a 'eureka' moment, a light-bulb going on in the mind of the victim of a police raid. It started, to be exact, at 8am on Saturday, 9 January 1954. On that bitterly cold morning, two Detective Superintendents, improbably named Smith and Jones, called on journalist Wildeblood at his home in Canonbury. They searched his flat without a warrant, denied him access to a solicitor, and arrested him 'for offences arising out of your association with Edward McNally and John Reynolds in the summer of 1952'. In addition to Wildeblood's arrest, this was also a trawling expedition, an attempt to get hold of the names and addresses of other well-known homosexuals in the hope of implicating them in illegal activities. As Wildeblood wrote:

> While Superintendent Jones was going through the contents of my wallet he found a number of visiting cards and telephone numbers, mainly belonging to business 'contacts'. Noticing one well-known name among them, he asked 'I suppose he's queer too?' I said that if they really wanted a list of homosexuals from me I would be happy to oblige, beginning with judges, policemen and members of the Government. I was beginning to feel slightly better. Very faintly, as though at the end of a tunnel, I could see what I must do. … I would simply tell the truth about myself. I had no illusions about the amount of publicity involved. I would be the first homosexual to tell what it felt like to be an exile in one's own country. I might destroy myself, but perhaps I could help others.[56]

And so it was that this rather feckless, charming, society gadabout, chum of debs, dukes and directors, acquired a kind of steel which saw him through trial, imprisonment and subsequent rehabilitation. His determination was born out of anger and disbelief that something that he thought only happened to others was now happening to him. Plus, be it noted, he was an only child, which is common to many of the early reform campaigners. One could speculate whether a solitary upbringing gives a child a self-sufficiency and resilience, not to mention a bloody-minded determination to get your own way, which are useful psychological tools when swimming so thoroughly against the conventional tide as Wildeblood, Grey, Horsfall, Martin Stafford and Brian Sewell did, to name but five.

5. Peter Wildeblood in 1951

Wildeblood claimed he was a victim of a witch-hunt which destroyed many reputations and ruined many lives. If the Second World War had effected a quiet revolution, in that it had reduced ignorance, at least among men of fighting age, of how the other half lives, the peace had also seen a backlash, an attempt to reinstate the old certainties and class barriers. Wildeblood's contact with young airmen McNally and Reynolds would have seemed utterly in tune with war-time Britain. Post-war, a civilian prosecutor could suggest that an association between Oxford-educated Wildeblood and two National Servicemen was *ipso facto* suspicious because it crossed the class divides.

According to Wildeblood, this change in attitude occurred in the early 1950s with high profile spy scandals. In the UK, Burgess and MacLean leaked NATO strategy documents to the Soviet Union before defecting to Stalin's Russia. In the USA, Communist infiltration of the State Department was alleged to be widespread, and President Truman instituted 'loyalty boards' which eventually investigated some 20,000 government employees. While people like Burgess seemed to reinforce the generally held conviction linking the Red and the Pink, the more general fear was that homosexuals were security risks, since they were likely to be blackmailed. Few if any made the connection that removal of criminal sanctions from homosexual activity would also remove the opportunity for extortion.

Cometh the hour, cometh Sir David Maxwell Fyfe as Home Secretary. In many ways on the right wing of the Conservative Party, Maxwell Fyfe had nevertheless drafted the European Convention on Human Rights (which elements in the Conservative Party were finding so problematic in 2014). On the other hand, he never seemed to consider that it might apply to everyone, including homosexuals. He also fiercely opposed the abolition of hanging. He was harried into setting up the Departmental Committee on Homosexual Offences and Prostitution (known as the Wolfenden Enquiry) and then cast as the principle opponent in the House of Lords to implementing its recommendations.

According to Wildeblood, the US State Department, in the throes of its witch-hunts, made representations to the British government that it too should purge its ranks of homosexuals. The Home Secretary, a Christian of a stern moral bent, leapt to their bidding with almost indecent haste. He in turn appointed Sir John Nott-Bower as Commissioner of the Metropolitan Police, the first serving police officer to hold the post. Nott-Bower's five-year rule seems to have been distinguished by nothing except his enthusiasm for getting queers into court.

This US-instigated 'drive against male vice' went unreported in the British press, save for lip-smacking accounts of 'indecency' cases in the courts. Again according to Wildeblood, it was left to the *Sydney Morning Telegraph** to blow the lid on it. According to their London correspondent, Donald Horne, the plan was a response to strong US pressure to weed out homosexuals from important Government jobs, because of the unacceptable security risks. Horne claimed that one of the Yard's top rankers, Commander E. A. Cole, 'spent three months in America consulting with FBI officials in putting finishing touches to the plan.' But this 'plan' – never spelt out in detail – was extended 'as a war on all vice' under Nott-Bower: Sir John swore he would 'rip the cover off all London's filth spots.'

> Sir John swung into action on a nation-wide scale. He enlisted the support of local police throughout England to step up the number of arrests for homosexual offences.

---

* According to Patrick Higgins, the name of the paper was *Sydney Sunday Telegraph.*

> For many years past, the police had turned a blind eye to male vice. They made arrests only when definite complaints were made from innocent people, or where homosexuality had encouraged other crimes.
>
> They knew the names of thousands of perverts – many of high social position and some world famous – but they took no action. Now, meeting Sir John's demands, they are making it a priority job to increase the number of arrests. …
>
> The Special Branch began compiling a 'Black Book' of known perverts in influential Government jobs after the disappearance of the diplomats Donald MacLean and Guy Burgess, who were known to have pervert associates. Now comes the difficult task of side-tracking these men into less important jobs – or of putting them behind bars.[57]

Both Wildeblood's account of his trial and his analysis should be taken with a hefty pinch of salt. The account in the Australian press, equally so. If true, it is startling that such a sensational British story can only be justified by citing one paper published thousands of miles away from where it was said to be happening. It seems more likely to be the result of a conversation between a journalist and a handful of homophobic coppers in a pub over a few beers. It has all the hallmarks of urban myth. The article also seems to think that Sir John, head of the Met, can somehow command the rest of a national police force, which is not true; and arrest figures give the lie to the assertion that his force had previously been 'turning a blind eye to male vice'.

Matt Houlbrook's analysis of London gay prosecutions shows a peak of 637 incidents in 1947 and a slight tailing off in the 1950s, suggesting a rather different story, one of a nervous tightening of morals after the laxity/liberation of the War. Wildeblood's own account of his arrest and prosecution doesn't tally with the theory, because the arrests were confined to the three associated with the incident in Norfolk, where a systematic trawl through address books and diaries would no doubt have produced many more arrests outside the county. Elsewhere in the country the overall figures for prosecutions did increase, but not to the extent of suggesting a mass pogrom suddenly introduced as a result of American pressure or moral panic about spying.

The figures for homosexual offences for 1930–53 issued by the Home Office also tell a slightly different story from Wildeblood's. These figures were used in the preparation of the Wolfenden Report. Yes, the number of homosexual sex offences 'known to the police' rises sharply in this period, but so do the number of heterosexual offences.* If the homosexual offences are

---

* Homosexual sex offences included:'unnatural offences', 'attempts to commit unnatural offences' and 'indecency between males'. Heterosexual offences included rape, indecent assault, defilement of girls under 13, defilement of girls under 16, incest and procuration.

expressed as a proportion of the whole, they rise to a peak in the immediate post-war period, and actually decline slightly in the early 1950s; the percentage of these sent to trial remains roughly constant. There are more detailed figures for 1953. Out of 2,166 sent to trial, 1,257 were found guilty (58 per cent). According to criminal justice statistics issued by the Ministry of Justice, conviction rates for sexual offences rose from 47 per cent in 2003 to 59 per cent in 2013. While most of the cases tried in 1953 have ceased to be offences now, the figures do not suggest that juries or magistrates were more vindictive or censorious then. This is not to belittle the tragic experience of those on the receiving end of the law or the many miscarriages of justice; in this year of 1953 146 men went to prison for more than two years.

Figures for offences

Year	Offences known to police		Homosexual as % of total	Homosexual sent for trial	% of homosexual offences sent to trial
	Homosexual	Heterosexual			
1930–39*	934	2,423	27.8	948	101.5†
1940–44*	1,651	3,112	34.7	672	40.7
1945–49*	2,814	4,010	41.2	982	34.9
1950	4,416	6,408	40.8	1,635	37.0
1951	4,876	8,220	37.2	1,942	39.8
1952	5,443	9,255	37.0	2,063	37.9
1953	5,680	10,135	35.9	2,166	38.1

* Average per year

† the figures for 1930–39 show more people going to trial for homosexual offences than were known to the police, which is a logical impossibility. This seems to confirm what many have said, viz. that there are serious concerns about the accuracy of Home Office statistics.

Historian Patrick Higgins in *Heterosexual Dictatorship*, his masterly survey of homosexuality on post-war Britain, is scathing about Wildeblood, describing him as 'uncharitable', and 'not particularly pleasant'.[58] He condemns what he takes as his cavalier presentation of the proceedings in his trial and about the so-called witch-hunt which Wildeblood claims followed in its wake. Higgins ignores however the purpose of *Against the Law*, which was avowedly propagandist and polemical. As such it was brilliantly successful, a key text to many young gay people in the later 1950s and beyond. and a game-changer in the reform movement. The very fact that so much of what Wildeblood wrote has been accepted and has entered into the received version of LGBT history, however inaccurate, is evidence of the book's effectiveness.

If Higgins and Houlbrook are correct in saying there was no witch-hunt, Wildeblood still had a right to feel paranoia, in that someone was clearly out to get Edward Montagu. Montagu had been tried less than a month previously for buggering a 14-year-old boy scout, the first noble not to be tried by his peers in the House of Lords.* The case in winter 1953 occupied the front page of the *News of the World* for weeks, and though Montagu was acquitted of the charge, his name was now nationally infamous. For many it was linked to their first awareness of the phenomenon of homosexuality. Michael Steed, Chairman of CHE in the 1970s, recalled learning a Rugby song when he was in his teens:

> On the first day of Christmas my true love sent to me
> My Lord Montagu of Beaulieu.†
> On the second day of Christmas my true love sent to me
> Two boy scouts and my Lord Montagu of Beaulieu.[59]

It was hard not to believe in some kind of frame-up when Montagu was arrested a second time so shortly after, especially since police officers had been heard to vow to 'get him' following the collapse of the first case.

However, if there was no general witch-hunt, at least in London, there was certainly an enormous increase in press interest in the subject, which created the impression among homosexuals themselves that there was. When it became common knowledge, in 1951, that Guy Burgess was homosexual, the phrases 'homosexual' and 'security risk' became inextricably entwined in the public mind, and homosexuals became even fairer game in the press. The press 'witch-hunt' began almost immediately.

Sunday Pictorial

The charge was led by the *Sunday Pictorial*, in a series of four articles by Douglas Warth in 1952. Warth it was who coined the phrase which would become a common cliché, 'These Evil Men':

> An unnatural sex vice is getting a dangerous grip on this country. I have watched it growing – as it grew in Germany before the war, producing the horrors of Hitlerite corruption. And as it grew in classical Greece to the point where civilisation was destroyed. …
>
> Most people know there are such things as 'pansies' – mincing effeminate young men who call themselves 'queers'. But simple decent folks regard them as freaks and rarities. They have become regrettably a variety hall joke. There will be no joking about this subject when people realise the true situation. Before the war, police reports assert, there were over a million known homosexuals in Britain. And both numbers and

---

* The right of peers to trial by peers in the House of Lords was abolished in 1948.

† Pronounced Bew-ley.

> percentage have grown steeply since then. Many, who have never been brought to book, are listed in secret police records as 'suspects'. …
>
> Three months ago a fifty-one-year old vicar was sent to prison for 15 years for 10 offences against boys. The police found a black book in his possession, containing the names of 850 boys. Against the names of 382 of them there were various symbols. One man, as Mr Justice Stabie said, had been able to corrupt many young people. 'Nobody will know how many ruined, broken lives you have caused.' …
>
> There is a freemasonry among them which brings the rich, pampered degenerates into touch with the 'rough' who acquired his unnatural habits from some corrupting youth club leader. …
>
> A number of doctors believe that the problem could be best solved by making homosexuality legal between consenting adults. … But this solution would be quite intolerable – and ineffective. Because the chief danger of the perverts is the corrupting influence they have on youth. So many normal people have been corrupted, and in turn corrupt others.[60]

It is strange how often the totemic 'black book' turns up in reports – often enough to acquire mythological status. Roger Casement had a 'black book' – the 'secret diaries'. In 1918 right-wing MP, homophobe and Hun-baiter Noel Pemberton-Billing wrote:

> There exists in the black cabinet of a certain German Prince a book compiled from reports of German agents who have infested this country for the last 20 years, spreading such debauchery and lasciviousness as only German minds can conceive, and only German bodies can execute. More than a thousand pages are filled with names. There are the names of 47,000 English men and women, practitioners of vices all decent men thought had perished in Sodom and Lesbia [*sic*]. All the horrors of shells and gas and pestilence introduced by the Germans would have but a fraction of the effect in exterminating the manhood of Britain.
>
> In this black book details were given of the unnatural defloration of children who were drawn to the parks by the summer evening concerts. Wives of men in supreme positions were entangled in Lesbian ecstasy, and the most sacred secrets of State were betrayed.[61]

There were to be many 'black books' produced in court in the 1950s, evidence of conspiracy deduced from simple address books. Special Branch had a 'black book' of known perverts, according to the *Sydney Morning Telegraph*.

Warth initiated another myth in his follow-up article, which dealt with the extent of the 'problem'. He outlined the state of gay life in the major cities (bizarrely citing Bournemouth as the homosexual resort of choice). The predatory and commercial aspects are particularly drool-worthy:

> There are boarding houses 'for men only' where they can take their customers for half an hour. One of these, which I hope to see raided soon,

> is just round the corner from Paddington Station. There is a man in Mayfair, nicknamed 'the Duchess', who acts as procurer for rich degenerates. He makes a weekly tour of all-night cafes, looking for new faces, making recruits. He looks particularly for ex-Borstal boys, for the appalling truth is that Borstal institutions tend to be veritable nurseries for this sort of vice. There is one ex-Borstal boy from the Midlands who has taught himself to talk intelligently about the ballet, opera, music and art – as part of his stock-in-trade.[62]

It is again noticeable how many 'Duchesses' turn up in court reports of the 1950s. Surely not *all* gay men of mature years gave themselves this nickname?

Warth's final article searched for a cure, and he enlisted the authority of psychiatrist Clifford Allen, an authoritarian Freudian who would be a bugbear of reformers and of gay activists for the next thirty years. Allen is quoted almost as a purifier of the race:

> There is no doubt that these perversions cause a terrific amount of biological WASTE, inasmuch as many desirable types fail to reproduce themselves. It must be admitted that sexual abnormalities do, in the main, occur in the more intellectual and artistic types whose abilities are so worth preserving in the future representatives of the race.[63]

Allen, like Warth, was vehemently opposed to legalisation. Yet prison was not the solution, since it created more perverts than it cured. In the 1954 adjournment debate in which MPs Robert Boothby and Desmond Donnelly pressed for a Royal Commission on homosexuality, Boothby said:

> To send confirmed homosexuals to prison for long sentences is, in my opinion, not only dangerous but madness. Our prisons today in their present overcrowded condition are factories for the manufacture of homosexuality.[64]

Despite Clifford Allen's enthusiasm for keeping the existing law, other doctors disagreed profoundly. One wrote in the British Medical Journal, 'It is as futile from the point of view of treatment as to hope to rehabilitate a chronic alcoholic by giving him occupational therapy in a brewery.'[65]

To get round this problem, What Warth proposed was a kind of medical concentration camp:

> A Broadmoor for homosexuals will enable the medical men to do the research that is needed. And if any pervert there failed to respond to treatment, at least society would know that he was not at large spreading his poison.[66]

This, it should be noted, was not just for those convicted of homosexual offences, but also those listed in the 'secret police records'. And the suggestion is that these should be detained indefinitely until they could be certified as 'cured'. Not the least of the questions begged is this: given on Warth's own admission there are a million perverts and rising, where on earth is the state to put them all, and who's going to pay for it?

Today it seems clear that Warth was barking, but there was sufficient public interest in terms of increased newspaper circulation for homosexual court cases to become a staple of the popular press. The *News of the World* at the height of this obsession in 1953–54 carried several articles every Sunday. This also had an effect on judges and especially magistrates, who, conscious of the eyes of the world on them, vied with each other to come up with ever more quotable denunciations.* No wonder that gay men felt persecuted by this snowballing interest. The cases were also reported in local papers on a weekly basis, usually giving the victims' addresses and often their employers for good measure.†

In implementing crackdowns in the regions, there were the enthusiastic bigots who leapt at the green light they had been given. C. G. Learoyd was adamant. Writing in *The Practitioner*, the journal for GPs, he was unequivocal: 'By far and away the most important part of treatment is preventive. Homosexuality is contagious. … A healthy and vociferous public opinion is probably the best preventive.'[67] The Chief Constable of Nottinghamshire, the splendidly named Captain Athelstan Popkess, was another such bigot:

> Homosexuality is beginning to eat into the very vitals of the nation like a cancer. The public would be horrified if they knew its extent, and it is on the increase. In one city, for instance, it has increased from 7 cases in 1938 to 62 cases in 1952, many of the offenders being non-residents who went there expressly to importune. The deuce of it, too, is that, in the main, homosexuals see no iniquity in it. And no wonder, when we read in the public press that a body styling itself 'The Progressive League' has expressed the view that, while recognising the need to protect minors, it

---

* Magistrate E. R. Guest, who heard the John Gielgud case in 1953, claimed he was hearing 600 cases a year. Given that, according to the Wolfenden Report, in 1953 there were 2,267 cases where court action was taken, it seems highly unlikely that 26% of all cases in England and Wales would turn up in front of the one magistrate at the one court.

† This practice was universally condemned and campaigned against by gay rights activists, but it did have one positive output. Following the law of unintended consequences, if addresses of alleged participants in a homosexual 'vice ring' appeared in the press, it meant that other isolated homosexuals in the locality now knew not only the names of other homosexuals, but also where they lived. As a result some men after conviction received letters from gay readers of the paper, with maybe a coded invitation to meet. They might even find one of the more reckless readers on the door step, though it was a high risk strategy to invite them in because of the possibility of police entrapment.

nevertheless calls for an amendment to the law so that homosexual practices shall not constitute a legal offence.* … In which direction do they suggest we should 'progress' if we legalised practices from which minors should be protected? The police know only too well the evils that would flow from such 'progress'.[68]

Celebrity court cases

In London, the Wildeblood arrest, and along with it that of Edward Montagu, third Baron Montagu of Beaulieu, and the Dorset landowner Michael Pitt-Rivers, was but the last in a series of high-profile celebrity busts. Nearly all were solo court appearances, or duos with their sex partner of the time.

Sir John Gielgud was perhaps the most famous, being arrested on 21 October 1953 for persistently importuning in a public lavatory in Chelsea. He got away lightly, under a false name and occupation,† with a fine of £10; but the police tipped off the Evening Standard and he was front page news. Gielgud was faced with the sack from the play he was rehearsing, until his brother Val applied some discreet blackmail on the producer, Binkie Beaumont, about his own private life.‡ It was left to Dame Sybil Thorndyke to rehabilitate him, when she led him onto the stage at the first night of *A Day by the Sea* in Liverpool, and orchestrated a standing ovation.§ It was in many ways Gielgud's case which spurred on the moral backlash, led by John Gordon in the *Sunday Express*, because he got off lightly, and because his career didn't suffer: 'In future the nation might suitably mark its abhorrence of this type of depravity by stripping from men involved in such cases any honours that have been bestowed on them.'[69]

Gielgud, author Rupert Croft-Cooke, Labour MP W. J. Field (who had to resign his seat), mathematician Alan Turing (who killed himself), the fifth Baronet Mowbray – all got their share of column inches. And although it was ordinary lower- and middle-class men whose lives were ruined in large numbers, it was the high profile cases of the well-known which generated outrage among the governing classes, and led to the setting up of the Wolfenden Committee. Wildeblood in *Against the Law* suggests that his and

---

* It is not clear why Captain Popkess caught up with the Progressive League twenty years late.

† *The Times* reported his case, with a straight face, as being that of 'Arthur Gielgud, clerk'. Allegedly, when Alec Guinness was similarly charged in 1946 in Liverpool, he used the name of his most recent film character, Herbert Pocket.

‡ Gielgud's partner, the glamorous John Perry, had previously left him for Beaumont.

§ This did not prevent Gielgud from having a nervous breakdown during the run, and leaving the cast after five months.

Montagu's trial were directly responsible for Wolfenden, but such an enquiry, particularly over such a then-controversial issue, would not have been produced out of a hat; there is evidence that the proposal for an enquiry was being developed in the Home Office throughout the autumn of 1953.

MPs Sir Robert Boothby, himself bisexual, and Desmond Donnelly,* pressed for an enquiry in the wake of these trials during an adjournment debate in the House of Commons, after the wheels were already in motion for an enquiry; when Home Secretary Maxwell Fyfe next met Boothby, he said, 'I am not going down to history as the man who made sodomy legal.'[70] Either he didn't know what his officials were doing behind his back, or he was party to it, seeing an enquiry as a way of kicking the issue into the long grass. For kick it into the long grass he did. When the Wolfenden Committee reported in 1957, Lord Longford prodded the government to take up its recommendations. Maxwell Fyfe, now Viscount Kilmuir and Lord Chancellor, replied:

> Her Majesty's Government do not think that the general sense of the community is with the Committee in this recommendation, and therefore they think that the problem requires further study. … Certainly there can be no prospect of early legislation on this subject.[71]

This first liberalising crack in the ice was one of many manifestations of a society becoming less rigid. As such it was also connected to the rise in youth culture and the increased economic power of teenagers; the invention of 'the homosexual' as a consumer in the 1970s had much in common with the invention of the teenager and 'youth culture' in the 1950s. It is emblematic of the changing times that in the week that the Wolfenden Committee first met, the Number One in the Hit Parade was Frank Sinatra crooning *Three Coins in the Fountain*. In the week that it reported, Buddy Holly was singing *That'll Be The Day*. Easy listening gave way to rock, conformity to transgression.

Impact of *Against the Law*

Peter Wildeblood's memoir of his trial experience, published in 1955, was hugely influential during the long haul towards changing the law on male homosexual acts.† It was a key piece of evidence to the Wolfenden Enquiry,

---

* Boothby, who had been Winston Churchill's secretary in the 1920s, was a Conservative. His various affairs, and his association with East End gangsters, were kept out of the papers. Donnelly at this time was a Labour MP, but changed his party allegiance four times in his career, ending up advocating the abolition of the Welfare State and a return to National Service. He committed suicide in 1974.

† *Against the Law* had a considerable influence on many early gay activists. Michael Steed, a crucial figure in CHE in the early 1970s, cites it as one of the half-dozen books which influenced his life. —Interview with the author, 23 May 2011.

and Wildeblood himself was the only openly gay man to appear before the committee.*

Against the Law was probably the best-known work on male homosexuality, along with D. J. West's *Homosexuality*, that was available to gay men seeking to read about their 'condition' in the late 1950s and the 60s. More than that, it made Wildeblood an international celebrity. He was discussed at ICSE congresses, and congratulated on his bravery ('he now needs to wear his mask no more'). The president of the Mattachine Society sought him out when visiting London, trying to find a representative and a resident correspondent for *OUT*. They did not hit it off.

There are several reasons why *Against the Law* carried so much weight. Firstly, it nailed its colours to the mast very clearly right from the start:

> I am a homosexual. ... I am in the rare, perhaps privileged, position of having nothing left to hide. My only concern is that some good may come at last out of so much evil. ... I do not pity myself, and I do not ask for pity, trusting that ... I can give some hope and courage to other men like myself, and to the rest of the world some understanding.[72]

It was difficult not to give such apparent honesty a respectful hearing, notwithstanding that it is an honesty which omits quite a lot. For example, in his desire to 'tell the truth about myself', he also wanted others to tell sometimes dangerous truths as well. He stood accused of buggering an airman; he himself knew this was a physical impossibility – and he wanted Patrick Trevor-Roper, who had shagged him, to testify as much:

> I knew Wildeblood quite well, and had a modest affair with him before. ... He was brought around by Ken Tynan, the man who you may remember did *Oh Calcutta!*. To see if I as a doctor could advise in relation to the fact that he was, as I had occasion to know, very passive in his sexuality. ... Anyway he was accused of buggering, which he said was just physically not possible. But of course there was no conceivable way I could give evidence of that, except if I said that in my personal experience he was incapable of

* Two other men known to the Committee to be gay also testified: Patrick Trevor-Roper was a Harley Street eye surgeon and brother of historian Hugh Trevor-Roper. He went on to be a founder member of the Terrence Higgins Trust. Carl Winter was director of the Fitzwilliam Museum in Cambridge, a last-minute substitute for novelist Angus Wilson. Wilson and Trevor-Roper seem to have planned the action to appear before the Committee as 'normal' homosexuals, either because they thought Wildeblood's testimony would be taken as special pleading as a result of his conviction; or that he would give a 'bad' image of homosexuals. Winter and Trevor-Roper testified to the Committee under conditions of confidentiality, using pseudonyms, and do not appear in Appendix 4 of the Wolfenden Report, which lists witnesses. Only Wildeblood was publicly identified. The ICSE offered to give evidence to the Wolfenden Committee but were rebuffed.

> doing this, they'd just say, well, you weren't exciting enough. It was no good.[73]

The idea that a cross-examining barrister would have the sang-froid to enter into discussion of how hot a homosexual lover Trevor-Roper was, is disingenuous to say the least. But it would have meant a very public coming out. No wonder he was scared. Wildeblood does not mention the way he desperately scraped round for a defence. He had to find a different way of facing his accusers.

Nevertheless, *Against the Law* was extremely well written, and, with a journalist's eye for detail, shone a light into murky corners where Middle England had never looked, and would probably have preferred not to look:

> One night when I had been working late at the office, I was walking along the Brompton Road towards my flat. Outside a closed public house in a side turning I noticed two men loitering. A man aged about seventy, with white hair, walked past them and went into a lavatory at the side of the public house. He was followed in by the younger of the two men. Almost immediately there was a sound of scuffling and shouting, and the older of the two … also ran into the lavatory. He and his companion dragged the old man out, each holding him by an arm. He was struggling and crying.
>
> My first thought was that they must be local 'roughs' who were trying to rob the old man, so I went towards them and shouted at them to let him go, or I would call the police.
>
> The younger man said, 'We are Police Officers.'
>
> A woman who had joined us on the street corner asked what the old man had done, and was told that he had been 'making a nuisance of himself'. He had now begun to struggle violently, and the two detectives pushed him up against the railings of the Cancer Hospital outside which we were standing. His head became wedged between two iron spikes, and he started to scream. The detectives asked if one of us would ring up Chelsea Police Station and ask for a van to be sent: 'They'll know what it's about.'
>
> The woman said: 'You can do your own dirty work, damn you.' It seemed to me, however, that the old man might be seriously injured if he continued to struggle, so … I telephoned the police station. … The van arrived almost immediately. The old man, who by this time was lying on the pavement in a pool of blood, was picked up and taken away.'[74]

The nub of the argument in Wildeblood is about love and affection, not sex. The key evidence in his trial was in love letters written to Eddie McNally, the young serviceman who turned Queen's Evidence and shopped him to the police. Wildeblood acknowledged these feelings, while at the same time showing contempt for the man who betrayed him: 'I remembered the loneliness and misery of the nights when I had written them, and my desperate hope that I could find, even in McNally, someone with whom to share my life.'[75] Wildeblood was scathing about those who didn't fit in with his idealised image of the love-sick homosexual – the 'pathetically flamboyant' pansies, the lovers of boys, the frequenters of the homosexual underworld.

The cumulative effect is to create a picture of 'the homosexual' as ordinary, with 'normal' feelings exactly paralleling those of 'the heterosexual'. Wildeblood emphasises that gay men come from all trades, and all classes of society. The rest of the world passes them in the street without noticing, and there is no sign of the 'maladjustment' so beloved of psychiatrists of the time. Paradoxically, there was, among members of the Wolfenden Committee, an unspoken assumption about what was a 'normal' homosexual. For the Committee, 'normal' meant upper class, or at least of the same class as Committee members. There were social ties between those who testified and those hearing the testimony. Others who wanted to testify were excluded as 'eccentric', 'cranks', or contaminated by the 'seamier side of things'.

The division between the 'respectable' and 'disreputable' homosexual made in evidence to the Committee is the same one, derived from 'invert' and 'pervert,' which will echo in many guises down the years through gay history. It dominated the debate up to the passing of the Sexual Offences Act 1967. It is the distinction between 'gay' and 'queer', between the Campaign for Homosexual Equality (CHE) and the Gay Liberation Front (GLF), between Stonewall and Outrage.*

Within CHE there have always been those who wished to embrace the rights of all deviants to deviate in their own chosen ways, as opposed to other members who attempted to define CHE's constituency by exclusion – it was not the organisation of the people who pick up men in toilets, nor the people who have sex with men under the legal age of consent, nor sadomasochists, nor transgendered people. Similar oppositions occurred on the international stage, in ILGA,† over the issue of paedophile organisation membership. These oppositions, which are sometimes creative, will surface regularly in this history.

The class issue was also extremely important in the 1950s, as one of the many myths surrounding homosexuality was that it was the pastime of the idle rich, who corrupted working class lads. John Gordon said as much explicitly in his Current Events column in the *Sunday Express*:

> An emotional crusade seems to be developing to legalise perversion and even to sanctify perverts. ... STUFF AND NONSENSE. Perversion is very largely the practice of the too idle and the too rich. It does not

---

* Stonewall is a UK lobbying organisation founded in 1989; Outrage is a UK LGBT direct action group founded in 1990 as a reaction to Stonewall.

† International Lesbian and Gay Association.

> flourish in lands where men work hard and brows sweat with honest labour.[76]

This was also raised at the Wildeblood trial, at the crucial moment when Wildeblood made his coming-out statement. The prosecution's language was straight out of the nineteenth century:

> Then Mr Roberts [prosecuting counsel] began talking about homosexuals, inverts and perverts, in a sudden access of scientific zeal. …You could see his trick questions coming a mile off, like flying bombs. I said, 'I think we all ought to agree on some kind of vocabulary. If I say somebody is a homosexual I am not necessarily implying that they indulge in criminal actions.'
>
> Mr Roberts brushed this aside and went on talking about inverts and perverts. I knew what he was leading up to. He faced me squarely, peering up at me under his wig, and demanded: 'Your character has been put in at its highest, and I agree in every way – nothing has ever been brought against your character. You can hold your head high. But you are an invert?'
>
> 'Yes, I am an invert.'
>
> 'It is a feature, is it not, that inverts or perverts seek their love associates in a different walk of life than their own? … I mean, for instance, McNally was infinitely – he is none the worse for it – but infinitely your social inferior?'…
>
> 'Nobody ever flung it at me during the War that I was associating with people who were infinitely my social inferiors.'[77]

The class element played a part in the formation of CHE, as contrasted with the HLRS.

Wildeblood's self-definition as an invert was also a defence. The invert could not help himself, all the experts agreed. He was, in a sense, not responsible for his actions. He was 'incurable'. Yet Wildeblood also drew distinctions between his kind of invert and the effeminate. If he was an invert, he was a 'normal' invert.

Wildeblood also developed the 'normality' argument in characterising the homophobes, effectively asking, 'Who is normal?' Writing about public reaction to his conviction, he deliberately invokes echoes of Oscar Wilde's ordeal by crowd on the platform at Clapham Junction. His is another monstrous martyrdom:

> That night, a woman spat at me. She was a respectable-looking, middle-aged tweedy person wearing a sensible felt hat. She was standing on the pavement as the car went by. I saw her suck in her cheeks, and the next moment a big blob of spit was running down the windscreen. This shocked me very much. The woman did not look eccentric or evil; in fact she looked very much like the country gentlewomen with whom my

> mother used to take coffee when she had finished her shopping on Saturday mornings. She looked thoroughly ordinary, to me. But what did I look like to her? Evidently I was a monster. I was quite sure that she had never spat at anyone in her life before. And yet, she had hated me enough to do this.[78]

Rupert Croft-Cooke

All Wildeblood's very considerable journalistic skills were brought into play, and one of the ways of measuring his effectiveness is to compare *Against the Law* with Rupert Croft-Cooke's *The Verdict of You All*, the other contemporary gay-written memoir of prosecution in the 1950s.

6. Rupert Croft-Cooke

Croft-Cooke's case paralleled Wildeblood's almost exactly. The locale for the alleged offences was identical – country house parties to which young men were invited from a variety of backgrounds, and often with armed services' connections. The police raid took place even earlier (2 a.m.), and each had a manservant who was also hauled off to the nick. G. D. Roberts, invariably known as 'Khaki', defended Croft-Cooke but prosecuted Wildeblood.

The charges were the same, indecency, Croft-Cooke's sentence half the length (nine months). Both men ended in Wormwood Scrubs, followed by Brixton prison, and the prison sections of their books highlight the same appalling conditions, and indeed feature several of the same prison characters. Although Croft-Cooke was convicted the year before Wildeblood, their books appeared almost simultaneously.

Croft-Cooke, however, was a coward. As soon as he was released, he fled to Tangier:

> I resolved to keep only my most intimate possessions and live in a country in which there was an adult and unpuritanical view of the way in which a man could conduct his own life.[79]

He also persistently claimed that the sexual offences charges, of which he protested his innocence, were merely a hook on which to hang small-town prejudices against his 'bohemian lifestyle'. He blamed:

> My own open and perhaps – as I see now – somewhat defiant way. Defiant not of law but of convention. …
>
> All I had sought to do was to live, eat, drink, laugh and make friends in ways of my own choosing. I had filled my home with cheerful young people indiscriminately chosen for their own qualities from among writers, politicians, gypsies, the services and the underworld. This had not pleased the residents in the more pretentious local houses, who were for the most part of the impoverished middle classes, pathetically clinging to the bourgeois traditions of an earlier age.[80]

This sneering assumption of superiority did not play well, and in some ways played to the prejudices of contemporary bigots – homosexuals as a secret society demanding special treatment for antisocial behaviour. It also seemed evasive and untrue – a man who picks up a serviceman in Piccadilly Circus and invites him to his country house, paying him money for fares in advance, is not likely to do so because he likes his conversation or his philosophy.

Croft-Cooke decided against an appeal, although still protesting he was not 'queer':

> Since mud always sticks, I realised, not without some amusement, that even after the charges had been thrown out, I should never escape from the reputation of a homosexual. … The fight is now for others, I have had enough.'[81]

No wonder that Wildeblood was not only the more liked; he was also the more credible campaigner. Though *Against the Law* contains its own evasions and untruths, they conform to what liberal people wanted to hear. Wildeblood now has something of a reputation as an Uncle Tom figure, but it is worth remembering both the constraints on self-definition around at the time, and also the sense that effective campaigning meant pitching the argument at the level of the listener. He was not the last reformer who would use such tactics.

Once released, he wrote *Against the Law* in white heat over less than four months, followed by a sequel,* and, in quick succession, by three novels of

* *A Way of Life* (1956).

Soho life, which played on, but never capitalised on, his low-life experiences as a gay man. Copies of his prison memoir were rushed to the fifteen members of the Wolfenden Committee, who were undoubtedly influenced by his forensic demolition of the supposed objectives of the supporters of the existing law, and the purposes of criminalisation. His arguments turn up in almost the same wording in the Wolfenden Report:

> I do not believe that a homosexual can be transformed into heterosexual overnight by the shock of prosecution and imprisonment. The most that can be expected is that he will, while still experiencing an attraction towards his own sex, refrain from giving way to it again. On the other hand, I have never met a homosexual who has resolved to mend his ways as a result of being imprisoned.[82]

Wolfenden Report

The Wolfenden Committee deliberated for sixty-two days, hearing witnesses on thirty-two of those. The members of the committee were drawn from left and right, churchmen, psychiatrists, academics, and the Vice President of the Glasgow Girl Guides. They were in no sense experts, they did no research, and those witnesses who were experts presented very scrappy accounts. Julian Huxley and Miriam Rothschild,* both highly respected scientists, sent in a couple of disorganised pages[83] which offered no evidence, only random thoughts.† Sir John Wolfenden himself, who lived with the secret knowledge that his own son Jeremy was homosexual and dreaded being discredited if this was discovered,‡ had a strong if unspoken sympathy for the homosexual's fear of blackmail. For two years he chivvied his charges towards a united front in their final report.

Despite this, there were three dissenting reports. Four committee members objected to singling out buggery for special treatment; two doctors on the committee wanted lower maximum sentences (two years instead of ten) for indecent assault; but all the dissenting members toed the party line on the

---

* Julian Huxley, brother of Aldous, was a cell biologist, first director of UNESCO and founder of the World Wildlife Fund; Miriam Rothschild was a zoologist and botanist, who also pioneered new approaches to schizophrenia.

† They made a joint submission, supported by a memo from the Institute of Biology, to the effect that homosexuality occurred in a range of other species from sheep to hamsters.

‡ It is noticeable that Wolfenden treats Wildeblood with barely concealed dislike and the most perfunctory introduction when he comes to testify. This is usually put down to distaste for a convicted criminal. In the light of the previous history of Wildeblood and Patrick Trevor-Roper, Wolfenden's favouritism becomes deeply ironic.

proposed age of consent – 21; only John Adair, former Procurator Fiscal for Glasgow, remained vehemently opposed to legalisation in any form.* It remains something of a mystery why the report, which is short, contains little new and is so timid, took so long to produce.

7. Sir John Wolfenden

The level of ignorance among witnesses was extraordinary. One thought that homosexual acts were currently legal and urged the committee to recommend banning them. However the most significant oppositional voice, in that it came from an organisation representing a group of people who could and did have a profound influence on the lives of homosexual women and men, was from the British Medical Association. The report they submitted in evidence to the Wolfenden Committee seems to have no medical basis whatsoever. It admitted that 'Homosexuals are often charming and friendly people, and many of them are well known to be of artistic temperament,' but nevertheless:

> Not only are their actual practices repulsive but the behaviour and appearance of homosexuals congregating blatantly in public houses, streets

* In his minority report, Adair wrote: 'The presence in a district of, for example, adult male lovers living openly and notoriously under the approval of the law is bound to have a regrettable and pernicious effect on the young people of the community.' He was correct about the power of example, though from our point of view, thinking of gay teenagers' need for role models, it is a wholly beneficial effect.

> and restaurants are an outrage to public decency. Effeminate men wearing make-up and using scent are objectionable to everyone.[84]

The BMA objected to relaxing the law but insisted they had the solution to homosexuality. Homosexuals would be cured if they found God. The medical basis for this prescription is unclear.

The Wolfenden report, published in September 1957, called for the decriminalisation of sex between consenting adult males in private, adult being defined as over 21. The Committee also took a firm, if controversial, line that the law had no place in enforcing or upholding morality in private behaviour:

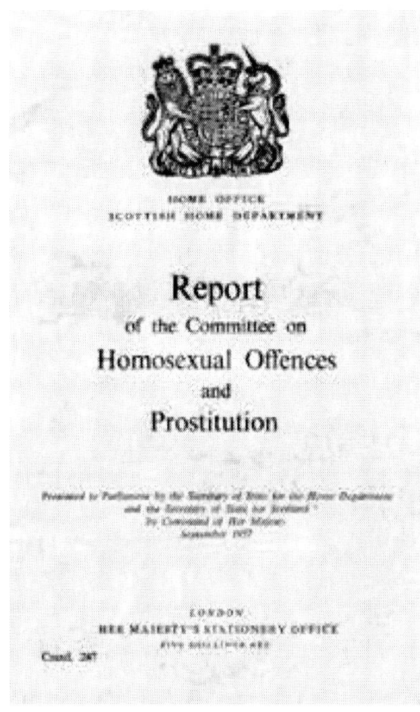

HOME OFFICE
SCOTTISH HOME DEPARTMENT

Report
of the Committee on
Homosexual Offences
and
Prostitution

LONDON
HER MAJESTY'S STATIONERY OFFICE

8. The Wolfenden Report

> The law's function is to preserve public order and decency, to protect the citizen from what is offensive or injurious, and to provide sufficient safeguards against exploitation and corruption of others. … It is not, in our view, the function of the law to intervene in the private life of citizens, or to seek to enforce any particular pattern of behaviour.[85]

Overall there were thirty-one recommendations, including one that would put a 'statute of limitations' on prosecutions for offences over a year old, and one which required the Director of Public Prosecutions to authorise all trials for gross indecency, thus ironing out inconsistencies in applying the law around the country. However, not all recommendations were in the direction of liberalisation. Proponents of the reforms were quick to offer a sop to the bayers for blood by pointing out that, where a man over 21 had sex with someone under 21, penalties would be doubled.

However, having commissioned the report, David Maxwell Fyfe, now Lord Chancellor (as Viscount Kilmuir), was determined to do nothing about it. The first Parliamentary debate on the Report, the first of no fewer than seven, was initiated by Lord Pakenham, later to become better known as Lord Longford, Aunt Sally of the gay movement for his obsession with pornography. On 4 December 1957 he told the House of Lords:

> When we reflect on what torture is being suffered by many decent citizens, along with others less respectable, of course, I hope that we remember the injunction, 'Blessed are the merciful'. One day this change will be wrung from us without, if it were long delayed, much credit to anybody. Let us take advantage of a point in time, while it is still in our power to do the civilised thing.[86]*

The debate lasted six hours; support for Wolfenden was led by the Archbishop of Canterbury, who had changed his mind over the previous four years. Perhaps surprisingly, he endorsed the Report's distinction between sin and crime:

> In general, however, a sin is not made a crime until it becomes a cause of public offence, although it remains a sin whether or not it be a crime. That is obvious enough but great numbers of people, having lost the sense of sin, have lost sight of this distinction, and it is most valuable that this Report should cast the limelight once more upon it.[87]

But perhaps the sanest, most humane speech came from the pioneering aviator and Cresta Run champion, 73-year-old Lord Brabazon of Tara:

> When we speak about the repugnance and disgust of the [homosexual] act we have to face the fact that all sexual intercourse, be it heterosexual or homosexual, if it is looked at anatomically and physiologically, is not very attractive. But along comes the glamour of love; and that is a mystical, creative, Divine force which comes over two people and makes all things seem natural and normal. And what we have to get into our heads, although it is difficult, is that that glamour of love, odd as it may sound, is just as much present between two homosexuals as it is between a man and a woman.[88]

---

* Later Longford was to oppose all further movement towards gay rights. He supported the introduction of Section 28, and opposed an equal age of consent. 'If someone seduced my daughter it would be damaging and horrifying but not fatal. She would recover, marry and have lots of children (as some such people do). On the other hand, if some elderly, or not so elderly, schoolmaster seduced one of my sons and taught him to be a homosexual, he would ruin him for life.'

—Hansard HL Deb 22 July 1998 vol. 592.

Brabazon was to be an energetic lobbyist behind the scenes for reform until his death in 1964, though he declined to be publicly identified with the HLRS.

Homosexuals and liberal heterosexuals had assumed that Wolfenden would be acted upon. But the Lords debate led nowhere. There was no sign of anything happening, and it became clear that if there was to be any action in Parliament, MPs and indeed Government would need to be prodded into it. What was needed was a catalyst to draw like-minded people together. It was not long in coming.

While Wolfenden and his colleagues were deliberating, and even after their report appeared, levels of convictions and imprisonment for homosexual offences continued to run into four figures per year. Police methods remained much the same – use of attractive young constables to entrap the unwary in toilets; trawling through address books of those picked up in order to find others in 'vice rings.'

Robert Reid

One such exercise was in Somerset. Dr R. D. Reid, a member of Wells City Council and a former public school headmaster, was so disgusted by the sight of consenting adults being dragged through the courts and pilloried in the press that he wrote a letter to the *Spectator*, which appeared on 3 January 1958:

> The pogroms … continue, one in this neighbourhood having started with long and weary police-court proceedings on the eve of Christmas, so that the Festival may presumably be spent in contemplation of the Spring Assize. And this for a lad of seventeen. The pattern is much the same in all these cases. The police go round from house to house, bringing ruin in their train, always attacking the youngest men first, extracting information with lengthy questioning and specious promises of light sentences, as they proceed from clue to clue, i.e. from home to home. This time the age range is seventeen to forty, which is about the average. Last time a man of thirty-seven dropped dead in the dock at Assize. Just because this happens in country places and at country assizes, it all goes largely unreported. We had hoped that it might be finished, but if it is to continue we desperately need some society to afford support and comfort to the victims and their families.[89]

'We' might be assumed to be a charitable liberal (presumed heterosexual) consensus. But Dr Reid had form. He had been convicted of importuning in 1936, and his reaction to his experience, which cost him his job and left him having to live off the rent from three small cottages, was to start campaigning. In 1938 he lobbied the Archbishops of Canterbury and York, urging that the church could not give homosexuals the pastoral care they deserved if the only advice was 'control yourself', with no indication as to how this was be achieved by frail man. More remarkably he gave in 1944 a lecture which is in effect the first set of modern demands to be articulated by a declared homosexual on behalf of all other homosexuals. In a lecture to the Prison Medical Reform Council he declared:

9. Dr R. D. Reid with Prince Amaha Desta, grandson of Emperor Haile Selassie, at King's College Taunton in 1937. The Emperor regularly gave out the school prizes on speech day.

> What do homosexuals want? Firstly, a repeal of the life sentence provision. Secondly reform of the law so that they suffer exactly the same penalties for sexual offences as their heterosexual brothers. Thirdly, a reform of police methods, including the even administration of the existing law. … Fourthly, they ask for public sympathy and toleration, and assistance in framing a reasonable code of behaviour. The present system is a potent cause of crime, since as long as homosexuals are denied intercourse among themselves, they are driven on to the streets, into the less desirable public houses and worse places, and into the hands of the blackmailer.[90]

Reid is primarily concerned with the working of the criminal law in relation to sex offences, but beyond that, he is also concerned, as a committed Christian, with the right to a moral life, and thus defining the homosexual man as more than the sum of his gonads. His conception of what it means to be homosexual is struggling towards a larger vision, and his language has extraordinary force and elegance, which was much in evidence in his correspondence to the papers.

It is worth noting at this stage that the early support for gay rights, at least in the limited sense of decriminalisation of male gay sex, came largely from, in addition to the Church, the political right, and the impetus came from heterosexuals. The *Spectator* was edited by Ian Gilmour, who was to become the arch-'wet' in the Thatcher years. This was the weekly magazine for the thinking Tory, and it became the platform for arguing the implementation of Wolfenden, with occasional forays into *The Times*. The *New Statesman*, on the opposite wing,* featured homosexual law reform comparatively rarely, though there was no doubt where its heart lay. Notable early supporters of implementing Wolfenden included the new MP for Finchley, Margaret Thatcher, and Nicholas Ridley, whose department was later responsible for bringing Section 28 to the Statute Book. In the 1960s Ridley was one of the sponsors of Private Members' Bills to decriminalise homosexual acts.

In the weeks that followed there were letters from E. M. Forster, Boothby, and a number of others, mainly agreeing with Reid. Among them was one from Peter Wildeblood. His contributions to the correspondence got rather bogged down in statistics and the finer points of Hansard's parliamentary reporting, but he did include his full address at the bottom of his letters: 30 St Paul's Road, Canonbury, N1. This was indeed brave – 'here's a homosexual and this is where he lives.' And it was to have consequences.

Dr Reid clearly had in mind a social welfare organisation for prisoners and their families, with little political dimension, but it was not long before the idea of an organisation widened in scope. A mere week later, a young assistant lecturer in English at Bangor University, A. E. (Tony) Dyson, also wrote:

> I agree very much with Dr Reid's letter, and would gladly belong to any society that existed to help the victims and their families of our homosexuality laws. But even more to the point would be the formation of a society concerned to work for a change in the laws themselves. …
>
> The present situation seems to be this. The fact that some people are homosexual is not in dispute, and it is generally recognised that if left to solve their moral problems in private, they would stand as much chance as anyone else of being decent and useful members of the community. The Wolfenden Committee has recommended a change in the law by a decisive majority of twelve to one,† and the responsible press has in general supported this recommendation, often in very strong terms. The conscience of the community as a whole is against the persecution of individuals simply because, through no fault of their own, they belong to a minority, and the Wolfenden Committee undoubtedly represents the good sense and humanity of most normal people.

---

* This characterisation of the two magazines as Left and Right is slightly simplistic, in that conservatives did sometimes write for the *NS* and socialists for the *Spectator*. Many people interested in politics bought both magazines, which each had much higher circulations than today.

† Two members of the Committee resigned in 1956, leaving thirteen members.

> All of which notwithstanding, the police round-ups continue, the advocates of the present law still regard themselves as instruments of moral justice, and the Government shows every sign of ignoring the findings of the Committee, which strong public opinion forced it to set up in the first place. Is it not time, therefore, that those who feel strongly on this issue should work together and attempt to make more widely known the compulsive moral and rational reasons in favour of a change in the law?[91]

Tony Dyson and the HLRS

Dyson was gay, and just turning 30. In this he was an almost exact contemporary of both Antony Grey and Allan Horsfall who were to carry his torch forward. He was also a very committed Christian, a lay preacher who later became a Canon of the Church of England, and one of the foremost English scholars of his generation. One gets the impression of an impatient, restless man, who must always be Doing.

Even as this initiative of homosexual law reform was getting off the ground, he was laying the groundwork for the magazine Critical Quarterly, which he co-edited for thirty years with C. B. Cox and was – is still – probably the most important cultural studies magazine in the country.

> My hope had been that a change of law, if accomplished, would return the subject to the realm of private life. I was concerned with liberty to live, work – without fear, without persecution – restoring normality to men who differed only in sexual orientation from their fellows.[92]

He seems to have had little sexual experience himself before making this exposed and then-dangerous commitment, his faith binding him to the pursuit of love rather than sex. It took the campaign he was initiating now, and the setting up of the first HLRS office in Liverpool Road in Islington, for him to come into contact with Camden local councillor, Cliff Tucker. They fell in love almost immediately, and set up home together in Hampstead, where they lived monogamously, at least on Dyson's part,* until Tucker's death in 1993.

Dyson was a high Tory of strong monarchist bent.† His motivation seems to have been fuelled, in addition to the libertarian concern with the protection of privacy, by Christian ideals of charity and love, and the deep conviction that those who conducted persecutions were as damaged by it as the persecuted:

---

* A letter from Antony Grey (17 October 1976) hints at Dyson's occasional unhappiness —HCA/DYSON/3.

† He refers to the 'martyred' King Charles I, and Cromwell's 'fanatical puritan generals' in his audio tutorial on poet Andrew Marvell. —BSA 29E NORWICH [20] 01.

10. Tony Dyson

> There was the persecution of adult human beings for private and chosen sexual behaviour, the disorder embodied in the law. During the campaign for reform the sponsors received various abusive letters, some of them merely obscene or coarsely brutal and clearly from people who were casualties themselves. But some came from people who were aware of being in whole or in part homosexual, and who felt that the law gave them some measure of protection from themselves. Some were from good-living family men who were often personally sorry for homosexuals, but feared that deviant sex was too dangerous to be tolerated by law. There were letters one could respect from parents who feared that if the law were relaxed, their own children might become inverts; there were letters from parents horrified to find this was actually so. I recall two parents who accepted that their 22-year-old son had been rightly imprisoned for loving physically a man of his own age and temperament, but thought the two-year sentence dangerously short.
>
> Is any of this in tune with the mind of Christ?[93]

Dyson began with a round-robin letter, asking for signatories to a draft letter to *The Times*. He mainly targeted actors, writers and academics he knew personally, doctors and psychiatrists, and bishops. Some of his targets reveal a naivety which shows a campaign virgin at work – no Government minister or Opposition spokesman was going to commit himself to homosexual law reform in a million years. Indeed, there is a wide-eyed innocent optimism about Dyson, which can also be detected in his voice, a slightly lisped drawl which nowadays we would call camp as Christmas. It was as if the demand for gay rights were being kicked off by Eric Blore, the comedy butler of those Fred Astaire and Ginger Rogers movies. There were rebuffs from figures as diverse as Sir Malcolm Sargent, chief conductor of the Promenade Concerts, who didn't believe that persecution happened:

> There are many things which have not been repealed but have simply gone out of use. The carrying of a red flag in front of a motor car is still a necessity but I have not seen anyone doing it lately. … To make the offence legal is more or less telling youth that it is no bad thing – rather like telling a boy he may smoke when he is twenty-one.[94]

and actor Donald Wolfit: 'I do not believe this sort of approach can serve any useful purpose. How *can* you avoid the controversial issue of sinfulness?'[95] Many objected to a reference to the Oxford Union in the letter, and it was dropped from the published version.* Recently-deposed Prime Minister Anthony Eden refused 'under strict medical advice'.[96] Nevertheless, when it appeared, on 7 March 1958, the call for Wolfenden to be implemented had thirty-three signatures, including the old Labour Prime Minister Clement Attlee, Bertrand Russell, J. B. Priestley and his wife Jacquetta Hawkes.† Among those who wrote to Dyson was Peter Wildeblood:

> I have for some time past been collecting the names of possible sponsors for such an organisation as yours. …
>
> I am entirely in favour of such a step provided that the 'Board' is really representative – preponderance of clergymen, psychiatrists or professional do-gooders (or indeed of homosexuals) would not be a good thing, though all of these categories should play their part. I am sure that Dr Reid would make an admirable chairman.
>
> My time is rather limited, but I do try to join in anything that looks productive, and I've been in touch with a good many prominent people about the Wolfenden Report, including recently the Archbishop of Canterbury, Lord Brabazon and J. B. Priestley and Jacquetta Hawkes. I've also made speeches to the Oxford Union, the Cambridge Liberal Society, the Haldane Society, the London University Debating Society, the Socialist Medical Association, the 'Grecians' at the Royal Society of Medicine, the Progressive League and the Islington Literary Society! Also articles in various magazines and letters to the *Telegraph*, *News Chronicle*, *Tablet* and *Spectator* which you've probably seen.
>
> More power to your elbow, and please let me know if there's anything I can do. Plenty of my correspondents have asked to be informed if any organisation was to be set up. …
>
> PS I'm also in touch with international organisations‡ in the US, Germany, France and Holland, which might be useful.[97]

---

* 'I don't think an undergraduate society, particularly such a frivolous one, can seriously count among the 'organs of informed public opinion.' A. J. Ayer (HCA/DYSON/1/12).

† Hawkes herself experienced strong lesbian feelings towards 'Amelia' (pseudonym) prior to her marriage with Priestley, although it is uncertain if these were consummated.
—*A Quest of Love*, 1980.

‡ See page 55. Wildeblood introduced the ICSE to the HLRS.

While there is an element of boastfulness here, of establishing credentials as 'Mr Gay Rights', there is also an energy, support and enthusiasm which the lone wolf Dyson desperately needed. There was no doubt Wildeblood was wholeheartedly committed. Most importantly, he contributed the most useful thing any journalist could bring to any campaign – his contact book.

11. Some who signed up in support of the HLRS: Michael Ramsey, Archbishop of York (Later Archbishop of Canterbury); Sir Julian Huxley, Scientist and Humanist; Earl Attlee, former Prime Minister

The approaches to the (presumably heterosexual) great and good continued. Which of the signatories were prepared to put their sweat behind their sentiments? It was becoming increasingly clear that few would be prepared to contribute more than their name on a letterhead, so the idea emerged of a two-tier organisation, involving an Executive Committee and an Honorary Committee. Wildeblood got to work with Dyson, rounding members up. Frank Pakenham (later Lord Longford) wrote to Dyson:

> Peter Wildeblood telephoned me this morning to say that you have not heard from me in answer to your very kind invitation to join the committee. …
>
> My Wife and I discussed the matter at great length during the weekend, and finally it seemed best that she should accept your invitation to join and that I should stay outside at this stage. …
>
> I feel, and I think that Peter Wildeblood saw the force of this, … that when the matter comes up again, I should probably be of more assistance if I was not regarded as the spokesman of an Organisation.[98]

By the time of the inaugural meeting of the HLRS, they had collected ninety-one honorary names for the letterhead.*

* Perhaps the most touching is the spidery scrawl of the 85-year-old composer Ralph Vaughan Williams, committing himself to the cause a mere three months before his death.

In some ways they were 'the usual suspects', the same kind of people who signed up to many a liberal-left cause at the time. The ninety-one members included Graham Greene, Maurice Bowra, Hardy Amies, publisher Victor Gollancz and Kenneth Tynan. It was a recurring criticism of the HLRS Honorary Committee, that it consisted of people who would put their name to anything, but they fulfilled the function of assuring the credibility of the organisation and the respectability of the arguments. The downside was that the HLRS was subsequently hampered by a sense of what it could and couldn't do, if it was to retain the support of the Honorary Committee.

The first meeting took place on 12 May 1958, at the Harley Street surgery of Dr Kenneth Walker. The 75-year-old Walker was both surgeon and psychologist, and was a pioneer 'sexologist' in the dark conformist days of the 1940s and 50s. He was to become Chairman of the HLRS and the Albany Trust for the next five years. There were only three people present, Walker, Dyson and Rev. A. Hallidie Smith, who would become the first secretary – Hawkes and Priestley sent their apologies. Their moment was well chosen. The objective was clear: law change. The lever was to hand: the Wolfenden Report. The incremental publicity of case after court case, and the increasing number of books which were appearing purporting to 'explain' homosexuality, all served to create a liberal, mainly heterosexual grouping disposed to bestir itself. Within a month, small ads had appeared in *The Times*, the *Daily Telegraph*, the *Daily Herald*, *Evening Standard*, *Sunday Times*, and *New Statesman*. In the first week there were 250 replies.

It was a grouping of the upper middle classes, especially from the South East. But small ads placed in the political weeklies and in the heavyweight nationals brought in additional enquiries and donations from all over the country. The HLRS had no membership, only supporters, which left the unelected Executive Committee, and its small staff, firmly in control. However it also left those outside of London with the feeling that they must Do Something, but frustrated as to what. No matter, one person was about to Do Something which would have far-reaching consequences.

Notes to Chapter One

1 Leila J Rupp, 'Persistence of Transnational Organising: The case of the homophile movement', *American Historical Review* 116/4 (2011), 1014-1039.

2 Seabrook, *A lasting relationship*, 177.

3 Ibid., 205.

4 Ibid., 166.

5 Young, Lewis and Donaldson, 'How ya gonna keep 'em down on the farm after they've seen Pa-ree?' (New York: Waterson, Berlin & Snyder, 1919).

6 Russo, *The celluloid closet.*

7 Ford and Tyler, *The young and evil*, 64.

8 Thomas Painter 'The homosexual' (1941), original typescript in Kinsey Institute Library, 18; cited in Clancy, *Gay New York*, 170.

[9] Alex Hill and J. M. Williams 'The stuff is here (Let's get gay)'. (New York: Northern Music, 1937).

[10] 'Jinis', 'GLF – What now?', *Come Together,* 5 (7 April 1971); 7 (July 1971).

[11] Allan Horsfall, interviewed by Jeff Evans, 9 March 2011. Tape in author's possession.

[12] Marshall, *Life's rich pageant*, 142.

[13] ICSE Archive in The Hague, cited by Leila J Rupp, 'Persistence of transnational organising: The case of the homophile movement', *American Historical Review*, 116/4 (2011), 1014-1039.

[14] Dent, *Mrs Patrick Campbell*, 78.

[15] Danny Brampton, 'Look to ourselves', *Lunch,* 2 (October 1971), 9-10.

[16] Mattachine Society membership pledge, 1950. Quoted in Alpert, *We are everywhere*, 284.

[17] 'Review of Michael Nelson's *A room in Chelsea Square*', *Der Kreis*, May 1960, 26.

[18] André Baudry, 'Mes chers amis', Arcadie circular, 1955. Cited in Jackson, *Living in Arcadia*, 11.

[19] United Nations *Universal Declaration of Human Rights*, 6 January 1948. www.un.org/en/documents/udhr, accessed 6 November 2014.

[20] Donald Webster Cory, Address to the ICSE Conference, Frankfurt, September 1952. Reprinted as 'Changing attitudes towards homosexuals', in Cory, *Homosexual outlook*, 431–441.

[21] Ibid., 7.

[22] *Der Kreis*, May/June 1951, 1, cited by Leila J Rupp, ibid.

[23] Grey, *Quest for justice*, 3.

[24] Nichols, *Father figure,* 112.

[25] Carpenter, *The intermediate sex*, 79.

[26] Quoted in Hyde, *The other love*, 107.

[27] Orwell, *The road to Wigan Pier*, 161.

[28] Donald Webster Cory, 'Changing attitudes towards homosexuals', in Cory, *Homosexuality: A cross-cultural approach.*

[29] Stuart Timmons, *The trouble with Harry Hay,* 28.

[30] Hyde, *The other love*, 107.

[31] Sigmund Freud, 'Letter to the mother of a homosexual', (1935), *American Journal of Psychiatry*, 107/10, (April 1951), 786–787.

[32] Carpenter, *The intermediate sex*, 57.

[33] Grey, *Quest for justice,* p.4

[34] '25 men in custody', *Altrincham, Bowden and Hale Guardian*, 31 July 1936, 6.

[35] Ibid.

[36] Ibid.

[37] Ibid.

[38] 'The Altrincham case: Two day hearing continues', *Altrincham, Bowden and Hale Guardian*, 7 August 1936, 7.

[39] Ibid.

[40] 'Seven years for Goldstraw', *Manchester Evening News*, 5 November 1936, 1, 5.

[41] 'Missing members of the gang: Altrincham case scandal', *Sunday Empire News*, 8 November 1936, 9.

[42] Allan Horsfall, 'The Altrincham lads'. *Gay life*, 5 (October 1986), 17, 19.

[43] R. D. Reid 'A human problem', *Daily Telegraph,* 2 November 1953, 6.

[44] 'A parish priest', 'A human problem', *Daily Telegraph*, 7 November 1953, 6.

[45] Church of England Moral Welfare Council, *The problem of homosexuality: An interim report* (London: Church Information Board, 1953), 13.

[46] İbid., 20.

[47] Most Rev. Geoffrey Fisher to Robert Reid, 'No to liberalisation'. 3 November 1953. HCA/EPH/1113

[48] E. M. Forster, 'A magistrate's figures', Ibid., 508–509.

[49] G. Gardiner, 'Society and the homosexual', *New Statesman and Nation*, 46/1183 (7 Nov 1953), 562.

[50] 'Scientist', Ibid, 563–564.

51 'A Lesbian', 'Society and the homosexual', *New Statesman and Nation*, 46/1185 (21 Nov 1953), 636.

52 'One of the anonymous', Ibid.

53 Grey, *Quest for justice*, 22–23; 38.

54 E. M. Forster, 'A magistrate's figures', *New Statesman and Nation*, 46/1182 (1953), 508–509.

55 'Appleby Assizes: Thirteen Kendal men accused', *Cumberland and Westmoreland Herald*, 17 January 1959, 2.

56 Wildeblood, *Against the law*, 55.

57 Donald Horne, 'Scotland Yard plan to smash homosexuality in London', *Sydney Morning Telegraph*, 25 October 1953, 7.

58 Higgins, *Heterosexual dictatorship*, 248.

59 Michael Steed, interviewed by the author, 23 May 2011

60 Douglas Warth, 'Evil men', *Sunday Pictorial*, 25 May 1952, 6.

61 Noel Pemberton-Billing, 'As I see it: The first 47,000', *The Imperialist*, 6/69 (26 January 1918), 3.

62 Douglas Warth, 'Evil men', *Sunday Pictorial*, 1 June 1952, 6.

63 Douglas Warth, 'Evil men', *Sunday Pictorial*, 8 June 1952, 12.

64 HC Deb 28 April 1954, vol. 526, col. 1751.

65 Dr Stanley Jones in the *British Medical Journal*, quoted by Boothby, ibid.

66 Douglas Warth, 'Evil men', *Sunday Pictorial*, 8 June 1952, 12.

67 C. G. Learoyd, 'The problem of homosexuality', *The Practitioner*, 172 (1030), 1954, 361.

68 Athelstan Popkess, 'Some criminal aspects of abnormalities of sex', *The Practitioner*, 172 (1030), 1954, 447–448.

69 John Gordon, 'Current events', *Sunday Express*, 25 October 1953, 6.

70 Boothby, *Recollections of a rebel*, 212.

71 HL Deb 4 December 1957 vol 206, col.763

72 Wildeblood, *Against the law*, 1.

73 Patrick Trevor Roper, interviewed by Margot Farnham, 1 August 1990. BSA C456/089/01-02.

74 Wildeblood, *Against the law*, 42–43.

75 Ibid., 67.

76 John Gordon, 'Current events', *Sunday Express*, 11 April 1954, 6.

77 Wildeblood, *Against the law*, 77.

78 Ibid., 84–85.

79 Croft-Cooke, *The verdict of you all*, 29.

80 Ibid., 12.

81 Ibid., 29, 88.

82 Wildeblood, *Against the law*, 183.

83 Julian Huxley and Miriam Rothschild, 'Submission to Wolfenden Committee', April 1955. HCA/DYSON/1.

84 British Medical Association, 'Evidence to the Wolfenden Committee'. HO/345/9/95.

85 Home Office and Scottish Home Department, Report of the Committee on Homosexual Offices and Prostitution, ['The Wolfenden Report'] (London: HMSO, 1957; Cmnd. 247), 10.

86 HL Deb 4 December 1957 vol. 206 col. 733.

87 HL Deb 4 December 1957 vol. 206 col. 754.

88 HL Deb 4 December 1957 vol. 206 col. 764.

89 'Vice Prosecutions', *Spectator*, 6758 (3 January 1958), 18.

90 Reid, *The Case of the homosexual.*

91 A. E. Dyson, 'Vice prosecutions', *Spectator*, 6759 (10 January 1958), 48.

92 A. E. Dyson, Covering note to Dyson archive, June 1990, HCA/DYSON/1.

93 Dyson, *Freedom in love*, 24–25.

94 Sir Malcolm Sargent to Tony Dyson, 'Refusal to sign', 18 February 1958. HCA/DYSON/1/8

[95] Donald Wolfit to A.E. Dyson, 'HLRS formation', 17 Feb 1958. HCA/ DYSON/1/6.

[96] Anthony Eden to A.E. Dyson, 'HLRS formation', 4 Mar 1958. HCA/ DYSON/1/28.

[97] Peter Wildeblood to A. E. Dyson, 'HLRS formation', 18 Mar 1958. HCA/DYSON/1/33.

[98] Frank Pakenham, 'Refusal to sponsor HLRS', 5 May 1958. HCA/ DYSON/2.

Chapter Two: North and South

Contents

Allan Horsfall – childhood and youth

Among those who followed the original 1958 correspondence in the *Spectator*, which led to the formation of the Homosexual Law Reform Society, was a prospective Labour Party council candidate in Nelson, Lancashire – Allan Horsfall. He wrote to Tony Dyson in Bangor, offering his support.

Horsfall was the antithesis of Dyson and of the kind of people who were involved in the HLRS. Where they were academics, he was working class, and the son of publicans. Where they were Liberals, he was of the old left-wing Labour Party. He was thirty years old, and had been in a relationship with a man twenty years his senior, Harold Pollard, for ten years.

12. The Emmott Arms, Allan Horsfall's birthplace

He was born in a pub, in 1927, making him an exact contemporary of Antony Grey. The Emmott Arms was the social hub of the pretty stone village of Laneshaw Bridge on the Lancashire–Yorkshire border, on the edge of the Yorkshire moors. His parents separated when he was six months old, so he never knew his father, Tom. His mother, Nellie, died when he was six, leaving Allan to be brought up by his grandparents in the pub. They too were dead before he was 16, leaving him with a guardian, also a publican, who was soon moved by his Brewery to another pub, in Burnley.

So Allan was an only child brought up by grandparents, who not only worked the all-consuming hours that running a pub required, but also viewed him across an age gap of more than forty years. This gave him a quietness and a gravity which often comes from having parents no longer limber enough to frolic with their children. He was also very much left to his own devices, and that self-contained quality was to stand him in good stead when he was out on a limb advocating law reform.

The close male camaraderie (no women) of the village pub left a strong impression, an image compounded of warmth, gossip, and community, which was to stand in stark contrast to the subdued bleakness of the standard gay bars he found in the 1950s. Jeremy Seabrook suggests in *A Lasting Relationship* (1976) that the search for a gay identity is looking for a kind of replacement for a geographic sense of community obliterated by the destruction of locally based industry and other work:

> With the removal of the intense awareness of place – and it was conditioned by knowing where we stood in relation to the process of production – we have to look elsewhere to find out who we are. We have turned inwards, to characteristics which will restore to us a feeling of communality, to reduce the sense of being stranded and robbed of identity. It is not surprising that sexuality should be one of the strongest sources of meaning that individuals can find within themselves.[1]

If sexual identity is to become the source of a general sense of self, then the gay club is where a sense of 'community of selves' ought to be expressed, as the village pub expressed the village. No surprise then that the relentless dehumanising commercialism of much of the 'gay scene' should cause such profound feelings of disappointment, even anger. Among other things, Allan Horsfall was trying to reconnect with his idealised version of the village pub when he took up the cause of Esquire Clubs in 1968.*

Horsfall was a bright lad, commuting to the Grammar School in Nelson. There were adolescent flings:

> I had sexual relations with lads who lived round about, one or two at school and one or two who lived in the neighbourhood, almost all of whom grew up and married. … I think I was probably the only one who grew up to be an acknowledged gay. … Despite the fact that they all married, and sometimes had families, they all remained on friendly terms when I met them as adults. So I suppose they were the ones who were going through a phase, and I was the one who wasn't.[2]

Homosexuality was something which was not talked about at all, even by those who practised it. It was 'a bit of fun', and some boys liked it and some didn't. If you approached someone who wasn't interested, there were no hard feelings. Also there was a kind of naivety on the part of the grandparents or guardians which could be turned to a boy's advantage.

> I don't know if it was indifference or naivety, if I took a lad home and said, 'Can he stay the night?' they'd let him stay the night. And nothing was said

---

* See page 174.

> about it or thought about it. …There was usually a reason, because he was a friend from the other side of town, and the buses had finished. … And occasionally that's what happened. And nobody read anything sinister into it at all.[3]

This homosexual activity was accepted as part of working class life. Lads went around in gangs, and the bonds between mates were strong, often stronger than relationships with wives and families.

Allan's part in school and gangs, however, was cut short by the urgent need to earn money when his grandparents died. In 1942, aged fourteen, he was cast into the wider world, and a series of office jobs followed in Nelson. Too young to go into pubs, and not aware of a cottaging scene, his sex life was largely put on hold apart from with a couple of old school chums. Call-up came right at the end of the war, as Allan joined the RAF. Most of his three years' service was spent in the ruins of Germany. Many gay men in the services found themselves and their sexuality during their service days, and some units were rampant with gay sexual activity. For his future partner Harold, who was an adjutant in a fighter squadron, gay sex was rife. After all, during the war these were young men facing each day as if it was their last, and grabbing any opportunity that life presented. This ethos continued even after the war, until there were efforts to crack down on it in the late 1940s. Allan himself was not so lucky in his personal encounters. Opportunities were limited in dormitories, where twenty men were packed in, allowing no privacy at all. But in Germany, in the British Army of Occupation, he got lucky, in that he was billeted in an ex-Luftwaffe barracks where beds were two to a room.*

> I was sharing with this lad … in this ex-Luftwaffe Barracks and we got one night to wrestling, as lads did to work off surplus energy, and I had him pinned down on the bed, fully clothed, and he grabbed my tie and pulled it, and said, 'It doesn't ring a bell, does it?' So I made a grab for his dick, and that was what he was hinting at. He went off to be a priest ultimately.[4]

This lad, and, the other gay man he met in the RAF,† didn't offer much in the way of hope for the future.

Harold Pollard – partner

After demob, like many ex-servicemen, Allan joined the local Royal Air Force Association. The RAFA club provided a place to meet new people and socialise. The secretary of the Burnley branch was a 40-year-old primary

---

* This is something which has always been anathema to British authority, which implicitly accepts that if two men share a room or a cell, sex is going to occur.

† See page 15.

school teacher, Harold Pollard. Harold was living with his family, but when his family moved to Devon, he had to stay behind because of his job. The sale of the family home left him without a roof over his head, and so he moved into the pub with Allan and his guardian.

13. Harold Pollard in 1972

It was a small pub, with cramped accommodation over the bars, and, as often occurred in working-class households, Allan and Harold had to share a bed. Where Allan had manoeuvred his school contemporaries into this situation knowingly a few years before, this was different: a man who was considerably older, met in 'straight' surroundings, an authority figure not obviously gay, and not obviously up for 'a bit of fun'. The passage of time had rendered Allan self-conscious.

It says something for attitudes to sexuality in the late 1940s that it took several weeks for Allan to realise Harold was gay and vice versa. Night after night they lay side by side in their flannelette pyjamas, wondering, not daring to ask, or to risk a first move. For Allan, with so little adult experience, it must have seemed unlikely that another gay man would be found so close to home. Gay men you met in toilets, maybe in a well-known local bar, but not at your own breakfast table. And Harold no doubt was wrestling with the fact that this boy whose breathing he listened to in the quiet of the night was twenty years younger than he was.

Eventually, it happened. They became an item. After some months Harold bought his own house in Burnley; Allan quarrelled with his guardian and moved in with Harold, and they lived there together for over five years. Harold got the headship of a primary school in Burnley. Allan started working for the Coal Board. Life went on with the two men living as a couple without noticeable hassle from the neighbours.

Local gay life

Allan was not a political animal, although forced by his sexuality into the position of a rebel and a criminal. In the early 1950s homosexuality came to public notice bigtime, first with the defection to the Soviet Union of spies Burgess and Maclean, and then, two years later, a series of highly publicised gay sex trials, and especially the two trials of Lord Montagu of Beaulieu.

> There was a whole feeling that things were getting a bit dangerous. Until Montagu, I'd never, and I don't think any of my friends had ever, thought that what we were doing was illegal. We never thought that anybody was going to get prosecuted for it. … If you put it in more adult terms, we thought that the law had fallen into disuse*. It was the Montagu case that proved this was very wrong. … It reminded people in a fairly sharp way that the law existed and could still be used.[5]

By the 1950s Allan's circle included gay friends. There were places in which you could establish some circumscribed gay space:

> There was a little gay coterie in the main pub in Nelson and the main pub in Burnley. The Thorn Hotel, Burnley. It always seemed to happen in the best hotels. It was never in a scruffy pub, because in the best hotels it was presumed you'd get a certain amount of tolerance. I suppose it was in the best hotels you didn't get so many people looking for trouble.† And in Nelson it was the Nelson Hotel, which had a Gents' Bar. Certainly in Burnley they were known about by all the other people in the bar, and they never objected. … It was used by solicitors, the editor of the local paper, all the local magistrates and bigwigs. Plus a few gays. And there was a general tolerance. If one or two of the gays got a bit tipsy and started sitting on one another's knee, the landlord would say, 'If you want to carry on like that, go in the upstairs bar'.[6]

In addition to corners in the local bars there was at least one fully-fledged establishment in Manchester, the Elgin,‡ and Allan would take the bus into the city on Saturdays. The Elgin was a rowdy affair, and, unlike the Nelson Hotel, not exactly discreet:

> It was heaving. When you were going to the gents you'd got to push your way through and push your way back. And you'd be groped for most of the way. It was male. I can't remember any women in there. … Anybody who walked into any of the Manchester pubs who knew anything at all

* Allan means since the war. He was all too aware of the Altrincham case.

† You were also much less likely to get a visit from the police.

‡ Now The Rembrandt in Canal Street.

> would identify it [as gay], within a couple of minutes. A lot of stereotypical gay people there. You'd only have to listen to them order a drink.
>
> [The bus home] got known as the buggers' bus because there were quite a lot of gays who used it, and after a fair intake of booze in Manchester they were pretty uninhibited on the bus going back, in conversation, camping it up. I remember there was a toilet half-way at Edenfield, and the ones who'd been drinking used to ask the driver to stop there, because they needed a pee. One time two lesbians got off and … [told the driver] they were going to the cottage,* and he drove off, thinking they were going to a country retreat somewhere. And they were left standing.[7]

Allan was not 'political', but read about homosexuality in the library. When he wanted to look at *Against the Law* (1955), the librarian wouldn't let him borrow Wildeblood's book; he had to sit down in a special section reserved for dodgy materials, and wear gloves as he turned the pages.

Books about homosexuality

There was now a steady trickle of books about homosexuality, the majority by doctors and psychiatrists. Mostly they talked in terms of disease, and cure. Charles Socarides was a notorious and unreconstructed American Freudian who led the American Psychoanalytical Association's rearguard action to prevent homosexuality being declassified as an illness.† Any homosexual reading *The Overt Homosexual* (1958) would have learned that he was suffering from impulse neurosis, a psychopathic personality, schizophrenia, paranoia, manic-depression, masochism, addiction and character disorders. His 'condition' was caused by an overpowering, cruel mother and a weak father. He was filled with aggression, destruction and deceit:

> A pair of homosexuals can sometimes succeed in living together in lasting fashion, but in … an infantile emotional state, in an atmosphere of petty quarrelling, compromises and sterility that is barely tolerable.[8]

This would have come as news to long-established gay couples such as Tony Dyson and Cliff Tucker, Harold and Allan, Antony Grey and his partner Eric.

Even sympathetic writers such as the influential Donald Webster Cory could give one strange ideas. According to Cory, the homosexual could be recognised by his well-fitting and expensive grey flannels, buttoned-down Oxford shirt, and black knitted necktie, and he lived in a rarefied atmosphere of good music, good art and good literature.[9]

---

* Gay slang for 'toilet'. Hence verb 'to cottage', to look for sex in public toilets.

† Socarides's son Richard is openly gay, and was principal White House adviser on lesbian and gay equality issues to Bill Clinton, 1993–99.

Clifford Allen,[10] the prominent English psychiatrist who assisted Douglas Warth and the *Sunday Pictorial* in 1952, was of much the same persuasion: 'If homosexuality is not to be regarded as a disease, then neither are such conditions as schizophrenia or manic depression.'[11]

Clifford Allen was to engage in acrimonious correspondence in the *New Statesman* and *The Spectator* over claims that he had been able to 'cure' homosexuals. What exactly constituted a cure was never defined, but cure them he had, he claimed. And when people weren't cured, it was simply because they didn't want to be cured or weren't trying hard enough, which was just another symptom of their perversion and lack of moral fibre.

One such recalcitrant queer was Ian Harvey, the junior government minister caught in 1958 *in flagrante* with a guardsman in St James's Park. He was fined £5 for breaking park regulations, a marked contrast to sentences meted out elsewhere, but it was enough to make him resign as a minister and an MP. In his depression afterwards he consulted a shrink, 'although all I had heard made me suspect them of being slightly more in need of attention than their clients.'[12] The shrink was Clifford Allen:

> He was clearly disappointed that I was neither on the verge of insanity nor desperately anxious to be cured of this terrible disease. If either had been the case he had a course clearly mapped out. As it was, he was confronted with a new situation and he was not helped by the fact that as we went along I both cross-examined and contradicted him. Quite clearly, the best clients did not do that sort of thing.[13]

Allen prescribed tranquillisers, then the latest thing from America. Harvey was told to take five a day.

> By the time I had taken the second pill I was sleepy. I took the third and a few moments later fell under my desk unconscious.[14]

He discontinued the treatment.

The first British book about homosexuality which might be described as in any way positive, or at least a plea for law reform on the grounds that 'they can't help it', was written by gay sociologist Michael Schofield under the pseudonym of Gordon Westwood. He published *Society and the Homosexual* in 1952. It was the first British book to try to discuss and 'explain' homosexuality to a general reader. The assumed name came from his publisher, the maverick Victor Gollancz. Gollancz was the third publisher he had approached*

Schofield's is a very Freudian view – dominating mothers, absent fathers. 'If I'd written it now it would have been less medical, because I was rather

---

* Victor Gollancz founded the Left Book Club in the 1930s and was later to become a member of the Honorary Committee of the HLRS.

taken with Freud, and it shows.'[15] As such, the main theme of the book is that homosexuality is a mental illness, and, as Freud said, it is cruel and irrational to punish people who are mentally ill. This pushes it into the field of advocating law reform, although Schofield denied any campaigning intention: 'I wanted to contribute to understanding, but I thought changing the law was a little far off.'[16] One of the disturbing aspects of the book, and a corollary of the 'mental illness' approach, is the way that it embraces the prospect of electric shock and chemical castration, and foresees the day of a Brave New World when all homosexuals will be able to be cured. In this it was only reflecting the desires of those considerable numbers of homosexuals tormented by guilt, who only wished for their shameful urges to cease, but it was small comfort for any homosexual reading the book who felt neither ill nor in need of a cure.

One off the stranger aspects of both *Society and the Homosexual* and of D. J. West's *Homosexuality* (1955) is that, although they are both written by homosexual men who were healthy, well-adjusted and fulfilled, they both wrote about homosexuality as if it were a mental illness. You have to ask, did they think that every homosexual was sick except themselves? 'I didn't reconcile these very well,' admitted Schofield. 'I suppose the true answer is that I thought I was on safer ground if I talked about it not as being illegal, but medical. But I didn't think I was sick personally.'[17] He blamed the excessive influence of Freud. West, more timorous, now describes this 'detached' viewpoint, distanced from his own experience, as his 'hypocritical style'.

This readiness to accept a theory which flew in the face of his personal experience came from acceptance that certain people were 'experts' – doctors, psychiatrists, priests – and that others weren't, least of all homosexuals themselves. Schofield came to the subject as an 'amateur', educating himself as he went along from the shelves of the Cambridge University Library: 'I was doing it a bit from "I'm gay so where does this come from?" It was partly an effort to understand myself.'*

As a result of the book, Schofield was deluged by letters:

> I got thousands of letters from gay people. Many letters, very difficult to reply to. They were all problems, and very sad stories, which struck to the heart. I wrote back with sympathy. It would have been a bad idea for me to refer someone to a psychiatrist.[18]

---

* Schofield was an early HLRS supporter, and became friends with Antony Grey. Grey thought he was too much in the closet, and encouraged him to come out more. As a result he joined CHE in 1970, and was prominent in both campaigning and talking to local groups.

Horsfall might also have found comfort in C. S. Ford and F. A. Beach's *Patterns of Sexual Behaviour*, also published in 1952. The book is an extended version of the kind of sociological overview of homosexuality as practised in societies round the world, which occurs at the start of both Edward Carpenter's and Havelock Ellis's works. Ford and Beach claimed to have studied 190 different societies, of which 64 per cent 'approved' of homosexuality. Courtship and same-sex marriage were common; in some societies the majority of males practised anal intercourse, and it was thought a bit weird not to. Disapproval of any form of homosexual behaviour as found in the UK 'differs from the majority of human societies'.[19] Ford and Beach argued for a natural universal bisexuality which was socially conditioned into heterosexuality:

> Men and women who are totally lacking in any conscious homosexual leanings are just as much a product of cultural conditioning as are exclusive homosexuals.[20] …
>
> Goethe wrote that homosexuality is as old as humanity itself and can therefore be considered natural, and human history lends his statement the ring of truth.[21]

Perhaps the most influential book by an 'expert' was D. J. West's *Homosexuality*, published in 1955 and quickly taken up by Penguin Books. Donald West was a psychiatrist based at the Marlborough Clinic in Hampstead.* He was gay, but had no casework experience of homosexuals himself; his work is entirely based on the fieldwork of others and notes from other people's cases at the Marlborough. Like Schofield, he was partly attempting to explain himself to himself. It is something of a mystery why his work, rather than anyone else's, should have been taken up for the mass paperback market. West, like others, bought into the notion that homosexuality was a problem, and that causes could be found for it, but he was refreshingly frank about the multiplicity of possible causes and the difficulties of finding them:

> Writers on the subject, even medical writers who should know better, carelessly throw out generalisations without an atom of validity. One reads that homosexuals are depraved or exhibitionists or (and this is usually from homosexuals themselves) that they are more 'alive' and 'sympathetic' than the humdrum mass of humanity. In reality some homosexuals suffer from neurotic fears and anxieties and some are self-assured and hard as nails, some are vain and ostentatious and some are shy and quiet, some are cowardly and some are heroes, some are effeminate and some are brutes.[22]

---

* Later, when he moved to Cambridge, his path crossed that of Michael Schofield occasionally, when they met at gay parties given by a Cambridge academic and his boyfriend at a farm outside the city. They remained firm friends for 50 years.

West was later to get a lot of flak from Gay Liberationists for his views, and indeed revised *Homosexuality* extensively in 1965; certainly he can be accused of excessive caution in his approach to the work of the law reform movement. Although he was a supporter of the HLRS, he declined to be named as such publicly, saying that he wasn't a celeb and the campaign needed celebs. This is disingenuous. He was scared that his professional reputation as a criminologist, and as an expert witness, might be undermined by a loss of respect if he was known to be homosexual; indeed there were grounds for him to believe that he had not been offered certain positions because he was not 'a safe pair of hands'. However, there were many who supported law reform – criminologists like C. H. Rolph, psychiatrists like Eustace Chesser – who were not themselves homosexual, and even so prominent a campaigner as Antony Grey was assumed by most to be doing it out of the goodness of his heart. By contrast with Michael Schofield, who was highly visible both in HLRS and later in CHE without damaging his professional reputation or his influence as a sociologist, Donald West's contribution was disappointing. Nevertheless, *Homosexuality* remained the first port of call for many a gay man coming out until at least the end of the 1970s, and, considering the company that it kept, it could have been a lot worse. Uniquely for a work of Social Science, it included a bibliography of novels dealing with gay themes and characters

West's bibliography shows that there was a spate of new novels to read. Rodney Garland's *The Heart in Exile* (1953) was a runaway best seller. Garland was a pseudonym for a gay expatriate Hungarian, Adam Martin de Hegedus, a former diplomat and journalist, and a friend of André Gide. After two more novels, he committed suicide in anonymous bedsitter land in 1958.

The masterstroke of *The Heart in Exile* was to make the central character a gay psychiatrist, Dr Page. The novel is a kind of detective story, investigating the death of an old school friend. But on the way the reader is led through the gay subculture of the time ('the underground', Garland calls it), which is painted in lurid disgust, a place where people only go because there is nowhere else, or because they are attracted to rough trade – Garland is frank about the class element. Dr Page can also generalise about the 'invert' in a way that educates the liberal, usually female, member of the Boots Lending Library:

> The trouble with all people like Julian and you and I is that life is extra complicated for us. We don't like people like ourselves. We don't want anybody who shares our standards, I mean, educated, middle class and so on. In fact we want the very opposite. We want the primitive, the uneducated, the tough. Then we are surprised that satisfaction is so difficult to obtain and that our affairs don't last. They don't last because we don't share the same culture. Things are far easier for people who are attracted to others like themselves. Possibly younger, but from the same background. They are usually happy. There are hundreds of dons, museum

> officials, clergymen, civil servants like that. They settle down to a happy married life with younger friends. I suppose they go to drag parties and dress up like Indian snake-charmers or Carmen Miranda, but they don't hunt and tour the pubs.[23]

It is uncannily close to Wildeblood, both in its division of the gay world, and in its insistence on the right to love, but goes further in maintaining that there is a role for casual sex, as part of the process of acquiring a real lover.

> Like eighty per cent or so of all inverts, I didn't consider myself an immoral person. I always felt that the invert was one of the least immoral people in a world that was more a-moral than immoral, perhaps because his own guilt feeling often forced him towards scrupulousness in all his dealings. I was not thinking of embittered inverts, of course, whom bitterness had pushed towards crime or just unscrupulousness. Perhaps because I believed in God, I was uneasy having sex with someone I didn't love, but I felt that perhaps the process was capable of reversing itself and I could afterwards in retrospect, fall in love with someone with whom I had had sex.[24]

Politicisation

But it was not homosexuality that politicised Allan Horsfall; it was the Suez Crisis. In October 1956 Israel, Britain and France invaded Egypt following President Nasser's nationalisation of the Suez Canal. It was a hugely unpopular action, both in the UK and internationally. Opposition came most vocally from the left of the Labour Party, but it reflected outrage in the country and a sense of betrayal – the Conservative Prime Minister, Anthony Eden, had misled Parliament about it, and the British action came seemingly out of nowhere. The response of Hugh Gaitskell, the Labour leader, impressed Allan, so he, along with many others, joined the Labour Party as a result.*

Horsfall was a natural doer and organiser, and it was not long before he was picked as a Labour candidate for the next local election, for a ward in Nelson. As a comparative newcomer he was allocated to a seat he was not expected to win, although Nelson Council itself was solidly Labour. The selection was a kind of political baptism. However, somewhat to his surprise, he was elected, on 10 April 1958, as a nation-wide swing helped to give Nelson a 100 per cent Labour council for the first and only time.

Shortly after his election Allan got in touch with Tony Dyson. By this time an anonymous donation of £250 had enabled the HLRS to set up an office in

* Antony Grey described a similar sense of outrage, but was careful never to reveal any party political affiliations.

Liverpool Road, near King's Cross, in the home of a very brave gay couple, Len Smith and Reiss Howard. 'What can I do?' Allan asked Dyson. 'Write to the papers. Write to your MP,' was the reply.

14. Allan Horsfall's election photograph, 1958

Allan's MP was Sidney Silverman, a left-winger remembered today, if at all, for introducing the Private Member's Bill in the House of Commons for the abolition of the death penalty. Silverman wrote back to Allan saying that of course he supported implementing the Wolfenden Report, and could be counted on to support any bill which did so. So that was that. Faced with such a push-over, there wasn't a lot more Horsfall could do in that direction as an individual. Convention required that a constituent could only write to his own MP.

That left writing to the papers, and there were many local papers around the mill towns of Lancashire. First off was the *Nelson Leader*, which had a particularly dotty medical correspondent. And then there were the nationals. The most obvious target was *Reynolds News*. This was the national paper of the Co-operative Movement, a mass-circulation left-wing Sunday paper with Labour MPs Tom Driberg and Desmond Donnelly as columnists, and a strong anti-nuclear stance. The new Councillor fired off a letter in the heat of the moment, almost without thinking about it.

Three weeks passed, and he heard nothing. He started to get cold feet. It began to hit home, what he had done. In the climate of the time, it was almost as if he had stamped the word 'Queer' across his forehead, and him an elected representative. He would be thrown off the council, he would be drummed out of the Labour Party, he would be a by-word in the local community, most of whom bought *Reynolds News* on a Sunday.

A visit to Peter Wildeblood

Riddled with doubt, Allan took his second thoughts to the only person he felt could understand, Peter Wildeblood. The *Spectator*, remember, printed Wildeblood's address, and Allan had all the old copies of the weekly lying around his and Harold's Nelson house. In June 1958, with Wildeblood's address in his pocket, he caught the train from Manchester to Euston, bought an A–Z, and hopped on a bus to Essex Road.

As he walked up the hill towards Highbury Corner, past the bomb site which still stood on the left hand side of the road, he was filled with trepidation. It was a bit much, calling on a complete stranger and dumping your problems in his lap. But on the other hand, Allan was so isolated. Even his partner was worried – as a teacher Pollard was vulnerable, and saw what Allan was doing as a potential threat to his position. His warnings of the consequences of Allan's actions were correspondingly exaggerated.

Number 30 St Paul's Road was a large early-Victorian terraced house, three storeys plus attic and basement. The contrast with Allan's world of red brick two-up two-downs and scrubbed front steps could not have been stronger. Likewise, when Peter opened the door, the contrast between the two men – Wildeblood tall and thin, with his clipped upper class tones and long aristocratic face, Horsfall short and stocky, with his harsh Lancashire rasp, his gabardine mac and homburg hat – was striking. But Wildeblood was a gentleman, and recognised a fellow-invert who was suffering.

'I suppose I was looking for reassurance,' said Allan. 'He wasn't at all put out. Maybe people were turning up on his doorstep all the time, I don't know. He sat me down, talked to me about things.' [25]

While Peter was in the kitchen fixing a drink against the chill, Allan looked round the high-ceilinged room. I like to think that on the table would have been some of the revisions to the lyrics for *The Crooked Mile*, Wildeblood's musical based on his best-selling novel of Soho life, *West End People*, due to open a couple of months later.*

There are no gay characters in *The Crooked Mile*, but the hero, an ex-con called Jug Ears who seems destined to end up inside again, draws on Wildeblood's prison experience, and this would have certainly have given a frisson to the first night audience who knew all about the author's past:

> You look through the bars
> And tell yourself that one day

---

* Wildeblood had not let the grass grow under his feet since his release from prison three years previously. In addition to *Against the Law* he wrote a sequel, *A Way of Life*, and two novels of low life, set in Soho, both of which sold well. The role of freelance author meant that there was never a question of him being ostracised or unable to find work.

You'll fly away
Fly far away
Up through the stars
As free as the wind you'll be
As free as the air
But deep down inside you
You know you belong right there.[26]

15. Peter Wildeblood's home at 30 St Paul's Road Islington

Or maybe Allan glimpsed the gossip song, which captures the reactions of all the Mrs Grundys who tut-tutted over the cons' (and Wildeblood's) 'dirty doings':

Other people's sins
It's sweeter than the sound of violins
When we hear about and disapprove of
Other people's sins …
Other people's sins

It brings a glow of virtue to our skins
When we rush to read about the capers
Featured in the Sunday papers;
Nothing puts us in such moral shape as
Other people's sins.[27]

For Allan, Wildeblood was a star:

> He sat me down, talked me through things. After all, he had bitter first-hand experience. I hadn't been given a rough time at all. He told me to be brave. And as for the future – what was the worst thing that could happen? I felt reinforced. I felt that if disaster fell, I could cope with it. Being rejected by the Labour Party was not at all the same thing as going to prison.[28]

Allan returned to Nelson reinvigorated, which was just as well, because there was scant support for him locally. The Wildeblood meeting was to see him through some dark days in the next few years.

> When I got involved in the campaign, I was shunned by local gay people. There was a very strong disapproval of what I was doing. People thought it would bring the police down on them, or they'd be found out too.[29]

With Allan as with others, the question arises, why did he do it? It takes a very particular kind of character to stick your neck out to this extent in such an unpopular cause. The key lies in a phrase he wrote in his chapter in *Radical Records*:

> All my inculcated respect for law and order never once caused me to consider whether a celibate existence might provide an acceptable alternative.[30]

So here, as in the case of Tony Dyson, is a deeply law-abiding person living with the burden of permanent criminality. And this stigma hovered over the love relationship which was central to his life. The thought was intolerable to him. Therefore, although he adapted to his situation as a well-adjusted gay man, he also needed at a very deep psychological level to adjust the situation to himself. In addition, as an only child and one brought up by grandparents preoccupied with running a large and demanding pub, he had the kind of stubbornness of one used to making his own way in the world. He needed all that self-reliance, because the ostracism was complete.

> Anyone who says he got involved before 1960 without trepidation is a liar. … Gay friends distanced themselves from me – I was a marked man. The man I lived with [Harold] was treated the same way. People would say, 'Please don't talk to me in a bar.' Someone he had known for years asked him, please, if he saw them in a bar would he kindly not speak to them there. I even found myself suggesting to him that it might be better if we were seen more often drinking separately rather than together.[31]

Pollard had his position as a schoolteacher to think of, and was not immune from social pressures. It drove them apart in terms of living arrangements. Having run a home together for nearly ten years:

16. Allan Horsfall's Coal Board cottage at 3 Robert Street, Atherton

> I could see that my pro-reform activities obtaining publicity were – not an embarrassment to him, but possibly putting his position in some sort of jeopardy, so I got a little separate house in Burnley, maybe just for presentation reasons really.
>
> I had an interview with the police, and I'd written one or two letters from there, to the press, and I had occasion to be talking to a senior policeman in the police station … and when he was opening his files on his desk, I could see he had a note of my new address … so I can only think that Special Branch were keeping tabs on me.[32]

From a separate address Allan could be less cautious. Soon he was to be moved by the Coal Board to Atherton, several miles away; the job involved accepting accommodation in a small tied cottage, and sharing it with a partner was not an option. By the time Harold retired and was free of constraints, he was too old and too settled to change. Allan and Harold lived apart for the remaining thirty years of their relationship.

As it turned out, the *Reynolds News* letter became a bit of a damp squib. The Features Editor rang up to say that they'd decided to publish it, but would have to edit it heavily. Did Allan still want his name and address on it? He decided he didn't, not because he was scared, but because he had no control over how the paper chose to edit him. So on 20 July 1958 in the Sunday Postbag, next to an advert for false teeth and a free booklet on Family Planning, appeared the following:

> The Wolfenden Report is now nine months old, and has not yet been debated by the Commons. The Government (and the Opposition) has a duty to lead the House in implementing the recommendations.
>
> If it doesn't do this, it is morally bound to give a reason.
>
> If the reason is merely that the issue is too controversial, is not this invalidated by the fact that the issue was referred to the committee in the first place simply because it was controversial?
>
> —A. H., Nelson, Lancs.[33]

It had all been a fuss over nothing.

Raising Wolfenden in the Labour Party

But there were other courses to pursue, and the most important was raising the issue within the Labour Party. Though some individuals were sympathetic, the grass roots of the Party were not. Or at least, that was the general belief. Allan remembered:

> I was at the Labour Party conference at Scarborough in 1959, and talking to some Labour members at the bar, when I raised the question of the neglect of Wolfenden's recommendations on homosexuality, and they said that whereas they were in favour of law reform, they were afraid of reactions in their constituencies. And I concluded from this that unless something could be moved in the constituencies, the MPs would remain inactive on this subject. And so I put down a motion for the local Labour Party Executive.[34]

What followed was a tale of procedural blocking at every turn. Allan himself wrote it up in *New Left Review*[35] and *The Guardian*.[36] At the beginning of 1960 his Ward Committee was going to pass resolutions to go forward to the Annual General Meeting of the local Labour Party Executive. If a resolution got beyond that stage it would go to the Regional Executive and then to the Party's Annual Conference in the autumn.

Allan wrote to a friend and fellow-councillor saying he intended to put a motion, urging the Parliamentary Party to work for early implementation of the Wolfenden Committee's recommendations on homosexual law reform. He expected support, but there was silence.

> Some days later I visited his home to test his reaction. We talked for an hour or so about anything and almost everything other than the content of my letter, until his wife had to leave the room to attend to the children. He then told me (in hushed tones) that of course he hadn't been able to refer to the matter in front of his wife but that he considered my intended action to be most unwise, since homosexuality was totally unsuitable for discussion by the sort of people who attended the Ward Committee.[37]

When Allan pointed out that this was the only way to get it to the Executive, his friend said that he didn't think it suitable for people who attended the Executive either. So, asked Allan, if not here, where was he to start? Answer came there none.

> I came away somewhat disheartened but a little wiser, having discarded my rather naïve assumption that, in any given person, prejudice was to be found in inverse proportion to intelligence. I consoled myself with the thought that if there was to be a fight, it is as well to know the territory on which the battle is to take place. It looked, in this instance, that it was to be in darkest John Gordon* country.[38]

Allan persisted in trying to advance his motion, though it took nearly a year to get it to the Ward Committee. Like all Labour Party meetings, this one was extremely long, and Wolfenden was way down the agenda. When the subject came up, two hours or more later, one member, a magistrate, objected to the discussion of homosexuality in mixed company. Allan pointed out that several members of the Wolfenden Committee had been women, so it had already been discussed in mixed company. In addition, many prominent women were involved in the campaign for reform. The objector persisted, and the meeting's chairman ruled a majority against discussing the subject, despite no vote being taken.

At the next meeting, Horsfall objected to the way the chairman had handled the issue previously, as an irresponsible piece of evasion, and demanded it be raised again. This time the objector wasn't present 'having succumbed to the superior attractions of an evening football match.'[39] The result was a complete change in the climate for the discussion. Allan proposed the motion, one of the women present seconded it, and it was carried unanimously. Having successfully negotiated the hurdle of the Ward, the motion could go now to the constituency Labour Party AGM.

The AGM took place on a bitterly cold night, and was not well attended. The woman who had been his seconder asked Allan to excuse her this time round, because 'she no longer felt capable of facing the ordeal'. The local

---

* John Gordon was first editor and subsequently columnist of the *Sunday Express*, whose rampant homophobia was expressed in his column from 1952 until his death in 1974. The tradition was continued by his successor, John Junor.

Councillors and Aldermen, not noted for attending these occasions, turned out en masse, showing how rattled the local party was.* They wanted to make sure that the local Party's Executive Committee voted the way the local politicians wanted.

> It soon became clear that sex, if it exists at all for these people, exists apart from life – something to be found in the jungle or the rabbit hutch or the farmyard, but never, never, perish the thought, in the lives of all the ordinary, decent respectable, hardworking people who send us back to the Town Hall year after year.[40]

Horsfall's resolution was the only one to be discussed; or rather, what was discussed was whether the substantive motion, the implementation of the Wolfenden Report, should be discussed at all. Allan wasn't called to speak, as the chairman simply asked for the wishes of the meeting. One Alderman said it shouldn't be discussed at all, and 'men should steer clear of politics until they had got all the sex out of their systems'.[41] Speaker after speaker said exactly the same thing, and clearly there was collusion. This time round it was suppressed by 13 votes to 6, with lots of abstentions.

Allan rang the constituency party agent to object to the way the meeting had been fixed. He was told 'certain people' thought that the motion was so important to the Party that there had been a private meeting to decide what should be done. Nobody would say who had been at this private meeting, or admit to having attended himself.

The agent was clearly unhappy, but 'asked me not to do anything rash without consulting him.' Allan reported back to his ward, with the agent in attendance. The ward took the view that the Party's Standing Orders laid a duty on the Executive to *consider* resolutions and therefore it had acted illegally in refusing to discuss Allan's. They were determined to put it forward again.

It came up in June 1961, nearly two years after Horsfall first raised it. This time the composition of the meeting had changed. Those who wanted to throw it out without discussion stayed away. 'The time for suppression was out, and evasion and misrepresentation were in.'[42] This time Allan got to speak for twenty minutes, and he was seconded by a young Councillor from another ward.

> Much sympathy was expressed for the homosexuals' dilemma, although in all but a few cases it was followed by the usual parade of humbug. …

---

* Paradoxically, these uptight Aldermen had presided over a comparatively relaxed police regime. According to Horsfall, Nelson boasted a particularly active public toilet which was well known to the town, and to the Council. And yet, in contrast to other towns in the area, there had been no homosexual prosecutions for 40 years.

—Allan Horsfall, interviewed by Paul Hambley, 12 May 2008. BSA C1405/05.

> Alderman A had attended a meeting where Sir John Wolfenden had spoken, and he was sure the Committee's recommendations were not for early implementation. Councillor B would be much more ready to support the motion were it not for the fact that at least some of the agitation for reform was organised by the queers themselves. [Here a meaningful look across the room at Allan himself, no doubt.]
>
> Councillor C said it would lose all the local elections for us. The only thing that wasn't suggested was that it would frighten new businesses away.[43]

The article concluded that the fight must go on, however difficult it was to galvanise the Labour Party dinosaur:

> It seems, then, that the British homosexual in his long search for justice and dignity will have to turn to the Labour Party – yes, even to this Labour Party – for his main support. My God![44]

Allan's experience was only a microcosm of the deep homophobia in the institutional Party. When the MP William Field was fined in 1953 on the word of a policeman that he had smiled at some sailors in a toilet, there was not a word of protest or support for him, and he had to resign. Even more shocking, George Brinham, the Chairman of the National Executive of the Labour Party 1959–60 and an executive member for over ten years, was murdered by a 16-year-old cellarman in 1962. The judge commented:

> I cannot see how any jury properly directed can fail to find there was provocation. There is the statement of the lad which shows quite clearly that this man attempted to make homosexual advances, and that in consequence Somers picked up a decanter and hit him on the head. I should think that is about as clear a case of provocation as it is possible to have.[45]

In other words, any homosexual who showed an interest in a lad deserved to be murdered.

The youth was discharged, sold his story to the *News of the World* for a tidy sum,* got hundreds of letters of congratulation, and was given a hero's welcome when he returned to his native Matlock. All the people who had

* 'If I hadn't done a bit of labouring with a sledgehammer and that, and a bit of bodybuilding, I mightn't have hit this fellow George so hard with the decanter. … But he made this pass at me, you see. It made me feel sick, but he tried to grab hold of me and press me against the bookcase. I put my hands behind my back, like a lever, to push myself forward. Then I felt this decanter. Heavy cut glass it was. Empty. … I hit him with it and he just stood there looking at me, then came forward. I hit him again. And again. It all took less than a couple of seconds. If I hadn't done a bit of slaughtering as well, pigs and things this blood might have panicked me. Made me vomit or something.'

—'The Night I Killed George Brinham', *News of the World*, 27 January 1963, 4.

known and worked with George Brinham and might have been thought his friends were silent in the face of an obvious mistrial and the vilification of a dead man's name. Gay MPs like the outrageous Tom Driberg were running scared. It was to be over twelve years before there was a Labour Campaign for Gay Rights.*

So Allan was under no illusions as to what it would take to get Labour to back a gay rights movement. But this experience was pivotal; from it came the germ of the idea that reform could only come as a result of local homosexuals organising themselves to lobby local party associations. This was to become one of the twin reasons for local CHE groups, along with the creation of that 'space to breathe' where people could find their identity as lesbians and gay people. Many of the hundred and more local groups formed a decade or so later assiduously cultivated and canvassed their local MPs.

Already, after his first rebuff by the Party, Allan had written to the HLRS asking for permission to set up a local group. They too were discouraging, wishing to keep total central control. Venetia Newall, a member of their Executive Committee, wrote to him in August 1960:

> Unfortunately, we always found in this office that although we get many splendid, able and willing volunteers, we always seem to get a percentage of crackpots and shifty types. I don't understand why but the office acts like a magnet to them, and one has to be very careful. Our work is so valuable, we don't want to endanger it in any way by taking risks. You will probably say that such people don't sit on committees, but the executive has certainly had problems of this kind to deal with in the past. I'm sure you will say that I am being unadventurous and much too careful, but I do feel very strongly that we stand to lose so much if we act unwisely, and we must get this terrible law altered.[46]

There was not a lot to do. Without that local organisation, there was no national organisation to contribute to, no lines of communication between homosexuals. Access to most media was denied most of the time. The only outlet for argument and persuasion was the local press, then much more widely read and therefore much more powerful, than now. Allan continued writing.

Parliamentary debates 1958 and 1960

During this time, while Allan was trying to work through the Labour Party, there were two debates in the House of Commons on the subject of the

---

* First called the Gay Labour Group. Subsequently the Labour Campaign for Gay, Lesbian, Bisexual, and Transgender Rights.

Wolfenden Report. First there was one to 'take note' of the Report in 1958. Then, in 1960, came the first serious attempt, by Labour MP Kenneth Robinson, to prod the Government into implementing it. These debates have been reported extensively elsewhere,* but it seems useful to include some examples of the debate in order to remind the reader of exactly how much a campaigner like Allan Horsfall was up against, and the frustration and despair which an MP like William Shepherd, member for Cheadle, could invoke.† Shepherd peddled himself as an expert, and drove Horsfall to almost incoherent rage. Lesser people than Antony Grey or Allan Horsfall would have given up.

The debates also had a knock-on effect on ordinary homosexuals. In much the same way as current debates about immigration and nationality serve to make non-British people resident in this country feel increasingly isolated and alienated, because of the terms in which they are couched, the debates of the 1950s and 60s only fuelled the belief among lesbians and gay men that the powers in the land would never understand them. Conspiracy theories were rife. The only difference between then and now was that the newspaper editorials were far more critical of government inaction over Wolfenden. Only the *Sunday Express* and *Sunday Telegraph* were against implementation.

In the sequence of parliamentary debates between 1957 and 1967 can be noted a subtle modification of tone between one debate and the next by the MPs, as well as a decreasing majority against reform. Because the subject was more to the fore, newspaper stories about the victims of the law came more to prominence, there was more awareness of the suicides and miseries caused by prosecution and conviction, the blackmail cases and the police corruption which came in the law's wake. These too chipped away at the monolith of prejudice.

The HLRS itself began to have some effect, lobbying assiduously. Behind the scenes, Wildeblood, Tony Dyson, Antony Grey and, in the Greater Manchester Area, Allan Horsfall, wrote to every MP in the Commons. In May 1958 as soon as it was formed and Wildeblood joined the team, the Executive Committee of the HLRS decided to commission him to write its first publication, a pamphlet 'about 5,000 words in length'; The work, *Homosexuals and the Law*, went to all MPs, and somebody else (Antony Grey didn't know who) also sent them *Against the Law* and Eustace Chesser's *Live and let Live*, hot off the press and with a foreword by Wolfenden. This blanket coverage backfired somewhat. In addition to stirring the backwoods, it opened the door to allegations of an all-powerful 'homosexual lobby'; pressure applied by

* Notably in *Peers Queers and Commons* (1991) by Stephen Jeffery-Poulter, a long-time CHE member.

† The anger was shared by the young Martin Stafford, who lived in Shepherd's constituency, and by Antony Grey, who had been brought up in it.

'legitimate' causes is acceptable, but when it comes to homosexuality, it amounts to a conspiracy:

> Over the last few months, honourable Members have been inundated from many sources with literature which, under the cover of stating facts, has in my view endeavoured to influence our opinions and to state the case for the homosexual. ... The suggestion is, 'Do not be frightened of him. He is really a decent chap.' ... In my opinion, in the general run the homosexual is a dirty-minded danger to the virile manhood of this country.
>
> —Godfrey Lagden, Conservative MP for Hornchurch[47]

This 'literature' was the last major involvement of Peter Wildeblood in gay rights campaigning. Having made a name for himself as a writer, he turned his attention to television, becoming a writer and producer with Granada in Manchester. Again in an echo of his past, his most successful achievements in British television were numerous scripts for the daytime favourites *Crown Court* and *Within These Walls*, a soap set in prison. Apart from *Against the Law*, the most commonly available Wildeblood book is another echo of his past, *Victorian Scandals*, a spin-off from yet another TV series.

He became an Honorary Vice President of CHE in 1971, the only recognition he ever had from the gay movement, and shortly after moved to Canada at the request of CBC, for whom he continued to produce television programmes.

Many found him uncomfortable, abrasive and difficult to work with, which is often the lot of the gay campaigner with strong convictions and the sense that there's no time to waste. Peter Tatchell has attracted similar criticism. But the push that Wildeblood gave law reform in five short years was a mighty shove indeed. When he had a massive stroke in 1994 which left him speechless, almost completely paralysed and quadriplegic, he learned to use a computer by operating it with his chin, and communicated by fax. 'After a lifetime of one-finger typing, I think I can master one-chin typing.'[48] That's the kind of man he was.

In 1960 again supporters, including Allan Horsfall, wrote assiduously to all MPs, friend and foe alike. Thus they roused opponents into attending a debate they might otherwise have missed. Nevertheless, it was the first time that an organised gay rights lobby had attempted to operate in the UK. In the 1960s lobbying was to become more targeted, and the voting figures improved. The operation became even more professional after Antony Grey took over as Secretary of the HLRS in 1962.

The first debate on homosexuality in the House of Commons was set up by the Government to 'take note' of the Wolfenden Report. In this it was asked to consider both Part Two (Homosexual Offences) and Part Three (Prostitution). The House was clearly far more comfortable with Part Three, which took up most of the debating time,* and that part of Wolfenden had a comparatively easy transit into law as the Street Offences Act 1959.

The debate was opened on 26 November 1958 by the new Home Secretary, R. A. Butler, who clearly had no intention of acting on the Report as far as homosexuality was concerned. His line was 'too soon … public opinion not ready … need for more research … etc., etc.'

Butler was later to claim in a BBC2 TV programme† that the government wanted to implement the whole of the Wolfenden Report; they had tried to find an MP who would sponsor it, but there were no takers. This seems highly unlikely. The government had always been deeply embarrassed by the subject, right from the moment when the Wolfenden Committee was being set up. The Committee has been erroneously described in some quarters as a Royal Commission, or as a Parliamentary Commission (not an English institution). To say that it was a Royal Commission is to misunderstand the politics at work, and to ascribe more 'clout' to it than it had. David Maxwell Fyfe, the arch-homophobe, was desperately keen that it should be a royal commission, and argued for this in Cabinet. If it had been a royal commission, it would have been chaired by a judge in all probability, and it would have had far more independence. Its status would have been more authoritative, but it would not have been something for which Maxwell Fyfe was personally accountable. Churchill, and Anthony Eden his Deputy Prime Minister, didn't relish the prospect of a commission over which there was less government control, and also calculated that it would get far more publicity, and be more difficult to stonewall, than a humble departmental committee. So a Home Office Committee was what it was.

In truth, the Labour Party's official line was no better; both parties were terrified of the electoral consequences of passing a 'Buggers' Charter'. Only the Liberal Party adopted implementation of Wolfenden as official party policy.

In addition to showing the mountain that reformers would have to climb for the next nine years, the 1958 debate also illustrates several strands of argument that would recur over the next twenty years and more. No vote was taken on this occasion, but it is clear that any attempt to pass Wolfenden into law would have been defeated by about three to one. 'Highlights' of the arguments from the opponents include:

> They are, in my opinion, a malignant canker in the community and if this were allowed to grow, it would eventually kill off what is known as normal life … I believe that humanity would eventually revert to an animal

---

* Part One was a general introduction.

† *A Question of Conscience: Consenting Party*, BBC2, 27 April 1972.

> existence if this cult were so allowed to spread that, as in ancient Greece, it overwhelmed the community at large.
>
> —Fred Bellenger, Labour, Bassetlaw[49]

Bellenger eloquently expresses the 'heterosexuality is so fragile that it has to be protected' school of argument. It would follow from this argument that homosexuality is so attractive that mere exposure to a homosexual man will send a straight male rolling onto his back with his legs in the air.

> We ought to face the fact that homosexuality is unnatural and that in the majority of cases there are prospects of people overcoming these tendencies. Incest is a much more natural act than homosexuality.
>
> —William Shepherd, Conservative, Cheadle[50]

Shepherd's remark about the naturalness of incest became notorious and came back to haunt him.

> One only has to look back into history to find that it was the condoning of this sort of offence which led to the downfall of the Roman Empire. I feel that it was the condoning of these offences which led to the fall of Nazi Germany. —James Dance, Conservative, Bromsgrove[51]

No-one picked up on the way that Dance seemed to consider the fall of Nazism a bad thing.

Many MPs opposed implementing Wolfenden on the grounds that their constituents would not like it, whether they had canvassed local opinion or not. This involved projecting into a future situation which showed homosexual couples 'insinuating themselves' into community life. In that this is what has happened in many communities in the last thirty years, it was actually prescient.

> I cannot imagine the miners' lodges welcoming a Report which will mean that it will no longer be an offence to procure an adult male and to set up a house in a mining village for a male friend.
>
> —Mrs Jean Mann, Labour, Coatbridge and Airdrie[52]

The mention of a mining village is significant, because the question 'How will this play with the miners?' was one many a Labour MP sponsored by a Trade Union or the Co-operative movement would ask herself or himself. The assumption was that the miners Wouldn't Like It. One of Allan Horsfall's strategies in locating the North Western Committee's address in his own house in a mining village, was to show in a very concrete way that the earth didn't cave in, and the miners didn't protest, when some homosexuals turned up next door to them.

> I found that it was remarkably easy to cure these people with the aid of hormone treatment which has been already mentioned today. By reducing

> sexual tension of the individual, provided he is under suitable treatment, this treatment can so suppress it that a reorientation of ideas has time to take place so that when sexual desires are allowed to return on the cessation of treatment they take a more natural form. Therefore, I say that it would be disastrous to abandon the law on that point.
>
> —Dr Reginald Bennett,* Conservative, Gosport and Fareham[53]

The arguments about whether homosexuals could be 'cured' or not raged throughout the 1950s and 60s. One of the reasons that people were keen to find the causes of homosexuality was that with causes came the prospect of cures. Conversely, the insistence of some campaigners that homosexuality *wasn't* a disease carried with it the implication that even looking for a cure for what wasn't an illness was futile. However, the medical model remained prevalent among most supporters and opponents of law reform alike until well into the 1970s. Causes attributed by psychiatrists were almost invariably those expounded by Freud, although hormonal imbalance was also a popular theory. The most common forms of 'treatment' were extensive courses of psychoanalysis, running into years, which even the most ardent advocates of turning gay men straight accepted was impractical for large numbers of people; and electroconvulsive therapy (ECT), sometimes accompanied by hormone injections and other drugs. Proponents of this claimed high success rates. Opponents pointed out that it was too soon for assessment of success in the long term, or indeed even to find an agreed definition of success. The best that could be claimed was that, in some cases where homosexuals were sufficiently disturbed by their sexuality to want a cure desperately, ECT and hormone treatment might render them asexual, at least for a while. ECT was loathed by the vast majority of gay men, especially those who had been subject to it and suffered serious mental damage. One of the earliest campaigns of both GLF and CHE was against the classification of homosexuality as a mental illness, and against the use of ECT and hormone treatment ('chemical castration'). The campaigns were finally successful when the World Health Organisation removed homosexuality from its list of mental disorders in 1990.† ECT, pharmaceutical castration and even real castration remain 'therapies' used in the 'treatment' of paedophiles. ECT is also sometimes given to people suffering severe depression or bipolar disorder.

Back at the first House of Commons debate in 1958, there was also the 'if you're not against it, you must be for it' argument. Very few on either side

---

* Dr Bennett was the only Tory practising psychiatrist in the Commons, as well as representing the UK in international yacht races.

† Although the WHO added by way of compensation something called 'ego-dystonic sexual orientation'. Don't ask …

dissented from the idea that you had to make a moral judgement about homosexual acts, and that judgement had to be negative:

> It is a well-known fact that homosexuals band themselves into groups, and I fear that if the law were changed so that homosexuals did not have this fear of punishment, those groups might elevate the practice of homosexuality to a cult. …
>
> Drinking parties have been organised as an introduction to the practice of homosexuality. I believe that the organisers have no sense of sin; they are homosexuals and they do not see that what they are doing is sinful.
>
> —Alfred Broughton, Labour, Batley and Morley[54]

It was – is – simply not true that prejudice is solely a result of ignorance. Several MPs such as Mann and Broughton showed prescience about the gay movement to come, though they expressed their prediction of the future in terms of absolute loathing. Homosexual men of the time would have viewed the prospects conjured by such MPs with delight, even if they didn't believe such a radical change of attitudes would come about in their lifetimes. Broughton again:

> I have a fear, based on what I know of homosexuals, that some, certainly not all, homosexuals will repress their homosexual feelings less. They may go to the extent even of showing some signs of the affection that they have for one another in public. I can envisage men walking along the street arm in arm, possibly holding hands, and at dances perhaps wishing to dance together and even caressing in public places.[55]

Men dancing together was to be one of the tests of whether a gathering of lesbians and gays constituted a disorderly house.

On the supporters' side, there was enlightenment in the speeches of H. Montgomery Hyde* and Peter Rawlinson†. Hyde quoted from letters he had received, and it is worth mentioning one to show the levels of low self-esteem which gay men were wrestling with at the time as a consequence of their social and legal stigmatisation:

> I do so want to try and make you people look upon this coming debate with kindness and sympathetic consideration and think 'There but for the

---

* Hyde was Unionist MP for Belfast, and was de-selected by his party at the 1959 election because of his speech in this debate, and also for being too often away from his constituency. Though there is nothing in his life to suggest he was gay, he became an expert in gay history and wrote several biographies of gay figures. *The Other Love* (1970) was the first history of homosexuality in the UK, and benefited from help from Antony Grey and the Albany Trust in finding case histories to cite, and to cover the modern period.

† Rawlinson was a barrister who had been Wildeblood's junior counsel at his trial. Later he was Attorney-General in Edward Heath's government.

> grace of God go I.' It is all right for people to condemn us so much, but they have no idea of the life of fear and dread we live all the time, in case our friends find out or we are caught. I know I did, and I know the hell I lived in when the police came to me, and I'm still living in hell now! You seem to be 'cut off' from everything, and can get no employment. Just because I was cursed with the homosexual trait, I was no more able to get rid of it than a man could get rid of cancer.[56]

Those who have labelled Wildeblood 'self-oppressive' because of the negative aspects of his portrayal of homosexuality should bear in mind the even more extreme negativity which saw homosexuality as a kind of cancer.

Peter Rawlinson drew on his legal experience:

> I can only say from my personal experience that I have left the court at the conclusion of some trials sickened by injustice, not so much of the verdict, but sickened by the injustice which does surround so many of this kind of crimes. To sit there and see a man, perhaps of talent and distinction, in the box, and to see the worthless wretched creatures being paraded there as witnesses for the Crown, pampered by the police as persons upon whom apparently there has been cast the mantle of perfection, is to feel that it is a mockery by society.[57]

Because it was merely a debate to 'note the contents' there was no vote in the Commons on this occasion. Eighteen months and a General Election later came the first serious attempt to get Wolfenden implemented, in a Private Member's Bill in the House of Commons, sponsored by the Labour MP for St Pancras North, Kenneth Robinson.* Robinson would have had a lot of contact with Tony Dyson's partner, Cliff Tucker, since much of his constituency covered Camden, where Tucker was now a Councillor. Though the HLRS had moved into the West End by 1960, its first office had also been in his constituency.

In the run-up to this debate, several important events occurred. On 12 May 1960, the HLRS held a public meeting at Caxton Hall in Westminster. Over a thousand people turned up, and a motion in support of implementing Wolfenden was passed by an alleged 1,000 to 3. It was the only large-scale public meeting the HLRS ever organised, in contrast to the Winter Talks which rarely drew more than a hundred people. In the columns of the *Spectator*, Dr Reid, who had lit the fuse for the reform movement in the same columns two years previously,† reappeared to train a spotlight once more on the disreputable behaviour of the police:

---

* Kenneth Robinson subsequently became Minister for Health in the Harold Wilson government and, on retiring from politics, Chairman of the Arts Council.

† See page 65.

> A friend of mine gave a lift to two men who sat in the back of his car. What took place there I do not know, but after police spies had appeared on the scene in a powerful and expensive limousine, a fine and binding-over were imposed on them. My friend, who was never accused of taking any part in the affair, was charged with being an accessory. He pleaded not guilty. For months the usual long and costly trials followed, ending with days of argument at Quarter Sessions, and a two and a half hour retirement of the jury. During this protracted period the accused understandably rather lost his head, and tried to commit suicide. He was for some time in hospital at the public expense. He was then found guilty and fined £10. The cost of all this to the State must have been several thousand pounds and we have the spectacle of a large number of presumably intelligent and highly paid men occupying themselves for days considering whether or not a man permitted an offence said to take place all the time at some schools and sometimes at all schools. …
>
> If anybody really wants to know how childish we are, I will take him to a public convenience in Bristol where a mirror is fixed to the ceiling so that a police spy may stand outside and see what is going on within. As any passing woman or child can take the place of the police, I complained to them, but no notice was taken, and this entertainment is still available to the citizens of Bristol.[58]

Three weeks later Ian Sainsbury in the same Letters Pages highlighted the ridiculousness of the use of criminal proceedings in the case of two young men in Glamorgan, who were convicted of homosexual offences *in a prison cell* while awaiting trial for similar 'crimes'.

And John Hunter pointed out that not all improvements were dependent on law reform:

> No legislation … would be required to end the degrading employment of young policemen as decoys and *agents provocateurs* to secure convictions. … The Home Secretary could issue orders that would put a stop to this revolting practice within twenty-four hours.[59]

But from a historical perspective, the most important letter was written by three undergraduates. They agonised over it for some time, before sending their letter to the *Daily Telegraph*, *The Guardian*, the *Spectator* and the *New Statesman*, who all hesitated before publishing it. In the event both *The Guardian* and the *Daily Telegraph* turned it down. It was that hot. They wrote, three weeks before the 1960 debate:

> Sir,
>
> We are homosexuals, and we are writing because we feel strongly that insufficient is being done to enlighten public opinion on a topic which has for far too long been shunned. Furthermore, because we deplore a situation which requires that most homosexuals who write letters for

> publication are obliged to do so under a pseudonym, we have determined deliberately to sign our real names, even though, by so doing, we realise that we are making only a token gesture which may well be foolhardy.
>
> Over the past few years an enormous amount has been spoken and written about the homosexual situation. Most of it has been realistic and sensible, some has been vicious and singularly ill-informed. But whatever its form we welcome it, because we must welcome anything which brings this topic, for so long taboo, into open discussion. Only in this way can prejudice, which is fear born of ignorance, be overcome. …
>
> Reform [of the law] though essential, is only a first step; there will remain the much larger and longer task of dissolving the centuries of accumulated and deeply ingrained misconception. We are under no illusions that this can be effected overnight, but we believe fervently that much can, and must, be done now by homosexuals like ourselves towards breaking through the barrier of public prejudice.[60]

This was the first time that ordinary gay men had 'come out' voluntarily and explicitly in print without the pressure of a court case. Here it was seen purely as an educational aid; later, when others took up the idea, it would be seen as good for the individuals who came out. The names of these brave boys were Roger Butler, Raymond Gregson and Robert G. Moorcroft.

Individual cases made great impact as well when they came to light. In 1959, when a man reported to the York police that someone was trying to blackmail him, he himself was tried, and sentenced to five years.

In the most widely publicised case of 1959, George Butler hanged himself in Durham jail while awaiting trial for gross indecency. He had been refused bail, and incarcerated for months. He was 17 years old. Mr Justice Elwes, who had been slated to hear the case, said:

> This is a disgraceful thing. In a decent world an adolescent would not be prosecuted on a criminal charge arising out of a sexual offence. He would be handed over to some intelligent sympathetic person who would help him out of his difficulties.[61]

Such cases would have impinged more on the consciousness of homosexuals in the regions, where the cases featured much more prominently in the local press, than in London. But one can be sure that supporters of the HLRS would have forwarded the press cuttings to their MPs, in case they hadn't seen them in the national papers or the capital's evening papers. In those, news-rich, stories such as these would merit only a few column inches on an inside page. In a local paper it would be front-page banner headlines.

It was in this context that the Commons held its second Wolfenden debate. MP Kenneth Robinson's moment came at 7 p.m. on 29 June, 1960. He opened, 'This is a subject which is distasteful and even repulsive to many people',[62] which set the tone of the following debate. There is a distinct air of the House holding its collective nose. Two of the usual suspects turned out again – Broughton, Shepherd – but the tone is slightly more moderate. Shepherd started his speech:

> I have a great admiration for those people, both inside and outside this House, who incur public stigma by supporting a policy which is contrary to public opinion, a great deal of which is ill-informed.[63]

This time around, his argument was that visibility and awareness of the subject had done harm to homosexuals; any publicity was bad publicity:

> I suggest that the last two years have, on the whole, made life exceedingly difficult for many homosexuals. Two or three years ago, the man who in middle age had not married would be able to say of himself, and other people would say of him, that he was probably a gay bachelor. With that rather light-hearted and probably quite erroneous assessment of his sexual nature, he would get away. Today, individuals know more about this subject. They have heard a great deal more talk about it and they say other things about the man whom they had previously called a gay bachelor.[64]

Shepherd here introduces into Parliament the word 'gay' in connection with homosexuality for the first time. The question – impossible to answer – is whether he was aware of the modern meaning of 'gay'. In the last sentence he almost seems to be bemoaning the 'corruption' of that 'innocent' word by nasty homosexuals – a recurring theme of newspapers' Letters Pages until very recently. On his own claims, Shepherd was widely read on the subject, and if his reading included any American literature it would have been impossible for him to avoid the American usage. It is unlikely, however, that many other MPs would have taken the point.

Where *Against the Law* had been the book of the hour in 1958, this time round it was Gordon Westwood's recently published *A Minority*. This was a series of interviews with 127 homosexuals which blew many stereotypes out of the water. William Shepherd had clearly done his homework in reading it, but twisted the intent to his own purposes. He seizes on statistics to 'prove' promiscuity ('If one reads this report one will see that 26% of homosexuals had between 12 and 24 partners during the last year.')* and proselytising ('It states that 20 per cent prefer to obtain partners who are not homosexuals and another 30 per cent are attracted by men who are not themselves homosexuals.') His main argument, however, is that changing the law will encourage bisexual people to act on their homosexual impulses rather than repressing them:

---

* And 32% were in a monogamous relationship, where another 35% had had a relationship lasting two or more years in the past.

> This book states that 20 per cent of the homosexuals who were interviewed had had regular heterosexual experience at some time during their lives. Therefore, we must not fall into the trap of believing that we are dealing with a helpless minority of men who have only one choice before them, namely, homosexual activity.[65]

Shepherd's arguments have become more sophisticated, which proves that the confirmed bigot becomes more dangerous with more knowledge. However, they were joined by some newcomers to the subject with more primitive attitudes:

> If we are to allow this sort of thing to occur, would my hon. Friend be happy to go into a public house and find a couple of hairy old males sitting on each other's knees and liking it? – Brigadier Terence Clarke, Conservative MP for Portsmouth West.[66]

On the positive side, the most notable speaker in the 1960 debate was Roy Jenkins, who would give tacit support for the Sexual Offences Act in 1967. And it took a woman, Eirene White, Labour MP for Flint East, to give a new twist to the Freudian approach:

> I believe that in considering the subject of male homosexuality a number of men consciously or subconsciously are moved to vehement condemnation by some feeling that they have to assert their own virility in the process.[67]

However, the Bill was defeated 213 to 99. It was all over in less than three hours.

Next time round, in 1965, with the more politically astute and cautious Antony Grey in charge of the HLRS campaign, the focus of lobbying would be more selective, on supporters and waverers; the backwoodsmen would be left undisturbed in their slumbers, in the hope that they wouldn't turn up.

Over the intervening years, there were two attempts to broker a compromise. Desmond Donnelly tried to introduce a bill to repeal the Labouchère Amendment, with its associated offence of gross indecency between males, but leaving buggery punishable with life imprisonment. Leo Abse tried to bring in a bill to reduce the penalties for importuning and gross indecency, and to get it enshrined in law that no prosecutions could take place without consulting the Director of Public Prosecutions. This would at least have had the effect of making sentencing more consistent around the country. But Allan Horsfall would have no truck with compromise. It was Wolfenden or nothing:

> It really is not good enough that it should be left to private members to seek to implement the findings of government enquiries. Mr Leo Abse's

> Bill … is totally inadequate. … A law which is bad is not made any less so simply because it is consistently administered.[68]

Though legislatively it went quiet in the early 1960s, there was one news story which brought the issue of homosexuality screaming onto the front pages again. John Vassall was a gay naval attaché who was set up by the KGB when he was photographed at a party having sex with several men, and subsequently blackmailed into spying. He provided information on British radar, anti-submarine equipment, torpedoes – several thousand documents, in fact.* In September 1962 he was arrested, and a month later was sentenced to 18 years imprisonment. This led to renewed hysteria in the press, of the kind that followed the Burgess and Maclean case. The *Sunday Mirror* ran a feature 'How to Spot a Homo', alongside an obviously faked photo of Vassall in his underpants [Caption: 'Vassall: a spy and homo – a gilt-edged specimen of his type']. According to reporter Lionel Crane, assisted by the shrink Clifford Allen, there were eight different types, from the unmarried middle-aged man who lived with his mother, through the crawler, 'the humble man with the fixed meaningless smile', to the one who is too clean and 'washes his hands a dozen times a day'. Rarely has the lack of hygiene of the traditional English male been so positively affirmed. The article concludes: 'Anyone with a grain of sense can smell the homos among these men.'[69] One would have thought it would be easier to smell the unwashed Heterosexual.

It was not the moment to try for law reform again.

By the time the Vassall spy story broke, Allan was out of local government. He had lost his seat on the Council in 1961, when the ward reverted to type and went Tory again. He had been moved by the Coal Board to a part of Atherton called Tyldesley† ('a godforsaken hole'). He was invited to get involved in the local Labour Party, and indeed to stand for a council seat again, but turned the offer down. He'd had enough of the politicking and hypocrisy, though he continued to offer the Labour Party use of his house at election times. In addition, doing his bit for the HLRS meant he was still writing to the local papers.

He was also, as all visible homosexual men and organisations were at the time, pushed into counselling and advising those deeply in the closet and filled with self-loathing. If you were a gay teenager in 1962, particularly in a small town, there was nowhere to turn to find out where to go to meet others. But if someone wrote to a paper, with their name and address attached, on the subject of homosexuality, with an appearance of knowing what they were

---

* The sheer number of documents suggests there was more than one 'mole', but this remains unproven.

† The address, in Robert Street, is sometimes referred to as being in Hindsford.

talking about, there was a contact. It could not be automatically assumed that writing about gay matters meant you were gay, but it helped. Allan never came out explicitly in print until much later, but he believed it was generally assumed he was homosexual. Certainly his letter-writing had a kind of vehemence and authority which would have implied it.

It did to Neil Makin,* a teenager in Blackpool. One of the the earliest items in the Horsfall archive in Manchester is this letter from Neil:

> To say simply thank you for your kindnesses and attentions these last few days seems rather empty sentiment, but I can assure you that I mean it from the very bottom of my heart, and I know that when my parents hear of what you have done, they will add their thanks to mine.
>
> To say that I was getting to the end of my tether is to use a hackneyed but never the less descriptive Lancashire term. However, what with your letter and the letter from Mr Grey I am beginning to feel that once more I am human and am looking forward to taking up a useful job again.[70]

Though coded, the reference to Antony Grey makes it clear what the 'hidden' subject is. When anyone wrote to the HLRS from 'the North', Grey generally referred them to Allan Horsfall, and Allan travelled hundreds of miles over the years to meet despairing correspondents, or they came to meet him. Reading between the lines, here is someone who has been paralysed with anxiety and depression, but has been relieved by the simple act of meeting another homosexual who has taken an interest in him. The reference to Neil's parents is interesting; we can't know for sure whether they were aware of their son's homosexuality and encouraged him to contact the HLRS, but the balance of probability is that they did. In this they were far from being alone. The furious incomprehending parent throwing out the errant offspring from the family home was not the only story.

Antony Grey

Antony Grey (real name Anthony Edgar Gartside Wright) was born just two weeks before Allan Horsfall in 1927. Before becoming HLRS Secretary he been a volunteer for four years. By his own account, he was a loner from an early age, the only child in an upper-middle-class household. His parents (accountant father and half-Syrian mother) had him quite late in life. So he was developing feelings he couldn't talk about and feeling unspoken and unrequited love for fellow students, when all that was on offer was adolescent sex play at his public school. Again by his own account, he decided before he was 20 that he wanted to do something to help change the law. He described

---

* Not his real name.

it as his 'life's ambition'. So here was another only child who had a compulsion to bring the world into alignment with himself rather than to adapt to the world:

> I am perhaps fortunate in never having experienced the phase of acute self-doubt, or even self-disgust, which so many young gay people pass through. [Being gay] was always so natural a part of my being ... that I couldn't understand how anybody else could doubt its validity, even if they didn't share the experience.[71]

17. Antony Grey in the 1960s

He studied history at Magdalene College, Cambridge, not an easy place to be gay in, before turning to journalism. He later had public relations jobs with the British Iron and Steel Federation and the London Press Exchange. This experience made him a very effective PR Officer for law reform, and taught him much that was useful for lobbying Parliament. As yet a campaigner without a movement, he was motivated to study for the bar in his spare time.

In private life, Grey lived suburbanly with his partner of 50 years, Eric Thompson, and they became one of the first couples to enter a civil partnership when partnerships were introduced in the UK in 2005. He was an accomplished amateur pianist with a penchant for showtunes of the 1920s and 30s, and a fondness for fine dining.* Ray Gosling says he was 'great, great

* Ray Gosling tells the story of him and Allan Horsfall inviting Grey out to lunch, many years later, expecting a modest cafe, and ending up in Soho with a bill for £100. Neither had enough money to pay for it, so Allan had to nip to a bank to cash a cheque.

fun', with a line in quite bitchy humour. It was a side of him well hidden from most people.

Gay Liberation Front pioneer Andrew Lumsden believes that Grey has been under-recognised in LGBT history. He was a friend of Lumsden's father, and they knew each other well.* Andrew points to the terrible price that Grey paid for his campaigning:

> Because he looked so straight, and because he was of a generation which thought in non-flower-power, non-love-in ways, he came across to the young as an elderly authority figure and even, to the most censorious, an 'Uncle Tom' because of the Parliamentary compromises he'd had to accept and endure just to cajole the House of Lords and MPs into a wording that would get a majority. … Yet he would get denounced to his face, or know he was being denounced behind his back, and later was sometimes denounced in print. … The more you learn of the compromises, agonising to himself, that he had to make to achieve the breakthrough that began the modern era, … the more you realise the heroic nature of what he did. He put up with the most horrendous attitudes in the 1960s, even from supporters, and often in ill-health, really damaged himself with the overload of work at the height of the campaign.[72]

But in public Grey vigorously denied any perceived weakness. He was an intimidating figure to many, with much in common with Wildeblood; he liked to get his own way, and was touchy about his position. He looked down through large thick-lensed glasses from his considerable height, and talked down to people in perfect Johnsonian sentences. He was dour. With his patrician, emphatic delivery, he always gave the impression that he, and the HLRS, knew what was best. And to be fair, he often did.

> He was very managing. And while he could of course make a joke like anybody else, it wasn't part of his campaigning style, so you got very much the committee man. And of course he could have been famous, had he wished, and had he had a different temperament. Had he been ceaselessly amusing in public like Clement Freud of the same generation, and still achieved what he did, he'd have become very, very well known and would have been adored at GLF as a character. But that personality was not his. Very severe glasses, horn rim often in those days.[73]

Allan Horsfall became a friend, though the friendship was tested several times over the years by disagreement. Allan was not one to be intimidated. After all, his partner Harold was a schoolmaster, with schoolmasterly manners, who

---

* Antony Grey's last holiday before he died was with Andrew, to Sirmione on Lake Como. Lumsden's book commemorating the visit, *Souvenirs of Sirmione* (One Roof Press, 2010) is a gay classic awaiting recognition.

likewise did not suffer fools gladly, and Pollard and Grey were two of a kind. Paul Temperton says of Harold:

> He ticked everybody off, all the time, in a slightly nannying way that schoolmasters have. But he knew a lot of things. He was quite wise in the ways of the world, even coming from a backwater like Accrington.[74]

But he could equally have been speaking about Antony.

Antony and Allan. It was a classic case of patrician London as opposed to the blunt, pugnacious North.

Witch-hunt in Bolton

In 1963 Allan had something to write about with a vengeance. The police conducted one of their periodic witch-hunts in Bolton, which was covered with relish by the *Bolton Evening News* on 26 June.

Opening the *Bolton Evening News* of 1963 now is like entering a lost world, as strange and distant as the Middle Ages. The small ads for ring spinners, doffers, slasher sizers, and one-card tenters speak of a vanished industry, the cotton mills. Letters are signed by imposing noms de plume: 'PUBLICUS', 'SIGNPOST' etc. Stories are an extraordinary mishmash. The resignation of the Prime Minister of Persia sits alongside a report of the Lady Mayoress going down the local pit. It had its share of scandal stories too. A year earlier it reported the Old Bailey conviction of a former local MP for indecency with teenagers. He had sat on the board of a local care home, and a string of liaisons went back four years or more. The accused, Sir Ian Horobin, said in evidence, 'Us poor devils are born like this and nothing can change me. It is natural for some men to love boys in this way.' He referred to his boys as 'sweethearts'. He got four years imprisonment.[75]

The moral attitudes of the time can be seen in the letters pages too, in all their busybody prurience:

> Some of the sex mad scenes [in the Peter Sellers film *Only Two Can Play**] I found absolutely disgusting. Is it any wonder there is so much immorality about when films like this are taken as a guide to life by so many young people?[76]

> When I visited a dance hall recently I was shocked to notice the number of married women there without their husbands. And people wonder why the divorce rate is increasing![77]

---

* X certificate, and the third most popular film in the UK in 1962. It is a highly moral film based on a Kingsley Amis novel, the adultery full of guilt and betrayal. In one scene a naked female is glimpsed very briefly from behind in a mirror.

On 26 June the *Bolton Evening News* was agog with the story of a 'homosexual vice ring'. Ten men, five of whom worked at Bolton General Hospital, appeared at the County Magistrates Court in committal proceedings to the Crown Court in Manchester. They were aged between 19 and 57. Prominent among them were John R., 24, an orderly, accused of fourteen offences with nine other men, and Vince L., 19 years old and a soldier, up on seven charges with two other men. The paper printed the names and addresses of all ten men.

They had been rounded up because they were all members of the Popular Pen Pals Club; police had got hold of the club membership records and taken it from there. This would have been bad enough, but what moved Allan was that at the core of this case was a true love relationship. John and Vince were obviously crazy about each other. As the prosecutor Cyril Morris said, 'So passionate was the affection between these two men that they wrote love letters to each other.' Vince was desperate to avoid being posted away with his regiment, and wanted to get out of the army in order to be with John. So he deliberately 'confessed' his homosexuality to his commanding officer in order to get discharged from the Service. His kit was searched, and the love letters were found. In the interrogation that followed, he described having sex with men in the toilets opposite the Town Hall. One of the detectives on the case said that John had admitted he was a homosexual, and that nothing anyone said was going to change him.

Then John came out in court with one of those simple, heart-wrenching statements which have echoed down the ages from time to time, from defiant gay men in the face of the law.* He said: 'You don't understand. I am in love with Vince. I don't think we did anything wrong.'[78] Allan was moved to write to the Letters Page in almost anguished tones:

> I have just learnt with horror of the recent homosexual witch-hunt in and around Bolton.
>
> Is there nobody in public life or in the Church in your town with the guts to speak out against this cruel and senseless injustice? I thought we had done with it, but if it is to go on then those who care about the difficulties of oppressed minorities will have to take a long hard look at the law reform movement in this country, and question whether, in this particular matter, it is any longer sufficient to await patiently the results of the dedicated efforts of a small and overworked London-based Reform Society.[79]

It was rare to find such passion in a letters pages devoted to the perpetual

---

* Cf. 'I think there is no crime in making what use I please of mine own body.'
—William Brown, July 1726.

sniping between ramblers and farmers and the like. It struck a chord. Rev. Kenneth Bishop, vicar of Deane, took up the explicit challenge to the Church:

> Mr Horsfall has challenged somebody in Church life to express his mind on the present law with regard to homosexuality. I accept his challenge, and say that, for the most part, I agree with his opinion.
>
> In these days, when there is so much sexual laxity, it may strike your readers as strange that a clergyman should appeal for a change in the law. Please do not misunderstand me. I believe, as the Bible does, that homosexuality is a sin.
>
> But I also believe that in this case the law treats it in a far harsher way than it does other sins which are worse, and I consider with Mr Horsfall that the sinners in this case are being treated in a way that is not very likely to lead to their reform, and which does them, and the hospital in which they have worked, a very great deal of harm.[80]

Of course there was the backlash. Miriam Greenwood wrote:

> Dramatic references to 'witch hunts' are ridiculous. Punishment is meted out to men who defile one another, and are not content merely to leer at innocent youth, whom we must protect from these perverts.[81]

But it was a backlash of only one. And it allowed Antony Grey to weigh into the debate with patrician disdain,* with a rebuke for Ms Greenwood and a plug for his organisation:

> Does she really consider that to punish grown men for acts of private immorality committed as long as six years ago, not merely with a court appearance but also with professional disgrace, the loss of their employment and the forfeit of pension rights involving, in at least one of these cases, the loss of 10 years' superannuation contributions, should be called anything kinder [than a witch-hunt]? If so, I would suggest she has a very defective sense of what justice is.[82]

It's clear from this that Horsfall was in regular contact with Grey, reporting on cases in the local area and sending copies of his correspondence. There was no other way Grey would have known of the case, since the HLRS had tried and rejected the use of a cuttings agency to trawl the local press for them.

With letters appearing at the rate of four to one in favour of law reform, Allan was emboldened to go and see the deputy editor of the *Bolton Evening News*, Michael Hope. This was at the suggestion of Grey, since Allan was at this time very much a foot soldier of the HLRS. Assuming the balance of letters reflected the paper's own liberal opinions, he asked Hope to run an article. Hope said he disapproved of law reform, and had in fact had many

---

* 'I would not have intervened in this local discussion, did I not feel that …'

letters of disapproval, but they had been phrased so violently that he'd returned them all to the writers and asked for rewrites. None of them subsequently appeared. Interestingly, the Bolton police also checked up with the editor to see if the letters reflected 'what the town really thought'. This suggests that they were concerned that their policing should be in line with public opinion.

The Bolton Ten case was far from being the only outrageous case in 1963. A 21-year-old Essex labourer and a 24-year-old black American airman were brought before the court for buggery and gross indecency. The 21-year-old had learning difficulties. Both were sentenced to three years, though the magistrate was of the opinion that 'there is no question of corruption, both prisoners being grown-up men.'

A local campaign – at last

By 1963, the atmosphere at the HLRS had changed. With Antony Grey now Secretary, well-meaning but ineffective do-gooders had been partly replaced by a professional campaigner. When Grey took over from Rev. Hallidie Smith as Secretary, he started the practice of putting supporters of the campaign in touch with each other if they lived in the same area. In this way small informal discussion groups popped up here and there, where maybe half a dozen supporters could meet. This was a strategy Grey initiated as a way of both broadening the campaign and dealing with the hundreds of requests which poured in to Shaftesbury Avenue, asking for help and advice.* A minute of the HLRS Executive of 26 October 1963 records:

> After some discussion, it was agreed to accept the Secretary's suggestion, which had been prompted by recommendations from supporters, that local committees should be formed in a limited number of provincial centres, and constitutionally affiliated to the Society's London office. … The Secretary was authorised to discuss this matter in Manchester with a group of supporters there who had requested him to do so.[83]

However, the HLRS laid down strict rules about what these groups could do. Its Honorary Committee of the great and good did not like the idea of groups over which it had no control. Ideally it wanted a member of the committee 'in charge of' each group. So groups were not allowed to publicise themselves, and they were most definitely not to be identified as gay. Gay people of course

---

* On 14 January 1964 Grey reported to his EC that the HLRS had received 900 requests for help in the last five months.

worked as volunteers in the HLRS office in Shaftesbury Avenue* but they were not put forward for the Committee or as spokesmen. Grey himself was never allowed to declare his sexuality, and only got the job of Secretary on condition that he did not use his real name.

18. Stanley Rowe's house in Moxley Road, where the early meetings were held

It was to take a year to set up the Manchester group. Grey kicked off by contacting his Manchester supporters. He wrote to Allan introducing Stanley Rowe:

> He and his wife said they would temporarily do secretarial work if need be, but of course it is impossible from Manchester. Recently he wrote saying that he had several teachers, social workers and probation officers interested in the idea of forming a local committee in Manchester. … If you would join, it would relieve my mind considerably, as I would feel that there was at least one member who has his head screwed on sensibly.
>
> There are a number of things such a group could usefully do, such as organising a public meeting, circulating literature etc, and if it were successful, similar groups might come into being elsewhere.[84]

Rowe, heterosexual, married, was a leader of the Jewish Youth Movement in Manchester. In due course he wrote to Allan to tell him of the group that had

* Among them was future CHE local group convenor and EC Member of over thirty years, Griff Vaughan Williams. Ken Plummer the pioneer sociologist, and GLF and CHE member Michael Brown also joined the envelope stuffers.

been meeting for a few weeks at his house; would Allan like to join them? Allan would, and his first meeting with them, on 4 June 1964, at 4 Moxley Road, near Heaton Park, might be described as the founding moment of the North Western Homosexual Law Reform Committee (NWHLRC), and therefore the start of CHE.* There were eight people present, according to Allan, although the minutes list only five, and only a couple were gay. Most probably the discrepancy indicates the trepidation with which people joined, fearing to be identified with such a cause and possibly even fingered as gay.

The minutes are headed 'Homosexual Law Reform Society – Manchester', but Grey was reluctant to let the group use 'HLRS'. They were not sufficiently under central control, and there was still fear in London that somehow the rough Northerners would let the side down. Grey insisted they find a different name.

Among the other heterosexuals was Colin Harvey. He was Scottish, young, and Senior Social Worker for the Church of England North West Board of Social Responsibility. Though married with two children, he had a profound conviction that the law needed to be changed as a matter of urgency and a matter of justice. He reported on the little discussion group to his Board, whose chair was the Bishop of Middleton, Ted Wickham.

Wickham was one of the few working-class boys to go into the Church of England, and one of even fewer who made it up the hierarchy to Bishop. Ray Gosling described him as a 'rough, tough East End cockney'.[85] He was one of the leading supporters of reform within the Church, and offered to facilitate the group. Colin and Allan set to work to get the inaugural meeting set up. They wrote to all Colin's social work contacts, to local vicars and other church leaders. At the time there were about thirty HLRS supporters in the area, and they too got the invitation. Significantly, they also recruited through the gay bars, especially the Rockingham, Matthew's and Club Rouge. All the owners were supportive, but they feared the constant plain-clothes police surveillance, and though willing to help they didn't want to do anything which could be seen by visiting police as somehow rocking the boat. The Rockingham displayed collecting tins for the NWHLRC – always the initials, never the word 'homosexual' – and promptly hid them if any police or council official visited. So Colin and Allan largely spread the word by buttonholing people. As a result, the NWHLRC had a grassroots constituency of ordinary gay people attending meetings, which the HLRS in London lacked.

Meanwhile in London Antony Grey reported to his Executive that 'he would be visiting Manchester to address the inaugural meeting of the North-Western Homosexual Law Reform Committee on 7 October.' This was

* Usually dated from the first formal semi-public meeting at Church House on 7 October 1964. A plaque outside Church House commemorates this.

indeed at Church House in Deansgate, although it was not really a public meeting, in that it was not publicly advertised as such.

19. Ted Wickham, Bishop of Middleton

The secretary was to be Allan; Tony said the meeting 'would discuss ... the question of contributions and its constitutional relationship with the Homosexual Law Reform Society'.[86] This relationship was one which exercised both parties. For those in Manchester, the bone of contention was the lack of democracy in the HLRS. Though both Grey and Horsfall referred to 'members' in Manchester, the HLRS legally had only supporters. The first North Western Chairman, Rev. Bernard Dodd, suggested Manchester should be represented on the London Committee, but this came to nothing.

There was to be a fee of £2/10/- (£2.50), and Grey suggested that £1 of this should be a levy for the national office. In fact, this Northern offshoot never contributed to the London parent beyond paying Grey's travel expenses. The traffic was rather in reverse, with the HLRS Executive Committee granting £50 to the North Western Committee immediately after it was set up. And the Christmas 1964 edition of *Spectrum*, the HLRS monthly bulletin, welcomed the formation of the 'North-Western Homosexual Law Reform Committee, which has come into existence to supplement the work of the HLRS by local effort'.* Allan remembers:

* The HLRS is confused over the precise name of the NW Committee. They were not the only ones, and it is referred to variously as the Northern, North West and North Western Committee, with or without a hyphen. The correct name, which appears on the letterhead and leaflets, is North Western Homosexual Law Reform Committee.

> The meetings were open in the sense that anybody was free to come. We didn't have members as such, we just had supporters and we didn't levy a subscription as they came or didn't come. Everybody on the mailing list was told when the meetings were.[87]

However, it's clear that the Bishop wasn't happy with the set-up. A Committee needed members, it needed minutes. Allan recalled:

> The Bishop of Middleton got a bit upset about this, and said it wasn't very satisfactory that decisions weren't taken in the name of a named and identifiable committee. After that we decided we must keep minutes and record who was there or not, and the result of that was a lot of people who used to come ceased to come because they didn't want to be identified even to that extent of being recorded in the minutes. That in itself is evidence of how delicate a matter it was at that time.[88]

20. The plaque commemorating the first formal meeting at Church House

Niel Pearson, a prominent local solicitor who was on the radio a lot, bravely became President, projecting the 'asexual' image at that point felt to be desirable.* But, though heterosexual, they were full of enthusiasm. First off, the Committee needed publicity. They wrote a pamphlet, *Something You Should Know*. There was a last minute problem with it: what was the contact address and phone number to be? Allan again:

> I had rather arrogantly assumed that since we were using the C. of E. boardroom for our meetings, that we would be able to use that address on

* Pearson was chairman of the commercial station, Piccadilly Radio, at its start in 1974, a governor of Manchester United and President of the Manchester Law Society. He was President of the North Western Committee for nine years, through its mutation to CHE, and then became an honorary Vice President. He died in 1975.

> our publicity materials, but the Bishop pointed out that that would be a step too far for the traditional wing of the church. So we were left with the whole thing set up in what had been hot metal, just waiting for an address so that it could go to the printers. And rather impetuously, I decided that they could print it with my home address, which was the coal board house in Atherton. And we sent it off and got 10,000 printed on rather good card.[89]

The use of a home address for such a controversial campaign seems like an act of almost reckless daring. Once the home addresses of campaigners such as Peter Tatchell become known, they can be besieged by anything from homophobic graffiti to shit through the letter box to actual firebombs. But Allan put 3 Robert Street, Atherton and his home phone number on the leaflet, with the sublime self-confidence of ignorance.

The leaflets went off to the local press. The new committee tried to place an ad in the *Manchester Evening News*, which turned them down. But smaller papers serving the satellite towns of Greater Manchester were not so illiberal. One which accepted the ad was the *Leigh Reporter*, and an eagle-eyed editor spotted the unprecedented content. As a result, Allan was door-stepped by a fresh-faced 16-year-old cub reporter, David Dutton, who wanted to interview him at home. Allan's first thought was that this was a police *agent provocateur*, but the boy was too young to be that. His next thought was that this was a joke set up by someone else from his committee, or that the boy had been sent from his paper as a joke by *his* colleagues, to embarrass him. What he didn't anticipate was 8-column banner headlines.

'That's the sort of headline you only get if war's been declared!' commented Allan. Under this banner ('Homosexuals and the Law', subhead 'Hindsford* man is heading NW Campaign') was a very respectable story:

> In 1957 the Wolfenden Report recommended that British Homosexual Law should be brought in line with those of almost all civilised countries … the leaflet goes on to say that homosexuals are vulnerable to young troublemakers.[90]

And so on over 100 column centimetres. And it gives Allan's home address.

The Coal Board Estates Manager who employed Allan found out what was going on when he opened his local paper. Allan had known enough not to ask the Coal Board, his landlord, for permission to use his home address, because he knew it would have been refused. Once he found out, the Estates Manager was very annoyed not to have been consulted. He summoned Allan to a meeting in his office. Allan thought, 'I haven't breached my tenancy

---

* Hindsford is a suburb of Atherton, but the actual address is sometimes considered to be in a different suburb, Tyldesley.

agreement, so if he wants to see me he can come here.' (This was purely symbolic, since they worked about ten yards apart.) But the manager never made the trip down the corridor, and Allan continued uninterrupted.

21. Allan Horsfall in 2008, with a copy of the Leigh Reporter

The sky did not fall in as a result of the leaflet. No groups of outraged miners marched on 3 Robert Street. There were no broken windows or abusive letters. The community received the news very calmly. According to Allan:

> The Coal Board house played a significant role in the gay campaign in a way that nobody had anticipated, because it emerged later that much of the opposition in Parliament had come from the miners' MPs, and various other people connected with the miners. … Mrs Jean Mann …was always sounding off in the Commons about how such a reform would not go down well with the Townswomen's Guild, or the Miners' Lodges. Similarly in South Wales the miners were construed as being opposed to it, which must have been an inhibiting factor for Leo Abse, who was a miners-sponsored MP.
>
> When articles appeared in the *New Statesman* saying how opposed the miners were to this thing, we were able to reply … that we'd been conducting a reform campaign from a miner's cottage in Lancashire, and had met no opposition at all over a period of eighteen months, and I think that had the effect of calming them a bit.[91]

The NWHLRC leaflets got around a lot. A thousand were distributed at the Labour Party conference and the TUC conference in Autumn 1965. One was picked up by Lancashire County Alderman Arthur W. Tack, who wrote to the Committee:

> Dear Sir, I think that homosexuals should be locked away from decent society. That is something *you* should know about (to quote your circular).[92]

In addition to the leaflets, the NWHLRC started producing a *Bulletin* for supporters on the mailing list. At first it was an occasional duplicated double-sided sheet, usually produced in the period coming up to some parliamentary debate on law reform.

Lord Arran and the 1965 debate

The next debate, five years after the last, was in May 1965, when the Earl of Arran introduced his own Sexual Offences Bill in the House of Lords.

Arthur Strange Kattendyke David Archibald Gore, 8th Earl of Arran, 8th Baron Saunders of Deeps, 4th Baron Sudley of Castle Gore, was a dyed-in-the-wool Tory and Government Whip in the Lords. Known to his friends as Boofy, he drank half a bottle of champagne every day before lunch. He also kept a pet badger and married a speedboat racer. Why this deeply eccentric figure, something out of PG Wodehouse,* espoused the cause of homosexual law reform seems something of a mystery, until you learn that his older brother was gay and committed suicide a mere nine days after inheriting the title; the suggestion being that the title would have brought with it an intolerable degree of public scrutiny to a very private man.[93] When Boofy became the 8th Earl, the sense of guilt must have been considerable. Having taken up the cudgels for homosexual law reform, he proved tenacious, if over-enamoured of his own daring.† With fellow-Tory Humphry Berkeley and Labour's Leo Abse in the Commons, he formed the triumvirate which piloted the Sexual Offences Bill through both Houses of Parliament over the next two years.‡ His years as a diplomatic Press Attaché gave him both an instinct for publicity and a sense of what would or would not 'play' with his colleagues in the Lords.

These contained some opponents so fervently bigoted as to drive the uncommitted into Arran's arms. They had not had the benefit, if such it can

---

* 'My father told me that if you saw a man in a Rolls Royce you could be sure he was not a gentleman, unless he was the chauffeur.'

—widely attributed to the Earl of Arran, but unsourced.

† 'My only fear was that because I was so outspoken I might get arrested.'

‡ His other interest was the protection of badgers, on which he was a great expert. When asked why his badger bill failed where his bill decriminalising homosexuality succeeded, he said, 'Not many badgers in the House of Lords.'

be called, of the previous debates and the lobbying that went with them. Lord Kilmuir, who as Home Secretary Sir David Maxwell Fyfe had commissioned Wolfenden, foamed at the mouth about 'sodomitical societies and buggery clubs'.[94] In fact 'a licence for buggers' clubs' became a kind of refrain during the House of Lords debate.

Viscount Montgomery, himself a deeply repressed homosexual,[95] played the xenophobic card: 'I have heard some say that such practices are allowed in France ... We are not French ... We are British, thank God!' He proposed an amendment that the age of consent should be 80, because:

> after the age of 80 it doesn't really matter what we do, and ... at least one has the old-age pension to pay for any blackmail that may come along. I regard the act of homosexuality in any form as the most abominable bestiality that any human being can take part in.[96]

Among those watching the debate were Michael Brown, a dentist, who was to become a member of the Gay Liberation Front, and later of CHE. Like many another gay man he asked his local MP to get him a ticket for the debate. Since he lived in Marylebone his MP was Lord Hailsham, who duly obliged. However, because of a mix-up, the ticket was not for the public gallery, but for the MPs' gallery, where members of the Commons could watch the proceedings of the Lords. Armed with a copy of Hansard and the order of proceedings, Brown took his seat aloft.

> I was in the front row, there were two gay MPs gossiping about the debate. I saw that, they were definitely gay. So this debate went on, and I had a Hansard, and ... Monty stood up and said, 'I have an amendment. I propose that the age of consent should not be 21, as suggested, but it should be 70.'* At which I got so angry I stood up and I shook my fist at him, and the Hansard flew out, and the leaves broke up, and fluttered down, and everybody looked up. Meanwhile I was sitting there and the gentleman ushers rushed upstairs. They looked in the public gallery and couldn't find me, because I was sitting with the MPs.[97]

It was a lucky escape. Boffing a national hero with a copy of Hansard, even lightly, would certainly have meant imprisonment.

The hysteria shown by Monty and his friends arose in part from the sense of the homophobes becoming an increasingly isolated minority. Society was changing, even MPs were changing gradually, which left the elderly Lords as the only defenders of so-called 'Christian' values. Even most of the bishops were changing and had deserted traditional morality in favour of legalising the buggers.

---

* Actually 80.

Eventually, on 28 October 1965, the House of Lords passed the Arran Bill by 96 to 31. However, there was no immediate follow-up in the Commons, although Leo Abse was trying to introduce another Private Member's Bill there. Abse was refused leave to introduce his Bill by 19 votes. Allan commented in a letter to Antony Grey:

> Very sad; even the BBC described it as 'surprising'; and now we must go back to the politics of the 'long haul'. The ludicrous position which now exists, with the Lords in favour and the Commons against, is bound to lend weight to the uninformed to the idea that homosexuality is the pastime of the idle rich.[98]

Parliamentary lobbying was not the only area of activity. Letter writing and public speaking took up a lot of time, whether there was a Parliamentary campaign in the offing or not. The May 1965 *Bulletin* reported correspondence in *Tribune*, *Peace News*, the *Manchester Evening News*, and various local papers in the Greater Manchester area. Allan also went to talk to student unions in Manchester and Lancaster. There were press cuttings to gather, to feed to Antony Grey in London. There was money to raise; several times the organisation threatened to die, starved of funds. The *Bulletin* appealed unashamedly for money from the start:

> We are grateful to those supporters who have given financial support, some very generously, but only a minority … have helped in this way and the flow of money has now dried up. Even a campaign without paid help can only be effective if there is money for stationery, postage, pamphlets, advertisements, meeting halls, etc.[99]

One of the first things they spent money on was an advert in the *Guardian*, in January 1965. Responses came from all over the country. Scrupulously Allan wrote to Grey that his Committee had got many replies out of their 'intended sphere of influence' and the writers of these had been asked to write directly to London.

Meg Elizabeth Atkins and the Trafford Estate

Some supporters undertook campaigning activities on their own. On the Committee were two heterosexual women. One, Meg Atkins,* had been a stable hand before moving to Manchester, where she was now working as a secretary, flitting between jobs to support her writing. She had had two or

* The other, Rosalind Hargreaves, became head of the Social Science Research Unit at the University of Kent, and helped to set up the Gaysoc there.

three novels published, most recently *The Gemini.** She got involved in the Committee because her best friend was a gay man:

> It seemed to me a total injustice that simply because of your sexual inclinations you should be criminalised.[100]

22. Meg Elizabeth Atkins c. 1980

She liked drinking in the Midland Hotel in Manchester, which had a gay bar. She told Allan that it was the only bar where she felt comfortable on her own. She remembered:

> I didn't used to go into bars on my own. I used to go in with my friend. I was a young woman, and I was quite attractive, and I couldn't go in many places on my own without people trying to pick me up.
>
> I met Allan there, and he was such a lovely man. Not a handsome man, but he had a very strong face. He was the driving force, but in the gentlest way. He was a gentle man. You warmed to him. I think it was his basic decency that powered the thing.
>
> I went to committee meetings. Everybody was so positive and active and engaged, and I thought, 'Well, there must be something I can do, instead of just being sympathetic. Put my money where my mouth is.' And it just occurred to me, I had a friend who'd been a welfare officer. And I thought, these were the sort of people who you go to with your problems and any difficulties. I mean, men were sacked for being gay. [101]

* *The Gemini* has a gay theme; later she repudiated the novel as an apprentice effort. Later she would specialise in crime fiction, with her series character DCI Sheldon.

The *Bulletin* of July 1966 reported that she:

> has been ploughing a lonely and courageous furrow around the large industrial firms in Trafford Park seeking interviews with Personnel Officers to tell them about the existence of this committee and the work it has been doing. In every instance except one she has been received with courtesy and interest and a desire to understand our work and the need it is meeting. Some of them had encountered homosexual difficulties in the course of their work in personnel management. Some agreed to display the Committee's literature on their works notice boards. … She is now enquiring into the attitude of various companies towards homosexual employees whose condition has become generally known, for one reason or another.[102]

Behind this lies a more human story. Meg Atkins was very, very glamorous. Tall, with a kind of clothes horse body made for modelling. High cheek bones, big brown eyes. Imagine Audrey Hepburn or Kay Kendall in full rig – picture hat and elbow-length gloves, a handbag over the arm. On one of the grimmest industrial estates in Greater Manchester – or, indeed, in the country. She told the author:

> The Trafford Estate was enormous. Every kind of manufacturing, every heavy industry. One of the most famous was Metrovicks.* I didn't go there. I felt it was too big to take on. I did the more hand-knitted stuff. Smaller ones I thought were friendlier. I had to psych myself up to do it. 'Right, I'm going to do it today.' And I'd do it.
>
> I'd always be very well dressed and presentable. Hat and gloves. I would go in and say, 'May I see your welfare officer, please?' So they thought, 'Well, she's not selling something.' They said, 'Who are you?' I said, 'I'm from the Law Reform Society.' If I'd said 'homosexual', I wouldn't have got in. But that was the attitude of the time. Once I was in, of course I came clean immediately. But I felt people should talk – nowadays we call it raising awareness.
>
> It was mainly men, though if there was a woman welfare officer, she was very sympathetic and understanding. The man would take me into his office. Sit me down. 'So you're from the Law Reform Society.' 'Well actually I'm from the Homosexual …' 'Oh.' Pause. A big pause. And then I just had to say that there is a great deal of pressure now for change in the law. 'You're probably aware of that.' 'Is there?' Or 'Yes.' Or 'About bloody time.' Or 'There shouldn't be.' The whole gamut of possible reactions. There was one guy who was very leering, very crude. Which was the kind of thing you would meet then. And another man tried to make a date with me. It was terribly funny. I wouldn't have been seen dead with him!

---

* Metropolitan Vickers made diesel locomotives for British Rail in Manchester.

> I would have to play it by ear to take it from there. If I had a totally unsympathetic person to speak to, I knew I wasn't going to get very far, so I'd just say, 'Perhaps you would be interested in this literature' and get out. Or 'Obviously I'm in the wrong place.' 'Yes you bloody well are.' Or I'd say 'Thank you for listening, thank you for your time.'
>
> But sometimes people were relieved to talk. Quite a lot of people did say to me, 'Well, we have had difficulties.' Of course it was illegal then, so they couldn't show support. I never had any tangible evidence of what effect it had, but it was just building contacts. It contributed to a climate of opinion. You've got to start somewhere. Mine was a tiny contribution to it.
>
> When my mother found I'd joined this society, she was speechless with horror. We didn't talk about it. And the boyfriend I had at the time that I joined, he said, 'You mustn't tell anybody.' I said, 'What do you mean? If I want to talk about it, I'll talk about it.' He said, 'You don't realise it would damage your reputation.' 'You mean as a writer? I've only just started, I haven't got a reputation yet, but I will have.' He said, 'Yes, it'll damage it.' The amount of prejudice was awful. It was hurtful. It used to hurt me.[103]

As a piece of campaigning this was years ahead of its time, but she was a determined and dedicated woman, working her way through the factories and workshops a few at a time. She regularly updated Allan with her progress report:

> I've been suffering a beastly bout of flu and am just coming to the surface. ... By a coincidence I went into Trafford Park but didn't feel well enough to make more than a couple of calls.[104]

Again, on 6 September 1966:

> I'm afraid holidays and many things have contrived to keep me from my 'beat' in Trafford Park since I last saw you; I'll try and work in the odd afternoon in the next couple of weeks.[105]

You can hear the county tones in that 'beastly bout of flu', and in the arch use of the word 'beat'.

By 1966, the character of the Committee was changing. There were between fifteen and twenty-five at each meeting. The heterosexuals were now well in the minority. According to Meg:

> It was largely made up of, it seemed to me, younger men. Very attractive young men! They were in their twenties. I think they regarded me as an alien species and were very ill at ease with me. They used to plan weekends together. Take over somebody's bed and breakfast place in Blackpool for the weekend. Which obviously left me on the side-lines. And they'd all go off and have these – orgies, I suppose. There was quite a group of them like that. It had become thoroughly evolved.[106]

Organising a Public Meeting

But the most important project of all was to get a public meeting organised, which Grey had floated as an idea a year even before the group started, and which is mentioned in the minutes of the first meeting in June 1964. The idea was to bring big-gun speakers from London to draw a crowd. It took over two years to come to fruition. Grey wrote to Horsfall on 15 February 1965:

> The Chairman* was very impressed with your pamphlet and has agreed in principle to arrange for speakers.

The speakers were an age in coming forward. First there was a problem with getting the venue. The Committee wanted the Lesser Free Trade Hall, which had dates free in early April, but this didn't coincide with dates when the Dean of Manchester would be free to chair the debate. Then there was the problem of getting a 'big name'; the Committee wanted three people – one from London, one from the North (Sidney Silverman?) and Grey himself. Londoners proved reluctant to volunteer, and MPs especially so. After all, the Labour government only had a majority of four, and an election could happen at any moment. They had to keep an eye on their seats and their majorities. Grey wrote to Horsfall at the end of March, apologising for Norman St John-Stevas, a new Tory MP:

> I wonder how much (if anything) he is in fact willing to do for us. He only joined the EC on the understanding that he wouldn't be able to attend many meetings, but I had hoped we might lure him onto a few public platforms. I think you may also find Jeremy Thorpe† a bit cagey about speaking on this.[107]

So then they started thinking about June, and then the autumn.

Over the months and years, the correspondence between Grey and Horsfall became quite intimate. They were similarly placed – lumbered with cautious, largely heterosexual, committees who wanted to move at a slower pace than they did. They could bitch about their own organisations to each other. Antony complained in April about his own committee, 'I'm beginning to wonder whether some of them aren't a rather doubtful blessing, even for the price of their names on the notepaper!'[108] And again in July about having continuing difficulties getting anyone to address a meeting: 'They really are somewhat of a dead weight and at times I feel a bit irked that everything is left to me.'[109]

---

* Philosopher Professor Sir A. J. Ayer, known to friends and colleagues as Freddy.

† Thorpe was positioning himself to take over the leadership of the party, which he did in 1967. Despite law reform being official Liberal Party policy, Thorpe was reluctant to advocate it in public – it was also a subject too close to his personal life.

Allan had similar feelings about his own committee:

> I am faced with a Committee which never consists of the same people at successive meetings; they therefore tend to reverse decisions. Last time I had an 'Anti-meeting' faction; they endorsed approval of public meetings in principle, but said that they did not want any until there was a definite prospect of the Bill going into the House of Commons. Sorry to be so unhelpful.[110]

This put the idea of the meeting on the back burner for another year. There were many in London who still distrusted this semi-independent group of bolshie Northerners and didn't think they could be trusted to get the right kind of publicity. Foremost among them was the criminologist C. H. Rolph,* Chairman of the Albany Trust. Antony Grey had to act as a buffer between the North Western Committee and the sceptics in London. He reassured Rolph:

> If the people here [Manchester] are going on with trying to organise a meeting, I would not wish to try and stop them. They are trying to get the Bishop of Manchester or the Bishop of Middleton to take the chair and this should do a good deal to counter the possibility of the press treating such a meeting as you fear they might.[111]

Apart from the practical difficulties of dates and times, this fear of bad publicity was the main reason for the reluctance of the bigwigs to head up from London to address the meeting.

Humphry Berkeley and the 1966 debate

The next debate found the issue back before the House of Commons. Six months after Abse's abortive attempt to introduce a bill in the summer of 1965, the liberal Tory† MP for Lancaster, Humphry Berkeley, came second in the ballot to introduce Private Members' Bills that session, and put forward another Sexual Offences Bill. Berkeley made little effort to conceal his own homosexuality, and was, according to Leo Abse, intensely disliked in the Commons.‡ On the other hand, Grey and Horsfall preferred Berkeley to

---

* Real name C. Rolph Hewitt. He had been a policeman for twenty-five years, rising to Chief Inspector, before turning to legal and criminal journalism. He was on the editorial board of the *New Statesman* 1947–70.

† Berkeley resigned from the Tories over their Vietnam policy, joined Labour, left Labour to join the SDP, then re-joined Labour when the SDP was debating whether to hook up with the Liberals.

‡ Abse is not necessarily reliable in this, as he was rather jealous of his position as the 'Legaliser of Homosexuality', and there was rivalry here.

Abse, as a man who would not make many compromises, unlike Abse. The January 1966 *Bulletin* urged supporters to write to their MPs once again, before the debate on 11 February:

> We have reason to hope that one or two might have shifted their ground because of our representations, but in the final analysis it is constituents who can most effectively do this work.[112]

The usual suspects – Shepherd, the two Cyrils (Black and Osborne) – were out in force, but the arguments were no different. Shepherd again found a text with which to bolster his prejudices; in this case, Richard Hauser's *The Homosexual Society*, which had been written with Home Office money and HLRS co-operation. Antony Grey, who helped with providing contacts and opinion, felt betrayed by the book. According to Shepherd, Hauser:

> knows of no minority … among whom self-pity and self-righteousness are so rampant. He knows of no minority which is so lacking a sense of values outside its own circle, no minority which is so bereft of loyalty to its country.[113]

To which one of the Doctors in the House, David Kerr, MP for Wandsworth, barracked: 'Speaking with what limited knowledge is available to me as a professional man in this field, I may say that this is one long string of claptrap.'[114] Shepherd did not have it all his own way this time, and he was unused to having his pose of being an expert questioned.

Shepherd always maintained he would have supported the repeal of the Labouchère Amendment, but he showed scant sympathy for blackmail victims. The reason they were blackmailed, he said, was because:

> homosexuals are so undiscriminating in their choice of partners. They pick them up here there and everywhere. Quite wealthy men get odd boys off the streets or pick them up in bars and clubs … and, if the boy makes off with the silver, it is not at all surprising.[115]

Leo Abse, who was to take the baton from Berkeley for the last and successful push to pass the bill the following year, opined in this debate that not passing this bill was creating a diversion from:

> the real challenge of preventing little boys from growing up to be adult homosexuals. How can we reduce the number of faulty males? How can we see that we have less of these individuals with men's bodies but feminine souls?[116]

Even the supporters were outrageously ignorant, their views of homosexuality still harking back to the 1890s and earlier.

The final flowering of prejudice came from Cyril Osborne, a man not noted for subtlety of argument:

> I am rather tired of democracy being made safe for the pimps, the prostitutes, the spivs, the pansies and now the queers. It is high time that we ordinary squares had some public attention.[117]

The distinction between 'pansies' and 'queers' is interesting, but it is not clear what he means by making it; when did he think that democracy had been made safe for 'pansies'? The Home Secretary, Roy Jenkins, congratulated the House for the reasonable tone of its debate.

One thing which had little impact on the debate, although campaigners feared it might, was the early 1960s panic about venereal disease.* The British Medical Journal drew attention to two West London hospitals which published findings that over 70 per cent of men with infectious syphilis believed they had caught it through homosexual activity. The gay man as source of infection would re-emerge as an archetype twenty years later with the onset of the AIDS pandemic, but many of the lines of battle were established in this period. 'The Homosexual and Venereal Disease' was a BMA pamphlet which promoted this line, but the counter-arguments came forcibly from Antony. Venereologists, he said, regard the law as a thoroughly bad one, because:

> it not only prevents many homosexuals seeking treatment when they badly need it, let alone regular check-ups; it also greatly inhibits the necessary spread of frank information about the subject, and it is consequently the case that many practising homosexuals are completely unaware of the fact that they can contract venereal disease in this way as easily as through heterosexual intercourse. ... I am in little doubt that the present state of the law is quite largely responsible for this.[118]

However the debate remained untarnished by VD. And Humphry Berkeley's bill was given a second reading by 164 to 107 votes – a significant advance. But it was to no avail. Less than three weeks later, Harold Wilson called a general election. The March 1966 *Bulletin* urged all supporters to write to their MPs to do everything possible to see that the Bill came back in the new Parliament. It listed the Pros (22) and the Antis (10) among the Northern MPs at the previous vote. But by far the greatest number – 60 – were the abstentions. Clearly the most important task was to get these 'don't knows' to turn out next time – if they could be persuaded to vote in favour of reform.

1966 general election

Horsfall had something of a dilemma. It concerned *bête noire* William Shepherd who as MP for Cheadle was on Allan's 'patch', and whose contributions to the

---

* Venereal disease, or VD, was the term then used for what are now referred to as sexually transmitted infections.

debates we have seen. He and Grey had always been particularly galled by Shepherd's combination of ignorance and stupidity on the one hand and his claim to be an expert on the other. Horsfall ground his teeth when Shepherd wrote to the North Western Committee as a response to being sent a copy of *Something You Should Know*: 'I'm afraid I am not impressed by this matter [the pamphlet], most of which I would contest, with, I may say, some knowledge of the facts.'[119]

Allan and Antony both crowed when they read of Shepherd's discomfiture at a student debate. In March 1966 the students of the London School of Economics* gave him such a hard time interrupting his speech that he walked out.

Horsfall desperately wanted to see the back of Shepherd in the 1966 General Election, and the candidate with the most chance of overturning his 9,000 majority was the Liberal candidate, Dr Michael Winstanley. However, the Labour candidate was a paying supporter of the North Western Committee, and Allan himself was of course Labour. Antony had asked him previously whether he could work for the Liberal candidate against Shepherd. At first, Allan was in favour. A few months later, he changed his mind. And then changed it again. By the time the election came, he was out on the streets in Cheadle for Winstanley, reporting gleefully:

> We distributed pamphlets at the Prime Minister's rallies in Manchester and Liverpool. Also at two public meetings in the Cheadle constituency. Shepherd seems very rattled and actually swore at us. He swept the proffered pamphlet aside with an angry gesture and said, 'Bloody homosexual law reform again!' I also had a row with his agent![120]

In the event, Winstanley crept in with a majority of 650. Immediately he wrote to the North Western Committee offering his support. Shepherd was not the only casualty; Humphry Berkeley also lost his seat, and blamed it on his work for homosexual law reform. Grey wrote to Horsfall, 'Also met Jeremy Thorpe and Peter Bessell who both said they lost upwards of 2,000 votes through it. This seems exaggerated to me.'[121]

Exaggerated or not – and with public opinion (as measured by both National Opinion Polls and Gallup) running in favour of law reform by two to one, it seems likely that it was exaggerated – this belief that gay rights was a vote loser was rooted firmly in the consciousness of most MPs and prospective MPs for years to come, even if they supported gay rights in principle.

For a Parliamentary lobby group, advocacy of what was seen as an unpopular cause could not have come at a worse time. Government majorities

---

* Soon to become the cradle of the Gay Liberation Front.

in the House of Commons were small from 1970 to 1979, and any of them could have been wiped out by bad by-election results – and there were eight or nine by-elections per year. Moreover the average majority of an individual MP was much lower, and therefore the number of marginal seats much larger. This problem was particularly acute during 1974–79, when Labour was first of all a minority government and then commanded an overall majority of five, which was steadily whittled away by just such adverse by-election results.

Public Education

The parallel work of public education continued alongside the parliamentary lobbying, for both Horsfall and Grey. The two Secretaries reported on meetings they had addressed. Meetings of small societies, student unions and church luncheon clubs were a small and steady, if unglamorous, platform. Even before the NWHLRC was formed, Antony relied on Allan to act as a deputy when he himself was snowed under with work. In March 1964 he despatched Allan to Ashton-under-Lyne:

> The vicar is quite young and was in fact with me in Cambridge (though he doesn't know it). .... The theme of the series of talks is Misfits in our Society. I know you don't like speaking on this subject, but I am sure you would do it admirably, and that you need have no fears about it being an unfriendly audience.[122]

In the event, there was protest. Allan reported back:

> To his [the vicar's] considerable displeasure, some of his disgusted parishioners, who had failed in their attempt to have my talk cancelled, had stationed themselves at the door and were turning away anybody from the youth club or scouts.[123]

The vicar, the Rev. Paul Bibby, apologised:

> The 'strong feeling' in fact only came from one man who refused to come into the discussion when youngsters were present. I'm afraid one gets that kind of thing from time to time and there is very little one can do about it. It was a very foolish attitude and it certainly wasn't subscribed to by any adults who were present. … I am sure the young people who were there benefited. I may very well get in touch with you again later on.[124]

This small incident illustrates the kind of battles which were going on for hearts and minds within the Church of England, however supportive senior clerics might be to law reform. It is also interesting that the vicar felt able to include teenagers in the discussion, evidently feeling they were in no need of protection from ideas about sexuality. Later in the year Bibby joined the

North Western Committee, and provided many of the contacts needed for invitations to its big public meeting, when it came.

In July Horsfall talked to thirty students at Lancaster University, 'which I thought was very good since we clashed with a meeting on Vietnam and the total strength of the University is only 300.'[125] Later, in October, Grey observed, 'I feel there has been a sea change in opinion, as my audiences are much more radical than we are!'[126]

The 'we' in that sentence is the HLRS, not Grey personally, who was himself far more radical than the Society allowed him to be. He often looked wistfully at Horsfall, envying his freedom to say things which he, Antony, would have loved to put forward.

In January Horsfall, deputising for Grey, proposed a motion to Nottingham University Students' Union that 'This House would reform the laws concerning homosexuality'. It was carried 124 to 2. In February he spoke to the Dean of Manchester's luncheon club: 'It was a starchy sort of gathering, but nobody openly opposed reform and I think we broke a little ice.'[127] Allan's tone was far more modest than that of Antony, who clearly relished being the public face of Law Reform in much the same way as Wildeblood did.

Policing other groups

Another job both men had was policing and checking out the claims of other groups and individuals. Now, and even more after the law changed, others were feeling the change of moral and political climate in the air, and coming forward to advance the case for equality in various forms. Both the HLRS and the North Western Committee were only later to become the dominant forces; initially they were only two among several. So it fell to the Secretaries to explore whether any group was worth joining forces with, or whether it was going to be off the wall and give the whole idea of homosexual law reform a bad name, or whether it was simply a front for selling pornography.

On 3 February 1963, just after lunch, the residents of the Riverside Gardens Estate by the Hammersmith Flyover were startled to have two leaflets shoved through their letterboxes from the Natural Law Religion Society:

> Angry Hammersmith parents read 'disgusting, obscene, crude and indecent' pamphlets which had been pushed through their letter boxes – and then threw them on the fire. Now they want to know why Hammersmith Council allowed a meeting – advertised on the pamphlets – to be held at the Town Hall. For the leaflets suggested that homosexuality should be encouraged, that it was something that was needed in Britain and should be made legal. …
>
> 'There is no sin, only ignorance. God and creation are bi-sexual. … There is only one Holy Book – the book of Nature. Physical, mental,

> spiritual, in that book homosexuality is not unnatural. It is not a sickness and should not be apologised for. It is a spiritual purpose which Britain needs at this time of crisis. The Law must be changed. The Natural Law Religion is a community of free men and women. We do not pry, or allow others to pry, into private lives. It helps you to live more happily and creatively.'[128]

The leaflet concluded, 'Help to change outdated laws. Meet new friends.' It turned out that the meeting was indeed held. The police kept a wary eye on the proceedings. One reader of the *West London Observer* complained about council premises being used for this kind of thing, but felt sufficiently aroused to attend the lecture:

> This was delivered by a Mr Webster, a representative of a body professing 'a natural law religion', whatever that may be. And in spite of the weather, a small audience turned up. It consisted almost entirely of men. I saw one or two arrive, singly, by taxi, and I must admit they appeared to be of a 'certain type'. Now we all know about the Wolfenden Report. That was based, I believe on an unbiased enquiry, and was, perhaps, necessary. This, however, seemed very different.[129]

The Council threw up its hands, protesting that they thought it was a religious meeting and knew nothing about queers. They vowed never to let the Town Hall to perverts again. And the Natural Law Religion Society passed out of history, leaving Grey none the wiser.

In January 1965 Allan alerted Antony to another possibly dodgy enterprise, which appeared in the small ads in *Private Eye*, giving a Bradford address. He told Antony, 'It's much the same wording as was used by the Minorities Research Group,* but directed to male homosexuals.'[130] Antony shared Allan's doubts:

> I myself wondered if this might not be a catch-penny – or possibly even a blackmail effort. I think it would be a very good thing if somebody with nothing to lose would write as a private individual sending the 2/6d† and seeing what transpires. Do you think Colin Harvey might be willing to do this?[131]

While waiting for action from Manchester, Grey wrote to the man in question. In reply he got the following from Myers Haines – probably a pseudonym:

> Unfortunately the laws of this land do not enable us to have any outlets, therefore I am organising the Club under my own initials … M. H. … to

---

* MRG was founded by two lesbians, Esmé Langley and Diana Chapman, as a charitable research/advocacy organisation to run as an adjunct to their monthly lesbian magazine, *Arena 3*. This advertised monthly in *Private Eye*, the *Spectator* and the *New Statesman*.

† 12½p.

> try to bring some sort of – um – relief to our feelings. Already I have had great response to my advertising and men from all walks of life, all ages, from all over England, have replied asking various questions.
>
> Our aim is to become a great big information centre. Where we will reply to any kind of problem. … First you are asked to fill in the particulars on the enclosed form, and send it with your remittance of One Pound to the above address. The forms will be carefully placed in our files with a card of your requirements in another appropriate file. As soon as the type of person comes along which will suit yourself, in the district required, cards will be sent to both parties in plain envelopes. It will then be up to both members to write to each other.
>
> ALSO I INTEND TO START A … PROBLEM PAGE … Which will be in the form of a circular. Members will receive our monthly issue of the pamphlet, on which we will print members' problems, answered by our … Myers Haines … who has known the problems of being homosexual for many years.
>
> I hope to bring hope to the many who join this organisation.[132]

This is very cautiously worded, and might have seemed even admirable, with its problem page. But the '– um –' is a dead giveaway. This is putting men in touch with each other for sex, and for no other purpose, and, as such, dangerous. Mr Haines didn't help his cover when he also sent pornography and an offer of cut-price contraceptives. At least, that's what Antony wrote when he reported back:

> I certainly did receive some very unpalatable literature. … I enclose a photocopy of the relevant document. I wrote him a very stiff letter, pointing out the dangers of blackmail etc. to which he was exposing all these people. He replied saying he was discontinuing the service and returning everyone's money. In view of the advert in *Films and Filming** this is obviously a lie.[133]

Allan went one further with 'somebody with nothing to lose.' He put one of the vicars on his Committee, Rev. Bernard Dodd, on the case. Meg Atkins remembered him as:

> always cheerful, always smiling, always helpful. He was always very supportive, always there at committee meetings, advising and helping. And what I always loved was, when they were fixing a date for anything, … he'd get his diary out, and every page would be crammed with hundreds of things to do. He was involved in everything.[134]

---

* *Films and Filming* was a monthly magazine founded in 1954 which became in the 60s a gay magazine in all but name. As well as production news, it carried liberal quantities of 'dolly boy' movie star photos (Alain Delon, Terence Stamp, etc.) as well as movie divas. And it had some gay personal ads from the mid-60s onwards.

In exchange for his 2/6d, Dodd got the offer of cut-price contraceptives and a form to fill in for a homosexual introduction service. Given that, less than two years earlier, the Bolton witch-hunt had started with a pen pal mailing list, this was highly dangerous, and Dodd took drastic action. The always smiling, always helpful Bernard turned up on the doorstep of a nondescript terraced house in Bradford to confront the man. The man did not want to talk about it, said he only discussed the business by letter. 'Apparently his wife was hovering in the background and this seems to have inhibited Bernard from having a real showdown with him.'[135] Nevertheless, the combined effects of Grey's letters and Bernard's visit seem to have warned him off this particular patch. There were no more adverts.

It was always the HLRS's intention to set up more local groups, and there was a prospect of one in Stoke-on-Trent, but the convenor, a Methodist minister, cried off. The same thing happened in Bristol. In Birmingham a local group project got further. Ivan Geffen, a local solicitor* who was convenor for the Birmingham branch of the NCCL,† agreed to convene. But pressure of work meant that it was six months before a meeting could be held to form the committee of the West Midlands Homosexual Law Reform Society.

It held a formal inaugural meeting in August 1966. There were messages of support from the Bishop of Birmingham, two local MPs (Renée Short from Wolverhampton and William Wells from Walsall), and from Dr Martin Cole.‡ Allan and Antony again came along. The group had an agenda very narrowly defined by HLRS, keeping a firm hand on its 'discussion group'. Antony floated publicly an idea which was to come into sharp focus immediately after the passing of the 1967 Act: 'Ultimately some socially acceptable situations must be provided in which homosexuals could behave responsibly as themselves.'§ Preferably under the supervision of the Albany Trust, and some responsible social workers.

But nothing much further happened. However, though the West Midlands

---

* The Geffen practice was the first port of call for any homosexual in the West Midlands in trouble with the police, and would remain so for many years; Geffen also wrote the constitution and the legal contracts for the Birmingham Gay Centre, set up in 1974.

† NCCL rebranded itself as 'Liberty' in 1989.

‡ Martin Cole was founder of the Birmingham (later British) Pregnancy Advisory Service and director of *Growing Up* (1971), a sex education film for teenagers which caused a huge controversy because it featured live actors, and was condemned by Mary Whitehouse, Lord Longford, and Margaret Thatcher. His Institute for Sex Education and Research used female therapists as surrogate partners to treat (heterosexual) men with erectile dysfunction, causing local MP Jill Knight to accuse him of running a brothel. He has a lesbian daughter.

§ 'Responsible' and 'responsibly' recur frequently in the publications of all reformist orgaanisations of homosexuals in Europe and America in this period. See Chapter One.

group was going nowhere, it contained the people to form a core of potential members in Birmingham and Wolverhampton, when CHE began the process of setting up local CHE* groups two years later.

Horsfall and Grey congratulated each other on the letters they wrote to the press. They bitched. Bryan Magee, a commercial TV presenter for the series *This Week*, made two documentaries, one on lesbians (1965) and one on gay men (1964). The HLRS furnished him with 'case studies', and Grey himself appeared on the male programme, albeit in silhouette. Magee turned the material from these programmes into the book *One in Twenty*, which attracted considerable publicity. 'I see you've got your knife into Magee,' wrote Allan. Antony replied:

> I don't think I was too hard on BM – he appears to be setting himself up as an 'expert' on the strength of his two television programmes! When I disputed some of his 'facts' with him over lunch some time ago he was quite off-hand, so I feel he deserves a public slapping.[136]

As far as Antony was concerned, there was only one expert.

The Secretaries swapped newspaper cuttings and stories. Allan was the HLRS's eyes and ears in the North. The clippings sped South: Brian Thompson got three years' imprisonment in Carlisle; again in Carlisle, a witch-hunt involving six men and a 17-year-old youth; another in Wales; another in Nottingham. Grey kept Allan supplied with copies of Hansard. They bitched about the idiot columnists who gave them their opening for firing off letters to the press.

The public meeting – at last

With the 1966 general election out of the way, the prospect of a new, younger Parliament and Leo Abse waiting to introduce the Sexual Offences Bill yet again, the time was once more ripe to fix up the long-postponed big public meeting. They found a hall, the Houldsworth Hall on Deansgate, in the centre of Manchester, a venue more accustomed to hosting the smaller rock bands. They pinned down the Dean of Manchester to a date when he could chair it; all they needed were the 'star' speakers. Allan insisted on Antony coming, so they needed two more. Humphry Berkeley was a possibility – though now out of Parliament, he was still a name and politically active; Winstanley, the new boy, definitely on the 'wanted' list. Alan Fitch, MP for Wigan, who supported the Committee and gave the lie to the idea that the miners wouldn't tolerate poufs or law reform, was:

---

* As they were called by 1970.

willing to give us a mid-week date, if we like, but there is this difficulty; Fitch is a government whip – so the normal pairing arrangements don't apply. If he was paired, and then a three-line whip came along, he would have to stay in London. Fridays are better for him, and he says that even if he were on three-line whip duty Friday morning, he would fly up to Manchester for a meeting. There is also the other factor that a meeting seeking to cater for a wide area will do better on a night when people don't have to work the following morning.[137]

PUBLIC MEETING

SOCIETY AND ITS HOMOSEXUALS:
WHY THE LAW MUST BE CHANGED

Speakers:
HUMPHRY BERKELEY
ALAN FITCH, M.P.
ANTONY GRAY

Chairman:
THE DEAN OF MANCHESTER
THE VERY REVEREND ALFRED JOWETT

FRIDAY, 11th NOVEMBER 1966, AT 7-30 p.m.
HOULDSWORTH HALL, 90 DEANSGATE, MANCHESTER.

Meeting sponsored jointly by the North-Western Homosexual Law Reform Committee, 460 Bridgeman Street, Bolton and the Diocese of Manchester Board for Social Responsibility, 27 Blackfriars Road, Salford 3.

23. Flyer for the 1966 public meeting

This pretty much clinched that it should be a Friday; 11 and 18 November 1966 were both Fridays, but Berkeley couldn't do the eighteenth. It was all getting to be a bit of a strain. In August Allan had to leave a conference early. 'I suffered what my doctor calls an anxiety seizure. I have had these before, but not for years. The truth is that I haven't had a proper holiday for about four years and it is now beginning to show.'[138] Both Horsfall and Grey demonstrated that intense campaigning is hazardous to your health. Still, Allan pegged away at it. What to call the meeting? He suggested 'The Homosexual in Society' but Grey wanted it the other way around:

> When I go round giving talks, I often call them 'Society and the Homosexual' – deliberately putting Society first, as I think it is a good idea to bring home to people that Society is largely responsible for the 'problem' and not the other way around.[139]*

Then there was the problem of how to pay for it. The HLRS was fully committed financially. It now had, in addition to Antony full-time, an office manager and two assistants on the staff, so it wasn't in a position to help. The North Western Committee itself didn't have subscriptions. It would obviously have to take a collection. Antony wrote, 'Do your collection boxes have provision for notes? I think we should try to get some paper money out of a gathering as rare as this!'[140] Still sponsored by the Church, the Committee got several of its vicar supporters to bring a collection plate. But help was also at hand from the commercial gay scene. On 18 October Allan reported that Reg Kilduff at the Rockingham Club 'has kindly browbeaten his club members into raising more than enough money to pay for the hall and he has also offered to help with food.'[141]

This close co-operation between clubs and Committee was a formative element in the character of the organisation in its early years.

Another reason for the meeting was to cock a snook at the local paper the *Manchester Evening News*. The *MEN* was especially homophobic in its editorial stance. It habitually used the terms 'pervert' and 'perversion' as interchangeable with 'homosexual' and 'homosexuality'. It spoke approvingly in an editorial of the National Cleansing Crusade, a new organisation with a strong right-wing, crypto-fascist agenda.

The NCC was the work of two men in Smethwick, near Birmingham. Alan Harris was a 23-year-old ex-Councillor who in 1966 had an almighty row with his party (Conservative) over fencing for demolition sites; there were hidden agendas about corruption. Two weeks after being defeated in the local elections as an independent, he joined forces with a local builder and estate agent, F. D. W. Tye. To quote Tye in their manifesto:

> Our nation is SICK, DESPERATELY SICK. Hospitals are full to overflowing. This is due not to bugs and germs, but to the breaking of God's Laws, principally the food laws as ordained in the scriptures.[142]

---

* The eventual billing, 'Society and its homosexuals' puts the responsibility for accepting 'its' homosexuals even more firmly on society.

Tye maintained that Britain was the custodian of divine law, which was proved by the white rainbow he saw in the sky at the D-Day landings. Together Tye and Harris became the NCC. The planks of its platform were 'To promote the restoration of capital punishment, the outlawing of sodomy, ... and a return to sanity and decency in our nation.'[143]

'Sodomy' in this case is not the sexual act, but homosexuality in general. The NCC joined up with a group called the Crown Covenanters in Birmingham, appeared on local television, and within a few months had several hundred supporters. Smethwick, the town where in 1964 the Conservatives had ousted the sitting MP, Patrick Gordon-Walker, with the slogan 'If you want a nigger neighbour, vote Labour', was fertile recruitment territory. As time went on, they became ever more hysterical. In 1972:

> We are a nation gone mad ... child rapists and killers live ... sodomy is legal ... sex taught in our schools ... with mongrelisation advocated ... and all because a handful of MPs and Bishops have forced these abominable laws on the decent people of Britain. Sex education is Communist-inspired. Shame to all men in Church and Government who degrade Britain through the Act of Sodomy.[144]

In the later 1970s the National Cleansing Crusade became absorbed into other groupings of the Far Right.

Abse tabled his Bill in May 1966. Harry Whewell in *The Guardian* quoted an NWHLRC Press Release:

> There is a feeling that July 5th could be make or break day. ... Unless the reformers can muster a vote sufficiently decisive it is quite possible that the chance for further progress will disappear until the 1970s.[145]

The Committee hastily produced another *Bulletin* for supporters: 'MPs who are definitely not hostile should receive as many letters of support as possible from supporters of this committee, and other sympathisers.'[146]

When Abse was given leave to introduce his Bill by a majority of 244 to 100 on 7 July, the *Manchester Evening News* went into overdrive:

> How can anyone talk of leadership in Britain, when in times of economic crises like these, another small group of MPs is to put forward a bill for sexual perversion between consenting male adults? Until it gets back to basic moral principles Britain is likely to remain 'the sick man of Europe'.[147]

In this it echoed its readers' sentiments, judging from the Letters Page ('Famous Postbag – Voice of the people with 2 million readers'):

> Our MPs certainly seem intent on making Britain a worse cesspool than ever. —Mrs C. R. Chinley, 8 July.

> Thank you for your leader article which quite properly and bluntly criticised those in Parliament who are wasting Parliament's time over dirty and perverted issues such as legalising perverted acts between males.
>
> —'Citizen', 8 July.

The same day, the paper reported that a pensioner got sentenced to just six months for sexually assaulting two girls, aged 4 and 5.

Slightly to his surprise, Allan Horsfall found that the *Manchester Evening News* published a letter of his – a lone voice in support of Abse:

> Your correspondents both claim that the Bill on homosexual offences is contrary to public opinion.
>
> The evidence is against them. The two major opinion-sounding organisations in this country, Gallup Polls and National Opinion Polls, both show that public opinion is now decisively in favour of a new deal for homosexuals. NOP published its findings on October 28th last year. The pollsters asked whether people agreed or disagreed with the following statement: 'Homosexual acts between consenting adults (21 and over) in private should be regarded as criminal.' 36 per cent agreed, 63% disagreed and 1% didn't know.
>
> The Gallup enquiry a month earlier produced similar results.[148]

But the paper only published this letter as a peg to hang its own survey on. It appended after Allan's letter:

> To test this claim for the North, the *Manchester Evening News* has done its own spot quiz of public opinion, which is quite different.
>
> In fact, 'definitely not' is Manchester's answer to the suggestion that Parliament should introduce a bill to legalise homosexuality between consenting male adults.
>
> In a four-part reader quiz, young and old – with one notable exception – condemned the idea. Among the 'mature' people quizzed in Manchester 80% of the women said 'definitely not' to a homosexuality Bill. Of the mature men, 70% opposed any such legalisation. Young women of student age, in their teens or early 20s, were 80% in favour of the bill, with 20% against, but among young men of similar age, only 40% favoured the bill ad 60% were against it.[149]

How many people were polled, how they were chosen and how the questions were phrased remain mysteries; the *Manchester Evening News* has no record of this survey, and the questionnaire itself has not been found. In this campaign, Allan claims, the paper went well beyond the bounds of journalism by reproducing its editorials as leaflets and distributing them in the streets of the city.[150]

No wonder Allan jumped at Antony's suggestion that the Committee should compile a collection of defamatory cuttings for display at the meeting, as 'an attack on the local press is one sure way of hitting next day's headlines.'[151]

But, surprisingly, the paper accepted a small box advert, which appeared on Monday 7 November 1966, advertising the meeting on the eleventh at the end of the week. Speakers would be Humphry Berkeley, who was flying up from London, local MP Alan Fitch, and Antony Grey, who would take the overnight train back to London to go straight to work as a jobbing sub-editor on *The Observer* next morning. This was how he bolstered his meagre HLRS income. Alfred Jowett, Dean of Manchester, would take the chair.

In the event there was a crisis. The weather was filthy, and Berkeley was grounded by fog at London Airport (as Heathrow was called then). It was far too late to find a substitute, and so the Dean got to speak as well as chair the meeting, and Antony padded his speech out, to fill the evening. Allan and the NWHLRC president Niel Pearson spoke from the floor, and there were only a few 'anti' comments from the 150-plus people there. It was only the second public meeting on the issue, the first for six years, and the only one outside London. Afterwards they all went to the reception laid on by Reg Kilduff at the Rockingham.

Letters flew back and forth afterwards between Grey and Horsfall, Horsfall and other supporters. Fellow Committee member Harry Eaves wrote to congratulate Allan:

> I think that Friday's turnout would exceed your expectations. It did mine. I'm surer that all the good work you must have put in was well rewarded. … The Dean of Manchester was outstandingly good, both as Chairman and Speaker. I liked the MP for Wigan. I had quite a chat with him before we left the Rockingham. We had quite a lot in common. … I think you will agree with my next comments. It applies to so many speakers that you would think that any one who undertakes to address the public from a platform would take a few lessons. Antony Grey's material was most interesting and helpful, but quite a lot came over to me as a blur. …
>
> The good news was of course that in six months' time alterations will be made to the oppressive law. And for that we must be grateful to a handful of folk who have dared to push things forward.[152]

Allan wrote back apologising for the length of Antony's speech – he clearly loved the sound of his own voice. This was echoed by several others, all of whom recognised that the meeting itself was a great success, and would not have happened without Allan.

One thing which clearly got the goat of both Allan and Antony was the attitude of the press. There were four or five reporters, and the *Daily Telegraph* man had dictated his copy on the spot from the back of the hall. But silence reigned in the news pages on Saturday 12 November. The only coverage was from the *Leigh Reporter*, and a bland paragraph in *The Guardian* in three column inches at the bottom of the Northern Page:

> Mr Alan Fitch, Labour MP for Wigan, said in Manchester last night there was little doubt that Mr Leo Abse's bill to reform the laws on homosexuality would be on the statute book 'by May at the latest'.[153]

Allan felt that the *Evening News'* failure to cover the meeting was 'unforgivable.' Unforgivable, but utterly true to form. Grey commiserated:

> They were obviously there to seek something sensational. One can perhaps understand the national papers ignoring it so long as things remained calm, but for the *Manchester Evening News* not to print a word looks very much like discrimination.[154]

He followed this with a guarded but revealing comment on his own loneliness:

> One does feel very isolated at times when faced with problems of great magnitude on the one hand and almost complete public (and professional) incomprehension on the other.[155]

If people moaned about Antony, Antony moaned about Alan Fitch:

> What struck me as the most significant thing about it was the way in which Alan Fitch almost appropriated the bill as part of the 'great Radical reforming Government's' social programme.[156]

In one sense Fitch's claim was justified. The passing of the 1967 Act was a partnership in which the Labour Government cleared the parliamentary time and provided the legal expertise to make the Bill happen. Such assistance also gave the government a considerable say in what finally went onto the statute book. Without Roy Jenkins the Bill simply would not have got beyond the second reading. It is also true that Jenkins saw himself as a great liberal reforming Home Secretary. Because of parliamentary convention, matters of conscience such as divorce and abortion had to be introduced as Private Members' Bills and passed on a free vote of the House, but in a way the social reforms of the 1960s were the result of Jenkins using the system, and using backbenchers to pursue his own agenda. If it helped to get the Bill passed, this was surely a good thing; but in stating it overtly, Alan Fitch belittled Grey's work.

The Home Service of the BBC did however pick up the story of the public meeting, with a short item on *Calendar*, the magazine programme which went out after the 6 o'clock news.

There were knock-on effects. The Committee was left pretty strapped for cash, with the result that begging letters had to go out pronto. Dr Burslem, a gynaecologist, sent in ten guineas. The HLRS sent a cheque for £25 from London. And there was an influx of new supporters.

Final Passing of Sexual Offences Act 1967

Abse's bill was put back, delayed again, and wasn't finally due for a second reading until 19 December 1966. As in previous debates, the public gallery was full of gay men, and if the atmosphere remained decorous by later standards, it was still electric. And somewhat cruisy, especially in the entrance queue. All the debates, like screenings of the film *Victim*,* were unacknowledged gathering places for homosexuals, who took advantage of the presence of large numbers of similarly-inclined people accordingly.

Griffith Vaughan Williams, later to play a very prominent part in CHE, tried to get tickets for that debate, but he left it rather late. Patricia Wolfson, Private Secretary to his MP, Michael Stewart, explained that nearly all tickets had been allocated but he could have two from 8.30 p.m. onwards; when he got into the public gallery Griff would have heard Eric Moonman (Lab, Billericay) have to stop in mid-sentence ('the example of the social worker who was asked to enquire about –') as the debate was adjourned on the stroke of ten o'clock, only to resume ten minutes later

Supporters were desperately concerned it would run out of time and they would be cheated again. Behind the scenes MPs horsetraded and plotted. The bill was already lumbered with a definition of 'privacy' which only applied to the subject of homosexual sex, and meant for example, that a hotel room would not be private, or a room in a house of multiple occupancy, or anywhere more than two people were present, even if they consented. As such it still left the door open for blackmail; Vassall would still have been in exactly the same position after 1967 as before.

Moreover, the law still offered no hope for young men in the process of discovering or determining their sexuality. Antony Grey wrote in a memorandum to Abse that the age of consent fixed at 21 and the increased penalties (five years' imprisonment instead of two) for gross indecency between a man over 21 and one under 21, 'make life even more difficult for young men in the 17 to 25 age group who are passing through a transient homosexual phase or having to adjust themselves to homosexuality as a basic life pattern.'[157]

Grey was not alone at the HLRS in his unhappiness with the way Abse was behaving and the concessions he was planning, but as the Parliamentary sponsor Abse had the right to do things his own way. No members of the HLRS were ever invited to a drafting conference by either Abse or Arran, who was now piloting the identical Bill through its stages in the Lords. The

* *Victim* (1961) was the first UK film to make its subject a homosexual relationship and the attendant blackmail. It painted a vivid portrait of the gay subculture of the time. It was directed by Basil Dearden, who ran ENSA during the war, and starred Dirk Bogarde, who was widely thought to have sabotaged his career in accepting the part.

HLRS was also constrained by the fact that Abse sat on its Executive and it would not therefore do to criticise him. Grey sent him a list of amendments he wanted, but with no lively hope that they would be acted on. He reluctantly accepted that Abse was out of control.

Abse gave further concessions so that the Act would not apply in Scotland or Northern Island. He wanted to make another exclusion, in the shape of the Merchant Navy. This seemed to bother Allan, because it betrayed the principle of equality, and he came up with a formula he floated in the *Spectator*:

> for including merchant ships in Section 1(2) of the Bill, along with public lavatories, as places in which a homosexual act would not be treated as being in private.
>
> Such an amendment to the Bill should allay the fears of those who now see it as a threat to naval discipline, and it would also avoid discrimination, since it would be no more unfair to homosexual seamen than it is unfair to heterosexual seamen that their wives or girlfriends cannot live aboard ship.[158]

This concern for equality, and an end to discrimination, is something comparatively new. It takes us beyond the compass of simple reform of one statute into an area which will affect not only the law but also other institutions, and the fabric of society itself. Again it shows the North Western Committee moving inexorably apart from the HLRS in London. Abse pleaded with Allan not to rock the boat:

> Perhaps refrain from writing letters on the seamen's question suggesting that a Merchant ship, if I understand your point of view, be treated as if it were a public place. I do not think this view would be considered. … I believe that we may be able to meet the disciplinary needs of the Merchant Navy without creating an anomalous situation where behaviour which would attract no penalties on land could attract heavy penalties at sea.[159]

In other words, the poor gay merchant seaman would not even be allowed to have sex when he was on shore leave. Not for the only time, Abse was using moral blackmail, to steer this bill through the House of Commons, saying any dissent might wreck its chances of getting through. He was adept at practising political passive aggression. Allan fumed to his President, Niel Pearson:

> Abse's bill, as it stands at present, is very unsatisfactory and falls very far short of the Wolfenden standard. The Homosexual Law Reform Society seems to be having some difficulty in getting an assurance from the sponsors that they will try to improve specific points in Committee.
>
> They are of course at something of a disadvantage in that Abse is a member of their Executive Committee. We, being free of similar involvement, may be better able to speak out in criticism of the Bill as it stands.[160]

Allan sent a memo to Abse as well, with barely concealed anger at the amount he was giving away:

> Insofar as some supporters of the reform in the House may have become complacent … I think it is important that it should be made clear during the debate that the law relating to private behaviour is far from dead. …
>
> [In Carlisle] Letters written to a seventeen year old journalist had fallen into the hands of the police. These proceeded, as is usual, from home to home and from clue to clue until thirteen or fourteen men were involved. The DPP decided that the youth and six of the men should be prosecuted. The Solicitor acting for three says the 'selection might have been made by drawing seven names out of the hat, for all he could see.' … Whereas the incidents may not all have been in private in the rather narrow sense laid down in the Bill, all took place either in houses or cars and there appears to be no question of outraging public decency.[161]

This letter shows the increasing impatience of the Manchester organisation, which was already by December 1966 planning what it wanted to do after decriminalisation. The increasing distance between North and South can be seen in a variety of small but significant details. Whereas in 1964–65 the Committee was describing itself as a subgroup of the HLRS, by 1966 Allan was saying that they 'worked in close co-operation' with it. In his mind it was a partnership of equals.

In becoming a gay organisation in the modern sense, the North Western Committee was becoming more radical. It rejected wholesale the idea that homosexuals were intrinsically ill or disordered. Even before the law changed the Committee 'took the view that homosexuality was not a medical problem; … what was needed was not more social workers, but more social facilities.'[162]

After the passing of the Act, Colin Harvey wrote to C. H. Rolph, the new Chairman of the HLRS, to explain that the North Western Committee was simply 'a collection of individuals, 95% of whom are homosexual'. This was seen as an outrageous admission. 'In fact my colleagues and I had not realised,' replied Rolph patronisingly, 'that the membership of the North West Committee was so predominantly made up as you state.' It seems he cannot bring himself to use the H-word. 'We thought it included a rather broader cross-section of people.' He conceded grudgingly, 'Of course a 'subjective' group of this kind has a useful and legitimate purpose to fulfil.'[163] But not in conjunction with the HLRS, it didn't. By 1968, the gap between North and South was pretty much unbridgeable.

But in early 1967, having surmounted the hurdle of the second reading, Abse was still piloting his Bill through the Commons, and Arran his through the Lords. Both were aware that time was of the essence. They could see the summer recess approaching apace, and if they didn't get it through all its stages by then, the Bill could be lost yet again. They were totally dependent on the goodwill of Home Secretary Roy Jenkins for making the time for it to happen, which also gave the Government a measure of control over what actually went into the Bill.

Allan might fulminate that 'If the opposition is allowed to go on saying that this, that and the other place is not private, they will not only mutilate the Bill, they will mutilate the language.'[164] Antony might declare that 'it will be most unfortunate if this reform is the occasion for a new legal concept to be introduced: namely that somewhere which is not a "public place" is not necessarily a private place either! The only people it is likely to benefit are the lawyers.'[165] But in practice there was nothing either of them could do about it.

Gay men sensed victory this time round, if only of a partial kind. Allan and Harold came down to London on 5 July 1966, to hear Abse introduce the Bill (and Cyril Osborne, as usual, oppose – they were the only two speakers). Grey got them tickets. The second reading resumed in early 1967. The HLRS was besieged with complaints from supporters, about how Abse was mangling Wolfenden, but Abse held firm: 'He would regard a proposal for its [the age of consent's] reduction from 21 to 18 as both politically dangerous and intrinsically undesirable.'[166] In other words, he was using realpolitik as a cloak for his own prejudices.

The committee stages took place in April 1967. During these, Nicholas Ridley mused:

> I wonder whether the right principle should not be to legalise them [homosexual acts] between consenting people of any age. It seemed anomalous to punish the person under 21 more heavily than the older person; in most other crimes the young offender was treated more leniently than the old hand. … To say that this behaviour was a crime before the age of 21 but not afterwards could make no sense at all in the minds of the young men who would grow up having to observe this law.[167]

Is Ridley seriously suggesting the abolition of the age of consent when he says 'people of any age'? Or are under-16s not considered as 'people'? In either case, the compassionate tone does not seem to belong to the same politician as the one responsible for introducing the Poll Tax under Margaret Thatcher.

In the Lords, Arran had got his second reading in May 1966, and his third a month later. The bigots had their final flatulent and ignorant roar:

> Lord Ferrier : The conduct we are discussing is a hideous sin – I nearly said bestial, but beasts do not do it. The homosexual is either mentally deranged… or he is a sinner in a sin which is bred from self-pity out of sadism. … The Bill offers a charter to the male prostitute …'[168]

> Earl of Dudley: 'I cannot stand homosexuals. They are the most disgusting people in the world. … I loathe them. Prison is much too good a place for

> them. In fact it is a place many of them would like to go – for obvious reasons.'[169]

Lord Saltoun, speaking to an amendment to raise the Age of Consent to 25, offered a fascinating glimpse of unknown gay history:

> When I was a prisoner of war … during the first world war, British seamen had to move around the prison in threes. … The homosexuals in the camp were extremely arrogant. Far from concealing their idiosyncracy, they were very proud of it, and boasted of it.[170]

The gay men in the gallery being showered with this testosterone would have chuckled at the counter-sally of Lord Snow:

> Some peers have spoken as if they had never met a homosexual, as though these were something like the white rhinoceros – strange animals, difficult to observe. Yet every one of you must have met many homosexuals, and many must have met some of the most distinguished and worthy of Englishmen.[171]

But for all the noise, the bill received its third reading in the Lords on 16 June, by 78 to 60 votes. When Abse introduced it back in the Commons, it was in the knowledge that when it finally went to the Lords after the Commons had passed it, this time it would go through on the nod.

Most of the arguments were pretty tired by now, but time was of the essence if the Bill was to become law. The North Western Committee put it succinctly in the *Bulletin* of May 1967. The second reading had passed unopposed in December due to the opponents' 'tactical blundering'; the committee stage was handled in one day on 19 April. The report and third reading were all to be done on 2 June. There were only two days left for Private Members' Bills in the parliamentary session, and David Steel's Abortion Bill was down for the same day. If it came up first, it would take all the available time.

> There is therefore a real possibility that the Homosexual Bill will fall, unless it can take its remaining stages in Government time. So far there has been no undertaking from the Government about this.[172]

Supporters had to pull their fingers out and lobby their MPs before 2 June. NCCL held an emergency meeting to try to put forward amendments through the Parliamentary Civil Liberties Group. The emergency meeting demanded that MPs lower the age of consent while maintaining protection of younger persons. Delete the definition of privacy, make the penalties less severe, prohibit prosecutions for conspiracy where the acts allegedly conspired about were themselves legal, and require independent corroboration of police evidence for public indecency or persistently importuning charges. It was far too late to take any meaningful action, and any attempt to do so risked scuppering the tight timetable. However, it laid down a marker for the next stage of liberalising the law.

Sexual Offences Act 1967 CH. 60 1

ELIZABETH II

1967 CHAPTER 60

An Act to amend the law of England and Wales relating to homosexual acts. [27th July 1967]

BE IT ENACTED by the Queen's most Excellent Majesty, by and with the advice and consent of the Lords Spiritual and Temporal, and Commons, in this present Parliament assembled, and by the authority of the same, as follows:—

1.—(1) Notwithstanding any statutory or common law provision, but subject to the provisions of the next following section, a homosexual act in private shall not be an offence provided that the parties consent thereto and have attained the age of twenty-one years. Amendment of law relating to homosexual acts in private.

(2) An act which would otherwise be treated for the purposes of this Act as being done in private shall not be so treated if done—

(*a*) when more than two persons take part or are present; or

(*b*) in a lavatory to which the public have or are permitted to have access, whether on payment or otherwise.

(3) A man who is suffering from severe subnormality within the meaning of the Mental Health Act 1959 cannot in law give any consent which, by virtue of subsection (1) of this section, would prevent a homosexual act from being an offence, but a person shall not be convicted, on account of the incapacity of such a man to consent, of an offence consisting of such an act if he proves that he did not know and had no reason to suspect that man to be suffering from severe subnormality. 1959 c. 72.

24. The opening of the Sexual Offences Act 1967

Even as the bill was being debated, a new prosecution blew up, in Sale in Cheshire, with many of the hallmarks of the Bolton case of three years before, which had indirectly led to the formation of the North Western Committee. Another police trawl had produced a 'homosexual ring' of twelve men, all of whom allegedly had sex in a public lavatory near Sale cemetery. It was a familiar story: police keeping watch late at night through a knot-hole in the cleaner's cubbyhole. As usual, the local papers published names, addresses and places of work. Allan was all for taking up this case, but Antony was cautious; it had been referred to the DPP before going ahead, according to the Home Secretary's guidelines; the police alleged that there had been numerous public complaints. Besides, these charges would still be offences even under the new Act.

However, there was a straw in the wind in this case, as gay men were beginning to gain the courage to protest about their situation. One was 33-year-old Stephen Harding, a sales rep:

> When he refused to be quiet after shouting 'This is a tissue of lies' and 'I am not going to listen to this claptrap,' Harding was hustled from a seat behind his solicitor into the dock.[173]

He pleaded not guilty – and was found not guilty.

Allan joined the fray by writing to the Editor of the *Manchester Evening News* protesting about the publication of personal details. 'I cannot see what earthly public interest is served by this practice.' The editor replied that it was necessary so that readers wouldn't think it was another man in the town who happened to have the same name. This right to privacy would be taken up by other campaigners, mainly in local groups.*

In fact the third reading debate was postponed. The simple cry, 'Object!' got it deferred without discussion. So it wasn't till 23 June that it came up. The opponents dragged out their speeches in filibuster, and the day dragged on. By close of play, there were still amendments to discuss. However the Government had, finally, agreed to give some extra time.

It took till 3 July 1967, and an all-night sitting, to get to a final vote on the third reading. There was a sense of occasion, for all that it was by now a foregone conclusion. The public gallery was packed with gay men wanting to see history in the making; at this point in time it seemed that the reform would solve most of the problems, once 'queers' were 'legal'. Among those present were George Tregaskis, Peter Norman and Griffith Vaughan Williams, all supporters of the HLRS and members of the same Albany Trust

* In Oxford the Gay Action Group got the practice stopped by writing to the editor of the *Oxford Mail* to congratulate him on publishing this information. Thanks to him, isolated homosexuals in the city would not only be reassured that there were others like themselves, but would know their names and where to contact them. By pointing out this unintended consequence, OGAG put the editor into a panic that he was actually committing a crime by facilitating sexual contact.

gay discussion group.* All three would become prominent in CHE. Peter Norman remembers:

> I went to the all-night debate in the Commons. … We had to queue up a long time to get in, but once we were in we stayed in, until five or six o'clock. And went to work the next day. It was absolutely packed, because we had to wait before we could get in, until the general public and the tourists came out. … It was exciting, because we knew it was going to pass by then. The danger was that the Bill wouldn't pass because of the time limit, but once it was agreed that there would be an all-night sitting, it was obvious it was going to go through.[174]

Admiral Morgan-Giles came up with the opponents' last new angle:

> What will be the effect of the Bill on public opinion abroad? … Catastrophic. One can imagine the headlines in foreign newspapers: 'Britain Votes for Homosexuality' 'Parliament Passes the Queers' Charter.' The Bill will be further evidence of Britain's degeneracy and loss of influence. [It] can only encourage our enemies … and dismay our friends.[175]

It finally passed at 6 o'clock on the morning of 4 July, by 99 votes to 14, and a red-eyed Leo Abse could stagger exhausted to a taxi. The Lords rubber-stamped it on the 21st. The Sexual Offences Act 1967 received royal assent on 27 July.

There was little celebration. For a privileged few gay men, it was not a cause for rejoicing; their exclusive club had been opened up, and the frisson of outlawry which added spice to their encounters had gone. For campaigners like Allan, it had been so long coming that the process of change had acquired a kind of inevitability: all the debates, some in the House of Commons, some in the Lords, each time with the majority against reform getting smaller and finally turning into a majority in favour of it. It was all a bit of an anti-climax.

There was also a sense that it was better to keep quiet about it. As Patrick Trevor-Roper put it:

> There were little celebratory parties, but everyone was feeling, 'We mustn't let this be visible to the public, because the image will be bad if we start rioting.' So it was more a clearing of the air.[176]

This was exactly what the Earl of Arran hoped for, because it fell to him to have the last word as the Act made its final formal passage through the House of Lords:

> I ask one thing and I ask it earnestly. I ask those who have, as it were, been in bondage and for whom the prison doors are now open, to show their

---

* See page 339.

> thanks by comporting themselves quietly and with dignity. This is no occasion for jubilation; certainly not for celebration. Any form of ostentatious behaviour now, or in the future, any form of public flaunting, would be utterly distasteful and would, I believe, make the sponsors of the Bill regret that they have done what they have done. Homosexuals must remember that while there may be nothing bad in being a homosexual, there is certainly nothing good. Lest the opponents of the bill think that a new freedom, a new privileged class, has been created, let me remind them that no amount of legislation will prevent homosexuals from being the subject of dislike and derision or at best of pity. We shall always, I fear, resent the odd man out. That is their burden for all time, and they must shoulder it like men – for men they are![177]

But even as he was speaking, others in Manchester were planning to put the cat among the pigeons as far as staying out of the limelight was concerned.

Notes to Chapter Two

1 Seabrook, *A Lasting relationship*, 7.

2 Allan Horsfall, interviewed by Paul Hamling, 2009. BSA C1405/05.

3 Allan Horsfall, interviewed by Jeff Evans, 9 March 2011. In the author's possession.

4 Ibid.

5 Ibid.

6 Ibid.

7 Ibid.

8 Socarides, *The overt homosexual*, 6.

9 Cory, *Homosexuality – A cross-cultural approach*, 389.

10 Allen, *Homosexuality – its nature, causation and treatment*, 72.

11 Ibid., 115.

12 Harvey, *To fall like Lucifer*, 113.

13 Ibid., 114.

14 Ibid., 114.

15 Michael Schofield, interviewed by the author, 20 December 2011.

16 Ibid.

17 Ibid.

18 Ibid.

19 Ford and Beach, *Patterns of sexual behaviour*, 132.

20 Ibid., 281.

21 Ibid., 132.

22 West, *Homosexuality*, 27.

23 Garland, *The heart in exile*, 77.

24 Ibid., 112.

25 Allan Horsfall, interviewed by the author, 10 April 2011.

26 Peter Wildeblood, 'Free' in *The crooked mile*, 1929. HMV CLP 1298.

27 Ibid., 'Other people's sins'.

28 Allan Horsfall, interviewed by the author, 10 April 2011.

29 Ibid.

30 Allan Horsfall, 'Battling for Wolfenden', in Cant and Hemmings, *Radical records*, 17.

31 Ibid., 19–20.

32 Ibid.

33 Allan Horsfall, 'Wolfenden', *Reynolds News*, 20 July 1958, 4.

34 Allan Horsfall, interviewed by Paul Hambley, 12 May 2009. BSA C1405/05.

35 Allan Horsfall, 'Wolfenden in the wilderness', *New Left Review,* 12 (Nov–Dec 1961), 29–31.

36 Allan Horsfall, 'Young Liberals in trouble: Scottish taboos', *Guardian*, 8 May 1960, 8.

[37] Allan Horsfall, 'Wolfenden in the wilderness', *New Left Review*, 12 (Nov–Dec 1961), 29–31.

[38] Ibid.

[39] Ibid.

[40] Ibid.

[41] Ibid.

[42] Ibid.

[43] Ibid.

[44] Ibid.

[45] 'Youth cleared on flat death charge', *The Times*, 22 January 1963, 5.

[46] Venetia Newall to Allan Horsfall, 'Local groups', 1960. MCA/GG/HOR/2.

[47] HC Deb 29 June 1960 vol. 625, col. 1474.

[48] Peter Thursfield, 'Obituary: Peter Wildeblood', *Guardian*, 16 November 1999, 20.

[49] HC Deb 26 November 1958 vol. 596 col. 416.

[50] Ibid., vol. 596 col. 425.

[51] Ibid., vol. 596 col. 437.

[52] Ibid., vol. 596 cols. 454-455.

[53] Ibid., vol. 596 col. 445.

[54] Ibid.

[55] Ibid.

[56] Ibid., vol. 596 col. 394.

[57] Ibid., vol. 596 col. 476.

[58] R. D. Reid, 'Homosexual prosecutions', *Spectator*, 6882 (20 May 1960), 729–730.

[59] John Hunter, 'Homosexual prosecutions', *Spectator*, 6883 (27 May 1960), 765.

[60] Roger Butler, Raymond Gregson and Robert G. Moorcroft, 'Homosexual prosecutions', *Spectator*, 6884 (3 June 1960), 800.

[61] NWHLRC *Bulletin*, April 1968. HCA/GREY/1/1/129.

[62] HC Deb 29 June 1960 vol. 625, col. 1453.

[63] Ibid., col. 1482.

[64] Ibid., col. 1483.

[65] Ibid., cols. 1484–7.

[66] Ibid., col. 1504.

[67] Ibid., col. 1468.

[68] Allan Horsfall, 'Action on Wolfenden', *Guardian*, 26 February 1962, 8.

[69] Lionel Crane, 'How to spot a possible homo', *Sunday Mirror*, 28 April 1963, 7.

[70] 'Neil Makin' to Allan Horsfall, 'Thank you', 1963. MCA/G/HOR/1.

[71] Edgar Wright (Antony Grey), 'Being rational about being gay', talk to the GLHA, June 1980, reprinted in Grey, *Speaking Out*, 96.

[72] Andrew Lumsden, interviewed by the author, 10 April 2014.

[73] Ibid.

[74] Paul Temperton, interviewed by the author, 28 March 2011.

[75] 'Knight on indecency charges', *Bolton Evening News*, 5 June 1962, 1.

[76] 'Signpost', 'Crude, vulgar and disgusting – no wonder it's popular', *Bolton Evening News*, 14 May 1962, 3.

[77] MJH, 'Is this the modern trend – and reason for divorce?', *Bolton Evening News*, 20 June 1962, 2.

[78] '10 accused of sex offences', *Bolton Evening News*, 25 June 1963, 1, 5.

[79] Allan Horsfall, 'This witch-hunt is horrifying', *Bolton Evening News*, 12 July 1963, 2; Select Trials, 1742, 2nd ed., 3, 39–40, quoted in Rictor Norton, *Homosexuality in 18th Century England.* http://rictornorton.co.uk/eighteen/brown.htm.

[80] Rev. Kenneth Bishop, 'Law is too harsh' *Bolton Evening News*, 15 July 1963, 2.

[81] Miriam Greenwood, 'Protect the young', *Bolton Evening News,* 22 July 1963, 2.

[82] Antony Grey, 'Outdated and evil', *Bolton Evening News*, 26 July 1963, 2.

[83] HLRS Minutes, 28 October 1963. HCA/GREY/1/1/49.

[84] Antony Grey to Allan Horsfall, 25 September 1963. MCA/G/HOR/1.

[85] Ray Gosling, interviewed by the author, 11 December 2010.

[86] HLRS Minutes, 2 September 1964 HCA/GREY/1/1/57.

[87] Allan Horsfall, interviewed by Sylvia Kolling and David Govier, 11 October, 2011. GB124.G.HOR/4.

[88] Ibid.

[89] Allan Horsfall, interviewed by Paul Hambley, 12 May 2009. BSA C1405/05.

[90] David Dutton, 'Homosexuals and the law', *Leigh Reporter,* 6 February 1965, 1.

[91] Allan Horsfall, interviewed by Paul Hambley, 12 May 2009. BSA C1405/05.

[92] Arthur W. Tack to 'Homo Sexual Committee' [About the NW Committee leaflet], 10 March 1965. HCA/GREY/1/15/235.

[93] G. Bedell, 'Coming out of the dark ages', *Observer*, 24 June 2007, Review, 4–7.

[94] HL Deb 24 May 1965, vol. 266, col. 656.

[95] Chalfont, *Montgomery of Alamein*, 274; Hamilton, *Montgomery: D-Day commander*, 12.

[96] HL Deb 21 June 1965, vol. 267, col. 342.

[97] Michael Brown, interviewed by the author, 1 July 2012.

[98] Allan Horsfall to Antony Grey, '*Sun* letter', 26 May 1965. HCA/GREY/1/15/200.

[99] NWHLRC *Bulletin* May 1965. HCA/GREY/1/15/203.

[100] Meg Elizabeth Atkins, interviewed by the author, 4 January 2012.

[101] Ibid.

[102] NWHLRC *Bulletin* July 1966. HCA/GREY/1/15/127.

[103] Meg Elizabeth Atkins, interviewed by the author, 4 January 2012.

[104] Meg Elizabeth Atkins to Allan Horsfall, 'Visits to Trafford', 21 May 1966. MCA/G/HOR/1.

[105] Ibid., 26 September 1966. MCA/G/HOR/1.

[106] Meg Elizabeth Atkins, interviewed by the author, 4 January 2012.

[107] Antony Grey to Allan Horsfall, 'Possible speakers', 31 March 1965. HCA/GREY/1/1/225.

[108] Antony Grey to Allan Horsfall, 'Committee members', 8 April 1965. HCA/GREY/1/15/222.

[109] Antony Grey to Allan Horsfall, 'Speakers for meeting', 9 July 1965. MCA/G/HOR/1.

[110] Antony Grey to Allan Horsfall, 'Thanks for donation', 17 November 1965. HCA/GREY/1/15/176.

[111] Antony Grey to C. H. Rolph (C. Rolph Hewitt), 'Manchester Public Meeting', 25 January 1966. MCA/G/HOR/1.

[112] NWHLRC *Bulletin*, January 1966. HCA/GREY/1/15/158.

[113] HC Deb 11 February 1966, vol. 724, col. 809.

[114] Ibid., col. 813.

[115] Ibid., col. 815.

[116] Ibid., col. 828.

[117] Ibid., col. 829.

[118] Antony Grey to Colin Harvey, 'VD argument', 14 February 1966. HCA/GREY/1/15/152.

[119] William Shepherd to Allan Horsfall, 'NWHLRC leaflet', 10 March 1965. HCA/GREY/1/15/239.

[120] Allan Horsfall to Antony Grey, 'Election campaign', 31 March 1966. HCA/GREY/1/15/144.

[121] Antony Grey to Allan Horsfall, 'Election results', 7 April 1966. HCA/GREY/1/15/143.

[122] Antony Grey to Allan Horsfall, 'Give a talk', 6 March 1964. MCA/G/HOR/1.

[123] Allan Horsfall to Antony Grey, 'Difficulties of talk', 23 March 1964. MCA/GG/HOR/1.

[124] Rev. Paul Bibby to Allan Horsfall, 'Apologies for behaviour', 23 March 1964. MCA/G/HOR/1.

[125] Allan Horsfall to Antony Grey 'Speech to Lancaster', 4 July 1965. HCA/GREY/1/15.

[126] Antony Grey to Alan Horsfall, 'Public reaction', 20 October 1965. HCA/GREY/1/15.

[127] Allan Horsfall to Antony Grey, 'Luncheon club meeting', 6 February 1966. HCA/GREY/1/15/156.

[128] 'Obscene leaflets at council estate', *West London Observer,* 8 February 1963, 9.

[129] 'E. H.', 'Reader complains of public lecture on homosexuality', *West London Observer*, 15 February 1963, 7.

[130] Allan Horsfall to Antony Grey, 'About Myers Haines', 25 January 1965. HCA/GREY/1/15/256.

[131] Antony Grey to Allan Horsfall, 'About Myers Haines', 26 January 1965. HCA/GREY/1/15/255.

[132] 'Myers Haines' to Antony Grey, 'Bradford Pen Pal Club', 17 February 1965. HCA/GREY/15/1/227.

[133] Antony Grey to Allan Horsfall, 'About Myers Haines', 22 March 1965. HCA/GREY/1/15/229.

[134] Meg Elizabeth Atkins, interviewed by the author, 4 January 2012.

[135] Allan Horsfall to Antony Grey, 'Myers Haines', 28 March 1965. HCA/GREY/1/15/226.

[136] Antony Grey to Allan Horsfall, 'Many thanks', 8 April 1965. HCA/GREY/1/15/222.

[137] Allan Horsfall to Antony Grey, 'Speakers for meeting', 24 January 1966. HCA/GREY/1/15/162.

[138] Antony Grey to Allan Horsfall, 'Anxiety attacks', end of August 1965 (undated). HCA/GREY/15/1/82.

[139] Antony Grey to Allan Horsfall, 'Title for public meeting',. 12 September 1966. HCA/GREY/1/15/121.

[140] Antony Grey to Allan Horsfall, 'Arrangements for collections', 13 October 1966. HCA/GREY/15/1/140.

[141] Allan Horsfall to Antony Grey, 'Financial arrangements for meeting', 18 October 1966. HCA/Grey/15/1.

[142] F. D. W. Tye, 'A programme for purity' *Smethwick Telephone and Warley Observer*, 30 January 1966, 7.

[143] 'Mandrake', 'For queen, country and the rope!', *Sunday Telegraph*, 6 February 1966, 7.

[144] Quoted in 'Wasps', *Muther Grumble*, 6 (June 1972). www.muthergrumble.co.uk/issue06/mg0605.htm (accessed 13/12/11).

[145] Harry Whewell, 'Homosexuals far too anonymous', *Guardian* 2 July 1966, 14.

[146] NWHLRC press release, quoted in Whewell, ibid.

[147] 'Even perversion', *Manchester Evening News*, 4 July 1966, 4.

[148] Allan Horsfall, 'Sex bill', *Manchester Evening News*, 13 July 1966, 4.

[149] Ibid.

[150] Allan Horsfall, 'Battling for Wolfenden', in Cant and Hemmings, *Radical records*, 18.

[151] Antony Grey to Allan Horsfall, 'A visit to Manchester', 1 November 1966. HCA/GREY/1/15/108.

[152] Harry Eaves to Allan Horsfall, 'Comments on public meeting', 13 November 1966. MCA/G/HOR/1.

[153] 'Homosexual law reform "by May",' *Guardian*, 12 November 1966, 4.

[154] Antony Grey to Allan Horsfall, 'Congratulations on meeting', 15 November 1966. HCA/GREY/1/15/100.

[155] Ibid.

[156] Antony Grey to Allan Horsfall, 'Alan Fitch' 15 November 1966. HCA/GREY/1/15/75.

[157] Antony Grey, memorandum to Leo Abse, 25 November 1966. MCA/G/HOR/1.

[158] Allan Horsfall, 'Sexual freedom', *Spectator*, 6 December 1966.

[159] Leo Abse to Allan Horsfall, 'Merchant navy exemptions', 30 December 1966. MCA/G/HOR/1.

[160] Allan Horsfall to Niel Pearson, 'Limitations of sexual law reform bill', 30 December 1966. MCA/G/HOR/1.

[161] Allan Horsfall to Leo Abse, 'Sexual offences prosecutions', 16 September 1966. MCA/G/HOR/1.

[162] NWHLRC minutes, 15 June 1967. MCA/G/HOR/2.

[163] C. H. Rolph (C. Rolph Hewitt) to Colin Harvey, 'Composition of NW Committee', 10 December 1968. HCA/GREY/1/15/22.

[164] Allan Horsfall to Antony Grey, 'Carlisle affair', 10 December 1966. HCA/GREY/1/15/82.

[165] Antony Grey to Allan Horsfall, 'Group cases', 13 December 1966. HCA/GREY/1/15/80.

[166] HLRS minutes, 30 January 1967. 'Antony Grey report'. HCA/GREY/15/1/1

[167] HLRS *Spectrum* 19, April 1967. HCA/AT/5/2.

[168] HL Deb 10 May 1966, vol. 274, col. 634.

[169] HL Deb 16 June 1966, vol. 276, col. 159.

[170] HL Deb 23 May 1966, vol. 274, col. 1171.

[171] HL Deb 16 June 1966, vol. 276, col. 167.

[172] NWHLRC *Bulletin*, May 1967. HCA/GREY/1/15/53.

[173] '12 sent for trial on indecency charges', *Altrincham Guardian*, 13 June 1967, 7.

[174] Peter Norman, interviewed by the author, 25 February 2014.

[175] HC Deb 3 July 1967, vol. 749 col. 1516.

[176] Patrick Trevor-Roper, interviewed by Margot Farnham, 8 Jan 1990. NSA C456/089/01–02.

[177] HL Deb 21 July 1967, vol. 285 col. 523.

Chapter Three: There's a Place for Us

Contents

Crises at HLRS

The passing of the 1967 Sexual Offences Act precipitated a crisis in the law reform organisations of both London and Manchester. The HLRS, with no membership and dependent on the random goodwill of supporters, found itself virtually broke. There were no meetings of the Executive after January 1967 for ten months. By the time it did meet again, it had no President. Freddy Ayer had written to Secretary Antony Grey to say that:

> he was strongly of the opinion that the Society had accomplished its purpose and should now be wound up. If the Executive Committee were to decide otherwise, he would not wish to continue as President.[1]

The liberal Bishop of Woolwich, John Robinson,* took over, but he had nothing like the kudos of Ayer. By January 1968, the Albany Trust was carrying an overdraft of £1,900, and the most recent appeal had only brought in £1,500. A benefit piano recital by Peter Katin† lost £231/-/9d.‡ By October 1968, the HLRS itself was down to £11/8/7d (£11.43) in the bank – with wages to pay and an office to maintain. Before the Act, any appeal for money had had a very clear object, and donations had come in with law reform in mind. Now it was by no means clear what the money would or should be used for.

In the area of law reform, everyone agreed that the Act as passed was unsatisfactory, and left much to be done. Grey reported that Lord Arran had

---

* John Robinson was most famous in the early 1960s for his book *Honest to God*, which expounded the idea of a 'religion-less' God and remains controversial. He also grabbed headlines by appearing for the defence in the trial of *Lady Chatterley's Lover*, and claiming on the witness stand that it was a book that Christians ought to read. This was twisted into a banner headline in the *Evening Standard*, 'A book all Christians should read'.

—C. H. Rolph, *The Trial of Lady Chatterley*, 72–3.

† Peter Katin, an internationally renowned pianist and acknowledged master interpreter of Chopin, became in 1958 the first British pianist to visit the USSR. He became a Vice-President of CHE in 1972, and remains one as of 2014. During the 1970s he gave several public recitals for CHE, and hosted further fundraisers for the local CHE group at his home in South Croydon.

‡ On 15 February 1971 (Decimal Day) the United Kingdom went over from 'old money', to decimal currency. The old currency was expressed in pounds, shillings and pence (£1/1/6d – one pound, one shilling and sixpence). Under the new system, a pound was worth 100 new pence. So the equivalent of a shilling (1/-) was 5p. In this book, currencies are expressed as they would have been at the time, and the equivalent in 'new money' is given in brackets afterwards. In the case of larger sums, the approximate contemporary value as of 2014 is given instead.

—Historic Inflation Calculator, www.thisismoney.co.uk

told him 'that he regarded the new Act merely as a holding measure and was interested in improving certain clauses.[2] He hoped 'that the society would remain in existence for the time being in order to hold a watching brief on the operation of the new law.'[3]

The context for further legal reforms was changing. Having used up so much Parliamentary and campaigning time and energy getting the Act passed, reformers estimated it would be at least fifteen years before another modifying bill would stand any chance of consideration. However, in the very week of the final passage of the Act, the Latey Committee* reported to Parliament, recommending a lowered Age of Majority of 18. This was brought in in 1969, and 18-year-olds were able to vote in a General Election for the first time in 1970. Grey in London and Allan Horsfall in Manchester both hoped it might be possible to sneak a lowering of the homosexual age of consent into the eventual bill that the Government announced in April 1968 to implement Latey.

Further, the Criminal Law Revision Commission, a standing committee of the Home Office with a brief to ferret out anachronisms and anomalies in the law, had recently announced it was to look at the whole issue of sexual offences, gay and straight. Leo Abse thought the HLRS should stay in existence to prepare a memorandum for this Commission,† and should then consider its future in a year's time. This more general concern became the focus of the HLRS, so much so that it dropped the 'Homo' from its name and became the Sexual Law Reform Society (SLRS) in 1970. This broadening of interest triggered the resignation of Angus Wilson, Jacquetta Hawkes and MP Chris Chataway. The Honorary Committee was now pretty threadbare. By this time, the Society had contracted from seven full-time workers in 1965–67 to the solitary Secretary, Antony Grey.

If there was uncertainty about the possibilities of, or a strategy for, further legal change, there was no doubt about the need for education. Richard Wollheim put the case succinctly as early as April 1958: 'There is little point in liberalising the law, if this merely means that the weapon of persecution is taken out of the hands of magistrates and placed in those of the mob.'[4] Since then, all campaigners had accepted that they needed to argue their case to the public. In this, British campaigners were in step with their counterparts in Arcadie in France and the Mattachine Society in America.

---

* Sir John Latey, a judge specialising in divorce and family law, was appointed by the government to investigate all aspects of the Age of Majority.

† In fact the Commission would not produce its report on the subject (its fifteenth report) until 1984.

Counselling needs and charitable status

The other need, which had been identified right from the start, was that of counselling and support for isolated gay men who were not comfortable with their sexuality. Within months of its formation, the HLRS was receiving nearly two hundred letters a month appealing for individual help. Michael Schofield says that he too was inundated with similar requests when he published his book *Society and the Homosexual* in 1952, as was Dirk Bogarde when the film *Victim* appeared in 1961. By setting up the Albany Trust as the charitable, counselling arm of the campaign, HLRS hoped to deal with this need as a separate issue.

As soon as the law was changed, the Albany Trust started placing advertisements in the Personal Columns of the national press and weekly magazines. A fortnight after the Act became law, the following appeared in *The Guardian*, *The Sun*, the *Daily Telegraph*, *The Times* and *Sunday Times*, *The Observer*, *Spectator*, *New Society*, *New Statesman*, *New Christian* and *Methodist Recorder*:

> HOMOSEXUALS – the law has changed but many social and personal problems remain. The Albany Trust (a registered charity)* exists to promote psychological health through education, research and social action, and is especially concerned with sexual deviation. Enquiries to...[5]

However, even this advertisement, so clearly targeted, was sailing close to the wind. The Trust was put into something of a straightjacket by its charitable status, which required it to provide counselling and support for people with all kinds of sexual difficulties, and not just homosexuals. Its association with the HLRS had already attracted the suspicion of the Charity Commissioners, as early as January 1967. Their tax inspector, C. P. Sherlock, wrote to them:

> My principal difficulty in looking at the Trust's tax claims has been to distinguish between those activities which seek to assist the individual homosexual [to] meet the psychological problems which arise from his condition and those activities which seek to advance knowledge about the nature and cause of homosexuality, both of which would I think be charitable, from the propagation of an ethical view that society ought to be conditioned to accept homosexual practices without attaching disapproval to them.
>
> I am assuming that the Trust has not sought to deny Society's right to disapprove of homosexual activities. ... Obviously the Trust's affairs must lie very near the border that distinguishes the charitable from the non-charitable.[6]

---

* The Albany Trust had become a charity in 1965.

For the cash-strapped Trust, there was a lot of money at stake – £2,500 in rebates on donations over three years. Potentially this was a financial lifesaver. But there was a price. Grey advised his executive, 'It is clear ... that in order to safeguard permanent recognition of the Trust's charitable status we shall have to ensure that all our activities remain clearly within the ambit of charitable objects.'[7]

The inability of gay organisations to obtain charitable status hampered their growth and development for many years. Some organisations such as CHE decided that they did not want to become charities anyway, as it would impose too much of a constraint on campaigning activities. Others, such as FRIEND, tried for many years to obtain charitable status, but were turned down because their beneficiaries were homosexuals. This was not deemed to fall into the definition of charitable objects. The prejudice was reinforced by the 1972 Law Lords judgement on the *International Times* appeal against conviction on conspiracy charges. In the words of Lord Reid, 'There is a material difference between merely exempting certain conduct from criminal penalties and making it lawful in the full sense.'[8] As a consequence of this, no gay organisation achieved charitable status in the 1970s. The first to do so was the Gay Bereavement Project, registered in August 1984. The counselling organisation FRIEND and London Lesbian and Gay Switchboard both achieved charitable status in 1987.

So the Albany Trust was only to survive as a charity by maintaining what was in essence a fiction, which was that its services were not provided exclusively for homosexuals. It started applying for grants. Four hundred applications went out to trusts, charities and government departments. Three responses were positive, 340 didn't bother to reply. It was noted in the minutes that it was being turned down 'because its aims suffered from too close an association with homosexual law reform.'

The Albany Trust was also prohibited from involvement in campaigning, and further constrained by the fact that, like the HLRS, it did not have an identified gay constituency. The Trust could not draw on the experience and opinions of its members to say with any authority 'what homosexuals want'. To fill this gap, and endow it with some of that authority, it sent out a consultative questionnaire, via other organisations, to gay bars, its supporters and ex-supporters. By the beginning of 1970 over 1,300 completed questionnaires had been returned, and the Trust hoped to get another two or three thousand from a tear-out in *Jeremy*, one of the main gay magazines of the time. Grey told Horsfall, 'The results should have excellent publicity value because this will be the first time, to my knowledge, that a representative section of the homosexual population have themselves been consulted about their attitudes and wishes.'[9]

Some of what was needed was clear from the Albany Trust caseload, which was growing rapidly – eighty enquiries in August and September 1967 alone. Sixty per cent of those contacting the AT for help were aged 21–39 and 'emphasising the need for positive social help'. Grey and sociologist Michael Schofield held talks with the Ministry of Health about the need for effective support for homosexuals in the provinces (as we called them then). They even got as far as mapping out a pilot scheme to establish a centre for advice and education; this was supported by the National Association for Mental Health, the Marriage Guidance Council and the Family Planning Association. The then Health Minister, Douglas Houghton, was sympathetic. But when the chips were down, there was no money.

In July 1968, Trust supporters, mainly professional people with an interest in social work, held a weekend study conference at Wychcroft in Surrey. As a result, private social gatherings of homosexuals started to take place at St Katherine's* in Limehouse. This was basically a discussion group at the start, mediated by clerics or social workers:

> We usually met on Saturday evenings. For the first year we wondered if we would be raided by the police, and a deliberately boring social work style handout was prepared, saying that we were helping lonely homosexuals who had come for counselling. … We all wore smart clothes, someone played the piano, and there was an improving talk for about thirty minutes. … The whole thing was conducted with great care and caution … but everyone had grown up in an atmosphere of complete illegality and secrecy. Potential members had to go through a vetting procedure. … Codes of behaviour were enforced and the existence of the group was kept in the early days very secret.[10]

It took a year to get a small unofficial bar opened – and to allow dancing, although even then some regulars voted against the idea. The result was a compromise: dancing every other week. This was a big deal, at a time when venues which allowed men to dance together were still being prosecuted for running a disorderly house. Clubs were all members-only, tiny, and offered either drinking or dancing. Dancing was allowed in a few small clubs, such as the Masquerade under a launderette in Earl's Court; but it was rigidly policed so that there was absolutely no touching., So when St Katherine's allowed dancing, there was a certain amount of trepidation about whether the police would raid; and indeed they did pay a visit after a year or so. They asked a lot of questions. Someone was arrested and carted away, leaving everyone else at the meeting very shaken.

---

* The Royal Foundation of St Katherine was an Anglican community dedicated to social justice. Its Royal patron was the Queen Mother, who was reputed to have personally approved the gathering. However the long shadow of Her Majesty did impose a certain caution and discretion.

There's no doubt that SK, as it was known, was a breakthrough, if of a limited kind. Very isolated gay men, whose previous contacts with other homosexuals had been confined to a grope in a cottage, found support, friendship, and information about a gay scene many did not even know existed. More, they found acceptance of themselves as people. On special occasions they held larger dances, and one of the rules of the group was that if someone asked you to dance you were not allowed to refuse.* This was in sharp contrast to the competitive sexual Darwinism of the few gay clubs.

However, none of this was anything like a real club – a place where homosexuals could chat and laugh and drink and dance and get a meal and bring their sister, which is what the boys in the North-West wanted. Even before the law was changed, they were on the move. Allan Horsfall wrote to Antony Grey in January 1966, 'I expect you will soon be hearing from Ray Gosling. We want to meet you about a joint project we have agreed in principle'.[11] This was to become Esquire Clubs.

Ray Gosling

Ray Gosling, who was just beginning to make a name for himself as a journalist with Granada Television, was a comparatively recent convert to the idea of law reform. The son of working-class parents in Northampton,† he was one of the new generation of Grammar School lads with opportunities for education and self-improvement un-dreamt-of by the previous one. But Ray was a free and restless spirit, a natural hedonist and anarchist who was potty about the new youth culture and gorgeous working-class boys. He dropped out of school as soon as possible, became a railway signalman, finished educating himself, started youth clubs – and started writing. He managed to place little bits of journalism here and there. They were noticed because of a unique literary style, by turns staccato and lyrical, combative and quizzical. An early piece, *Dream Boy*, in the *New Left Review* from May 1960, comes with the editorial introduction: 'In this article, a young signalman, who has organised the first Youth Venture Clubs‡ in Leicester, writes a manifesto for the scheme.'[12] Not so much a manifesto as a love letter to unobtainable youth:

---

* The *Arcadie* club in Paris operated a very similar convention, as well as an elaborate ritual, the *danse de tapis*, which licensed strangers to approach each other, kiss and then dance.

† Some sources suggest he was born in Chester, but his birth certificate gives his place of birth as Weston Favell (a former village, now an area of Northampton).

—Brixworh District Registry of Births, Vol 3b, p.136

‡ Youth Venture Clubs had been founded by Lord Longford.

> In an age of sexual muddle, his common charm has attracted the society moll and the homosexual. ... The boy stands up in his sexual and phallic dress, a rebel against a sexless world of fear, and from his own he has made gods. In his dress, his walk, in his whole way of life, he makes a private drama for the world that failed him to take note of. ... He is constantly pleading for help, for understanding; and yet he is incapable of returning that love.[13]

25. Ray Gosling, around 1982

Certainly he attracted this particular homosexual, who concluded, 'His world awaits a new culture, a new art in the age of the common man.'

The *New Left Review* was the latest, most exciting intellectual magazine. Founded by pioneering sociologist, Professor Stuart Hall, it boasted the best cultural commentators of the left – Richard Hoggart, Raymond Williams, E. P. Thompson, Arnold Wesker and (in September 1960, something of a coup) Fidel Castro. It's not surprising that Ray should gravitate to its tiny Soho office, hustling for commissions. The one thing he was never short of was chutzpah. After all, this was a man who published his autobiography at the age of 24.

Allan Horsfall too got into Hall's pages. In May 1961, he wrote a piece on the chasm of a class divide opened up by a new hotel in Burnley, 'As conspicuous and self-conscious as a brand new car upended on a scrap heap.' The manager turned away a pre-booked twenty-first birthday party because they were not wearing evening dress. 'He couldn't afford to have the town's butchers' boys and bakers' boys mixing with the type of people his hotel catered for.'[14]

By November 1961, Allan had tried and failed to get the Labour Party to adopt the Wolfenden Report. Seething with frustration, he poured the whole sorry saga onto paper for the *New Left Review*. Stuart Hall, when he saw the article, knew he had to make an introduction. Ray Gosling remembers:

He says to me one day in Soho, he says, 'I've got this piece come in from this guy up North, have a look at it.' He would have known I was queer. I was always picking up boys in Soho and going off with them. And bringing them along with me in tow, that sort of thing. And he said, 'Have a look at it.' And it was about changing the law. … And I said, 'Well, you'll have to publish it, Stuart, because it's a good piece.'

But I said, 'I disagree with it. I don't think the law should be changed.' I said in some anarchic, mad young way. I said, the thing that's got to be done is people have just got to get out and bloody do it…. They've got to go round Piccadilly Circus picking one another up and going to bed with one another and falling in love with one another. You don't want to change the bloody law, I said. … What happens when you change a law is, suddenly everything gets legal, but there are so many restrictions that The Life goes.

And that is what happened. Allan wrote me a private letter, and he said, 'I think we ought to meet.' He didn't give me his address or anything, not at that stage. So I went up to Manchester, and the Bishop of Middleton provided us with an office. And we met and had a very, frosty meeting. Cos I said he was wrong, and the law didn't need to be changed, and he made out a very good logical case for the law to be changed, and he had a lot of case histories going back to Altrincham in the 1930s, where people had been picked up and prosecuted. I went away. Thought nothing of it.[15]

R. v. Ray and Clarkson

It took a Nottingham court case in 1965 to bring Gosling round to the need for law reform. Billy Ray, 28, had been living with 19-year-old John Clarkson for two years when Clarkson was done for shoplifting. He was fined £5, but something about him, or about the relationship between the lads, made the police suspicious. They came to the flat the couple shared, ostensibly to look for more stolen goods, but became inordinately interested in the bedroom. They found a couple of very suggestive Christmas cards, according to PC Colin Kilbourn's deposition to the committal proceedings:

EXHIBIT 1. A Christmas Card 'To Billy – all my love as ever – John.'

'Do you care to explain this?'

'I only sent it because Billy sent me one.'

KILBOURN: 'I also found a piece of white towelling, which had a damp patch on it [Exhibit. 4], and also a tin of Talc de Cety Powder* [Exhibit 5] and from a pile of clothing in front of the wardrobe I found another piece of white towelling which was stained [Exhibit 7]. In the bathroom

* Coty was/is a well-known international cosmetics manufacturer; it is possible that 'Cety' is a misprint.

> I found on a small line which was erected two pairs of small pink briefs [Exhibit 8].'[16]

The police kept hinting at a homosexual relationship. They took away other items which would later be produced in court. John was bullied into admitting that he slept with Billy. Held separately and incommunicado at the police station for several hours, each being told that the other one had confessed, eventually they both allegedly gave statements incriminating themselves. John said:

> I had better tell you all about it. For the past three years I have been having sexual intercourse via the rear passage with Billy. ... The last time was about four weeks ago. It started with masturbating each other. I want to get the other matter cleared up. Will you put it down in writing for me?[17]

It is unlikely that this is what he or Billy actually said, since Billy ends his statement identically: 'I want to get the matter cleared up. Will you put it down in writing for me?'[18] The police also pursued the 'domino effect' in questioning them about previous relationships. Clarkson claimed only two, and those casual, and neither was pursued. Two of Billy's affairs were followed up, and questioned. Neither was charged, although as a result Billy faced an additional charge of buggery with one of them, an actor.

Having got the statements, the police claimed to be 'bailing'* them when they let them go on condition that they didn't see each other and John went back to live with his parents. Two days later they had to submit to medical examination by a police doctor, who reported to the Court 'I found that two fingers could be inserted into the anus without causing undue discomfort. The sphincter grip was less than normal. I formed the opinion that buggery could have been committed with this man as passive partner.'[19] They also gave samples of head and pubic hair (Exhibit 12). When the police drove them back to the flat, they took the opportunity to seize the sheets off the couple's bed.

The HLRS became involved with the case when a distraught John wrote to John Robinson, Bishop of Woolwich, immediately after the arrest. Dr Robinson had recently been urging the Church to make a large regular donation to the Albany Trust, and this got newspaper publicity. John told the Bishop:

> I was until the beginning of this year living in a flat with my partner whom I love dearly. All our furniture, our personal effects and all our money were shared equally, but most of all our two lives existed as one. We have

* There was no bail document signed.

> irrevocable faith in each other, we both have the same likes and dislikes… and everything we did we did not for ourselves but for each other. …
>
> Now I am compelled to reside with my parents and not at my rightful home. To date the police have not charged us with a crime and we are left in a state of ignorance about what is to happen. For me and my loved one the past six months have been sheer agony. Life has not seemed worth living. …
>
> I am unable to concentrate fully on my work or on anything. Each new day is another day of anguish. … A part of my life has been taken away from me and thrown on one side.[20]

Robinson put the case in the hands of Antony Grey, who tried to find them a good local solicitor through the NCCL, and counselled them most forcibly to say nothing and plead not guilty. Unfortunately the NCCL had no lists of recommended solicitors, and so the two men settled for a rather docile and ineffectual local firm. In any case, the damage was already done, in their naïve confessions.

Not surprisingly, John couldn't stand being at his parents' house, and one night returned to Billy. Immediately his mother told the police, who came round at 11.15 that night. The police threatened them because they had 'broken bail', although they soon changed tactics when the couple said there was no bail agreement, and drove them back home. When it came to the committal proceedings John Clarkson's statement was defiant:

> By now we were in love with each other and frequently showed it by holding hands and kissing each other on his mouth, shoulders, legs and backside or any other place we could. … At this stage we both fully understood what we were doing was by the antiquarian moral British Code illegal, although in our own minds we both knew to ourselves that we were doing right. And to date our views about each other and what we were doing have never changed. Our affection for each other strengthened to the thought of separation being unbearable. … We have both been blissfully happy.[21]

As part of his watching brief – watching, in that he couldn't talk directly to the solicitors John and Billy had chosen – Grey got in touch with Ray Gosling and asked him to report on the committal proceedings for the HLRS:

> The proceedings filled me with a mixture of uncontrollable laughter and rage. Never tears. It was not a sad occasion.
>
> A PC in his early twenties: handsome and cool as if he was reading a script – gave evidence first, and the bizarre items were produced.
>
> From the dresser: one partly used jar of Astral cream
> one soiled piece of towelling
> One tin of talcum powder

> From the wardrobe: three tins of Nivea Cream
> another stained piece of towelling
> From the bathroom: 2 pairs of small pink briefs.

What the PC had to say, more than is usual, seemed a set, carefully rehearsed piece of monologue. In cautioning Clarkson, 'From enquiries I have made and information I have received…'

> How, I kept asking myself, had this happened? Why did they submit so passively to the police enquiries?[22]

Later Ray Gosling recalled:

> But they did during the trial the most amazing, humiliating things I'd ever seen in my life. Two ushers came out in proper suits, and held up the bed sheets. And then a clerk came out and pointed out to the jury where there stains of spunk and a bit of what is politely called a skid mark. The jar of Nivea was passed along the jury – 'Notice the pubic hair.' I thought, this is awful. This is absolutely awful. … They were twelve good men – I think it was only men then. But they went to prison. John went to prison for two years.* And the lad went to a Borstal, it would have been called then, for two years as well.
>
> I wrote Allan a letter the night that trial finished. And I said, 'I'm coming back to Manchester to see you.' I went back and saw him, again in the Bishop of Middleton's office. And I said, 'I'm with you. Count me in.'[23]

And so, in the summer of 1965, Ray became a supporter of the North Western Committee. Once in, Ray threw himself into campaigning by dashing off a letter of protest to the Chief Constable of Nottinghamshire about the case. It hasn't survived, and Ray doesn't remember it, but it seems clear that it was one of those 'Why don't you prosecute me too?' letters, no doubt laying out chapter and verse of the basis for the charge. Grey wrote to Allan:

> Ray Gosling sent me a copy of that letter, and, while I doubt the wisdom of his opening paragraph, I cannot help admiring his guts. I should hate to think that this will lead him into trouble.[24]

For Ray himself, there was never any sense that he was putting himself in danger. He was a buccaneer, a wanderer, his own man.

The growing number of TV commitments kept Ray from any significant involvement in the campaign for a while, but when it came to social clubs, this

---

* In his article on the John Clarkson website, Ray says the sentence was three years. But he has confused the two defendants. In fact John was 'the lad' who went to Borstal, and for six months. Billy Ray went to prison; his sentence was the more severe because the prosecution attributed Clarkson's defiant words to him.

was right up the party animal's street. By the beginning of 1967, there was a strong sense that law reform was just around the corner, and it was time to plan ahead.

A need for social clubs

Pressure was growing within the Committee. They wanted social clubs.* There was Allan's dream of the Working Men's Club for homosexuals, owned by its members. Others had been on holiday to Amsterdam, or, if they hadn't, were familiar with the COC club in Amsterdam they had heard about, or read about in newspapers, whether in the prurient reports in the *Sunday Pictorial* or more considered articles such as one which appeared in *The Observer* in January 1963:

> A meeting place not only where homosexuals gather openly but to which they are directed by the police – this may sound unbelievable to English people but it exists in Holland. … In allowing inverts all legitimate freedom consistent with public decency, Holland's attitude is broadly similar to that of Belgium, France, Denmark, Sweden, Spain and Italy.[25]

The reporter wrote of COC: 'It has gathered a unique body of practical experience on helping the homosexual to accept himself and his situation, and to adjust sensibly to society.'[26]

The Dutch organisation boasted 4000 members of whom 500 were women; it was run by a council of ten and held an annual conference to form policy, employing a full-time permanent office staff of four. The COC Club had a dance floor, bar and meeting rooms. Here Dutch homosexuals could find social activities, discussion groups, play readings, music groups, and lectures. Bob Angelo,† the chief officer since 1948, was quoted: 'Our whole aim is to encourage members' capacity to form lasting relationships.'[27] This was to become a recurring theme in the arguments for social facilities, and for CHE groups. The article concluded by addressing the issue of corruption of minors: 'They are punctilious about excluding under-21s, and everyone knows by then [whether they are homosexual or not].'[28]

COC was not the only gay club in Europe by any means. Arcadie had been going since 1957, and in 1952 GLF and CHE activist Michael Brown went on holiday to Zurich purely because he'd heard of *Der Kreis*, and the club of the same name there. However, it was Amsterdam which most English homosexuals knew, and COC which had the most efficient PR operation. Further

---

* They were not the first in this. The very first issue of the pioneering lesbian magazine *Arena 3* in spring 1964 had floated the idea of lesbian social clubs.

† A pseudonym for well-known Dutch TV actor Nico Engelschman.

publicity was given by Bryan Magee's 1964 *This Week* documentary,* in which he interviewed British homosexuals (in silhouette) and Dutch members of COC (full on). A minute of the NWHLRC of 15 June 1967 records:

> It was felt that a series of clubs for homosexuals, similar to the ones existing in the Netherlands, would be of great value in this country. It was decided in principle, as soon as the law is changed … that the Albany Trust should be asked to sponsor a similar club movement in this country.[29]

So Allan wrote to Antony asking him to put it to his own committee, 'I told them I don't know whether your constitution would allow the Trust to do this, or how far you might be restricted by your position as a registered charity.'[30] By August 1967, Allan was reporting that he was having difficulty keeping his committee under control. They were straining at the leash:

> A considerable number of people there now lean to the view that the homosexual community is frustrated rather than maladjusted and it was only with some difficulty that they were persuaded against some sort of precipitate action on clubs.[31]

Esquire Clubs

But the HLRS and the Albany Trust, as has been seen, were in chaos; their committees didn't meet for nine months between January and October 1967. So the Mancunians went it alone. Sometime in the summer of 1967, Esquire Clubs was set up as a private limited company with six directors – Allan Horsfall, Allan's partner Harold Pollard, Ray Gosling, Colin Harvey, Jack Jackson (another North Western Committee stalwart) and Reg Kilduff. President Niel Pearson provided the legal expertise.

Kilduff was the owner/manager of the Rockingham Club and the Rembrandt Hotel in Manchester. He seems to have alternated between extreme caution and enthusiastic support for the aims of the NWHLRC and Esquire Ltd. His first contact with homosexual campaigning was a visit to Antony Grey in 1965. Antony wrote to Allan:

> He came to see me because some of his clients apparently want to know why they can't have dancing. We discussed the matter at some length, and I told him it would be most unwise unless he had taken some very knowledgeable legal advice beforehand (and that even if he did it would still probably be unwise). But he is willing to help with the proceeds of collections and raffles. I told him about the formation of your committee, and he said he would very much like to meet you if you would get in touch with him sometime.[32]

---

* See page 141.

Not the least of Antony's talents was effecting useful introductions, and this particular bit of matchmaking paid dividends. Kilduff gave supporters of the Committee free membership of the Rockingham, as an incentive for new members to sign up. He helped to finance the big 1966 public meeting* – paid for the hall, organised security, provided the food, and put up Antony Grey when he stayed overnight for a talk he was giving locally. Allan, who was wined and dined, was very taken with him: 'His entertaining is lavish and generous and far beyond what I am used to or able to return. I think he will certainly be able to help in all sorts of ways and he is certainly keen to do so!'[33]

Reg started to display collecting boxes for the Committee – but discreetly.† According to Allan:

> He was very cautious about advertising it within the club, in case the police could use evidence. He used to put collection boxes for our campaign on his counter, but he always insisted that the full name didn't go on the boxes, we had to have initials, which everybody knew, but it couldn't be used in evidence. That's the way clubs used to be conducted in those days, everybody was tiptoeing on eggshells.[34]

One of the mysteries much discussed in gay circles in Manchester was why the Rockingham was untouched by the police, where other clubs and bars were subjected to raids and prosecutions. Reg ran a very clean and tight ship, but that wasn't the only reason. Allan remembered:

> I remember once being in the Rockingham … at a time when everything was illegal, and I was talking to the proprietor, and his manager came up and said, 'Excuse me, but your usual Monday night visitors are here.' So the proprietor said, 'Excuse me, Allan, I must just go and have a word', and when he'd been away a while, I went to the gents and I found him halfway down the corridor, looking very puzzled, and I said, 'What's to do, Reg? Who are your Monday night visitors?' And he said, 'Oh it's the police again, and I'm just wondering whether to give them spirits on this occasion or cash.' Obviously they were coming in every week for a bit of dosh for – their way of saying, we know what you're up to, and if you want to carry on unmolested, you know …[35]

Reg became the friendly face of the commercial scene, to whom uncertain homosexuals were introduced when they wanted to dip a toe into its waters, and in turn referred to Horsfall those people he had talked to at the club who seemed to be in need of more support than the Rockingham could offer. It was largely thanks to Reg and his contacts that the North Western Committee was able to claim the constituency it did.

---

* 'Society and its Homosexuals' – see page 141.

† See page 120.

The foundations for Esquire Clubs were being laid in the summer of 1967, almost before the Sexual Offences Act received the royal assent. On 11 August, Allan was writing to the Borough Planning Officer about 191 Bridgeman Street, Bolton, next door to the Corporation Bus Depot, shortly to be vacated by the Labour Club. He wanted to know what the plans were for it. He wanted a temporary club – ideal site for a pilot scheme. They needed to get some expert advice from people who had been in this situation before, and that meant the Dutch. Martin Stafford* went down to London to meet Jan de Groot from COC, in the Albany Trust Office in Shaftesbury Avenue. He wrote back to Allan:

> This was in some ways disappointing. Nothing was said that has not been said before. Antony Grey says that while the Albany Trust may help to inaugurate clubs like COC, it is outside the scope of the Trust to establish them by itself. … I will make an informal report at the next meeting, though it is hardly worthwhile to say very much about it; we have heard it all before.[36]

It was increasingly clear that, if they wanted something done, the Committee couldn't look to the Albany Trust to do it as originally intended: they would have to do it themselves.

Persecution of gay clubs

Just what they were letting themselves in for is made clear by a story which appeared in *The People* on 24 March 1968. The paper said that it was following a tip-off from the Leeds University Student Union which feared for the purity of its members. Denis Cassidy reported:

> A place like the Hope and Anchor might have an adverse effect on curious, impressionable youngsters. I saw men—
>
> DANCING CHEEK TO CHEEK to the music of a juke box.
>
> KISSING PASSIONATELY on the dance floor and in secluded corners
>
> HOLDING HANDS, PETTING and EMBRACING unashamedly in the packed room.
>
> There were men heavily made up and smelling strongly of perfume. Others were in women's clothing and wore charm bracelets and rings on their fingers. They giggled and talked among themselves in high-pitched voices.
>
> I watched effeminate-looking men disappear into the 'Ladies' to titivate their appearance and tidy their waved dyed hair. … Girls too danced

---

* See page 243 for an introduction to Martin Stafford.

> together and kissed. Many of the girls wore men's hair styles, suits, shirts and ties.[37]

Within the limits of the times, the landlady, Cathy ('whatever you do, point out I'm normal') Wilson, offered a strenuous defence, and a glimpse into a gay lifestyle which could just have easily been a description of an eighteenth-century Molly House:

> About 90% of my customers are queer or lesbian. They spend all their time and money in here. If I threw them out, where would they go? They come in here because they regard it as their pub, and I get no trouble. I would rather run a pub like this for these people than have a pub full of some of the normal types we have in Leeds. …
>
> They live in a world of their own and they are no trouble at all. They have really nowhere else to go without getting ridiculed. They take themselves very seriously and there have been several 'weddings' among regulars. We've even had 'brides' in here in their wedding dresses on the night of the ceremony.'[38]

Her gay customers, however, in some respects hardly presented the kind of image that the North Western Committee would have been keen to promote.* Mr Cassidy met Kevin and Jane. Jane said:

> My real name is James and I work in a mill, I'm wearing women's tights and a kaftan back-to-front so it looks like a dress. I'm an exhibitionist … I like to be looked at … I don't mind what people call me. I've been bent ever since I was interfered with as a nine-year-old child. I don't want to change. I enjoy being what I am. I like girls for company but not for sex. I have lots of boyfriends and I even have some normal friends.[39]

The article concluded:

> It's about time the authorities took some notice of the Hope and Anchor. It's about time, in fact, that the police put a stop to the odd goings-in there. … Do we really want pubs like this? Even in this so-called enlightened and permissive society?[40]

The *People* article was disingenuous. Like other papers, it had stringers trawling through local and specialist press, looking for potential stories. These included student papers, and one of the best, twice winner of *The Guardian*'s Student Newspaper of the Year Award, was *Union News*, put out by the University of Leeds. However, the idea that the story was appealing for police action to protect the innocence of its readers was very far from the truth. Guy Thornton, who became CHE's international liaison officer in the 1970s, as well as chairing the NCCL Gay Subcommittee, puts the record straight:

---

* They may of course have had their words twisted.

> We had a sit-in Leeds in 68 when we took over the Brotherton Library. And we were producing daily editions, emergency editions. But we also did an award-winning article on the Hope and Anchor, which was a gay pub in Leeds, and this was a pub which was being victimised by the NF and skinheads. They were laying in and trying to gay-bash it.
>
> Our article was very much pro, and 'Why aren't the police in there? Why isn't anything to be done to stop this victimisation? Why aren't the police in there protecting these people who are only doing what comes natural to them, as it were?'[41]

The fiery left-wing radical editing this paper throughout the sit-in, and supporting gay rights? *Daily Mail* editor, Paul Dacre.

As if they needed any telling, the article in *The People* showed the Committee exactly how fraught the whole business of running clubs was. Two court cases in 1968 also brought this home. In September, Eduardo Verguillas pleaded guilty to 'permitting dancing of a nature likely to cause a breach of the peace' at the Club Rouge, the second most important gay club in Manchester. He also pleaded guilty to selling alcohol out of licensing hours. The club had already lost its Special Hours Licence and its Supper Club licence, so the police clearly had their eye on the club. To the local paper, the homophobic *Manchester Evening News*, the most disgusting aspect of the case was that a plain-clothes policeman was forced to dance with another man in the line of duty:

> Throughout the evening there had been a constant procession of men to the dance floor. They were seen to kiss and hold each other in passionate embraces. No restrictions had been imposed on this kind of dancing by the management. … On the first visit, the observing officer became so conspicuous because he was not engaging in this kind of behaviour, that when he was approached by a homosexual he was obliged to dance with him, or risk being signalled and having to discontinue his observations.[42]

The image of the plod trying to imitate gay dancing in his regulation police boots would be funny, were not the consequences so serious. Esteban was fined £30 and £5 costs. The magistrates seemed to accept, at least in part, the defence argument that 'it is better to have these types concentrated in one club than spread them over all the clubs in the city.' At least he didn't lose his licence entirely.

Even more serious was the prosecution of George Smith, owner of the Cresta Sports and Social Club, popularly known as the Flamingo Club, in Wolverhampton. Smith was a pensioner, a retired hotel manager who had sunk his entire life savings of £1,500 (£25,000) into buying and improving the club. In the winter, plain-clothes police had put the club under observation and saw, according to the prosecution:

> behaviour between homosexuals which would in any view outrage public decency. There was no attempt to conceal an orgy of disgusting revelries which existed in the days of Sodom and Gomorrah. … Men were dancing together and fondling each other. Some men were dressed as women. Outside the club men were behaving indecently in parked cars.[43]

As a result, 35 police raided the bar in April 1968. They took names, addresses and occupations, removing the membership register and guest book. Subsequently they went to people's houses, alleging they had information about sex involving under-21s (although nobody was charged with any sexual offences as a result of the raid.) However, the club seems to have fostered an extraordinarily strong atmosphere of solidarity, because a group of members got together to write to Antony Grey and state their case:

> We feel that the honour of the proprietor and club members has been jeopardised by the action taken, by the police, and furthermore that they are attempting to restrict the liberty and rights of the members, because in the main they are homosexuals or persons who enjoy the pleasant and, up to now, free atmosphere of the club. However, since the raid the pre-October 1967 atmosphere has returned …
>
> We the members are of the opinion that the overall conduct of the police … has been to shew prejudice towards people of the highest ideals and in many cases of the highest professional standing. They also shew contempt for general civil liberty. We feel this is yet again another strike against a free and healthy and democratic society. …
>
> The police have called on several members at least once. … Their attitude has been authoritarian, frightening and possibly damaging to innocent people.[44]

They concluded with an appeal for help from the Albany Trust. In this letter it is clear that Smith fully intended to rebut the charges. However, by the time it came to trial, he had changed his plea to Guilty. Grey put the Club and its members in touch with Ivan Geffen, solicitor and abortive convenor of a West Midlands group.* Geffen seems to have taken the view that only by pleading guilty could Smith hope to retain his licence.[45] This was no small consideration when life savings were involved. When it came to trial, the police went into lurid details:

> When a police officer first visited the club, he was charged 12/6d [62½p] for entrance. He saw about 250 people there, including 5 women. Nearly all those dancing were men. All were behaving familiarly with each other and some were dressed as women. On another occasion the same officer again went and paid 2/6d [12½p] after signing an application form. Only two women were among the 150 in the main dance hall. One woman was

---

* See page 140.

> dancing and a man was interfering with her. In turn the man was being interfered with by another man. The same activities were taking place on the third visit made to the club. …
>
> On March 29th, 60 people were dancing and there were only four women present. Smith was present for some time in the dance room as these activities went on but did not pay any attention to it.[46]

The case was covered extensively in the local paper, but a fuller record survives, in that the supporters of the club sent a transcript of the proceedings to the Albany Trust, perhaps in the hope (unfulfilled) that they would organise an appeal. The remarkable thing about the trial is the number of club members who were prepared to come forward and say that nothing untoward was happening, even if this meant implicit identification as homosexuals and possible risk of losing a job. So, when Smith said that he had started the club as a sports and social club in 1965, but 'from February 1967 it had been run as a homosexual club with a discotheque', the implications for witnesses who were long-standing members were clear. For example, Brian Carleton, a schoolmaster, said he had been a member of the club for over a year.

> He had visited the club every two or three weeks before and since the [police] observations. Homosexuals met there to talk, dance and drink. He saw no disgusting conduct there. … The club served a useful and desirable purpose for homosexuals and he had never witnessed anything indecent either in the toilets or on the dance floor. He had seen men dancing together in a modern style where they did not touch. The kind of dancing which went on was what one would see in any ordinary club and nothing more. He had seen some men in the club who were dressed as women.[47]

Clifford Smith (address given in the paper) said he had been a member of the club for 15 months.

> He visited the club twice a week – many of the members were homosexual. There was a friendly, happy atmosphere and he had never seen any disgusting conduct. He visited mostly on Saturdays, sometimes on Fridays. He thought that homosexual clubs were essential for the relaxed atmosphere which they provided. … Smith had excluded undesirables before and since.[48]

Cannily, the defence also produced a female witness, name not given, who:

> stated that she was married with two children and had gone to the club as a guest of members. She knew the nature of the club and that most of the members were homosexual. She had seen no disgusting conduct, but men danced together. She had continued to visit the club since the charges were brought, and would not have done so, as the mother of two children, if she had considered anything to be improper.[49]

In essence both prosecution and defence seem agreed on what they saw, but differed radically in what it meant to them. A police witness had alleged that an act of indecency was committed only five feet from the bar while Smith was serving drinks; the act of indecency was that a man took off his shirt. To the defence witnesses, men dancing together was perfectly natural and healthy; to the prosecution 'the fact that there was a homosexual club and that men were dancing together was enough in itself to constitute a disorderly house.'[50]

Smith was an old man with a good war record in the RAF; his former employers thought highly of him; he had no criminal record; he was married with grown-up children. He had built up the club himself with no outside support, and now he stood to lose everything. He said, quite rightly, that the police hadn't told him about goings-on in the toilet, and if they had, he would have stopped it; and that he wasn't responsible for what went on in cars parked on a public street. The recorder, Christopher Oddie, was having none of it:

> I think you knew much more about what was going on than you admit. You were prepared to shut your eyes, so long as you made a profit. What was going on was intolerable by any standards, homosexual or hetero-sexual.[51]

Despite his excellent character, it was only Smith's age that kept him out of prison. Instead he was given a £500 fine (£7,900 in 2014 money) and three months to pay, or face nine months inside. This was far more than he had. The club went out of business.

Dancing has always acted as a focal point of symbolic sexuality – or at least sensuality – from the Bacchic frenzy of Greek ritual onwards. The church and other moralists have seized on it since the Middle Ages as an activity where passion is manifest, and if in one sense it is checked by stylised movement to music, the very act of containing it while at the same time expressing it heightens its intensity. As St Francis de Sales said:

> Balls and similar gatherings are wont to attract all that is bad and vicious; all the quarrels, envyings, slanders, and indiscreet tendencies of a place will be found in the ballroom. While people's bodily pores are opened by the exercise of dancing, the heart's pores will also be opened by excitement, and if any serpent be at hand to whisper foolish words of levity or impurity, to insinuate unworthy thoughts and desires, the ears that listen are more than prepared to receive the contagion.[52]

For the spectator at a nineteenth-century dance performance, the free-flowing and often skimpy clothes allowed women to show and men to view their bodies in ways which meant that 'ballet girl' became synonymous with 'whore'. In film musicals of the 1930s–50s, under the repressive Hays Code, dancing becomes the metaphor for sex and sexuality. A Fred Astaire and Ginger Rogers routine begins with circling, testing for compatibility, and builds to a synchronicity which is discreetly ecstatic.

Participation dances have routinely been condemned when a new dance appears. The Waltz, with its close contact, was considered 'riotous and indecent' in the early 1800s, inflaming inappropriate feelings – a condemnation echoed in the popular press by articles on the Charleston (kicking legs up and showing knickers), the Lindy Hop, and Rock and Roll in the 1950s. Dance was never 'only a dance'.

26. Dancing together

When tyrants fall there is dancing in the streets. Specific dances are associated with specific rebellious or counter-cultural movements, like the association of raves with eco-warriors and 'Stop the City'. The very word 'disco', which was so central to gay culture of later 1970s and early 1980s, has its origins in resistance. 'Discothèque' was a slang French word coined to describe the underground dance dives in Paris patronised during the war by the *zazous.** … *Zazous* were young anti-Nazis who expressed their opposition through zoot suits, the banned American swing music and the associated jive and lindy hop dances. When Jews were forced to wear yellow stars in France,

* The name comes from the 'za-zou-za-zou' phrasing of scat singing used by the likes of Louis Armstrong, Ella Fitzgerald and Cab Calloway.

zazous appeared publicly with yellow stars that had the words 'zazou' or 'swing' superimposed. Racially mixed, compounded equally of young men and women, discothèques were also safe havens for homosexuals. Notable among them were Pierre Seel, who was deported to a concentration camp for his homosexuality, and a sixteen-year-old leader of the French Resistance known only as 'The Colonel'. As his party piece the Colonel liked to pop out his glass eye into a girl's cocktail, to scare the pants off her. He turns up as a series character in several Boris Vian novels.

So there was something atavistic, almost, about the desire of gay men to dance with each other. It was one of the primary objectives for lesbians and gay men when trying to create 'a space to breathe', or to 'be oneself'. It was a way of touching (in some forms), of expressing sexuality, and also of allowing inhibitions to crack through the combination of music and movement. Equally atavistic was the response against it.

The issue of men dancing together – was it or wasn't it legal? – would remain alive for many years, resurfacing through local by-laws in some parts of the country against 'licentious dancing'. In 1973 the DJ Tricky Dicky (Richard Scanes) was charged with allowing it in Camberwell in South London; in the early 1980s the born-again Chief Constable of Manchester, James Anderton, used licentious dancing by-laws to prosecute local gay clubs.

The North Western Committee would have been aware of the implications of cases like the Flamingo, and were kept well informed via Antony Grey and solicitor Ivan Geffen in Wolverhampton, who forwarded newspaper cuttings. They were treading on eggshells. And not only did they have to deal with the law and police corruption, there was the small matter of actually running the club, staffing it, finding a brewery to supply it, and getting the members in.

Nevertheless, by early 1968 Horsfall and his fellow directors were fully committed to Esquire Clubs and finding premises. Allan wrote to Ray Gosling in November 1967:

> Grey is coming to the next [meeting] and I have a feeling it might be a bit turbulent. Reg and I and one or two others are now committed to a project for promoting clubs. The idea is that these will not be proprietary clubs, but will be members' clubs, each controlled by an elected committee and inter-affiliated, with profits going for development.
>
> The idea is to proceed by stealth, but only so long as this is necessary and possible.[53]

Antony Grey was indeed present at the meeting, and unenthusiastic:

> He could not envisage a single national organisation working on COC lines since there were now no provincial committees except ours. He thought that any moves in this direction should be made openly – that police attitudes should be known and that the idea should be cleared at least at

> Chief Constable level, and if possible, at Home Office level. Clubs should not operate as ghettos but as agencies of social integration.[54]

Feedback from supporters and contacts made with the new series of advertisements* suggested that although the main need was social meeting places, there were also some, desperately unhappy with their sexuality, who needed support of a more organised kind. With these two needs identified, the logical thing to do was to combine them, and use the clubs both to finance counselling activity and to provide a base where advice and counselling could be given. Again, the COC clubs, with their combination of activities, provided a possible example.

Building support for clubs

The promoters were not naïve, and knew what opposition they were likely to face. Allan wrote to all the vicars and other Great and Good who had supported the North Western Committee pre-legalisation. They were circulated an information sheet in July:

> The need is not for exclusive queer clubs but for intimate clubs with a gay informal atmosphere where homosexuals could meet, bring their sister to, their friends both homosexual and heterosexual. It would also be a place *where they are not obliged to buy a drink* – as is the case with most of the bars where they meet now. … On humanitarian grounds alone, they have the right to be able to meet in decent surroundings.[55]

The leaflet refuted the 'dens of vice' idea – why should homosexuals be any more promiscuous or wicked than heterosexuals?

> There would be strict rules of behaviour – no gambling, for example – and a high restrained tone throughout. The North West Committee has encouraged the formation of Esquire Clubs Ltd independent company formed for:
>
> The provision of food, friendship, drink, dancing and entertainment, cultural activities, discussion groups etc.
>
> The provision of a counselling service for homosexual people, members and non-members alike.

The money for counselling would come from profits from other activities, especially bar takings.

Horsfall wrote personally to those with whom he had local connections, through giving talks or knowing them in Leigh and Nelson. To Rev. John Rogan, Leigh:

---

* See also Chapter 4.

> You will appreciate that a project such as this is likely to be widely misunderstood or misrepresented by that section of the community which still regards all homosexuals as wicked, and it is for this reason that we are trying to gather the maximum responsible support right from the beginning.[56]

In drumming up the respectable support needed, they recruited as Honorary Vice Presidents the General Secretary of the NCCL, Tony Smythe; Antony Grey as Secretary of the Albany Trust; Rev. Basil Higginson, National General Secretary of the Samaritans; and Rev. George Henshaw, Director of the Manchester and District Samaritans. They also acquired a reputable address, which they shared with a number of other voluntary organisations, at Gaddum House. The Gaddum Charity was the oldest and most respected of social work and healthcare foundations in Manchester, having been founded in the wake of a cholera epidemic in 1833, and counting the novelist Elizabeth Gaskell as one of the earliest supporters.

From this they launched into action. In order for the idea to work, breweries needed to be involved. In order to get breweries involved, they needed to be convinced that there were going to be enough members to make the investment pay. So Esquire Clubs went into business as a membership organisation, and it was the Club membership which was to form the basis of the CHE membership. When the North Western Committee changed its name and turned itself into a national organisation, Esquire had already been advertising nationally. In Issue 177 of *Private Eye* appeared the following: 'A social club for homosexuals in your area? Write Esquire Clubs Limited, Gaddum House, 16–18 Queen Street, Manchester 2.'[57]

The choice of *Private Eye* was shrewd. For all the homophobia of then-editor Richard Ingrams and the relentless jokes about 'pooves', the magazine had a large gay readership, as evidenced by other small ads at the back – for 'Ultrabrief briefs from Carnaby Male', for the lesbian magazine *Arena 3*, or 'The Boy – Photographic Essay – Joys of Boyhood crystallised. 400 plates Sebastian D'Orsai Ltd.' (February 1966). Esquire followed its Private Eye ad with others in the *New Statesman*, *New Society* and *Spectator*.

In addition to drawing in new members, Esquire tried to enthuse existing North Western Committee supporters about the project. With the April 1968 *Bulletin* came a leaflet:

> We have agreed to take over the Rockingham Club in Manchester and negotiations are being completed.
>
> We have looked at premises, suitable and available; and we want to take options in BOLTON, BURNLEY, LIVERPOOL, BLACKPOOL, LEEDS and SHEFFIELD.
>
> The Breweries want and are willing to provide the financial backing. What they want to know? What we do? The purpose of this letter to you –
>
> IS THERE A DEMAND? DO YOU WANT …

And then on the back, a membership form which you had to send in along with 30/- (£1.50) as a subscription valid until October 1969.

Reg Kilduff had indeed offered to turn over the Rockingham Club to Esquire, but his motives were not entirely idealistic. The lease on the premises had only three years to run, and the area was scheduled for redevelopment. He would be well off out of it, and was also expecting to make substantial money from the deal. But to Allan and Ray it presented a unique opportunity to get something up and running with a minimum of effort. It also created a certain amount of urgency, whatever Antony Grey might say, with the lease getting shorter with every week that passed and the fear that Reg might change his mind. By September 1968, Esquire Members were being offered free membership to the Rockingham and special offers for entry to the new club, Matthew's. But it was clear that things were not going smoothly. The leaflet, written in Ray Gosling's inimitable style, was in two parts; the first was to members:

> Thank you. God bless you for the faith you showed us with your thirty shillings. We believe ESQUIRE is worthy of that faith; that you will be proud and pleased to have been one of the first members. …
>
> Unfortunately our negotiations to take over the Rockingham have reached an impasse. …
>
> ESQUIRE have begun talks in other towns in the North, in the Midlands, in the South and West and in London, where we hope to have an ESQUIRE affiliate very soon.*
>
> Have you a talent? Can you help? These clubs will be yours, so if you think you can help in your area, have energy and ideas, write us now.

Part Two was to non-members, and was sterner, almost to the point of hysteria:

> What's the matter with you then? You have put us to shame by your lack of faith. You can't be all THAT mean. Or can you? At one stage we had more members from Wrexham than from Manchester. At this time of writing we have only one member in Cardiff! … We have to convince the Breweries there is a demand. The thirty shillings is the only way. Come on. Don't delay any longer. Come off that fence. Take a little courage. …
>
> We want your talent, skill and local knowledge. We want a magazine, writers – is there a cartoonist? We want interior designers to make these clubs exciting and different. So tell your friends at home, at parties and in the bar – pass the word and the leaflet.
>
> Only you and they can make it happen.[58]

---

* This would have been the A & B Club in Wardour Street. Short for Arts and Battledress, which indicates its wartime origins, the A & B had a reputation as one of the friendlier gay drinking clubs in the West End.

The level of response can be gauged by the Esquire accounts. By October 1969 the membership income was precisely £61.[59] With membership fees at £1/10/- (£1.50p), that means there were about 40 paid-up subscribers, way short of the thousand which the breweries were seeking. The identity of the breweries was a strict secret at this stage, because everyone was terrified they would back out if they got bad publicity. But there were three interested – the Mansfield Brewery and Walker's in Warrington, both small local breweries, and Charrington's. And the money on offer wasn't peanuts.

There was also the prospect of a chain of clubs. Those who'd tried launching similar schemes in other areas were invited to the Committee meetings of May and June 1968. John Holland came from MANDFHAB in Wolverhampton, where he'd been trying to get a group off the ground, and Peter Spencer from Nottingham.* The Committee noted that a Midlands branch of Esquire looked particularly promising.

Also present was Tom Frost from Coventry, a city which had been credited with setting up 'Britain's first club for homosexuals ... where homosexuals can meet and feel free to talk'.[60] Frost was a heterosexual social worker, attached like Colin Harvey to a church diocese. He set up 'Homosexuals Anonymous' with Canon Stephen Verney, and with help and support from Antony Grey and the Albany Trust. However, despite covering the formation of the group as a news story, the *Coventry Evening Telegraph* refused to take its adverts. But then, the *Daily Mirror*[61] and the *Daily Express*[62] picking up the local story, reported it more accurately as a 'clinic' and an 'advice centre'. As a result Frost was inundated with enquiries, most of which he referred to the Albany Trust. Scared by the publicity, the Provost of the Cathedral issued a statement that there would be no club for homosexuals at Coventry Cathedral while he was in charge. Instead, the local Council for Social Service (CSS) offered a telephone line, an answering service and an interview room. At this point Tom got interested in Esquire Clubs for providing social activities.

All was not plain sailing. As word went round, there were hoaxes; people who were booked for an initial interview with a social worker took fright and failed to turn up. People came once, but didn't return.

> A kind of 'Gresham's Law' operated, so that the more noisy, gregarious members tended to drive out the shy, retiring people, for whom the project was really intended.[63]

Ultimately attendance dwindled to only three or four people, and the group folded. It did not lead to a CHE group, unlike those in Nottingham and

---

* For more details about these groups see Chapter Four.

Wolverhampton, and it was not until 1974 that Coventry CHE was founded as an offshoot of Birmingham CHE.

There were also groups meeting specifically about clubs, in the Wirral and Nottingham at least. Ray convened his chums at his house in Mansfield Road on 3 July 1968. Though they were friends, it was all very formal and carefully minuted; though minuted by someone who was not experienced, almost as if he was playing at being a Secretary. 'T. Crook, N. Harrison, M. Alge, R. Gosling …' The meeting noted that those present represented 'a wide range of ages and general outlook.'[64] Ray announced he was thinking of forming a club within the Esquire framework in Nottingham. Everyone agreed it was a good idea, but there was a need for 'an air of stability':

> Now with such a great change in social opinion there was less need to resort to special public houses and other places far less pleasant. It is quite obvious in the not too distant future there is going to be a considerable number of very commercial clubs opening all over the country and obviously they will be successful.[65]

But Nottingham's Esquire Club will be something more: 'A club that will when necessary of [*sic*] social services and a club that will in no way be an embarrassment to the general society.'[66]

One issue surfaced, which would continually preoccupy gay organisations through the next few years; this was the position of under-21s 'who obviously need some help and guidance and yet at the moment as the law stands they are in great difficulty.' They decided to take legal advice about whether they could admit teenagers.

But though everyone agreed Esquire was a good idea, nobody seemed willing to take it on. Ray explained:

> It was absolutely disastrous, because this was my town and they were all my mates, and I just knew during that meeting that they weren't going to go through with it. They were not prepared to come out and say, 'I'm gay'. They became frightened.[67]

Ray was the public face of Esquire, and spent a large amount of time going to meetings of local members, trying to ginger them into action:

> I was always doing meetings. Once, twice a week. Wolverhampton, Bournemouth, Southampton, Norwich. All meetings of gay people. And they would all be very enthusiastic to begin with. … When they'd talked about it a little bit, and you wanted their name on the committee, because you wanted local committees, they all started to pull out.[68]

It was too big a responsibility; they weren't experienced; and most importantly, if you put yourself up for being a director, or a committee member, you were identifying yourself as homosexual.

Esquire wasn't the only game in town. Others, post-legalisation, saw commercial potential. Antony Grey reported to the Albany Trust Board that in January 1968 he'd been approached by a Mr Davis to give advice on the setting-up of a COC-type club in London, and later visited by his partner Mr Marshall. A group of businessmen were interested, and there was talk of an investment of £50,000 (£790,000). Grey stalled, saying he'd like to see more advanced plans. Nothing further was heard from them, but in the meantime, the knowledge that this rival scheme was in the offing, and much better funded than Esquire, both spurred and threatened. Ray in particular was insistent that only Esquire could provide the solid respectability and high moral tone needed for the enterprise, and poured scorn on this 'group in London wanting to set up an enormous hotel which would be like a vast brothel.'[69]

Opposition from the HLRS and Albany Trust

Through all this, Antony Grey was doing a difficult balancing act. Privately supportive of the principle, he was deeply concerned about the strategy, and he also knew that his committee, and particularly Leo Abse, would not stand for it in any way, shape or form. He offered to go and see the Home Office to sound out the official attitude towards the idea of clubs, and indeed did go, along with the HLRS Chairman, C. H. Rolph, and sociologist Michael Schofield. The discussion was strictly informal, but very high-level. Rolph wrote warningly to the North Western Committee Chairman, Colin Harvey:

> I think you should know that Antony Grey, Michael Schofield and I have had a confidential off-the-record discussion with Lord Stonham (Minister of State, Home Office). While this discussion was intentionally informal and non-committal, Lord Stonham did authorise me to tell you, and anyone else interested in promoting social clubs for homosexuals, that in view of the still controversial nature of this subject, he felt that it would be common prudence for anyone doing so to consult beforehand the Chief Constable in any town where they propose to operate. Lord Stonham also … felt sensationalism could only be harmful and that it would surely be better for things of this kind to happen gradually and without the lurid publicity which might all too easily be attracted.[70]

From all sides the North Western Committee was being advised that if it wanted to get anywhere, it needed to contact the police, the local council, anyone in authority who might cause trouble for the project. But when they tried to follow the advice in Manchester while the Rockingham Club deal was in the air, there was just one problem; the police wouldn't talk to them. When Allan Horsfall asked the Chief Constable of Manchester and Salford for a meeting, he was turned down flat. Later, in Bolton, it would be the Council which gave him the cold shoulder.

However Allan by now felt that his Committee could stand on its own two feet, and could go over the head of Chief Constables. By the time Grey got his meeting with Lord Stonham together, Horsfall had already got the Wigan MP, Alan Fitch, to approach the Home Secretary on their behalf, armed with the first outline proposals for the club. Grey was most put out when he made his offer to approach the Home Office, to be told, 'Oh, we've done all that already.' And, through Fitch, at a higher level than Grey was able to reach. Despite being told this, he still went ahead with his own meeting with the junior Home Office minister as described – an indication of the lack of trust Grey felt towards the North Western Committee.

Antony was no longer in control, and it irked him. Over the next year or so, relations between the two organisations steadily deteriorated. One action of Allan's was guaranteed to put the cat among the pigeons. In April 1968 he asked Leo Abse to become an Honorary Vice President of Esquire Clubs.

It was an act of incredible naivety to assume that support for decriminalisation equalled support for clubs for homosexuals. Any study of Abse's speeches would have shown that this was a non-starter. For two years the MP had been pushing his reforms in the face of people who at every turning had been raising the spectre of 'buggers' clubs' mushrooming all over the place as a consequence of his reform. And now here were the buggers' clubs in prospect, to prove that the opponents had been right. Worse, they would let in young, illegal, gay men, since nowhere on the Esquire publicity leaflet was the redeeming phrase 'Over 21 only'. Abse was incandescent. His response was to call a meeting of the Executive of the Albany Trust, wanting to make sure that the club movement was strangled at birth.

The minutes of this meeting[71] reveal some interesting divisions. Grey had prepared a memorandum 'Social Organisations for Homosexuals' in advance. This outlined the COC project in Holland, but again stressed that it was too soon in the UK, and needed Home Office approval. This was endorsed by Freddie Ayer and MP Christopher Chataway. Mr Frankland (the Trust fundraiser) was even more emphatic:

> While reasonable, liberal, middle-of-the-road opinion would be prepared to support the counselling, research and educational work of the Trust, such support would be lost if the Trust became involved in the setting up of homosexual clubs; these were likely in any event to prove dangerous and uncontrollable and association with them on any level … could gravely prejudice the Trust's charitable status.[72]

And he threatened to resign from the HLRS if there was any sign of support in that quarter. The actual homosexuals on the Honorary Committee were understandably more generous. Angus Wilson thought the Trust should support clubs,

> but not the Esquire Clubs as present constituted; any appearance of flouting the newly-reformed law in the matter of age-limits or public behaviour was to be deplored. While a suitably structured organisation could be a valuable force for good, he was strongly of the view that the ultimate aim must be the integration of homosexual people into the total community.[73]

Only sociologist Michael Schofield said unequivocally that the Trust should support the scheme, even in its present form:

> Any group or club wanting to be responsible would want to work with the Trust, and the Home Office would prefer to know that there were more reliable centres of social contact, and the Trust would set standards and be a guarantor. It should not brush aside responsibility by only giving secret advice. It was part of the Trust's job to see that such clubs were responsibly run.[74]

But it was Leo Abse who had the ultimate deterrent as far as the Albany Trust was concerned. There was, he hinted darkly, a real chance that Esquire Clubs would provoke a backlash which could lead to a repeal of the new Sexual Offences Act:

> The Esquire proposals would give those hostile to the recent liberalisation of the law ample grounds for saying their worst fears were being realised. Certainly the admission of those under 21 combined with the provision of dancing could be interpreted as a defiance of the law. … He thought that national organisations of homosexuals were highly undesirable: heterosexuals did not go around looking for exclusive clubs before they felt they 'belonged'.[75]

All of which led to the question of Grey's position as a Vice-President of Esquire. Should he resign? Albany Trust Board members were threatening to resign if he didn't. It was a moot point whether he had actually accepted the position, since, he maintained to his Board, his acceptance was conditional on their approval. If he did resign, it would indicate that he disapproved of and rejected the idea of clubs, which he did not. The Esquire board had requested a meeting with the Albany Executive – couldn't he defer a decision until after that? No he could not, the committee decided by a slim majority. So Grey reluctantly resigned from Esquire, saying that it was not for lack of personal support on his part, but because the Trust had decided to research the whole question of social adjustment more deeply.

Reasons for disapproval

The phenomenon of Esquire Clubs threw up many issues which set alarm bells ringing. If the position of under-21s in Esquire was one, another was the idea that these clubs would openly advertise themselves as places where homosexuals could come and meet. It was flaunting it, when people like Lord Arran and Abse firmly believed that homosexuals would melt into the background after they were decriminalised. Not only was it flaunting it, it was setting up separatist ghettos when what was needed was integration. And even worse, they wanted *dancing*.

At almost the same time as the Albany Trust meeting, the Esquire Club directors were taking more advice. They invited Jan de Groot from COC, whom Martin Stafford had met the previous year, to visit Manchester for a long weekend at the beginning of June. Antony, anxious to keep tabs on developments and get an outside opinion, asked him to act as an Albany Trust spy and report back. The report, in slightly stilted Dutch English, was scathing:

> They received us very cordially and every-body has been very friendly. But the whole programme has not been organised very well. Knowing that our visit must cost them a lot of money I had expected that they had took more advantage of our visit. … They really made very little out of it.

On the Saturday of de Groot's visit, there were two meetings. In the afternoon he met a few social workers, a few members of the Committee, a psychiatrist from the University and the Esquire directors.

> There were not more than 18 people I guess. I held two speeches about COC and *Dialoog*,* followed by a poor discussion. In the evening there was a meeting in the Rockingham Club for Esquire Members. There I held a speech about the COC only, followed by a lively discussion, And that has been all! I had expected a work-meeting with all the Committee members, at least. I hardly met the secretary. So most of the talkings were between Colin [Harvey] and Us. I met Mr Frost† (and Martin S. who I think is in better condition than in September last).
>
> I found out that there does not exist a clear planning nor a clear policy. There exists enthusiasm to do something but it is more a vague dream than a real plan. …
>
> We talked with one of the owners. He wants to sell the club to Esquire. He is commercial interest by doing so. He assured us that the profits are for Esquire when they take over the club; The club is situated in a building which will be broken down within 2 or 3 years. The Esquire members know that. They are aware of his commercial interest. There is a growing tendency not to accept the offer. …
>
> I fear that Colin is not a strong person. I did not find any trace of the wish to leave behind a monument, as you suggested. I got the impression

* *Dialoog* was a Dutch Lesbian and Gay magazine which ran briefly in the mid-1960s.

† Tom Frost from Coventry.

> that he realises it is not so easy after all. He said that he believes that their plans are too ambitious and that they have to change all.
>
> During our conversation I perceived the fear of being threatened by you. I perceived competition feelings by several Manchester people. It seems to me that this is completely wrong and incorrect. …
>
> There is a disorder in communication between you and Manchester. That is clear! I would ask you to analyse how far your own approach, remarks or way of acting contribute to this communication disturbance. I noticed that you are irritated by their way of acting. But is it good to show this irritation so much that it is a hindrance for the contact?[76]

Grey did not take the well-intentioned advice, and his reply shows a revealing petulance:

> It appears the group is not stable or mature enough to see realistically what it is possible for them to do at the present time and what is too ambitious. … I am afraid that better communication is in fact impossible until they are ready to listen more realistically to what I have to say. Meantime they must learn from their own mistakes.[77]

Up until now, Esquire Clubs had progressed, if at all, on the quiet. Esquire publicity went out of its way to reassure, with its talk of respectability, somewhere to take your sister, provision of counselling and the involvement of social work agencies. But the more people Allan and Ray contacted, the greater the danger that someone would talk to the press and blow their cover.

Going public

Sooner or later, Pandora's Box would have to be opened. By July 1968, Allan was convinced that the Press had got hold of the story, and the cat would soon be out of the bag. Further, Esquire needed more members and that meant advertising publicly. He decided to launch a pre-emptive strike, and released the club plans to the press. The *Burnley Evening Star* reported that Esquire was 'hoping to take an option on premises in Burnley for a nightclub.'

> Facilities will include a dance floor, bar, restaurant and a counselling room where homosexuals can bring problems to a panel of social experts including lawyers and doctors. … Alan [*sic*] Horsfall, secretary of the company, has said that control would be strict and there would be no bedrooms, no gambling and no indecency. 'We hope that the clubs will be such that members will bring their sisters and heterosexual friends along.'[78]

BBC Radio Sheffield followed it up with an interview and an offer to devote one of their religious programmes to the social needs of homosexuals.

What is interesting about the *Burnley Evening Star* story is the almost total lack of response it provoked. Only one comment appeared on the Letters

Page, and that was in favour of the idea. Three years later, Burnley was to be the site of a pitched ideological battle over the 'clubs issue', when indignation was worked up by a local Christian coalition at the prospect of a local club for homosexuals. The only other paper which seems to have picked up on the story is the *Sunday Telegraph*, which covered it in very similar terms and phrases.

One of the arguments used frequently to justify both legalisation of homosexual acts and the plan for clubs was that homosexuals only behaved in a 'promiscuous' and 'degraded' way because they had nowhere to meet properly. Given the chance, they would develop friendships and fall in love like everybody else, and the need for sex in toilets and bushes would disappear. So believed liberal social-working heterosexuals. Although homosexuals themselves realised that the truth was more complex, it was necessary for them to concur as part of the hypocrisy attendant on the ideology of 'normality'. Later it would become clear that, even when there were many more outlets and meeting places, there was still a significant number of gay men who enjoyed the anonymity and danger of public casual sex for its own sake. Even Antony Grey, the respectable 'front' of homosexual law reform and in a stable, loving relationship, was known to appear from time to time in the West Hampstead underground station toilet a few yards from where he lived.[79]

The most extended statement of the case for clubs came from Ray Gosling, in an article for *New Society*.[80] He opens with the observation that so far emancipation, such as it is, has been achieved by heterosexuals on behalf of homosexuals. This was not a new observation, and had been made in the past both benevolently and malevolently. During the third reading of the 1967 Bill, Harry Gurden, Conservative MP for Selly Oak, observed:

> According to the figures we have heard and seen published, there is quite a percentage of people who practise homosexual acts. It would be strange indeed, in a place of 600 members, if there were not some here, but I have not heard anyone declare such an interest.[81]

His implication was that the whole reform movement was a conspiracy of closet cases; and any supporter of the Bill might be 'one of them'. Some journalists made the same point in a more thoughtful way. As early as October 1963, in a *Spectator* Afterthought, Alan Brien floated the idea that:

> the great weakness of the homosexuals' campaign for freedom to behave as they wish in private is that they lack that sense of solidarity any mass movement needs to change public opinion. … I am not sure that the only worthwhile move for homosexuals isn't to identify themselves, and in enormous numbers. It would be an act of impressive and almost unimaginable courage.[82]

Homosexuals were caught in a double bind. If they campaigned in heterosexual camouflage, they were open to the charge of hypocrisy; if they campaigned as gay men or lesbians, they were indulging in special pleading and part of a queer conspiracy. Or, as Wolfenden pronounced on the hundreds of unsolicited submissions from homosexuals which poured in to his Committee, they were 'exhibitionists', which was enough for him to discount their evidence and make no reference to it in his Report. All this was changing, now that the door was, if not open, slightly ajar. According to Gosling's article, Esquire was only one response of many to legalisation, and was part of a movement to identify openly as homosexual:

> Independently of the NW Committee and the Albany Trust, people are using and abusing the new law. Like mushrooms, 'poove n' perve' magazines appear, many from Soho. *Camp*, by Cottage Productions, a publication for the consenting adult. 'Well educated young man wishes to meet riding master who is strict. Interested in leather and domestic correction'
>
> In Nottingham two young men form a group. The duplicated application forms show off the enthusiasm of a young minority. 'Complete in duplicate. I am single/married/divorced please cross where applicable.' … Misspellings. The dry grammar. The phoney legal jargon and the attempts at big-time bureaucracy. It reminded me of when I ran a loco spotters' club and had ideas above my station
>
> The floodgates are open as those who fought against reform predicted. From the Church of England and the porn pushers of Soho, from wide boys and from social workers, from dedicated committed young homosexuals a demand is going to be supplied. Something more sophisticated than cruising the public urinals. Pressures mount. …
>
> Esquire chewing off a little at a time, extending from the North West into the Midlands, … is an adventure, honestly begun and bravely continued. Would they be dating centres? No – oddly, a club, unlike a public bar, is a difficult place to make any sexual pick-up. Go to the club with your friends. Take your sister, to meet your friends and their friends. … The one sure place where homosexuals need not be afraid.[83]

The most remarkable thing about this article is that it is, in its delicate way, a coming-out article. Self-revelation in journalism at this time was rare, but to those who could read it, it would be clear: homosexuals used to have others to speak for them, now they are doing it for themselves; Allan Horsfall, the Esquire Secretary, is specifically referred to as 'a bachelor', and this can only be for one reason; and now here am I, the famous Ray Gosling, declaring I am a director of this scurrilous enterprise, and *we* want to create 'a proselytising sodomite society'.

BBC Radio 4's flagship news programme, *The World at One*, picked up on the article and tied it in to a report on the first anniversary of decriminalisation. As for so many liberal heterosexuals, the nub of the problem was integrating homosexuals into society, although it was clear that many did not want to be integrated, and why. An anonymous voice:

> We're homosexual, and it's not as such my society. The heterosexual finds us repugnant and nauseating. Well, we're not bothered what they think. We don't affect them and we don't think they should affect us.[84]

Gosling was interviewed too. He saw that this argument between wanting a ghetto to escape to and a desire to integrate was a false dichotomy, because nobody would be living in that ghetto for more than a few hours a week:

> We don't want these clubs to encourage homosexuality at all. We want them to be places where a minority can feel free, can feel they're not going to be persecuted and where the majority of people can come and see that the minority are not some sort of animals but are ordinary normal human beings. … Every minority wants its own little world which it can work in, and the balance is to keep that little world and to keep it part of the big world. If you're a member of the Pigeon Fanciers Club, you want to belong to a Pigeon Fancier's Club. That doesn't mean you're going to cut yourself off from the rest of the community.[85]

Certainly the self-revelatory nature of the *New Society* article seemed clear to the young Ken Plummer, a hugely influential pioneer of Queer Theory, and in 1968 a sociology postgraduate, who had met Ray in Nottingham that spring, when he came to make contacts for his upcoming PhD. Ken had been one of Antony Grey's office helpers in the dingy HLRS offices on Shaftesbury Avenue, braving the disapproving stare of the commissionaire in the doorway, and putting up with the stench of the always-leaking lavatory at the end of the corridor. For four years, 1966–70, he dutifully stuffed envelopes while trying to fend off Grey's advances:

> I knew Antony Grey – at one point too well. He was a wonderful man. He was absolutely dedicated to it. He was the power and force behind the whole law change movement. But he was rather a morose man. Dour. He wasn't a laugh a minute, that's for sure. He was a bit of a lecher too. I found myself lured into a little trap of his making. Being only 21 and fairly naïve.[86]

Here Plummer remained, working as a volunteer, until the advent of GLF towards the end of 1970 offered a much more congenial and exciting prospect of action, right on his doorstep in the London School of Economics where he was working. But in September 1968 it was natural for him to see Ray's article in *New Society*, to which as a sociologist he subscribed. He wrote to him at the end of October, acknowledging this element of 'coming out' – his verdict on Grey at the time was less kind:

> We've all been given the most outrageous deluges on Esquire from TG [Tony Grey], who means well but can't cope alone. … But a few of us are beginning to tire of hearing abuse of Esquire from second hand, and feel that if there's any hope at all for a homophile organisation in this country – then its growth just can't be fragmentary, competitive and unplanned. We must work together.
>
> Hope all goes well with you, *especially after sticking your neck out so bravely* with the article. [author's italics][87]

Not all received Ray's article so enthusiastically. Grey fired off a letter of reply to *New Society* for the next week's issue:

> Clubs can undoubtedly help in this respect, but only if the provision of a physical meeting place is not regarded as the be-all and end-all. Much more immediately important is the need to build up new personal and community attitudes, which will replace the common cynicism and loneliness of the sexually different with a new sincerity of comradeship and concern for one another. …
>
> We hope the energies of others who are concerned to improve the lot of the homosexuals in society will not be confined to the establishment of clubs – which, with or without drinking, dancing and dating, may unnecessarily arouse public alarm.[88]

For the first time, sections of the Gay Rights Movement were washing their dirty linen in public. Two organisations were effectively having a row publicly in a general magazine. The tone was polite, the criticism reasoned, but the schism was apparent for all to see.

In addition, there were bad practical consequences from Gosling's article and the follow-on publicity.* Those who were in local Esquire working groups, already nervous, now scattered like a covey of partridges. A disappointed and bitter Peter Q. Rhodes wrote from Wilmslow in Cheshire:

> The aim of Esquire clubs in this area to establish clubs for homosexuals is seriously set back by the kind of reaction that Ray Gosling's article attracts. What a pity that men of the calibre of T. Colin Harvey and Allan Horsfall should be associated with Gosling's hysterical, publicity-seeking methods. It is now too late for a discreet approach to this problem.[89]

Clearly there had been a Cheshire group working on a local club, but Rhodes' hard work was out of the window as others fled under the glare of the publicity. If Rhodes had sound reasons for resenting Gosling's article, other homosexuals with no vested interest were also scathing simply because they felt that their own safety in the closet was threatened. A correspondent,

---

* Pieces appeared on BBC Radio 4: on *The World This Weekend* on 1 October and on *The World at One* on 4 October.

tellingly 'Name and Address supplied', called the idea of clubs, 'the most nauseating and degrading suggestion that I, as a homosexual, have yet come across. If there is one thing the homosexual does not want, it is organised tolerance.'[90]

What Name and Address Supplied *did* want is unclear. But the biggest blast came from Lord Arran, one of the two prime movers of the 1967 Act, who did not hesitate to use his kudos to add weight to his condemnation. In his regular Opinion Column in the *London Evening News*, he said:

> Had I known that this would be the result, I would never have introduced William.* … The setting up of these clubs is an open flaunting. … Moreover the organisers of these clubs would do well to remember … the clause in William which makes a homosexual act in the presence of a third party a crime.[91]

The contradiction in Arran's article was quickly pointed out by the pianist Peter Katin, who was still a supporter of the HLRS and in correspondence with Tony Grey:

> It is not true that the setting up of clubs should be in any way an 'open flaunting', even though I agree that the Esquire project has probably been too hasty. However, Lord Arran contradicts himself by saying subsequently that he is sure the proposed clubs would be 'most respectably run'. If so, there can be little excuse for his original outburst, which can cause nothing but ill feeling.[92]

But Grey's hostility was by this time increasing, as he saw Esquire threatening to undo what he regarded as all his good work. He was equally scathing about both sides:

> I am far from happy about the activities of Esquire Clubs. I think they are ill-timed and badly planned. … The best remedy … is to talk about the whole matter as little as possible. … His [Arran's] uncalled-for mention of the clause making homosexual acts in the presence of third parties a crime seemed to me to imply (whether intentionally or not) that the promoters intend to run a brothel or something orgiastic, and was reminiscent of the hysterical rubbish about 'buggers' clubs' with which the late unlamented Lord Kilmuir and others degraded the House of Lords debates.[93]

Antony protested to Arran with a telegram expressing alarm at the damage he was doing by stirring controversy.

> He replied, not very euphemistically, 'Balls'. I must say this strikes me as a new low in communication between public people over a serious matter. It

* 'William' is the jokey name by which Arran always referred to his Sexual Offences *Bill*.

> reflects the less agreeable side of His Lordship's complex character. I had fondly imagined, after all the hard work he and I did on law reform (which I had been engaged upon for some years before he entered the scene) that Lord Arran was in some sense a friend of mine. It appears I was wrong – which is a pity, because this whole sorry episode has considerably increased my own personal feelings of isolation and stress.[94]

This revealing letter shows not only Grey's sense of his own worth, but also a sense of betrayal, and a degree of depression. It is one of the few occasions on which he admits the considerable personal cost of his campaigning. Perhaps this also accounts for the way his attitudes towards clubs seemed to change constantly, depending on who he was talking to.

The defence of clubs

Others came to the aid of the cause of clubs. David Tribe, president of the National Secular Society and with Grey a member of the NCCL Executive, wrote to Arran privately, sending a copy to Grey – his covering note saying 'Dear Edgar,* I hope this meets the bill.' While emphasising the social aims of Esquire, Tribe goes further than most by insisting that existing clubs are harmless anyway:

> At least in London these have been in being for a very long time. As a writer I have been invited over the years to half a dozen or so of these places. I may say I have never seen anything improper taking place there – unless dancing be so regarded – and the curious dress of some of the members is a commonplace of our streets today. Far from flaunting themselves to the public gaze, they tended to be in windowless and airless rooms which made them a positive firetrap. … I have little doubt that good sense will prevail in these new clubs, the proprieties be observed and the only result the provision of more aesthetic meeting-places than the average club today.[95]

For a letter to the *Evening News*, which was not published, he was pithier:

> The best way to avoid seeing sinks of iniquity is not to peer into other people's sculleries. Those whose imaginations colourfully speculate on what may go on inside such places ought to see a psychiatrist – or join one![96]

Another source of comfort and inspiration was American activist Frank Kameny, who co-founded the Washington DC Chapter of the Mattachine

---

* Referring to Grey's real name Edgar Wright. Only a very few close friends were ever allowed to call him Edgar.

Society in 1961. Kameny, who was sacked as a government astronomer, took his case all the way to the Supreme Court; although he lost, he set a precedent for contesting employment discrimination. He was an ebullient man of huge energy, who brought renewed militancy to the gay civil rights cause. In 1965 he organised a picket of the White House under the slogan 'First Class Treatment of Homosexuals'. Inspired by the Black Panthers' 'Black is Beautiful', he coined the phrase 'Gay is Good', which was a slogan of the LGBT movement for many years.

Clearly gay rights campaigners in England and Scotland were in touch with the Mattachine Society, and the CHE *Bulletin* was sent regularly to Washington. Kameny watched the prosecutions of bars and clubs in the UK and the opposition to Esquire with horror. The lack of an aggressive response disturbed him. He wrote to Ian Dunn, his personal friend in Edinburgh who was starting the Scottish Minorities Group with Colin Harvey:

> WHY are they [Arran and Abse] opposed to clubs, etc.? I would suggest that as homosexuals, acting on behalf of homosexuals, you ask them, – and make the request a firm one – for appointments to discuss with you (pl.) the question of clubs and – more broadly and importantly – general questions of the creation of rewarding and satisfying lives for homosexuals as homosexuals in a pluralistic society.
>
> They are public officials; their very *raison d'être* (*inter alia*) is to engage in just this kind of discourse with the citizenry whom they are supposed to serve. Again – what – VERY specifically was the basis of Lord Arran's objection to the clubs?
>
> I feel that *is* very much in the interest of homosexuals themselves to join organisations of self-declared homosexuals. This is part of the *Gay Is Good* approach.
>
> A concerted effort should be made to have homosexuals *as homosexuals* appear on radio and television programs throughout Britain, so that people can see that we are just like everyone else. You would be surprised how much that helps. …
>
> I suppose I'll have to come over there, dance at a club, get arrested and appeal the matter up to the Queen. She might have some sense. Should be fun. I am shocked that the owner* pleaded guilty. We would *never* do that – on principle. … For heaven sake don't back down on these things!!![97]

Ian forwarded this to Allan, and no doubt this spirited support and urging on fed into the increasingly confident character of the Committee, and the decision to fight over Burnley in 1971. Mattachine ideology reinforced and helped to develop CHE's stand of 'human rights for the homosexual minority'.

---

* Referring to George Smith of the Flamingo in Wolverhampton.

Allan did his best to defend the Esquire position in a variety of newspapers, bending over backwards to accept the basic tenet of integration. He wrote to the *Evening News*:

> We at Esquire Clubs regret that it is necessary for minorities to be organised in this way, but homosexuals at the moment are misunderstood and misrepresented to such an extent that they need the particular support and protection that only the proposed clubs can give them. We will continue to work and pray for the time when the clubs are no longer needed and then the homosexual can take his place in the wider community.[98]

Given the kind and level of opposition they faced, it is not hard to see why the Esquire organisers, and Ray Gosling in particular as chief publicist, emphasised the respectability of the clubs – what he often referred to as the 'high moral tone'. But this was not just a strategic ploy; it represented a genuine desire for something better:

> We had an idea of clubs that would be more than just clubs, a bit more like, I suppose, a St James's posh people's club, or working man's club, a miners' institute club of South Wales. There'd be a library there, there'd be books there, we didn't want just dancing and a room at the back where people went and fondled one another and fucked one another, we wanted something more than that. So, yeah, we wanted a high tone, we weren't doing that to impress anybody. … We thought that gays should have the best.[99]

A setback: the Rockingham falls through

But the spotlight played on Esquire exposed more cracks in the dream. Grey had been forced to resign as a Vice President of Esquire in May. Now, on 10 October 1968, came another resignation:

> Dear Allan
>
> When I agreed to support Esquire Clubs it was under some pressure from Colin [Harvey] and although I had reservations about the project, I thought it best … to trust Colin's wisdom.
>
> Subsequent developments seem to show that this was a mistake. In my view there is little hope of getting either official sanction for or public acceptance of a chain of clubs. … I feel compelled to ask you to withdraw my name from the list of Vice-Presidents.
>
> Yours sincerely
> George Henshaw,
> *Director, Manchester and District Samaritans*[100]

The General Secretary of the Samaritans, Basil Higginson, wrote on similar lines:

> I am very disturbed because the Samaritans have been associated with the development in 'Esquire Clubs' without consultation. … I must ask you to delete my name from the list of vice-presidents. I'm sorry if this is an unhelpful action but I cannot … have the Samaritans associated with this controversial matter through myself as the General Secretary.[101]

Worse, Esquire, having widely advertised Gaddum House as its address, was about to lose it. On 21 October, Jane Gaddum, the secretary of the Family Welfare Association which ran the building, wrote to Allan complaining about the advert which had appeared in the *New Statesman.* The advert gave the impression that the Club was actually situated in Gaddum House and 'had we been consulted beforehand this might have been avoided.' There had been complaints from tenants, 'the most important being from one of the youth organisations'.

> As you will appreciate, most of our tenants have been here for many years and, whatever our own views, we must take their views into consideration. When we first agreed with you for the postal arrangement which we are operating, the possibility of the present situation arising did not occur to us.
>
> The Committee would like you to make some other plan if you can. Is it not possible to get the Post Office to deal with the post for you in some manner? … We want to be as helpful as we can, but … I hope you will appreciate our position.[102]

Gaddum House was liberal, but not *that* liberal.

In truth, the original promise of the Rockingham, and the first Esquire Club being open by the autumn, had evaporated. On 26 May 1968, all the Directors had agreed to get an independent valuation on the club. On 6 June the valuers went in. On 12 June, the valuer wrote to Allan to say that he was instructed by Reg Kilduff not to sell the club. There was no discussion about it; Reg wanted more money than the valuation offered. The figure he suggested was £7,000 (£111,000). In view of the short life of the premises, this was exorbitant, and was rejected. It couldn't realistically be covered in three years without charging commercial prices, which defeated the whole purpose of the exercise.

Relations between the Committee and Kilduff deteriorated further. Free admission to the Rockingham was cancelled, and Esquire members found themselves being turned away. Reg remained unobtainable, sending an employee to a Committee meeting of NWHLRC on 4 October to say he was terminating the association. A meeting of the Esquire board on 11 October agreed to ask for his resignation, but he'd already sent it in, his letter arriving the next day. The October Esquire Newsletter reassured members that they could still get into the other club, Matthew's, but soon after, the police raided it and the club was closed down.

> We all knew from the beginning that we should not be able to launch an important and much needed social venture such as this without encountering considerable difficulty and opposition. We expected that the howls of protest would come from the traditional moralists and the 'thou shalt not' brigade. What we did not anticipate was that our first major crisis would be precipitated because of faint-heartedness among the reformers and treachery among the commercial operators. …
>
> Unless the support of the homosexual community is forthcoming in ever-increasing numbers we shall ultimately be forced … to fold up our tents and steal away. If that should happen … there is no possibility of establishing clubs for many years … WE JUST HAVE TO SUCCEED – NOW.[103]

The bitterness is palpable, but still Esquire looked forward. If a club couldn't happen in Manchester, there were many satellite towns in the Greater Manchester area which still offered possible venues – and the smaller the town, the greater the need. The laid-back response from readers to the *Burnley Evening Star* item gave hope that here was promising territory. The same Esquire October newsletter reported that 'Full, frank and friendly discussions with the Burnley police proved extremely useful and informative and we are convinced that we can make early progress there given the support of the local homosexual community.'[104]

Possible premises around Manchester

The main challenge was to find suitable premises. Allan scoured the estate agents and the property pages of the local papers. By the beginning of 1969 the focus was on Bolton. Allan discussed with Ray Gosling the idea of floating a separate company – Esquire Clubs (Bolton); the existing directors would be on the board, plus anyone who guaranteed £100 would have one share, £200 two shares, and so on.

Another Esquire newsletter went out. In February 1969 it reported that the directors had taken an option on large club premises. The club would be in a basement area on the Parade. There was a call to a special meeting in Bolton 'to assess the strength of support for this new move. Please attend and bring as many interested people as you can.'[105]

The meeting was on 21 February, in the Crofters Hotel. Presumably there was enough support at it, because by August there was a planning application in to the local council. The process of applying necessitated going public, and that meant coming to the attention of the local press. The *Swinton Journal* reported:

> Teenagers attending Swinton's town centre Precinct Youth Club would be in danger of becoming perverted if a club catering for homosexuals was

> opened nearby, a meeting of the town's planning committee was told this week.[106]

Councillor R. Beech opposed the application:

> 'These people might be very nice. I don't know and I don't want to know. ... But what about the youngsters in the youth club there? They might go down to have a look and a giggle, but some of them might become perverted.'
>
> He called on the committee to send a 'letter of disgust' to the developers, Dunlop, Heyward and Co, for allowing the application to go forward. ... Councillor K Clements added, 'I think Dunlop Heyward's have a damned cheek.'[107]

The Town Clerk suggested the developers might not know what kind of a club was intended:

> These people might say that they are perfectly good tenants and that it would be a good establishment and cause no trouble. And so, bearing in mind this possibility, if you are going to turn this down, it might not be a bad idea to hear what these people have to say. They could have applied to us to get this as a night club and then let it be used in this way later, and we could do nothing about it. But they did not. They have not tried to hide anything at all.'[108]

The Licensing Committee ignored their Town Clerk's advice, refused to meet with Allan, and rejected the application by eight votes to one. Similarly a plan to convert the Westminster Bank in Eccles was turned down, after a long meeting with the Borough Surveyor, the Chairman and Vice-Chairman of the Planning Committee.*

The letter to members following the Esquire AGM in October 1969 makes it clear that there were other obstacles – cash and membership. Breweries, which had been seen as a source of easy finance at the start, had to take back many of their promises because of the credit squeeze in the autumn. And by this stage Esquire was short of money – if indeed it had ever had any. There was £400† (£6,000) in the bank, which was about £2,000 (£30,000) short of what was needed. They were short of members too – 300 by now, where 1,000 were still needed to make the project credible to breweries. A letter went out, appealing to members to keep faith, renew membership, canvass their friends, and lend or give what they could.

Meanwhile, Grey and others kept sniping at the idea. In *New Society* he and criminologist D. J. West laid out the integrationist arguments against clubs, very much looking down their noses:

---

* The bank remained empty for several years after.

† Including interest-free loans of over £300.

> It may be mistaken at this stage to concentrate upon advocating a beer-and-skittles approach to the homosexual's problems.
>
> In the present state of opinion, is it really in the best interests of homosexuals themselves to allow their clubs to become officially labelled, or to join organisations of self-declared deviants? The stigma attached to homosexuals may be unfair or exaggerated, but it exists. However matters may turn out in the distant future, affected individuals have still to contend with it today. … Most homosexuals, when in normal company, find it best to conceal their deviation.[109]

But the tone of confident superiority, the language of deviance, the insistence on secrecy and the continued use of 'them' for homosexuals, were all already beginning to seem out of date. And the continuing refusal to countenance clubs led to ever-widening rifts between the NWHLRC and the Trust. The North Western Committee's Counselling Secretary, Martin Stafford, who might be thought to be in sympathy with the Albany Trust's approach, severed his links with the Trust. He wrote to Grey:

> I was profoundly disappointed when your Trustees elected not to support Esquire Clubs. … I firmly resolved that while the Trust withheld even its moral support from that worthy enterprise, I should withhold my modest financial support from the Trust. You have always maintained that your organisation would not be prevailed upon by the opinions of its members, and on this account it is no surprise to me to learn that your supporters have fallen off. …
>
> As for expanding your work, you'll get not a penny from most people. Unless you make them see sense, the end of the Albany Trust is indeed at hand; nor will it be a great loss if its members aim to do nothing.
>
> *Exam Question:* Place the following passage in its context and comment on any points of interest. 'The early establishment of such a (counselling service) is only one of the Trust's aims. It also hopes that changing legal and social conditions will open the way for a much more positive community approach to the social needs of homosexual men and women, and that these needs can be provided for in positive ways.'
>
> This passage comes from pages 5–6 of a pamphlet called *The Albany Trust and Its Work*. The necessity for clubs is patently obvious to anyone of the meanest intelligence who is conversant with the facts. AT will become an absolute laughing stock if it continues to abrogate its own aims and fail in its self-appointed task. If your lot think that all homosexuals are inherently wicked, they are not worth helping, so why not pack up right away and close the office down?[110]

On the other hand, Grey was fending off enquiries from the many people who confused the Albany Trust with Esquire Clubs: 'We are in no way connected with, or wish to imply approval of, that organisation.'[111]

The club in Burnley

And in 1970 and 1971 there was also Burnley. In February 1970 Allan Horsfall found a promising location in a former Mormon church in Liverpool Road. The price of the lease was £5,500 (£79,000): for this you got a main hall 39 feet by 33 feet with a platform, a small hall, five meeting rooms upstairs, a gallery overlooking the hall and a kitchen. 'Do we apply for planning permission, just for the hell of it?' he asked Ray Gosling. Clearly, given the state of the Esquire finances and membership, and the difficulties over buying the Rockingham, support from a brewery was essential. This sort of money was out of the question without it. According to a letter which went to members in September 1970, a new brewery was interested, and even got to the point of a verbal agreement to support the project in any town where the police were co-operative. But they backed out. No Mormon church, then.

The scale of the difficulties was becoming more and more apparent. The members' letter[112] admits that when they started, no one knew what was involved in setting up and running such clubs. There were legal difficulties and contracts; fire regulations; location; parking. As Roger Baker, CHE's Press Officer, pointed out in 1972:

> It was necessary to get four sets of permission before opening a club – from the local town hall (planning permission), from the fire authorities, from the police and from the breweries. Not once did they acquire all four.[113]

At least, not at the same time. But now towards the end of 1970 it seemed as if a new possibility was opening up. The Pendle Co-operative Society wanted to sell the lease of an upstairs café in a parade of shops* in the centre of Burnley. By now Allan was getting almost reckless in his attitude to premises; putting in planning applications was becoming a kind of consciousness-raising guerrilla activity. In October 1970, he reported to Ray Gosling that he was starting negotiations with the Co-op. The only problem was that there were no directors for the local club. It was always the intention that individual clubs would be separate legal entities with separate boards of directors. This would protect the overall project from any individual financial failure, and allow for local membership accountability. However, without a Burnley board, there was no-one to take legally binding decisions there. Who should he ask? Would Ray do it? He would. Another who responded was Ken Pilling, a 34-year-old licensee who ran the Merchant Hotel in Blackburn.

Allan was desperate to sign people up as members as well as directors. The existing board of directors of Esquire Clubs was not very keen on Burnley as a

---

* in Hammerton Street.

location, so Allan – a one-man band as so often – was hoping to present them with a *fait accompli* at the next board meeting in January 1971. He wrote to all the members of CHE groups within a fifty mile radius, among them Peter Norman in Liverpool:

> Burnley Corporation has given me Planning Permission for a club in the town centre. This leaves me a bit out on a limb as the Esquire Directors are not all that keen on backing a development in Burnley. But there is an Esquire meeting in early January and if by then I can present them with a list of 25 founder members (which is the minimum the law requires for a registered members' club) – preferably all from Lancashire – I think I could persuade them to act on it.[114]

He assured Peter and his Liverpool CHE group* that no money was needed at this stage and there need be no financial obligation in future. Plus there was a written assurance from the Clerk to the Burnley Justices that the members' names would not be made public. Peter was cautious. What was the structure? Who would the directors be? How would they be held to account? How much could it cost later? Allan said they would buy some off-the-peg club rules from the Law Society Stationers, and he enclosed a membership application form to join, not Esquire Clubs, but the Crucifer Club. The origin of this name is a mystery; perhaps they had already bought a ready-made company, which just happened to have that name. It could not have been a worse choice. A crucifer is someone who carries a cross in a Catholic religious procession; to name a club for homosexuals 'The Crucifer' was guaranteed to cause outrage to any Christians who found out about it – especially Catholics.

Negotiations continued with the Co-op into 1971. When the planning application had been sent in earlier to the Town Hall, the purpose was described as a 'social club', no mention of 'homosexual'. Allan had learned the lesson of the Swinton and Eccles applications: if you're not asked, don't tell. Likewise a discreet silence in the licensing application to the Bench. That application was passed in early May. And at this stage, the proverbial shit hit the fan, when the true nature of the club and its clientele was revealed.

It came out in a two-minute interview on Radio Blackburn on 26 May 1971. No-one remembers why Ken Pilling was invited on the programme, or why he talked about the club at this stage. Maybe there was a feeling that it was in the bag, since the licence had been granted. Maybe it slipped out in a general outline of the problems of isolated homosexuals. But he told the interviewer that Esquire was trying to acquire premises 'by stealth but without deceit'. The interview was followed by a short vox pop, in which only one

---

* For a list of all CHE groups formed up to May 1973, and the dates of their foundation, see Appendix B. The formation of the Liverpool Group is discussed in Chapter 4.

person was against the idea. Two days later it was picked up by *Late Night Extra** and the next day by the *Today* programme. Then it got TV exposure on Granada, on *Newsday*. In a discussion chaired by local journalist Michael Parkinson, Ken Pilling complained of the pressure: 'You can't win. If you talk about it, you're "encouraging people to flaunt their homosexuality", if you refuse to talk, you're "setting up secret societies".'[115]

The local press had to follow the story through. There were two papers in Burnley. The *Evening Star*, the more liberal, had publicised the first intentions for a Club nearly three years previously, with no adverse reaction. Now the far more reactionary *Burnley Express and News* got the story. It is not clear whether they got it from looking at the agenda of the planning committee, or whether the indiscreet and over-enthusiastic Pilling was the source; Pilling is the one quoted most extensively in the first article:

> Blackburn licensee Mr Ken Pilling, Northern convenor† of the Committee for Homosexual Equality stated this week that negotiations are under way to open the first club for homosexuals and lesbians in Britain, at Burnley.
>
> Mr Pilling, aged 34, of 1 Clay Street Burnley, said yesterday that it was not yet certain where premises for the club would be leased in Burnley, but an address in Hammerton Street or another in Colne Road were possibilities.
>
> An application would still have to be made to the magistrates' court for a drinks and music and dancing licence, he said.[116]

It was a small story, only three column inches, and hidden away on Page Three. There was no indication of how much it would grow. For two weeks there was silence. And then the backlash. The *Express and News* reported:

> An action committee has been formed against the plan for a club for homosexuals and lesbians in Burnley. The decision was taken at a protest meeting held at the 110 Club. Father John Neville of St Mary's Roman Catholic Church demanded 'protection' for the town's children and told the meeting that the common good denied the right of the local authority to allow such a club to open. …
>
> 'We have the right to demand that our community legislators protect our children in this matter.'[117]

The paper was clearly on the side of the protesters, unlike the *Evening Star*. Insidiously, in its headlines, it always put the word 'club' in inverted commas, as if suggesting it was a front for something much more devious and disgusting. The *Burnley Evening Star* also covered the formation of the Christian

---

* *Late Night Extra* was a long-running evening chat show on Radio 2, whose early presenters included Bob Holness and an unknown Irishman, Terry Wogan.

† The post of 'Northern Convenor' did not exist, and was a fabrication of the paper.

group, but after a brief summary of its aims ('we realise that these people have a problem, and on other occasions we would shout out in their defence'), allows far more space to Pilling as Esquire Clubs' spokesman:

> The club will be affiliated to the Committee for Homosexual Equality,* and this respectable body has support from the National Council for Civil Liberties, prominent citizens like former MP Dr Michael Winstanley and churchmen like the Bishop of Salford, the Right Reverend Thomas Holland. The club will be very strictly run and closely supervised, and profits will immediately be ploughed back into the club. I don't know why we weren't invited to this protest meeting to put forward our point of view. … Children are influenced in all sorts of ways. You have only to look at the latest reports advocating the prescription of contraceptive pills to youngsters. Our club will not be a bad influence on youngsters. And surely any comments on the club being a bad influence should only come after it has opened, not before.[118]

Among the founders of the 'Stop the Club' campaign were several local councillors, and it was not long before the Council's Development Committee was debating whether to ban the club. Both Labour and Conservative councillors vied with each other to condemn the project in the most extravagant terms. Cllr Wilfred Roberts (Lab) was afraid 'Queer bashing could start up if a new club for homosexuals was established in town',[119] thus neatly blaming violence on the victim rather than the instigator. There was backing from Mrs Edith Roberts (Con) who called on the Council to oppose the club 'with every means at our disposal'.[120] Cllr Hudson: 'We can sympathise with this problem or sickness, but it's not up to us to promote it.'[121] Frank Bailey (Con) suggested that the Corporation should buy the building, so that queers couldn't use it. Cllr Baldwin (Con) agreed: 'I think the ratepayers of Burnley are prepared to pay a little bit to keep them out of this town.'[122] Labour leader of the Council Alderman Gallagher: 'Segregation of homosexuals from the rest of Burnley is only going to bring trouble. Years ago this was the case when homosexuals frequented certain pubs.'[123] He said he did not want to see punch-ups on the streets between rival gangs of homosexuals and other youths, as has happened in the past. 'This club will bring no good either to the people who want to use it or to anyone else.'[124]

The notion of roving gangs of homosexuals is rather pleasing, if unlikely. However, the Town Clerk, Mr Thornley, stepped in to pour cold water over

---

* The North Western Homosexual Law Reform Committee became the Committee for Homosexual Equality in 1969, and officially the Campaign for Homosexual Equality in April 1971. Pilling was therefore slightly out of date in referring to the Committee in June. Although notionally separate from Esquire Clubs, most of the Club directors were involved with CHE, and in practice the boundaries were blurred.

all the zeal. The council had already passed the planning application; it would be accused of pre-judging the issue and showing prejudice if it recalled the application and now rejected it, which would leave it open to legal challenge.[125]

Frustrated, the worthies promptly went to the next General Purposes Committee meeting, and passed a unanimous resolution, deploring the fact that they didn't have the powers to boot the perverts out, and calling for an urgent review of the 'problem' by the Home Office. They also warned the owners of premises to beware of possible future applications from suspicious characters.

But even as the Councillors were debating, the Pendle Co-operative Society had already done their work for them. Scared by all the negative publicity, they withdrew from negotiations. The CEO, Mr Cornfield, explained to the *Express and News* that his Board hadn't known of the nature of the club:

> They were told that the premises would be used as a social club. Neither our agents nor I knew anything about it. … It would seem that quite a number of the population in Burnley were against this sort of thing. … We don't want the society involved in any controversial subject such as this.[126]

The Council also 'made it plain that the local authority was not informed of the intended use of the club premises when they recently approved a planning application for it'.[127] The application was purely for a private licensed club. Stung by allegations of skulduggery, CHE responded in a press release written by Allan Horsfall:

> In applying for planning permission, the Committee fulfilled all its legal requirements. …
>
> In our negotiations we answered every question honestly, but it seems we are condemned because we didn't answer questions that were never asked. The implication is that the homosexual has fewer rights than other people and is bound to declare his homosexuality even when not asked. … This club could have been opened by stealth quite easily. Honesty apparently does not pay.[128]

But Esquire and CHE were not going to let the matter rest, especially since the controversy was still raging all over the pages of the local papers. Horsfall emphasised in a letter that:

> There is no intention of abandoning the plan, and we shall go on with our campaign until homosexuals in North-East Lancashire are permitted the same kind of civilised social facilities as the rest of the community.[129]

The arguments continued to rage on the Letters Page of the *Express and News* long after the Co-op's decision. The priests who had set up the campaign, Fr

John Neville and Rev. J. L. Sullivan, maintained a more-in-sorrow-than-in-anger, love-the-sinner-hate-the-sin approach, maintaining it was in the homosexual's own interests that he shouldn't be 'segregated':

> There has been condemnation of the proposition to open a club for homosexuals. This does not imply a condemnation of homosexuals and lesbians. It does imply a condemnation of homosexuality. … Speaking as a professional counsellor with experience of assisting homosexuals, I would no more suggest a club for homosexuals than open a bar for alcoholics, a roulette room for gamblers, or a smoke room for 'pot' addicts. I might well suggest a clinic.[130]

Others were far less temperate. 'Taffy' was a regular correspondent in the Express and News, clearly a man with hang-ups:

> I sincerely hope we don't have to read any more letters on this disgusting subject. … The very fact that you seem to need a club would suggest to anyone with a grain of sense that you deliberately want staring at. … On the recent television interview it was stated that these unfortunates were being driven into dirty little out-of-the-way pubs. This surely is the place for people of this type. They will get exactly what they want, that is to drink, without being stared at by bigots. Believe me, we bigots don't want to see them at all.[131]

The corruption issue was well to the fore, in a letter, among others, from 'Horrified Mother of Four':

> I know I am not alone in deeming the proposed opening of a club for homosexuals and lesbians in our town to be a retrograde step when efforts are being made to salvage the lowered moral standards of today.
>
> We in Burnley do not want an establishment devoted to the promotion of immoral and unnatural practices.
>
> It is unfortunately true that some individuals are born with unnatural tendencies, but surely these should be cured, if possible, and not fostered. … How many of our young people are going to be lured into vice if this scheme goes through.[132]

On the positive side, there were plenty of liberal heterosexuals to pick up on the civil liberties issues:

> There are thousands of genuine homosexuals in every walk of life. They have no problem. They cannot be cured because there is nothing to cure. They are as they are. …
>
> I have never believed a 'normal' man or boy can be tempted. There are splendid-looking men who are genuine homosexuals and will never marry. They will take no notice of you, why not do the same and take no notice of them?[133]

But it also brought people out of the closet, and in particular one lesbian, writing as 'Unashamed', making a spirited defence both of her own lifestyle and that of her gay brothers:

> As a member of the lesbian community may I ask the exalted pillars of our society just what their objections are?
>
> Do they visualise orgies of unspeakable sin and sex going on behind its doors? Do they see their children molested every night of the week? I suggest they read their daily papers and find out who molests the most children – the so-called queers or the so-called normal men.
>
> Do they know for sure whether or not any member of their own family is homosexual, or whether, indeed, their children will grow in that way?
>
> Some of us have had the same partner for years, and I defy any of the 'anti' group to keep up our high standards, both morally and sexually.[134]

PUBLIC MEETING

HOMOSEXUALS
AND CIVIL LIBERTY

Speakers:

RAY GOSLING
IVAN LIMMER
KEN PILLING
MICHAEL STEED

BURNLEY CENTRAL LIBRARY
FRIDAY - 30 JULY 1971 - 8 p.m.

Sponsored by:
THE CAMPAIGN FOR HOMOSEXUAL EQUALITY
28 Kennedy Street, Manchester, 2 with the
NATIONAL COUNCIL FOR CIVIL LIBERTIES

Lords Printers Limited. Tel. Burnley 24277

27. Poster for the Burnley public meeting

The Burnley public meeting

In response to the furore that had been unleashed, the EC meeting on 26 June 1971 agreed a high-risk strategy. They would hold a public meeting in Burnley and confront their detractors. They would prove that the opposition to the club was whipped up by a minority, and that the majority of the town was either indifferent to the issue, or would positively welcome a club. And since the Council had been so vehemently opposed to the club, they would hold it on council premises – Burnley Central Library.

It was not an easy decision, because this was really Esquire Clubs' business, not CHE's. But they were goaded into it by one of their newest and most radical members. Nick Stanley was a young sociology lecturer at Birmingham Polytechnic, who was also convenor of the local group in Birmingham, and involved in Birmingham GLF. Michael Steed remembers:

> I think some of the older members, the more C. of E. Board of Social Responsibility members, weren't sure if we needed it. You see, we had no need to be involved. CHE as such was not involved. But [Nick Stanley] challenged us and said, 'Well, are you serious? This is your chance to stand up and be counted.' And I responded to him by saying 'Yes.' … And we carried the committee. … But many were fearful. … We didn't know if we'd be howled down at the meeting. We didn't know that a load of London GLF people were going to come up and back us.[135]

In the discussion Nick or Paul Temperton would have pointed out that CHE had just changed its name* from a Committee to a Campaign; what was the point if there was no campaigning? As soon as Paul Temperton secured the two-hundred-seat hall on the first floor of Burnley Public Library for the evening (at a cost of £3.25), the Executive wrote to all members:

> The prospective landlords chickened out in the face of a vicious and bigoted anti-homosexual campaign mounted by 'The Burnley and District Christian Group' – a committee which is Catholic inspired and specifically formed to prevent the opening of the club. … We are to hold a public protest meeting in Burnley on 30 July. … We hope you will do all you can to make it widely known and gain maximum support. Meanwhile the search for alternative premises will go quietly on. … The name 'Crucifer Club' has been abandoned in favour of 'Esquire Club'. We remain grateful for your support and patience.[136]

That so many out of an essentially cautious and closeted group of people responded is a testament to the importance of the issue in people's minds at the time.

The same meeting also discussed a proposal, from the Think-In† organised by Gay Liberation Front Leeds the weekend previously, that CHE and GLF

---

* From 1 April 1971, with the adoption of the first Constitution – see Volume Two.

† A very 1960s term for events of varying sizes combining a conference, brainstorming and consciousness raising.

should meet up to try and find ways of co-operating. Representatives of the two groups were due to meet a fortnight later, on 10 July, and Glenys Parry was one of the CHE contingent. Glenys was a 19-year-old psychology student and secretary of CHE's Manchester University Student Group. She was to play an increasingly important part in CHE over the next five years, ultimately becoming Chairwoman.

From the EC came the idea that Glenys should talk to one of the GLF mass meetings in London and appeal for people from GLF to come to Burnley to give moral and physical support at the public meeting. After all, nobody had any idea what would happen; Burnley was a National Front stronghold, and the meeting might easily be attacked. She went along on 28 July – it was the first mass meeting at All Saints Church Hall in Notting Hill after GLF transferred from Middle Earth* in Covent Garden. The Burnley meeting was only two days away – there was no time to lose.

The large GLF weekly meetings were not easy to take part in. Even attendance could be intimidating, as playwright and polymath Alan Wakeman remembers:

> There were a group of radical queens who saw themselves as leading GLF. And they would all sit on the platform swinging their high heels, and making sarcastic, caustic remarks to anybody who spoke. So you had to brave that, to speak. And a lot of people didn't speak. And I think they didn't speak because they were terrorised by these drag queens. … There were some who were really vicious. I don't think in my life I ever heard them say anything good about anybody. It's just part of the way they were. But we needed them because they were incredibly brave.[137]

At the end of the GLF meetings there was always 'Any Other Business'. People gave out information about what was happening during the week – zaps and the like. The chair introduced Glenys as 'someone from CHE who would like to talk to you all.' Given CHE's reputation in some (but by no means all) quarters of GLF, it was not the ideal intro to guarantee attention. Glenys came up from the well of the hall, and sat on the edge of the stage, swinging her legs quite nonchalantly. No sign of nerves or of how much was at stake. She braved any barracking; she was a person who radiated warmth and generosity. She explained that this group had tried to start a club in Burnley, and they'd got as far as getting premises, a drinks licence and a club licence before a local Catholic priest had started a hue and cry. She appealed for help. Her friend Andrew Lumsden remembers her at the GLF meeting:

---

* Middle Earth was a disco/alternative/performance space in a basement. For several years it was known as the Arts Lab. Covent Garden at this time was awaiting re-development, and the old fruit and vegetable market was in its last days.

> She was the most at-ease person with GLF from the second she walked in. She showed no conflict between CHE and GLF, saw it all as one vast river of effort. And on this particular occasion she needed help from the GLF bit of the River Amazon, and just came and asked for it. And that's when I met her and I admired her immensely for doing so. For many CHE people found GLF deeply frightening. Glenys never showed the slightest fear. And she described the situation at the town hall, Burnley, and we thought, yes, this is something we must do.[138]

28. Glenys Parry in 2012

Unlike the Christian group, which had never bothered to contact Esquire Clubs, CHE issued invitations to their opponents, showing again its remarkable liberalism – in Richard Wollheim's terms, the Amiability of its Warriorhood. Glenys wrote on behalf of the EC in sprightly tones to Alderman Gallagher, as leader of the political opposition. There seems to have been a bottomless fund of naïve goodwill in the belief that enemies were what they were purely out of ignorance, and it would only take reasoned argument for the scales to fall from their eyes. Gallagher refused the challenge; others, such as Cllr Edith Roberts, said they would come. It was the first meeting of its kind since the passing of the 1967 Act, the first the Campaign had held since 1966.*

---

* See page 141.

The EC took adverts out on local buses for two weeks, at a cost of £2.50 a week. There was an advert in the bigots' paper, the *Express and News*, under the Public Notices on Page 3.[139] And an enthusiastic group of seven students, led by Glenys and all from university groups of CHE, descended on the town to distribute 4,000 leaflets to Saturday afternoon shoppers on St James Street. The leaflet was mild in tone, very much a continuance of previous literature:

> WE BELIEVE: that the club would not corrupt the youth of the town, and that such a suggestion is a result of ignorance and misunderstanding. Homosexuality is NOT an illness NOR unnatural, but a viable alternative to normal sexual patterns. It means the ability to *love* one's own sex.
>
> WE ASSERT: that homosexuals have a right to the same social facilities as heterosexuals.
>
> WE KNOW that there are at least 4,000 homosexual men and women in Burnley – many of whom are forced to hide just because of the prejudice and hostility shown by the public.
>
> WE WILL STATE OUR CASE at Burnley Central Library. Come and Talk to Us![140]

Nevertheless it was too much for the secretary of the Christian Group, Fred Evans, who spluttered to the *Evening Star*:

> This literature belongs in a sealed brown envelope for adults alone. … In one case a teenage girl was given leaflets. … To assert this is an open invitation to youngsters. It is a clear attempt to corrupt. The objective of sexual relations is to produce a child. Anything else is therefore unnatural.[141]

The battle lines were drawn. The weather on Friday 30 July 1971 was vile. It was hot as hell, and thundery with it. 'The atmosphere was electric. Electric in every sense,' remembers Michael Steed, one of the speakers that night. The rain poured down as over two hundred people dashed up the steps and through the neo-classical portals of the library.

No-one is sure quite how many GLF people went to Burnley. It was somewhere between fifteen and twenty. Alan Wakeman hired a minibus, and there was at least one car as well. They motored up, exuberant and chatting, sharing spliffs. There was no planning – the last thing they talked about was anything gay. It was a holiday, a day out. Then they arrived outside. Alan Wakeman remembers:

> It was a very impressive Victorian pile*. I remember going in and thinking, 'My God, it's almost like church.' … There's a flight of steps leading up,

* Actually 1920s.

> and at the foot of the flight of steps there's a bunch of skinheads, all standing there looking very aggressive. And sort of speaking to people as they were going in, and saying. 'Don't worry, we won't get you until you come out.' And I remember thinking, 'This is quite a scary way to start a meeting.' … The meeting gradually filled up, and the skinheads came in, and they sat at the back on the left hand side, and I thought, 'Make a note where our enemies are. There's a little cohort there and a little cohort there, so if we need to make a quick getaway'– I did think in those terms, seriously.[142]

29. The lecture hall in 1956

The lecture hall on the first floor was packed, with people standing all round the edges. There were councillors, magistrates, social workers. There was no attempt to segregate the 'sides'.* One JP, stiff and sweating in a three-piece suit and bow tie, was sandwiched in among the GLF members, who'd arrived during the afternoon. According to Ken Plummer:

> There was a danger of violence, but I don't think it actually happened. The actual meeting was very fiery from what I remember. I think I'd have remembered if there was, because I always avoid violence. I remember it

* There was one 'fifth columnist' in the Christian ranks. Ken Plummer, in the middle of his PhD on the subject of homophobia, or homosexual taboos, had joined the Christian Action Group incognito, in order to write them up as a project. 'I was drinking in a Catholic Drinking Men's Club hearing them, all their stories. I didn't find it very easy. … So I was actually in the meeting when GLF zapped it. And I was in a really anomalous situation because I was hoping I would not be spotted by my friends. … I was in a very ambivalent position.' —Interviewed by the author, 31 January 2012.

> being overwhelmed by the visitation from London. Whatever was going on, it was thrown into disarray by this outside group, it was agitprop as we say now. They were dressed up, radical drag. Banners, yes.[143]

The radical drag doesn't seem very radical now. According to a local paper, one person wore a purple ladies' hat* and another a black vest. Ray Gosling was to chair the meeting, and he would have his work cut out to prevent the sides from coming to blows – or at least drowning each other out. He remembers taking a taxi from Manchester at a cost of £100:†

30. The lobby of Burnley Central Library, where the bovver boots were left

> It was an amazing, amazing evening. I'd been doing live telly in the North West for Granada, and I was massively famous in Granadaland. I was the voice of the people, I was the common man. That particular night it finished quite late for me, it was tight. … And I got out of the taxi, and I knew we were in trouble. The police were all lined up outside. And the police knew me, and an inspector came across and he said, 'I've had all the lads take their boots off, Ray.' And it was the time of bovver boots, those big, red – and he'd got them all to take their boots off, they could go into the public meeting.[144]

---

* Andrew Lumsden.

† It is highly unlikely that in 1971 even an unscrupulous taxi driver would have charged £100 (£1,350) for a journey from Manchester to Burnley, a distance of under 30 miles. This makes Temperton's version the more plausible, but may not invalidate Gosling's other memories.

Paul Temperton, by then the full-time, paid CHE General Secretary, remembers slightly differently:

> In fact I drove Ray Gosling to it over the moors from Manchester. He didn't drive I think. And it was a filthy night, pissing with rain, and dark, and there was Ray Gosling and his then boyfriend – at least I took him to be his boyfriend – sitting in the back. I have this distinct memory of wondering whether we were ever going to get to this godforsaken place in the rain.[145]

As they arrived, they would have seen the rows of bovver boots in the lobby by the front entrance, along with scores of umbrellas – the police also confiscated these as potential offensive weapons. The meeting kicked off with the speakers, all very calm and reasonable. Michael Steed:

> I remember saying something like, 'I live in Todmorden, and opposite me there is a Polish ex-servicemen's club. And round the corner there's a Ukrainian shop and there are Ukrainian social clubs. Having clubs for people who have something in common is a natural part of the way we live.' I came at it that way. I don't recall a hostile reaction. … I spoke about it very much as a political, social, liberty-type issue. As did Ivan Limmer.[146]

Limmer was a field officer for NCCL, and a councillor on Burnley Rural District Council: 'If civil liberty is threatened in Burnley, it is threatened all over the world.'[147]

After the speakers, the discussion was thrown open to the floor. Father Neville spoke for the Catholics. It comes as something of a shock to see pictures of Neville – reading his words you get the impression of a stereotyped elderly cleric, but he was young and remarkably handsome, with full, sensuous lips; he bore a strong resemblance to Montgomery Clift in Hitchcock's film, *I Confess*. He worried that youngsters would try homosexuality out of curiosity. The GLF people roundly abused him: 'You'll have trouble getting to Heaven, man,' one shouted at him. 'Fascists' and 'Paisleyites', the GLF-ers chanted. Glenys Parry remembers:

> There were some people making the most outrageously homophobic and completely mad statements about corrupting the youth of the town, but we would heckle and then we'd cheer – it was all done in the most light-hearted way, and yet it was deadly earnest at the same time. … It was a bit of a lark, that sort of mixture of deadly serious campaigning but also having a bit of fun. The opposition, the Christians, were actually rather disconcerted by that.[148]

The meeting developed into a consciousness-raising coming-out session. At one point one of the Christians asserted that there was no demand for a club in Burnley.

Andrew Lumsden put up his hand and said, 'May I ask a question?' Andrew was wearing a purple hat, he always wore a big hat as his gesture on demos. He said, 'You seem to be speaking as if there were no homosexuals in the room. I would like to ask everyone who's homosexual in the room – well I am homosexual, and I'd like to ask all the other homosexuals here, 'Will you please stand up.' All the GLF people jumped up like that, defiantly, immediately, and then very gradually the whole room stood up, until the only groups that weren't standing up were the Roman Catholic priest and his cohort, and the skinheads. And so suddenly we felt very powerful. It was one of the most interesting moments of my whole life, watching people gradually thinking, 'I think it's safe to stand up.' Bit by bit by bit. And it turned out some of them were not gay, they were the parents of gay people, but they were standing up in support. That came out in the discussion. … The most interesting thing was as we were leaving, the skinheads were waiting back where they were, but they were saying 'Right on, mate. We didn't realise you get treated the same way we do.'[149]

This mass coming out was only possible because of the groundwork CHE had done. The publicity had worked in the paper to rally homosexuals to defend the scheme, and the mailing to Esquire and CHE members produced a turn-out of people who desperately wanted the clubs. The effect of this public declaration was of enormous importance psychologically to CHE, in increasing the confidence and radicalism of the members, and it contributed to a surge in radicalism in groups from Liverpool to Leeds.

The word had spread. I think there were gay people in the audience from all over Lancashire. … There was a sense that people had come from far and wide.
—Michael Steed[150]

What was also very, very moving was some local people stood up who weren't out already, some people in the audience we didn't know.
—Glenys Parry[151]

One of them was a young male nurse from Southport. He challenged Neville, who claimed to be a counsellor, to advise him how to live as a homosexual. He said he had tried to commit suicide three times before accepting himself.

Andrew himself does not remember calling on people in the meeting to come out, although he knows it was something he did on other occasions. Other witnesses say that it was Allan Horsfall; however Alan Wakeman's account is the most detailed and circumstantial, and it seems likeliest that the gesture came from GLF rather than CHE. Andrew makes the point that it could have been any one of them:

GLF had got into the swing of how to handle public occasions where we wished to be hostile to those who were running them. We hardly had to

> discuss tactics really. We had to find out what was going on, and swing into the choirettes routine. I remember doing something we often did, and that's simply saying, How many of us here are gay, because there was a platform there talking to us as if there were two gay people in Burnley, and five in Lancashire, and everybody in the hall would be straight. And I thought, looking around, 'There's an awful lot of us here'. I think something like half or three quarters of the hall stood up, to I believe the consternation of some on the platform. … It could have been anybody, because by then we were developing tactics, and that was one of the obviously subversive tactics, to show the people to whom homosexuality is a theory, to show them faces. … the word I'd use is 'lively', It was intense, the feeling in the room was very, very strong. The anxiety to get something achieved out of this situation. Politics at its best.[152]

In the jargon of the time, it was a zap, part of the GLF arsenal. Alan Wakeman:

> If you went to a meeting where there was hostility, you would zap it. For example, we might all go on the platform, say 'We're taking possession of this microphone, and we're going to hold an open meeting where anybody can speak. Who would like to speak from the audience?' I went to several meetings where we did that. Initially it took huge courage to do that, but gradually you began to think 'Why am I scared? They're just people.' And I lost my fear of people.[153]

Fred Evans, the Christians' secretary, was enraged by the demonstration of solidarity. 'Homosexuality is a filthy practice,' he shouted, almost drowned in the uproar. One young woman supporter had to be dragged off him by her friends.

If the declaration of the homosexuals at the meeting gave them the feeling that they were winning the argument and had the Christians on the run, this is not confirmed by the press reports. Nor was it shared by Ray Gosling chairing the meeting and desperately trying to keep order. Then from the platform he spotted a woman in her 60s, with dark glasses and a crisp perm – Mrs Swindlehurst. Ray Gosling saw her from the platform:

> I remember looking around the hall, and it was clearly going against us. The Catholics were clearly winning. 'We'll have no buggers' clubs in Burnley.' One after the other, 'We don't want this sort of thing in Burnley. Let people go to Manchester if they want that sort of thing.' It was going terrible. …
>
> And I looked down that hall … and there was this blind white-haired woman with a stick. She'd got her hand up, like this, only half up, only a little bit, she wanted to say something, and I said, 'Come on, everybody, lady half-way down. Blind lady, she wants to say something.'
>
> I had no fucking idea what was going to happen. She half-stood up,

> and she said, 'My son killed himself, because he was a queer, and he was ashamed. If there had been something like one of these clubs, where he could have gone, and had a good time, he would be alive today.'
>
> You can feel a meeting. I remember looking at Allan, and Allan would have looked at me and said, or thought something like, 'You fucking lucky bugger.' But I knew it was all over. Roman Catholics nil – Queers, seven. It was all over.[154]

That there was no violence was largely due to the chairing of Gosling, who was praised in the *Express and News* report of the meeting for maintaining an order which was 'precarious at times'. Ken Pilling disarmed the skinheads: 'It is ridiculous to suggest that skinheads would move in and beat us up. Skinheads are quite decent lads.'[155] Faced with this emollience, the skinheads restricted themselves to a sly 'Whoops, dearie!' when the policemen weren't looking.[156] Sitting at the back, they were one of the more orderly sections of the meeting.

In the end, there was little meeting of minds, and those opinions which had been firmly held weren't shifted one bit. Some waverers came over to the CHE side. The audience picked up their umbrellas and left, leaving the organisers and their supporters to celebrate in the bar the simple fact that they'd managed to pull the meeting off:

> It gave us a tremendous fillip. Before it happened we just didn't know, we could have had hardly anybody turn up, if the opposition had boycotted it, if we hadn't gone about publicising it the right way, if the GLF contingent hadn't turned up. —Michael Steed[157]

After this, the GLF contingent drove back to Glenys Parry's shared house in Victoria Park in Manchester to crash on the floors. Suspicious of two vehicles crammed with flamboyant queens, the police stopped them.

> We were in one car and Stuart Feather was in another. I remember Stuart coming up to our car and saying, 'Keep cool, keep cool. These cars are ripped off.' We were absolutely horrified, we didn't want to know really, but somebody had used a credit card or something to hire these cars and … there was some fraudulent deal, and he was very worried the police would find out.* But they didn't, and they let us go on. I remember being quite shocked at the time, in my slightly provincial sort of way.'
>
> —Glenys Parry[158]

* Alan Wakeman, who hired a minibus, is insistent that he would have paid for his minibus; he had a considerable income at the time from his pioneering language study courses. This suggests that two GLF groups responded to Glenys' appeal independently (quite possible, from a rowdy meeting of 400), and made their own arrangements unbeknownst to each other.

More surprises awaited Glenys back in Manchester:

> It turned out my parents had come on a surprise visit to see me, without giving me notice, and had pitched their tent in the garden. So there was this surreal situation where there were all these half-naked GLF guys wandering around, with my dad trying to make breakfast and looking rather disconcerted.[159]

As parents, the Parrys seem to have been remarkably accepting for the time. However, nothing could have dampened the exhilaration of the meeting.

31. The Burnley Library meeting: top left Fr Neville (Roman Catholic) top right Ken Pilling, Ray Gosling, Allan Horsfall; bottom left Fr Cayton (Anglican); Bottom right Michael Steed, Ken Pilling, Ray Gosling

Michael Steed describes the decision to stage the Burnley meeting, and his appearance on the platform, as a personal Rubicon. It was the first time he had had to find the personal bravery to stand up and be counted. He was not alone. In many ways it was the moment at which CHE grew up. It had established full independence from Antony Grey and the Albany Trust. It had proved it could organise large-scale public meetings. It had proved that it could take on the bigots and run a full-scale public relations campaign. It brought other homosexuals to join the organisation, and engendered a burst of self-confidence which would lead to increasingly articulate demands nationally. The confidence and articulacy also rubbed off on the proliferating local groups. For Allan Horsfall, it was the most successful meeting CHE ever held.

The fallout from Burnley

The issue rumbled on afterwards. There was extensive coverage in the gay press, such as it was, in the UK and elsewhere. Perhaps the most detailed account was in the American paper, the Los Angeles-based *Advocate*, which gave the incident a whole page and quoted Nick Stanley in fighting form:

> It made no difference whether those writing to the papers claimed to be our friends or opponents, neither group dealt with us as people, only as walking (or rather stalking) stereotypes. … Nearly all the articles and letters … spoke of sickness, or imbalance. …
>
> If for the moment we are denied a club in Burnley we do not intend to crawl under the nearest stone. On the contrary we propose to draw the maximum attention to what has happened, and why. The campaign in Burnley has armed us with concrete evidence of the way our opponents move against us, and demonstrates, to those who have forgotten, that all is far from well for homosexuals in England, in spite of limited law reform.[160]

Burnley Borough Council pursued its own agenda, putting a motion to the Association of Municipal Corporations' General Purposes Committee. They got the brush-off: 'We do not consider that the establishment of a social club of this nature presents a problem requiring local authority control.'[161]

The local paper carried more letters. The Burnley Local Medical Council welcomed the failure of the club because it would have caused 'some latent homosexuals to become active (as noted last week at the BMA scientific meeting this DOES lead to an increase in VD).'[162] This brought a response from Horsfall which is worth quoting at length because in many ways it prefigures the arguments over AIDS/HIV in the early 1980s, when many were in favour of penalising sufferers, and gay men in general.

> I wondered how long it would be before someone dragged venereal disease into the many spurious arguments advanced against 'that club'. … If homosexuals run a greater than average risk of contracting VD (and – along with immigrants and teenagers – they do) this is because society as represented in the outmoded thinking of bodies like the Medical Committee … forces them into a life of furtive, fleeting and anonymous sexual encounters in which the chances of contracting the infection are increased, while the possibility of tracing contacts (which is the most important aspect of the control of VD) is rendered hopeless. …

> The VD problem would diminish if more homosexuals were able to establish stable relationships, but this will not happen so long as they are denied – as they are now in Burnley – the same kind of stable social institutions as the rest of the community.[163]

There was also a blistering response from Paul Temperton, who issued this press release:

> It is high time that the myth that ordinary doctors know everything was well and truly exploded. Homosexuality is NOT a medical matter and this group of GPs is no better placed to comment on the issue of homosexual clubs than any other member of the community, particularly since medical training at the moment includes almost no balanced information on homosexuality and the average doctor's knowledge of the subject is therefore based largely on his experience of the highly unrepresentative minority of homosexuals which he sees as patients.
>
> For the Burnley Local Medical Committee to dictate what is best for the homosexual men and women of Burnley is an act of the most appalling arrogance. Whether or not there should be a homosexual club in the town is a matter for the homosexuals of Burnley, and nobody else. [164]

GLF and CHE continued to take action jointly on the issue. Together they penned a letter to the *Express and News* as a personal appeal to Fr Neville. This drew on the parallels between the persecution of early Christians and the current persecuting of the homosexual minority:

> It [persecution] is a word that Christians once had much on their mind. … Those Christians were unable to openly call themselves what they were. They were slandered and people were frightened that Christians would corrupt their children. … It was not the authorities of the day that Christ asked to be his friends, but outcasts, slaves, the miserable, the poor. … Homosexuals wish, as the early Christians did, to come out into the open, to be seen for what we genuinely are and not for what slander has made us seem, and be free to assemble as others, including Christians, have long been free to assemble.[165]

They went further, in taking a joint complaint to the Press Council.* There had been two reports of the meeting in the national press; Robert Chesshyre in *The Observer* gave an accurate summary, but Colin Dunne in the *Daily Mirror*

* The Press Council (1962–91) was replaced by the Press Complaints Commission, which in turn gave way in 2014 to the Independent Press Standards Organisation. It was a voluntary, self-policing body made up of 80 per cent newspaper employees and 20 per cent lay people, and funded by newspaper proprietors. There was widespread criticism of its ineffectiveness, and in 1980 the National Union of Journalists withdrew from it, saying it was incapable of reform or effective action.

did not. He represented it as a fight between the people of Burnley and the intruding metropolitan queers:

> Ken Russell could have made a torrid film about it. Later, when feelings have cooled, it could make a first class Brian Rix farce. And in another twenty years or so it could have all the ingredients for a nostalgic musical. But right now, the story of how the citizens of a sturdy provincial town fought off a fifth column in their midst, hangs somewhere between the wildly funny and rather sad.
>
> Burnley is one of those smoky northern towns that hasn't seen a lot of excitement since the Luddites left town. And it was about the time of the annual Wakes holiday that the honest ratepayers, their traditional pallor vanished from a week in Whitby or Majorca, returned to realise the full horror of what was happening to them.
>
> A group of homosexuals were planning to open a club smack in the middle of town. In the old Co-op, to be precise, where curlered heads, which have never known an indecent thought, have long queued for the divi. So far Burnley has gone along with society's new freedoms. Saucy bookshops? Certainly. Strip shows? Why not? But Nancy-boys? Burnley held up one hand very firmly: The permissive society stops here.[166]

It's a jokey, almost sniggering piece, but it also makes fun of the ubiquitous Fred Evans, who is quoted:

> If you ask me, most of 'em weren't genuine homosexuals at all. Perverts, I'd call 'em. One of these fancily-dressed fellers at the back of the hall was kissing a girl. A girl! Now that's not normal, not for them anyway. … Just look at Burnley. The textile industry's gone for a burton. So has coal. The football team has been relegated. What are we going to be famous for? A club for queers?[167]

Truth to tell, the article was equally insulting to the Christians and the gays. But the central assertion that 'the town' was on one side and 'the queers' were on the other was simply untrue. The idea of complaining to the Press Council seems to have come from Andrew Lumsden, then working on the *Financial Times*, and shortly to leave to become a co-founder of *Gay News*.

The submission to the Press Council, which ran to eight pages, was highly professional and very detailed. In the summary, Andrew wrote:

> We consider the *Daily Mirror* article we complain of to be the worst case in some time of prejudicial reporting on a subject of acute and serious concern to society. The author attempts to make into an entertainment a meeting of 250 people at which a priest declared that many young men in his care had killed themselves as 'a result of corruption by older men'. The deaths of these young people, however, whatever the truth about the reason why they died, should alone have been enough to make a

> responsible newspaper give serious and well-researched coverage to the matter, always provided that the reporter describing the meeting was actually present. …
>
> The writer gives a misleading impression of the dates on which events occurred, and fails to mention the crucial part played by local clergymen both in opposition to a homosexuals' club, and in the public meeting at Burnley library; he misrepresents the behaviour of the police and the character of local young people at the meeting. … We call on the Press Council to require the Editor of the *Daily Mirror* to print an updated and properly balanced account of this matter of strong regional and national interest.[168]

This was merely the first of many CHE complaints to the Press Council over the next ten years. They all fell on stony ground.

The search for premises continued. Paul Temperton wrote to the Co-op, asking whether their withdrawal from negotiations was just for these premises, or would they be prepared to consider another building? Maybe in another town? The Co-op HQ in Manchester replied that they'd be prepared to consider applications for lease of property in other areas. But there was no property in other areas. Privately, Ray and Allan were breathing a sigh of relief that they'd had a narrow escape. In Ray's words:

> The last thing me or Allan wanted to do was to run a bloody club. I was writing, I was doing radio, for Radio Four, I was doing telly for Granada, I wouldn't have had any time to run a club. My life was absolutely chocker. I had no time for anything like that.[169]

This does not mean that they entirely gave up on the idea. Michael Steed, CHE Treasurer and later Chairman, remembers looking at buildings in Todmorden and Littleborough. They got as far as obtaining planning permission and having a structural survey done on a redundant church in the former, and a chapel in the latter. The Littleborough chapel was riddled with woodworm. Since there was no income from Esquire after 1969 and all subsequent projects required financial outlay, the only conclusion to draw is that Allan and Ray stumped up the cash for these activities from their own pockets.

A plea from Allan appeared in the September 1971 CHE *Bulletin*: Did any local group feel strong enough to take on the running of the club? Can we look for premises? Preferably of a club which had closed and wouldn't need planning permission? Preferably to lease? There were no takers.

However, if clubs couldn't be created in Manchester or the Midlands, perhaps they could happen in London. By 1972 there were thirteen local CHE groups in London, and a London Co-ordinating Committee. Much energy was devoted to raising money and trying to find premises for a London Club over the next two years,* and well into the late 1970s, the establishment of social centres was one of CHE's primary aims.

From Esquire Clubs to Gay Centres

Equally, GLF tried hard to get clubs off the ground. Like CHE, they set up a fundraising group after a think-in at the LSE in September 1971; they organised jumble sales, and put on benefit concerts and discos. David Bowie was scheduled to perform on 4 October 1971 at Seymour Hall off Edgware Road, 'Proceeds to go to founding a community centre for all our sisters and brothers.' However, shortly before the concert the police alleged that GLF were associated with the Angry Brigade and its bombing campaign in London. Bowie withdrew from the concert, claiming GLF were 'too aggressive'.†

The GLF premises group paralleled the London Clubs Working Party in CHE; nobody could accuse them of not thinking big:

> We ought to look round for a disused church, preferably with a crypt if possible, a church hall attached and with hopes of a vicarage also being attached. It was thought that the church could be used for GLF weekly meetings. If not used by us every night of the week, it could be let out to other organisations for a reasonable rent. The crypt could be a media workshop centre for the making of saleable things to make it become self-supporting. The church hall could be used by street theatre group for rehearsals, also by theatre work group for making scenery etc. etc. The vicarage, should we be lucky enough to have one, should become our second commune at say two a room. With common TV lounge, quiet room, library, dining room, general lounge. Upper rooms to be used as bedrooms for sisters and brothers. If there was a basement this could become a washing and ironing and drying room, with perhaps a table tennis room, and billiard room, with a hobbies work shop room. ... We would like to see as soon as possible a premises account being opened at a bank to which any Sister or Brother who could afford it would be able to send a donation never mind how small.[170]

It was insanely, outrageously ambitious, and, as CHE also found, it was impossible to raise enough money. The fundraising group issued appeals for 'names of wealthy gay people outside GLF'.[171]

Nobody came forward, and house price inflation pushed the dream ever further out of reach.‡

---

* See Chapter 5.

† Handwritten note from John Chesterman in the Chesterman section of the Hall Carpenter Archive.

‡ Nationally, house prices doubled between 1970 and 1973.

Meanwhile, with GLF fragmenting into local groups, Camden GLF was looking for its own centre in its own area, nothing grand, just a house scheduled for demolition in maybe two or three years' time, big enough to run a coffee bar in, and have meetings. And a library. And an arts and crafts room. Oh, and somewhere for dancing. And a cinema. And an information office with a pay phone. And maybe living accommodation. It was going to have to be a rather large house. They agonised over whether to buy or rent, but decided high-mindedly to rent because of the dangers of creating 'a vast property-owning bureaucracy pandering to the institutions we are trying to destroy'.[172]

However, in January 1971 the group had its chance, with an old café opposite the Roundhouse in Chalk Farm. The co-operative that owned it was so keen to let Camden GLF have it, they offered two weeks rent free. The catch was, the offer had to be taken up immediately. Another fundraising jumble sale; another urgent appeal, this time for volunteers for painting the premises over the coming weekend. Again, not enough people, not enough money. It too came to nothing.

The centres which did work, and for a surprising length of time, were the ones created by collective squatting, thus bypassing problems of money, management and structure. East London GLF, in the shape of the Bethnal Rouge collective, took over an agitprop bookshop, selling gay, feminist and children's books. They told the local CHE group, 'There's plenty of room here for people to relax, chat and have coffee, so come on round.'[173] Bethnal Rouge's reputation was somewhat hard line, but they embedded themselves into the community remarkably successfully. They held dances in the local church hall:

> It's taken the vicar some time to get it together and come over to the shop and speak to us. He suggested we wrote something for the parish magazine instead of paying the usual £12 fee for the hall. … Our local pub around the corner is run by two gay women. … When we had trouble with the rates we went over to the solicitors opposite and they've been giving us free legal aid. … There was this E2 festival for the East End and we had a stall there. It was like … incredible, all the people and the kids. We were putting make up on them, the kids!! They took lots of pictures of us too, and they're going to have them displayed in the library in Bethnal Green Museum.[174]

But there were also the bricks through the windows, and the attacks with broken bottles.

South London GLF also ran a successful Gay Centre at 78 Railton Road in Brixton, surrounded by a whole parade of gay squats. Icebreakers ran its phone service from the same 'complex', and there were women's organisations and black groups too. South London GLF also held dances in Lambeth Town Hall, and organised the 1976 Gay Pride Week and Pride Parade from the Centre. It fielded two candidates for Lambeth Council in the 1974 local elections, running on a gay rights ticket. They did not do well; unlike Bethnal Rouge, the Centre was not popular locally, and did not get good publicity:

> Men fondling each other in the saloon bar of the 'Windsor Castle' has led to homosexuals being banned from the pub. For the last 18 months it has become a meeting place for people using the nearby Gay Community Centre in Railton Road. The 'Windsor Castle' publican, Mrs Ann Collyer, has decided that she doesn't want their custom any more because of their 'suggestive behaviour'. 'The way they act in front of other people is not very nice. They seem to think they can do exactly as they like. I have seen them kissing and canoodling. They are trying to take over my pub. … When this came up before I defended them, but I am not running my business to suit the gay community centre.'[175]

Despite incidents like this, the South London Gay Centre stayed in business for over four years.

Esquire itself continued in existence. By 1974 Paul Temperton and Michael Steed were listed as new directors. Allan at some point resigned in a telegram to Ray Gosling (date uncertain): 'As acting chairman please accept my resignation from Esquire. Stop. Present set-up not viable.'*[176] In 1976 Ray was still getting requests to go and talk to a group in Bournemouth about setting up a club. But really it was a dead duck.

Meanwhile, someone had quietly gone and set up exactly what Allan and Ray were planning – a member-owned club in Shardlow, deep in the country six miles from Derby. Ike Cowen was already CHE's Legal Officer by 1971, but he kept his club interests strictly separated from his CHE work. Ike had come to Nottingham in the mid-1960s, having been introduced by Antony Grey to Rev. Barry Hodges, who ran a club called Night Off. It provided coffee evenings, with occasional talks by doctors and social workers:

> Night Off was not ostensibly a gay organisation, not as far as I knew at that time. Barry Hodges had certainly not told me he was gay. However, one night at this Night Off meeting, we had a talk, I think it was by a doctor, somebody not a member of the group anyhow, who came along to give us a talk about homosexuality. And he talked such a lot of cobblers that I got so angry about it that when he'd finished and asked if we had any questions, I stood up and said, 'I'd like to say that he's been talking a lot of

* It's not clear what was so urgent that required Horsfall, normally very careful with money, to send a telegram.

> bloody nonsense, and I can tell you this with authority, because I'm gay.' It was the first time I'd ever come out openly in front of a group of people by saying I was gay. And I could have bit my tongue off, because I didn't intend to do it, but there it was, it was done.[177]

Ike was using the gay scene in Nottingham, in particular the Flying Horse, but getting increasingly irritated by the prices being charged, the police harassment, and the unfriendly attitudes. He claims to have had the idea of a club independently around 1968, although it is more likely, given the publicity around Esquire in 1968, that it was 'in the air', and he picked it up maybe even without realising it.

> Eventually I came to see that things were wrong, that we had to rely on pubs that overcharged, that we were tolerated not accepted. I didn't like this, I was very militant. So I had a brainwave. Using the college Gestetner I ran off a series of pamphlets – 'Are you fed up with being ripped off in pubs? If so, come and meet me at …' And I had an arrangement with a Probation Officer I knew, to use his office in Mansfield. … I think twenty people turned up. And I outlined to them what my idea was, to form a club which would be run by its members, it would run on non-profit lines, and it would be open to gays only. Anyway, 20 people turned up, and I ended up with twenty pounds.[178]

For the next two years this little group met, slowly evolving and expanding, They met in a series of pubs and clubs, holding raffles, making small profits from running their own bars, collecting subscriptions. In this way they raised enough to be able to put a deposit on premises. This was a cricket pavilion which had been found by the Club Treasurer:

> [He] found this ideal place, this old – I think it was a cricket pavilion or tennis pavilion, something of that nature. It was a little hut, quite a pleasant place. You'd go up a long path from the main road. And we could have this for a reasonable price. … Then things began to go wrong. First of all, I was very disappointed to find you couldn't trust gays. There were so many gays who couldn't be trusted. We were ripped off right, left and centre. We had two treasurers who interfered with the money; we had barmen who left with our takings.[179]

Like Allan, Ike had adopted a policy of not volunteering information in his applications:

> You see, when I applied for a licence in the first place, I'd gone along to the court in Derby and asked for the licence, and when I was asked, what was the purpose of the club, I honestly didn't know what to say. And the Chairman of the Bench said, 'Is it a social club?' and I said, 'Yes, sir!' And that was the end of that.[180]

Fortunately there were no blabbermouths to the local media. The club thrived over several years as a male-only club. (This was to be a bone of contention with the local CHE groups, which campaigned for several years to get a mixed night for their own members.) Operating deep in the country away from any residential area, it developed into quite a hot spot:

> [There was] drinking after hours, things happening in the toilet, and one day I got a call to go and see the Chief Officer of Police for that area of Derbyshire. I've forgotten what his rank was but he had a lot of pips on his shoulder. And he said that he'd heard about all this, and I started to say, 'Well I don't know anything about this, and I'm sure this doesn't happen, we don't drink after hours.' And he said, 'I would prefer that you didn't tell me any lies.' … Anyway, the writing was on the wall. Without drinking after hours in those days it was impossible. We couldn't get a late licence even if we'd asked for one.[181]

Extremely fortunately under the circumstances, there was a fire at the Pavilion within a month. The members patched the Pavilion up again, but within another month it burnt down completely.

> You know what gays were like in those days – nobody ever came out on a Saturday night before eleven o'clock. And if they couldn't drink after eleven o'clock they wouldn't come. Also it was becoming difficult to drive out to Shardlow because of the drink-driving laws. The breathalyser had come in, we had no car park, we used to borrow the car park of a café on the opposite side of the road. And [the owner], realising he had us over a barrel, was putting his prices up every time we asked him. So we were on the verge of being extinct anyhow. So the fire in fact did us a good turn, because we got £16,000 in insurance.[182]

However it ended, the Club had served its purpose for over ten years. The insurance money was put into a Trust, charitable status then being withheld from gay projects, for the benefit of gay people living and working in Nottingham, Leicester and Sheffield. It financed a lot of AIDS work in the 1980s and 90s, and survived into the 21st century.

In parallel with the Pavilion Club, another members' co-operative club, the Nightingale in Birmingham, opened in 1969 on Camp Hill in Bordesley, and survived as such until it was threatened with liquidation in 2011 and sold to a commercial operator.*

Neither the Pavilion nor the Nightingale conformed very closely to the Esquire ideal, beyond being member-owned. They didn't have a 'high tone'. There were no libraries, no restaurants, no film or theatre shows, no advice sessions or formal support as Allan and Ray envisaged, or as COC offered in

---

* It subsequently moved to Kent Street in Birmingham's gay quarter.

Amsterdam or Arcadie in Paris. Yet the idea of Esquire Clubs lived on, transformed into the concept of Gay Centres. London CHE tried seriously for one in the years 1972–74. Edinburgh got its Gay Centre in 1974, Birmingham in 1976, Manchester and Bristol in 1978. Tyneside CHE tried to start one in Newcastle, Chester CHE got one in 1979. And although a CHE Club in London failed to materialise, a Gay Centre did, in 1985, with a grant of three quarters of a million pounds from the Greater London Council.

It is perhaps idle to speculate what might have happened if Esquire Clubs had taken off when it was proposed. However, it stands as a paradigm of a golden opportunity lost, one of the great 'what-might-have-beens' of lesbian and gay history. Esquire's founders stipulated that the takings would be ploughed back into more clubs; however, with the increasing involvement of CHE in 1971, it also offered a huge potential source of campaign funds. With a successful Esquire movement, there needn't have been the series of financial crises which bedevilled CHE for the next twenty years, hampering its campaign work and taking up precious energies in fundraising, energies which might have been better channelled. Ultimately all successful campaigning depends on money. It was not until the advent of Stonewall in 1989, with its supporters' network of the great and good with almost bottomless pockets, that serious and effective mainstream lobbying became a reality.

However, the failure of the Esquire project had a profound effect on the future shape of CHE. The loss of the Rockingham in particular necessitated a complete strategic rethink, for although Allan and Ray and Michael Steed kept looking, suddenly a Centre was much further off in the future, and the needs of isolated homosexuals were pressing. If social centres were not to offer the gay space which people craved, there had to be another way to provide it. A way which was cheaper, easier to set up, more flexible, and more modest. If gay space could not be fixed to bricks and mortar, it would be mobile. It would reside in gay people themselves, created by the very fact of coming together, in local groups. At a conference in July 1970 Martin Stafford, then Counselling Secretary of CHE, made the connection very explicitly:

> The committee's activities have increased considerably in the last ten months or so; I think this is due to the dormancy of Esquire. … Since Esquire was unsuccessful we sought alternative means of achieving the aims which Esquire was created to promote, with the inauguration of local groups instead of large social centres, and the emphasis has come to be on local groups, and these can be established with little financial outlay.[183]

The process by which these came into being is the subject of the next chapter.

Notes to Chapter Three

[1] HLRS, Minutes of meeting of 11 October 1967. HCA/GREY/1/1/81.

[2] Ibid.

[3] Ibid.

[4] Richard Wollheim, 'The road to toleration', *Spectator*, 6771 (4 April 1958), 435.

[5] Albany Trust 'Homosexuals', advertisement in *The Guardian*, 11 August 1967, 2.

[6] C. P. Sherlock to Albany Trust, 'Tax status of donations', 3 February 1967. HCA/AT/4/4/48.

[7] Antony Grey to Albany Trust trustees, 'Covenanted donations', 15 February 1967. HCA/AT/4/4/67.

[8] 'Magazine publishers win appeal in part', *Times*, 15 June 1972, 10.

[9] Antony Grey to Allan Horsfall 'Correspondence clubs', 15 January 1970. HCA/AT/7/60.

[10] Walton, *Out of the Shadows*, 9–10.

[11] Allan Horsfall to Antony Grey, 'Possible clubs', 23 January 1967.

[12] Ray Gosling, 'Dream boy', *New Left Review* 3, November–December 1960, 30-31.

[13] Ibid.

[14] Allan Horsfall, 'The pub and the people', *New Left Review*, 9 (May–June 1961), 56–57.

[15] Ray Gosling, interviewed by the author, 11 December 2010.

[16] PC Colin Kilbourn, deposition to Magistrate's Court committal proceedings, 14 May 1965. HCA/AT/10/23.

[17] John Clarkson, Deposition in case of *R. v. Ray and Clarkson*, 1965. HCA/AT/10/23.

[18] Billy Ray, Deposition in case of *R. v. Ray and Clarkson*, 1965. HCA/AT/10/23.

[19] Dr Allen, Deposition in case of *R. v. Ray and Clarkson*, 1965. HCA/AT/10/23.

[20] John Clarkson to Rt Rev. John Robinson, 'Police behaviour', 21 February 1965. HCA/AT/10/23.

[21] John Clarkson, Deposition in case of *R. v. Ray and Clarkson,* 1965. HCA/AT/10/23.

[22] Ray Gosling, Report on Clarkson and Ray committal for Albany Trust, 1965. HCA/AT/10/23.

[23] Ray Gosling, interviewed by the author, 11 December 2010.

[24] Antony Grey to Allan Horsfall, 'Visit of Reg Kilduff', 15 January 1965. HCA/GREY/1/15/262.

[25] Roy Perrott, 'A Club for homosexuals', *Observer,* 13 January 1963, Weekend Review, 12.

[26] Ibid.

[27] Ibid.

[28] Ibid.

[29] NWHLRC Minutes, 15 June 1967. HCA/AT/4/4/40.

[30] Allan Horsfall to Antony Grey, 'Sponsorship of clubs', 18 June 1967. HCA/GREY/1/15/39.

[31] Allan Horsfall to Antony Grey, 'The need for clubs', 28 August 1967. HCA/GREY/1/15/28.

[32] Antony Grey to Allan Horsfall, 'Visit of Reg Kilduff', 15 January 1965. HCA/GREY/1/15/262.

[33] Allan Horsfall to Antony Grey, 'Niel Pearson involvement', 20 January 1965. HCA/GREY/1/15/259.

[34] Allan Horsfall, interviewed by Paul Hambley, 12 May 2009. BSA C1405/05.

[35] Ibid.

[36] Martin Stafford to Allan Horsfall, 'Meeting with COC', 23 September 1967. MCA/G/HOR/1.

[37] Denis Cassidy, 'Do we want pubs like this?' *The People*, 24 March 1968, 6.

[38] Ibid.

[39] Ibid

[40] Ibid.

[41] Guy Thornton, interviewed by the author, 5 April 2014.

42 'Why a policeman had to dance', *Manchester Evening News and Chronicle*, 9 September 1968, 11.

43 'Orgy in club: £500 fine', *Wolverhampton Express and Star*, 24 July 1968, 1.

44 G. A. Smith, et. al. to Antony Grey, 'Police raid on the Flamingo Club', 21 April 1968. NTU/GE/161/82.

45 Allan Horsfall to Antony Grey, 'Flamingo Club trial', 21 September 1968. HCA/GRAY/1/15/34.

46 'Revelries of Gomorrah', *Wolverhampton Express and Star*, 25 July 1968, 34.

47 *R v. Smith and The Cresta Sports and Social Club* (unreported) [Wolverhampton Quarter Sessions, 24 July 1968]. Transcript by Allan Horsfall. NTU/GE/161/81.

48 Ibid.

49 Ibid.

50 Ibid.

51 Ibid.

52 de Sales, *Philothea*, III, 100.

53 Allan Horsfall to Ray Gosling, 'Proposal for Esquire Clubs', 26 November 1967. MCA/G/HOR/1.

54 NWHLRC Minutes, 18 December 1967. HCA/GRAY/1/15-2/3.

55 Esquire information leaflet, 1968. NTU/GE/161/82.

56 Allan Horsfall to Rev. John Rogan, 'Support for Esquire', 23 January 1968. MCA/G/HOR/3.

57 'Esquire: A club for homosexuals', advertisement in *Private Eye*, 177 (17 September 1968), 6.

58 Ray Gosling, Esquire Clubs Limited leaflet, September 1968. NTU/GE/161/82.

59 Esquire Clubs, Accounts accompanying leaflet, 1968. NTU/GE/161/82.

60 'Canon forms club for "lonely men",' *Coventry Evening Telegraph*, 10 January 1968, 9.

61 Paul Connew, 'Special "clinic" for homosexuals at a cathedral', *Daily Mirror*, 12 January 1968, 18.

62 'Cathedral clinic for lonely men', *Daily Express*, 12 January 1968, 4.

63 Tom Frost, quoted in Antony Grey, 'Memo to Albany Trust', 2 May 1968, HCA/AT/2/15.

64 Minutes of Nottingham club group, 3 July 1968. NTU/GE/161/81.

65 Ibid.

66 Ibid.

67 Ray Gosling, interviewed by the author, 11 December 2010.

68 Ibid.

69 William Hardcastle, *World at One* [radio broadcast], BBC Radio Four, 1 September 1968.

70 C. H. Rolph to Colin Harvey, 'Meeting at the Home Office', 12 September 1968. HCA/Grey/1/15-2/63.

71 HLRS Minutes of meeting of 14 May 1968. HCA/GREY/1/1/84.

72 Ibid.

73 Ibid.

74 Ibid.

75 Ibid.

76 Jan De Groot to Antony Grey, 'Esquire Clubs', 11 June 1968. HCA/GREY/1/15-2/57.

77 Antony Grey to Jan de Groot, 'Esquire Clubs', 18 June 1968. HCA/GREY/1/15-2/55.

78 'Burnley may get club for homosexuals', *Burnley Evening Star*, 9 September 1968, 1.

79 Michael Brown, interviewed by the author, 1 July 2012.

80 Ray Gosling, 'Homosexuals now', *New Society*, 309 (29 August 1968), 293–294.

81 HC Deb 3 July 1967 vol. 748 col 1478.

82 Alan Brien, 'Afterthought', *Spectator*, 7061 (25 October 1963), 541–542.

[83] Ray Gosling, 'Homosexuals now', *New Society*, 309 (29 August 1968), 293–294.

[84] William Hardcastle, *World at One* [radio broadcast], BBC Radio Four, 1 September 1968.

[85] Ibid.

[86] Ken Plummer, interviewed by the author, 31 January 2012.

[87] Ken Plummer to Ray Gosling, 'Esquire Clubs', 27 October 1968. NTU/GE161/81.

[88] Antony Grey, 'Homosexuals now', *New Society*, 310 (5 September 1968), 349.

[89] Peter Q. Rhodes, 'Homosexuals now', *New Society*, 311 (12 September 1968), 384.

[90] Anon, Ibid.

[91] Lord Arran, 'The Arran Column: Shocked' *Evening News*, 4 September 1968, 10.

[92] Peter Katin to Antony Grey, 'Esquire Clubs', 14 September 1968. HCA/GREY/1/15-2/4.

[93] Antony Grey to Peter Katin, 'Esquire Clubs', 18 September 1968. HCA/GREY/1/15-2/39.

[94] Ibid.

[95] David Tribe to Lord Arran, 'Esquire Clubs', 18 September 1968. HCA/GREY/1/15-2/42.

[96] David Tribe, 'Esquire Clubs', Letter to Editor, *Evening News* (unpublished) 7 September 1968. HCA/GREY/1/15-2/46.

[97] Frank R. Kameny to Ian Dunn, 'Prosecution for men dancing', 17 June 1969. MCA/G/HOR/Uncatalogued.

[98] Allan Horsfall, 'Arran's wrong', *Evening News*, 19 September 1968, 3.

[99] Ray Gosling, interviewed by the author, 11 December 2010.

[100] George Henshaw to Allan Horsfall, 'Esquire Clubs', 26 October 1968. MCA/G/HOR/2.

[101] Basil Higginson to Allan Horsfall, 'Esquire Clubs', 15 October 1968. MCA/G/HOR/2.

[102] Jane Gaddum to Allan Horsfall, 'Gaddum House', 21 Oct 1968. MCA/G/HOR/2.

[103] Esquire Clubs Newsletter, October 1968. NTU/GE161/81.

[104] Ibid.

[105] Esquire Clubs newsletter, February 1969. HCA/GREY/1/15.

[106] 'Club could "pervert town's youths",' *Swinton Journal*, 9 September 1969, 3.

[107] Ibid.

[108] Ibid.

[109] Antony Grey and D. J. West, 'Homosexuals: New law but no new deal', *New Society*, 339 (27 March 1969), 476.

[110] Martin Stafford to Antony Grey, 'Resignation', 13 December 1969. HCA/AT/7/60.

[111] Antony Grey to several enquirers, 12 May 1970. HVA/Grey/1/15-2.

[112] Esquire Clubs, Letter to members, September 1970. NTU/GE/161/81.

[113] Roger Baker, 'The yellow brick road to Oz', *Contact*, 1/3 (September 1970). HCA/CHE/Chesterman/14.

[114] Allan Horsfall to Peter Norman, 'Membership of Burnley club', 18 December 1970.

[115] CHE *Bulletin*, June 1971, 1. HCA/CHE/4/18.

[116] 'Burnley site for new "club",' *Burnley Express and News*, 26 May 1971, 3.

[117] 'Group forms to fight "club",' *Burnley Express and News*, 11 June 1971, 2.

[118] Ken Pilling, quoted in 'Burnley drive to halt club', *Burnley Evening Star*, 9 June 1971, 1.

[119] 'Club "could bring queer bashers to town",' *Burnley Evening Star*, 24 June 1971, 6.

[120] Ibid.

[121] Ibid.

[122] Ibid.

[123] Ibid.

[124] Ibid.

[125] Ibid.

[126] 'Co-op stops club talks', *Burnley Express and News*, 18 June 1971, 1.

[127] Ibid.

[128] 'Fight for club will continue', *Burnley Express and News*, 22 June 1971, 1.

[129] Allan Horsfall 'Help welcome', *Burnley Express and News*, 25 June 1971, 7.

[130] Rev. J. L. Sullivan, 'Only the plan to open a club is condemned', *Burnley Express and News*, 25 June 1971, 7.

[131] 'Taffy', 'Hopes for end to subject', Ibid.

[132] 'Horrified Mother of Four', 'Please stop this club', *Burnley Express and News*, 15 June 1971, 7.

[133] D. Smith, 'No problem for them', *Burnley Express and News*, 18 June 1971, 7.

[134] 'Unashamed', 'Just what are the objections?', Ibid.

[135] Michael Steed, interviewed by the author, 23 May 2011.

[136] CHE letter to members, 'Come to the public meeting', undated. HCA/CHE/Norman/5.

[137] Alan Wakeman, interviewed by the author, 15 April 2014.

[138] Andrew Lumsden, interviewed by the author, 10 April 2014.

[139] CHE, 'Public meeting: Homosexuals and civil liberties', advertisement in *Burnley Express and News*, 27 July 1971, 7.

[140] Student leaflet, 'Public meeting about clubs for homosexuals', July 1971. HCA/CHE/Norman/5.

[141] 'X-certificate plea for leaflets', *Burnley Express and News*, 30 July 1971, 5.

[142] Alan Wakeman, interviewed by the author, 15 April 2014.

[143] Ken Plummer, interviewed by the author, 31 January 2012.

[144] Ray Gosling, interviewed by the author, 12 December 2010.

[145] Paul Temperton, interviewed by the author, 27 March 2011.

[146] Michael Steed, interviewed by the author, 23 May 2011.

[147] 'The action group meets challenge: tempers fly at "club" meeting', *Burnley Express and News,* 3 August 1971, 1.

[148] Glenys Parry, interviewed by the author, 27 August 2012.

[149] Alan Wakeman, interviewed by the author, 15 April 2014.

[150] Michael Steed, interviewed by the author, 23 May 2011.

[151] Glenys Parry, interviewed by the author, 27 August 2012.

[152] Andrew Lumsden, interviewed by the author, 10 April 2014.

[153] Alan Wakeman, interviewed by the author, 15 April 2014.

[154] Ray Gosling, interviewed by the author, 12 December 2010.

[155] 'The action group meets challenge: tempers fly at "club" meeting', *Burnley Express and News*, 3 August 1971, 4.

[156] Colin Dunne, 'The permissive society stops here', *Daily Mirror*, 11 August 1971, 11.

[157] Michael Steed, interviewed by the author, 23 May 2011.

[158] Glenys Parry, interviewed by the author, 27 August 2012.

[159] Ibid.

[160] 'British gays hold public meeting attempting to enlighten bigots', *The Advocate*, 71 (October 1971), 8–9.

[161] Association of Municipal Corporations (AMC), Ruling of 18 November 1971. HCA/CHE/5/70/28.

[162] 'Burnley LMC GPs strongly against "club",' *Burnley Express and News,* 6 August 1971, 7.

[163] Allan Horsfall, 'Reply to GPs', *Burnley Express and News,* 10 August 1971, 8.

[164] Paul Temperton, 'Press Release about bigoted doctors', August 1971 (undated). HCA/CHE/Norman/5.

[165] CHE and GLF, 'Open letter to priest', *Burnley Express and News*, 6 August 1971, 11.

[166] Colin Dunne, 'The permissive society stops here', *Daily Mirror*, 11 August 1971, 11.

[167] Ibid.

[168] Andrew Lumsden, Submission to Press Council over *Daily Mirror* article 'The permissive society stops here' (11 August 1971): Summary. HCA/CHE/5/66.

[169] Ray Gosling, interviewed by the author, 10 December 2010.

[170] GLF Premises Group draft report, 28 October 1971. HCA/GLF/1.

[171] GLF Fundraising Group 'Appeal for donors', GLF newsletter, 10 May 1972. HCA/GLF/1.

[172] Camden GLF newsletter 12 Jan 1972. HCA/Chesterman/2.

[173] Bethnal Rouge circular (undated – 1972?). HCA/CHE/5/54/5.

[174] 'People: Bethnal Rouge', *Lunch,* 22 (October 1973), 18-19.

[175] ' "Kissing, cuddling" men are banned from pub'. *South London Press*, 10 June 1975, 1.

[176] Allan Horsfall to Ray Gosling (telegram), date illegible. NTU/GE/161/82.

[177] Ike Cowen, interviewed by David Edgley, undated 2000. Tape supplied by DE.

[178] Ibid.

[179] Ibid.

[180] Ibid.

[181] Ibid.

[182] Ibid.

[183] Martin Stafford, 'Introduction to CHE' (Transcript of the proceedings of the York Conference on the Social Needs of the Homosexual, 10 July 1970). HCA/AT/11/20.

Chapter Four: Going National

Contents

Martin Stafford

On a fine spring evening in 1967, while Leo Abse's bill was still winding its tortuous and uncertain path through Parliament, Allan Horsfall opened his front door to find a young man in a smart suit standing on the step. He was slight, quite short, his name was Martin Stafford, and he was revising for his A-levels. He was the first of a handful of teenagers who would shape what was to become the Campaign for Homosexual Equality. Martin remembers:

32. Martin Stafford in 1975

> The preponderance of correspondence in the *Manchester Evening News*, which was the main local paper, [was hostile] and occasionally Allan Horsfall would write letters countering the arguments that were raised by the people who wanted to oppose law reform. So that's how I knew he existed, and he gave an address, and I think one Sunday I went up to Bolton just to reconnoitre the area, to find out where the letters came from, and then I wrote or phoned him, asking could I come and speak to him some time.[1]

However, if Allan agreed to this, he had forgotten about it by the time Martin arrived. 'He turned up unannounced on my doorstep, a 16-year-old from Stockport Grammar School. I thought he was a set-up by one of the papers.'[2]

In fact Martin was 18, but looked younger than his years. There was enough prejudice about homosexuals, and the corruption of youth, for Allan to be understandably cautious, as he had been when cub reporter David Dutton had doorstepped him two years previously. Was it a wind-up or a trap this time around?

Allan needn't have worried. Like him, Martin was deeply serious. He also had remarkable self-confidence. He had started to tell friends at school that he was homosexual when he was sixteen and a half. He had had a crush on another boy, but where most people would have buried the information deep in unrequited love, Martin chose to tell:

> He didn't react with horror, or run out of the house, or not want anything more to do with me. … I can't remember what he said. But he'd suspected it for some time. Because I think the nature of my interest in him was probably self-evident. He didn't stop being my friend. … And that emboldened me to tell other people. I subsequently told someone else at school, who was a friend, and then I gradually told others of my contemporaries at school. By the time I left school there were maybe half a dozen who knew.[3]

He also told his mother in May 1966:

> That was quite easy, because the subject had been discussed … with various relations, some of them sort of hostile, others not. Two of them worked in television … and they were explaining there were men who were just not interested in women, you could have a troupe of dancing girls going down the stairs, and they wouldn't take any notice. And there was a reaction. 'Get away! That can't be true!' 'But it is true.' … Someone else said, 'They're dirty buggers and they should be shot.' And my uncle said, 'Don't be stupid. It's silly, they're not doing you any harm.' That sort of attitude. At some point in this conversation, my mother said to me that if *she* had any such inclinations, she'd be very annoyed if anybody tried to frustrate them. …
>
> And this one night – I can remember exactly where it was – it was in her room at my parents' house – she was doing the ironing. It was a great shock to her, but it shouldn't have been. … There was a woman that she worked with, who was lesbian, and my mother had once said to her … that I'd said I had no intention of ever getting married, and I think she said something to my mother to the effect, well maybe Martin knows that he isn't going to get married for the same reason that I did. … But … she thought it cast a great cloud over me, that my life would be ruined.[4]

Allan could not help being impressed with Martin's commitment to 'the cause'. He was reading all the letters pages of the local papers, and following the parliamentary debates on law reform in *The Times* and *The Guardian*, borrowed from the school library. He already had a record of activism, having led a campaign to preserve his local railway line. Plus he could talk the hind leg off a donkey. Words rolled out of his mouth in great natural balanced eighteenth-century periods, learnt from the philosophers he'd been studying for his A level, and for pleasure. His writing was equally elegant.

In addition to his talents, Allan also detected in Martin a kind of mutual sympathy. They were both very matter-of-fact people, resolutely unglamorous, concerned with substantial argument rather than presentation. Both had an uncritical faith in the power of reason. Even their voices, flat and stressed, sounded similar. With his usual gift for gathering useful talents around him, Allan co-opted Martin onto the North Western Committee on the spot. His first meeting, in the panelled Boardroom of Ted Wickham's Diocesan HQ, was on 15 June 1967. He was still just short of his nineteenth birthday.

He would have found the meeting largely taken up with the issue of Esquire Clubs. But he would also have found the germs of a growing confidence on the Committee, which would not allow the social workers, now a minority, to dictate the agenda for what was becoming a genuine organisation *of* rather than *for* gay people.

Counselling

In tandem with the need for clubs went a need for support which was still seen as the province of heterosexual 'experts'. This paralleled the agenda of the Albany Trust in London, which was similarly driven by the concerns of various kinds of (mainly heterosexual) counsellors.

Of the heterosexual social workers in Manchester, Colin Harvey was the most vocal; at the previous meeting he'd forecast that after any change in the law the demand on social workers would become intense, although the welfare facilities that existed were already woefully inadequate. At that meeting the Committee had decided in principle that it would be a good idea to convene a meeting of social workers and possibly doctors, 'to examine how help can best be mobilised'. As Allan explained it to Dr Maurice Silverman, a Vice President and a consultant at Blackburn and District Hospital:

> Our last meeting … was concerned mainly with the question of providing help for maladjusted homosexuals. I think the committee has in mind the creation ultimately of a new agency which could advise people not considered to be in need of medical treatment, as well as providing some support for the medical services.[5]

The Albany Trust offered to co-sponsor a conference if another 'problem' area was included – drug dependency lumped in with homosexuality. The June Committee meeting, Martin's first, dug its heels in. It talked about self-help for homosexuals, whereby counselling could best be given by those with first-hand knowledge of the subject. Silverman insisted that only qualified medical professionals could do this kind of work. In the face of these demands, the Committee asserted itself:

> In considering Dr Silverman's fears about homosexuals being counselled by non-medical personnel, the Committee took the view that homosexuality was not a medical problem. It also concluded that the role to be played by Social Workers in making the homosexual condition more tolerable was limited.[6]

Though limited by its acceptance of pseudo-medical terms like 'condition', and of the idea that homosexuals are inherently unhappy through the use of 'tolerable', this is the first of a series of declarations of independence from the 'do-gooders' and an assertion of the Northern values of self-help and self-improvement.

There were to be many ideological conflicts and arguments over strategy within the Lesbian and Gay movements, and the first was over the role of 'professionals' and 'professionalism' in offering support to isolated homosexuals. To Allan and the gay men on the Committee it seemed that the greatest gift that could be given from one homosexual to another was friendship, and the only knowledge needed to support and encourage the insecure came from being homosexual and having experience of gay life. But to doctors especially it seemed obvious that the medical profession knew best. This conflict was to surface in a slightly different form, with the establishment of the counselling organisation, FRIEND, in 1971;* it also became a running argument among the telephone advice services which proliferated from 1973 onwards.

Aims of NWHLRC after 1967

Much of 1967–68 was taken up by the business of getting Esquire Clubs off the ground, as discussed in the previous chapter; this was a comparatively clear, almost self-contained, project. However, the realm of counselling and support led to discussion of the future, more general, aims of the organisation. The most crucial decision was that, unlike the HLRS in London, the NWHLRC actively committed itself to a future. A newsletter went out in April 1968, the first for nearly a year, apologising for the long silence:

> This is not because we have been inactive, but because we have been seeking out new directions for the Campaign† and new ways of providing help and support for the minority with which we are concerned.[7]

* See page 379.

† With a capital 'C' - the first recorded use of the word, as opposed to 'Committee'.

The passing of the 1967 Act rendered its existing publicity, the leaflet *Something You Should Know About* (1965), obsolete. It fell to Martin to draft the next one, *After the Act* (1968). Although modified somewhat by committee, the style is pure Stafford. Within the framework of its time, it gives a clear sense of an organisation gearing up for work. It asserts its respectability with its array of officers brandished like a shield – Chairman, Vice-Chairman, President, three Vice-Presidents* and Secretary – with their MAs, MDs and DScs. It opens:

> After the first Reform Act† in 1967, the Committee, conscious of widespread and desperate problems of isolation, anxiety and guilt, was convinced of the need for a permanent body to advise and help homosexuals and to promote further public education. …
>
> Most people give no serious thought to this subject. They accept the prevalent fallacies that homosexuality is a vice freely chosen‡ and involves merely sordid sexual participation;§ that homosexuals constitute a threat to children; that all homosexuals are effeminate.
>
> PREJUDICE: It is in such misconceptions, rather than in malice, that prejudice is rooted. This prejudice can be dispelled only by enlightenment – preferably through conscious association with homosexual people.[8]

The corollary of being able to know homosexual people is, of course, that homosexual people can be known. This leaflet is the first assertion of the importance of 'coming out' since that of the three undergraduates in the *Spectator* in 1960, as a political act for the benefit of the heterosexual majority, rather than for oneself and one's own mental health:

> FACTS: Homosexuality denotes not a course of action, but the involuntary and usually irrevocable state of being attracted sexually AND EMOTIONALLY towards members of one's own sex rather than to those of the opposite sex. The vast majority of homosexuals are in all other respects ordinary people. That is why so few incur suspicion.[9]

The legal situation may have loosened somewhat, but 'numerous personal problems, induced by social attitudes rather than inherent in the condition

---

* Dr R. W. Burslem, previously a Committee member; Professor Colin Adamson, a psychiatrist; the Dean of Manchester.

† Note the automatic assumption that the 1967 Act is only a stepping stone – not an assumption shared by many. Also the phrase 'Reform Act' echoes the historic struggles for the vote in the nineteenth century.

‡ 'Vice freely chosen' – the inversion is pure eighteenth century, with even biblical echoes.

§ The issue of 'sordid' sexual activity was one which would greatly preoccupy Martin over the next few years, and bring him into conflict with most of the organisation.

itself, continue to confront the homosexual.'*

There is a gradual externalisation of the 'problems', from 'inherent in the condition' to a 'creation of society'. The emphasis on emotions, capitalised, was an important shift in the on-going campaign. Inevitably discussions during the debates on the 1967 Act focussed on what gay men did for sex. However, the development of the campaign into a struggle for equal rights beyond the merely sexual also necessitated defining homosexual women and men as whole people. Not that this view is entirely consistent yet. The first aim of the newly-focused campaign is to provide a counselling service 'for the alleviation of problems arising from the homosexual condition';† the old view of homosexuality as inherently problematic died hard. Attitudes do not change overnight; and in the process of change sometimes a person can hold two contradictory opinions or beliefs simultaneously before they are brought into alignment. And there was no doubt that counselling, however defined, was needed:

> The response to our advertisements in local newspapers reveals an urgent need for such facilities. Fearful that admission of homosexuality will entail rejection, many refrain from consulting friends and relations about their personal problems.
>
> Reluctance to confide in General Practitioners indicates that a panel of sympathetic doctors is essential to help those who feel they need medical advice. There is need for a similar panel of legal advisers also.[10]

Martin Stafford by now was becoming a key figure on the Committee. He had drive, intelligence, articulacy, and he was beginning to formulate both a coherent platform and a strategy. He would be especially important in the moves towards becoming a national organisation. He had recently been appointed Counselling Secretary, although he remembers doing little counselling. One counselling case came very early, before even the advertisements appeared. Allan wrote to Dr Maurice Silverman about the 'client' in April 1967:

> I have been seeing a young homosexual who seemed reasonably well adjusted to his condition and whose main problem seemed to be one of social isolation. He is twenty-one years old, pleasant disposition, well-educated and from a good family. His father is dead and he lives with his mother, who is aware of his condition and is not unsympathetic towards his difficulties. …

---

* Despite the suggestion that it is important for people to know homosexuals, the leaflet fights shy of saying that the North Western Committee is a body of homosexuals.

† This rather contradicts the previous assertion that social attitudes are responsible for the problems.

> A number of sexual encounters recently have failed to lead to the kind of permanent relationship which he is looking for and feels that he desperately needs.
>
> I now find that he has persuaded a GP to refer him to Crumpsall* for aversion therapy. I have made my own views about this very clear while emphasising that I am in no position to give a medical opinion.
>
> He has asked me to consult a medical member of the committee about it, and I should be most grateful for any help or advice.[11]

Silverman's advice was not what Allan wanted to hear:

> It would be extraordinarily difficult, if not impossible, to draw any line between homosexuals 'not considered to be in need of medical treatment' and others who are seeking help or advice, … and I do not think I would be in favour of non-medical personnel … trying to do this.
>
> I am by no means against utilising aversion therapy in appropriate problems. The problem, as always, is the expert assessment of the individual case.[12]

Not for the last time, homosexuals discovered that if they wanted a thing done according to their beliefs, they were going to have to do it themselves. So Allan drafted Martin in, as someone nearer the boy's age:

> He was three or four years older than I was, and at that time he was considering undergoing a course of aversion therapy. Allan was very unhappy about this. We told him it wasn't really the answer. … You give people either nausea or electric shocks. They had nausea-inducing drugs, so that you looked at attractive guys, and then if you find them attractive you're given an electric shock. And then you're encouraged to look at girls, and then you don't get a shock. It was all very very crude. …
>
> I didn't counsel a lot of people, though I did counsel this particular fellow. I can remember him perfectly well. And I suppose since we did discourage him from having aversion therapy, we were successful. [13]

The mere fact of meeting up with other homosexuals seems to have been enough to discourage the troubled boy from aversion therapy. He came to Committee meetings, and never said a word. It was enough comfort to him to sit in the presence of other homosexuals and know what was going on. However, the experience of this man and others like him prompted the committee to pass a resolution:

> Concern was expressed at the continued use of aversion therapy as a 'treatment' for homosexuals. It was agreed that so long as the treatment

---

* Crumpsall Infirmary in North Manchester grew out of the old workhouse under the Poor Laws, and by this time had beds for 600 people with mental health issues. It was prominent in the use of ECT and drug therapy for behaviour modification.

> was undertaken voluntarily it was a matter for the individual, but that it became highly objectionable when the treatment became compulsory as the result of a court order.[14]

The battle to suppress the use of aversion therapy, and, beyond that, to get psychiatrists to realise that homosexuality was not an illness, was one of the major CHE campaigns* of the 1970s, and one which was of deep personal significance for many who had fallen into the hands of shrinks before they found their self-respect and joined CHE. Perhaps only the education campaign aroused more passion, as all members had experienced sex education at school, or the lack of it, and knew how deeply it stigmatised vulnerable gay adolescents.

First adverts

The Committee decided in early October to put ads in selected local weekly papers, 'to find out how great was the need for a counselling service, and a small case committee was elected to deal with people with homosexual problems.'[15] Nowadays, with the prevalence of the internet and the decline of print journalism, it is difficult to remember the sheer power which local papers wielded until the 1980s, the size of the readership, the eagerness with which they were bought and read, the reliance on them for communication.† It was the only way to reach like-minded people, apart from word of mouth. Word of mouth largely depended on having at least one meeting-place where homosexuals actually talked to each other, which meant larger towns. In the sticks it was impossible.

The North Western Committee didn't have a lot of money for advertising, since there was no formal subscription system, and the Committee was still purely dependant on donations. So it was only possible to place two- or three-line ads in the Personals – a shilling spent here, half-a-crown there, with the occasional foray into an extended series.

The first ad appeared in *The Chronicle (Oldham and District)* on 23 October 1967, for one week only:[16] 'Have you a homosexual problem? Ring Bolton 62783‡ or Manchester 832 5253.'§ It was followed by a rare display advert in

---

* The Gay Liberation Front had a parallel campaign.

† Of the newspapers used here, for example, *Bury Times* had a circulation of 28,000 out of a population of 150,000; *Bolton Journal* 94,000 out of a 200,000 population. In 2011 they could muster less than half these figures. Today most local newspapers are web-based, and count their circulation in terms of hits, rather than copies sold.

‡ Allan Horsfall's number.

§ Diocesan Board of Social Responsibility – Colin Harvey. Later a third number, Burscough 2001, was added. It belonged to Rev. Alun Williams, Committee member and

the University's *Manchester Independent* on 24 October; unusually for these ads, the word 'homosexuality' screams out loud and clear, centred and in bold type. This was followed by the *Bury Times* on 28 October,[17] again a one-off. Then in quick succession there were the *Rossendale Free Press*,[18] a month of repeated adverts in South Lancashire Newspapers' *Reporter* Series,[19] the Tillotson group of *Journal* newspapers,[20] and the *Stockport Express*.[21]* One of the reasons that advertising was still strictly confined to the Greater Manchester area at this stage was because the Albany Trust was still advertising nationally. In 1967–8 there was still a certain amount of deference to the senior organisation.

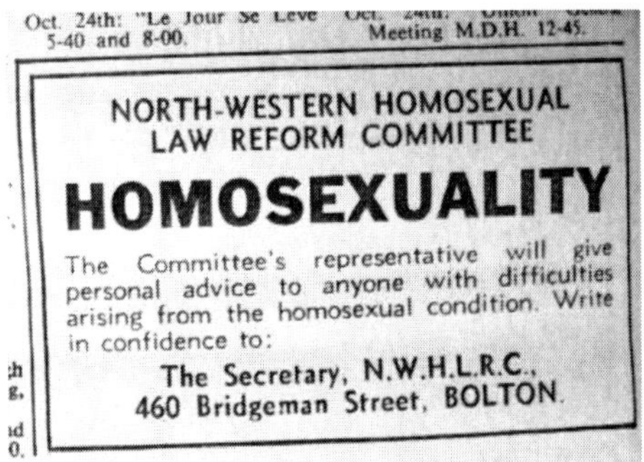

33. NWHLRC advert in the *Manchester Independent*, 24 October 1967

The NWHLRC adverts were not exactly eye-catching, sandwiched in between the many pages of used car sales, estate agents, and situations vacant. It was not always clear from the wording of the advert exactly what was on offer. Paradoxically, the people who had the confidence to respond to a newspaper advertisement were not the kind of people who defined themselves as having a 'homosexual problem'. They wanted involvement in a different way:

> On the whole … they didn't want counselling. …Certainly the kind of people who were willing to get involved didn't need counselling, they were reasonably confident about being homosexual, and wanted an opportunity to meet others. Possibly for sexual encounters but also for social encounters and whatever led on from that.[22]

In April 1968 supporters read in the latest *Bulletin*:

> The response to these [adverts] was immediate and universal, so much so that we had to deliberately limit the advertising in order not to be

---

later a vice president. Although he was Counselling Secretary, Martin's number could not appear because he and Paul did not have a phone.

* The *Stockport Advertiser* was also on the list of papers to be used, but nothing appeared in this period, suggesting that it was the first of many papers to refuse gay ads.

> overwhelmed. The picture which emerged was one of widespread anxiety, despair and isolation. …
>
> There is some evidence that the homosexual in this country has become a little more relaxed and a little less apprehensive since the law was changed last year. The time is ripe for a move into more congenial surroundings, but this cannot take place unless the facilities exist and are known to be available.[23]

'Sympathetic' doctors were also seen as a priority. Not necessarily because they knew better than homosexuals themselves, but because everybody had to go and see a doctor at some time, and many had had very bad experiences, especially if it involved having to 'come out'. Many were scared that if they went to their family doctor, the rest of the family would find out. Rules of confidentiality were not nearly so strictly enforced in the 1960s and 70s. Martin envisaged a network of sympathetic medics across the country forming doctors' panels. He wrote to the medical journals to try to recruit them. *The Lancet* quoted from his letter:

> Among those who approach us with problems arising from the homosexual condition are a few who desire advice from a doctor but are reluctant to consult their own G.P.s, either because of their association with the family or because they fear that revelation of their homosexuality would meet with an unsympathetic reaction. Accordingly we are seeking to contact G.P.s in all areas of the U.K. whose attitude towards homosexuality is tolerant and informed. … Their services would be required only very infrequently; it is primarily a matter of knowing they are there when required.[24]

This, coupled with an article in *The Guardian* which picked up on the *Lancet* piece, resulted in a response from perhaps a score of doctors, not enough for a network and too scattered for a panel. But many joined CHE because they were themselves gay, and in years to come some local groups would find a GP among their numbers to whom other members could turn.

But greater far than the need for counselling or doctors was the need for 'more congenial surroundings', as the *Bulletin* said. This is reflected in the struggle for Esquire Clubs already chronicled, and in the second aim listed in *After the Act*:

> To support the inauguration of new SOCIAL CENTRES where homosexuals and others can meet in congenial surroundings. … We would support the provision of facilities to meet the social and cultural needs of the homosexual, so that he may develop more stable personal relationships.* The present inadequacy may well account for some of the public

---

* 'More stable' and 'depravity' are words which again indicate the hand of Martin Stafford.

> soliciting which results from sheer desperation and loneliness rather than depravity.[25]

This moral agenda, the idea that improved conditions would lead to 'better' behaviour and 'better' homosexuals, with monogamous aspirations akin to heterosexual marriage, was current for many years in the campaign for equality, although most campaigners could see from personal experience that improved facilities or indeed stable relationships did not necessarily mean the end of cottaging or casual sex. Indeed, many long-term gay couples attribute their longevity to having degrees of openness in their relationships. There was a kind of hypocrisy of normality in the PR. Nevertheless, the prospect, though unrealistic, was an attractive one to liberal heterosexual supporters.

The third aim of the North Western Committee was the one which would lead furthest:

> To eliminate prejudice directed against homosexuals, and to assert that the homosexual has an equal right to self-fulfilment, and can make an equally positive contribution in our common quest for the betterment of society and the happiness of all.[26]

This self-conscious echo of the preamble to the American Declaration of Independence, and commitment to the pursuit of happiness as a universal right was a further milestone on the road to equality. Beyond the limited issue of legal sexual rights, it would lead into the fields of employment, housing, civil contract, and access to goods and services. There is a direct line of descent from this modest pamphlet to the full-blown equalities legislation of the early twenty-first century. The leaflet closed with an appeal for donations:

> We have no paid staff and all work undertaken by officers and members of the committee is voluntary. Nevertheless the unavoidable expenses of promoting and making effective a campaign and service of this kind have proved far too great for our present resources to bear. We have no Government grant, nor any support from the large charitable foundations. We are, and always have been, dependent on the generosity of our supporters. … Donations of any amount will be most welcome.
>
> If you would like to help us or us to help you …[27]

With only the resources to print the one leaflet, the Committee somehow had to combine an appeal to reason among the powers-that-be, give notice of its existence and agenda to social service providers, and both recruit from and offer help to a homosexual readership. Initially they printed ten thousand, and duly circulated them to local Labour parties, doctors and priests, their supporters and local bars and clubs. A few brave souls left copies in libraries and, surreptitiously, on buses.

Through 1967–8, the Committee was essentially playing a numbers game, gathering supporters who would provide both the management and the clientele for the clubs once they got off the ground. There was no membership system, no formally arranged meetings beyond those of the North Western Committee itself.

Apart from talking about Esquire Clubs, the Committee monitored the effects of the 1967 Act. To their surprise and consternation, they found that police activity was increasing rather than diminishing, and more cases came before magistrates that would previously have gone to Assizes. The twelve men who came to trial in Sale did so months after the Act became law.* The Committee noted its concern, but didn't suggest any further action; there was not much they could do.

Police raids on correspondence clubs

One way in which the police went trawling for evidence for 'sex crimes' was through raiding the offices of 'correspondence clubs'. Suspects were normally rounded up on the basis of appearing in the address book of someone who had been arrested for cottaging. Alternatively, the police might have found actual correspondence. However, 'correspondence clubs' could lead to the start of a chain of cases without an initial incident to set off the round-up.

When the smiling Bernard Dodd traipsed over to Bradford in 1965 to confront Myers Haines,† Haines was running an isolated effort. But by 1968 there were a number of these pen pal clubs run for commercial gain all over the country, more than the Committee could check out. These operated by subscription, in exchange for which members would get the addresses of other members, supposedly with the object of becoming pen-pals but really to make sexual contact. Members might also buy pornography from the facilitators of these clubs. In August 1968 Antony Grey wrote to Allan Horsfall that several people had been in touch with the Albany Trust over one such police trawl:

> We have had a half a dozen cases within the last two months of people who have been prosecuted or questioned by the police in connection with their membership of the 'Gayplume Pen Pals Club'. The police seem to be going to quite extraordinary lengths in questioning people – some of them elderly – about letters which they wrote to other members of this organisation as long as 18 months ago. I really do think that such things are extremely risky unless administered with the utmost discretion, and even then the position would appear to be doubtful, since one cannot control what individuals are foolish enough to put into their letters.[28]

---

* See page 153.

† See page 138.

On the strength of this, the Committee agreed that supporters should be warned of the dangers of joining such clubs, and Allan wrote back to assure Grey that they had no intention of 'going into the pen pals business'. Despite this, the Committee would 'go into the pen pals business' within eighteen months, with trepidation, but convinced that there was a real need for it as a way of ending isolation.

Bulletins now became more regular. They had appeared from May 1965 for supporters from time to time, mainly alerting people to a possible need to write to their MPs when parliamentary activity was in the offing. These early *Bulletins* were usually four sides of duplicated foolscap* paper. In April 1968 they started appearing again after an absence of nearly a year. Most of the *Bulletins* for the rest of that year were taken up with Esquire Clubs, as were the Committee meetings.

Paul Temperton

A new name appeared on the minutes of the meeting of 28 June 1968, held at the Rockingham Club. It was Paul Temperton, three months past his nineteenth birthday. Paul was a softly-spoken, smooth-faced young man with a conciliatory manner and a talent for playing the organ. He had left school at fifteen, and was living alone in a bed-sitter in Chorlton-cum-Hardy. He'd been working for two years in an advertising agency, Royd's, whose biggest customer was Beecham's Pills. This experience was to come in extremely handy when it came to developing a national CHE. Paul had a political background, but not a party-political one – the British Humanist Association, the Manchester Non-Violent Action Group, NCCL, the Anti-Apartheid movement.

Paul was in the process of developing a political awareness, as well as a growing awareness of his sexuality. Like Martin, he came into CHE and gay politics with little or no sexual experience and no knowledge of a gay 'scene':

> I remember talking about Civil Liberties … I'd read … in *The Guardian*, about outrageous cases of injustice, and I'd get very steamed up about them over the dinner table. And my mother said, 'Well, life isn't fair,' or words to that effect. I did have this very strong sense of injustice about things. I was certainly aware of the debate about gay law reform, but I hadn't been following it closely. … I had come to a growing realisation that I was gay, and that the state of affairs in the world, not just the legal situation, but more generally, was unsatisfactory. …
>
> I was hinting it [that I was gay] to one or two close friends, without going into any details. I think I allowed it to be rather obvious in some

* 203 x 330 mm, rarely used now.

> cases. There was one young chap that was at university with my elder brother, that I was quite fond of. He must have realised that I fancied him, but … it was a completely unrequited love. … I wasn't trying to hide the fact that I was gay, I just wasn't going around talking about it in explicit terms.[29]

34. Paul Temperton in 1973

Paul's route to CHE was via the NCCL. He went to a public meeting in 1967:

> It wasn't specifically about gay rights, it was about civil liberties generally. Tony Smythe, the general secretary [of NCCL], came, and gay rights was, I think, one of the things mentioned at the meeting. … Somebody said at the NCCL meeting, 'There is a meeting of the North West Committee.'[30]

To go along to a Homosexual Law Reform meeting was a very scary experience. Paul said:

> It was almost like a coming out, because you had the feeling that it was going to put a label on you if you were seen going in and out of the meeting. I went along with enormous trepidation, not knowing what to expect at all. And I think Martin sort of pounced on me when I turned up, and introduced himself to me, and I suppose if he hadn't have done, I might have gone away and never come back again.[31]

Martin was only a few months older than Paul, and they were both by several years the youngest people at the meeting. Martin was the intellectual, the leaflet writer, with all the arguments for homosexual equality at his fingertips. He was talkative, persuasive and knowledgeable, unlike the shy new boy Paul. Martin was at University studying Philosophy while Paul had left school after O Levels. They were both sexually and emotionally inexperienced, and they were both looking for a relationship.

It is not surprising that they became an item very quickly, or that Martin was the dominant force at the start. He introduced Paul to books about homosexuality, gave him a crash course in gay politics. Paul moved in with Martin, at Martin's parents' house:

> My mother was quite happy to let Paul move in with me. My mother liked Paul, and I think she took the pragmatic view that it was far better to have this sort of arrangement. Given that things were quite likely to happen anyway at my age in any case, it was better that they happened in an environment over which she exercised control.[32]

This appears not to have been discussed with Martin's father, who, despite the activity at the house, didn't discover his son was gay until 1972.

They were to stay here for just over two years before striking out to a flat of their own in Whalley Range. It is one of the more striking facts of the early days of CHE that the growth into a national organisation was plotted and steered by two youngsters who were themselves 'illegal', from the parental home of one of them.

Sex and love are the elephants in the room in most discussions of lesbian and gay politics. Many people over the years were to come to CHE in search of sex, and, despite official playing down of this aspect, many people found what they were looking for. Members formed relationships with others they met in CHE, at local groups or at national meetings, and many of these became long term partnerships, surviving thirty years or more. At conferences and National Councils some delegates would always stumble drunkenly into bed with each other after the disco, and orgies were a feature of at least some gatherings; a whispered word of a time and a hotel room number being enough to set the ball rolling. All of these things created positive dynamics, binding people together within the organisation, and generating goodwill towards it. Conversely, if there was a falling out, it could on occasion become extremely destructive towards the organisation. The personal was political in more senses than one.

Their relationship gave Martin and Paul the motivation to do something about the absurd legal situation, and the energy and mutual support to bring those tenets into their own lives. Martin had already realised the strategic importance of publicly identifying as homosexual, as well as telling friends and family at an early age, and Paul quickly took this on in his own life:

> There we were, both under 21, which at the time was illegal, and it seemed completely preposterous, absurd that … what we were doing could be deemed even theoretically to be against the law. But more than that, Martin himself must have politicised me a great deal, because I'd never come into contact with any explicitly gay person before. I obviously got straight from him the idea that, really, gay people needed to come out, although we

> didn't use that phrase at the time. That came along later. But to declare oneself as far as possible, to one's family, maybe, or to close friends, because if lots of gay people didn't do that, we would never get anywhere. … My mother was – not entirely unsympathetic, but just thought that it was going to make life very difficult. In unspecified ways. …
>
> With my brother, it was about the time he got married, and I made a bit of a fuss about asking Martin to come with me to the wedding. And my brother wasn't having any of it, and in the end I didn't. So there was a bit of friction about that. I think in retrospect I was probably being unreasonable. At the time I expected people to go too far too soon … it was a bit too revolutionary for them at that time.[33]

For Martin, emotionally conservative and with a liking for stability and order, the relationship, extremely intense at least at the start, confirmed his belief that what homosexuals wanted and needed was lifetime partnerships, and that the purpose of law reform was to make these more possible. This in turn would pave the way for more general acceptance in society, when the world saw that homosexuals were just like anyone else save in the small matter of sexual preference.

He was both protective of his relationship and insistent it was acknowledged. In his letter cancelling his subscription to the Albany Trust, he wrote touchingly to Antony Grey about it, and its importance:

> I am not lonely any more. Eighteen months ago I met Paul, who is six months younger than I am … after we had known each other for two months he came to live with me at my parents' house. We were going to share a larger flat, but it is difficult finding satisfactory unfurnished flats, and my mother thought we might as well live at home. Since I met Paul I have been much happier, but I still remember how lonely I used to be in my first year at University.[34]

He and Paul travelled everywhere together, to meetings and conferences, and Martin was quick to chide those other gay people and organisations that did not seem to recognise it. When Ike Cowen invited him to a conference in York in 1970, he wrote back, 'I was rather surprised that I was invited but Paul was not; it is unlikely that one of us would attend without the other.'[35] To which Ike hastily replied that of course Paul was welcome.

Most of 1968 was taken up with Esquire Clubs, in which Paul and Martin played little part, but there were two unintended consequences of the Clubs project. Firstly, there were moves, almost unconscious and certainly not thought through, towards a membership system with regular subscriptions. In the *Bulletin* of January 1966, the Committee had expressly ruled this out, but with the proviso that 'only those who have subscribed a minimum of ten shillings [50p] will be eligible to vote at annual general meetings.'[36] Since the NWHLRC had no constitution and no structure at this stage, nor indeed had even discussed one, it is hard to see where an AGM would have fitted in with the organisation. The *Bulletin* often concluded with an appeal to keep the money coming rolling in, to continue the work of public education, but it did not, and the *Bulletin* of January 1969 reported:

35. Ike Cowen in 2002

> Perhaps not unnaturally, our financial support has dwindled since it became apparent that the law would be changed. The total response to our last appeal amounted to a little over eight pounds. Accordingly we have decided that in future it will only be possible to forward bulletins and other publications to subscribing supporters. The subscription has been fixed at ten shillings per annum, which we hope will at least provide enough to keep the Committee in existence.[37]

It was a modest sum, and at this stage financed modest aims. However, by the summer it had built up into a usable war chest.

Esquire had subscribers too, some 300, and when it became clear by the end of 1969 that no immediate club was in the offing, people were offered instead automatic subs to the North Western Committee for a year, until something more concrete turned up. Only forty people took this up, but it all swelled the numbers. It also became increasingly difficult to think in terms of anything other than memberships.

Committee for Homosexual Equality

There was also the small matter of what to call the Committee, since the HLRS and Antony Grey were extremely agitated about all the publicity over clubs that the Northerners were getting. Once it was clear that the Albany

Trust and the HLRS were not going to support the clubs it became a matter of urgency to put some clear blue water between the two organisations. The HLRS Chairman, C. H. Rolph, urged this on his opposite number, Colin Harvey:

> Those of us who have borne the brunt of the law reform campaign and are still concerned to improve the position of homosexuals in society, feel very strongly that the North Western Committee's current preoccupations and activities are quite inappropriate to its name, and that if it wishes to continue its existence as a 'law reform committee' it ought to confine its attentions to the legal aspects and leave *social* developments to 'Esquire' or to some other more socially orientated body.[38]

The patronising assumption that all the campaigning work had been done in London and somehow the Mancunians were riding irresponsibly on the back of it would have irritated Allan Horsfall intensely. If the Southerners were getting fed up with the Mancunians, the feeling was mutual:

> We had come to see that law reform, even if it had been achieved in total, which was far from the case at that point, was anyway not by any means the whole story. And we wanted to make that an explicit radical stand. To sort of show that we weren't going to go along with Antony Grey and his very gradualist, apologetic approach, we felt we didn't have anything to apologise for, and we were going to stand up and be counted really.[39]

By February 1969 Horsfall reported to Grey that he was canvassing opinions about possible new names, and he was able to report, in a PS which reads like a casual aside, 'From 1st April we shall be known as the Committee for Homosexual Equality,'[40] to which Grey replied that he liked the name and applauded the objects.

Not everyone was so enthusiastic. The Bishop of Middleton, Ted Wickham, had his doubts, which had to be taken very seriously since he was still hosting committee meetings in Salford. These doubts were not about the basic principles, but whether the Committee knew what it was doing:

> Is the change of name the proposal of a national organisation of which the NW Committee is simply a local expression, or does the proposal stem from our committee? I also wonder whether the new name would connote in the public mind the kind of objectives you set out. … Certainly 'equality' is not a very useful concept unless it is spelt out in specifics that can be embodied or defended in law. I suggest you should be very careful in changing the name.[41]

The phrase 'embodied or defended in law' shows that the Bishop is still thinking in terms of legal action, where the committee had already gone some way beyond that. As Allan explained:

> While we shall be working towards equality in law for homosexuals ... we shall also be working for equality in such non-legal matters as housing, employment, mortgages, hospital visiting rights, etc. This Committee is entirely autonomous, and the decision is entirely our own, but it will help to avoid confusion between the Homosexual Law Reform Society and this Committee.[42]

Wickham returned with another name suggestion – Committee for the Defence of Homosexual Rights. He argued 'Equality – in some senses of the word at least – is not possible in the nature of things.' This is an interesting philosophical argument which might have merited development on both sides; however, it was too late, Allan told him. The Committee had agreed the name change on 14 March.*

The new letterhead was in use by May, and the name change seems to have given CHE (as it now was) a new rush of energy. The August 1969 *Bulletin*, the first under the new name, reported:

> We feel that the old North-Western Homosexual Law Reform Committee did useful work in its time, but it was always looked on in some quarters as an appendage of the Homosexual Reform Society [*sic*], which of course it never was. Now, at a time when the Homosexual Law Reform Society remains silent, and the Albany Trust moves into the field of drug addiction and transvestism, we feel that there is a need for a new national body to concentrate exclusively on the problems of the homosexual, both in pressing for further improvements in the law and seeking solutions in the many areas – other than the law – where homosexuals face discrimination and persecution.[43]

To pursue these aims, the Committee set up further sub-groups, for social, medical and legal issues, plus one for literature. The suggested donation† was raised to £1, to employ a press cuttings bureau. A 'limited' advertising campaign was to start to attract new supporters, and:

> There will in future be regular meetings open to all subscribers. These will be held in Manchester for the time being, but we are looking at holding meetings elsewhere or setting up local committees in various areas.[44]

The use of the phrase 'Homosexual Equality', and the removal of the words 'Law Reform', are explicitly acknowledged here as taking the concept of gay rights a step beyond the narrow confines of the old HLRS-inspired remit. It acknowledges that there are vast areas in which discrimination follows from sexual preference, and that 'equality' may have multiple meanings. The North Western Committee had already attracted casework relating to the medical

---

* This however is not recorded in the Minutes.

† Fixed at 50p since January 1966.

profession, and to discrimination by employers. They were only too aware of how the police behaved and how the legal system treated gay men and lesbians. All had experience of the inadequacies of sex education, in the home and at school. Discrimination in housing was soon added to the list. And under the influence of Martin Stafford, the whole question of legal recognition of homosexual relationships would soon be open for discussion. It was a piecemeal development, and for many the equalisation of the Age of Consent remained the core objective, but the elements were gradually being assembled to create a platform for demands for total equality throughout society, only a few of which were reflected in the explicit aims expounded in the literature CHE put out.

The 'hardworking Committee' had a new chairman. Heterosexual Colin Harvey had left in the summer of 1968, moved to Glasgow, and by Autumn 1969 was busy setting up with Ian Dunn the Scottish equivalent of CHE, the Scottish Minorities Group (SMG). In his place, rather reluctantly, came Allan's partner, Harold Pollard, now retired from schoolmastering.

Meetings were now in earnest. Allan was still secretary,* but the bulk of the work to set up 'local committees' was done by Martin and Paul. The key to it was advertising, and now Paul's special expertise as an advertising agency employee came in handy. In the summer of 1969 he placed the first national adverts, in magazines such as the *Spectator* and papers such as *The Observer*. The *Spectator* notice, just three lines in the personal columns, marked a step forward, in that the word 'problem' was dropped: 'Committee for Homosexual Equality invites enquiries. Write BCM/Box 859 London WC1.'†[45]

This appeared for four weeks, at a cost of £1/4s (£1.20) per insertion. It was hardly an advert to leap out of the page at a reader, but nevertheless got twenty replies a week. CHE opened a BCM box to receive the expected deluge of enquiries, since it would be Martin and Paul handling the replies, and Martin did not want large numbers of letters pouring through his parents' letterbox. Soon the BCM number was used for all kinds of correspondence, and appeared on the letterhead. The days of operating out of Allan's house were over. Martin remembers the morning post:

> Any correspondence would go to the BCM Box number, in London, and every morning a big envelope, varying in size depending on how much mail there was, would come through our door in Bredbury with the letters that needed to be answered.[46]

---

* When Harold Pollard resigned as Chairman in April 1970, Allan Horsfall became Chair, and Paul Temperton succeeded him as Secretary. When Allan had a massive heart attack in May, the weight of all the organisation fell on Paul and Martin.

† The wording reflects the growing assertiveness of the organisation. By July 1970 the ads say, 'HOMOSEXUALS. FIGHT prejudice, join local and university groups.'

Expansion of membership

The effect of this advertising was to boost middle-class representation in the organisation, since the readership of these publications was itself middle class. More importantly, it was spread all over the country. As enquiries built up, it became important to offer subscribers – still not members – something concrete for their money, and this led to a commitment to produce a regular *Bulletin* on a monthly basis. The new-style *Bulletin* was a mixture of news and comment on the organisation, leavened by book reviews by Paul, Allan or Martin. They ran it off in the Bishop of Middleton's office in Blackfriars Road, Salford. Envelopes were stuffed and addressed by hand in Martin and Paul's home, a task which became increasingly arduous as the membership expanded to several hundred.

36. Former Bishop of Middleton's office, 27 Blackfriars Road, Salford

The confidence induced by expansion can be seen in a letter Allan Horsfall wrote to *Peace News* in November 1969. The story started with *Private Eye*, in an article of 7 November headed 'Poove Power':

> The hour is past, loves, for parliamentary agitation. The struggle for what we want must now be fought for on the streets.
>
> If you see a heterosexual grabbing your job or your house or your boyfriend, KILL HIM with a look; HIT HIM with your handbag; or even write nasty words on his car with your lipstick. CUT HIM DEAD and walk away. …

> Mass Mince-in in Hyde Park. We will all assemble at the Dilly and then troll off en masse to Hyde Park where we will all lie down on the grass. Then the boys in Blue will come and carry us off in their big strong arms. Whoopee! Don't be late. (If it's a rainy day we'll all stay at home and get on with some things around the house.)[47]

It's a moot point just how homophobic this might be. In a bizarre way it foreshadows the Gay Liberation Front. *Private Eye* had a good record for publishing gay-themed advertisements, including a regular one for the Albany Trust and for the lesbian magazine *Arena 3*, which had appeared since 1963. It was, after all, a satirical magazine, and this piece, to our more relaxed eyes, is no more scabrous than many another, and even in a way affectionate. On the other hand, editor Richard Ingrams was personally notoriously homophobic, and arguably minority groups were entitled to different treatment from that meted out to Government ministers. Certainly 'John Ball', who had a regular column in *Peace News*, took the latter view, and castigated *Private Eye*:

> I'm not homosexual. But some of the people I most respect, admire and like are, and a brutal and pointless attack like this sickens me. It isn't just that it will hurt homosexual readers who have done *Private Eye* no harm – after all, homosexuals have to get pretty well inured to that kind of thing. What *Private Eye* is helping to do is to substitute for the old incomprehending intolerance an equally incomprehending sneering 'tolerance'. As if anyone had the right to 'tolerate' what a neighbour chooses to get up to sexually.[48]

This gave Allan Horsfall the perfect opportunity to plug the newly militant Committee:

> The emergence in this country – which John Ball envisages – of a movement fighting to establish and defend homosexual civil rights has already taken place. We are working to establish regional and local committees which will be part vigilante, part crusading and part social. At the moment we are short of people willing to act as convenors … and we should be pleased to hear from any *Peace News* readers who feel they can assist in this way.[49]

This indicates that the idea of local groups was crystallising well before any individual groups were started in CHE. In contrast to groups that others, such as Night Out, had set up, CHE groups were to combine social and political activity. The use of the phrase 'local committees' is still a hangover from the HLRS, but it was not long before the advertising man Paul Temperton realised that it was hardly attractive: 'groups' became the favoured alternative.

According to the *Bulletin* of November 1969, the response to adverts was good in quality – everyone wanted to join local groups – but poor in quantity. Potential convenors for local groups were too few, and badly distributed. The committee decided to continue advertising to get a better geographic scatter.

A strategy began to emerge. Respondents would be recruited nationally, and asked whether they would like to join a local group in their area. When they had agreed to this in sufficient numbers, and there was a cluster in one part of the country with a convenor willing and competent to organise them and invite them to a meeting, their names would be forwarded to him or her, and an advertisement placed in one or more local papers. Convenors would decide where to hold the meeting (usually in the early days at their own house or flat) and send out invitations to those on their mailing lists. It needed comparatively few people, sometimes only half a dozen, to set a new group in motion.

Difficulties with placing adverts

In practice this scheme of things would have certain weaknesses. For a start, though many local papers would accept advertisements, many would not. Throughout the first five years of CHE, Paul would face a constant battle to get insertions into the local press. Acceptance was entirely on the whim of a paper's business or advertising manager. For example, the *Bath and Wilts Evening Chronicle* took advertisements in June 1970, but a year later, J. R. Simonds, Classified Sales Manager, wrote almost apologetically, 'Thank you for sending us your advertisement for the North Somerset Weekly Group. Unfortunately it is now not the policy of this newspaper to accept advertisements such as yours.'[50] He had been overruled by a new evangelical Christian boss.

Again, in November 1969, Allan approached the *Oxford Mail* to advertise. The advertising manager, E. D. Dore, wrote back, 'I would be grateful if you could let me know the purpose of this advertisement and the aims of the committee.' Allan sent a copy of the *After the Act* leaflet and explained, 'The purpose of the proposed advert is to gather sufficient support in Oxford to set up a local committee.' There was no response, and two months later Allan sent a polite nudge to Mr Dore. Back came the familiar response, 'I regret that we are unable to accept your advertisement for publication in our newspapers.'[51] And yet just over a year later there was a reversal of the decision, no reason given but gratefully accepted, and no questions: 'Homosexual Equality Group to be established in Oxford.' This appeared in April 1971, but then, after it appeared, there were again rejections as renewals were turned down:

> It was not realised at the time [we accepted the ads] that you were using an accommodation address in London, which is of course a realistic thing to do. But I must point out that it is the policy of this paper not to publish advertisements with accommodation addresses, but rather if necessary advertisers should use the newspaper's own box number facility.[52]

Mr Dore amended the ad and charged 20p for forwarding the replies, on a one-off basis. However, fear of breaches of confidentiality at the paper prevented CHE from placing any more adverts there.

The most common newspaper strategy was to ignore letters, in which case Paul would send a gentle reminder and a repeat request three months later. This too might be ignored, in which case there was little more that could be done. Most commonly, the explanation would be that 'ours is a family newspaper'. In late 1969 an offer from Norwich to convene a local group seemed promising, but the *East Anglian Daily Times and Evening Star*, *Eastern Counties Newspapers*, and *Southend News Review* all refused to take ads. The January 1970 *Bulletin* commented wryly:

> One wonders – and doubts – whether it ever occurs to these people that homosexuality is often a matter of family concern, or whether their regard for their readers' delicacy prevents them reporting local court cases involving homosexuals.[53]

Usually when refusal came, it was bald, no reasons given. V. N. Brooks, Advertising Manager of the *Bucks Herald* series: 'We regret that it is the policy of this newspaper not to accept it [the advert] for publication.'[54] To which Paul responded, sending as usual some CHE literature:

> As we now have an organiser for our proposed Chilterns Group we are anxious to advertise as widely as possible in the area, and to be denied access to your readers is a serious handicap to the development of this group.[55]

There was no reply, despite several prods.

General Manager Alan Elliott of the *Waltham Forest Guardian* series: 'After due consideration I regret to inform you that we are unable to accept your advertisement.'[56] Again, Paul followed it up:

> This is most surprising in view of the sympathetic editorial coverage which you were kind enough to give to the group.* The group cannot develop unless we are able to advertise its existence locally, and therefore the success or otherwise of the venture depends to a considerable extent on the co-operation of the local newspaper.[57]

Again, no reply. And so it goes on. *South Wales Evening Post*, *Croydon Advertiser*, *Shropshire Journal*, etc. Other refusals were not so polite. J. Carr, advertising manager of the *Billington Express* and the *Stockton Express* simply returned the advertisement ['Committee for Homosexual Equality seeks to establish Teesside group'] with a hand-written note scrawled across it, 'I have no intention of accepting any such advertisement.'[58]

---

* Waltham Forest CHE is covered in Chapter Five.

These refusals could inhibit development for years. In Cumberland both local papers turned down ads, and Cumbria CHE did not properly get off the ground till 1974, despite having had a convenor ready to start a group for nearly two years.

In April 1973, trying to put an ad in the *Lancashire Evening Post*, Paul walked into a local row. Barry Askew, the editor, wrote to him:

> You will be interested to know that I am currently in correspondence with your Preston chairman, demanding from him an apology for accusations in a recent letter that I was guilty of suppressing information about the Campaign for Homosexual Equality organisation. I am still awaiting his apology. (13 days after letter)
>
> So far as advertisements are concerned it may well be true that we do not move quite so quickly from the position of a respectable, circumspect family newspaper as some of the other publications you have listed. We shall continue to exercise discretion.[59]

In other words, 'no ads'. Which rather proved the Preston chairman's point.

There were interesting variations on the 'refusal' theme, and sometimes there was compromise. When Liverpool CHE was trying to attract more women, Paul tried to place an advert in the *Liverpool Echo* which read 'LESBIANS: You can now join an established Liverpool group for homosexual women and men',[60] Back came the reply from A. H. Draper, Advertising Control Manager, 'We feel that the word 'lesbians' would cause offence to some of our readers; consequently we would require the advertisement to be reworded'.[61] Paul Temperton again:

> I must say I cannot see why the word 'lesbians' is any more likely to cause offence than the word 'homosexuals', but if that is your policy I am quite willing for the advertisement to be reworded.[62]

Substituting 'homosexuals' rather undermined the point of appealing to women.

Mr P. E. R. Cutter of the *Stafford Newsletter* objected to the word 'socials'. The advert was to have read, 'Homosexual women and men* join the Campaign for Homosexual Equality. Stoke-on-Trent local group now meets regularly for socials/informal discussion and political action.'

But Cutter, who had evidently read the leaflet accompanying the ad quite carefully, ruled, 'Referring to section (e) of the paragraph headed 'The Law' in the leaflet you sent to me, I must insist that you remove the word 'socials' from the advertisement.'[63] This was a new response, but Paul took out the offending word, and offered only discussion and political action instead.

---

* Note the order 'women and men'; by 1972 the influence of feminism was being felt in Head Office, largely the work of EC Member Liz Stanley.

In July 1971 the London *Evening Standard* was equally cautious about socials, presumably on the same unspoken assumption that get-togethers were purely for the purpose of men picking each other up. The advertising manager, C. R. Shrewsbury, wanted a list of places where the socials were held, so that he could check them out. Paul replied that it was difficult to give the information, since there were now so many that he couldn't keep up with them. However, the Chairman of the London Co-ordinating Committee, Tony Ryde, went to see Mr Shrewsbury, and must have reassured him, because the advertisements appeared in August, at a cost of £9.

In the case of the *North East Evening Gazette* advertisements were meant to appear in October 1970. Paul heard nothing, so wrote back on the assumption that the paper had refused them and was simply being rude. An aggrieved T. F. Cassidy replied, of course they had appeared, and then helpfully suggested why they might not have had a reply. Maybe there was no call for it; maybe Teesside homosexuals were shy; maybe there wasn't enough information; maybe the ad wasn't large enough, or hadn't appeared often enough.

An apologetic Paul wrote back that they had received one reply after his previous letter, and hoped for more:

> We are finding that there are inexplicable differences between the levels of response in different parts of the country; however, I expect I shall be writing to you again soon to have another try on Teesside. In the meantime, your co-operation is greatly appreciated.[64]

From then on Paul kept Mr Cassidy abreast of progress, and was able to report after the third appearance of the advertisement that he'd had four more enquiries. Obviously there was some kind of delayed action effect, but CHE now had the nucleus of a Teesside group, thanks to the *Gazette.* Mr Cassidy later gave a talk to the local group, and the paper featured it handsomely in the editorial pages.

Sometimes refusals reflected splits within the staff of a paper, which could be exploited. Agony aunts were good allies. Jean Austin was one such, syndicated through the Newsquest Group. The Chilterns group in 1970 was having problems with getting adverts in the *Berkhamsted and Hemel Hempstead Gazette*, so Paul wrote to Ms Austen, reminding her that she'd had information from CHE, sending the latest *Bulletin* and asking her to mediate. She wrote back:

> I showed both the note and the pamphlet to my editor and he expressed some surprise that it should be banned, and could not think, immediately, who would ban it. I left it with him to pursue, though that does not mean that it will be accepted. If I hear anything I will let you know.[65]

They did eventually appear, but not till over a year later. Rejections were so frequent, and the process of arguing for inclusion so frustrating, that in December 1970 the Committee agreed to complain to the Press Council.

The Press Council

CHE was not the first gay organisation to make such a complaint. *Arena 3*, the lesbian magazine, had met rejection in late 1969 from *The Times*, the *News of the World*, *The Scotsman* and the *Yorkshire Post*, all of which choked on the idea of a lesbian magazine.* In response they formed the Press Freedom Group, whose leading lights were *Arena 3* co-editor Jackie Forster and her then partner Babs Todd. They were both to become important figures in CHE. The PFG met at the Plough, and later in the Museum Tavern, in Bloomsbury – Jackie always liked meetings in pubs. A colourful, feisty and forceful woman, she braved the enemy in Fleet Street in a way that CHE rarely did.

> In sheer terror some of the Admen surrendered with barely a squeak. Others stood fast. Undaunted, Mrs F composed a powerful complaint to the Press Council (the amount of time, work and sheer hard labour involved in this would leave the average £5000 a year male executive fainting in coils).[66]

Jackie had done this in early 1970, but the complaint was turned down. The Press Council process was however revealing, in that the papers had to justify themselves, and their weasel words were duly recorded in the Press Council adjudication:

> One expressed sympathy with the complainants but said his newspaper and many others did not accept advertisements soliciting money by post for magazines unknown to them. A second said that had the complainants explained their purposes more fully, the newspaper would have given the matter more consideration. The wording of the advertisement was not such as to indicate that there was a serious-minded organisation behind it. A third stressed that the complainants were offered a chance to submit a re-worded advertisement but this was not taken up. A fourth said he felt the purpose of the magazine 'not informative but intrusive'.[67]

The Press Council judgement was unequivocal. 'The question of accepting or not accepting advertisements is in the discretion of each individual Editor, and the complaint is rejected.'[68] The magazine commented:

> Although the Press Council has rejected the complaint, it has done so on the merely technical ground that editors must be allowed to decide what advertisements they wish to accept. The 'reasons' given for rejecting our ads are not only feeble but in some cases dishonest. No offer to send in a reworded ad has ever been turned down by *Arena 3*. … In short, the excuses of the enemy admen are really quite contemptible, and the press council report makes this lucently clear.[69]

---

* The *Daily Telegraph*, *Sunday Telegraph* and *London Weekly Advertiser* all accepted adverts if the wording was changed from 'lesbians' to 'homosexual women'.

The Press Council rejected the CHE complaint as well, as it was to reject all complaints from gay organisations for the next ten years.*

Paul Temperton's experience was not however all rejection. The list of publications that would take advertisements by the end of 1971 was impressive.† Further, when requests to advertise came in, good editors saw opportunities for getting interesting copy, in the form of visits to the groups or interviews with convenors. So, when Paul placed an advertisement for a Group forming in Reading, the editor of the *Reading Evening Post* wrote that CHE didn't need to pay for ads in advance, and asking for some of the committee members to contact his features writer, David Rose, about getting some editorial coverage.

Difficulties finding convenors

Then there was the problem of convenors. Advertisements would only be placed after someone had come forward who was prepared to do the legwork. Many wrote in who wanted to meet others, a few who wanted to 'do something', but translating that into practicalities was another matter. Faced with what was involved, many fled. Some were too cautious, closeted, and felt that as convenors they would be too publicly exposed. Others simply thought it was too much work. One such was Angela Williams, in Bury. In the months that it took to place adverts and find suitable meeting places, some potential convenors would find their work transferred them to another part of the country. Some found when they met other possible helpers in their area for the first time that they couldn't stand them at any price. At least one possible convenor died of a heart attack before the group could get off the ground,

* There was however support from the NCCL, which passed a motion in 1973 condemning the refusal of newspapers to take CHE ads.

† When arguing with newspapers, Paul cited those other papers which had accepted adverts. By January 1972 he was able to say the following were currently willing to accept advertisements: *Liverpool Echo*, *Newcastle Evening Chronicle*, *Hull Daily Mail*, *Bournemouth Evening Echo*, *Bristol Evening Post*, *Lancashire Evening Telegraph*, *Yorkshire Post*, *Watford Observer*, *Teesside Evening Gazette*, *Belfast Newsletter*, *Oxford Times*, *Western Daily Press*, *South London News* group, *South London Advertiser* Group, *Manchester Evening News*, *Halifax Evening Chronicle*, *South London Press*, *Huddersfield Daily Examiner*, *Burnley Evening Star*, *Birmingham Post*, *Birmingham Evening Mail*, *Wolverhampton Express and Star*, *Cambridge Evening News*, *Slough Evening Mail*, *Bucks Examiner*, *Yorkshire Evening Post*, *Reading Evening Post*, *Darlington Daily Despatch*, *Northern Echo*, *Sheffield Star*, *Middlesbrough Evening Gazette*, *Belfast News Letter*, *Belfast Telegraph*, *Havering Express* series, *Brentwood and Shenfield Argus*, *Oxford Mail*, *Lancaster Guardian* series, *Watford Observer*, *East Lancs Press* group, *Darlington and Stockton Times*, *Berkhamsted And Hemel Hempstead Gazette*, *South East Essex* group, *The Times*, *Sunday Times*, *The Sun*, *News of the World*, *New Statesman*, *Spectator*, *Sunday Telegraph*, *Daily Telegraph*, *The Guardian* and *The Observer*.

another was incapacitated by a stroke.

There was also the question of suitability. The Committee decided very early that nobody should be vetted for membership, but becoming a convenor was a different matter; they would have a responsibility for vulnerable people. Not everyone could be vetted, although Paul made efforts to meet volunteers who lived reasonably close to Manchester. In December 1969 he and Martin went to Shrewsbury to meet a student member from Aberystwyth, Roy Payne; no group materialised, but a general half-price student subscription rate did, in response to Roy's plea of poverty.

Still, there were offers from many people that Paul had to take on trust, judging personalities only from their letters of introduction. This could have disastrous consequences, as Peter Norman, in his role as local groups' organiser, warned Trevor Locke in 1973 when Trevor was trying to set up a Cornish group:

> Some strange people have offered to, or have in fact, convened meetings in the past (e.g. a middle-aged man living with a boy of sixteen who arranged meetings which consisted of blue film shows, an alcoholic who chaired a meeting when drunk and insulted members by calling them 'old queans' [*sic*], and married men whose wives didn't know the score, but who invited other unsuspecting members to their homes. Such situations are embarrassing, even dangerous, and certainly lose members.[70]

Some convenors slipped through the net, appointed but not always especially suitable. Some used the situation to furnish themselves with bed partners, to get the 'fresh meat' before anyone else did; this was not necessarily a bad thing if done with grace and a spirit of encouragement. After all, it was what some lonely and frustrated enquirers were hoping for when they came to CHE. Other convenors created personal miniature 'empires'. Some either couldn't or wouldn't be other than one-man bands, which meant groups collapsed as soon as they left. Perhaps most seriously, a few took it on themselves to vet members or turn people down for no good reason other than the fact that they didn't like them.*

Nevertheless, progress was being made. By December 1969 there was the student group, the Manchester Homophile Group, which Martin Stafford had set up and was the first of its kind in the country. By April 1970 there were groups meeting regularly in the East and West Midlands, and moves to set up further student groups in Oxford and Sheffield. Bristol had just had an inaugural meeting, and there was one group in London. These were groups which supported the aims of CHE but without the formal membership struc-

---

* Very occasionally, there were people who were so seriously disturbed or needy that they had to be turned away for the sake of the group as a whole. See page 297 onwards.

ture which would make them CHE groups, since there was no framework in place within which this could happen. The EC was starting to address this.

Right from the start of expansion, there was concern about structure, and an attempt to impose some kind of centralised communication system, if not actual control. The Committee realised it would have no way of knowing what was going on locally, unless locals told them. Setting up lines of communication seemed to take priority even over what groups should actually do, what they could offer to members. By March 1970 it was agreed that convenors' names and addresses should be published, and that the groups should be autonomous as long as they were run 'in accordance with the general principles of the Committee'. The *Bulletin* opined:

> The scope for local groups is vast. It is on strong local groups that a national executive can best be based. It is envisaged that once a sufficient number of local groups are set up and functioning, these groups would be able to send delegates to convenors' meetings where experience and advice can be shared.[71]

Stylistically, the *Bulletin*, with its ponderous passive constructions, its inversions and its concern for form rather than content, already showed the lack of a common touch as far as communication was concerned, and an incipient bureaucratic approach which would come to alienate many.

MANDFHAB

The CHE group in Wolverhampton, started early in 1970, was not the first attempt to get a group for homosexuals off the ground in that town. In January 1968 the *Wolverhampton Express and Star* ran a full-page interview conducted by reporter Ray Seaton with 19-year-old John Holland,* who lived on a council estate and worked as an accounts clerk for a steel firm. John showed amazing frankness and self-confidence for the time:

> [The 1967 Act] does not go far enough. I believe it should have legalised the act in private for homosexuals under 21. Its great advantage is that it curbs blackmail. The Act shows that the community is at last beginning to accept us as human beings and realising that we are not freaks or perverts.
>
> There was a time when you never dared admit you were homosexual. Now we need not be so ashamed. I have told my colleagues at the office where I work as an accounts clerk and a short while ago I wrote a note to my mother to tell her I am a homosexual. Her reaction is that I am going through a phase but, of course, that is not so. I am a passive homosexual and will be until I die.

---

* Referred to only as John, and photographed from behind.

> I began to suspect when I was ten years old and knew for certain by the time I was 15. I was taunted by other boys. Most of the teachers, I'm afraid, took their side. I was very shy and very lonely. … I was often in tears. I felt alone in the world and withdrew into myself.[72]

This interview drove a coach and horses through any kind of belief in the 'corruption' of young men by older, or in the possibility of cures. The interview is worth quoting at length; in its freshness and personal immediacy it is far in advance of almost anything that had appeared by this time in the UK. It also set the template for many interviews with other homosexuals in the early 1970s. John found his salvation in the gay club in Wolverhampton, the Silver Web. 'In Wolverhampton we have the best social club in Europe with 550 members drawn from all over the country. Before the club opened I was extremely lonely. Now I have several friends.' – But no girlfriends? – 'That doesn't mean I will not marry. I may marry a lesbian.'[73]

One lesbian he could have married was his best friend, Elizabeth Cook. Unlike many gay women of the time, she was unafraid of the word 'lesbian'. If John and Elizabeth were agreed 'lesbian' was a fine word, they despised the word 'queer':

> It's a nauseating word. There is nothing queer about us. If you believe in God, you must believe he created everything, including me as I am. It would be indecent and callous if I adopted sexual habits alien to me. People who condemn us and claim to be Christians are hypocrites. We do the community no harm. I fact, we do it a service by keeping the birth rate down. …
>
> It is not just a sexual matter. There are eight sexes – two heterosexual, two bisexual, and four homosexual, active and passive. Love between two men, or between two women, is the same as that between a man and a woman. It begins with physical attraction and develops into true love. Two homosexuals can be happy together in old age, long after physical passions have gone. But it is no use us trying to be close friends with heterosexuals. We are virtually a separate species, an underworld with our own language.[74]

One may raise an eyebrow at the idea of eight sexes, but Holland is blowing a big raspberry at ideas of what is 'unnatural', and also at the idea of integration in society, as espoused at the Albany Trust and by people such as Martin Stafford. And then John launched into his big campaign strategy, for the formation of MANDFHAB (Male and Female Homosexual Association of Britain):

> [We have no] freedom of speech. There is hardly a paper or magazine in the country that will accept our advertisements. Society will not allow us to communicate.
>
> We need to improve our public relations, make sure that our talents are

> not wasted, and establish a better image. The best way is through organised groups. Some of us are prepared to parade with banners proclaiming our homosexuality if it will help. We are in the position of the old suffragettes, struggling for our democratic rights. …
>
> We are planning through MANDFAB [*sic*] to raise money to buy a large house which we could convert into an office, clubroom, library, restaurant and bar. We need £5,000 or £6,000. We want to live our own lives in our own way. We are content to live apart with our own places of entertainment. Please, do not condemn us because we were born an oppressed minority.[75]

The letters which appeared in the paper in the two weeks following were mostly supportive.

The *News of the World* picked up the story and ran with it a week later. This time John was interviewed with his friend Elizabeth, a 'blonde and pretty' 28-year-old who looked much younger in her expensive suede jacket, and clutched a white miniature poodle called Britt. They had met in 1967 through the Samaritans. She told the paper: 'I enjoy men's company a lot as long as it is just social. It was when they tried to kiss me goodnight that I couldn't stand it. I can't bear to have a man touch me.'[76]

The article concluded, rather wistfully: 'Our aim is to relieve loneliness and show the world what we can contribute.'[77]

The two articles sent Antony Grey and supporters of the Albany Trust apoplectic. As they told Esquire clubs, it was their belief that any club scheme must get police and home office approval in advance – even to the extent of submitting proposed club rules of conduct. John Holland and his like would only give clubs a bad name. And the worst of it was, not only did he talk 'twaddle' (Grey), he was also only nineteen. Local Albany Trust supporter David Buckle told Grey when he alerted him to the article:

> I must confess I was horrified. I just could not understand a man of Ray Seaton's intelligence discussing such an important social problem with a boy of 19. I have already written Seaton a very strong letter of protest, asking why he did not get in touch with a more informative person over the age of 21. I also said how foolish such an interview was, and nothing but trouble can arise from this article. … I can tell you this from the people I have spoken to already the most understanding sympathisers are very annoyed and shocked. … The most damning part of course was the boy's age, not being a consenting adult. … I sincerely hope this foolish boy's silly talk will not make all that much difference to the Home Office/Police decision.[78]

As Grey put it, 'He might have waited till he'd got his nappies off.'

John came down to London to see Antony Grey for advice, but must have quickly realised he was going to get no help and nothing but condescension, for he did not return. Grey told a journalist a few months later:

> We made very little headway at this meeting: although a sincere and well-meaning young man, he was very naïve, unsophisticated and self-opinionated. He refused to contemplate a minimum age limit higher than 16 for his club's membership and appeared adamant in his intention to proceed along these lines. We offered to assist him with case referrals (he was receiving numerous requests for help from lonely and disturbed people). … We told him that if he wished to refer anybody to us who had problems or difficulties … he was at liberty to do so. On the strength of this he made the claim about 'working in close co-operation with us' – although we have in fact never heard from him again from that day to this.[79]

Given the way he was patronised, it is unsurprising that Holland didn't come back. He got his membership application forms printed, distributed them in the Silver Web and sent them out to enquirers (there were hundreds after the articles appeared). These forms are more than an application; they are a manifesto:

> We aim to end discrimination against homosexuals; to prevent loneliness; and to end the sordid activities which have given homosexuals a bad name. We can put members in touch, if required, with qualified psychiatric advice, and we work in close co-operation with the Albany Trust. We publish a monthly magazine *Gay Today* to keep members in touch. We organise social events (which must be self-sufficient). … We cannot make introductions for illegal purposes, and when we have premises they must not be used for illegal purposes.[80]

The aims and activities are very similar to those of CHE, though anticipating CHE by a year or more. The warnings are similar as well. However despite the caution, the form is quite clear that MANDFHAB is open to anyone over sixteen.

By the autumn of 1968, the Association had foundered. Elizabeth Cook had left, and the demand for its services had swamped John's ability to keep up. It was not true that all publicity was good publicity. He told Allan Horsfall:

> Thinking the publicity would help us launch the organisation I conducted an anonymous interview for the *Express and Star* in which I was (unintentionally) grossly misquoted and quoted out of context. We were then subjected to an onslaught by the lowest form of Press 'life' and as a result of this unwarranted intrusion into our private lives, Miss Cook left me holding the baby. I was then swamped with literally hundreds of enquiries and about a dozen actual memberships. Postage alone exceeded the subscriptions and with other expenses involved I was put heavily in debt. At this point I decided … to suspend the organisation as I was in

trouble with my health. ... It was perhaps inexcusable to have also to stop communicating with members.

The next blow was an article in a 'sophisticated' magazine.* This unsubstantiated 'article' (which I heard about from a subscriber to the magazine) published comments and opinions about myself and my organisation without any reference to me. It was read by an in-law and has since caused me considerable trouble at home. It was impossible to make refunds, but I was determined to honour the guarantee I had given. I took a part-time job and now have cleared the debts and repaid all the subscriptions. I have learned a lot by this misadventure and I think I have been a help to some at least.[81]

But the story did have a happy ending. 'I now have all I want – a husband and a future. Society's memory is short and I have sunk into anonymity although I would still like to better the lot of the homosexual.'[82] He signed off 'disillusioned but hopeful'.

Wolverhampton CHE

Whether he was still with his husband a year later is not known, but in February 1970 fifteen people met to start a Wolverhampton CHE group, and the convenor was the same John Holland. Supporters came from Birmingham and from as far as Shrewsbury 'pending the setting up of a separate group at Oswestry.'[83] This Oswestry group never materialised.

At first it was called West Midlands CHE, since there was nothing else for fifty miles. Its meetings were held initially at Atkinson's Corner House, which was a rundown pub in a rundown suburb, miles from the centre of town. The number slowly rose. The first minuted meeting, in May 1970, records that they agreed a letter of introduction to send to enquirers, and decided to ask permission to place their own newspaper adverts. Just who placed adverts and how they were worded was a bone of contention, since Paul Temperton in Manchester thought in terms of a national organisation, and wanted to keep track of enquirers through a centralised system, which would allow them to be chased up for national subscriptions. In the early days, too, it was the national organisation which was paying for the ads, and the system had to be such that CHE could try to ensure it had a return on its money, through membership fees. The same minutes recorded:

> A member of the group had received a letter from the retiring National Chairman [Harold Pollard] advising caution in the case of admitting 16 to 21 year olds to membership. ... It was agreed that the exclusion of this age group would imply that the group's activities were other than wholly

* It has not been possible to identify this magazine.

> legitimate. The group reasserted its intention that all its activities should be 'above board'.[84]

It continued to admit anyone over sixteen, in line with Holland's MANDFHAB policy, although most members were in their 20s. The issue of whether to admit people between the ages of sixteen and twenty-one was one which exercised many groups over the next few years, and could cause some controversy. The Wolverhampton group described itself, as many did, as 'homophile' rather than 'homosexual'.

The group had contacted the Samaritans, the Brook Centre and Open Door, a young people's counselling organisation, hoping to wrest referrals from straight organisations and 'contribute to the adjustment of homophiles unaware of the existence of others, or of groups.' However, although the Samaritans remained almost invariably the first port of call for new groups starting outreach, both the Wolverhampton and Birmingham branches were found to be offering less than satisfactory help for homosexuals. They discussed this at their July meeting, and agreed that anyone getting bad advice in future from a Samaritan should go straight to the Director of the organisation. More helpful was the Brook Centre, which also suggested contacting an advisory service for homosexuals in Walsall.*

At first, the very fact of being with other homosexuals was exhilaration enough in itself. The mere existence of gay space – that is, space which was controlled by homosexuals on their own terms, in which assumptions could be shared, a common language developed, and guards could be dropped – allowed people, in the commonest phrase, to 'be themselves'. But gay space was more than that; it allowed people to *become* themselves, to find out who they were, to develop emotions and thoughts previously stunted, to find and sustain friendship networks.

At the same time, the first steps of many groups were characterised by a curious shyness. Years later Terry Sanderson pinned this down, describing the early days of Rotherham CHE: 'It was a fraught time. We were all very wary of each other, not really knowing what we wanted, what was possible, or even what gay people could do together besides have sex.'[85]

In this process of self-discovery, discussion of homosexuality was the first step: what caused it, if anything; whether it mattered what caused it; how to live and love; the social position of homosexuals; legal constraints; religious and psychiatric options. It was only after such issues had been 'talked out' that the realisation dawned that being homosexual was not in itself enough to bind a group together, and as a shared commonality it was rather narrowly confined.

---

* The author has been unable to find any information about what this might have been.

By August 1970 the West Midlands group had become big enough to split into two, one group based in Birmingham and one in Wolverhampton. Initially this was just an arrangement to hold meetings in different parts of the West Midlands, so people didn't have to travel so far, but over two or three meetings there was a *de facto* separation into two catchment areas.*

The Wolverhampton group had a far stronger working-class element within its ranks, which in 1972 led to the formation of a specific offshoot, the Wolverhampton Workers' Group. Peter Norman as local groups organiser was suspicious of it because of the element of selection it would involve – who decides who's a worker? On the other hand, where were potential members to go who felt uncomfortable with the atmosphere of their local CHE group? As founder John Cleary put it:

> Whether we like it or not, a class barrier does exist within the homosexual community as in the heterosexual community; it is part of our daily life, you have only to look around yourselves in work and in social attitudes – the basic working class person enjoys doing different things and going to different places. …
>
> CHE as it now stands is basically middle-class. I do realise of course that with any national organisation you will always have this middle-class attitude, and if it wasn't for this then CHE would not exist.
>
> What I want to do is to overcome this class barrier so that everyone will be accepted and treated as an equal and to attract the basic working class homosexuals into joining CHE.[86]

When it started in September – subject of the first meeting's discussion, 'Class Distinction' – the group attracted a dozen men and a couple of women. Alternating between Cleary's flat and the Silver Web, it showed a fondness for stereotypical 'working class' sporting activities such as ten-pin bowling, table tennis and ice skating, but also confounded stereotypes with chess evenings and a trip to see *King Lear* at the Birmingham Arts Lab.

Most members of Wolverhampton CHE remained in the closet and reluctant to get involved in any active campaigning. However, in July 1971 an issue arose which gave rise to much heart-searching. The American play *The Boys in the Band* played at the Birmingham Rep, provoking a string of letters of complaint in the *Wolverhampton Express and Star*. How were the local group to react? The group secretary told Paul Temperton:

> It was the wish of the group that you should write a letter to the newspaper, should you desire to do so. … I myself would welcome a letter from you speaking in the name of CHE as a whole.[87]

---

* For the Birmingham group, see page 284.

The slightly humble tone, the hesitancy and uncertainty with which they deliberated and came to the conclusion to ask someone else to do the campaigning work, speaks of a group with very low political expectations or expertise. Paul excused himself, being in the middle of the Esquire campaign in Burnley,* getting out an edition of the *Bulletin* and setting up a new membership card index system. His letter is also a gentle hint that the group itself could do better:

> It seemed very difficult because the opponents of the play didn't appear from the press reports to be on about the homosexuality of it specifically, just the four-letter words; And it would have been impossible to reply to such an unspecific attack without appearing to defend the play itself, which I wouldn't want to do because it is an appalling play and one which we really ought to be attacking ourselves for the highly misleading impression it gives of what homosexuality is all about.[88]

The 'we' of the last sentence is a reminder that they can't expect to have everything done for them. John Holland has left by this time; it's hard to imagine him asking others to do his fighting for him. In his place came Dennis Platt, a more emollient figure. Birmingham lost its radical edge.

MAF-MAN

The East Midlands CHE group was in Nottingham and also came out of an earlier organisation. Peter Spencer got in touch with John Holland when MANDFHAB hit the headlines in 1968, hoping to set up a Nottingham branch. However, he had a major falling out with Holland over the involvement of under-21s, and set up his own, similarly named, MAF-MAN.† He wrote to Antony Grey explaining: 'We in Nottingham … feel we cannot put our names to the contract‡ as it stands, … and must therefore on a point of principle dissociate ourselves,' and asking his advice 'if we are correct in taking a stand with regards to the minimum age of a homosexual organisation.'[89] He offered half the group's income to the Albany Trust. His membership form was something of a manifesto as well:

> This association offers tremendous opportunities to enable the homosexual to lead a much more fuller life [*sic*], such as has never been known in this country before. If you are a homosexual, male or female, this is your association and we want your support; … have the feeling of belonging,

---

* See Chapter Three.

† It isn't clear what the name MAF-MAN stood for, if anything.

‡ Filling in the MANDFHAB application form was entering into a contract.

> security, friendship and the knowledge of not standing alone in a somewhat cruel society.
>
> The members of this association must all be prepared to help each other, give of their talents and efforts. ... Even by joining forces together it can only be what the members make it themselves; everyone must be prepared to help.[90]

MAF-MAN proclaimed itself a social organisation for homosexuals, but offered in addition access to advice on 'legal, medical, psychiatric and personal problems.' Like MANDFHAB, it set its fees at £2/10s per annum (£2.50), twice that of CHE. In addition to being for over-21s only, it bowed to the 1967 Act in denying membership to serving members of the armed forces. It also denied bisexuality insofar as it refused to accept married members. On the positive side, it was the first organisation to show any awareness of equal opportunities, being 'for homosexuals, no matter what sex, nationality, profession or social status.'

Like MANDFHAB it found it impossible to take out newspaper advertising. It met in people's houses, but was more than a discussion group. It offered a telephone advice service, and answered a number of desperate letters, which came in increasing numbers through 1968. It's not clear when MAF-MAN became a CHE group, or indeed whether it ever did in any formal sense. However, the Committee claimed it for their own, and when Nottingham-based law lecturer Ike Cowen reported its collapse in mid-1970, Paul took it on himself to ask Cowen to kick-start it again as a definite CHE Group.

It was not the only activity in Nottingham. Ike, who was in the middle of setting up the Pavilion Club* was also getting together Night Off (A night off from pretending to be heterosexual; a night off from searching for a partner or partners). Ike described it as meeting:

> fortnightly in premises obtained through Nottingham Council of Social Service. The group consists of people of both sexes, who do not like the idea of a gay club or a gay bar. Some are simply too shy and some have not sufficiently arrived at a recognition or acceptance of their condition. Meetings take the form of informal discussion; most people repeat the experience and many gain sufficient confidence to go along to the Club. We think that this group provides a valuable outlet for the many isolated and lonely homosexuals in this area. Recruitment is through personal contact, CHE, Samaritans and the CSS. ... We are not very militant, but can claim, however to have improved the quality of life for a large number of homosexuals.[91]

---

* See page 232.

He described this group in 1971 as having 'no specific orientation to either CHE or GLF, but contain members of both groups.'[92]

None of the early groups kept minutes or produced newsletters. Little was reported to the national office in Manchester, and the only references to them, in Committee minutes, national bulletins and occasional letters, are sporadic and tantalisingly vague.

Bristol CHE

Bristol, for example, had a group about to start in March 1970, and Paul Temperton put several advertisements in the *Bristol Evening Post* which produced 45 enquiries. By September 1970 it claimed 40 members, and in December 1970 'FB' (the first convenor, Fred Blackburn) reported in the *Bulletin* that they were meeting in flats and about eighteen people were turning up. They had elected a four-person committee and appointed a press officer.

> Anyone who says he cannot adjust should take a leaf out of our book and make the effort; it is a very rewarding venture to achieve. … It is up to everyone to pull together and make every evening a succes … A lot of people are less lonely than before, and can meet and talk without looking over their shoulders to see who is listening.[93]

The record for the rest of the year is shadowy.

Student groups

The strategy for developing local groups was very much Martin Stafford's. Robin Bloxsidge, shortly to co-found the Liverpool group, remembers:

> Paul Temperton was actually running it [National CHE], with his boy-friend, Martin. Paul was very susceptible to anything Martin wanted to do, so in some ways, Martin was more important than Paul … he did the work, but he was pushed a lot by Martin. But Martin was a very, very difficult person to get on with.[94]

Student groups have been mentioned. Martin Stafford commuted to Sheffield to do his MA in the autumn of 1970, but had 'cased the joint' and laid the groundwork for a group before starting his course. He wanted to repeat the exercise he had already carried out in Manchester University to advertise a homophile society. He described the problems of starting a group in Sheffield, when he went to an Albany Trust conference in July 1970:

> I placed in the Sheffield Union university newspaper, an advertisement which we had placed previously in the Manchester University newspaper which never attracted any enquiries at all. This advertisement suggested

> that the Committee would give help or advice to people on problems connected with homosexuality, or invited them to write to the Committee if they were interested in its aims. Well, this brought in only one letter from Sheffield. … We consulted the Director of the Student Health Centre. … He was worried by the problem of homosexuals meeting at the University, as many of them would be under the age of 21, and he asked me what my attitude was to this, and how we proposed to resolve any difficulties. … We thought that we should not commit ourselves too much on this. … I certainly won't condemn relationships between people under 21 and he apparently wanted me to say this. …
>
> We now have a group of seven or eight people, and one or two joined and then left. So at least in Sheffield we have a beginning. It's going to be called the Homophile Society.[95]

He also got support from 'Off the Record', a counselling service for young people. The Committee discussed the position of under-21s once more. It was clearly a nonsense to have university groups which didn't include under-21s, but the issue of sex between members under 21 was particularly acute in their minds:

> Although those under 21 should clearly be permitted to join the group, there was some discussion about what would be the Committee's attitude to any illegal relationships which might develop as a result. It was agreed that although the law relating to those under 21 was unreasonable, unenforceable and unlikely to be adhered to, the Committee could not officially condone the transgression thereof.[96]

Among those who were prominent in Sheffield was Bob Elbert. A second-year student, he had joined CHE nationally in response to an advert by early 1970. At this stage the number of new members coming forward was small enough for Martin and Paul to give some at least their individual attention. Martin visited Sheffield to meet him in February. He came and stayed with Paul and Martin at Easter. As a result, the Sheffield Homophile Society had its first meeting in June 1970, and was officially recognised by the University in October – the first gay group in the country to be so. Bob later became a key figure in the Bristol Group after he graduated, and the partner of Trevor Locke.* Bob, with Martin's encouragement, was Sheffield's driving force. He was a much more political animal than some, and among other things invited a student psychiatric counsellor to talk to the group. Martin Stafford recalls, 'She was given a rough ride. One young man who had been considering aversion therapy subsequently joined the group. A very satisfactory result!'[97]

Martin was keen to expand the student network, and went to Bristol to

---

* Trevor Locke's role in CHE is covered more fully in Volume Two.

visit a student in the summer of 1970. This was Robert Palmer, later to become Chair of the national organisation in 1978, and to buy *Gay News* from Denis Lemon in 1982. What was set up as a result of this meeting, the Gaysoc, had no connection to Fred Blackburn's town group, and was predominantly a social group until the arrival of Trevor Locke in 1972 brought a more political dimension.

Stafford and Horsfall also tried to start a group in Oxford, but were stalled by the *Oxford Mail's* refusal to take adverts. They did however have an ally, and an outlet, in John Rose, a classic extrovert Oxford eccentric who founded *Daily Information.* This was a brightly coloured double-sided A2 sheet – a different colour for each day of the week – which was posted and fly-posted all around the university. Big, bearded and loud, John Rose could be seen cycling round the city laden with bags of the freesheet and with an origami *DI* hat on his head, bellowing, '*Daily Information*! *Daily Information*! Read it as a newspaper, wear it as a hat!'* *Daily Information* brought twelve enquiries from one insertion, among them the composer Stephen Oliver, busy working on his first opera, *The Duchess of Malfi*.†

By May 1970 there was quite a large group meeting under the convenorship of Robin Robbins, a Balliol College don whose estranged wife Anna was fond of proclaiming that he had a very large penis. Within weeks they were approaching college deans and chaplains to find out those who could offer the most sympathetic personal advice, while Paul Temperton contacted Oxford Samaritans to ask for referrals; to this extent they were still operating within a model which associated homosexuality with problems. The group remained a university group, meeting in college rooms, and people from the town were *de facto* excluded because it was only university-based publications which would take adverts. In any case, the social chasm between Town and Gown was wide, there was no gay pub to bridge it,‡ and the only place students and 'townies' would meet was in public toilets. Oxford CHE acquired a reputation for being extremely closeted and cliquish, and was cast into the shade in 1972 by the more active and inclusive Oxford Gay Action Group. A separate Town CHE group started in late 1971, paradoxically by a university member, William Berry, who was doing a postgraduate Law MA at St Catherine's College.

Martin's student/university groups continued over time to exist in their own bubble, and as CHE groups they rather died the death, not least because

---

* Author's memory.

† Oliver would go on to write over forty operas, as well as music for the Royal Shakespeare Company (*Nicholas Nickleby*), TV (the BBC complete Shakespeare) and radio (the 13-part *Lord of the Rings*). He found a more popular audience with *Blondel*, the musical he co-wrote with Tim Rice.

‡ The Gloucester Arms by the bus station had a small gay corner.

they came into being at a time when the membership system was haphazard, and because there was in the nature of student groups a yearly turnover of people. However, through Bob Elbert and later his partner Trevor Locke, they were very important to the later establishment of the Gaysoc movement in Universities, with the official recognition of Gaysocs by University Unions. This in turn led to the National Union of Students becoming one of the earliest, largest and most vociferous organisations allied to CHE in the struggle for gay rights.

The Manchester Committee was conscious how ramshackle its own arrangements were, and how little input supporters had. They sought ways to bind a national organisation together. They organised an open meeting on 25 April 1970 at the Houldsworth Hall, where the NWHLRC public meeting had been held in 1966, but there was so little interest that only two people turned up. However, before the public meeting there was a get-together for people interested in starting local 'committees' (they were not yet habitually referred to as 'groups'). In addition to Holland (Wolverhampton), Spencer (Nottingham), Elbert (Sheffield) and the very attractive* Nick Stanley (Birmingham), there was Wilf Hunter from Preston. Paul Temperton had gone to Preston to meet Wilf in March, to assess whether he would make a suitable convenor. However, Wilf would not manage to get a group going in his area for three years.† Allan, ever with an eye for talent, co-opted both Stanley and Hunter onto the Committee, 'to get their names in the minutes and keep the Bishop happy.'[98] Wilf, tall, bespectacled, in his late twenties, was a TV repair man who also bought and sold second-hand TVs. As Martin Stafford remembers it, the contrast between Nick Stanley and Wilf Hunter could not have been stronger.

> [Wilf] was a dyed-in-the-wool Tory and had little sympathy for the hard-up people who were constrained to sell him their TVs for next to nothing. They had, he maintained, mismanaged their affairs and this rendered them ripe for 'exploitation'. Despite this, I found him a pleasant and jovial man.[99]

Wilf doesn't seem to have contributed greatly to the Committee, but he did at least come in handy for repairing Paul and Martin's TV.

---

* Paul described him as a 'dolly young man', a phrase new to Martin. Martin saw the phrase in *IT* and had to ask Paul what it meant. He said, 'Someone like Nick Stanley.'

† There was already an informal group meeting in Preston, but it took three years before Wilf could persuade them to have anything to do with CHE, and the local papers turned down adverts.

Birmingham CHE

By contrast, Nick Stanley was a young (25) sociology lecturer at Birmingham Polytechnic, and very left-wing for CHE. This was at a time when conflict in Northern Ireland was at its height, and there was daily coverage of it in the press. In England too people felt obliged to take sides. A convinced republican supporter, Stanley always referred to the 'six counties', never to Northern Ireland. From the point of view of the Committee, he was an asset as a lecturer who had easy access to meeting rooms, and also connections with Birmingham University for when it came to larger gatherings such as conferences and National Councils. If ever two people illustrated the breadth of opinion which CHE had to reflect, it was Wilf Hunter and Nick Stanley.

Although Nick was listed as a group representative, he was at first more of a convenor-in-waiting. By July 1970 the West Midlands group was ready to start the process of splitting into two, and although Nick was both ready and capable of starting it, political sensitivities dictated that West Midlands CHE should be seen to initiate it. They negotiated with the Friends Meeting House for a meeting place, and ads went into the *Birmingham Post* and the *Evening Mail* in September. They invited a member of the Executive down, 'in view of the importance of interesting new members and getting them to contribute enthusiastically'.[100]

The adverts paid off, and five new members joined. West Midlands CHE also put up posters and handed out leaflets in the Birmingham clubs and pubs.* From the first meeting in September, the group met fortnightly on Wednesdays in Dr Johnson House, and a special meeting on 7 October 1970 formalised the two groups and the split. They agreed that the West Midlands group would cover Tipton, Cannock, Walsall, and Bloxwich, while Birmingham would take people from Sutton, West Bromwich, Birmingham, Solihull, Redditch, Halesowen and Bromsgrove. This division was largely academic, in that individuals were free to go along to whichever group they liked – or, indeed, both.

This progression, and the amoeba-like splitting of groups in two as they expanded, was characteristic of CHE as it developed. It also worked in reverse, as groups contracted and amalgamated in later years when CHE went into decline.

Birmingham CHE was one of the first to use the media skilfully. By September 1971 they had featured in an article in 'a local paper', and got themselves onto a programme on Radio Birmingham called *It's a Gay World.* They appeared on a live BBC Midlands TV programme in November 1971,

---

* Birmingham had two gay clubs, the Nightingale in Bordesley and the Grosvenor in Hagley Road. There was one gay pub, The Jester, in the city centre.

along with members of the Birmingham Gay Action Group, 'confronting liberal experts and closeted gays'.

The release of the film *Sunday Bloody Sunday* provided another opportunity. John Schlesinger's film was about a bisexual triangle, with Glenda Jackson, Peter Finch as a gay Jewish doctor, and Murray Head as the bed-hopping eye candy in between. Though Schlesinger was openly gay, studio pressure prevented him from treating the two relationships even-handedly, and it was this that CHE members objected to. The audience coming out of the cinema were confronted with leaflets which drew attention to the discrepancy between the handling of the heterosexual and homosexual relationships (the homosexual one was decidedly coy, although a lot of attention focused on the single melodramatic Finch/Head kiss, the sole expression of gay sexuality). The leaflet also gave information about Birmingham CHE, guessing, correctly, that the audience would contain a large number of gay men.

Tony Newton* and Nick were not the most efficient of people, as Paul kept getting letters of complaint from local people who had sent in their applications, asking why their local convenor hadn't been in touch. Sometimes this was a more than casual complaint, and reflected real need:

> I would like him to contact me soon, as I am going through a period of stress and very much want to meet other people of a similar nature to my own, hoping that it will help me to make new friends and have a steadying influence on my life.[101]

By April 1971 they had also found a meeting room in Handsworth where informal gatherings happened on Tuesdays and Fridays, between 7.30 and 9.30 p.m. This was a lot more frequently than most groups met, and the combination of the local group and various activities for National CHE induced a severe case of overload for Nick. Plus he was living with his boyfriend Karl, who worked for Rolls Royce and always required a meal on the table when he got home from work. Nick wrote to Paul almost humorously, but there is a certain desperation underneath: 'I try to keep things one jump ahead of our members' boredom tolerance. Numbers increase all the time. The only disquieting factor is people who come once only'.[102]

Sometimes Paul would receive testimonials or complaints from people who had visited or joined groups, which gives a glimpse into what the group was like, and what it did for people. One such came from A. J. Yorke, who visited the Birmingham group. Clearly he was worried that people would try to pick him, or each other, up, but:

---

* Secretary of Birmingham CHE.

> I felt quite at home, despite the rather mixed bag of folk there, and although I know that a good deal of the matters discussed are now old chestnuts and perennials, at least the concept of *an actual social group* was formulated. … As long as it remains only social at the meetings anyway, all will be well, and there is nothing to indicate that it could be otherwise, for everyone behaved themselves beautifully. In fact, in comparison with some of the people *I* have met (one was a compulsive importunist and I couldn't have taken him anywhere), everyone seemed very ordinary* and well-behaved. I hope to go along again soon, and feel that my own viewpoint, that there is a very real social need for such groups, is amply confirmed. It is a relief after all to just meet people with whom one can speak freely instead of having to watch oneself all the while for the false word, or the slip of the tongue. This in itself imposes often an intolerable strain on those in isolated situations in society as it is. I mentioned that contrary to what some members said, I had not met with much hostility in general life. This is of course untrue. I have met a great deal of hostility, but only when I have attempted to discuss homosexuality in a rational way. It is of course more or less social suicide to discuss it sympathetically and on any subjective basis.[103]

The pattern of what a local group was, and how it should function, was slowly solidifying. It would bring people together to alleviate loneliness; it would encourage and support individuals in gaining self-confidence, with the ultimate aim of getting people to come out; it would develop a social alternative to the commercial gay scene, where there was one, and provide a gay scene where none existed already; and it would campaign to further the aims of CHE, which it would share.

And here was the central paradox of CHE, a conflict which caused endless tension between the 'socialisers' and the 'campaigners'. For in order to campaign effectively, a local group needed to enlist the support of at least most of its members; but these were the very people who lacked the outlook, skills and self-confidence to be effective campaigners. No doubt the circle was squared in the minds of the Committee by imagining the progress of a typical member from hesitant, closeted, self-oppressed and inexperienced newcomer to confident and politicised member over a period of time. This is indeed what happened to some people, but many more remained stuck somewhere along the journey. As a result, the ordinary membership of CHE remained much more cautious and conservative than the Executive; and the active campaigning remained always the preserve of a committed minority, many of whom had the double burden on their time of also running their local group, and nearly all of whom felt held back by the apolitical CHE masses.

---

* Only for reformist groups like CHE and Mattachine Society, could 'very ordinary' be an accolade.

Standardising groups

Groups as they developed adopted some kind of formal constitution. At first they wrote their own. A standard version of this emerged gradually, as the national organisation itself crystallised – and only later would there be a model constitution, drafted by Ike Cowen as legal officer, which ran to four pages. The constitution laid down (in its model version) that there would be convenors to meet people joining and provide a kind of induction service; there would be a secretary to take minutes of meetings, a social secretary to organise events, a treasurer to look after the money.

Money procedures were quite vague when local groups started to spring up. Groups could charge admission to meetings, or take a hat round at the end, or set up a formal local subscription. It was assumed that people coming along would have made first contact with the National Office and paid their £1 subscription there. The reality soon became more complicated. As word of mouth spread, or groups did their own advertising, people would start to go along without ever having been in touch with Manchester. Nor did the convenors always put them in the picture about needing to be a member of National CHE in order to benefit from the local group; probably many convenors thought that asking for a quid would put people off returning for another meeting, probably there was the simple English embarrassment about mentioning money. Whatever the reason, the actual number of people involved in CHE throughout its history was impossible to give accurately; to just count those on the membership database at Headquarters was to under-estimate by anything between 30 and 60 per cent. Throughout the seventies and eighties CHE was bedevilled by financial crises which took much time and energy to deal with, and severely limited its activities. These were partly as a result of setting membership fees far too low to cover the cost of servicing the members, and partly because there were thousands of people using local groups but putting nothing back into the national kitty. The other consequence of this haphazard entry into CHE was that many members of local groups had only the vaguest idea of what CHE stood for.

The four officers – convenor, secretary, social secretary, treasurer – would make up the basic minimum committee, which would form on a self-selecting volunteer basis to start with, but then become democratically elected once the group was up and running. The convenors' contact details would be circulated within the organisation, but it was left to individuals whether they wanted their phone numbers or addresses more widely publicised. There was a furore when Paul gave the convenors' contact list to the new national listings

Broadsheet in 1971, and it was passed on to members of the *Come Together** editorial collective. Paul wrote to one of their number, Bob Mellors:

> Most of the names and addresses of CHE group convenors on the list you enclosed are very out of date. Actually you should never have had the list in the first place. … I suppose it was those naughty people in Leeds who passed it on the GLF. … Please ensure that you've destroyed the list unless you have their permission individually to use their address.[104]

The magazine had a comparatively limited circulation, and the level of exposure was hardly sufficient to warrant the hysterical reaction of some convenors. Temperton by contrast seems almost amused, certainly affectionate about the 'naughty' *Broadsheet* compilers. For much of its history, many of CHE's local groups were only contactable through the national office, and this remained true into the 1980s, despite a decision in 1977 that it was a condition of being a CHE convenor that you agreed to let your contact details be publicly available.

Liverpool CHE

Two other regional groups emerged in the spring and summer of 1970, both of which were, if not started, at least booted into life by people associated with the old HLRS. Liverpool CHE took off with an offer of premises by an actor, Ralph Hallett. Ralph's family had a cake shop, and over the shop was a large sitting room which he suggested was suitable for meetings – it was also used for the local Labour Party committee meetings. In a letter to Paul Temperton in August 1970 he offered this, and also a list of five people who were willing to help. Paul already had the details of Peter Norman, a former supporter of the Albany Trust and the HLRS, who had moved from London to Liverpool a couple of years previously to take a job in the Planning Department. Peter was also involved in Medical Aid for Vietnam and was chairman of the local branch of the NCCL. Peter had contacted Paul because his friend George Mortimer was the first convenor of CHE London groups, and so he was kept up-to-date with what was going on in the dynamic new organisation which was rapidly taking over from the one he previously belonged to. He was also seconded from Liverpool Council to the Ministry of Housing. This meant that he was travelling down to the capital several times a month, on which occasions he stayed with Mortimer.

When he contacted Paul in May 1970, Peter Norman offered to be convenor for any new group in Liverpool, and indeed was natural Convenor

* Magazine of the Gay Liberation Front. Sixteen issues were printed between November 1970 and July 1973.

material, far more so than Ralph. But in May there were only five paid-up National CHE supporters in the area, and none of them was living in Liverpool itself. There needed to be more people to establish a momentum. Peter certainly helped to create that, because he notes in his diary that he spent his twenty-eighth birthday in the local gay bar, the Lisbon, with Robin Bloxsidge, and afterwards gave out CHE leaflets to the people he invited back for coffee.

Robin, later to be Liverpool CHE's convenor after Peter and also a member of the EC, was Peter's 'affair' at the time. He was a school friend of Peter's younger brother, studying in Liverpool, and Peter's only gay contact when he moved to Liverpool in 1967. It was to be two years before the pair gelled into a couple, but it became quite intense.

Peter met Hallett with Robin and a couple of others in mid-August, and the first thing Hallett did was to fall for the very youthful-looking, blond, blue-eyed Robin. He wrote Robin a 'rather gushing' letter, the first of many, which he and Peter bore with good-humoured equanimity. It didn't bode too well for Ralph as convenor, but it was containable.

37. Ralph Hallett

Faced with a choice between Peter and Ralph, Paul offered them a joint convenorship, although Ralph remained the one he corresponded with. He sent Ralph the contact details of nine more people in the area who wanted to join a group, Bloxsidge among them. Paul advised Ralph:

> It would probably be best, if you had the time and patience, to see these people separately in the first instance; I will of course be referring more people to you as and when they join. At the full inaugural meeting you could, if you wish, go through the motions of electing officers or you may prefer to wear all those hats yourself for the time being. … Whether you wish to be democratic or not about this is really up to you and Peter [Norman]. In any case I don't think it's a good idea to get bogged down in too much 'procedure' – my experience is that unless such formalities are kept to a minimum, people's enthusiasm tends to wane. …
>
> As I mentioned on the phone, local groups are supposed to be self-financing once they have got going; this can be achieved either by having an entrance charge or a collection, or an actual local subscription.[105]

Seeing fourteen people individually was a lot of work, and there was one problem with Ralph: he was not very well. He suffered from hepatic fibrosis, a liver disease, often hereditary but sometimes related to cirrhosis, which results in the build-up of scar tissue in the liver. As a result his mobility was severely restricted, and one of his motives for starting a group was probably to get gay people to come to him, since he couldn't go to them.

He was a larger-than-life figure who had worked at the Shakespeare Memorial Theatre in the early 1950s. Here he struck up a friendship with Richard Burton, no doubt cemented by booze-fuelled nights around the town. In the late 1950s he turned up in minor parts in a couple of BBC-TV play adaptations – *A Man for All Seasons* and Shakespeare's *Henry V*. However, he was forced to retire through illness – there is a suggestion of some kind of nervous breakdown. Retirement did not bring hardship, as the Hallett family business was successful enough to support him. He also had a gay brother, Martin, who was sexually very active around Liverpool until he found Jesus in 1972.

Peter Norman remembers Ralph as 'a rather overwhelming sort of character, quite a bit older than us. … I went to meet him, and I thought that he was a bit off-putting.'[106] For example, Ralph told a story about how he had tried to attract the attention of a young man by standing naked in a window where he could be seen exposing himself. Peter wasn't shocked by the exhibitionism so much as the fact that Hallett seemed to regard this as a perfectly natural thing to do.

There was also the mysterious 'dossier', which Peter refers to several times in his diary but now can remember nothing about. Ralph had a 'dossier', which worried people. Peter records that he discussed the 'Ralph Hallett problem' both with his friend Alan Swerdlow and at the National Committee. First the Vice Chairman Alun Williams and then Paul and Martin came across to Liverpool to discuss what to do about this. Ralph was refusing to hand it over, and it got into the hands of someone else, Derek Eaves. He proved willing to destroy it, and so the problem was solved. Peter told the author:

> I do remember there was a kerfuffle about Ralph and the way he handled things, but the problem went away because he got so ill he wasn't able to attend meetings, even though we went on using his room.[107]

Nobody else in Liverpool now remembers what the contents of this mysterious dossier were either. The most likely answer is that they were connected with the Correspondence Club* and its address list, the security of which Robin was to raise as an issue later when he was convenor. Whatever the contents were, the protracted negotiations over the dossier show that Ralph was clearly not the easiest of people to deal with.

38. Alan Swerdlow in 2012

The second key figure in Liverpool CHE was Alan Swerdlow, who was in his early thirties and had studied graphic design as a student at Liverpool College of Art in the year above John Lennon. In 1970 he was combining graphic design with work in the family catering equipment business. By the time he came to be involved in CHE, he was a successful independent businessman† with his own catering equipment company, with a number of gay friends, and had experienced a couple of deeper gay relationships. In short, here was a confident man who sought nothing from the group personally, beyond the sense that he was helping others, and furthering homosexual equality in

---

* See page 322.

† He kept his hand in with graphics, though, and was responsible for the design of the CHE letterhead and a number of posters and leaflets.

society.

Once again the ties between CHE and the old HLRS were strong. Alan had supported the HLRS since 1960, and received their mailings, although he discreetly arranged for them to go to a different address, in case his family opened them by mistake. Antony Grey passed on his address to Allan Horsfall when the Mancunians were organising their first public meeting in 1966, which he went to:

> I remember feeling very brave going in through the door, rather like when you went to the cinema to see one of the Oscar Wilde films at the time.* You thought everyone would guess why you were going to see that film. Of course it was complete nonsense.[108]

Alan also followed Esquire developments, and gained a reputation as a tough cookie for asking awkward questions about the project.† (His reservations turned out to be amply justified by events.)

Alan was not a 'scene' person. With his circle of friends and relationships to sustain him, his public gay life was largely limited to one place, the Basnett Bar. Alan remembered:

> It was a London-style oyster bar. Plates of smoked salmon, or plates of rare roast beef, and very good pints of Guinness. Long and narrow, with mirrors. Marble-top. It's where people like Brian Epstein used to go. … Everyone kidded themselves that it wasn't a gay bar, but without the gay clientele it would have closed. I went there most evenings on the way home from work for a drink. I had my own pewter tankard. It wasn't a sort of pick-up place, it was more a social place.[109]

He met Paul Temperton and Martin Stafford in person at the Albany Trust conference on homosexuality, in York in July 1970, which led to the formation of the National Federation of Homophile Organisations.‡ It was an occasion which also brought several other key people into the CHE ambit. Within a month Paul and Martin were visiting Liverpool to talk to him about

---

* Two Oscar Wilde biopics were released in 1960. *Oscar Wilde*, in black and white, starred Robert Morley, who had played Wilde in 1936 at the Gate Theatre Club. Though the play had to be given a private performance in the UK because of its subject matter, it was a huge success on Broadway. Morley spent twenty years trying to bring it to the screen. *The Trials of Oscar Wilde*, in widescreen and starring Peter Finch, was edited in four editing suites while the filming was still going on, in order to rush the film into cinemas the same week as Morley's more deeply-felt offering was released. As a result the flashier film eclipsed the other.

† In this he was prompted by Antony Grey, who wrote him an extended critique of the weaknesses of the Esquire project in December 1969.

‡ This is covered in the Chapter 'Them and Us' in Volume Two.

setting up a local group. Swerdlow, although not a CHE member, had already gathered around himself a circle of other non-CHE people who could form the basis of a CHE group. He was also involved with the Samaritans, which gave both an interest in the support and counselling side of a group, and experience of a voluntary organisation. Paul clearly thought Alan would be one of the keys to getting the group off the ground, because, having secured his involvement, he took out a series of seven adverts in the *Liverpool Echo*, starting on 17 July 1970, to which twenty-eight people responded over time.

The fourth interested party was 22-year-old Robin Bloxsidge, an academic researcher at the University of Liverpool.

Unlike Alan, Robin was a 'gay scene' person. According to him, in the late 1960s and early 70s Liverpool's gay clubs and bars were quite advanced – far ahead of those in Manchester:

39. Robin Bloxsidge in 2012

> Manchester, which became the great gay mecca of the North, in those days was very, very backward, and the police, who were much more backward even than they were here, wouldn't even let same-sex couples hold each other when they danced in clubs. They would be split up. But in Liverpool they didn't do anything like that, and to that extent it was a fairly advanced gay scene at the time. There wasn't a lot of it, but I mean it was fairly advanced in that sense, and coachloads of people all came from Manchester on Saturday nights, rather than the other way around. …
>
> I was more interested in the campaigning side. Though of course it was also very necessary to have something which could bring people out who

just had no interest in a pub and club scene and were too scared to go to it anyway.[110]

Alan Swerdlow remembers one such person, albeit from Merseyside FRIEND a while later, particularly clearly:

> I remember one elderly gentleman who lived with his sister, and it was only when the sister died that, at the age of late fifties, early sixties, he decided he could do something about it. And when he came to these meetings it was the child in the sweetshop; he had to be taken aside and told, just because all these people are gay, doesn't mean they're all on offer.[111]

So much repression, such a long-term dam on pent-up feelings, created the same kind of desperation in many callers and newcomers. It was quite common for people joining groups to fall in love with the first other gay person they met, simply because they were gay. This was often the convenor or secretary. So in addition to organising social activities, meeting places, campaigns, writing letters, sitting on committees and reporting to the national office, convenors would find themselves having to fend off unwanted advances without hurting feelings or crushing embryonic self-confidence. Robin remembers:

> I just wouldn't do it [have sex with newcomers]. I don't think there's necessarily any harm in it because a lot of people joining CHE did it because they were looking for sex. … And there's nothing wrong with them having got it, as long as it didn't mess up their lives or something. But I just found it easier to say, No I don't do it, because sometimes you could get people who just became obsessed with you and it made your life impossible.
>
> Well I had one lad, actually, called Barry, who … was about seventeen when he first started throwing himself at me, and he used to turn up out of the blue, even his dad used to drive him to see me, which was the most extraordinary – he said, 'I must have caused you an awful trouble, all those years ago.' And I said, 'Well it wasn't so much an awful trouble, but it was a sort of worry, because it was an obsession. I was the first person you'd met, and you just couldn't decide to do it with anyone else.' So I always had this thing that I wasn't going to do it. But other people certainly did it. Some people … with a cynicism which was not really desirable.[112]

Influence of singles clubs

The first hurdle any new CHE group had to surmount was, what would it actually do? They were feeling their way, to some extent, because there was no formal precedent to follow within the organisation, and groups could be what they wanted to be. Gay men themselves often had little experience of relating to other gay men apart from in a sexual context, where contacts were largely wordless in any case. When these early CHE members found themselves in their first meeting, their awkwardness was more than a self-consciousness about effectively 'outing' themselves in this situation; they literally did not know how to talk to each other.

However, there were models within the heterosexual 'singles' world, a world which Peter Norman had experience of. Innately shy, he was the kind of person whose homosexuality, or sense of 'difference', had fenced him off from casual friendly interaction. He needed groups, both political and social, to provide a formal channel – an excuse, if you like – through which to interact with others. So when he first came to Liverpool, knowing no-one and nowhere, the advertised heterosexual organisations were the first port of call:

> I looked round for how I was going to meet people, and I found an organisation called the Intervarsity Club. It was formed of people who had graduated from universities in various places, and it formed a social network. ... But of course it was mainly for people to pick each other up. It was a singles club. So although I quite enjoyed some of the things it organised, ... there were far more women than men, so you were sort of ambushed by all these twenty-somethings on heat. That was a bit trying. The other thing I tried was a group called the Octopus Club, which was much better. It wasn't so rooted in university graduates, it was much more varied. It was basically a semi-arty social group for professional-type people, but not exclusively, and it had interesting discussion meetings and speaker meetings, and various social events, and things like theatre visits. And I quite enjoyed that.[113]

He brought that experience to bear when, in October 1970, he, Alan and Robin met to cobble together their first programme. Before the meeting, Peter mapped out his ideas in the form of notes:

> Re future programme: Need to take bold steps now in conjunction perhaps with further advertising, in the hope that new members will join and then remain. Compare social groups and clubs that exist in the outside world. .... For example, the Intervarsity Club and Octopus Club which function in Liverpool. Came across them on first coming to Liverpool. Exist basically to provide single people mostly young but some widowed, divorced etc. with opportunity of finding a mate. Tend to be youngish single footloose professional type members on the whole, nothing basically in common. IVC runs events most nights of the week – bridge, play-readings, rambles, theatre trips, car rallies, table tennis, coffee parties, etc. Has largish membership. Octopus has Wednesday meetings, Thursday socials, darts, chess etc., and Sunday and weekend rambles, also swimming Monday nights. Obviously couldn't imitate that straight away, but surely need for similar facilities for homosexuals to get to know people more

> than on the whole shallow bar relationships. Obviously nobody would want to participate in all activities, and spend their whole time in homo-company. If that is the aim, what should be the early steps? Ask for ideas.[114]

And afterwards he noted in his diary that 'I think my view of a sort of Octopus organisation may have prevailed.'

This meeting was a matter of days before the first gathering of convenors from all the groups, held in Birmingham (24 October 1970). Here for the first time local organisers could meet each other and exchange information and ideas, something which would become the staple of National Councils when they were set up a year later. People came from London, Bristol, Birmingham, Wolverhampton, Liverpool, Nottingham, Cambridge, Oxford University and Sheffield University, and there were others interested in starting groups from Leeds, Teesside and Chilterns. Peter took along his newly-formulated, recently discussed ideas, and no doubt other local convenors, as well as Paul and Martin, took them away to their own groups, or to suggest to new convenors.

It would have been skirting the borders of legality to suggest in 1970 that a gay organisation was modelling itself on heterosexual societies aimed at finding people mates. Nevertheless, this kind of pairing up was implicit in the set-up, and explicit in the minds of Peter and his fellow organisers.

> The hetero equivalents work through putting people in a situation where they meet and socialise, and things develop from there if both parties wish it. And I thought the same thing would happen in CHE.
>
> I don't think I would advocate that people should join specifically to pick people up, no. 'Come to the meeting, go home with somebody that night' – that wasn't what I had in mind.[115]

In this way, as Working Men's Clubs were a model for Esquire Clubs, heterosexual singles clubs were models for local groups, at least outside London. No social organisation ever comes into existence in a vacuum.

Vetting members

Liverpool, like all early groups, was in its first stages extremely insecure, and one of the ways in which this manifested itself was in discussions about how or whether to vet new members. It was always national policy that groups should be completely open to all but the most destructively sociopathic, but to those on the ground and hesitantly dipping a toe in unknown waters, threats from people they didn't know were potent, even if they were more imaginary than real. Although it is easy at this distance of time to ridicule this as elitism, or perpetuation of the closet, it must be remembered that not only were conspiracy laws lurking at the back of everyone's minds, the strangers who were being drawn into the group were being invited into people's flats and houses. It was all very personal.

> There were people who thought, 'My goodness. ANYBODY might come. We're meeting at our flat.' Looking back, I think it was a bit the fear of the unknown. Don't forget a lot of gay people then knew no or hardly any other gay people at all. There were the beginnings of a pub scene, and you'd see all kinds of people in the pub, some of whom you wouldn't want to associate with. Probably people felt, we don't know who we might get, they might be all sorts of nasty people. There was a lot of self-oppression, of course, in those days. A sort of feeling at the back of some people's minds, 'Well I'm not too bad, although I'm gay, but there are lots of gay people who are really awful.' But the general view of the group was not to vet people.[116]

Under Alan Swerdlow's first constitution, membership was open to anyone who paid their subs, but when Liverpool came to revise its constitution in 1972, there was an attempt to introduce vetting through having a Membership Committee which would interview newcomers. Peter Norman advised that the wording be changed and that the Membership Committee should not 'interview and accept (or reject)', but should 'meet and welcome'.

It seems as if in some respects the suspicions were justified. Brian Sewell held tea parties for London Group 3, and always checked the spoons afterwards. Another CHE host, Kenneth Jameson, told Jeremy Seabrook in 1974:

> I used to hold parties here for CHE, the London main group* as well as the local branch. But people will steal things. I suppose we all need so much love, don't we? But there are some people who steal things presumably because love is lacking is in their lives. I don't mind, only it's boring when they do. So lately I've been inclined to withdraw even from that.[117]

In rejecting vetting, Liverpool was also going against the feeling of the workshop on social groups at the Albany Trust Conference in York, for which Alan Swerdlow had taken the notes a mere four months previously. That workshop had expressly advocated screening new members, in the name of group safety. It had also recommended separating out 'problem homosexuals' – married lesbians, transvestites – into different social groups.

However, whatever the official policy, vetting was certainly going on, and in January 1972 Keith Brook complained about it to local groups organiser Peter Norman. In particular, he was concerned about the behaviour of John Lear, a previous organiser for the St Katherine's (SK) Group in Docklands, who brought the SK habit of screening members for suitability with him when

---

* It isn't clear what he means by 'the London main group'.

he became convenor of South Herts CHE:

> I first met John Lear last summer at his home in Radlett, when he was interviewing prospective members of the South Herts CHE group. … I asked him how many members there would be in the group, and … he said he wasn't accepting for membership all the names he had been given. I … said that I thought group membership should be open to all CHE members in the district. His reply was that he proposed to hold meetings in his own home and there were certain prospective members he didn't wish to invite. …. I raised the matter again at the first meeting of the group, to make sure I hadn't misunderstood the situation, and in the hope of getting some kind of discussion going. John again said that he had been given the names of people he wouldn't wish to invite into his own home, and added that one of these was an Indian.
>
> At a party at Roger Baker's flat at the beginning of October 1971 I asked Roger how many people have been rejected for membership in London CHE groups. He was emphatic that no-one had ever been rejected. … It occurs to me that there can't be so many Indian CHE members in this area that identifying the one who was refused membership should present any difficulty.[118]

Confrontation is never easy, and accusations of racism are not always easy to substantiate. A short-handed voluntary organisation is always tempted not to antagonise the volunteers it depends on in case it drives them away. 'Better a volunteer with – ah – eccentric views than no volunteer at all'. Peter Norman had been founder/chairman of the NCCL in Liverpool and as such had taken up the issue of the rights of gypsies; he had been involved in the anti-apartheid campaign, and Amnesty International. He was keenly aware of the implications of the accusation. Nevertheless he delayed on the issue, preferring it to be subsumed in a wider discussion of vetting in general. He wrote back to Brook:

> There have been a number of developments bearing on this lately, and I wanted to see how they would turn out. I think it is too late to consider raking over the coals in Hertfordshire, but since then a similar problem has arisen in Teesside, and another, slightly more complex, in South Hants. Also Ike Cowen, who as well as being an EC member is also a barrister, drafted a model constitution for local groups which included a clause permitting the exclusion of prospective members without reason; this caused quite a lot of controversy at the EC, and we decided to allot some time for a discussion of the whole question at the next NC [March 1972].* Personally I think that to be worthy of the name 'campaign' it is crucial

* The National Council discussion of vetting is covered more fully in Volume Two.

> that we are ready to accept all comers, but the feeling of the meeting on this remains to be seen.[119]

In the event, the need for confrontation was taken out of Peter's hands when Lear stepped down as convenor to concentrate on St Katherine's, shortly after the NC in question. He was replaced by John Kernaghan, a graduate of London Group 10 and a friend of Peter Norman's partner. No more vetting went on in South Herts CHE.

Another group which vetted was Guernsey CHE, a slightly later formation, where there were complaints from women that they were being excluded. This was taken seriously enough for the CHE women's officer, Liz Stanley, to investigate. She was more proactive than Norman, and reported to the EC:

> Some time before Christmas I reported to Howarth* two complaints about the Guernsey group from CHE members (both women) who I met in Leeds. They had been in Guernsey for six months and had tried to join this group.
>
> They were told that they could *apply* for membership but it was very unlikely they would be *accepted* because the group accepted mainly professional people. (One of those women was told that the group had in it a number of local government officials and they had to be protected against discovery.)† One of the women was working in a hotel, the other in a shop; both were put off and didn't bother 'applying'. It was lucky for them that they were together – what would have happened to them if they had been alone and in a strange place for six months? As we all know, gay women don't grow on trees.[120]

The General Secretary Howarth Penny wrote to Kaye le Cheminant, the convenor, but got no reply. Guernsey being so far away, it was easier to ignore it than to act. Then another case came to Liz's attention:

> On Saturday 22 June I was phoned by a woman living in Guernsey who got my phone number from *Gay News*, and who wanted somewhere to stay in Manchester when she came to visit her parents. During the course of the conversation she told me she had wanted to join 'Kaye's group' but hadn't been allowed to 'because the women in it are too masculine for you'. (She is bisexual and has never met a gay woman apart from Kaye). She has since met a few gay men from the group and gets on well with them – so even if the women in the group are a load of old dykes I can't see why she shouldn't go and associate with the gay men. Kaye herself was 'feminine' enough, and I suspect she is being kept out because she's bisexual, something an alarming number of members and groups do. …

---

* Howarth Penny, Paul Temperton's successor as General Secretary, 1973-4.

† Homosexuality was not decriminalised in Guernsey until 1983, or in Jersey until 1990.

> Obviously the situation stinks. 1) The group (or Kaye) excludes all 'undesirables' – like people in non-professional jobs, and bisexuals. CHE is supposed to be open to all gay people; this doesn't do our image much good, as, for e.g., other non-CHE women in Leeds are now saying that we're a bunch of closetty middle-class shits, basing this on the experience of those women in Guernsey (and the equally awful Leeds group). 2) Gay men who are excluded from this group have the clubs and bars to go to (they may not like them but they are there for men): gay women have *nowhere* else. And a high proportion of gay women are Bisexual.[121]

The admission that a large number of groups effectively excluded bisexuals is significant, coming as it does from a member of the EC with her ear to the ground, especially with regard to women members. However, it is in the nature of the operation that such exclusion would have been clandestine, and there is little other evidence of such exclusion at this early stage of the organisation. It was also something vehemently denied by Roger Baker, the London organiser, when Laurence Collinson suggested that this vetting was responsible for CHE's 'middle-class' image:

> Collinson implied that members of CHE are vetted in some way to make sure they are suitable and 'unlikely to present an awkward or embarrassing image of homosexuality to the "straight" world.' This is not true, the only qualification required is that he or she supports the aims of the organisation. There is, I know, a still small voice within CHE that wishes to see some sort of selection system introduced ('to keep out the mad and the smelly' is the exact phrase) but the National Executive will not tolerate such an idea, nor, it is hoped would local convenors or chairmen.[122]

If it was happening however, one of the outcomes would certainly be to weaken the working class representation over a period of time, and to exaggerate the middle class elements. Middle class people were in any case more likely to read the *Spectator*, *Private Eye* and so on, where adverts appeared, and were more commonly 'joiners' of associations; from the middle classes came, as usual, the reformers, and now the middle classes were in a position to start perpetuating themselves within the organisation. In this way the essentially working class origins of CHE would become, if not lost, smudged over a period of time.

Liverpool social activities

Unencumbered with such class distinctions, or any exclusions save of people under 21, Liverpool CHE started its social meetings above the cake shop. However, unlike other local groups, Liverpool had a clear formal structure pretty much from the start. Peter Norman explained:

> Basically I suppose nobody had much experience of it [running a group], we did it how we thought we would do it. And of course we did it in what today people would think is a rather fuddy-duddy way of proceeding, where we had a constitution and rules and elections. We devised this ourselves because there wasn't a kind of national model. Alan [Swerdlow] was a business man, and ... he was involved much more in very middle-class organisations and I think that he would've seen that as how to do it. It wouldn't occur to me to have a constitution.[123]

At only its second meeting in October, which was a party, it set up a committee of five, purely from people who wanted to get involved. Alan, Ralph and Peter were all members. Robin, less of a 'joiner', wasn't. This small group was converted into an elected committee in early 1971, which Peter wasn't on because he was away in the United States at the time. On his return in May 1971 he was both co-opted and elected convenor, when Ralph's health finally forced him to retire.

The advertisements continued to appear, but it was the word spreading on the grapevine which drew most people in:

> Once we'd got the initial membership, more people were coming by word of mouth. In the first year or so, I would think we got more people by word of mouth than anything else. And they were people really who were sort of hidden in the community. Nobody knew them, but they knew other people. It was like a hangover from gay life being a secret society. ... And after a while people began to come to CHE who were pub and club people, because they had found out about it and, although they might continue being pub and club people, they quite liked the social aspect, the fact that you can actually talk to people.[124]

So meetings grew until the sitting room could take no more people, and they had to find other premises. New members were introduced at dedicated meetings where three or four newcomers met a couple of committee members. Activities diversified into more and more people's houses, but the main monthly meetings had to find somewhere much larger. By the middle of 1971 they were claiming 100 members. They abandoned Ralph's family's sitting room, and went briefly to a Friends' Meeting House, where one of their speakers was Ray Gosling. However, Friends' Meeting Houses are not noted for their comfort, and they were relieved to move on again into – a cake and coffee shop. It was open until one in the morning, which was as late as anything stayed open in Liverpool in 1971, and as long as the group bought cakes in sufficient numbers, the owners were happy. By this stage there were also several sub-groups of a kind which would be more elaborately diversified in London:* play-reading, music, rambling, an action group (rechristened Task Force,† and then changed back because *Task Force* was a popular TV series).

The range of activities which the group developed can be seen in the report which appeared in the first issue of the Leeds *Broadsheet* in October 1971. There were speakers from a variety of sources, from Doreen Cordell of the Albany Trust to Edsel, a pink-haired proto-punk from the Gay Liberation Front in London. Peter Norman noted that Edsel generated 'a good discussion, involving a good number of members'. Local MPs were invited, and of course canvassed. Their reaction was usually pessimistic. When Dick Crawshaw,‡ Labour MP for Toxteth, came to the group, although he had voted in favour of the 1967 Act he said that he 'could not foresee any future reforms on this subject [age of consent] or others raised, such as equal social rights and equal job opportunities, for at least ten years.'[125]

40. Liverpool CHE canal trip, 1972, Paul O'Grady third from left§

* See Chapter Six.

† Not to be confused with the London 'Task Force', which turned into FRIEND.

‡ Lt Colonel R Crawshaw, OBE, TD, DL, MP. Later he became Baron Crawshaw of Aintree and a patron of Friend Merseyside.

§ Judging by my dishevelled state I'd say that I was 'with drink' at the time and had been obviously up to no good below deck on that boat. I recognise nearly everyone on that

One group of speakers provided possibly more regular subject matter than any other, and those were vicars, Catholic priests and other religious representatives. The dialogue between homosexuals and various religions has always been fractious, but a sizeable proportion of CHE members belonged to churches, or at least felt the pain of exile from them. Visiting clergy provided an opportunity to chip away at institutional homophobia, to canvass friends within the churches, or to attack the enemy. And many clergy derived their own comfort from visiting CHE groups. Alan Swerdlow remembers:

> Catholic priests came to talk to us and I think most of the ones who claimed they weren't gay were gay, but they just came and talked, and I think it was as much as anything a support for them as an interesting evening for us.[126]

The group organised larger-scale public outings. There was a boat trip along the coast to Llandudno:

> While on board don't sit on the Capstan. And leave the rollocks alone. It is not allowed to warm your bummel on the funnel. Sorry, no feeding arrangements organised. Have a nibble at each other, or munch a banana – very sustaining.[127]

The same newsletter announced:

> August meetings will also be out-of-doors if possible. We want to see those sunburned arms and legs, not to mention torsos and midriffs. See those bronzed faces and laughing eyes, sparkling with *joie de vivre* from dazzling Liverpool sunshine. … Barbecue on Formby Beach followed by Rounders.[128]

---

photo, we'd had a day out on a canal somewhere and the girl standing next to me with the short hair is Cathy Cowley, she was a very good pal of mine at the time and we were forever on demos and protesting about something and I remember nearly getting arrested outside Liverpool Town Hall during a 'sit in'. It was a real Sodom and Gomorrah… —Paul O'Grady, e-mail to the author, 20 October 2014.

41. 1972 Liverpool v. Manchester football match

The tone is flippant, but these outings, these large parties of openly gay people, combined personal pleasure with something more serious. As Robin Bloxsidge put it, 'A lot of things like that even, which were social events, were actually good in terms of influencing the public, because they were things that were taking place in public.'[129] On one memorable occasion in 1972, there was a football match between Manchester Homophile Society and Liverpool CHE, a match undertaken more in a spirit of camp than competition. Manchester was the first gay group ever to announce the formation of a football team, in October 1971. ('Don't worry, no-one else knows how to play. No-one actually knows the rules. But who needs rules?')[130]

> In an attempt to free ourselves from a particular 'gay' image the society has formed its own football team. Whilst not quite up to Man. United or City standards yet – those readers who cried, 'What standards?' should kindly leave the room! – we hope to take on Leeds GLF and London GLF in due course and expect to give them both a good licking! (They mean win the game – Ed.)[131]

The 1971 season was spent learning how to kick a ball. But 13 May 1972 was announced as 'the campest day of the year'. The local derby was held in Heaton Park in Prestwich, a suburb of Manchester, and it was the first public gay football match in the UK. Glenys Parry was the sole woman playing, and managed to score the only goal of the match. Robin Bloxsidge remembered the occasion well:

> The police came and watched, hiding behind bushes. I don't know what they thought we were going to do on the football pitch! But clearly they

didn't believe we were only going to play football.[132]

Police surveillance of the most innocent CHE activities was something which several CHE groups were subjected to.

Liverpool Youth Group

Liverpool's November 1971 meeting was to have implications for the future of the group, which was split over the issue of admitting under-21s. In the first constitution, presumably at Alan Swerdlow's insistence, the group was only open to over-21s, something which Robin was passionately opposed to, and campaigned to have overturned. As part of this campaign, Ike Cowen of Nottingham CHE, and CHE's legal officer, was to speak 'on legal aspects, after which we [Liverpool CHE] may or may not alter our age limit to admit under-21s.'

Ike didn't convince the group to change. The teenagers were not accepted into the group, but in order to provide some facilities rather than turn them away completely, CHE started a separate Youth Group. In fact it would take Robin two years to get his way, and for the Liverpool group to admit teenagers.

> It always seemed to me absolutely wrong that if you were campaigning for equality [you should exclude under-21s]. But I had a terrible time driving that through. 1973 is when they did it, against any advice nationally. I just said I'm not going to have anything more to do with it unless it's over 16 people can come in. It caused a terrible row … it got very acrimonious. We had a meeting to pass the change of the rule, 'cause we had the constitution, and I was accused of driving it through, which I suppose I was. But I mean I could only drive it through if I persuaded enough people to vote for it. But there were so many people against it, it was a very big row for a long meeting. But then, when it did go through, we actually lost quite a lot of members. Maybe about twenty or twenty-something members went. Ironically some of the principal opponents of this were what you'd call 'chicken hawks', really, who thought it was alright for them to go hunting young people for sex, but you weren't allowed to have them in this respectable organisation. But we did begin to get quite a lot of young people in after that.[133]

When the vote was finally cast, Robin wrote jubilantly to Paul Temperton:

> Well, we finally did it – last night the Liverpool Group resolved to change its age limit to 16 by a majority of 2 votes! A close-run thing! Actually, I wanted no age limit at all but it's the next best thing and having taken 2 years with 4 separate votes on the subject I wasn't going to quibble.[134]

In fact there were sufficient youngsters to start a youth group, which aroused opposition from the same people who opposed the lowering of the entry age.

> A lot of these people who were opposed to it were saying, 'Oh, you're going to get police attention and people are going to come round.' But the police never took any notice of it at all as far as I can see. At one time in its history, for quite a long time, it met in a gay club, on an early weekday, when they weren't getting any other customers. The youth group was sixteen to twenty-one, but these people were drinking too, of course, and the police used to come to every meeting. And all they did was say hello, and some of these kids would buy the policemen a drink, and then they'd go on their way![135]

The contrast between the Liverpool police force and the spying Manchester force is revealing, and affected the local gay cultures of the early 1970s.

As a spin-off from this decision, Robin appointed a 17-year-old assistant convenor, Dave Evans. Dave's role was to welcome new members by letter, and invite them to a new members' meeting. Robin remembers:

> This role, quite possibly because of his age and because some people mistakenly believed I had promoted him because we were having an affair, was somewhat controversial with existing members, but I think the new members were generally quite pleased to be greeted by an attractive young man. … Dave had been referred to CHE by the Samaritans, who he had phoned not because he felt a problem about being gay (he was moderately confident) but to ask how he could meet other gay people. This was in the late summer/early autumn of 1971 – I had clearly known him a little while by the time that he wrote to me in November that year – and I remember being a little taken aback when I'd arranged to meet him in a pub and he turned up in school uniform! Not that anybody seemed to notice.[136]

If Dave Evans was appointed assistant convenor at the age of 17 in 1973, this means he must have been barely 15 when he contacted the group in the first place. Robin and members of the group must have offered very strong support if he remained within the friendship circle, if not the actual group, for two years until the rules were changed.

Among the other young people who came along as a result of the rule change was 17-year-old Paul O'Grady, later to find fame first as drag act Lily Savage and then in his own persona as a TV and radio presenter. Paul had a troubled bisexual sexual history, and had accidentally fathered a child, although he felt himself predominantly gay. He read a CHE advert in the back of *New Musical Express*. It gave a London number, so it was presumably placed by the London groups. They in turn gave Paul a Liverpool contact number, so Paul phoned Robin Bloxsidge. He gives a graphic account of meeting up with Robin in the first volume of his autobiography, *At My Mother's Knee – and other low joints*:

> He sounded enthusiastic and invited me to attend the next meeting. 'Oh before you hang up,' he added cheerfully, 'What's your name?' I didn't want to give my real name in case these people expected me to come out and run through the streets of Liverpool screaming, 'I'm gay.' I wasn't ready for such extremes just yet. Best to give an alias, I thought, until I see what they're like.
>
> 'Simon,' I answered. 'Simon King.'
>
> The day of the meeting I was beside myself with anticipation. Would it be an orgy of unbridled lust and passion, I wondered (I'd read one of my ma's Angelique books), and if so, what would happen if I didn't want to participate? Would I be drugged and gang-raped while unconscious or just thrown out into the street and mocked for being uptight and inexperienced? …
>
> I arrived at Robin's flat three quarters of an hour early. He opened the door to me wearing nothing but a short towel, confirming my earlier suspicions about an orgy. Thank God I've had a bath, I thought to myself as I nervously entered this den of iniquity. It transpired that this wasn't Sodom and Gomorrah: Robin had been in the shower when I arrived as he wasn't expecting anyone until eight, but he kindly showed me into his untidy front room, left me with a copy of Gay News and went to get dressed. …
>
> When everyone had finally arrived we were given tea and biscuits, not what I'd expected at a bacchanalian orgy – but then nor was the group. I was discouraged to find that they all seemed perfectly ordinary and unexciting. I was by far the youngest in the room, and looking around, there was certainly no one that I fancied. … It was all so pleasant and genteel, we could've been at a 1930s WI meeting in Tunbridge Wells. The atmosphere was far from predatory or threatening, and after our initial shyness wore off we talked freely and openly among ourselves, which made me regret using an alias. These were nice people and I wouldn't mind coming back to attend further meetings.
>
> A guy named Steve, who up till now hadn't had much to say for himself, offered me a lift home. He was older than me, with sly eyes and a small moustache, and he only came up to my shoulder; not really my type, although I was still unsure what my type was. But since the alternative to a lift meant having to stand at a bus stop on Upper Parliament Street, then a notorious red light district at eleven o'clock at night, I accepted the offer.
>
> 'We'll stop off in New Brighton and have a drink at the Chelsea Reach first shall we?' He said innocently, failing to add 'followed by a session in the back of my van on Egremont Promenade.'
>
> I wasn't agreeable to this suggestion at first, but it's amazing how a combination of cider and persistent persuasion can weaken the resistance of a lad who's far too well brought up to say no.'[137]

So whatever was going on within the respectability of the group meetings, it's clear that outside there was more stereotypical gay male behaviour. However, the very respectability was a two-edged sword. On the one hand reassuring, on the other it quickly palled.

> It was beginning to bore me because it was all talk, talk, talk and not enough action for my liking. … None of the CHE lot were scene queens, and rarely if ever went to the gay pubs and clubs in town. This left me feeling very frustrated and wishing I had the bottle to go in on my own, but I didn't, so that was that.[138]

Liverpool campaigning

Coupled with this social life, there were campaigns. This took some time to get off the ground, and was not to the fore up to May 1972, when Robin Bloxsidge became convenor. The group until then was too occupied with establishing itself and creating some kind of group spirit and identity. Peter Norman justifies this:

> Except that you had to campaign to stand still, in the sense that when we lost the use of Ralph's large room, we had to find somewhere else to meet. I don't know who suggested it, but someone suggested we might approach the Quakers for the use of their meeting room, or a room somewhere. And that was agreed, and I wrote to them. And then I found that the person in the Quakers who was responsible for dealing with bookings, the secretary or whatever, was actually a member of the team I supervised at the City Planning Department. So he came up to me and said it would be all right, in the office. I thought it was an interesting variation on where people are afraid to come out to the boss, I came out to the staff! It related to campaigning in the sense that the simplest thing was in a sense a campaign, because you had to go to people and say who you were and what you were up to, and even by doing that you were making waves, or could be.[139]

Despite the size of the Liverpool group, most campaigning was done by a hard core of some half a dozen people – the Action Group. Some campaigns were local and some co-ordinated through the national office. Local campaigns were very much at the discretion of local groups, and could probably be more accurately labelled outreach. At its most elementary and reactive level, it was simply a question of telling people that the group existed. In this way, Liverpool started getting referrals from the Samaritans and from Social Services. Other institutions were tougher nuts to crack. It took months of letters and meetings to persuade the probation service to use the group; even longer to get visiting rights to prisons. Bloxsidge was keen to support prisoners:

> We just kept bombarding these prison governors, saying that we've got to do it, that it was just if a gay prisoner wanted somebody gay to go and see them, we could fix it up. In the end they said yes, and we had a great response from prisoners. At one time we were visiting quite a lot of prisoners and we had four or five people visiting prisoners quite regularly. Even to the extent – I don't know if this happened more than once – that Nick [his partner] and I had one prisoner to stay with us on home leave. I mean, he didn't have a home, but the prison allowed him to have us as his home leave, preparatory to his release.
>
> Some of them were there because of gay alleged offences, or they might just have been gay people who didn't have any other contact.[140]

Many CHE groups had 'campaign specialities' and prison visiting was one of Liverpool's. Other groups around the country took inspiration and advice from this project and started knocking metaphorically on the door of their local prisons.

Talks given to other organisations were important too, and, like other local groups, Liverpool wrote round to local Women's Institutes, Rotary Clubs, Trade Unions, church groups, schools* and colleges. The Group talked to trainee social workers at the Josephine Butler College in early 1972. Since public opinion was far in advance of what Press and Parliament thought it was, visiting speakers were in the main surprised at the lack of hostility. There were however exceptions:

> I remember the Widnes Rotary Club, of all places, where there were about thirty-five people. Men, of course. We had a meal, and then I gave this speech afterwards. And then they asked questions and made statements. A lot of them were statements rather than questions. They didn't accept anything I'd said! It was a very nerve-racking thing in a way, just standing up and being attacked left, right and centre. But you always got a little response, and after this one everybody went except five people came to the bar with me and carried on talking, which was a good thing. And for quite a few years after that I saw one or two of these people who used to just stop in the street and speak generally. So you were getting through gradually, inch by inch, to people, really.[141]

The media were important. Every group tried to get articles into the local papers. Sometimes the press handed a group an opportunity on a plate, as with the *Liverpool Daily Post* and its full-page interview with 'Albert' in 1971. The subhead of the article tells readers that:

> The Medical Research Council's Clinical Endocrinology Unit at Edinburgh has, after concentrated research, suggested that it may be as wrong to

---

* Schools campaigning is dealt with separately in Volume Two as a national campaign.

> stigmatise the homosexual as it would be to victimise the congenitally blind, the deaf or the dumb.[142]

The rest of the article continues very much in the 'Pity the Handicapped' vein. In some ways Albert conforms to the stereotypes: he is someone with a physical revulsion for all women except his mother, who was a saint. He is a 'passive queer' who has been living with his 'husband' for 18 years. However, in other ways he blows the stereotypes apart:

> He is not effeminate. He is stocky, very broad, good-looking in a mannish way and as tough as they come. He looks as though he would be extremely handy to have around in a pub brawl. He is in fact a club barman. 'It was not unusual to be picked upon as a punch-ball by a few louts who found out that I was 'one of those'. I learned the hard way to look after myself.'[143]

'Albert' is at great pains to assert the 'normality' and 'harmlessness' of The Homosexual; in this he pursues the common strategy of separating the worthy from the unworthy homosexual, a parallel with the deserving and undeserving poor, which characterised much of the more cautious reformist movements of the 1960s and 1970s. Albert told the reporter, Don Smith:

> The true homosexual hates the flaunting, effeminate, brightly dressed, painted and long-haired type. They are in a minority but get the majority a bad name. Lower down in the strata of homosexuals is the sort who deliberately antagonises the public. They are usually youngsters who haven't grown up. … The lowest form of homosexual is the type who hang around public toilets and the like. They are, to us, revolting. They are male prostitutes and complete degenerates. To a true homosexual the idea of love between two men is a wonderful thing.[144]

This led someone from the group to take the unusual step (for CHE, and for the time) of defending the outlaws on the wilder shores of effeminacy. Because it was so controversial, the letter appeared anonymously:

> I was amazed that such a person as 'Albert' should have been chosen to put forward the case for tolerance for homosexuals. While it is obviously more acceptable to society that homosexuals should not be extrovert and effeminate in their mannerisms, it is ludicrous to plead for tolerance and in the same breath state that 'the true homosexual detests the flaunting, effeminate, brightly dressed, painted and long-haired types.' These people are just as much homosexual and perhaps even more in need of understanding than the less overt types.
>
> —A non-effeminate homosexual.[145]

Apart from this unacknowledged sally, Liverpool CHE was not conspicuously successful at publicity in the paper, although it was on the receiving end of some unwanted press intrusion when it organised a conference for social workers in the precincts of Liverpool Anglican Cathedral,* in the teeth of opposition from members of the congregation. [146] On other occasions press coverage of homosexuality was violently negative:

> On the other side of the vice problem is homosexuality. ... It is still only legal between consenting adults. What no-one knows is whether this has led to an increase in the practice or whether it has brought it into the open. Their old haunts have either been demolished or closed, so the 'gay' population have spread out to fresh fields. ... There are a few pubs and clubs which actually cater for them and at least one where the normal male is regarded as an intruder.
>
> I asked the licensee of one of these pubs why he openly encouraged them. His reply was straight, if nothing else: 'They spend well and they never cause any trouble. ... And don't get the idea they can't look after themselves. ... Many are ex-seamen and know how to handle themselves in a punch-up.
>
> The main difficulty I found was that, with the current trend towards long hair and more flamboyant clothes, it was difficult to tell who was queer and who was normal.[147]

This was the second article on the subject by Don Smith, author of the 'Albert' interview. There was a space of two and a half years between the two pieces (April 71 to November 73), in which great strides were being made socially. But not for Mr Smith. Whether it represents a hardening of attitude or a cynical pandering to readers' prejudice is hard to say. The article goaded Liverpool CHE to a demonstration outside the offices of the *Liverpool Daily Post*. Needless to say, the papers didn't report that. The group did, however, get airtime on magazine programmes on BBC Radio Merseyside;† Robin Bloxsidge first broadcast in July 1971, a few days before the Burnley public meeting.

There were more public forms of outreach. Stickers became popular. The idea was first floated in March 1970 when Martin Stafford suggested that 'small stickers be printed for sticking up in public places, but this method of publicity was thought disreputable and rejected'.[148] But by 1971 all groups were issued with a sheaf of stickers, to be stuck up in phone boxes, lavatories and anywhere else with a smooth surface which would take the adhesive.

---

* See page 313.

† BBC Local Radio started in 1967, but was initially hampered by a requirement that it should be funded jointly by the BBC and local authorities. As a result, only eight stations got off the ground. The funding requirement was dropped in 1970, and as a result a further twelve stations started broadcasting that year. Liverpool CHE broadcast on BBC Radio Merseyside in phone-ins four times in the years 1971–73.

These gave basic information about how to contact CHE. But even on so banal a subject there were rumblings of discontent, which Robin as convenor dutifully noted to Paul Temperton in a letter of April 1972:

> There were some mumblings about the new stickers. Not because of objections to sticking stickers, although there is a feeling that some members could be more discriminating in where they stick them. More that people seem to think they're likely to be ineffective. A fair number of members have voiced the same opinion – some, but a 'pacifiable' minority, I think – that they're likely to be counterproductive in that they're irritating things to have to remove. The group committee seemed to think there was much more point in the Manchester Students' 'Homosexuals were here – Did you notice?' stickers and would welcome an issue of these as they made a real point.[149]

There was leafleting as well. Robin remembers:

> We did a huge thing at one time with not very many of us handing out leaflets in Liverpool city centre. We didn't get any really bad reaction, but a very surprised reaction from people that these people would be out giving them leaflets saying 'Why are you against gay people?' And we wore badges which said, 'How dare you presume I'm heterosexual'. I remember, in Lewis's department store in Liverpool, a man coming up to me and saying, 'How dare you presume that I presumed you were heterosexual!'[150]

The largest single education project undertaken by Liverpool CHE was the teach-in for local social workers and probation officers, in September 1972, held in the Western Rooms in Liverpool's Anglican Cathedral under the auspices of the Dean, the Very Rev. E. H. Patey. The group had already had experience of organising large-scale events: in March 1972 it had hosted a quarterly National Council for CHE representatives from all over the country at the same venue.* This stood it in good stead. This time they actively courted press publicity. Robin Bloxsidge recalls:

> A small announcement in the *Liverpool Echo* a couple of days before started complaints against the use of a place of worship for a meeting on such a disgusting subject. The protests were spearheaded by the Secretary General of the Christian Political Union, and hit the front page of the *Liverpool Daily Post* on the day of the teach-in, and was given prominent coverage in one of the suburban weeklies. There were demands that the meeting be called off. Because of the protests, interviews with the convenors of the two

---

* The National Council had attracted no adverse comment because it was not a publicly advertised event (and plans to film it for television had come to nothing: see page 512). For more about CHE's quarterly National Councils, see Volume Two.

> Merseyside groups and the CPU were broadcast on Radio Merseyside the next day and a short report appeared in the *Liverpool Echo*.[151]

When people complained to the Bishop, he referred them to the Dean, who in the Anglican church is a kind of cathedral manager. 'This meeting shouldn't be happening in the Western Recital Rooms,' one protester said. 'Well, where else in the cathedral do you suggest they hold it?' replied the Dean.

The conference was extremely successful. Modest in scale, in that it only attracted 35 delegates, it nevertheless targeted them very carefully. There were representatives of schools, youth clubs, the probation service, voluntary and local authority social services, Anglican and Roman Catholic clergy, Samaritans and magistrates. To get such a cross-section, especially from schools and magistrates, in 1972 was no mean achievement. Alan Swerdlow spoke, as did Michael Butler from the Samaritans, and there was a panel of speakers answering questions in the afternoon, including Antony Grey and Rev. Dennis Nadin, who spearheaded CHE's campaign within the churches and was to join the Executive two years later. There was a lot of debunking of myths, talk about the legal position, and explanation of the need for counselling services – at the time, CHE's counselling wing, FRIEND, was just being set up.* Out of the day came contacts, further discussion of ways to help homosexuals, and, because of the outcry in the papers, a stark awareness of exactly what gays were up against. Robin concluded in a *Gay News* article, 'It was expensive and time consuming to arrange, but it paid off in all sorts of ways.'[152]

In 1972 the Group also canvassed their local MPs. This was a regular exercise conducted by many local groups, co-ordinated nationally at times of General Elections. It was however more unusual between elections, and Liverpool CHE was the first group to undertake the exercise. In an accompanying letter they described the group as having 100 members, 25 per cent of whom were women, and an autonomous sub-group in Wirral. They had been out to speak to local colleges. Then they set out their stall:

> There is no logical or proven medical reason for supposing that young men are at any special risk if the age of consent is reduced. … I am writing to ask what your opinion is on this subject and on the possibility of a further bill to amend and equalise the age of consent for homosexuals and generally overhaul the sexual laws. … and the important matter of clearer directions to the police.†[153]

The replies are preserved; they present a depressing picture for those eager for

---

* See Chapter Five.

† Entrapment being still a common police practice.

further law reform. Tim Fortescue, Conservative MP for Liverpool Garston with a special interest in disability issues, was deeply pessimistic:

> There is almost no possibility of a new Bill on Homosexual Law Reform being introduced into the House of Commons this parliament and, if it were, even less possibility of it being carried. As you well know, the current Sexual Offences Act was bitterly contested on its passage through the House and, in the eyes of very many people, liberalised the law to excess. ... The time has not yet come to flout majority opinion again.[154]

It was, of course, a myth that majority opinion had been against law reform, inside or outside Parliament, and CHE spent much energy trying to get this point accepted. Despite these and other negative replies, Paul Temperton sent Robin an upbeat acknowledgement:

> From my experience, for a reform campaign these are the most sympathetic and forthcoming replies I have seen. While it would obviously take two or three years of campaigning to make the need for further reform a live political issue, I think you can draw considerable encouragement from this batch of responses.[155]

This so flies in the face of the content that one wonders what fantasy world Paul inhabited. Or maybe he just wanted to boost local morale.

The size and strength of Liverpool CHE made it particularly fecund in spawning subgroups. Wirral CHE was active by the end of 1971, when the main group, seventy-strong, got too large to organise. Later Paul O'Grady joined it, and remembers it as New Brighton CHE. They used to go to the bingo at the Empress Ballroom on Wednesday nights. Judging from its newsletter, it was quite a radical group. When David Holbrook wrote a crazy article for the *Guardian* claiming that homosexuals had a 'malignant condition', and that there was a gay conspiracy to suppress criticism and prevent him from publishing his books, the newsletter editor commented, 'If you were a publisher, would you publish anything by this silly little man?'

The same newsletter had a problem page ('I am a frozen OAP eating cardboard and ragged Axminster. What should I do?') and gave out prizes for 1972:

> Star of the year award goes to the Conservative Party for keeping one million people unemployed and enabling the privileged 3% of the population to still own 95% of the land and wealth of the country.

The newsletter shows them campaigning vigorously into the late 1970s. Chester CHE in turn grew out of Wirral CHE in 1974.

Blackpool CHE was going to be an offshoot of Liverpool, and its first meeting was convened by a woman member, Jane McEvilly, in October 1972.

However Manchester CHE took over as the 'parent group', which was important when members of the all-women committee had an almighty bust-up, and a new woman, Shirley Oxley, was installed as convenor. The female presence remained strong for several years. Many members of Blackpool also attended Preston, convened by Wilf Hunter from 1972 onwards. The nucleus of the group was a pre-existent social set, but Wilf was able to radicalise people to the extent that they became campaigners throughout the 1970s.

Chilterns CHE

While Liverpool was setting up its group, George Broadhead and Roy Saich were also trying to get one off the ground, but in very different circumstances. Based in Chesham in Buckinghamshire, they wanted to set up what would be the first rural CHE group – Chilterns CHE. Or at least, semi-rural, because its catchment area would include places like Amersham and Harrow, which were on direct and easy train lines to central London, with all the rival attractions which the Big City would offer.

Roy and George were – as of 2014 still are – partners. They were relocated Londoners, and, with Robin Bloxsidge, were the first local organisers to come to the role after a full experience of the commercial gay scene. George had a sexually active but very discreet boyhood in the Isle of Man, a Crown Dependency far more reactionary than the UK on which it depends.* University at Keele and a teaching job in Italy allowed George the chance to let his hair down, and in the late 1950s he found himself teaching at the Language Tuition Centre off Oxford Street. Most of the teachers were gay, and one offered him an introduction to the various seedy gay clubs of central London.

* Male homosexual acts were not decriminalised in the Isle of Man until 1992; capital punishment was abolished in 1993. Man is not a member of the EU.

42. Roy Saich and George Broadhead at their partnership ceremony, 2010

He met Roy, six years his junior, in London's most famous gay pub, the Coleherne, in early 1965. Love at first sight prompted George to whisk Roy away from living with his mother in Essex to a bedsit in Frognal. They've been together ever since. They moved to Chesham in 1969, Roy working for an insurance company, and George, still commuting to London, at a prep school in Hampstead. Like many teachers, he found his profession imposed severe constraints on how public he could be as a homosexual.

Although he was younger, Roy was the more politically experienced. Like Alan Swerdlow in Liverpool, he'd been a supporter of the HLRS, but it was a July 1970 newspaper advert which prompted him and George to get in touch with Manchester and offer to start a Chilterns group. They had been beaten to it by an offer from someone else, but that person chickened out on realising the work involved. However, on the strength of the offer suddenly withdrawn, Paul Temperton had started generating publicity. When adverts appeared in the *Bucks Examiner* (31 July 1970) and the *Bucks Advertiser & Thame Gazette* (23 July), resulting in nine enquiries, there was the basis of a group but no convenor. As it turned out, Roy and George's timing couldn't have been better.

There was something of a hiatus before a group solidified in November. For a start, Roy and George were uncertain what a group could or should actually do. Neither had any experience of anything similar. Then there was the problem of where to meet. It needed more than a member offering his or her flat, it had to be somewhere that all the other members could get to. Dr Beeching had axed local branch railway lines, some buses only ran once a day, or even once a week, and most never ran in the evening. This was probably the time of the worst quality local public transport in the twentieth century, as the transport planners saw the car as the mode of the future.

What they needed was some inspiration, some framework, and some experience to share. Roy and George found all these at the meeting for convenors and would-be convenors already referred to. This was organised in Birmingham by Nick Stanley, and there were about 15–20 people there. Allan Horsfall, still vulnerable to illness following a serious heart attack back in May, was bedfast and not able to go to the meeting. But he had clear ideas about what they should be talking about. He wrote to Paul:

> Obviously local groups fulfil a useful function if they only operate to bring members together socially, but if we are to develop as an affective agency of political and social change, then local groups will need to be more than this. What is needed will differ from place to place, but we badly need to find new areas in which the oppressive majority can be challenged and changed. Just as one example, there is a pub somewhere on the East Coast (I think in Hull) which forbids 'queers' amongst others (women also). Local groups should be encouraged to ferret out this kind of thing and fight it.[156]

While Allan had his political ideas, Peter Norman had his social model. So Roy and George went away from that meeting with a much firmer idea of what the group might do. They needed to contact the local members, they needed to write to doctors and lawyers for more referrals, they wanted to get in touch with the local women's organisations, they wanted more newspaper ads, and they needed somewhere to meet. Bob Greenwood, a warm, very camp man in his 50s, offered his sitting room in Berkhamsted. Paul again sent his blueprint for a successful group:

> The group will need to come to some decision about finance; local groups are self-financing and either a local subscription, or some other system of contributions, should be used to cover all local costs such as postages, cups of tea, hiring rooms, etc. … New members should be asked to a preliminary new members' meeting in groups of a few before being absorbed into the whole group. (This is not essential but it is desirable). At such meetings the new members would meet two or three responsible officers of the group who would explain everything to them. And perhaps weed out 'undesirable' people if really necessary, although it is unlikely to come to that.[157]

That Paul should give such 'official' advice about 'weeding out', even if only as a remote possibility, rather dents any claims for total inclusivity. Roy and George got out their bus timetables and their maps. As Roy wrote to Paul:

> I have consulted the local maps and timetables and it seems to us that the largest towns which should be tackled, with the most likely first, are: Bletchley, Leighton Buzzard, Aylesbury, High Wycombe, Watford, Harrow. However, from the point of view of membership of CHE the last

> two may be the most rewarding, but we feel that members living in these areas may prefer to join one of the London groups.[158]

Paul took their target towns and identified the papers from the Press Gazette: Home Counties Newspaper Group, *Buckinghamshire Advertiser*, *Bucks Examiner*, *Bucks Free Press/Watford Observer*. He forwarded the addresses of the people who replied. These included people in Bletchley, some 25 miles away, because it was on a direct train route to Watford. Roy and George suggested adverts in the *Bucks Herald*, but that organ had already turned Paul down. These were all weeklies, whereas evening papers, read at times when people would feel especially lonely and had possibly had a drink or two to give courage, were much more likely to produce a response. *Berkhamsted and Hemel Hempstead Gazette* took an ad, as did the *Watford Observer*. Everyone else turned them down.

They met on 9 November, just informally, a bit uncertainly, then, much more businesslike, a fortnight later. Roy reported to Paul Temperton that this was quite successful:

> from a therapy point of view. Some are, however, already members of London groups, but I told them there was no reason why they should not belong to more than one group – I hope this is right – but we don't want to poach members from others.[159]

Here they also elected Roy as Convenor and George as Secretary, although in practice most correspondence came from Roy. They agreed to have a constitution, and to set the age limit at 21+. This caution characterised the group. They were not markedly into political action. But they did have a cracking social programme.

Like Liverpool CHE, they met in people's houses, mainly those of Bob Greenwood and Norman Boyce. Boyce was a teacher like George, albeit of pottery at a local secondary school. A big bearded man, very much looking the artist, he had a large house, big enough to have his own pottery kiln, and since he lived in Amersham he was comparatively well served by transport. In addition, members with cars regularly offered lifts to those without.

Meetings were fortnightly, and initially hosted talks by CHE and the usual other gay worthies: John Holland from the Albany Trust (not the John Holland from MANDFHAB), Ike Cowen, Paul Temperton and Martin Stafford together. Between times they held car rallies, pub visits to Thame, Dunsmore and Maidenhead. On Friday nights they went together to Pan's Club in Dunstable. They visited other groups as they formed, especially Windsor CHE and Reading Gay Action. They made theatre trips to London.*

* In October 1971 they went with Windsor CHE to see Alan Bates in Simon Gray's gay-themed *Butley*.

They organised exchanges with the CHE groups in Bristol and Manchester, going for weekends and then hosting in return. Members of the group put up visitors in their spare beds, or on sofas. These exchanges between CHE groups were extremely popular around the country, offering visits to new gay pubs and clubs, new faces – and sometimes, at the end of a long night's clubbing, a new sex partner.

Their calendar became an object of emulation for other groups. William Berry, wanting to start an Oxford Town Group, came to visit and wrote to Paul:

> I have seen a well-conducted and thoroughly respectable group operating in the Chilterns and have nothing but praise for the enterprise of Roy Saich in organising so many interesting lectures and discussions for the members. He has also arranged cinema, theatre and restaurant outings and has personally taken much trouble to make these events successful. I trust the Oxford Group, when it is inaugurated, will be as creative.[160]

By 1972 there were seventy members of Chilterns CHE, and the group had become too large for a private living room. Attempts to hire halls were fruitless. Roy Saitch explained:

> People wouldn't let you hire halls, public halls. They'd always have to refer it to their committees, and the committees always said no.[161]

However, there was a pub in Beaconsfield, the Beech Tree, which, if not precisely gay, had a gay barman or landlord, and two Chilterns CHE members were regulars. As a result, the upstairs room at the Beech Tree was theirs. Here Roger Baker twice came to give his regular talk on drag,* and they also heard the gay publisher Anthony Blond, who brought out the novels of Simon Raven and Jean Genet among many others.

They went to the Thame Fair, an annual carnival which takes over the High Street for several days. *Gay Scene* dutifully recorded that they went on the roundabouts, the 'lightning swirl' and 'Messrs Pettigrove's old time roundabout, with its galloping horses and 'Black Forest' organ.' Nobody won a goldfish.

The group's attitude to campaigning can be seen in the replies to a survey Roy Saich put out to his members in August 1972. Only seventeen questionnaires were returned out of fifty, and of these nine people said they didn't want any campaigning locally.

---

* The Chilterns newsletter *Gay Scene* (July 1973) wrote up this visit, commenting: 'Note for local transvestites, "Esquire" shop at Oakfield Corner, Amersham-on-the-Hill, invariably has under a large sign saying "Men's Wear" a delightful display of dresses and women's clothes.'

Nevertheless Roy and George found themselves contributing their modest mite to the cause. They wrote to all local doctors in 1971, informing them of the group's existence and inviting referrals. This was a standard practice for local groups, along with letters to local churches, magistrates, colleges, and social workers. Each of these exercises involved an enormous amount of work, especially for groups which had no access to duplicators and had to write each one by hand. For example, in 2013 there were fifty-eight doctors and surgeries in Buckinghamshire alone – forty years earlier, before amalgamation into clinics, there would have been at least double that number to contact. There was little feedback from these letters. However, they contributed to the drip-drip effect of gradually raising awareness that there were homosexuals in every community, even in the Chilterns, and that they were reasonable people.

Chilterns CHE organised a group library of gay fiction* and non-fiction.† Their magazines included the lesbian *Arena 3*, *Lunch*, GLF's *Come Together*, the Albany Trust's *Man in Society*. Self-publicity was itself a campaign. While Paul Temperton crossed swords with the newspapers trying to place advertisements, Roy and George argued about getting their posters and leaflets into libraries. It took nearly two years. They appeared in a feature in the *Bucks Examiner*, which carried their adverts (and had since 1970), and, later, in the *Thame Gazette*, which did not.

The *Thame Gazette* reporter came to a meeting, appropriately in Gayhurst Road, High Wycombe, and reported in a full-page spread:

> I walked up the stairs to the flat and paused before knocking on the door. Should I feel so apprehensive, even nervous? ... The door opened, not on scenes of wildest imagination, but on a welcoming convivial atmosphere. ... Everyone I met that evening behaved perfectly normally. There were members and friends. ... Some were homosexual – they use the word gay – others were not, and it was impossible to distinguish one from the other.[162]

---

* E.g. Alberto Arbasino *The Lost Boy* (1964); James Baldwin *Giovanni's Room* (1956); Lennox Cook *No Language But a Cry* (1958); Ford and Tyler *The Young and Evil* (1932); Rodney Garland *The Heart in Exile* (1953); Martin Goff *The Youngest Director* (1961); Neville Jackson *No End to the Way* (1967); Noel Langley *The Loner* (1967); Roger Peyrefitte *Special Friendships* (1944); John Rechy *City of Night* (1963); Mary Renault *The Charioteer* (1953); Angus Stewart *Sandel* (1968); Gore Vidal *The City and the Pillar* (1948). It was an adventurous collection of the limited literature available at the time.

† Gordon Westwood (Michael Schofield): presumably *Society and the Homosexual;* D. J. West *Homosexuality*; Peter Wildeblood *Against the Law*; Bryan Magee *One in Twenty*; Michael Davidson *The World, The Flesh and Myself*; Angelo d'Arcangelo *The Homosexual Handbook*; D. W. Corey *The Homosexual in America*.

This article conforms to the format used by many local papers in covering their local CHE groups. A reporter asserts his heterosexuality, his nervousness, and is then reassured by the 'normality' of what he finds. The message is both disconcerting – they are everywhere and you can't tell who they are – and reassuring – actually they are no different from anyone else. The degree of closetedness is shown by the fact that no names are used, except one first name, Geoff. References to a prep school master and an accountant indicate that George and Roy were there, but certainly not identified. 'We do tend to be a bit clandestine about it,' said one member. Another confirmed a stereotype: 'There is a weakness in homosexuals that they find it difficult to form stable relationships.' One of the manifestations of self-oppression is belief which flies in the face of evidence: there were several couples, including Saitch and Broadhead, who had been together for years. Despite this, the stereotype persisted; self-oppression was rife. Though the article was sympathetic, there were still no ads for the group in the personal columns of the *Gazette*.

Their first newsletter, *Gay Scene*, appeared in December 1972, a basic diary with few additions. One political action happened when Roy wrote to the BBC to protest about the schools' programme *Looking at Life 6: What are friends?*:

> The point being made seemed to be that single sex friendships were very fine, provided they were not homosexual. This could only cause unhappiness to children hearing the programme who would find as they grew older a friendship developing on this basis. Would it not have been better to stress, as was done about friendship leading to marriage, that if a friendship did develop into a homosexual one, this could add to the friendship, and that this is the best way for homosexuals to enter into a relationship?[163]

The reply, from assistant Ruth Udell, was bland and missed the point. As was so often the case, institutional culture was impervious to protest.

For a joint meeting with Windsor CHE in 1973 they invited all the main political parties to come and discuss law reform; only the Conservatives bothered to reply, and they pleaded a clash with another event. The meeting had to be cancelled.

It is perhaps worth noting what they didn't campaign about. While Gay Cambridge was fighting police tactics of covert surveillance in public toilets,* the Thames Valley police openly admitted they were using exactly the same methods. In a 1973 court case which came to Aylesbury Magistrates, Det.-Con. David Beeching gave evidence that 'he was keeping watch on two cubicles from a loft and from two holes in the roof he had a 'good clear view' of both compartments'.[164] From Chilterns CHE, not a peep.

---

* The is covered in detail in Volume Two.

As more groups formed and the London commercial gay scene burgeoned, membership declined in the face of the competition. By November 1974 only twelve people could be mustered for a meeting to decide whether the group should continue. By this time George and Roy had left. George Broadhead went on to found and become the Secretary of the Gay Humanist Association. Chilterns CHE continued, with a purely social programme, until the early 1980s.

The Correspondence Club

While those lucky enough to be within the catchment areas of groups had somewhere to go, there were many more who did not. By October 1970 there were over 600 members, but of those, more than two-thirds were still stuck in isolation. To help these isolated members the Committee developed, with great trepidation, a correspondence club. The trepidation was because of the situation created by a legal case, *Shaw v. DPP* (1960). Fred Shaw published a 'Ladies Directory', which was a list of names and addresses of female prostitutes, who paid for the privilege of being included. It also contained nude photos of some of the sex workers, and lists of the kinky things they'd be prepared to do at a price. It was published weekly, and at most sold about 80 copies, at 2/- (10p) a copy. He made about £250 (£5,000) a week from it, mostly from his exorbitant advertising rates. Because of this he was charged with living off immoral earnings, but he was also charged under the new Obscene Publications Act with publishing an obscene publication, and, most dubiously, with conspiracy to corrupt public morals. His appeal was rejected on all three charges, but he was given leave to appeal to the House of Lords on the conspiracy and immoral earnings charges, because of the legal points involved.

Shaw argued that he wasn't living off immoral earnings; he was charging for advertisements and delivering an advertising service. Would the chemists who supplied contraceptives to the prostitutes or the landlords who charged them rent also be living off immoral earnings? The argument held no water for the judges:

> His occupation of gathering and publishing these advertisements would not exist if his customers were not prostitutes. He was really no more than a tout using this means of bringing men to the prostitutes from whom he received money.[165]

The issue became whether he lived 'parasitically' off the women; whether he had other sources of income, and whether he charged a premium because of the nature of their business. No he didn't have other income, and yes he did charge a premium. Bang to rights.

The conspiracy charge had serious implications for others. There was no criminal offence of corrupting public morals, but, as Viscount Simonds in the Law Lords admitted, bringing conspiracy charges was a way of getting round the uncertainty of a conviction under any other law:

> It may be thought superfluous, where that Act [Obscene Publications Act] can be invoked, to bring a charge also of conspiracy to corrupt public morals, but I can well understand the desirability of doing so where a doubt exists whether obscenity within the meaning of the Act can be proved.[166]

The Law Lords in this case were not upholding the law, they were upholding Christian morality, and bending the law – or creating law by extension – to fit the case:

> In the sphere of criminal law I entertain no doubt that there remains in the Courts of Law a residual power to enforce the supreme and fundamental purpose of the law, to conserve not only the safety and order but also the moral welfare of the State, and that it is their duty to guard it against attacks which may be the more insidious because they are novel and unprepared for. That is the broad head (call it public policy if you wish) within which the present indictment falls. It matters little what label is given to the offending act.[167]

The Lords supported this dubious judgement by 4 to 1; the dissenter, Lord Reid, having severe doubts about the propriety of their Lordships usurping the powers of Parliament.

Despite the ruling, the CHE EC very early on decided to pursue the idea of a correspondence club.* In late 1969 Paul Temperton wrote to all members outlining the idea. Members would be able to sign up for membership; they would have to agree to their address being circulated to others on the list; the lists would be circulated every three months. They could then write to anyone on the list, which would be kept strictly confidential. Comments were invited. In January 1970 the Committee heard that no-one had opposed the idea: 'Various dangers such as blackmail and commercial exploitation were mentioned, and the legal aspects discussed at some length.'[168]

In March they decided that nowhere would the word 'homosexual' appear in the text, it would not use Committee headed notepaper, and a copyright clause would also appear. Everyone agreed that advertisements should avoid the suggestive content of the gay contact ads in *International Times*, which had just been found guilty in a magistrates' court, charged like Shaw with Con-

---

* By this time *Arena 3* had been running a correspondence club for lesbians for years. Although lesbian sex was not illegal, the magazine could still have been open to conspiracy charges.

spiracy to Corrupt Public Morals. In April 1970 the EC discussed the issue again:

> It was agreed that persons under the age of 21 must regretfully be excluded from the list. John Holland expressed misgivings about the legal aspects of the scheme but AH pointed out that this had been thoroughly investigated and that supporters had been informed that a slight element of risk might be involved.[169]

And in May, when they received the latest Committee for Homosexual Equality *Bulletin*, supporters also got an application form, a declaration that 'I would like my name to be included on the restricted list of members wishing to correspond', followed by personal details to be filled in – age, occupation, interests. The covering letter, headed only with a typewritten 'C.H.E' and a box number, explained that this plain typewritten style was what would be used throughout.

In an age long before emails, before most people even had a phone* and when for those who did the cost of long-distance calls was prohibitive, letter writing was an accepted part of a week's routine. Many people regularly devoted an evening or a weekend afternoon to correspondence. A six-page letter was not unusual. It was a genuine way of communicating news, emotions and ideas until at least the 1980s. Pen pal clubs were popular, particularly for literate children who would exchange weekly letters with others across the globe. So for isolated homosexuals to communicate in this way would not have seemed in any way odd, but offering genuine relief from isolation. At the same time, gay men being gay men, many members of the scheme would use it for finding sex. That at least was the unacknowledged belief of the Committee, which was to be proved right in at least some cases.

Not only was the spectre of conspiracy, as so recently invoked by the courts, hanging over what the Committee did, the 1967 Act had specified a penalty of two years' imprisonment for 'procuring'.† As long the list was being used to find sex partners, and the Committee knew this, they were wide open to prosecution for publishing it, despite all disclaimers to the contrary. In addition they had received frequent reports of the police using address lists from correspondence clubs to trawl for potential 'sex offenders'.

There were problems with the scheme right from the start. Though

---

* In 1970 phone ownership was 35 per cent of households. There were also long waiting lists to have land lines installed. The person whom CHE needed to have a phone most urgently, Paul Temperton, had to wait several months in late 1970 and early 1971 before he was connected. At first the Post Office told him that the waiting time for a phone was nine months.

† Specifically procuring 'another man to commit with a third man an act of buggery'.
—Sexual Offences Act 1967, S4(1).

Temperton might ensure addresses were confidential at his flat in Deerpark Road, once a list went to out to subscribers, there was no knowing what any one of them might do with it. The system was about as confidential as posting on Facebook, and inhibited only by the fearful and secretive natures of most of the Club members. Less than a month after the scheme started, a member on the supporters' list from Sheffield rang up Paul to complain that his parents had been subjected to anonymous telephone calls as a result of some-one getting hold of his details from the Correspondence Club. Paul could only say, 'Well, we told you there was a slight risk …' Others got hold of the list quite innocently although they weren't even official supporters of CHE. Anyone receiving a letter from Neville B. and checking the name against the list they had, would have discovered he wasn't on the list, triggering instant fears of blackmail or police infiltration. And yet Neville had crossed the path of a bona fide Correspondence Club member, Derek X.,* in a completely different context. Derek took the list with him to London, and lost it out of his suitcase. Somehow Neville found it and just took the chance to make some new pen friends. Paul ordered Neville to return it. He did. On this occasion the system of self-policing was effective.

On others it wasn't. Often members complained of unspecified 'abuse' of the system. In April 1972, Robin complained to Paul Temperton, and asked the EC to take action:

> I have received complaints that the correspondence list is being used as a sexual contact machine – I suppose that is inevitable – and in particular that people receive letters of a 'crude and vulgar' type (I quote!). I have seen some of them, and tho' I find them amusing, I can see that some people might find such letters upsetting. Is that a risk people take? The point is, is the correspondence list:
>
> A sort of pen-pal list for members not in groups for some reason or other, or in different parts of the country, *OR*
>
> Is it a sexual contact list, *OR*
>
> Something that is expected to fulfil both functions?
>
> It ought really to be made clear what it is.[170]

Some subscribers were persistently importunate. When Tyneside CHE was minded to exclude 'KP' from group membership, they wrote to the EC explaining that when he came to meetings he kept pestering people for sex, and had almost blagged his way into getting accommodation sharing the flat of a particularly vulnerable member. 'KP' was also recklessly indiscreet with people's personal details. The Tyneside convenor Richard Webster mentioned in passing that KP had already been dropped from the correspondence list

* Names have been changed as this letter is covered by a 50-year confidentiality clause.

once because of similar behaviour, but subsequently readmitted, and was now about to be dropped from it for a second time.

Paul Temperton again tried to get the scheme shut down in October 1972. To him it was nothing but a time-consuming nuisance. He briefed the Executive:

> It was started when there were hardly any local groups, with a view to alleviating isolation. There are now local groups all over the place. There is plenty of evidence that it is used primarily as a sexual contact list (which it isn't supposed to be) and very little that it provides any significant degree of real relief from loneliness and isolation, which are problems now better dealt with by Friend anyway. Complaints about misuse of the list are not infrequent and sometimes cause resignations.[171]

It seems from Temperton's comments that a kind of Gresham's Law was operating, the 'bad' correspondents driving out the 'good'. The actual complaints were vague. It seems clear that mostly they related to delicacy and timing. If a writer wanted sex, the sensible thing would have been to establish a pen pal relationship before introducing a sexual element into the correspondence, and then to do so by indirection and hints. Only then when there was some kind of positive response should he or she have arranged to meet. All this was possible without any overt sexual reference at all.* But if a correspondent was isolated, sex-starved and/or inexperienced, it was all too easy to freak out his reader by coming at the subject bull-at-a-gate. Not for nothing had the Albany Trust been advising for years that you shouldn't keep diaries or retain letters.

Despite this, the scheme was retained for several years. It remained surprisingly popular, even with people who would seem from their addresses to have access to a local CHE group and commercial bars. Group convenors and committee members used it. Anyone thinking that CHE was an exclusively middle class organisation would be swiftly disabused by the Correspondence Club mailing list. Yes, there are architects, lecturers and accountants; but also postmen, machine operators, lorry drivers and caretakers. In December 1972 there were over 220 members, of whom about 10 per cent were women. The ages ranged from a declared 21 to 70.

The eventual upholding of the *IT* verdict† caused further heart-searching, but in 1973 the Executive agreed to keep it yet again. However, it decided, regretfully, that the lower age limit for it had to stay at 21, although paradoxically it also decided to stop asking people their age. This seems both a tacit

---

* Some of the letters sent to Griff Vaughan-Williams through the Correspondence Club survive, and clearly indicate this kind of careful progression.

† The *IT* trial and consequences are covered more fully in Volume Two.

admission of the sexual purpose of the scheme to some, and to invoke a 'Don't ask–don't tell' policy.

The final confirmation of the *IT* verdict made them doubly cautious. As it stood, the whole Committee could be vulnerable if prosecutions were in the offing. To counteract this, the EC set up a panel of three as figureheads of the scheme, people who were prepared personally to make test cases of the issue, at whatever cost to themselves. One of the panel was Michael Steed:

> We said, CHE as an organisation perhaps couldn't take the risk, because if it got taken to court, all its members' funds could be confiscated. So we agreed that the four of us would be the names on that list, so if they wanted to prosecute, they would have to prosecute those four. One was Ray Gosling, one was Ian Harvey, the former Conservative MP who had had to resign in 1959. One was myself. I can't remember the fourth. And that in a way was a personal act of, well, 'I can stand up and be counted'. And I reckoned that – Ray Gosling was a broadcaster, I was already doing election broadcasts, and stood for Parliament twice, Ian Harvey was a former MP. We probably wouldn't be touched.[172]

Nevertheless Steed, Gosling and Harvey were sticking their necks out. Like appearing at Burnley, it required great courage.

All this bother with the boys rather obscures the importance of the Correspondence Club to gay women. Women members never constituted more than a quarter of the membership of CHE, but there were significant numbers up at least until the late 1970s. These tended to be even more isolated than the men, many trapped in marriages contracted when they didn't know better. Liz Stanley, CHE women's officer 1972–75, told the Committee that the Correspondence Club was probably the best thing CHE offered isolated women at that moment.

She was one person who argued consistently in favour of the correspondence club. She was aware of the number of lesbian and bisexual women who were trapped in marriages, and others who for a variety of social and economic reasons found it hard to travel to meetings; or who, having got to a meeting, were deterred by the predominantly male atmosphere. For such women, writing and receiving letters was a far more crucial link to others than it would have been for most men. She urged that not only should it be kept, it should be marketed to women as one of CHE's unique selling points, and in her own publicity for the organisation it featured strongly. Despite this, the women's membership of the correspondence club remained about the same proportionately as of CHE as a whole.

Tony Ryde, chairman of the London Co-ordinating Committee and one of the few long-term strategic thinkers within CHE, agreed that the list should be marketed as one of the benefits of membership. In early 1973 he proposed an expansion of the scheme. Why not publish it monthly instead of every three months? Why not have volunteers run it, instead of it falling on Paul Temperton's already overburdened shoulders? Can we computerise the membership list, separate from the organisation's membership list? Why not charge for it as a separate service? Why not help the most closeted by offering to run it through a box number service, and using only first names?

The EC were convinced of the need to keep the scheme, but not for monthly updates; they despaired too of finding someone sufficiently reliable and discreet to run it outside the office. They rejected the idea of paying for it separately. How could you charge separately for something which was also advertised as a benefit of CHE membership? Tony Ryde insisted:

> More important is the principle: why victimise the most isolated, those for whom the correspondence list is second best to group activities which are not available – and in many cases won't be for ages?[173]

However, they did start to solicit donations for it. They agreed to canvass the users about using box numbers.

And so the Correspondence Club continued, although it never had the publicity that it needed to expand as Ryde envisaged. This was partly because the scheme was a loss-maker, and tied up so much administrative time, but also because there always remained a kind of vestigial embarrassment around the scheme, because of the knowledge of how it had been used in the past. It was finally wound up in 1979, more on grounds of cost than anything else.

The success of the first groups, and of the correspondence scheme in the first instance, had to be balanced by the failures. In mid-1970 adverts were placed in the *Aberystwyth Courier*, *Darlington & Stockton Times*, *Hull Daily Mail*, *Northern Echo*, *Southern Evening Echo* and several papers in Newcastle. This argues that plans were sufficiently advanced for potential groups in these papers' circulation areas to at least have had a convenor. Someone had written from Hull in February 1970, and Paul and Martin went there to see him:

> The Hull man we went to see has turned out to be a dead loss. … Another member in the area has written to say that only one meeting was convened, in May, but when he got there it was cancelled and nothing has happened since.[174]

From Southampton Alan Seagrove complained in May 1970 that he'd offered to convene months previously and no-one had come back to him. Paul replied that there had been two people offering to convene, and he needed to sort this out. Since he seems to have made no effort to do so, unlike in other towns, the only conclusion to draw is that he didn't think either of them was suitable, but was too diplomatic to say so.

Newcastle adverts didn't get the replies – 'the people in Newcastle seem to have been overcome by chronic inertia' – so that temporarily killed a group on

Tyneside.

All these initiatives cost time and money, and often arguments with advertising managers. When they came to nothing it was deeply frustrating, and Paul worried that members would start to leave if there was nothing for them locally. There had been a phenomenal growth in the six months to October 1970, but it was far from secure, and he feared CHE was stalled for lack of resources.

However, what happened in London from the autumn of 1970 onwards was soon to dispel those fears, if only to replace them with others.

Notes to Chapter Four

[1] Martin Stafford, interviewed by the author, 11 January 2011.

[2] Allan Horsfall, interviewed by the author, 10 April 2011.

[3] Martin Stafford, interviewed by the author, 11 January 2011.

[4] Ibid.

[5] Allan Horsfall to Dr Maurice Silverman, 25 May 1967. MCA/G/HOR/1.

[6] NWHLRC *Bulletin*, June 1968. HCA/Grey 1/15-2/3.

[7] NWHLRC newsletter, April 1968. HCA/EPH/93.

[8] NWHLRC *After the act*, 1968. HCA/Grey 1/15.

[9] Ibid.

[10] Ibid.

[11] Allan Horsfall to Dr Maurice Silverman, 'Advice about aversion therapy', 6 April 1967. MCA/G/HOR/1.

[12] Dr Maurice Silverman to Allan Horsfall, 'Aversion therapy', 5 June 1967. MCA/G/HOR/1.

[13] Martin Stafford, interviewed by the author, 11 January 2011.

[14] NWHLRC minutes, 3 August 1967. HCA/Grey/1/15.

[15] NWHLRC minutes, 6 October 1967. HCA/Grey 1/15.

[16] NWHLRC, 'Have you a homosexual problem?', *The Chronicle,* 23 October 1967, 2.

[17] NWHLRC, 'Have you a homosexual problem?', *Bury Times,* 28 October 1967, 18.

[18] NWHLRC, 'Have you a homosexual problem?', *Rossendale Free Press*, 28 October 1967, 16.

[19] NWHLRC, 'Have you a homosexual problem?, *Leigh Reporter* etc., 2–23 November 1967, weekly, 10.

[20] NWHLRC, 'Have you a homosexual problem?', *Bolton Journal and Guardian* etc., 3 November–29 December 1967, weekly, 8–10.

[21] NWHLRC, 'Have you a homosexual problem?', *Stockport Express,* 7 December, 5; 14 December 1967, 2.

[22] Martin Stafford, interviewed by the author, 11 January 2011.

[23] NWHLRC *Bulletin*, April 1968. HCA/Grey 1/15-2/3.

[24] Martin Stafford, 'Medical advice for homosexuals', *Lancet*, 25 July 1970, 218.

[25] NWHLRC, *After the Act*, 1968. HCA/Grey 1/15.

[26] Ibid.

[27] Ibid.

[28] Antony Grey to Allan Horsfall, 'Warnings over correspondence clubs', 19 August 1968. HCA/Grey/1/15.

[29] Paul Temperton, interviewed by the author, 28 March 2011.

[30] Ibid.

[31] Ibid.

[32] Martin Stafford, interviewed by the author, 11 January 2011.

[33] Paul Temperton, interviewed by the author, 28 March 2011.

[34] Martin Stafford to Antony Grey, 'Resignation', 13 December 1969. HCA/AT/7/60.

[35] Martin Stafford to Ike Cowen, 'Conference invitation', 18 August 1970. HCA/CHE/5/2.

[36] NWHLRC *Bulletin*, January 1966. HCA/EPH/94.

[37] NWHLRC *Bulletin*, January 1969. HCA/Grey/1/15.

[38] C. H. Rolph to Colin Harvey, 'Composition of NW Committee', 10 December 1968. HCA/GREY/1/15/22.

[39] Paul Temperton, interviewed by the author, 28 March 2011.

[40] Allan Horsfall to Antony Grey, 'NWHLRC name change', 18 March 1969. HCA/GREY/1/15.

[41] Rt Rev. Ted Wickham to Allan Horsfall, 'NWHLRC name change', 6 March 1969. MCA/G/HOR/uncatalogued.

[42] Allan Horsfall to Rt Rev. Ted Wickham, 'NWHLRC name change', 11 March 1969. MCA/G/HOR/uncatalogued.

[43] CHE *Bulletin*, August 1969. HCA/CHE/4/18.

[44] Ibid.

[45] *Spectator*, 30 August 1969.

[46] Martin Stafford, interviewed by the author, 11 January 2011.

[47] 'And now it's poove power', *Private Eye*, 7 November 1969, 7.

[48] John Ball Column, *Peace News*, 1742, (14 November 1969), 12.

[49] Allan Horsfall, letters – 'Homosexual equality', *Peace News*, 1743 (21 November 1969), 9.

[50] J. R. Simonds to Paul Temperton, 'Advertising refusal', 2 June 1971. HCA/CHE/70.

[51] E. D. Dore to Paul Temperton, 'Advertising refusal', 13 January 1971. HCA/CHE/5/65.

[52] E. D. Dore to Paul Temperton, 'Advertising refusal', 20 April 1971. HCA/CHE/5/65.

[53] CHE *Bulletin*, January 1970. HCA/CHE/4/18.

[54] V. N. Brooks to Paul Temperton, 'Advertising refusal', 20 July 1970. HCA/CHE/5/65.

[55] Paul Temperton to V. N. Brooks, 'Advertising follow-up', 14 November 1970. HCA/CHE/5/65.

[56] Alan Elliott to Paul Temperton, 'Advertising refusal', 8 December 1970. HCA/CHE/5/65.

[57] Paul Temperton to Alan Elliott,' Advertising follow-up', 11 December 1970. HCA/CHE/5/65.

[58] J. Carr to Paul Temperton, 'Refusal of ad', 9 November 1970. HCA/CHE/5/65

[59] Barry Askew to Paul Temperton, 'Advertising refusal', 15 May 1973. HCA/CHE/5/65.

[60] Paul Temperton, Letter to *Liverpool Echo*, 15 May 1971. HCA/CHE/5/65.

[61] A. H. Draper to Paul Temperton, 'Advert refusal', 18 May 1971. HCA/CHE/5/65.

[62] Paul Temperton to A. H. Draper, 'Uses of word "lesbian",' 3 June 1971. HCA/CHE/5/65.

[63] P. E. R. Cutter to Paul Temperton, 'Advertising refusal', 22 August 1972. HCA/CHE/5/65.

[64] Paul Temperton to T. F. Cassidy, 'Replies to adverts', 14 November 1970. HCA/CHE/5/65.

[65] Jean Austen to Paul Temperton, 'Help with adverts', 10 December 1970. HCA/CHE/5/65.

[66] 'The Press Council decision', *Arena 3*, 8/4 (June 1971).

[67] Ibid.

[68] Ibid.

[69] Ibid.

[70] Peter Norman to Trevor Locke, 'Weekend at Dorbet Guest House', 24 May 1973. HCA/CHE/7/43.

[71] CHE *Bulletin,* 3 (1970), HCA/CHE/4/1.

[72] Ray Seaton, 'There is nothing queer about us', *Wolverhampton Express and Star*, 8 January 1968, 4.

[73] Ibid.

[74] Ibid.

[75] Ibid.

[76] R. Mount, 'A very strange club', *News of the World*, 21 January 1968, 12.

[77] Ibid.

[78] David Buckle to Antony Grey, 'John Holland', 14 January 1968. HCA/AT/14/75.

[79] Antony Grey to W. D. Thomas, 'MANDFHAB', 16 September 1968. HCA/AT/14/46.

[80] John Holland, 'MANDFHAB membership application form', 1968. HCA/Grey/1/15-2.

[81] John Holland to Alan Horsfall, 'Closing down MANDFHAB', undated [end of 1968]. MCA/G/HOR/uncatalogued.

[82] Ibid.

[83] CHE EC minutes, 20 March 1970. HCA/CHE/EPH93.

[84] West Midlands CHE, Minutes, 10 May 1970. HCA/CHE/5/55/104.

[85] Terry Sanderson, 'Faltering from the closet', in Cant and Hemmings, *Radical Records*, 85-93.

[86] John Cleary, 'Wolverhampton Workers Group', *Bulletin* August 1972, 4. HCA/CHE/4/1/46

[87] Geoffrey N. Baggott to Paul Temperton, '*Boys in the Band*', 11 July 1971. HCA/CHE/7/130.

[88] Paul Temperton to Geoffrey N. Baggott, '*Boys in the Band*', 17 August 1971. HCA/CHE/7/130.

[89] Peter Spencer to Antony Grey, 'About MANDFHAB', 9 March 1968. HCA/Grey/1/15-2.

[90] Peter Spencer, MAF-MAN membership application form, 1968. HCA/Grey/1/15-2.

[91] Ike Cowen, Leeds *Broadsheet*, 1 (October 1971). HCA/CHE/7/156.

[92] Ibid.

[93] 'FB' [Fred Blackburn], CHE *Bulletin*, December 1970. HCA/CHE/4/1/9.

[94] Robin Bloxsidge, interviewed by the author, 28 August 2012.

[95] Martin Stafford, 'Proceedings of the York Conference 1970', Albany Trust transcript. AT/11/21.

[96] CHE, EC minutes, 25 April 1970. HCA/CHE/2/1.

[97] Martin Stafford to the author (by e-mail), 'Reply to questions', 4 July 2013. HCA/CHE/5/1/73.

[98] Allan Horsfall to Paul Temperton, 'Co-options', 26 April 1970. HCA/CHE/5/1/73.

[99] Martin Stafford to the author (by e-mail), 20 September 2013. HCA/CHE/5/1/73.

[100] West Midlands CHE, 'Letter to members', 1970. HCA/CHE/8/55/102.

[101] Anonymous to Paul Temperton, 'Request for contact', undated [1971]. HCA/CHE/2/17/72.

[102] Nick Stanley to Paul Temperton, 'Group update', 6 January 1971. HCA/CHE/2/17/53.

[103] A. J. Yorke to Paul Temperton, 'Visit to Birmingham', 8 May 1971. HCA/CHE/2/17/63.

104 Paul Temperton to Bob Mellor, '*Come Together* and related issues', 5 November 1971. CHE/HCA/5/4/2.

105 Paul Temperton to Ralph Hallett, 'How to develop a group', 8 August 1970. HCA/5/55/136.

106 Peter Norman, interviewed by the author, 25 February 2014.

107 Ibid.

108 Alan Swerdlow, interviewed by the author, 10 September 2012.

109 Ibid.

110 Robin Bloxsidge, interviewed by the author, 28 August 2012.

111 Alan Swerdlow, interviewed by the author, September 2012.

112 Robin Bloxsidge, interviewed by the author, 28 August 2012.

113 Peter Norman, interviewed by the author, 25 February 2014.

114 Peter Norman, 'The future programme', 1970. HCA/CHE/NORMAN/5.

115 Peter Norman, interviewed by the author, 25 February 2014.

116 Ibid.

117 Kenneth Jameson to Jeremy Seabrook, in Seabrook, *A lasting relationship*, 33.

118 Keith Brook to Peter Norman, 'South Herts convenor', January (?) 1972. HCA/CHE/5/55/23.

119 Peter Norman to Keith Brook, 'Action on John Lear', 14 February 1972. HCA/5/55/28.

120 Liz Stanley, 'Report on situation in Guernsey' to the EC, 24 June 1974. HCA/CHE/7/33.

121 Ibid.

122 Roger Baker, 'Dear Sir', *Lunch*, 6 (March 1972), 31.

123 Peter Norman, interviewed by the author, 25 February 2014.

124 Ibid.

125 Peter Norman, Leeds *Broadsheet,* 1 (October 1971), 3. HCA/CHE/7/156.

126 Alan Swerdlow, interviewed by the author, 10 September 2012.

127 Liverpool CHE, Newsletter, July 1972. HCA/CHE/5/55/146.

128 Ibid.

129 Robin Bloxsidge, interviewed by the author, 28 August 2012.

130 Manchester Students Group, entry in Leeds *Broadsheet,* 2 (November 1971), HCA/CHESTERMAN/20, 4.

131 'News: No clouds over Manchester', *Lunch*, 6 (March 1972), 17.

132 Robin Bloxsidge, interviewed by the author, 28 August 2012.

133 Ibid.

134 Robin Bloxsidge to Paul Temperton, 'Age of admission', 5 October 1972. HCA/CHE/5/55/136.

135 Ibid.

136 Robin Bloxsidge to the author (by email), 'More about Liverpool CHE (3)', email, 5 July 2014.

137 O'Grady, *At my mother's knee*, 281.

138 Ibid, 284.

139 Peter Norman, interviewed by the author, 26 February 2014.

140 Robin Bloxsidge, interviewed by the author, 28 August 2012.

141 Ibid.

142 Don Smith, 'I feel the world is out of step but I accept I'm a queer', *Liverpool Daily Post*, 21 April 1971, 8.

143 Ibid.

144 Ibid.

145 'An effeminate homosexual', 'Homosexuality and the need for tolerance', Letters, *Liverpool Daily Post*, 28 April 1971, 8.

146 'Group "not accepted by society",' *Liverpool Echo*, 21 September 1972, 11.

147 D. Smith, 'City after dark', *Liverpool Daily Post*, 20 November 1973, 5.

[148] CHE, EC minutes, 20 March 1970, HCA/EPH/93.

[149] Robin Bloxsidge to Paul Temperton, 'Campaigning matters', 17 April 1972. HCA/CHE/5/55/156.

[150] Robin Bloxsidge, interviewed by the author, 28 August 2012.

[151] Robin Bloxsidge, 'Liverpool teach-in', CHE *Bulletin,* Nov–Dec 1972, 4.

[152] Robin Bloxsidge, 'CHE talks to Liverpool', *Gay News*, 10 (November 1972).

[153] Liverpool CHE, Questionnaire to local MPs, 1972. HCA/GRAY/1/17.

[154] Tim Fortescue MP, reply to Liverpool CHE questionnaire, 1972. HCA/G GRAY rey/1/17.

[155] Paul Temperton to Robin Bloxsidge, 'Completed questionnaires', undated [1972]. HCA/ GRAY /1/17.

[156] Allan Horsfall to Paul Temperton, 'Local convenors' meeting', 18 September 1970. HCA/CHE/5/1/73.

[157] Paul Temperton to Roy Saich, 'How to form a group', 13 November 1970. HCA/CHE/7/27.

[158] Roy Saich to Paul Temperton, 'First Chilterns meeting', 11 November 1970. HCA/CHE/7/27.

[159] Roy Saich to Paul Temperton, 'Second Chilterns meeting', 27 November 1970. HCA/CHE/7/27.

[160] William Berry to Paul Temperton, 'Formation of Oxford Town Group', 17 April 1971. HCA/CHE/7/137.

[161] Roy Saich, interviewed by the author, 30 January 2012.

[162] Antony Seib, 'Gay's the word for this group', *Thame Gazette*, 13 November 1973, 4.

[163] Roy Saich to Producer, Schools Programmes, 'Protest letter', 19 December 1972. HCA/CHE/7/137.

[164] 'Acquitted of gross indecency', *Thame Gazette*, 18 September 1973, 3.

[165] Lord Reid, *DPP v Shaw,* 1961. HL/PO/JU/4/3/1089.

[166] Viscount Simonds, Ibid.

[167] Viscount Simonds, Ibid.

[168] CHE EC minutes, 20 February 1970. HCA/CHE/2/1.

[169] CHE EC minutes, 24 April 1970. HCA/CHE/2/1.

[170] CHE EC minutes, 17 June 1972. HCA/CHE/2/1/75.

[171] Paul Temperton, 'Briefing to EC', 14 October 1972. HCA/CHE/2/1/91.

[172] Michael Steed, interviewed by the author, 23 May 2011.

[173] CHE EC minutes, 10 February 1973. HCA/CHE/2/1/120.

[174] Paul Temperton to Allan Horsfall, 'Local groups report', 27 July 1970. HCA/CHE/5/1/73.

Chapter Five: London Particular

Contents

London's special situation

Homosexuals in London were different, part of the vast army of singles in bedsits and flats, in Notting Hill and Earls Court, Fitzrovia, Pimlico and Bloomsbury. A significant number of them were not native Londoners, but had come to London as adults: partly for work, but also partly to find a life for themselves as homosexuals. People who had got as far as recognising that they needed to get to a big city in order to find that space to breathe, and had made the move on their own initiative, were not the same sort of homosexuals as the lonely, isolated people that the old North Western Committee adverts were aimed at. Some had a history of involvement with campaigning, through support of the HLRS and the Albany Trust. Those in the inner city could feel themselves 'in the action', whether buying clothes by John Stephen in Carnaby Street, seeing the latest Alain Delon movie at the Electric Cinema, or following debates from the public galleries in parliament.

They had a level of sophistication, of emotional and sexual experience, denied to those whose horizons were circumscribed by small towns. They also had in London a gay scene of restaurants, bars and clubs which post-1967 was comparatively free of police action, if not surveillance. This did not make the streets less dangerous, the toilets less risky or the insults less offensive. The expansion of possibilities did not necessarily make people happy; it made it possible to be unhappy in different ways.

At the core of London unhappiness was dissatisfaction with what was on offer in the available social spaces, variously described as predatory, shallow, expensive and dirty:

> In the last hour before closing time there is always an increase in tension. … Most people find it a strain to spend the whole evening in a pub, if they are intending to meet someone casually. Even those who say they are not concerned about whether they pick anybody up or not, or who claim to be there for a friendly drink, are seldom unaware if there is somebody who takes an interest in them… Among those who remain talking together, conversations become increasingly distracted, as people look through transparent interlocutors, over shoulders, above heads, through lifted elbows, while trying to maintain a polite interest in what is being said.[1]

It seemed equally impossible to be yourself in gay clubs or bars as constituted, as it was among uncomprehending heterosexuals. The irony of which so many were unaware was that those who complained of the superficiality and aridity of the bar scene were often just as much part of the problem as those they scorned. After all, it takes two to connive at a shallow exploitative relationship just as much as to create a deep and meaningful one. So when those who came to London CHE groups looking for something more satisfying failed to renew their subscriptions or even to return after their first visit, part of the reason was that a CHE group could not magically change who they were. Wherever you travel, you always take yourself with you.

Those in the outer London suburbs were perhaps another matter, and recognisably kin to the more isolated provincials. While the Sixties swung for a tiny minority in the centre of town (and Brighton), for the rest the Sixties did not come until well into the Seventies.

George Mortimer, who accepted Allan Horsfall's invitation to start groups in London, found when he started a small but ready constituency, receptive to 'the message', but it would turn out to be rather more bolshie than he would like.

George Mortimer

George Mortimer was a wine merchant, though you'd never think it to look at him. Tall, stooped and lugubrious, he looked, in his forties, more like a Funeral Director. Or perhaps, with his glasses, something in academia. His 'Old Chelsea Wine Stores' was in Lamb's Conduit Street, near Bloomsbury, close to his flat, and Bloomsbury was the scene of the first tentative growth of CHE in London. For Mortimer was the first London Organiser, and during a brief period in the summer of 1970 kick-started the first London CHE groups.

In the mid-1960s Peter Norman became George's lodger, soon after he finished his MA at the University of London.

> My view was that I was going to be a lodger; I think his view was that I was going to be a lover, but he was very nice about it. He didn't force himself on me in any way. He was very very avuncular. For a period of a few months we got on really quite well. He said, 'This will be your own room, make yourself at home.' But it was hopeless because it was absolutely stuffed with all his books from floor to ceiling, and there was just a bed in the middle. And he wanted me in his bed anyway, which I did a few times. I liked him but I didn't fancy him at all. … He had this huge collection of books. Every wall in his flat was lined from floor to ceiling with bookshelves, you could hardly get through in places. And he would keep buying new ones – well, old ones actually.
>
> It was interesting because he was the first person I formed a friendship with who was not of my generation. … He was somebody who'd built a life and a business. So I think I looked up to him quite a lot.
>
> He introduced me to [the music of] Bob Dylan and he was very keen on that sort of thing. And he used to take the *Village Voice*, which told us all about life in Greenwich Village, and he was a very keen cook and *bon viveur* in the sense he used to go to posh restaurants and told me he knew the owners, and I think he did. And it all seemed a very cosmopolitan and grown-up life.[2]

George had been a supporter of the Homosexual Law Reform Society, a friend of Antony Grey, and an occasional speaker on homosexual law reform to outside organisations. He also had some responsibility for fostering local discussion groups for the Albany Trust.

Albany Trust discussion groups

The Albany Trust discussion groups had started in 1965. The active supporters of the HLRS and the Albany Trust were always pushing to be more involved and more helpful, whereas the parent bodies wanted a straight and straight-laced image, in which concerned liberal heterosexuals were working on behalf of those poor benighted people who couldn't help themselves. Antony Grey when he arrived reconciled the two by deciding that the HLRS would start discussion groups, and when they clustered in sufficient numbers, they could form HLRS Area Committees. The new NWHLRC could be a model for just such a committee. The Albany Trust was already running seasons of lectures, 'Winter Talks', and discussion groups were a logical extension to those – seminars maybe, rather than lectures. Forty volunteers came forward. It was enough to set up two groups. Peter Norman remembers:

> I went to a series of lectures the Albany Trust organised at the Alliance Hall, somewhere in Westminster. … It was a slightly strange sort of meeting, because the people who were there were, I suppose, almost all gay, certainly the vast majority were men, and yet officially it was a meeting of a charitable trust, or possibly you could say it was the HLRS, in that case it was a body which was campaigning for a change in the law on behalf of 'these poor people'. So nobody was admitting they were gay, but there we all were. … One thing that spun off from that was a series of discussion groups. … We met in people's flats.[3]

The discussion groups were labelled as Albany Trust groups, and it's a measure of the inextricable confusion at grass roots level between the Trust and the HLRS, through the person of Antony Grey, that the members of the one were also asked to be letter-writing campaigners of the other.

The discussion groups were intended for members to improve themselves as homosexuals. It was a plank of the campaigning platform of both the HLRS and early CHE, as of Arcadie in France fifteen years earlier, that not only the public needed educating about homosexuality, but also homosexuals themselves, who remained pitifully ignorant about their 'condition'. One group minuted:

> I think it was agreed that we are in ourselves the principal problem, our attitudes to society in general and above all our attitude to others of our

> own kind. … A common meeting ground for the exchange of ideas and feelings just does not until this moment exist. We partly fail to accept the idea that we are as other human beings, but differ in only one fact.[4]

Two discussion groups started in May 1965. A third was formed in October that year. They were rigidly controlled by Grey, through what he described as the 'syllabus'. This consisted of topics and literature chosen by him for discussion on a fortnightly basis, and although lip-service was paid to the group's freedom to talk about other things, it was generally assumed that the chairmen (they were all men) of each group would keep things marching to the right drum. George Mortimer was a member of Group A, as were Peter Norman, Griffith Vaughan Williams and George Tregaskis.* The organiser was Dr D. R. G. Neaumann-Cooke.

The topics were quite literary and intellectual; often members were given a reading list in advance of a meeting, which they were expected to have worked through. There might be papers trailing a bibliography of a dozen books and articles, including some only available at the Bodleian Library. Members of the group had to work hard. When it came to discussion of gay marriage, Neaumann-Cooke produced for the meeting a closely-argued, densely typed position paper of six foolscap pages (about 4,000 words) on the secret of creating a long-lasting 'affair':

> Success in an affair is much more than a matter of finding the right person; it is a matter of being the right person. … It takes two to make an affair, and an affair is what they make it. … The male who wants to be a good 'wife' should, therefore, keep well in mind that he is a 'wife' only by virtue of having a 'husband'. …
>
> Happy lasting affairs involve a sound adjustment between two persons. And this adjustment, contrary to impressions held in some quarters, is not entirely a sexual one. Generally sex plays a part. But there is more to it than sex. Indeed it is possible for an affair to be happy without sex directly entering into it in any degree worth mentioning. …
>
> It is an old question, which partner is more responsible, the active one or the passive one for the breakup of an affair? They are about equally responsible. The numbers of active and passive men who count as the 'guilty' parties does not affect the issue. Going to bed is very rarely the real grounds for a split up. It may provide the excuse for it, but the real causes are much deeper, which are connected with an ill-adjustment to the affair itself.[5]

---

* George Tregaskis was a lifelong friend of Griff Vaughan Williams, member of CHE London Group 1 and later the West End Group. Member of the CHE EC for thirty years.

The absolute division of male and female roles in a relationship seems to be taken as a given. Elsewhere the piece refers habitually to 'gay men', a phrase not very common in Britain until after the arrival of GLF; it suggests that the group was heavily influenced by American usage and literature.

The chairman also laid down strict rules. Personal problems, if relevant to the subject, could be discussed at the chairman's discretion; ten minutes was allotted to this if necessary at the end of the meeting.[6] So there is a distinct nervousness about any kind of 'coming out', or sharing personal experience in what would be regarded as a consciousness-raising way a few years later. To talk 'on a personal basis' would also involve the personal admission of homosexuality. There were constant reminders of the high-minded nature of the project, as if any intrusion of the personal would put that in jeopardy; it was as if self-confessed homosexuals were unable to be 'high-minded':

> We must have ever present in our minds that we are not a law unto ourselves but are part of a group of people who are trying very hard to create something that has never before existed in this country. We have a great work to do if only we can instil the right spirit of *esprit de corps*. There is a lot we can do to help ourselves and others in the same position, but it will not develop fully as it can if we are constantly seeing the personal view only.[7]

Subjects included 'D. H. Lawrence and Sex', the 'Kama Sutra', 'The Homosexual and the Woman', 'The Homosexual, Transvestite and Pederast in the Cinema', likewise on 'TV', 'The Homosexual Problem', 'Psychiatry', 'Promiscuity', 'Montesquieu' and 'the Salvation Army'. At the end of the 'course' of fortnightly discussions, members would have emerged, if there had been an exam, with something like an A-level in Queer Studies. Although the discussion groups had this aura of academic rigour, Peter Norman felt that they were also awareness groups almost in spite of themselves. Two things marked out these groups from the HLRS, and provided a bridge into the London CHE groups. Firstly, they gradually acquired a social cohesion which expressed itself in trips out to theatres and restaurants; second, unlike at the Winter Talks, it was permissible here to say that one was homosexual, if only briefly or indirectly, and people did.

> Some of the subjects were a bit abstruse, but some of them were much more personal, where people could relate their own views and experiences if they wanted to. … When CHE was forming, and people joined CHE, people … wanted to explore the nature of being gay and how they felt about it before they could do anything else. But I'd already done that bit, at least in an academic and theoretical way.[8]

Mortimer fostered the three discussion groups for over four years. Although a 'faint spark' of a possible group in Bristol came to nothing, he did address a meeting in Burnley in April 1966.*

Mortimer was a close friend of Labour MP Gwyneth Dunwoody, and active in the Labour Party. Allan Horsfall knew him personally, both from Party conferences and through Antony Grey. He told Paul that George 'might be very useful to us in sorting out the London problem.' In this way, at Horsfall's behest, Mortimer became the first London Organiser – not a convenor, but someone who helped to set up a group, and then, having got one off the ground, moved on to start another one once the first had enough members to function and officers to organise it.

Kingsway Group into London I

The London 'problem' which Horsfall referred to was a London group which existed before CHE established a presence in the city. It was called the Kingsway group, and was organised by Terry Whittaker, a CHE member. Whittaker first appears as a member of something called the Talbot Square group, which asked to affiliate as a group to CHE in February 1970. Terry was its liaison officer with CHE. Little is known of the group before this moment, but over the next few months George Mortimer probably visited the group and talked about CHE; Paul Temperton would have mailed his thoughts to Terry, about how meetings and local groups might develop. There was a kind of 'firming up' process at work.

As the Kingsway Group it held its first formal meeting in May 1970. Though it called itself a CHE group, and Whittaker claimed to speak on behalf of CHE, it was at best semi-detached from the Committee. It met in the Kingsway Hall, owned by the Methodists and home to the West London Mission. It was best known for its main meeting hall, which functioned as a recording studio, home to many great EMI recordings from the 1920s to 1970s. However, the mission itself had a maze of meeting rooms, a youth club and a luncheon club. Donald Soper, a pacifist and an outspoken supporter of homosexual equality, had been minister there for 35 years, and it was through his offices that Whittaker secured use of the Hall. The meetings attracted very large numbers, seventy to eighty at a time. George Mortimer wrote in the August 1970 CHE Bulletin that there had been speakers every month – Lord Soper, Spartacus publisher John Stamford and gay journalist Roger Baker are mentioned – but on the whole the meetings were rather stuffy and formal. Things loosened up a bit when members went off to a pub after the meetings.

* This suggests a substantial and interested homosexual community in Burnley, one which CHE drew on to fight for Esquire Clubs a few years later at the public meeting described in Chapter Three.

The 'problem' Allan referred to was, how to rein in this group and make it a formal part of CHE?

Having been set up independently, the Kingsway Group was suspicious of becoming part of a national organisation, especially one based in Manchester. Manchester was equally suspicious of it. Mortimer proposed an amalgamation between the people he had been inducting into CHE so far with the intention of forming a group, and the existing Kingsway group. But all was not well with the Kingsway group, for reasons which are not clear. After a telephone call from George mid-July, Paul Temperton told Allan:

> I have a nasty feeling that very strange things are going on in London, because Nick Stanley has fed back to me some extraordinary things which Marchant from IHWO* has told him about how CHE is regarded in London.[9]

Any suggestion that the group was misbehaving in some way would have been anathema to Mortimer. He was in some ways deeply conservative, despite his political affiliations, and also something of a snob. His conservatism manifested itself in the way that he introduced new members to CHE at induction meetings. According to Roger Baker, his successor as London Organiser:

> George appeared with his old AT [Albany Trust] entourage being rather *de haut en bas* to the rest of us fledgling campaigners, and then read us the Sexual Offences Act; occasionally pausing to say how ill he was and how many injections he'd had that afternoon, which achieved a fairly harrowing effect. Everyone brightened up later however as we toddled across to the pub and got down to what is laughingly known as socialising.
>
> George also passed round a sort of certificate which we had to sign and which stated we were not gathering for an immoral purpose, and if we were under that impression we could have our money back there and then. An unnerving thing, I thought, casting a slightly furtive air over the proceedings. I wouldn't have thought that anyone who had got that far, after all our screening process, would have been still under the impression

---

* International Homosexual World Organisation, started in 1954 by one of the founders of the Danish Forbundet af 1948, Axel Axgil. It originally operated as a correspondence club for individuals. After liberalisation of Danish pornography laws in 1967, it started to publish its own magazine, *UNI*, which featured numerous contact advertisements world-wide. It was also a shipping agency for other magazines, for pornographic photos and film, as well as offering film processing services. It ceased trading and other activities in 1970. Given the IHWO brand, it is not clear what it would take for a group to get into bad odour with them, unless it was a financial scandal of some kind. It was unlikely to have been sexual.

it was going to be lights out and knickers off, but G does have these neuroses.

George is very nervous of the press and the police as you know.[10]

43. Roger Baker

This is not necessarily personal prudishness, as Roger implies. After all, George subscribed to *Village Voice*, and introduced his lodgers to Bob Dylan. Rather it is a hangover from the ethos of the old Albany Trust discussion groups, where high-mindedness reflected the importance of the work being done as well as fear of the pre-1967 law.

No wonder, then, that George freaked out even more at the Kingsway Group inviting the editor of *Spartacus* magazine, John D. Stamford, to speak to them. *Spartacus* was one of a new generation of gay magazines, with little awareness of political issues, a few articles, extensive personal ads, a problem page, mail order porn, and pictures of dolly boys, some of them very young.* George did not at all approve. He wrote to Horsfall:

> However, by the very nature of local groups, the whole movement could be set at peril by one group going 'rogue' and acting out of line with the rest of the other groups. At this moment I see great danger because I understand one or two people – no doubt for laudable motives – are

*Stamford attempted to justify this, rather bizarrely: 'If the inclusion of pictures of young models around 15 years of age makes any contribution to the prevention of seducement of these boys, then I think it is worthwhile.' —*Spartacus* 17, Editor's Letter, 4.

> toying with the idea of obtaining publicity from magazines which would certainly arouse suspicion in the eyes of the general public and possibly result in police action. … There may be room in the homosexual law reform movement for people willing to urge reform in unconventional ways, but I myself am only willing to participate on the lines set out in your published pamphlet.[11]

This is a clear dig at Whittaker, who had written something about CHE for the semi-pornographic *Spartacus*.

Roger Baker, however had a much more holistic view of what CHE should be doing. Of Mortimer he said:

> Educating the homosexual about his position regarding the law is very much a George Mortimer hobbyhorse; but it's only one of a whole host of things which ought to happen more or less unconsciously (otherwise it sounds like evening classes).[12]

Roger lived round the corner from George's shop in Bloomsbury, in a tiny flat piled high with books and records in Great James Street. They shared similar tastes in gourmet food as well as both being great readers, and became firm friends, although otherwise temperamentally chalk and cheese. He got to know Mortimer as his customer, being a great lover of wine. He records that George sold him two bottles of very good red at an excessively cheap price – as a preliminary to talking him into a case of something much more expensive. Mortimer and Baker had a stormy relationship, of violent quarrels and equally violent reconciliations, both fuelled by alcohol.

Baker's relationship with alcohol was certainly not out of control, in that he led an extraordinarily diverse and productive life both in work and play. However, it could affect personal relationships, and within the enclosed, sometimes hothouse, world of CHE there could be ramifications. Alan Wakeman describes the effects:

> At a party Roger would drink very sensibly, but he would gradually get drunker, and drunker, and once you knew him well, you had to look at him, because he would suddenly change colour, and he would become a beetroot colour, and that point you had to avoid him, because he would start attacking people. And at my fortieth birthday I saw him turn that colour, … and at that exact moment he got his glass of wine and tipped it over the head of the woman he was talking to. Then she hit him. And then he hit her back. And I remember thinking, 'Oh God, this is my 40th birthday, and all I wanted was for them to love one another,' and I fled out the flat and went downstairs. …
>
> Roger said to me, when I saw him next time, after a party, 'So who did I insult last night? Who's never going to speak to me again?' But once I'd seen that happen a few times, I thought, really he needs protection. He needed someone to say, 'Come on Roger, you've got to go home now.'[13]

So if George was something of a puritan, Roger was a hedonist. Where George was severe, Roger was a charmer. And it fell to him rather than George to charm Terry Whittaker back into the CHE fold. Both he and Nick Stanley in Birmingham were showing dangerous signs of independence. There were sighs of relief when Stamford turned down a Whittaker article for *Spartacus*, which he'd written without consulting anybody. Stamford asked Baker to do it instead. The Kingsway Group was also charging only 2/6d (12½p) entry for the meetings instead of the recommended 4/- (20p), and ran no formal membership system. As a result national CHE wasn't seeing any money from the people going along to the group,* and had no idea who they were, or how many there were. Though individuals had become members off their own bat by writing to Manchester, there was no attempt to enrol from the meetings, or to insist on CHE membership as a condition of going along.

At the start of his charm offensive, Roger invited Whittaker over for a chat: 'I contacted Whittaker who burbled affably over the phone and now comes to see me. (I do like holding court in my own house – talk about a tyrant queen!)'[14] They came to an agreement. Roger would go along to a meeting and harangue the group about the benefits of being an individual CHE member. This he did in October 1970:

> My confrontation with the Whittaker Group last night was fascinating. I kept my cool and sailed through it rather well, I thought. At one point I was almost voted out of office. Had it come to the point I wouldn't have let them, but fortunately some more sensible person pointed out they couldn't do that!
>
> However the main thing is that everything is now sorted out and everyone is happy. They are No 1 group, they are part of us and will be brought in to all CHE activity in London. They will supply me with a list of their members. I didn't make any strictures about their financing, I simply pointed out that they were, like the others, an autonomous group. So everyone agreed to forget the past and I was quietly apologised to afterwards by a number of people for the bitterness and acrimony. So you need lose no more sleep over that lot.[15]

Though Baker talks of Kingsway 'becoming' London 1, Mortimer had already started a London 1 group, and the two joined forces as Allan had suggested back in July. London 1 started with members of all the old Albany Trust discussion groups brought together. The upshot of amalgamation was that Terry Whittaker slipped quietly out of the picture, and with him went any money that the Kingsway group had made up to this point. Group 1 members took over the running of the combined group.

---

* It's not clear where this recommendation of 4/- per meeting came from; there's nothing in the archives to support it.

London Group I

Laurence Collinson became Secretary of London Group 1. Known as Laurie, he was a considerable literary figure in Australia, where he wrote for television and radio as well as editing journals. He came to the UK in 1964 at the age of 39, and had three television plays broadcast by ITV in the late 1960s. He lived in a very modern flat in the Barbican which he was inordinately proud of. This was paid for by working for the romantic publishing house, Mills and Boon, whose stereotyped fictions contradicted everything he personally believed in. He became involved in GLF, when it started a few months later, and used that experience to start a Group 1 awareness group, designed to examine the concept of self-oppression and to raise personal esteem.* This became a prototype for other awareness groups within CHE.

Collinson also became the first of the new-wave gay British novelists with the publication of *Cupid's Crescent* (1973), which caused considerable controversy and there were half-hearted attempts to ban it. His play *Thinking Straight*, directed by Roger Baker, was part of the first Gay Sweatshop season in early 1975. His papers are in the National Archive of Australia.

He was very interested in transactional analysis, an amalgam of psychology and psychotherapy developed by Eric Berne and popularised through his book, *Games People Play*. From this position he critiqued much of conventional psychoanalysis. The 1971 GLF conference on 'Psychiatry and the Homosexual' was largely organised from Collinson's flat by members of the GLF counter-psychiatry group.

The new Treasurer of Group 1, Teck Ong, tried to collect any money the Kingsway Group had taken, pressing Whittaker for a statement of accounts. When letters went unanswered, Group 1 discussed taking legal action, but decided against it. Eventually, some months later, Whittaker sent in figures which conveniently showed a loss of £1/6/1d (£1.30p). Given that the nine meetings in the period covered had reportedly attracted up to eighty people, membership fees (only £19) and collections were suspiciously low and catering losses were suspiciously high. However Group 1 realised they would never know the truth, and there the matter rested.

Soon they had enough members to want to start their own club night. In October 1970 they secured Sunday nights at the Paintbox Club,† and David Forsyth of Group 1 appealed in a circular:

---

* His awareness group met with hostility from the London-wide Task Force, shortly to become the counselling service, London FRIEND, on the grounds that it was trespassing, and duplicating their efforts.

† The Paintbox was a tiny club with a stage in Foley Street, near Broadcasting House. In the early 1960s it was a haunt of Stephen Ward, who killed himself in the aftermath of the Profumo scandal.

> Many CHE members have expressed a need for a regular social meeting place, and we are pleased to be able to tell you that this now seems possible An existing club has offered us Sunday evenings for the exclusive use of our members beginning Sun 25 Oct. At the moment this is an experiment running for three consecutive Sundays. If they are successful then there is every possibility that they will become a permanent feature of CHE's social calendar. …
>
> This is not an official CHE enterprise but only CHE members will be admitted. Each member may bring one guest for whom he must take responsibility. … This is a serious attempt to set up a regular meeting place and its success depends on your support.[16]

It was open from 7.30 to 11.30 p.m., cost 10/- (50p) including a light supper. However, it came with a warning that drinks were at 'familiar West End club prices'. It would be an expensive night out. There were not enough takers to make it financially viable.

It is an indication of the ambiguous attitude the average CHE member had towards commercial establishments, that on the one hand clubs are criticised for being soulless, and on the other hand, one of the first things many CHE groups tried to do was to start their own club nights. But for every member keen to prove that a club could be friendly if it had the right attitudes and the right people, there was another too scared of being identified as gay to dare to go into a known gay venue.

John D. Stamford and *Spartacus*

By August 1970, the advertising in London was kicking in with a vengeance. The spate of enquiries from the national adverts of July was supplemented by the free publicity in *Spartacus*. John Stamford had started *Spartacus* in 1968 as a small (roughly A5) glossy fashion/entertainment/pin-up magazine with its face resolutely set against anything political. An editorial in July 1970, a year after the Stonewall Riots in New York, marked the anniversary:

> Thankfully we haven't had any kind of the militancy here that has happened, and is still doing so in America.
>
> In my opinion, this sort of semi-violence belongs very much to the stage and screen – it may be ideal in a camp farce, but not in real life. It is impossible to imagine anything more horrifying, and more inherently comic, than a march of queans on Whitehall or Buckingham Palace, chaining themselves to the railings and chanting slogans.
>
> The only revolution is a fashion revolution, a Carnaby Street revolution.[17]

However, Stamford was not a natural journalist. He was a lapsed Catholic priest who ran a guest house in Brighton.* A distinctly shady character,† he was more interested in the business than the quality of the copy. The magazine was really a hook to get people to buy from his mail order business. This was brought to the attention of the local paper in Brighton by some outraged straight men who received unsolicited catalogues of gay materials through the post. Stamford was in the habit of buying mailing lists off other concerns, this being the days before Data Protection Acts. The *Brighton Evening Argus* promptly set up a 'probe', and interviewed Stamford, who readily cast himself in the roles of victim, honest trader and fighter for gay rights. The paper frothed:

> A 'sex shop' catering for homosexuals is operating in Brighton and illustrated literature is being sent unsolicited through the post to single men living in the town. ... Brochures picturing nude male models offer photographs of boys in sets of six assorted poses for £2/10s. The 'homo' shop is above a betting office in Preston Street, which for some years has been known as Brighton's 'street of shame'.[18]

And they drew attention to how well he was doing out of the business, with his Rolls Royce and Mercedes parked outside. However, Stamford was full of bluff self-justification:

> I make no secret of the fact that I am 100% homosexual. This business, of which I am the sole proprietor, is highly profitable, but I am not concerned with making money. I am concerned with defending sexual equality. ... My organisation is affiliated to the Committee against Sexual Discrimination.‡
>
> I purchased a list of 18,000 names of people said to be homosexual three months ago and have been circularising them in batches of 6,000. Of the people we have circularised, 80% have placed orders with us,§ 15% have asked us to remove their name from the list and 5% have not replied.
>
> Every home is equipped with a dustbin and if I received something I considered offensive I would put it in my dustbin. People who shout the odds about 'filthy queers' usually have a guilt complex and something to hide, and I feel sincerely sorry for them. I am not afraid to admit I am homosexual. If God made me this way he must have a reason, and who am I to dispute it?

---

* Le Chateau Gaye. 'We try to create an informal home-from-home atmosphere, everyone uses first names and guests come and go as they please. ... We do everything we can to give you a really fabulous time.'

† In later life he was pursued by the Dutch tax authorities for millions in back taxes, and also spent some time in prison for running a ring of underage rent boys.

‡ This presumably is the Committee for Homosexual Equality.

§ This seems an impossibly high response to a mail order circular.

> You can describe me as a wealthy businessman with interests in men's cosmetics and the film industry. I do a lot of social work advising people on homosexual problems. Our customers include many who are household names. We try to help them adjust to their condition.[19]

The story of the 18,000 names and addresses so alarmed CHE that Paul Temperton was forced to reassure members in a letter to the paper, and in the CHE *Bulletin*:

> In case any of our own supporters should wonder where this list came from, I would like to point out that our mailing list is very strictly confidential and in no circumstances would we reveal the names and addresses of our supporters to anyone.[20]

It is strange that when interviewed John Stamford makes no mention of his magazine *Spartacus*, which was comparatively innocuous in its content and its visuals, offered some lifestyle and relationship advice, and might have been seen as a demonstration of his purity of intention.

Having admitted that editing a magazine was outside his skills range, he brought in Roger Baker, officially as features editor, in practice, editor; this was extremely useful to CHE, providing instant access to the press. The editorial line became CHE's, particularly on the importance of coming out:

> The Committee for Homosexual Equality do a certain amount of campaigning for the cause, but really, very few ordinary men working in offices and factories would have the courage to be honest with their closest friends. … We have still a long way to go to be accepted and we will never become accepted as normal rather than queer unless those of us who are indistinguishable from heterosexuals in appearance and manner are prepared to be honest.[21]

There were free adverts, constant references to CHE, and, in February 1971, a densely-argued two-page feature about why people should join:

> 'Congenial surroundings' … does not necessarily refer to carpets and curtains, but to people. … The gay bar or club is, for many people, the only place they know where they can go and meet other homosexuals. Their intent may not be sexual, but merely social, and they are doomed to another miserable evening. A CHE gathering cuts this away with one stroke; it is somewhere to go to meet other homosexuals, not as a sexual object, but as a person. …
>
> Nor does CHE reject any applicants. What happens is that potential members screen CHE rather. … In fact CHE can provide a means of contact between homosexuals which is just not available anywhere else, where the middle-aged introvert can talk to the outrageous effeminate with neither fearing nor hating the other.[22]

Others might want to vet potential members as described in the previous chapter, but Roger's vision of CHE was humane, sociable, tolerant and inclusive. He was an ideal London Organiser.

Roger Baker

At this point Roger Baker was 36 years old. He had come to London in 1960. His background was solid working class, his father a mining electrician on shift work down a pit. His mother was determined that he would not suffer the same fate, and pushed him to grammar school and the University of Nottingham. He realised he was gay when he was 12, but suffered the common dislocation between his experience and finding the words and labels to define it:

> The concept of homosexual as applied to myself didn't come till much later. One talked about queers. … As in all the industrial Midlands, there are lots of local legends and scandals about men who had been sent to prison for interfering with small boys. They were defined as a separate category of people. I had lots and lots of gay sex when I was in my teens. … I discovered the local cottage in Mansfield quite by accident. … I couldn't keep out of it. When I think back now … all those miners who were cruising in those days to come across this 16, 17, 18 year old boy who was quite willing and happy to do anything they wanted. It must have been quite a bonus for them. … But during the three years I read English at university I absolutely conformed to the style of things at Notts university at that time. I had girlfriends – fucked girls. But it didn't mean anything.[23]

The cash-strapped family situation meant that Roger had to go to work immediately after leaving university, to bring in some income – no time to look around or build a career. He worked in a cigarette factory:

> There was a man in the factory who went round banging the wall and shouting … it was sheer frustration. I read *Gone with the Wind*, *War and Peace* and *The Good Companions*, which were the three longest novels I could find, and did all the workload that was required.[24]

In desperation he applied to the *Nottingham Evening Post*, and, rather to his own surprise, was taken on. Now, with independence, his gay life could begin:

> When I started working on the *Nottingham Evening Post*, I was astonished, absolutely astonished, to find there was a gay scene in Nottingham. … I remember moving into a bedsitter, and there was a boy living in the bedsitter next to mine who was gay. He knew the scene and he took me out. I'll never forget my first night out in gay Nottingham. I'd been living there for four years.[25]

After three years, he got a job on *Tatler*, at a time when, thanks to the likes of actors Albert Finney and Richard Harris, working class accents became fashionable. All the best magazines – *Queen*, *Man About Town*, *Nova* – had at least one tame 'pleb' on the staff. Now *Tatler* had Baker.

For all his comfort in his skin by this time, the first year in London was very intimidating. He felt socially ill at ease in most clubs, and reverted to old ways:

> I was very unsure, very insecure. I was in my mid-twenties. All sorts of strange things happened. I did a hell of a lot of cottaging. I was hauled up at Bow Street, fined for importuning. I was beaten up. I was blackmailed. I was robbed. … When I was actually arrested, I had to have time off work to make my sensational appearance at Bow Street, so I had to go and tell the editor what it was all about. …
>
> I picked up this guy in the cottage at Islington Green and went back and had sex with him, and he said he wanted money. I said I hadn't got any money; he said he wanted some money by Friday or else he would do all sorts of things; he wanted ten shillings. I gave him ten shillings and that was that. I never heard from him again.
>
> I also got VD twice. I didn't know what I'd got. I just knew that something messy and unorthodox was happening to my cock. I rushed off to my local GP who of course knew immediately what was happening. I went off to St Bartholomew's, which is the nearest hospital to Islington. It was very cold and unpleasant indeed; the doctors were … making put-down remarks; there was definitely an edge there. They whisked me off to some well-meaning lady social worker. I couldn't understand why it was any business of hers that I was gay, I'd just got VD.
>
> So all in all that first year was pretty harassing.[26]

Tatler went through an ownership change and a rebranding in 1965, and Roger found himself thrown into the choppy seas of freelancing. To plump up his CV and make himself more employable, he wrote *Drag* (1968), a history of female impersonation in the arts. This was pre-GLF, pre-feminist almost, and the book is almost a marker on the borders of gay awareness. In the introduction there is plenty of non-judgemental discussion of the relationship between homosexuality and drag, which manages also to convey some of the prejudice gay men faced. Clearly Baker describes drag parties with an insider's knowledge. He also quotes the now-well-known but then revelatory accounts of the Mollies Club in *The London Spy* of 1709, with their elaborate cross-dressing rituals, and the raids on the Clare Market queer clubs of the late eighteenth and early nineteenth centuries:

> The participants were hauled through the streets in open carts and the population would crowd the routes and pelt them with anything to hand. On one occasion when a particularly notorious club was raided, dung,

> rotten fruit, stinking fish and brick-bats were sold in the streets for ammunition.[27]

Despite the obvious potential for political commentary, Baker remains neutral:

> A talented homosexual may decide to earn his living by doing professionally what he has been doing with apparent success at private parties. But that need not concern us. … A professional female impersonator working on the stage may be homosexual, heterosexual, bisexual or asexual, just as a wrestler, a policeman or a plumber may be. The assumption of outward sexual characteristics by no means implies the equal assumption of that sex's function or desires.[28]

For the rest of the book, drag is treated purely as a particular aspect of show business, requiring particular skills. At the time, and in the shadow of the libel laws, it would have been hard to cover the subject any other way.

He was to give many talks on the subject of drag to CHE groups over the years. He followed *Drag* with three cookery books* that mined the 'cooking-for-idiots-who-live-on-their-own' vein pioneered by Katherine Whitehorn's *Cooking in a Bedsitter*, but his books were squarely aimed at the young single males (implied 'gay') who constituted a burgeoning market. These books also provided Roger with material for his cookery columns in the developing gay press in the 1970s and 80s.

It was against this background that Roger went to *Spartacus*, growing from contributor to editor, and during this time, he became aware of gay politics and gay liberation:

> What happened was that a friend of mine who was a journalist was asked to edit a magazine called *Contact*, and it was to be a sex magazine without photographs. He asked me if I would write an article for its first issue, on drag. … and after that he asked me to do an article every month. …
>
> Then one day he said, there's this Gay Liberation thing going on in the States, why don't you write an article about the situation of homosexuals in Britain. … I realised I knew fuck-all about it. All I knew was that I was gay and lived my own life. I didn't know anything about anything at all.
>
> So I had to tackle it like any other feature, and I had to research it, and my researches took me, of course, to Antony Grey and various other places, and I began to learn for the first time about the Wolfenden Report, the lobbying of the sixties and the Albany Trust, … and eventually I got this article together. … I decided we needed a good gay magazine, a gay organisation which could socialise gays, … there was no socialising force, which was very important. I also felt we ought to have a spokesman –

---

* *Cooking for One*; *Cooking With Wine*; *Cooking Out Of Cans*.

> some grey-suited, white-shirted individual who would appear on television and say nice things.
>
> But this is absolutely true, I wrote the article and took it out to post, and met a friend of mine* in the street, who said, 'Oh Roger would you be interested in a gay organisation,' and I said yes, And he introduced me to CHE, … and I took over, and set up the first ten London CHE groups.[29]

The first job of the London organiser was to meet new enquirers, to tell them about CHE and what it could offer, and then to organise them into groups. From August 1970 to June 1971 it was an extremely demanding job. The first article in *Spartacus* produced over 120 enquiries, and from then onwards regular adverts in *The Observer*, *The Guardian*, and the *New Statesman* would routinely produce 50 responses apiece.† At least 50 per cent of these were from people in London. In this period membership nationally rose from 400 to 1,000 and in London from about 50 to 350.

It was to Roger's tiny flat that the new enquirers came for their induction. Often there would be ten or fifteen people crammed in, sitting on the floor and drinking Roger's best claret. As Roger explained the aims of CHE, how the social side worked and what people might get out of it, it was a convivial atmosphere. People could talk if they wished to about what they wanted from the group, and how they came to be there. It was the original icebreaker, before the group Icebreakers started.‡

Inductions were supplemented by parties. Lunch parties, tea parties, night-time parties. Roger loved to have his flat filled with noise and laughter. The air would be thick with smoke, and Maria Callas would sing in the background. Andrew Lumsden remembers one such:

> His parties were very sensational and splendidly indecent. I was slightly surprised because I thought I was going round for afternoon tea or something. I think I put on lace gloves. But then it turned out that his version of afternoon tea wasn't exactly the same as Miss Prism's. … He was very well regarded.[30]

Michael Moor and London Group 2

Other CHE newcomers came along singly. Among them was 22-year-old Michael Moor, working for Camden Council on his first job since studying

---

* This must have been George Mortimer.

† One of the charges levelled against CHE is that it was a 'middle-class' organisation. However, this was not for lack of trying. Adverts were placed regularly in *The Sun*, *The Daily Mirror*, *Evening Standard* and *News of the World*, but they produced nothing like the response that came from *The Observer*, the *New Statesman*, *Spectator*, or *Private Eye*.

‡ When Icebreakers started in 1973, Roger was one of its first members.

sociology at the LSE. Like so many, he had ruthlessly repressed his gay feelings, until a trip with some friends to Amsterdam after finals had opened his eyes. He had stumbled on a gay bar in what was then the gayest city in Europe, and instantly realised that this way of life was for him. He returned to London in the summer of 1970, determined to do something about it.

He threw himself into the gay scene, such as it was, becoming a regular at the A & B club, the Festival Club just off St Martin's Lane by the London Coliseum, and at the Catacombs, a subterranean dive near The Coleherne in Earls Court. All of these were members' clubs, and deeply respectable. Michael remembers the Catacombs:

> It was a very strange environment in that it was all gay men there, but you were not allowed to touch anybody. I mean, not only not touch in a sexual fashion, but you weren't allowed to even hold their shoulder, or their earlobe, or anything at all! The proprietors obviously were concerned about what they might face from the police.[31]

There were also the magazines, available from some news-stands if you knew where to ask. In addition to *Spartacus*, there was *Jeremy*, a much more fashion-conscious, trendy affair than John Stamford's magazine. It was published by a 25-year-old photographer Peter Marriott, who raised the necessary capital by taking out a bank loan. Just before the first issue appeared in August 1969, he and the editor, Christopher Jones, gave an interview to the *Daily Mirror*, which was open but also defensive. Marriott said:

> *Jeremy* will be designed to appeal to gay people and bi-sexuals. It will not be at all crude, but very sophisticated and camp. And its motto will be, 'Who cares about sex?' ... *Jeremy* will feature art, fashion and culture reviews, male (but not fully nude) pin-ups and girl pin-ups too. And it will carry interviews with stage people, a guide to homosexual pubs and clubs, and a fashion feature on a pop group member. ... *Jeremy* will avoid the seedy classified advertisements for liaisons which appear in some publications. Instead its advertising will be slanted towards way-out fashions and cosmetics (for men). That is an area where there are hundreds of thousands of men with no mortgages, no kids, and plenty of surplus money to spend.[32]

In saying this, Marriott was one of the first people to articulate the concept of the Pink Pound, the idea of homosexual men as an identifiable consumer group. However, the 21-year-old editor, Jones, was more defensive: 'Smaller minority groups have their own papers. I mean, the coin collectors are well catered for, aren't they?'[33]

Michael Moor saw an advert in *Jeremy*. He also made personal contacts through the magazine. One way or another, he found himself on the phone to Roger Baker:

> I phoned him up and he said why don't you come round and talk about it? So I went round and saw him on my lunch break. He explained that he was forming these groups in London and the number one group was full and so he would have to start off a number two group. He obviously didn't know quite how big this was going to be.
>
> I don't actually remember what we talked about. But I remember him being great in terms of confidence-boosting, because he said to me very clearly when I arrived, oh, it's really good of you just to come round and see somebody you don't know about something that is quite personal. And just to be open and friendly about it, that was actually a big confidence boost for me. He was pleased that I saw it as something fairly natural and normal for me, I'd literally gone along, rung a doorbell and gone upstairs to see him, not knowing what I was going to find.[34]

London Group 1 being full, it was a question of waiting until there were enough people to form London Group 2. Once there were enough people, there was then the question of where to meet. Roger, convivial soul, was concerned to wrest the groups away from Kingsway Hall, with its overtones of social work. In any case, there were too many other activities going on there. George Mortimer reported in the August 1970 Bulletin, as he was handing over to Baker:

> We are now setting up a series of new groups in London and members are flocking to join. Two, if not three, groups will be definitely opening in September, and should open monthly throughout winter. While London has a profusion of specialist pubs and clubs there is obviously growing dissatisfaction with the social life which they offer. People want to talk seriously, and the new groups provide them with an opportunity to do so. Many also of course welcome the companionship offered by groups. All great cities have a higher suicide rate in all age groups than smaller towns and country villages. … But we must make it clear that they do not exist to provide casual sexual adventures and membership is not confined exclusively to homosexuals.[35]

The reference to suicide is typical Gloomy George, as is the warning away from 'casual sexual adventures'.

These new groups worked to a template devised by Mortimer. The ideal size for a group, he suggested, was twenty-two, though why this precise figure was chosen is not clear. From this is was assumed fifteen to eighteen people would come to each meeting, which was a number that could be comfortably accommodated in a smallish upstairs pub room of the kind to be found in Central London. There would be one formal and one informal meeting a month, alternating fortnightly.* And if attendance at one group started falling

* This was the same format Mortimer's former lodger Peter Norman worked out in Liverpool, but it is not clear whether they evolved them independently, or talked it over.

off, it could be topped up and morale stiffened by importing people from another – always assuming that members were prepared to be moved around in such a regimented manner.

At the meetings, there was to be a short talk by a member or a guest, followed by twenty minutes questions and twenty minutes discussion. An hour in total, followed by an hour's drinking and socialising. This was schematic, but at least somewhat less regimented than the old Albany Trust discussion groups, in that it did not work to a curriculum, but followed members' interests. Early subjects tended to be similar, group to group: theories of homosexuality; sex and partnerships; psychiatry; social work; gays and religion. This was part of the mission to explain homosexuals to themselves. Those who had never had intellectual or serious social engagement with other homosexuals often had little sense of self, and without a sense of self there cannot be self-confidence. These meetings and their subjects provided the basic building blocks for self-awareness. To those who were already self-aware, they could be boring.

The groups would be self-financing, members being expected to pay, in addition to a national subscription, £1 a year, and 4/- (20p) every time they went along, to cover the cost of room hire. The groups would keep and administer the proceeds.

By September 1970 it was Roger doing the legwork. He was self-confident enough to be able to approach pub landlords about upstairs meeting rooms, and thick-skinned enough to take rejection.

As the enquiries poured in, it was only a matter of weeks before Michael found himself going along to the Pig and Whistle.*

> I suppose the most difficult thing for people, including me, was walking into a pub saying, I've come for a meeting that I think's happening upstairs, or whatever. Later we used to arrange for people to meet new people, and bring them along.[36]

London Group 2 first met on a Friday night – 4 September 1970. Roger reported back to Paul Temperton:

> Last night's meeting was a success and a good start. Angus is first rate, an excellent chairman, affable, witty and in control. Also full of good ideas – just the right sort of man to keep everyone enthusiastic and together. There were about 15 there – those who couldn't come sent apologies and in three cases £1 each, which indicates good intent, I think. Everyone was relaxed and chatted happily but no actual swords were crossed.[37]

* He recalls it as being at the at the junction of South Molton Street and Davies Street, near Bond Street tube. Not to be confused with the Pig and Whistle in Little Chester Street, Belgravia, which was a Sunday lunch time gay watering hole somewhat later.

Angus Forsyth, however, proved to be temperamental. By November Roger could write:

> Angus arrived of course, and was very sour indeed, full of gloom and bitterness. … He was very low-keyed, and the tone of the discussion was rational. He is not particularly well-liked but the points he made did cause a considerable amount of concern among those present. Already it is going to take quite a bit of talking to undo the damage that Angus has already done – for you must remember that the 100 or so CHE people in London see each other a lot and talk spreads very fast. … I have been forced into a corner rather.[38]

This meeting was the first gathering of the first six London convenors, of which more anon. The precise bone of contention is not clear.

As the number of groups grew, Roger would allocate the new ones to a different night weekly at the same pub. The Pig and Whistle did not last long, as it had the reputation of being a bit of a dive, and people were not coming back. In early 1971 two pubs came to the fore, home to different groups on different nights. Over a period of time the Coachmaker's Arms, near Bond Street, hosted London Groups 1, 4, 12 and 13 as well as meetings of the CHE Poetry Group and rehearsed readings by the Drama Group; while the Two Brewers in Monmouth Street hosted Groups 2, 3, 8, 9, 10, and 11. There was at this stage no attempt at geographic separation of members into genuinely local groups reflecting where people lived. From all over London they poured in to what would become by 1972 London Group 1 to London Group 13. This arrangement had the major advantage, for people who were still in the closet, of allowing them to seek out other homosexuals away from home, and at a venue not generally known to be gay, where 'discovery' seemed less likely.

On the other hand, it also ruled out much campaigning, in the sense understood by groups in smaller towns, where members could take collective action on their own 'patch'. In order for groups in London to be effective, they needed to combine together, and that would not happen until May 1971, with the formation of the London Co-ordinating Committee (LCC).

By May 1971 Michael Moor was secretary of London Group 2, with responsibility for organising social and discussion events. London Group 2 was something of a family affair, convened by Angus Forsyth, with his partner Keith as Secretary. This was the group which Roger Baker himself belonged to, and when Angus left shortly after, he was succeeded as chairman by Gavin Clare, who was Roger's partner. Michael Moor in turn succeeded Gavin. This comparatively high rate of turnover suggests some malaise within the group, perhaps related to its meeting place at the Two Brewers. When, shortly after, they tried to start a second night in the same pub on Saturdays, by the third Saturday only one person showed up. Roger Baker admitted the arrangement wasn't working:

> We did pick about the grottiest pub in the West End … also there weren't so many members as now. The gay club we patronised for a time was considered too expensive (it wasn't actually – but gays are notoriously out of touch with the cost of club living in London). I have not yet come across any gay club that is more expensive than its heterosexual counterpart.[39]

Brian Sewell and London Group 3

London Group 3 followed hard on the heels of London Group 2, at the beginning of October 1970. Its first convenor was Michael Thomas, a pipe-smoking Liberal, small, avuncular and bookish. He was quickly replaced when he moved to Bristol by an equally dynamic figure in the shape of Brian Sewell, who was the *Evening Standard*'s art critic for thirty years. He is also the author of two volumes of autobiography.* These paint a portrait of a man of enormous learning, almost fanatically dedicated to Art and the History of Art, who in private life enjoyed a cheerfully promiscuous life of casual encounters in heroic numbers. Not greatly favoured in romantic entanglements, he nevertheless emerges as a man of great loyalty and kindness allied to the gift of friendship. So when he joined CHE, Brian was not a man with a strong need for a gay social life, unlike many others. His motive for joining was primarily to make an impact politically. At the time he was working precariously as a freelance art dealer. His involvement in CHE came about as follows:

> It was an advertisement, I imagine in *The Times*, in the personal column. There was repeatedly this two or three line, very very small advertisement, and I was getting angrier and angrier. I knew exactly how it felt. Because the Wolfenden Report was being rather half-heartedly accepted, but there was a great deal of fierce and rather beastly opposition in the House of Commons, much of it led by Gwyneth Dunwoody, who would castrate them, and if that doesn't work, hang them. I was so angered by her that I did what I'd never done before, I wrote a letter. And I said, I thought you ought to try to have some understanding of the situation, rather than wanting to castrate everybody. And she wrote back an obviously secretarial letter, one line, 'I have read your letter with interest. Yours sincerely, Gwyneth Dunwoody.' And I wrote back and said, 'This isn't good enough, I wanted an answer. It's quite clear from my letter and my arguments that you should respond to them.' And I got a duplicate letter. And then I got very angry and she responded the third time with, 'This correspondence is now closed.' This correspondence had not even begun to be a

---

* *Outsider* and *Outsider II* – see Bibliography.

correspondence.* And I thought, if this is the kind of person who is in Parliament making decisions about my life, then something has to be done. So the campaigning wish was there, and then there was CHE, waiting.[40]

44. Brian Sewell in 2012

Initially, Brian would have written off to the CHE British Monomark box number (BCM 859), and the letter would have been forwarded to Paul Temperton and Martin Stafford's flat in Manchester; Paul would then have passed Brian's details back to London, to Roger Baker,† and then there would have been the phone call, and the invitation to Great James Street for induction. Like Michael Moor, Brian was seen alone:

> I don't know if it was the same for [others], but induction by Roger Baker meant being left alone with an awful lot of really filthy magazines, of the kind which were outside my experience, while he went off and made tea or something. I had to make a very positive leap beyond that. This is only one person. This person doesn't necessarily represent [CHE] – because this I

* This account is somewhat hard to square with Dunwoody's record on gay rights. Arriving in the Commons in 1966, she supported Leo Abse's Bill through all its parliamentary stages, staying until after 4 a.m. for the final cliffhanging vote on 3 July 1967. Her friendship with London Organiser George Mortimer has already been mentioned. She did, however, blot her copybook as far as LGBT rights are concerned somewhat later in her career, by voting against Edwina Currie's amendment to the 1994 Criminal Justice Act, to equalise the age of consent at 16. Ironically, her appetite for casual sex, according to Peter Robins, producer of Radio 4's *Today in Parliament*, was as great as her correspondent's, albeit in a heterosexual direction. No parliamentary assistant was safe from her advances.

† British Monomark's HQ was about 400 yards from Roger's flat.

> think may have been an aspect of the campaign that I didn't want to have anything to do with. I wasn't into pornography in any serious sense.*
>
> But things expanded really remarkably fast. Because I was told to join a Tuesday or Wednesday or whatever it was group, and this unhappy gathering of twenty or so people, in a bleak room above a pub. There was a whole series of these things. And they were always in bleak rooms above pubs. It was quite a wide spread of people. Which was why the thing had to be, 'I can only do it on Wednesday, because that's the night my wife goes out to bridge' or whatever. There were quite a lot of those problems. And people came, and then they went. … Because all they've had is this awful room, for two hours, with people talking to each other. And the talk was never in any way productive.[41]

It is clear from Brian's interview that his abiding memory is one of frustration, and of wasted potential. In the second volume of his autobiography, *Outsider II*, he is if anything even more scathing about CHE:

> This I found to have its headquarters in Manchester (then, and still, another country) and to be run by the kind of men who are always dubbed 'old women'; a pro-London coup engineered by a handful of members of whom I was one, more or less succeeded in achieving independence, but then it too succumbed to what we unkindly called the 'couch parties' – the uncomely middle-aged and middle-sexed, turgid of mind and body, who wanted every word of every meeting addressed to the chair, and who would never reach agreement without setting up a working party. I and the other revolutionaries left and CHE eventually died of self-inflicted suffocation.[42]

This is slightly unfair, both to CHE and to himself. What is remarkable is the extent to which Sewell and others threw themselves into making London CHE work over the next two or three years. To dismiss the organisation out of hand both devalues his activity and ignores the effect that process can have, irrespective of outcome.

As chairman† Brian assiduously organised social activities. These included generous garden parties at his house in Castelnau, which were watched from behind lace curtains by his mother upstairs, recording her disapproving comments on Brian's visitors in her diary.

---

* Nor would Brian have approved of the indecent display in the toilet. Alan Wakeman remembers: 'There was a boy's toy called Action Man at that time, and he had two Action Men who were on the ledge in the bathroom, and when people went for a piss, they rearranged them into various inappropriate positions. Every time you went for a piss they were doing something different.'

† Because Roger Baker was the pan-London organiser and therefore inductor of new members, London groups didn't have convenors like provincial groups, but Chairmen (they were usually *men*).

London v. Manchester

Under Sewell's chairmanship Group 3 became the centre for a critique of the Manchester leadership and a generator of innovative ideas for the London membership. Dissatisfaction with the national organisation was widespread, and fuelled both by the lack of information in the *Bulletin* which went to every member, and a sense of the remoteness and unaccountability of the national headquarters. In 1970–71 the *Bulletin* was a very basic monthly account of a few social groups and isolated activities, interspersed with some indifferent book reviews. Roger Baker was alarmed enough to give Allan Horsfall a warning: people in London want to know – what are the Executive actually *doing*?

> More and more people are asking me this and I cannot tell them because I do not know. …
>
> There are reasons for this. One is that the groups already formed have settled down and got used to each other and enjoy their meetings. But while this largely pastoral activity is much appreciated, members are wondering how they relate to the main committee, wanting to be part of something bigger than their immediate group. …
>
> At the moment there is a strong feeling that the CHE London, South East and Home Counties groups could break away from Manchester, form their own committee and finance their own advertising and action. … A split would be disastrous but unless some sort of closer identity with Manchester happens, weight of opinion might make this more than a hypothesis.[43]

The antagonism continued for some time. Peter Robins joined CHE about six months later, becoming chairman first of Group 9 and then of Group 11. He joined forces with Brian and the two became known in Manchester as the Terrible Twins. Paul Temperton recalls them both coming to his and Martin's flat in Whalley Range for a meeting which was 'slightly acrimonious … not very productive. … There was a certain amount of mutual misunderstanding.'[44] The antagonism was also rooted in the history of the North Western Campaign and the HLRS, and in the very concept of a national organisation and what it should be. Peter Norman, who moved to London in May 1972 to shack up with London Group 10 convenor John Saxby, saw this conflict from both sides:

> The [NWHLRC] was originally part of the HLRS. And when the law was changed the HLRS effectively stopped. But the North West group thought, we haven't got there yet, and we need to carry on. And they did carry on. And they regarded themselves as having been betrayed or cut off by London. And they regarded themselves as having to take the lead … there was always this feeling that London had dropped the ball. They'd had

the chance, and then lost it, thrown it away. So whenever the London view began to express itself, there was this automatic reaction from the North Western people. 'You had the chance, and you didn't do it then, and we're doing it now, so shut up!'

45. Peter Robins in 2012

The other part of it was the fact that people who lived in London and joined CHE in London were very unused to the concept of an organisation whose headquarters wasn't in London. Nowadays I think it's not quite so bad. There are some bodies – for example the National Trust doesn't have its headquarters in London – but in those days you expected the national headquarters to be in London, especially if you lived in London. So I think they just thought it was odd. … If you've got a body that's seeking changes in the law, for example, traditionally they need to be in London near Parliament and all the rest. And if you want to get publicity the traditional place to be is London.[45]

If it was partly historical, it was also partly cultural; Peter Norman was to discover when he moved back to London that CHE was different 'down South':

When I moved to London I found the CHE set-up there very different from what I'd been used to, and I didn't like it very much. It was ponderous. There was the London Co-ordinating Committee, and the London Management Committee, and then the groups, and CHELIC* –

* CHE London Information Centre; see page 408.

> and there was a lot of trouble at CHELIC when it started because of the personalities involved. But mostly what I didn't like was the London people seemed to be much more well-heeled, or pretentious or middle class or something. I can't quite put my finger on it. It wasn't universally true, of course, obviously some of them weren't. … I just couldn't relate to a lot of these people. They weren't my kind of people. I'm a grammar school boy from the sticks, I just couldn't relate to these airy-fairy people who liked to have Chopin recitals. I couldn't get on with this. … It made me feel that the organisation's head office was better somewhere else.[46]

Peter Norman's memories raise quite explicitly one aspect of the homosexual rights movement that has been little studied – the historic part played in the dynamics of LGBT liberation by class. CHE came to have a reputation as 'middle aged and middle class', but it was certainly not always so. The Manchester–London divide was in some respects a class divide, and within London there were groups in the suburbs – notably in East London – which were significantly more working class and also more radical than those in the West End. In Wolverhampton the Workers Group was started in reaction to the bourgeois atmosphere of the main local CHE group. Groups in the North East and the North West of the country also retained some working-class spirit. Oldham CHE boasted of the extent of its working-class membership, for example. What happened in CHE, with the increasing professionalism of the organisation through the 1970s and its slow abandonment by most women by the end of the decade, was a kind of creeping gentrification of protest. The same class tensions also happened to some extent within GLF, most specifically between the college-based and the non-university groups, between the hippies and the Marxist intellectuals. However, the subject of GLF is outside the scope of this book.

It should not be assumed, however, that there was nothing but antagonism between London and Manchester. There were strong personal links at many levels. Liverpool's Peter Norman met London 10's John Saxby at a party after a London CHE meeting, an encounter which blossomed into a relationship sufficiently strong for Peter to relocate back to London. Robin Bloxsidge while serving on the National EC found himself having a fling-ette with Roger Baker, after they too met at a meeting:

> We went out to a dinner in a restaurant, which is something I couldn't afford to do in those days, at this time I was actually unemployed … well we had the Chicken Kiev – this was a smart dinner for me at that time, I'd never had a Chicken Kiev, and dug my knife into it and the butter just spurted up all over me. I suppose that might have been an excuse to get my clothes off. But Roger had this – it had never happened to me before and has never happened to me since – thing of having two single beds in his bedroom and you had sex and then you went to your single bed.[47]

Unfamiliar sleeping arrangements aside, it was a sufficiently pleasurable experience to be worth repeating several times.

Even if sex was not involved, there were strong personal friendships developing, particularly among those who travelled regularly from Manchester to London or vice versa. Glenys Parry in particular, a pauperised student not yet twenty, found herself taken under the wing of Tony Ryde and Michael Launder:

> It sounds as if it was a bit hostile, this London/Northern thing, but it wasn't really. … We would have people we would be slightly kind of at odds with, like Peter Robins and Griff, but there'd be other people in London like Tony Ryde and Mike Launder, we were very close to them and to Roger Baker. … I used to stay with Roger at his flat and to me he was the height of London sophistication, he and Andrew Lumsden and Tony Ryde. These were people I sort of – not idolised but – looked up to, and found them, you know, witty, interesting, intelligent, fascinating. For a young woman who had no London history at all, being a child of the Midlands, Burton-on-Trent, I ended up mixing in these circles and finding it absolutely brilliant. So I wouldn't like you to think there was, on a personal level, any deep-rooted anti-London hostility at all.[48]

Tony Ryde and London Group 4

The formation of Group 4 followed almost immediately on the heels of Groups 2 and 3. Its chairman was Tony Ryde, who was also to become Chairman of the LCC and later to be on the National Executive. Treasurer was John Saxby, later convenor of Group 10. The Group 4 Secretary was Ryde's partner, Michael Launder, who would go on to found the counselling organisation, FRIEND. Tony and Michael were something of a Golden Couple in early CHE. Young, attractive, and with seemingly limitless energy, they took a sometimes dithering group of people by the scruff of the neck.

They had met at a Promenade Concert at the Royal Albert Hall in August 1968, and fallen in love to the sound of Stravinsky. Michael was slightly younger than Tony, although more sexually experienced, having lived with a farmer in Devon for five years since the age of 16. Michael was a trainee social worker, Tony an up-and-coming senior executive for BP, responsible for selling oil in South America. After they had been together for six months, Michael moved into Tony's flat in Bloomsbury, not far from where Roger Baker lived.

There was (is) a famous old real ale pub in Lamb's Conduit Street, The Lamb, which had a significant gay clientele, attracted as so often by a friendly gay barman. It was Roger's local, and George Mortimer's, but Tony found it by accident, in 1967:

> I went into the pub with a female friend from university, who got in touch with me – she was always trying to get off with me. And we went into the pub together and during the course of the conversation she said, 'Good gracious I know that chap, he's queer.' And I said, 'My god, how disgusting. In Bloomsbury? Really!' But I noted his expression and his face, and when she disappeared, I came back the next night and introduced myself. Because I was the classic, repressed, young, male gay, up at university, full of unrequited boyhood love affairs, getting nowhere, couldn't accept anything.[49]

46. Tony Ryde and Michael Launder

Tony gradually found himself with a circle of gay friends, including an alcoholic composer and his boyfriend, who dragged him to the Proms – and his fateful meeting with Michael. This was the start of a partnership which lasted 45 years, until Michael's death in 2013. Unlike Brian Sewell, Tony Ryde when he joined CHE saw it as having a mainly social function:

> It was definitely a social enterprise. Helping gay people to meet each other in a safe, pleasant environment, usually pub rooms, branching out from that into other social activities, walking groups perhaps, theatres, what have you. The social side was the bedrock. I think really from the beginning we were saying, well, those of us who are interested in campaigning, that's fine to be encouraged, but it's quite ok if you just want to meet people in a relaxed atmosphere and to explore all aspects of being gay. … I was very receptive to the idea of trying to do something to make it easier for other people to come out and accept themselves than it had been for me.
>
> What I was going to get out of it and what Michael was going get out of it was, I suppose, some social pleasure, but … we felt that, as young,

moderately attractive, outgoing people, we could offer something to others to be a sort of nucleus for the formation of groups.[50]

When it came to forming Group 4, Tony was the natural person to ask to convene it. According to *Lunch*, CHE's semi-independent, semi-in-house monthly journal, 'This group, I am told, is a bit argumentative, and meetings get a little contentious, as is to be expected from lively alert minds.'[51]

Certainly it seems to have attracted an intellectual class of guest speaker, and to show a collective sense of curiosity that was absent from some others. When the president of the Adlerian Society came to speak, the discussion with him about Adler and Freud continued into the small hours, after the meeting adjourned at pub closing time to a member's flat. In 1972 they had Quentin Crisp* as their guest, and 'He admitted beforehand that he hoped to provoke a reaction in his audience. This he certainly succeeded in doing. One could not but admire his courage in retaining his individuality amidst some barracking.'[52]

Unlike previous groups, Group 4 attracted from the start a considerable number of women, including Jo Batchelor,† first convenor of the London Women's Group, and her partner Gini Stephens, editor of *Lunch* for much of its existence. Jo and Gini in turn invited Jackie Forster, one of the most prominent lesbian activists in London and founder of *Sappho*, which was both a magazine and a support network. Also in Group 4 was her then partner, Babs Todd, who became convenor in 1972. Sue Gilbert, a librarian, and her girlfriend Jane, who lived in Highbury, joined shortly after.

Jackie Forster

Jackie Forster was the Scottish product of two of the most expensive girls' public schools in the country, which showed in her emphatic aristocratic drawl. She came from a very privileged home background. Her father was a surgeon brigadier who was imprisoned by the Japanese for much of World War Two. It was during the war that Forster played lacrosse for Scotland, at a time when all sports teams were depleted by call-up.

The absence of the Brigadier left behind a mother who had to develop her own organisational skills and independence, bringing up two children to be equally independent, articulate and questioning. Jackie became an actress, and for a period in the late 1950s and early 1960s a highly successful TV presenter

* Quentin Crisp had published *The Naked Civil Servant* in 1968, and this with the subsequent media publicity turned him into the first 'professional homosexual'. His views however were deeply controversial among gay activists, e.g. 'If as a homosexual person you regard yourself as part of a group, the first thing you must do is behave nicely everywhere, all the time.'

† Real name withheld by request.

both in Britain and Canada.* It says something for both her quality and her confidence that she felt able to turn down a weekly slot on the Ed Sullivan show, produced by CBS in America and one of the most popular and influential TV shows of all time. Her TV specialisation was what was termed at the time 'visual reporting'; she would cover events not from the press box, but from a worm's eye view, getting vox pops from the public, and then acting out both the event and the popular reactions to it, mime, accents and all. It was a unique style of performance, funny, charming and slightly surreal.

She had married Peter Forster, a TV and theatre critic, in a marriage which seems more companionate than anything else, and sealed with large quantities of alcohol. Her affair with Hattie,† Managing Editor of *Harper's Bazaar*, was intense, fraught with deception, and ended in devastation when Hattie found someone else. For the next few years Jackie managed a string of heterosexual affairs while presenting a series of one-woman shows, which she described as lectures, on one night stands across America and, from 1961, Canada. She worked for CBC in Toronto for three years as actress and presenter, during the course of which she met another actress, Babs Todd. Mrs Todd was married to the CBC Head of Scripts, Lyon, and had two daughters, Marie and Hilda. Intense passion led Babs to follow Jackie back from Canada, and the two set up home in a run-down town house in Connaught Square, which they bullied Duncan Sandys'‡ private secretary, Theodore Fitzgibbon,§ into selling to them. Among the horde of students crashing there unbeknownst to the estate agent was Richard Branson, 18-year-old editor of *The Student*. The paper was produced in the basement, until Jackie and Babs gave him his marching orders a few weeks later. The same space – and some of the same equipment – was subsequently used to produce *Arena 3* and *Sappho*.

Jackie was a member of CHE but with a nodding acquaintance of GLF – she sold *Arena 3* at the weekly meetings – and a strong commitment to feminism, through the Camden Women's Group. Babs had become the chair of the weekly *Arena 3* social/planning meetings at the Museum Tavern, opposite the British Museum, mainly because she had trained as an actress, and could project her voice over a very noisy refrigerator. This was to stand her in good stead in Group 4 after she became chair of that as well, taking over from Tony Ryde. The Group moved out of the Coachmaker's Arms to *Arena 3*'s old haunt, and again someone was needed to drown out the fridge.

As so often in London, Jackie and Babs got into CHE by word of mouth.

---

* Under her maiden name, Jacqueline Mackenzie.

† In interviews in later years Jackie never referred to her except by her first name only, perhaps for reasons of discretion.

‡ Shadow Colonial Secretary and Winston Churchill's son-in-law.

§ Brother of the controversial right-wing historian and novelist, Constantine Fitzgibbon.

Jackie remembered:

> There were two women who came to Arena 3 then, who were called Gini and Jo, and they said to Babs and me, 'You really ought to come and join CHE, because this is really political and campaigning, and doing things about the age of consent and all sorts of laws.' So Babs and I went along to a meeting in a pub off Wigmore Street, … dressed as conservative wives. … And it was an astonishing evening, because speaking that night was Ian [Harvey] and he was a Junior Minister in the Ministry of Defence and he fucked with a guardsman in St James's Park, and was picked up by the police. And I remember being married and Mrs Forster, and sitting in my flat with my husband reading this in the paper, and saying 'How disgusting! These sort of people blah blah blah.' That must have been about 1958, and here am I all this time later facing this man. … And I was so amazed at the complete reversal. I could hear my voice saying this all those years ago, And I thought, this is a wonderful group, I'm going to join this. And we were the only CHE group which was actually 50% women, 50% men.[53]

The whole thing was growing so rapidly that by November 1971 Roger Baker could report in the *Bulletin* that:

> as London organiser I am now meeting an average of 15 new London members a week and if this level of interest is maintained then it is safe to prophesy that at least one new London group can be set up each month through the winter.[54]

His prediction of one new London group a month for the duration of the winter was slightly over-optimistic, mainly because even in the heady early days there was a significant drop-out rate. Over the longer period the prediction was more than fulfilled. By August 1971 there were ten London groups, by March 1972 there were fifteen.*

They were being drawn from areas as far away as the South Coast, Essex and Hertfordshire. In the wake of this expansion in London, there was clearly a need for more out-of-town groups. If only the convenors would come forward…

London Group 5

London Group 5, which came into being in January 1971, was the Youth Group. As we have seen with Liverpool, one of the dilemmas imposed on CHE by the anomalies in the 1967 Act was how to cater for people under 21, without running foul of conspiracy laws. In theory, local groups could be prosecuted if accepting people under 21. One solution was to tell under 21s

---

* See Appendix B.

that they couldn't join an ordinary local group, but they could join a student or youth group. Many of the youth groups within CHE were the liveliest and most radical, with extensive contacts with both the Gay Liberation Front and other gay student groups and Gaysocs. Group 5, which was open to people under 25, students or not, set the template for this in many ways. It was founded by David Porter, whom Brian Sewell remembers as:

> A rather good-looking, quite bright, menacing young man, who came from round the Vauxhall Tavern, Camberwell area, who was really only interested in boys, not old fogeys like us. And he wanted to start a junior section, and I think that started at … the quiet one at Camberwell Green,* whatever it was. And there was a user-friendly landlord, who didn't mind teenage boys coming in and being picked up. The rest of us had quite serious misgivings about that. Because he was definitely going for people under age.†[55]

They were enthusiastic leafleteers and stickerers, distributing 1,000 CHE publicity hand-outs in March 1972 to pubs in the East End and in Earl's Court, outside Whitechapel tube station and at one of the Essoldo cinemas which was showing *Some of My Best Friends Are…*‡ 'This proved good fun even though we were ejected from London Transport's property by a big butch policeman.'[56]

Group 5 were good-time guys, with an anarchist streak. They had frequent meetings at the Rehearsal Club§, staying on to party afterwards, and were regular visitors to the Father Redcap in Camberwell, where Tricky Dicky ran some of the first gay discos.** They were also famous for their own wild parties. They changed their name first to the London Student Group, and then, in 1972, 'Internal politics finally reached a climax, resulting in a revolution. Heads rolled and the group has been totally reconstructed.'[57] The

---

* The Father Redcap.

† Brian means under the age of consent as it was then, i.e. 21.

‡ A 1971 film starring among others Royal Ballet Principal Dancer David Drew, and Candy Darling. Although this post-Stonewall conversation piece had limited release, it was seen as a political advance on the roughly contemporaneous *Boys in the Band.*

§ The Rehearsal Club was at 3 Archer Street in Soho from 1967 to 1973. It had a large dance floor, and was one of the few places in London where men could dance with men at the time. Because it was a 'mixed' club, same-sex dance pairs were not that easy to spot in the dark.

** Tricky Dicky (real name Richard Scanes) also provided the disco at many CHE events. In 1973 he was prosecuted for running a disorderly house because he allowed men to dance together at the Father Red Cap. Unfortunately the pub was used at lunch times by the magistrates and staff from the nearby court, and it is believed that the police were pressurised into taking action by magistrates who felt contaminated by association.

result was the London Youth Group, whose activities in the name of integration with straight society were similar to GLF's in some respects:

> A decision was taken to invade a straight dance at the first opportunity. A disco to be held at the Commonwealth Hall on March 17th gave us our first chance to practise corporate integration. … All told 17 members went along to the Commonwealth Hall disco (two went to the Commonwealth Hall in the middle of Holland Park, where they found themselves less integrated than ever). … We certainly managed to dominate the scene. …
>
> However, the dark forces of discrimination unfurled their banners towards the end of the evening – perhaps they hadn't found the courage, or hadn't recovered from shock earlier in the evening – and various officials decided to make flutterings to protect the sensibilities of their young wards. According to a 'spokesman', some twenty young ladies had complained about the behaviour of young men at the dance. … Unfortunately the young ladies weren't around to testify. Perhaps we should come to the conclusion that they were young men who had been transsexed in order not to make the spokesman look ridiculous. … Active resistance to insistence on desistance made our point to the various officials, and the evening ended an enormous and enjoyable success.[58]

Winter in Walthamstow

In addition to London Groups 1 to 5, which were all in place by the end of 1970, there was one 'rogue' group, in Walthamstow, convened by Mike Winter. This group was referred to variously as Walthamstow, Waltham Forest and East London CHE. Winter was an energetic, short-tempered and headstrong man who had the deepest suspicion of any kind of national or pan-London organisation. He ran a mobile disco unit, and was referred to in *Lunch* as 'the non-stop disco king of the East End'. Given his attitudes, it's surprising that he should identify his group as a CHE group. He seems to have gathered it together, sometime in the autumn of 1970, by personal contact in the area in the first instance, and subsequently by advertising in the local press. Roger Baker referred to him as 'the celebrated Mike Winter of Walthamstow who seems to have his neck of the woods thoroughly taped already and only needs the authority of CHE to get smartly off the ground.'[59]

One of the first articles in the mainstream press about CHE in general, and local groups in particular, appeared in the *Waltham Forest Guardian* in December 1970:

> Help is on the way for voluntary welfare organisations in Waltham Forest – from a group of homosexuals. The local branch chairman of the Committee for Homosexual Equality, a two-year-old body affiliated to the National Council for Civil Liberties, has already received partial agreement

> to the scheme from leading welfare workers in the borough. …
>
> A recruitment campaign is planned for the borough within the next few weeks, together with the scheme to introduce CHE members to social and welfare work. Although he does not wish to be identified at this stage the chairman told the *Guardian* why he was launching the help-your-neighbour project.
>
> 'The main aim of the group is to re-educate people on the homosexual. We want to show that he not a person to be frowned upon, and he can have a good place in society. We are not exclusively a homosexual group. There are some female members and some married couples.' He added that he had found difficulty in obtaining a meeting place in the borough … but had now secured a church hall just outside the borough. There are so far 15 members.
>
> Mrs Kathy Latreille, Chairman of Waltham Forest Health and Welfare Committee said, 'I think it is a good thing. They do not force their views on anybody. They are trying to be accepted into society as responsible citizens.'[60]

This group went its own way. Winter refused any involvement in any London-wide committee of CHE chairmen, and insisted that he wanted to do his own advertising using his own contact details. Effectively this put recruitment in the hands of the local convenor, and Paul Temperton in Manchester depended on Winter to tell him who had become a national member, and to forward honestly the subs he had collected. Where London 3 grumbled about Manchester in a general way, Walthamstow kicked against something specific which smacked of a diktat from the centre. Paul was not the only one to feel uncomfortable, Tony Ryde did as well:

> I was glad to see that Mike Winter is still being kept down to size. Maybe I'm paranoiac about this fellow, but … I know I am not alone in my misgivings. What worries me now is his local advertising effort, and my fear that replies are not being channelled through the Box Number and therefore you. Are these fears unfounded? If the NATIONAL character of CHE is to be maintained (and I firmly believe it must be) then it is clearly imperative that all advertising be conducted by you. … This is the system I believe must be followed everywhere – otherwise the organisation will simply crumble.'[61]

Paul replied:

> I have already made it clear to him that any advertising in CHE's name must carry only CHE's national address. This is in accordance with a clear ruling by the EC many many months ago and I shall therefore continue to implement this policy until such time as the EC orders otherwise.[62]

Despite this, Winter remained a cat walking by himself, pursuing his social work agenda. In the winter of 1970 he set up an 'advisory board' of local GPs, a mental health worker, a vicar, a probation officer and two council social workers. He contacted Michael De-la-Noy, who had become Secretary of the Albany Trust after the resignation of Antony Grey:

> I am going ahead with our plans for the setting up of a referral agency here in East London. It has been decided that our group will remain outside the jurisdiction of Central London and act independently of them. We of course look towards Manchester for our guidance. We would very much like to see a connection between CHE and the Albany Trust and we feel it is essential that we work in close co-operation with both of them. This group at present will have boundaries from Aldgate to Romford and as far West as Barking and East to Hackney and Chingford.* I am at present writing to the authorities in these boroughs and also to other organisations. … It is hoped to supplement the 'panel' with befrienders, and also to gather in information that will be passed on to Manchester and yourself.[63]

This sense of difference from the national organisation in matters of policy aims as well procedures was underscored by their constitution, an amateurish document clearly drawn up by Winter. He lists the aims as:

> a) to re-educate and inform Local Authority Agencies and the public at large with regards to homosexual matters generally;
> b) To operate an advisory agency and to include a panel of sympathetic and qualified people supported by a force of volunteer 'befrienders';
> c) To assist those in the field of law reform by gathering information concerning homosexual matters in general.[64]

Uniquely, the group had a provision to expel members for 'behaviour likely to draw the group into disrepute', trying to follow Quentin Crisp's dictum that homosexuals 'must behave nicely all the time'. It also gave Winter a deal of personal power. The divergences in aims were enough to get him and his group discussed at the CHE EC, where the advice and befriending aspects were seen as a direct challenge to the work which Michael Launder was beginning to do in London in setting up FRIEND. As a result the EC passed a resolution 'That Mike Winter be sent a letter reminding him that he holds no official position in CHE and he has no brief for recruiting members other than through the Manchester Headquarters.'[65] This seems to have had no noticeable effect, and independently he organised the printing of CHE key rings and badges. In October 1971 convenors were writing to Paul complaining that they'd ordered goods and sent money, and never heard anything more. Paul could only commiserate. He seemed to think that Winter had conducted a scam:

---

* Winter's sense of direction is erratic, since from Walthamstow Barking is in the East, Hackney to the South-West and Chingford, North.

> The Waltham Forest group doesn't exist any more and it doesn't in the least surprise me that the goods you ordered never came. He had no right to produce CHE material on his own initiative like that, anyway. Of course, if he has already cashed the postal order, the counterfoil won't do you any good.[66]

Like many forceful convenors, Winter left in place no structure to bring out his successors, and it was left to others to start again in East London. Not for the last time, CHE would have to start again from scratch.

The first mass meeting (April 1971)

With six groups, there was clearly a need for some kind of pan-London co-operation. The solution to London organisation initially was to set up a mass meeting for the London membership, which was held in April 1971 at the Holborn Assembly Rooms. On the platform were four of the London chairmen, and Paul Temperton and Martin Stafford from Manchester. Roger Baker chaired.

There were 120 people there, over a quarter of the London membership. Because it was the first, it mainly transacted rather boring business, despite an entertaining zap by members of GLF protesting at the fuddy-duddy nature of the occasion. Having made their point, they ate all the biscuits and left. Once they were gone, Paul and Martin were left to take the brickbats about lack of democracy. 'There's going to be a constitution,' assured Paul. 'And elections. Have patience.' Grudgingly, and with mutterings about the slowness of Manchester compared with the dynamism of London, the meeting was won over.

Most importantly, the meeting laid the foundations for London activities for the next several years. There would be monthly mass meetings, with guest speakers.* There would be a London Co-ordinating Committee (LCC) of all group chairmen, plus the leaders of any Working Parties set up, plus a Secretary, Treasurer and Chairman. At this time in 1971, that would mean a total of thirteen members,† although the Constitution specified that all future London groups would be entitled to representation. There was some discussion of what constituted a London group. Croydon, it appeared, did, but Ilford did not.‡ In practice this would become a cumbersome set-up in that anything which was brought to the Committee would then have to be taken

* In practice, these became bi-annual. In the heat of the moment, CHE's reach exceeded its grasp.

† Mike Winter from Walthamstow refused to take part.

‡ Croydon quite quickly decided it was not a London group, and withdrew from the LCC in 1973.

back for discussion in each of the groups, before returning to the Committee; this insistence on representative democracy meant that any policy could only move at the speed of the slowest, most disorganised group.

The situation was made more bureaucratic and the process became slower when, for no very good reason, the LCC also set up a London Management Committee, a kind of sub-committee of Ways and Means, with six members chosen from the LCC. As a result demarcation lines and responsibilities became blurred, ordinary members were confused, meetings proliferated and only the most die-hard addicts of internal politicking derived any satisfaction from it.

There would be working parties, some of which fell by the wayside but others led to long-lasting and worthwhile projects.

A Clubs Working Party, led by Mike Thomas of Group 3, would 'look into the possibility of establishing a London CHE club, preferably with its own premises, and search for pleasant meeting places for individual groups.'[67] In April 1971, it looked as if a first club was already in the bag, in Burnley, so there was a real feeling of optimism in the air about getting premises.

There would be a Speakers Working Party, which would recruit and train people to go and speak to outside organisations. This would be led by Roger Baker. There was a skills shortage, in London CHE as elsewhere, and so training members in the art of public speaking would be vital. Only four other people volunteered. They met at Roger's flat, they each drafted separately what they would consider their standard speech, and then collated them into a template. They discussed the awkward questions they might be asked, which in turn led them to query some of the basic assumptions of a reformist organisation, such as the role of 'ordinary-ness':

> In speaking to the general public – let's say those who've made no special study of political/social issues, it's right and necessary to emphasise how ordinary we are. Because there are still a fair number of people who believe we're all sex-crazed maniacs who have little boys on toast for tea, or at least that we all wear mascara and carry handbags.
>
> With people at a liberal conference we don't have to start the argument that far back. – in fact the danger I foresaw was that we might sound off about being very ordinary, but a bit oppressed, and the reaction might be, 'OK, we more or less go along with that. Now what?'
>
> Well, we're not ordinary people at all. A lot of our members are trying to kid themselves they are, as well as other people. They think they want to meet Mr Right, then they'll settle down and everything will be wonderful. … But we have to question our most basic assumptions about people and relationships. If society ever does come to accept us (not just absent-mindedly tolerate but positively accept) that too will be a different society from what we have now.[68]

47. *Lunch*, issue 1

Roger was to allocate speakers to meetings as requests came in, depending on their experience and the size of the meeting they were going to speak to. (Roger anticipated audiences of anything from 20 to over 100.) Not many requests came in; it was however very useful background when the opportunity came very early in 1971 to start appearing on local radio. From this also evolved a group which took on the daunting task of visiting Speakers' Corner* every other week and advocating for lesbian and gay rights in front of one of the most intimidating crowds possible.

* A designated area on the North-East corner of Hyde Park where traditionally anyone can turn up to speak on any subject. Although held to be symbolic of the right to free speech, speaking at Speakers' Corner confers no special privileges or protections of free speech.

Another Working Party, led by David Hyde of Group 3, would 'consider the possibility of producing a magazine or bulletin on a local or perhaps national basis, in liaison with Manchester.'[69] The magazine, which quickly launched in July 1971 with Hyde as first editor, was called *Lunch*, a whimsical phonetic portmanteau of 'London CHE'.* Given the inadequacies of *Jeremy* and *Spartacus*, the only other magazines around at the time, a serious news and features magazine would fill a real gap in the market.

There was a pan-London Social Activities Working Party, which would put members with shared social interests in touch with each other, and 'arrange theatre parties, shot-putting contests, etc.' This was seen almost immediately as a great way of raising money for the London Centre.

There was a Liaison Group, which was to establish contact with international and other national gay groups. CHE nationally had always had international contacts, with, for example, the Mattachine Society in America, with COC and DOK in Holland, Arcadie in France and Det Norske Forbundet av 1948 in Norway; now the burgeoning gay liberation movement led to new groups springing up in Italy, Germany, Spain and the rest of Scandinavia. Bringing all these together was to be a huge challenge. There were a couple of false starts at creating a transnational organisation, with gatherings in Bologna and Edinburgh which exposed more differences than similarities between lesbian and gay organisations. It was not until the CHE Conference in Coventry in 1978 that thirty people from fourteen countries laid the foundations of the International Gay Association (IGA), which has grown into the International Lesbian, Gay, Bisexual, Trans and Intersex Association (ILGA), with consultative status at the UN and the EU, and over 1,000 member organisations in over 120 countries.

FRIEND

Perhaps the most important Working Party set up in April 1971 went by the dynamic but vague name of the Task Force, under the leadership of Tony Ryde's partner, Michael Launder, of Group 4. The mission was clear:

> To set up a team of members willing to visit homosexuals in prison or hospital, and to befriend and advise homosexuals in trouble. This prompted considerable discussion and the terms of reference of the task force will have to be clearly defined so as to avoid competition or conflict with other specialised organisations such as the Albany Trust, Samaritans etc.[70]

---

* Peter Robins of Group Nine naughtily suggested it be called 'Meat and 2 Veg', but the women were having none of that.

Launder, with his dual role of social worker and local group secretary, could see very clearly that there was a two-fold problem. CHE advertising was attracting enquiries from people who had personal needs which could not be met by a simple social group. Often these people would be extremely time-consuming for already hard-pressed convenors, and demanding and disruptive within a group. Moreover, convenors and group members did not have the skills to offer the kind of support and help that such people needed. Peter Robins, who became later convenor of Group 11, remembers one such example:

> Wherever this particular meeting of my Number 11 group, or the Tuesday group, was, there was a phone in the corner. And there was a young gentleman from North London who'd rushed into a telephone box [to call us] and said, 'I'm going to kill myself. I've had enough, I can't find anybody, I'm going to slit my throat in this telephone box.' And I'm saying, 'Well don't, don't do that, come in a little nearer where we can come out and pick you up, you see.' And he made his way to the meeting from the telephone box in less than ten minutes.[71]

This kind of incident was not the most useful thing to happen in the middle of a meeting.

Tony Ryde found his attention similarly demanded. On one occasion in 1971 he was rung up at work five times in a single day by a demanding recruit who couldn't raise him at home. Convenor phone numbers were meant to be confidential, so how this lad got hold of Tony's was a mystery. The Albany Trust was the prime suspect, and duly reprimanded.

The story illustrates how influential and supportive the best, most active convenors were. They were aware, from the start, of the importance of coming out as gay, both politically and for self-esteem. Tony Ryde recalled:

> John Haygarth was probably late thirties, early forties, and he wasn't outgoing, and he was exactly the sort of person I thought I'd been a few years ago. He turned out to be a lot more so than I realised, because [when] he came to the flat,* he took quite a lot of persuading over the telephone to come. He was very presentable, but he was just absolutely paranoid about being gay. There were at this induction meeting perhaps half a dozen people, but the whole thing very much focussed on him, trying to draw him out and make him comfortable, with the idea of going forward and joining the group.
>
> And right from the beginning he said, 'I absolutely can't be involved in public because if my employer found out my career would be ruined. I'd be sacked.' And we sort of talked around the subject and eventually I said to

---

* When Tony took over as London Convenor, he held inductions in his own flat.

> him, 'Look John my employer is not the sort of company you would associate with being pro-gay, but I've absolutely no problem. John, what is this company, do you wanna tell me?' And he said, 'I work for BP.'
>
> And I said, 'Well I work for BP. I've worked for BP for years. I've been out in BP for two years. I know lots of gay blokes in BP. So … think about it, it's not that awful.'
>
> And he says, 'Oh no I'm different.' But he did think about it and became quite active in CHE.[72]

If John Haygarth was a success story, David Latimer* was not, according to Ryde:

> David … was seriously deranged, and he insisted on my reading a manuscript, a treatise on the theory of relativity, which he said was his contribution to making a complete nonsense of Einstein. And I found this quite difficult, and I had it in a bottom drawer in the flat for about two years wondering what to do with it. … He was seriously something. I don't know how to put the right label on. He was probably someone behind the thought of setting up FRIEND, but much too complicated for FRIEND to deal with.[73]

The Task Force, as FRIEND† was initially called, is an outstanding example of what CHE was always best at: letting someone with a vision, who knew what they were doing, get on with it. Launder's vision was of a service run by trained volunteers. These would not necessarily be gay, although the bedrock of the service would be provided, at least in the first instance, by lesbians and gay men, mainly from within the ranks of CHE. They would be vetted for suitability, and have some kind of basic training which would enable them to act as befrienders. The object was either to equip the 'client' with the social skills and confidence to forge a gay or lesbian life for themselves, or, in more serious cases, to refer them on to other services which could better help them with their problems. For this he needed three things – premises, volunteers and a little money. As he explained in his report to the 1974 Malvern Conference:

> My ideas were fluid: I thought that a collection of people without any special skills but with consideration and kindness could satisfy the need. It was not long, however, before we learned how naïve that view was. The

---

* Surname changed.

† The name change came in October 1971, the result of a tortuous acronym dreamed up by Michael Launder: Fellowship for the Relief of the Isolated and Emotionally in Need and Distress. This became a source of embarrassment and was quickly forgotten, leaving a perfectly good descriptive name.

> complexity of the problems that FRIEND was being asked to handle was such that simple friendship alone was not enough.[74]

Once he realised this, the choices were stark. Either FRIEND had to restrict itself to the simplest cases, ones which could probably be handled in the social groups anyway, thus making FRIEND itself redundant; or it had to select volunteers more carefully and recruit people with special skills. Again, CHE found itself with ambitious plans but a skills deficit which prevented the Campaign from implementing them. What made Launder unique was the systematic way he went about dealing with the deficit.

The first step was to look around at what was already available. In addition to government-funded Social Services, there were two other organisations already in the field. It was not an impressive array:

> The findings were not encouraging. The Samaritans' ability to help varied widely, in some areas excellent help was offered to gay people but they were hopelessly overworked, in other areas Samaritans were ill-informed about homosexuality and less able to provide the help gay people needed. ... We were faced with the plain fact that if we did not do the job, no one else would do it for us.[75]

The Samaritans was a telephone helpline which had been founded by Rev. Chad Varah in 1952 as an emergency service for those at immediate risk of suicide.* The Task Force saw itself offering a similar kind of service, and looked to the Samaritans for its training model. The Samaritans had offered assistance to homosexuals through the Albany Trust since the mid-1960s, and its senior figures were entirely supportive. When a new CHE group started up, its first port of call when telling the world of its existence was almost invariably the local Samaritans group. However, on the ground the quality of Samaritans varied considerably, as Launder discovered. At worst they were actively homophobic. Most crucially, the Samaritans did not offer personal contact, which was what isolated homosexuals needed more than anything; in meeting someone from FRIEND, a client would often be meeting the first other lesbian or gay person they had ever known.

The other similar organisation was the Albany Trust, which had only a tiny number of people to draw on, totally inadequate to the demand. It was also exclusively London-based, and had no facilities to offer in the rest of the country; as a result, anyone wanting to take advantage of Albany Trust counselling services had to ring, and usually make the effort to come to, London. Michael made noises about not wanting to tread on the Albany Trust's toes, and went out of his way to cultivate the Trust's Secretary, Michael De-la-Noy.

---

* In 2005 the Samaritans become more of a general support for people in emotional distress, and Varah left the organisation in disgust at this dilution of purpose.

He wrote to De-la-Noy in June 1971, asking for co-operation, in the form of use of his office:

> The Task Force ought to be more available to deal with casual callers, and it would be advantageous to share in some way the facilities of the Trust's offices. What we had in mind is that, say, two volunteers should be available in the evenings to chat to people who drop by or call up the Trust. If the callers wanted counselling the volunteer should take details and it could be decided thereafter if it was something we could handle or yourselves.
>
> If the service were available it would enable CHE in London to make known a telephone number (which might in the wee small hours be diverted to some Task Force Saint!) and would of course help people who find it difficult to get to the Trust in normal office hours.[76]

De-la-Noy had to decline, because the Trust's landlord closed the building promptly at 6.30 p.m. Nevertheless, over the next few months he began to refer Trust callers to the Task Force. Increasingly, with the mushrooming of CHE across the country and the Trust's continuing struggle to keep afloat financially, FRIEND emerged as the dominant organisation in the field.

Michael Launder's appeal for volunteers went out in the CHE *Bulletin*, and in *Lunch*. There was an immediate response, and not just in London. However in the first instance, lacking anywhere to either train people or to operate from, nothing happened. After a couple of false starts, an offer of premises came from Rev. Peter Royston-Ball, who ran the CENTRE, a community counselling project just a few minutes from Marylebone Station. Royston-Ball offered a telephone, and rooms which could serve for interviews or group work, or as an office. However, the telephone was a shared line, which stymied any thoughts of advertising a direct contact number. Tony Ryde also recalls a sense of unease at the atmosphere in the CENTRE. It did a great deal of work around youth activities, and Royston-Ball seemed to be unusually close to some of the lads who came into the Centre. Inappropriate behaviour seemed a distinct possibility. However, FRIEND was in no position to challenge or argue, being dependent on goodwill until it found its own home.

Having secured a base of a kind, Michael called his volunteers together at Kingsway Hall in October 1971, some of them a little peeved at having been kept waiting for months. As in many voluntary organisations, the grassroots desired instant results, and couldn't understand why the leadership had been hanging back. Michael assured them that he hadn't been dragging his feet.

> There were murmurs from some who felt disgruntled because although they had volunteered to join the group, they had been given nothing to do, and were ignorant of anything Task Force had achieved in the way of befriending. It was explained that so far Task Force had not been given

> enough to keep all its members occupied, as CHE itself was so little known at present, it had not yet succeeded in creating a sufficiently widely known and favourable image of itself to attract many homosexuals with problems. He [Launder] quoted the distressing fact that he had written to two dozen organisations about FRIEND and only two had bothered to reply.[77]

Despite the initial lack of response, Michael persisted. He found allies in the probation service, but none in the prisons:

> The Prison Service is very much against homosexuals, so that it is not yet possible for members of FRIEND to visit homosexual prisoners simply as members of CHE; they may only do so if a prisoner writes directly to them.[78]

There were, however, sympathisers in ACCESS, a Home Office approved prisoner support and counselling service run by Doreen Cordell, formerly of the HLRS and Albany Trust:

> It was made clear that some homosexuals who appealed to ACCESS might have greater associated problems than FRIEND, as at present constituted, had resources to deal with, but that others could be befriended by our members. It was urged that members of FRIEND should follow a Counselling and Befriending course, under the auspices of ACCESS, consisting of evening sessions once a week for a month. Counselling is dealing with a person's problems in depth, taking detailed notes, which may be handed over to a specialist helper, if such is needed. …
>
> Some people present felt that there was no way in which a person could be taught to be a friend. Michael concurred but pointed out that though our experience of our common condition gave us an advantage over trained social workers, the assistance to be gained from a course of training by ACCESS would be of added value. Since April, thirty homosexuals have been 'dealt with' and, although some had problems greater than could be dealt with by CHE unassisted, none had been turned away.[79]

The Task Force/FRIEND meeting at Kingsway Hall passed a resolution approving training, but it was to remain a bone of contention. There was suspicion of top-down leadership, of authoritarian control from the centre, which paralleled the CHE local groups' suspicions of the National Office. In spite of this, Michael had very clear notions of what befriending involved, and why it was important to achieve a certain standard of 'professionalism' if FRIEND was to gain respect and attract referrals. But he also knew that he must have more counsellors than the professionals could supply.

He drew heavily on the Samaritans and their London deputy director Rev. Michael Butler, both to draw up guidelines for choosing volunteers and in the first instance to staff the phones.* He reported to the EC, of which he was

* In April and May 1972 only Launder and Butler answered the phones at the CENTRE.

now a member, in May 1972:

> I would like to draw the attention of the EC to a problem which has been bugging me for some time. It is not possible to accept all the volunteers who offer their services. Thus there must be some form of selection, which can be seen by both outside agencies and members to be reputable and impartial. To this end, I am urging existing groups to gradually adopt a procedure similar to the one I used for the London group. This is simply to use a written questionnaire followed where appropriate by an interview with the local organiser and an experienced advisor with some recognised, relevant qualification or expertise. I think this is the only way to avoid accusations of bias or unsuitability. It will also serve to bring some uniform standard to the operation. …
>
> FRIEND will stand or fall by the calibre of its volunteers and the success of the service it operates. Its development must inevitably be cautious and gradual. To launch a nationwide advertising campaign at this stage would be clearly disastrous in that we could not possibly cope with the response. … Above all Friend must be carefully co-ordinated and its progress regularly evaluated. This presupposes a much greater degree of centralised organisation than the rest of CHE requires.[80]

Previous meetings with prospective volunteers which had tried to explain the importance of selection had not gone entirely smoothly. In February 1972, there were two recruitment meetings on successive Mondays and fifty people turned up. They all had to fill out questionnaires, on the lines of what they could bring to FRIEND and what they hoped to get out of it. At the second meeting, these questionnaires came back to haunt them. There was a power cut, so the meeting started by candlelight. First they discussed how FRIEND would be structured, 'which did not really get down to brass tacks':

> Then, during the final part of the 2nd meeting, we were thunderstruck to discover that the questionnaires were to be used, not simply as a think-tank, but as a basis for the selection of suitable befrienders – and that some had already even disqualified themselves by their answers. There was to be no discussion of the ideas and trends emerging from the questionnaires. … Michael Launder then informed us how, in fact, CHE Friend would be run. Quite a number felt they'd been hoodwinked over the questionnaires, and even asked to have them returned; while the sudden change from the cumbersomely democratic to the brutally autocratic angered others. …
>
> It seemed highly ill-advised that the feelings and expectations of those volunteering for FRIEND, which after all makes its appeal to the idealistic and compassionate in us, should be treated with so little regard. After the power cut was over those present still felt left in the dark.[81]

At this stage, most volunteers coming forward had only a hazy idea of what befriending might involve, in any practical sense. As the commitments became clearer, through practical experience, the need for training and supervision largely sold itself. Michael Butler laid it down most clearly in a talk covered in *Lunch* in June 1972:

> Befriending is not the same as friendship. It is rather helping a person who may have lost the gift of reciprocity, to 'thaw out'. …
>
> The distressed homosexual can exhibit panic or paranoid symptoms; he may have nightmares, pathological or religious guilt and a sense that 'No one has done or felt as I do, and what's more, nobody cares.'
>
> They may become clinging, demanding or wildly promiscuous. Consequently the befriender needs protection, so that he need not become overloaded, too involved or emotionally drained. … A good befriender would allow the client to grow away from him at his own pace. Details of the befriender's own private life should not at first be given, or money lent, as this makes for continued dependency. The befriender should not make decisions for the client. It is a mistake to patronise the person befriended. … The befriender should be … humble, recognising that it is a privilege to have the happiness of some fragile person entrusted to his care.[82]

Michael Launder was equally adamant about standards:

> Although it was recognised that FRIEND groups must be free to respond to local needs using the resources available to them, it was also realised that certain basic standards of help must be provided by every FRIEND group. A prospective FRIEND group must earn recognition by its ability to provide caring and responsible help for the lonely and those in trouble.[83]

The key here is the word 'recognition'. From the start Launder realised that success depended on acceptance by other social work entities as a similarly bona fide support group. Without recognition there would be no referrals. Without recognition there was no access to any pots of money for the voluntary sector; a sector which FRIEND, unlike other parts of CHE, felt it belonged to. Without recognition, there was no chance of offering training in issues related to homosexuality to other organisations, which Launder had clearly identified a need for, and which might also attract funding. Nobody was going to call on the services of FRIEND simply because it was 'gay'.

From taking ten calls a week at the start of the service, FRIEND had grown to forty calls a week by January 1972. The danger was that demand for the service would outstrip the ability to supply it. The rudiments of a service outside London were also beginning to come together. Michael Launder went to the major cities to tout the idea and explain it. Groups in Manchester, Liverpool and Cambridge sprang up, and there were individual befrienders dotted around the country as well, too spread out to form groups yet. These presented a particular problem, because there was little control over them, and there were only superficial ways of vetting them in advance, except by questionnaire and the most perfunctory of telephone conversations. It took some time for Launder to persuade CHE to insist that all organisers (the FRIEND word for convenor) should come to London for induction – after all, CHE had never insisted its convenors should be subject to such controls. Launder also insisted that local groups should set up proper local training programmes, to be run on broadly similar lines to what he had done in the capital. Eventually, sometimes reluctantly, local groups accepted the need for selection of volunteers, which was usually done by the local organiser paired with an experienced counsellor from an outside organisation.

There was certainly a need for vetting and monitoring, in that solo befrienders could be a law unto themselves. The same sex-starved people who previously would have button-holed CHE convenors now came to FRIEND, and some befrienders were not averse to responding* to such propositioning. Alan Swerdlow in Liverpool remembers it as a FRIEND conference topic on more than one occasion:

> There's no doubt that people were making relationships. … The Friend conference every six months or so took a topic, and one of them was sex with clients. Should you or shouldn't you? And the thing that struck me there was, if it's alright to have sex with Client A, who's cute, and Client B is an elderly gentleman who's not too – well, not looking after himself, if the therapeutic side of having sex with clients is real and proven, you should be prepared to go with either of them. And of course that cut right through the waffle.[84]

It was a topic which brought disagreements between the male and female volunteers into sharp focus. Sue Wise, organiser of Manchester FRIEND from the later 1970s, recalled: 'There were some tensions, sort of, between me and some of the guys, who thought that it was appropriate to fuck people.'[85] Her partner, Liz Stanley, who also worked on Manchester FRIEND, was equally appalled:

> They were privatising eleven- and twelve- and thirteen-year-olds for their own particular purposes and not telling those people about this huge number of gay people who went to the discos, groups that had a hundred and fifty people going to them, et cetera. … There were very, very exploitative things that happened, and if you thought they were exploitative and you said it, you got it in the gob.[86]

---

* Icebreakers, the London phone line which grew out of the GLF counter-psychiatry group, certainly put no barriers in the way of volunteers having sex with callers; to some it was an affirmative act which helped to reinforce callers' sense of self-worth, as callers themselves testified. This view was shared by some volunteers both in FRIEND and on the various LGBT Switchboards which were set up around the country throughout the 1970s.

This should not however be over-emphasised. The vast majority of FRIEND volunteers were deeply conscientious about their work, and scrupulous in their concern for the welfare of the client. Despite this, there remained resistance and resentment over the training issue from the out-of-London groups. Centralised control was symbolised by the fact that organisers had to come down to London for the vetting. In one way it was a replay of the Manchester v. London conflict, but in reverse. Launder being a Londoner and the service being most developed in the capital, it was natural that FRIEND should have a London base; but for established CHE groups out of London, used to Manchester being both the hub and more local to them, subservience, as they saw it, to those snotty Londoners raised hackles. Robin Bloxsidge put it this way:

> FRIEND became the great CHE dictatorship. A FRIEND group had to be formally recognised. You had to go and be interviewed, and go through a procedure to run it. … Alan Swerdlow and I were interviewed, 'cause we became joint organisers at first. And we had to go to London to be interviewed by people. … FRIEND, in its very early days, was absolutely dictated centrally. FRIEND was doing something, I think, that they [CHE] were slightly frightened of, and they were determined you weren't going to do it wrong, if they had anything to do with it. In fact in practice, like everything else, once it was up and running there wasn't anything they could do about it at all. …
>
> In Liverpool we set up other training, as well as the national training – all these funny things like role play and shouting at each other and things like that. It had to appear to be sort of professional. And to some extent it did have to be.

'To some extent' indicates considerable reservations; there were always debates about whether the pluses of uniformity outweighed the minuses of stifling local initiative.

From 1972 to 1975, FRIEND was identified completely with CHE. It was CHE groups who set up FRIEND branches around the country, CHE who provided the seed money, and CHE members who staffed the phones.* Throughout the 1970s and 80s, local CHE groups all over the country organised fundraisers both for their local group and the National Office. However, even as early as 1973, Launder was aware of the dangers of this:

> There are certain major problems for FRIEND while it remains a part of CHE. Firstly, there is the confusion for non-CHE members as to the

* FRIEND did however have significantly more women members than CHE, some lesbian, some heterosexual. Though lesbian members of CHE volunteered in considerable numbers, the difference was made up by heterosexual women friends recruited largely by word of mouth.

> relationship. This creates a second problem, that of convincing outsiders, and particularly statutory bodies, that FRIEND is not a subtle kind of recruitment agency for CHE. The third and most difficult problem is that as long as FRIEND is within CHE it cannot have charitable status.[87]

At the same time, FRIEND needed CHE for equally fundamental reasons:

> FRIEND may be trying to heal but CHE must find the cure. Without an active political pressure group at its side, FRIEND would be nothing more than a do-gooding welfare agency working in a void and quite powerless to fight the root cause of the problem.[88]

The model at the back of people's minds was the Citizens Advice Bureau service. CAB headquarters ran a formidable social policy unit, which advocated for social and legal change, on the basis of a huge number of case studies taken from the problems that individuals presented in their bureaux. Perhaps CHE advocacy could be informed by similar casework coming from FRIEND. Others were equally suspicious of the possibility of a split between the two functions, campaigning and supporting. As Bernard Greaves, EC member at the time, put it:

> It was fragmenting what ought to have been a coherent campaign. The original concept was of a holistic campaign that was addressing issues across the board. My experience of that was, when I first started campaigning in Cambridge, there was no telephone helpline of any kind, [but] my telephone started ringing. So I could see the link between the two. That when you campaigned, people got in touch. … The campaigning brought people in, and it provided them with a social outlet but some of those people became campaigners. So I saw the two, right from the start, as linked.[89]

This dilemma was not resolved until FRIEND split from CHE in 1975–6.

Launder's talk of charitable status and relations with outside bodies shows that he, uniquely in CHE enterprises, had a comprehensive development plan for his 'baby'. Phase One dealt simply with new CHE enquirers, who were referred to the CENTRE when their needs were beyond the capacity of existing groups to meet. This was the basis on which FRIEND was set up, and by May 1972 was dealing with fifteen clients a week.

Phase Two would happen once the London phones and office were staffed five days a week, and there were half a dozen regional groups or so. Then the service would be advertised to all CHE groups, to encourage convenors to refer 'clients' from the existing membership as well. In one sense advertising had already happened, since Groups had been asked to cough up funds, and fundraising appeals are themselves a form of advertising. But Phase Two, in addition to giving more detailed information about what

FRIEND has done so far, would create a more binding tit-for-tat, offering groups a service they could use in return for their donations.

For Phase Three, FRIEND would go public and national. In Launder's own words:

> Advertising FRIEND to the general public cannot be contemplated until we have a national network which is under-utilised. I don't think we'll reach this point for at least a year. In the meantime, we will get referrals from specialist agencies (e.g. the Inner London Probation Service, which has asked us to contribute a page in their monthly newsletter) on an increasing scale.[90]

CHE groups and their members seized on FRIEND as something simple and practical to which they could give their support. Setting up a FRIEND group was almost the first thing a CHE group would consider, once it was viable socially. Not everyone could qualify as a counsellor, but anyone could raise or donate money, or write off to tell social agencies of a local FRIEND group's existence. In this PR work they were sometimes more enthusiastic than skilled. At the NFHO Befriending conference of September 1972, Michael Launder was complaining of the reluctance of professional people to be associated with homosexual organisations.

> Some of the professional people made the point that the manner of approach was crucial. One said that his Director of Social Services had received a letter from a local CHE branch asking what his department was doing for homosexuals. As the answer was 'very little, if anything' the recipients felt threatened and instinctively sought to avoid the issue.[91]

By November 1972 there were fifty befrienders nation-wide, supported by twelve professional therapists; the London operation at the CENTRE was open seven nights a week, plus there were branches in Manchester, Liverpool, and Cambridge, with Cardiff and Leeds in the offing.

The new branch in Manchester was well aware of the tendency for over-self-confidence, or, in the flush of enthusiasm, for a volunteer to bite off more than she or he could chew. There was a leaflet of advice for trainees:

> The befriending service is not a counselling service. Befrienders are not qualified to counsel people with serious personality problems. ... People that we are best equipped to deal with are either those whose homosexuality has caused them to be lonely or those who are unnecessarily worried about their homosexuality. To these people we may be able to offer friendship, reassurance and sympathy.
>
> The Befriending service is *not* an introduction bureau and this is explained to applicants in our first reply.[92]

In January 1973 FRIEND was strong enough to hold its first national conference. By mid-year there were twelve local FRIEND groups,* with London providing the national enquiry line and Michael Launder formally in charge of National Development. A considerable number of befrienders still lacked a local group, and 10 per cent of callers were met by one of these individually. There was a sub-committee for maintaining standards of local groups, and in February noises were being made about setting up a separate management committee. At the same time, FRIEND was branching out:

> FRIEND has provided support where an individual's lifestyle has been threatened by the possibility that the custody of children may be lost as the result of matrimonial proceedings, or in the legal proceedings which follow an arrest charged with sexual offences. … We intend to increase our visits to gays in prison, but this will depend on our ability to obtain information about gays who are currently imprisoned.[93]

For a while, things drifted. When Michael Launder resigned in March 1973, Ted Clapham replaced him as national organiser, with two assistants – Manchester's Barrie Kenyon and Vivian Waldron in London. However, while it thrived and expanded locally, it stagnated nationally. Everyone could see that the need for FRIEND, and the only way to finance it was to go independent and get grants. Yet independence carried risks – was it strong and confident enough to survive alone? It was all very frustrating.

One way to acquire the stability and structure it was looking for would be to take over wholesale the structure of another organisation. If FRIEND sought charitable status it could take forever and there was a real possibility that they might not get it. However, there was another charity to hand. The Albany Trust had also set up the Albany Society Ltd, which already had charitable status, as well as being a limited liability company. The Society was not controlled by the Trust but by its members, who elected a Council of Management. Some of the members were also members of CHE, which gave CHE a foot in a very inviting door. Since there were no other members apart from the Council of Management, who could co-opt and invite to membership at will, it was a wonderfully self-perpetuating system. However it was dependent on the Trust in that it had no money of its own. At this time there was talk of the Albany Trust transferring all its assets and making over its covenants to the Society, and running the Trust down, which would effectively rationalise the situation and bring everything under the charitable/limited liability umbrella.

Michael Launder wanted a part of it. He held talks with Antony Grey and Michael Butler, and Grey proposed that the Society should apply for money

---

* London, Bradford, Croydon, Leeds, Merseyside, Sheffield, Liverpool, Cambridge, Manchester, Cardiff, Birmingham, Sussex.

on FRIEND's behalf, for a full-time professional organiser/administrator. Since this would leave the notionally independent FRIEND financially beholden to the Society, Launder and Ryde were dead against it. Gradually the whole situation was turning into a power struggle between Grey and Launder over the future of homosexual counselling services across the country. Ryde sensed an opportunity and proposed a strategy to take control of the Society. First the two of them went to a meeting of the Society's Council of Management. As he reported to the February 1973 CHE EC meeting:

> FRIEND would effectively take over the Albany Society structure, with the AS limiting its role completely to counselling/befriending plus *related* education and research. The idea was well received, although strongly opposed by Tony Grey, and I have agreed to put forward firm proposals written within the next two weeks.[94]

Grey was on a hiding to nothing, in that a majority of members of the Council of Management were, in Ryde's words, 'intimately involved with FRIEND'.

> As for the Trust, I am certain it will gradually die anyway. Its assured income from existing covenants cannot support its ridiculous overheads and the Trustees (whose liability is not limited) are clearly very worried. With diplomatic handling I believe we could get a major part of the recent four figure legacy directed to the Society; the Trust would then become a grant giving body with no staff. Merely distributing existing income to for example SLRS,* NFHO,† Albany Society.[95]

While exploring other forms of co-operation between FRIEND, the Trust and the Society, Ryde made clear he preferred a wholesale takeover. The new Council of Management would consist of four people from FRIEND, three outside professionals for credibility, three officers and a couple of representatives of CHE and the Scottish Minorities Group (SMG).

> FRIEND would come equipped with existing local organisers, and a national voluntary organiser who would serve until a grant was available. I consider FRIEND could at the outset contribute at least £1500 from its own resources; perhaps the Trust could match such a sum.[96]

It was news to many EC members that FRIEND had so much money at its disposal. However, they agreed on the basis of the report that Ryde, Launder and Ike Cowen as Legal Officer should start negotiations.

Three months later, in May 1973, there was finally a meeting. Tony Grey put forward his own proposals for revamping the Society with a new Council

---

* Sexual Law Reform Society, successor to the Homosexual Law Reform Society.

† National Federation of Homophile Organisations – see Volume Two.

of Management, which Launder and Ryde rejected. When their own proposals were put forward, Grey and Michael Butler said they didn't have any authority to comment on them. There was a hopeless stalemate, and a few days later David Kerr, the Chairman of the Albany Society, wrote to say that 'as a result of Michael Butler's report of this meeting he was forced to the conclusion that 'for the moment at any rate we should postpone the pursuit of closer co-operation.'[97]

This debacle was not unconnected with the loss of the CENTRE as a base of operations. In May 1973 Royston-Ball threw FRIEND out, and resigned as its London Organiser. To the membership this was mysterious, and when Martin Stafford tried to get at the truth behind this sudden move, EC member Ted Clapham told him 'it was for confidential reasons'. However, the resignation occurred so quickly on the heels of the attempt that it is clear that Royston-Ball's disapproval of the manoeuvres was so strong, as a trustee of the Albany Society, that he felt he had to sever relations. Equally, given Michael Launder's uneasiness at aspects of the way Royston-Ball ran the CENTRE and related to his charges, FRIEND was glad to be out of it. As a result, observers felt FRIEND was in 'a sorry state'. It necessitated some makeshift arrangements, and a quick drawing-in of horns. From August 1973 the postal address became ℅ 44 Earls Court Road; the phone number quickly changed to 01 603 6293, open for two hours nightly. This was based at 14 Gwendwr Road in Barons Court, about a mile away. This large Victorian villa also provided a drop-in centre for the same hours. However, these were private houses, offered out of individual generosity; it was no permanent solution for a rapidly growing national organisation. The hunt for grants for permanent premises was now in deadly earnest.

Rejection, however, also spurred FRIEND finally to formalise its own independent management committee structure, and to work more closely with SMG. The Albany Trust suffered increasing marginalisation, and after some years reinvented itself as a small semi-commercial (fee-charging) relationship counselling service, which as of 2014 operates out of a part-time office in Balham.

Despite this setback, FRIEND continued to grow and diversify. By 1973 it was offering training, in London and on a local level, to social work agencies. Bristol CHE ran a ten-week evening course on ten aspects of homosexuality, which was open not only to potential befrienders but also to other local support groups and social workers. This covered sexual health; religion; parental attitudes to homosexual children; integration and social problems; transvestism and transsexuality; homosexuals and the law; employment; housing; psychological problems; and counselling techniques. Liverpool and Manchester, too, ran training courses. FRIEND had become, by any standards, a resounding success, and a recognised social work resource.

A club for London

FRIEND came from the first London mass meeting in April 1971 and the Task Force which the meeting set up. It was not the only initiative which had some success. The COC-style club beckoned invitingly, always on the horizon. At first, raising the money needed for a Club seemed achievable. One way of doing it was through breweries, and the LCC approached them in the same way as Manchester had done. However, there was the same sticking point, in that they would not consider investment in a members' club – not at least until a large enough membership was signed up to make the deal financially viable. It was a Catch-22 situation.

The other way to raise money was through wealthy individuals. Patrick Trevor-Roper, the Queen's eye surgeon who had given evidence as an openly gay man before the Wolfenden Committee, coughed up £100. Angus McGill, a close friend of Michael Launder, was a columnist on the *Evening Standard* responsible for many years for producing their annual Good Pub Guide. He also co-wrote their long-running cartoon strip 'Clive'. A convivial man, he introduced Tony and Michael to some of his extensive contacts, with the result that the pair found themselves wining and dining the more glittering of the capital's discreet fagarati.

One such was the fashion designer John Stephen. He had almost single-handedly created the mass market for men's fashion in the late 1950s, and put Carnaby Street on the map as the epicentre of the Swinging Sixties. He was known as 'The Million Pound Mod.' So here there was a prospect of serious money. Tony remembers:

> Michael and I went to dinner with John, and … we got to the point where he was pretty much saying, 'Look, I will back you if you can get some structure together.' And particularly, 'If you can highlight some potential premises.' It ended up in us both being sick in his Rolls Corniche as he was driving us back to North London. John had been an alcoholic and had gone completely straight, and he took great pleasure, not being able to drink, in making sure that those he was entertaining drank too much. Even at the expense of mucking up his Rolls.[98]

In 1971 pan-London activities and fundraising were sporadic and disorganised. Individuals arranged the occasional spectacular which, if successful, was readily incorporated as a repeat performance into a more coherent plan for 1972 – Chris Brocklesby got together a riverboat trip in August 1971; taking a leaf out of GLF's book, there was a disco at Kensington Town Hall in September; and there was a Winter Fair, held in November. Peter Robins, then convenor of Group 9, claims to have had the original idea for the fair, and Group 9 was the main organiser:

> I was having a bath, and an idea came to me, as it does when one's in one's bath. Eureka, you see. We organised this … at the gay cathedral, Conway Hall.* And it was amazing. We were still in a state of – not fear and trepidation, but slight apprehension. Would the local yobs come rushing in? What did come rushing in were dear old ladies at four o'clock at the chance of a bargain.[99]

The discos and the Winter Fairs were to become London CHE's major fundraisers for the next few years. Roger Baker reported for *Lunch* on the first Conway Hall Fair. Groups had been preparing for this for months, each deciding on a specialism. Group 3 organised the raffle, Group 6 indoor plants, Group 7 'Good as New', Group 8 scatter cushions, Christmas cards and calendars, Group 9 hardback books, Group 10 candles. There was a buffet run by Groups 6 and 9. Brian Sewell was able to use his contacts to get a David Hockney† print to auction. The report in *Lunch* conveys the humour, the endearing amateurism and the camaraderie of what was in all other respects a village fete:

> Considering everything, it was a great success – in financial terms, which is important, but in social terms too. It was just great to see so many members and friends wandering around the stalls creating a really great, relaxed atmosphere. …
>
> The earliest arrivals found Tony [Ryde] looking casual but chic in a brown pully at the door and Peter [Robins] looking fantastically smart at the hardback bookstall where there were some real bargains going, including a mint copy of Roger's book,‡ which got snapped up a darned sight quicker than Roger.
>
> John was discovered behind a stall full of long, hard, coloured candles and looking suitably flattered by such a setting. … I vividly remember the district correspondent of a provincial newspaper I once worked for, writing a report of a church Garden Party and saying, 'But the hit of the afternoon was the vicar with his balls in a bucket.'
>
> Alas, there were no such delights for us, but the hit of the afternoon was probably Tom who hid behind a curtain and told fortunes non-stop for hours. …

---

* Conway Hall is the headquarters of the South Place Ethical Society and had been since 1878 a noted chamber music venue. It had moved from its non-conformist religious roots to a secular humanism, and provided both a shelter and a platform for radical groups in this period and beyond.

† David Hockney returned briefly to live in the UK 1968–73, and during that time was a discreet but reliable funder of both GLF and CHE, as well as giving uncompromising interviews about his gay life.

‡ Roger Baker's *Drag*.

> There were vast bottles of WINE, a very sexy record from Denmark and yet another copy of Roger's book to be won. … Norman had a dazzling display of glassware, and Chris stood slightly defensively behind a stall laden with skin bracer – which no-one admitted they needed.
>
> Tony [Ryde] won the Hockney (engraving) but instantly auctioned it again, making another £27.* … There was a photographer, and a lucky dip, and David selling some pottery and mint copies of Ian's book.† The student group added glamour to the scene, and also made a lot of money on paperbacks and records.
>
> A GLF contingent arrived complete with furry coats and a baby; they sold lots of copies of *Come Together*,‡ handed out leaflets, and spent a lot of money, largely, it seems, on cakes.[100]

In just five hours, and with no advance publicity, they raised £360 (£4,900). The LCC opened a Building Fund account to deposit the money in. There were five Trustees, and Ike Cowen from Nottingham was invited to join, as Manchester representative and because of his experience with the Pavilion Club. He does not seem to have responded.

The LCC was also blessed with an energetic and intelligent fundraiser, William Blackledge. He was very bullish: 'With the envisaged growth of membership in the near future, a target figure of something like £10,000 in the next two years should be attainable, if not doubled.'[101] For 1972 he produced a list of proposed London-wide activities which would give CHE members something more exciting to do than visit a West End pub:

Jan 28:	Grand Masked Ball
Feb:	Victorian evening (complete with cockle and whelk stall)
Mar:	Easter Exhibition and sale of members' work (art, sculpture, photography)
Apr:	Wine and cheese to inaugurate CHE Film Society
May:	Garden Party and sports day, followed by barbecue
June:	1) Riverboat trip; 2) Cricket match
July:	1) Summer Ball and fashion show; 2) Car Rally

* He was not best pleased. 'Of course I couldn't have it, because I was chair of the co-ordinating committee at the time, and so I put it back into auction and we resold it. But that was the nearest I ever came to owning a Hockney! I would love to have that now.' – Interview with the author, 5 December 2012.

† Ian Harvey's autobiography, *To Fall Like Lucifer*, was published in October 1971, and Harvey sold large quantities of it through CHE. Harvey was a minor member of the Macmillan government who was fined £5 for breach of park regulations in 1958, when he had sex in St James's Park with a Coldstream Guard (see page 85). He resigned from government and Parliament, although there appears to have been little pressure on him to do so.

‡ Issue 10 appeared that month.

Aug:	Canal boat trip and Car weekend to Amsterdam
Sept:	1) Coach trip to stately home; 2) CHE soccer team opens season
Oct:	1) Ideal home exhibition inc. cookery demo; 2) Halloween ball
Nov:	1) Play; 2) Inauguration of classical disco
Dec:	1) Winter Fair; 2) Christmas party

48. Flyer for Masked Ball

A letter went out to all convenors:

> These are being staged *by* you, *for* you. They are intended to serve a dual purpose 1) to bring together London members who would not otherwise meet because of the group system, and 2) to build up the basis of a fund to provide us with Club premises.
>
> It is the general consensus of opinion that we badly need premises of good quality that we can call our own. But these premises will become reality mainly through our own efforts. … Supporting our own social events is one way in which we can express our opinion in a constructive

> way. … Consider the events as opportunities for you to contribute to the Club Fund account.[102]

The Masked Ball, the Summer Ball and the Halloween Ball all happened, all at Fulham Town Hall. They were hugely popular, and there was enough demand to put on extra dances. These Balls were following in the footsteps of GLF, which pioneered them at Kensington Town Hall in December 1970, and both groups continued to mount them regularly. There was a CHE riverboat trip again, and a 1972 Winter Fair.

Winter Fairs continued until the 1990s, later in conjunction with GALHA* and, as the more elaborate Winter Pride in the University of London Union, with the Pride Committee. There were Fairs in 1972 and 1973, each more elaborate than the last. CHE Groups from outside London started contributing – Chilterns in 1972, Windsor and Surrey in 1973.

> We then had a second winter fair, and this was on a much larger scale. And some of them were larger, the groups, by this time. I can remember the Windsor Group rang me and said could we come? And I said, yes of course you can. We'll find a corner. Well they were there at eight in the morning, and opened up [the hall], and we opened [to the public] at ten. By nine o'clock you'd never seen anything like the corner that they'd managed, they did flowers and potted plants and bulbs, and God knows what – lovely! … Somebody came up to me and said, 'Look over there. You see that woman?' I said, 'Yes, I know that face. I also know that autumnal two-piece that she's wearing, and the hat'. And it was the actress Coral Browne. Mrs Vincent Price. Who was wearing still the brown tweed that she wore in a very famous horror film called *Theatre of Blood*.[103]

The 1972 Fair had 16 stalls, plus bingo, hot food and fortune-telling. This year the raffle had serious prizes, including a fortnight's Mediterranean holiday for two: 'It would have warmed any vicar's wife to see preserves and cakes on sale, lucky dips, seemly games of chance, though the rummage stall labelled 'Drag' might have raised an eyebrow or both.'[104]

> There were lots of little stalls which were selling everything from cakes to antiques, naughty pictures to second-hand clothes, and even one of those old-fashioned gramophones (without the dog). I was selling candles, which was rather fun, except for all the rude comments. You know what a prude I am! The big candles (at £1 and £1.25) sold very well but no-one seemed very interested in little ones for 30p. We're going to melt down all the ones left over to make a big one in the shape of Georgie Best, so that's something to look forward to next year. … I did win a tube of Rowntrees Fruit Gums (worth 2p) on some silly game where you had to pull straws

---

* Gay and Lesbian Humanist Association.

> out of a box, but as I had spent 5p on the ticket I didn't exactly jump up in the air with delight. … Peter Norman* kept telling the piano player to 'shut up' while he made announcements from the stage, and later when he announced that we'd made over £1,000 (£12,000) we were all so delighted that the mutual embracing, back-patting and various other things went on for several minutes.[105]

However, the big innovation was evening entertainment (20p entrance to the fair, 40p day and evening). The newly-inaugurated CHE Players mounted a triple bill of N. F. Simpson and Harold Pinter, while Roger Baker devised and appeared (in drag) with members of Group 10 in a reworking of *No, No, Nanette*, entitled *Yes, Yes, George*. A few hearts fluttered at the spectacularly handsome Canadian tenor, an equally astonishing 'castrato', and 'CHE lost quite a bit of its square image in a marvellous combination of handbags, wigs, falsettos and dubious dancing sequences.' It was left to Ralph Norton to review Baker's performance, not entirely seriously, in *Lunch*:

> Suddenly out of the wings there came bursting upon us a great strapping blonde of a woman with gilded shoes and the street-walk of a strumpet. And her voice! Rich, dark and tarty; a bass-contralto; a feminine bassoon of a voice; a vehicle for the expression of inexpressible innuendos; a deep siren woodwind, fit to hail mariners to shipwreck; a randy-rousing, organ-raising, codpiece-busting vulgar-prompting sonority; an ancient whore of a voice which cannot have changed its intonation since Babylon. … Men of my years are of course, liable to strange fancies and bizarre desires, but, oh the shame of it! What can I do now except hang about the Ladies at Paddington in a faded rubber mackintosh. … Truly the plight of the aging hetero-perve is a sorry thing.[106]

Henceforth every Fair had its accompanying performance; in the later 1970s these were provided by Gay Sweatshop, Britain's first publicly-funded lesbian and gay theatre group. For the moment, the Centre Fund was doing nicely.

The Working Party on Club Premises chaired by Mike Thomas was at first optimistic. Since Mike was from Group 3, it became something of a pet project for that group, something which convenor Brian Sewell in particular was passionate about. But Thomas left London for Bristol shortly after, and so the working party came to nothing. By the time Brian sent round notice of the second mass meeting in October, he was forced to admit, 'Some working parties were still-born and we shall attempt to set them up again: the saddest of these mortalities was the club, and we must make an urgent effort to get this under way.' They did. Brian tried hard to inject some urgency into the proceedings, with an article in *Lunch*:

---

* Probably a mistake for John Saxby.

> The question of club premises constantly recurs at any meeting of Group 3, and I sense a mounting impatience among members with our failure to put down roots. Money is obviously going to be the stumbling block, but without some preliminary work and the presentation of some definite proposal, money will be difficult to raise. We need a working party made up, not of enthusiastic amateurs, but of members with useful professional experience – estate agents, solicitors and accountants, and anyone who can deal on their own level with the police, licensing authorities, local government, planning authorities and so on, and who can also give us advice on fundraising, the benefits of registering CHE as a charity* and the financial administration of a club.
>
> As far as the premises themselves, these should provide at least an office for CHE administration, a small room for the meetings of committees, working groups, and a large room for mass meetings, parties, balls and whatever other bun fights may be devised.
>
> Coffee, soft drinks and alcohol should be on sale at reasonable profit-making prices. … If it develops along those lines, we should find ourselves with an organisation not dissimilar to COC in Amsterdam. …
>
> When the crunch comes, funds will have to come out of members' pockets: donations, covenants, bonds, the sale of shares on some kind of ordinary share basis. … We need help at that sort of level with the decoration of whatever we get; and here we shall have to form another working party of plumbers, electricians, decorators and builders to control the enthusiasm of those of us who can only wield a brush. …
>
> Access to public transport is essential. One idea that has come up is the use of some unloved Wesleyan (or any other denomination) chapel scheduled as an ancient monument and not to be knocked down – one in Putney is now used as a youth theatre and club. Has anyone the ear of Lord Soper or the Church Commissioners?
>
> This really boils down to a cry for help. My own group has ideas but no expertise … may I appeal to anyone with usable professional qualifications to come forward and form a working party? And will you all keep your eyes open for possible premises.[107]

An almost aching longing is palpable. Behind that, Sewell also had a sense of structure, of the process which the project needed. Plans, proposals, fund-raising, premises. In that order. In *People not paper*, the policy document he produced for the LCC in the summer of 1971, he is even more explicit about what the club should contain:

> A Quiet room/library/writing/members
> B Committee Room

* An impossibility with the words 'campaign' and 'homosexual' in its title; Sewell was being naïve to even think it was a possibility.

C A quiet games room (Bridge/Draughts)
D Noisy games room (Darts/ Table Tennis/Bingo)
E Snack bar (soft drinks/evening snacks)
F Bar
G Shower room (key with secretary or duty officer)
H Recruitment secretary's office (phone)
I Counselling room
J Recruiting secretary's bedsitter.[108]

Brian was also spot-on in his assessment of the range of skills and the number of people necessary to bring the idea to fruition; skills which were never forthcoming within CHE. Nevertheless, fundraising at local group level continued. For a fleeting moment, the Putney Youth Club seemed a genuine possibility. There was talk of employing 'two girls working up to twenty-five hours a week as part-time secretaries – the cost and running expenses of which would amount to £500 a year.'* But this would only have been the running costs of a London office. There was a clear distinction between long-term owned club premises and a leased office. Putney was an office and funds for it would have to be raised separately as a short-term project. A suggestion for auctioning a signed copy of Ian Harvey's *To Fall Like Lucifer* was greeted with derision, if only because at this time the unsigned copies were rarer. Instead the Committee decided to raise an office levy of £1 a head on all London members, and Group 1 started rattling the collection plate for the Putney office, only to be rapped over the knuckles by the LCC.† David Smith, the then Chairman of Group 1, told the Treasurer:

> I understand Group One is on the carpet. … Apparently John Hidgson was naughty in asking for donations for the dead issue of the Putney Office. Other schemes are afoot – and in any case money for the forthcoming office, club or whatever will be submitted as a group donation to the LCC. I … would like to speak with you about it so that I can have some clearer idea what it is we are supposed to have done wrong![109]

A London club or a National CHE Centre? There were those, of whom Tony Ryde was the most eloquent, to whom a national centre was the priority, and a key to financing CHE's development. He wrote a very detailed proposal for employing a fundraiser, with the centre/club as the most attractive option to raise funds for. A less divisive figure than Brian Sewell, and one with more

---

* The 'girls' would have been two of CHE's women members, Jo Batchelor and Gini Stevens. They met as married women in Australia, and came to the UK as a couple to escape the social climate Down Under. Jo Batchelor was the first convenor of the London Women's Group (1971–72) and Gini was the editor of *Lunch* from Issue 6 to Issue 21.

† It is unclear why Putney fell through. Perhaps it was not thought central enough.

extensive contacts on the EC as well as being LCC chair, a proposal from Tony carried far more weight.

> In the long term the only way to finance CHE's wider programme is to offer something in return for which there is an undisputed demand. A CHE centre would also be infinitely more marketable as an objective, even though it would cost far more to set up.
>
> What would it involve? Obviously bars and dance floor as the main money-spinners. But far more than this limited concept of a club. Offices, for national and local work, meeting rooms, a library, a point of contact and a centre of recruitment, the nucleus of legal and aid services in general, and Friend (Task Force) in particular. In time it would become the centre for projects such as housing associations, charter flight holidays, Help the Ageing [*sic*]. …
>
> It would have to be in London, where 25–30% of membership concentrated. But it would have to be a CHE Centre which happened to be in London, rather than a London club which happened to be run by members of London CHE. This is a most important distinction which is critical to the future development of CHE. …
>
> The CHE Centre would be an ambitious project, but perhaps an organisation like ours will die unless it does set its sights high. The initial stage alone could cost £20,000–£30,000, financed by existing and future members, the fundraising campaign and commercial loans. But this is unquestionably what is needed to enable CHE in London not just to grow, but [even] to survive. Is it what is needed for CHE nationally? …
>
> This could mean moving the CHE office to London in the near future, rather than waiting for the Centre to be established in perhaps a year's time. If we accept that a CHE centre located in London does not mean London CHE doing its own thing and saying 'bugger the rest', then it must make sense, if only because only the availability of man and woman power in London CHE can keep the problem of administration nationally within manageable proportions.[110]

Though it piggy-backed on Sewell, it was far, far more ambitious than Sewell had allowed himself to imagine. It also cast CHE not only in the role of campaigning organisation and social support provider, but also a kind of co-operative society providing a whole range of member benefits in much the same way as a Trade Union does. It allied itself with those who argued that the headquarters should be in London, not as part of some abstract cultural power struggle, nor from the point of view of proximity to the corridors of power and to media influence, but as an essential part of a financial strategy for survival and development.

The National Executive discussed the proposal in some detail in January 1972. Michael Steed, the Treasurer, gave it the thumbs-up, repeating Ryde's arguments and sometimes his words:

> The London club project will go ahead anyway. … But to set it up from the outset as a national enterprise would widen its appeal and in my view help to tie London in with the rest of CHE, whereas a London club in the limited sense would work in the opposite direction. Of course, CHE nationally would have a say in the development of a National Centre in London, both as a project and subsequently a club. The club idea is not new, but central, to CHE and I believe of great psychological importance even for those who could rarely use it.[111]

Michael was politically astute enough to see that in any case a successful London club would be a challenge to Manchester's claim to be the national headquarters. If London could establish and run a successful club where Manchester had signally failed to in Burnley, it would become very clear who could 'get things done' and who couldn't. The EC took its cue from Steed, and passed a resolution that tried as hard as possible to tie the London development in with Manchester and the National Office:

> The EC welcomes news of London's plans to establish a club, and hopes that this will be set up as a registered members' club and projected as a national centre for CHE, potentially the first of many around the country. The EC emphasised the importance of involving members from all over the country in the project and suggests that methods be explored of involving such members as early as possible in the formative stages of the project.[112]

However, it did not take on board the integral element of the strategy which involved moving to London, nor did it agree to Tony's proposal for employing a fundraiser; thus its endorsement was meaningless without accepting the necessary consequences. To the many committee members based locally in the North West, a move would not only be inconvenient, it would change the nature of the organisation, cut it off from its roots, make it more middle-class and managerial in outlook. And so there was stasis.

By July 1972, the more extravagant fundraising ideas were dead. Those working on it were convinced that thousands of pounds were simply undeliverable within the foreseeable future. While its work on events had brought in some money, the Club Working Party knew that the real finance would have to be raised elsewhere. It was left to Michael Moor, echoing Brian Sewell's first article, to carry the banner for the project. He still talked up the possibilities:

> It is not easy to convince the wealthy few who will ultimately provide the wherewithal, without having something more tangible to offer than an idea. We have to show that we really want our own place, that we can run it, and that it will be as different as we say it will be from the ordinary commercial scene. …

> We need to know who we can call on for financial backing, primarily loans and guarantees, possibly donations. We need to know who will be ready to man the office, to work behind the bar, to paint walls, to prepare accounts, to give furniture. And if any of you own an empty boutique in Carnaby Street or a warehouse in Covent Garden … now is your chance.[113]

Towards the end of 1972 there was a balance of £1,500 (£18,500) in the account. Despite this, the Club Working Party, desperate for progress, thought the only way forward was to involve CHE nationally as Tony Ryde had suggested. The LCC reported in November to the EC, who had been kicking the idea round for over a year:

> With perhaps close to a thousand members within the Greater London area, and a far larger potential, a central club is not only urgently needed, but should also be a source of strength to CHE as a whole. The basic requirement is a congenial place where members and their guests, from London and beyond, can meet informally whenever and as often as they like. This would be complementary to the organised social activities which have become a feature of London CHE, many of which would benefit greatly from being able to use the club's facilities.[114]

The report went into some detail about the running of the Club. It would be a registered members' club, membership of CHE conferring automatic club membership. This would give the club a built-in clientele of up to a thousand to bring into the building and persuade to spend money. There would be an elected members' club committee, and that would be the National EC, which was already elected by the membership:

> This will automatically allow us a licence, but we shall also aim for the right to stay open beyond normal hours on the more popular nights to maximise use of the facilities. Obtaining the necessary permits should be straightforward. … As a matter of principle, and in order to attract as many people as possible, we decided that membership of the Club should be a right of *all* paid-up CHE members, and that membership of CHE should be a condition of entry to it (apart from members' guests).[115]

If this and subsequent clubs were run directly as part of CHE, profits could be channelled back to the organisation without paying corporation tax, which any profits donated from a separate company would attract.

> The cash flow of this one venture alone will be several times greater than that of CHE nationally. … The purchase of a 5/10 year lease and equipment of the club may come to around £10,000.* Some £1,400 has

* This is considerably lower than the earlier Ryde estimates, which were for a more ambitious project which involved owning the premises. The LCC was drawing its horns in.

> been raised already in London and the rest will have to be mobilised very quickly. We plan to do this by obtaining gifts and loans from a handful of individuals, the latter on a short-term basis to give us time to fundraise from the membership as a whole, for a reality rather than an idea, and to utilise the Club's profits, which should be substantial.[116]

The EC would not buy this. They had already stalled Tony Ryde's proposals earlier in the year, after a certain amount of heart-searching. This time they were not being asked to move, but the consequence was that they would not be in effective control. No way were they going to accept legal and financial liability without some control over the project when so much money was involved.

For a start, a scheme this size would have seriously unbalanced CHE's social/campaigning mix, as they saw it. It would be a devourer of time and attention; it would also saddle whoever were the named directors with individual personal liability if things went wrong. Having already advocated that the club should be national, the EC, by refusing to take this on, laid itself open to a charge of at best lack of bottle and at worst hypocrisy. It was wanting all the benefits while someone else took the risks. It was this refusal which gave 'Manchester', in the eyes of 'London', its reputation as a brake on the organisation. Again there was serious talk of secession. Brian Sewell remembered:

> I remember we discussed this very clearly, because there were those who said, 'Let's break away', and there were others who said, 'Well, before we break away, let's try not to. Because the movement will be very much stronger if it is national than if it is just local. So it is much better if we can get Manchester to agree.'[117]

London ploughed on. They looked at premises on the market in Soho, but thought them unsuitable. They gave their minimum requirements to an estate agent, and told him to be on the lookout. They needed a bar area to accommodate a hundred and to seat at least fifty; a meeting room to seat fifty; a kitchen to serve simple meals; and two offices of 100 square feet each. The ambitions were being scaled down even further. They started to go cap in hand to breweries, but still there were doubts about demand and viability.

By February 1973 the working party had involved David Offenbach, a gay solicitor who handled many cases of gay men prosecuted for sex offences, and was regularly invited to talk to gay groups. He was charged with working out the best structure for managing the Centre, and charged in turn £250 for the service.

It's an indication of the poor relations between London and Manchester that Ike Cowen didn't get to set it up as he had the Pavilion Club. Skills came expensive when they were not in-house, and there were all too few skills within CHE. In this case they didn't even use the skills that were available.

But in addition to the skills shortage, EC reluctance and a dearth of suitable premises in Central London, another barrier erected itself. By a miserable stroke of fortune, house prices in London doubled in the two years 1972–73, with a corresponding rise in the cost of leases and rents.* However quickly they raised money, it couldn't keep up with house prices, and in any case study groups working on the legal and financial intricacies were slowing everything down.

Eventually, in March 1974, the Working Party effectively threw in the towel, at least until someone else could raise the money; clearly they had lost all heart for the project, however pious their vague wishes for the rest of the year:

> The cost of acquiring property is beyond the present means of London CHE, and … the working party feels that with the finance at present in our bank accounts the club premises idea must remain a castle in the air. … The working party also fears that as CHE members can find almost anything they want in the existing haunts … any CHE Club might be a seven-day wonder. …
>
> Lack of funds makes the search for suitable premises extremely difficult. … Consideration of buying or renting larger premises (than CHELIC) must be put off until a series of money-raising efforts have really brought in the cash. … Funds should be built up first during a period of concentrated effort. … Perhaps 1974 should as a whole be a special year with a financial target set.[118]

They had missed the boat for several reasons. Paradoxically, the very opening up of possibilities for gay socialising, which CHE was contributing to, gave others with more of an eye on profit an opportunity as well. The day of the Pink Pound was not far off. Tony Ryde acknowledged this:

> I think it didn't happen because nobody really could come up with a viable proposition. Not because it couldn't be done but because we couldn't do it. Possibly there wasn't the expertise, the commitment. By the time we really started trying to do this in earnest, the commercial scene was opening up, and there was a great deal of, 'Well why do you need to do it on a non-commercial basis?' Because now people had the option of going to 'swinging' clubs. And I think that was probably the thing – had we been three or four years earlier, it probably would have happened. But we just decided in the end, probably with potential backers, that actually the

---

* Inflation was running at roughly 9%. In 1974–77 it averaged over 16% a year, though house prices became comparatively cheaper. It remained over 10% until 1982.

commercial sector was going to meet this need rather quicker and more effectively than we could. 'Cause we very much saw it as a fundraising thing. To generate the income to keep the organisation and the social side going, as well.[119]

An office for London

London CHE also undermined its own club project with diversions. Collectively, like the White Queen in *Through the Looking Glass*, CHE sometimes seemed capable of believing six impossible things before breakfast – or at least, believing that they could accomplish things which were completely incompatible. The first mass meeting in Holborn wanted not only a London centre, it wanted a London office. The working party concentrated exclusively on its search for a club, believing that was where the office would be located. However, young and impatient Derek Brookfield of the London Monday Group (previously London Group 10) took it on himself to bring the office into being, whatever the Working Party was doing.

> Where does this leave the urgent call for an 'immediate' CHE office? In my lap. … This is a direct appeal to anyone with contacts with estate agents, London boroughs, especially central ones (which tend to have properties under shadow of demolition within a year or so) and constructive ideas to join my working party. It isn't a talking shop; what we need are people who are determined to work flat out to realise the unequivocal call of the Holborn Congress – we want a London office NOW![120]

Tony Ryde agreed. For over a year he'd wanted an office more than anything. Desperately overworked as chair of the LCC, London Organiser (and therefore chief inductor) in succession to Roger Baker, and member of the National Executive, he saw a London office as a way of channelling work away from himself and parcelling it out more effectively. He put the case when he was guest speaker at Group 1:

> He spoke of the pressing need for a central CHE office to be set up in London to channel the enormous amount of administrative work (for which he was finding himself responsible) to the various groups and working parties in the most efficient manner possible. The office would take over induction administration and the answering of general enquiries from outside organisations, would receive callers by appointment, undertake interviews by Task Force and be a clearing house and information bureau generally. The members present agreed in principle that such an office was necessary.[121]

So Brookfield ploughed ahead. In July 1972 he put adverts in *Gay News*, which had hit the streets in June. The premises they found were in the basement of the former headquarters of the National Union of Journalists. Its phone number was very similar to the London Palladium's, and many wanting to book for Bing Crosby, or Tommy Steele in *Hans Christian Anderson*, were surprised to be greeted by, 'Hello, this is the Campaign for Homosexual Equality.' By the end of August, they were advertising that the London Information Centre (CHELIC) was open, at 22 Great Windmill Street, W1, from 12 to 3 p.m., Monday to Friday. It was in a dingy backstreet tucked off Piccadilly Circus. An LCC motion to ask Manchester for money towards the office was defeated by 8 to 6, probably because of the fear of 'interference'. Despite this, the tardiness of some London groups in coughing up their share of the rent meant that in October the LCC was forced to try to tap Manchester for money; Manchester drove a hard bargain. Many EC members were against it, and said the organisation couldn't afford it. Michael Steed, CHE Treasurer, produced a very cautious briefing:

> I feel that any national CHE contribution should be clearly related to any expected benefit to CHE nationally and not regarded as a grant towards a regional enterprise.
>
> I do not think that there are any major office functions which could satisfactorily be devolved from the national office. Not only is hiving off of odd jobs over several hundreds of miles liable to create as many problems as it solves, but the actual office facilities … are cramped. Encouraging its use as a reception point and meeting place may also detract from the efficiency of the use of the office.
>
> The centre should boost recruitment of CHE members, though it is impossible to guess how much. However, advertising currently costs us 55p per member joining. … A CHE contribution of £5 per month in the hope of a net additional couple of dozen other recruits seems not unreasonable.
>
> The centre's use as a reception point and meeting place will be overwhelmingly for London members. But a number of non-London CHE members visit London on business and could be glad of a place they could drop into, ring up for information etc.[122]

This placed an onus on those running CHELIC to keep a lot of statistics about membership and visitors, to send monthly to Manchester. They also had to submit quarterly accounts, have an annual audit, an EC member on the management committee running the centre, and to agree to consult Manchester when they wanted to spend any non-routine money. Despite the restrictions (and grumbles of 'more interference'), London agreed.

Number 22 Great Windmill Street offered the absolute minimum needed for an office. It was never a very nice place to hold meetings. Many objected to its location in the seedier part of Soho, next to a load of strippers in the famous Windmill Theatre, and underneath a travel agency, Morocco Bound. There were more genteel places to get cheap offices then in Central London – Bloomsbury, or Kings Cross, for example. The office can be seen in the 1974, CHE-made, episode of London Weekend Television's community programming series, *Speak for Yourself*.* There was hardly any natural light, and the furniture in the main room was a set of twenty lurid orange plastic stacking chairs.† You entered down a flight of steps into a semi-basement; on the right a tiny cubby-hole which housed a desk and a kettle and served as an office; on the walls a map of the UK, with pins showing where the CHE and FRIEND groups were; a threadbare carpet; a small stand with leaflets. It had a depressing, run-down feel about it. However, it was only £65 per month, including rates and heating. Despite its gloom, it was to serve as a meeting room for the LCC, several of the Central London groups‡ and also some of the SIGs which mushroomed in London in 1972–74.

> CHELIC isn't just an office, there's a lounge where visitors can relax and enjoy a cup of coffee or tea and talk. Small Groups can hold their meetings here, and friends can meet before going on to a show. Telephone messages and letters can be held for you. A notice board lists coming events, and also has a section devoted to members' accommodation needs. Tuesday night is ladies night.
>
> Urgently wanted please! Has any reader any spare Easy Chairs? We are trying to make CHELIC a pleasant place to visit, and great changes have already been made. If you have a chair or two, please let us know and someone will arrange to collect it/them from you.[123]

From the start, CHELIC was caught in a dilemma. On the one hand it wanted to be a shop window for the organisation, with all that this implied – smart, well-decorated, an efficient office, steady opening hours, a reliable welcome. On the other, it had little in the way of money to lash out on décor, and was entirely dependent on an erratic volunteer force to keep the place open.

The first requirement was decoration. The London Monday Group, one of the groups most enthusiastic about the Centre, pitched in with a Scrubbers Party:

> Whatever the eventual fate of the London Information Centre may be, it still needs cleaning. Howarth Penny§ is finding out what has to be done so

* Available to view at the National Film Theatre's Mediatheque on the South Bank, London.

† These replaced the original tube train seats.

‡ The Women's Group, The Youth Group, London 1, Piccadilly and West End Groups were regulars.

§ Howarth Penny was Social Secretary of the group. He moved to Manchester in September 1973 as successor to General Secretary Paul Temperton.

> contact him about taking along sponges, Flash, squeezy mops etc. Whatever else we need, booze will be on tap after the work. The more people there, the more time for drinking.[124]

Less than six months into its existence, CHELIC was already in trouble. Derek Brookfield was the first, unpaid, manager, and in October 1972 CHELIC's opening hours were extended to 10 a.m. to 10 p.m, seven days a week. He identified totally with his project. Peter Norman, who was on the Working Party to sort out the mess he left behind, remembers:

> He was quite young. I didn't know at first, but he had some sort of mental problem – depression, or something – and he threw himself into the CHELIC business, and got it running and started, and everything was going fine. But he got so involved with it, he stayed there all the time, and he slept there, and regarded it as his personal fief. And in the end he had to be told very firmly that this wasn't on, and I think he went off in a huff. … His heart was absolutely in the right place, but there was something about him that sent him a bit off the rails and he couldn't cope.[125]

There was no way that CHE could produce the volunteers to sustain the opening hours. Half the time the office did not open; and when it was open, the lack of consistent office systems meant administrative chaos.

Among all the other things it was supposed to do, CHELIC was a recruitment centre. People were meant to be able to come in off the street, find out about CHE and join up. Having done so, their forms would go off to Manchester for processing and their cheques for banking, and in due course they would get their membership cards and copies of the CHE Bulletin. That was the theory, but Paul Temperton found it impossible to find out how many London members CHE had, at least until Michael Yelland* took the card index system by the scruff of the neck:

> I'm afraid rather too many people have had a hand in this particular pie in the past for efficiency to reign. You may not believe this, but the cards are arranged in 25 different sequences (by groups and other oddities) with a rather inadequate index, so that it was next to impossible to check on individuals.[126]

It took him two months to sort out the mess. Still the problems kept coming. Martin George was secretary of Group 2, a leading light of the Motoring Group and a senior contract co-ordinator overseeing the installation of BT telephone exchanges. He became CHELIC manager in December 1972, when Brookfield's head rolled. Yet members were still complaining that they'd joined CHE at CHELIC, and then heard nothing further. Blame piled on Paul

---

* Treasurer of Group 3 and a Trustee of the Building Fund.

Temperton and National Office. 'Not me, guv!' protested Paul:

> All new memberships are always dealt with within a week of receipt here, usually sooner; so all these stories about 3-month delays and so on can absolutely be discounted as far as this office is concerned. These reports about people joining at CHELIC and never hearing anything subsequently keep on coming up and I really do wish something could be done about it; complaints on this score are never heard from any other new members except those joining at CHELIC. … It annoys me that people are allowed to get the impression that the national office is inefficient, when it isn't the national office's fault at all.[127]

Nor, insisted Martin, was it his fault. It turned out that there had been fraud at work. Peter Robins:

> I was working at Broadcasting House, I just came down Regent's Street and could just pop in. The idea was that if you were interested in joining CHE, you went there. And you met this man, who was office manager, and filled in your form, and gave him your annual subscription, and he would send it all to Manchester. Now I went to a Sunday afternoon meeting at John Saxby's flat at South Ken* … and John came back from the kitchen, bearing a great tray of tea for us, and said, 'Now there's something I think you all ought to know. … The forms and the money are not managing to go from Piccadilly London to Piccadilly Manchester.' And this guy was on the fiddle. … There were these poor souls going in and paying their ten quid for their subscription for the year or whatever it was, ten quid in today's money. And it never got there. He was using the subs to go out and pick up rent boys in Piccadilly.
>
> So then there was a dreadful meeting, somewhere in Pimlico. John Saxby was sitting next to me, and at this point Griff Vaughan Williams emerges as a person. This poor creature is hauled in front of us, and Griff then is Prosecutor General. 'Did you or did you not …?' Someone said, 'When did you last see your father?' And the man broke down in tears; he would repay every penny, and I said, 'You'll be lucky if you see a ha'penny.' And they never did.[128]

Brookfield is recorded as owing CHE £140 (£1,600) in April 1973;† he had also taken £20 from Haringey CHE, but returned it when confronted. By now he was definitely *persona non grata* at CHELIC, and posters and notices for other groups he belonged to were torn down.

Martin George in turn came under heavy pressure because of the amount of time it took to keep the centre open. He too retired, hurt and burnt out, in late 1974. Before that, he relied heavily on Audrey Barry, elected as joint

---

* John Saxby was convenor of London Group 10 from its formation in August 1971.

† LCC Minutes, 24 April 1973.

manager. The very manner of their appointment was fraught, as the Kensington CHE newsletter records:

> At a recent LCC meeting Kensington Members seemed very thick on the ground. One item on the agenda was CHELIC. This brought accusations, excuses, counter accusations and resignations which resulted in a vote of no confidence in the CHELIC working party being carried. Control of the information centre was given to Martin George and Audrey Barry. We pledged our group's support, so now will you please back us up with your offers of help. It doesn't matter how little, an offer to sweep out the office once a month would be welcome.[129]

This duo also came to feel beleaguered, as a member of Wandsworth CHE reported to his Chairman in January 1974:

> I must say however that things are not at all easy there. I have a very good ring-side seat really since I see quite a lot (and hear!) and don't get too involved. There is still a great deal of bad blood between Martin G. (and his companion in arms Audrey) and Bill Barron* and Tony Naylor.† The trouble is, Martin really isn't very good at politics. He seems to think that simply because one has an apparently good idea, that in itself will be sufficient to convince others of one's ability. Nothing infuriates people more than that you ride roughshod over them in pursuance of your own plans. However good they may be. I think Martin must find that out for himself.[130]

Audrey too put people's backs up. An undated letter from Peter Norman is accusatory:

> It appears that you have taken it on yourself to hold the keys to this office, and also that you are not allowing people to man this office, thereby causing a great deal of ill-feeling to those willing to man the office and whose good-will we should lose. It is wrong that the public phoning up for information cannot be helped because you have locked the steel cabinet with all the information inside. How can we operate as an information centre if it is not manned? This is most unsatisfactory. To the best of my knowledge Martin has not given you permission to do this.[131]

No doubt Barry was motivated by security considerations – Great Windmill Street in the heart of Soho was vulnerable to break-in, with its shared entrance. The compromise arrangements were elaborate. Peter Norman sent round a note to all volunteers:

---

* London Monday Group.

† Croydon CHE.

> Some of you arriving for a turn at the office recently have found the downstairs CHE door closed, and the ground floor Windmill office which keeps the keys for collection, also closed. And infuriating it is. The problem is due to the Windmill office closing early. I have now asked the Windmill office to leave the keys with the downstairs Morocco Bound office if the Windmill closes first. So remember to ask for the keys at Morocco if the Windmill's shut.[132]

The financial difficulties continued, even if they stopped short of fraud. Local groups began to question whether the £5 a month levy they were meant to pay was really worth it. The London Youth Group thought it pointless; in 1974 the once-keen London Monday Group withheld money too:

> The main reasons are i) Chelic is operationally insolvent and no sensible plans have yet been put forward to remedy this. ii) the objectives and plans for the centre are not being directed by those raising money for it and seem to be at odds with the existing arrangement of a national head-quarters in Manchester and iii) it is not right that we should have money we are misusing in London while Manchester is desperately short of funds.[133]

CHELIC started dipping into the Building Fund. Its Management Committee borrowed £250 from National Funds. The promised audited accounts for presentation nationally never materialised. Costs, especially rent, doubled to some £1,500 per year. The levy from local groups remained at £5 a month, with many groups withholding it. When Barrie Kenyon took over as treasurer in 1975, he reported that there was just £400 in the bank in the Building Fund, and if the Winter Fair didn't raise £2,000 they would either have to close CHELIC or look for somewhere cheaper and better value for money.

> The books were not consistently kept prior to his appointment as treasurer and there were a number of discrepancies. … A financial drain existed on the CHELO funds which could not be taken into account, i.e. irregularities with the sales of *Gay News* … he was not indicating that fraud had taken place.[134]

It was all a huge drain on time and money, and brought in very little in the way of membership. August 1975, when CHE was still in its heyday, brought in fifty enquiries, forty from non-members. Only eight people joined London groups through the Centre, compared with 27 via National Office. With costs running at £125 a month, 8 members and 50 enquiries wasn't much of a return on the investment. Brian Sewell analysed it in terms of expanding a business:

> Trying to expand a business, when you're being reasonably successful, somebody says, why don't you employ somebody, and why don't you

> employ more? Why don't you have three lorries instead of one? The answer is because of the great leap that is required, and it also requires change in your own mentality and the way that you do things, if you have then to hand over to deputies and get them to do what you want to do in the way that you want it done.
>
> And as far as the office was concerned, we didn't really make that leap. We couldn't because we didn't have enough money, and we didn't have anybody reliable to take it over, and we couldn't have paid them properly. It was a jump too soon.* And all it would have proved was that we'd got an office, with somebody running it. The moment you have your own bureaucracy you have your address, which has to be paid for. You have to have office equipment, you have a telephone. … Everything that was done before was done out of our own pockets. …
>
> But the moment you have an office, then having a summer fair and making eight hundred quid, is gone in a month. … And it hasn't done anything for the membership. It hasn't improved anyone's lot.[135]

It was inevitable that the National Office would eventually in the late 1970s put CHELIC out of its misery, and appropriate the tiny remnants of the Building Fund, thus again confirming its image as the authoritarian bully of gallant little groups.

Lunch

Alongside FRIEND and CHELIC, the original mass meeting also proposed a new magazine, *Lunch*, which came into being remarkably quickly. From May 1971 a working group was meeting in Roger Baker's flat. By June they were soliciting adverts from the Albany Trust. The first issue was planned for July, but there were more arguments about finance, and the amount of subsidy it might require to get off the ground. The budget was rejected, and the LCC would only agree to subsidise it by a maximum of £17.50 (£230). Each group would guarantee to buy one copy per member, at a cost of 5p each, and it was then up to the group to recoup its costs from its members. Under the editorship of David Hyde, the first edition appeared in September 1971. It was quarto-sized,† had fourteen pages, and ran for twenty-four issues until the end of 1973, when it was killed off by the larger, better financed and better distributed *Gay News*. From an initial print run of 800 it grew to a circulation of 3,000 at its height.

From the start its aims were somewhat contradictory. On the one hand it

---

* Despite the reservations of hindsight, both Brian Sewell and Peter Robins voted in favour of acquiring the office at the time.

† 23 cm x 30 cm.

was meant to be an in-house journal for CHE members. The mass meeting voted 'To consider the possibility of producing a magazine or bulletin on a local or perhaps national basis, in liaison with Manchester.'[136] However, Manchester wasn't interested, and said that it must be clear that it was a London magazine, and not a reflection of national CHE.

On the other hand, *Lunch* wanted to reflect all shades of opinion within the gay movement, welcoming contributions from members and non-members alike:

> Founded primarily to serve the group interests of CHE at a more personal level, its wider aims now are to provide a platform for all shades of opinion within the homophile community of Great Britain. ... Opinions expressed in *Lunch* are therefore not necessarily those of CHE itself; contributions are accepted from any source. This way it is hoped to build up a truly representative magazine. ... *Lunch* remains an independent publication with no axe to grind.[137]

This openness was to be tested with Issue 5, which carried an article from Laurence Collinson, who was a member of GLF as well as CHE. It is a fierce critique of the structure, campaigning and membership of CHE.* It provoked a furious response from the LCC, which demanded an assurance from the new editor, Gini Stevens, that she would publish no more pieces by Collinson. She gave no such assurance, and many readers rushed to her support. Laurence's own Group took up the cudgels in a letter, published in Issue 7, written by their Chairman, David Smith:

> This action quite simply constitutes a form of censorship and is not to be tolerated. There are, admittedly, arguments in favour of having an editorial policy for *Lunch*, but we feel most strongly that such a policy should be exercised by the editor of *Lunch* alone and not interfered with by a body of people who may or may not have vested interests in what is published in the magazine.
>
> It may be said that Mr Collinson's article was extremist in tone, misleading in content and arguable in its conclusions. This it was undoubtedly meant to be, and strikes us as a very good reason for printing it.[138]

Gini was a fine editor, and wisely printed a response from journalist Bob Sturgess, as well as numerous letters. The subject was closed in Issue 7 with two summaries, pro- and anti- CHE, from Sturgess and Collinson. There was no more editorial interference, and the magazine grew and throve. By the beginning of 1972 it had developed ambitions to be a national magazine. In the February edition of the Leeds *Broadsheet* it advertised:

---

* The actual article, and the response it triggered, is considered in Volume Two, in the chapter 'Them and Us', along with the many other articles covering GLF.

> In order to expand *Lunch* into a truly nationwide magazine, we wish to appoint a number of area reporters and photographers. They would contribute regularly on a monthly, bi-monthly or quarterly basis, and on special occasions from their part of the country. *Lunch* has big ambitions, and it can succeed by creating a team to cover the whole of Britain.[139]

The main feature in each issue was an interview between the editor and a 'celebrity', something which no previous gay magazine had achieved. Starting with Rose Robertson of Parents' Enquiry* (April 1972), it also featured jazz singer and surrealist expert George Melly:

> Personally I find the idea of picking people up in 'cottages' squalid and rather smelly but if that's other people's particular thing, I don't mind. But these places are open for big game hunting on the part of the law, who are handsome young fellows who cruise about smiling provocatively at nervous elderly gentlemen, then jump on them. This seems to me a most cruel activity, … a monstrous thing to do – an exploitation of people's needs, most of which are harmless.[140]

Writer Maureen Duffy† in Issue 9 related the gay struggle to class issues; Quentin Crisp (Issue 10) proved characteristically out of step:

> As regards Gay Liberation – I think it's a movement towards separation, which is bad, when the merging and rubbing out of the line between other people and homosexuals had grown blurred. I think movements are misplaced because the thing is moving itself; you only have to stand still now. … When I ask 'What do the letters CHE stand for and you say 'It's a Campaign for Homosexual Equality', with whom do you wish to be *equal*? Isn't this the failure of Women's Lib? Why be equal with dreary old men? In fact, if there was a rule of life, it should be, 'NEVER SEEK TO BE ANYBODY'S EQUAL – SEEK TO BE YOURSELF.'[141]

These were all substantial, meaty five- or six-page in-depth discussions, something the new *Gay News* was not yet capable of. 35-year-old David Hockney ('He looks like a wise blond owl') got the treatment in September 1972; he was both supportive and frank:

> I feel one should stand up and be counted and do one's bit occasionally. … When I first went [to California] I was promiscuous because that's the way people lived. You really had to live like that and I didn't know

---

* See page 447.

† Duffy wrote pioneering lesbian novels in the 1960s, most notably the thinly disguised portrait of The Gateways club and its members, *The Microcosm*. Her play, *Rites*, commissioned by Joan Plowright for the National Theatre, had an extended run in 1970–71, and she wrote early episodes of *Upstairs, Downstairs*.

> anybody … and that's the way you get to know people. But later on it got a bit boring … also, it interfered with work. …
>
> I met Peter nearly six years ago. … I led a kind of stable married life. I'd never lived with anybody before. … I can cope with that situation better because I can work better, than having to spend all night out looking for somebody which really takes up too much time in the mornings![142]

Jimmy Savile, then a Radio 1 DJ, pioneered the coverage of social issues and group access programmes within a popular music format, through his programme *Speakeasy*, of which more in Chapter Six. His interview in February 1973 manages to show a breath-taking egotism as well as hinting at a darker side:

> It's one of me failings that I've never lost me temper in me life. I've been attacked by people, jumped on physically, when I was a dance hall manager and wouldn't let people in. They've spat at me and I've said 'Bullseye!' and I've also had them murdered afterwards. Because I'm the greatest Al Capone at organising things. I've got a team, second to none, that works for me. I can arrange to have dreadful things happen in London when I'm in Edinburgh and I've got no compunction either over doing that. …
>
> I spend a day or two a week at Broadmoor. I've got me own room there. … My regular deal is that I record *Top of the Pops* on Wednesdays every fortnight, drive down there and watch it with the maximum security wing, sitting on the floor with them all. We have a fantastic time, and specially the new girl patients. … I'm the only civvy there who's got his own keys.[143]

This seems an astonishing thing to admit in the light of our own hindsight.

Lunch featured personal stories, stories of coming out and tales of the most horrific medical 'treatment'. Perhaps the most moving of these is by 'B. M. M.', a married woman struggling with her feelings, her own ignorance, medical brutality and the most appalling luck. Illegitimate, she grew up in an orphanage, fell in love with a girl at school. The girl was killed in a road accident. With no sense of self-worth, she discovered that she became popular with boys if she agreed to have sex with them, with predictable results. She got pregnant. Her child was forced from her into adoption, and her parents threw her out. Several suicide attempts followed, and a brush with cancer. Eventually she married, into a numb life in which she had three children because she was desperate to keep the affection of the one man who had shown her any respect. But the resulting depression, and another suicide attempt, led her to seek 'treatment'. From this point it is worth quoting her words at length, if only as a reminder of the shadows in which lesbians as well as gay men thrashed around, whatever their comparative legal status; also as a memorial to a woman who can only be called heroic:

> I saw the psychiatrist once a week, who prescribed tranquillisers, until on one visit he gave me an injection and under this drug I told him the truth. Then, for the first time in my life, I was told about homosexuality. Until then I had thought I was the only one who felt this way. But now it was explained to me, even knowing there were thousands like me, didn't help. I was frightened to death now. …
>
> The psychiatrist admitted me to the psychiatric wing of the hospital. Here it was decided to cure me of being a homosexual. I was given treatment. An electric current was attached to my wrist by means of a leather strap that looked like a dog collar. Attached to this strap were wires that led to a control box. This box controlled the extent of the shock to be given. I was then placed on a bed, soft lights were switched on and sweet music played, all to give it a romantic atmosphere. I was shown highly colourful pictures of women scantily dressed, then, when in the opinion of the doctor I had looked long enough to cause a sexual arousal, the electric shock was applied. This treatment was applied two or three times a day, for several weeks, until at one session I could stand the pain and torment no longer and I wrecked the control box. After this the treatment stopped for a while.
>
> Then I was moved to a room which I shared with another woman; she was very feminine, married with children. As I got to know her better she told me she was a lesbian. We became very close, and the doctor, realising this, moved her to another hospital. Now the treatment took a different form. Instead of pictures, I was asked to think of this women while suggestive ideas were put to me. Any response on my behalf resulted in a severe electric shock. This treatment carried on for weeks, each session making me more and more agitated, until once again I became violent, wrecking everything. Two days later I was transferred to a hospital in Southern England, where, on admittance, my nail file, scissors and any other sharp objects I had, were removed from my possession. I was placed under constant observation, only being allowed to mix with the other patients if a nurse was present.
>
> Over a period of months I was given hypnosis, tablets to remove any sexual feelings, injection upon injection, abreactions, until I couldn't even think straight. By the end I had no feelings and my spirit was broken. They had won.
>
> They were sure I was cured. Just one last test. Ink blots on cards were given me. I had to say what they looked like. I couldn't help it if the last one looked like two naked women facing each other, he'd asked me what I saw. He just smiled. Next morning I was informed I was being sent to a Civil Mental Hospital where I would be committed. My husband, on hearing this, immediately took me home.[144]

The family moved. There was a divorce. She got a job, met a gay boy who gave her some support, and then at work found another divorcée like herself:

> We were members of a local group and very active in organising fundraising events. For two years we were very happy, and then out of the blue we were asked to resign from the local committee. It was felt that we had been too close (though we had been very discreet for the children's sakes). We objected strongly but to no avail. At the same time I was working in a junior school, and the headmaster received a letter stating that it wasn't nice for me to be in such close contact with young girls, and unless I was dismissed the mothers would keep their children home. I lost my job. Teenage boys in the area started to make our lives hell. Whether I was with my friend or alone, they would call out loud enough for everyone to hear, 'Lesbian', 'Queer' and stand in a group making it impossible for us to pass, pulling at us, and making suggestive remarks. My friend had a nervous breakdown because of this and left the district, not only ending our relationship but also our friendship. Several months later I left the district myself.[145]

The story ends on a muted note of happiness and a remarkable lack of rancour:

> My children know I'm gay now. They don't love me any the less. They've seen what my life was like before, and the change in me now. I'm happy. I have peace of mind. I haven't got a partner or a special friend. I may never find one, but for the first time in my life, I belong. It may only be to a minority, but I belong.
>
> Even after all many ups and downs, I have only one regret, that I was never told the meaning of homosexuality while I was at school. Life has been a hard teacher and it would have saved myself and my family so much heartache and despair.[146]

As a woman editor, Gini was always anxious to include as many articles by women as she could. She herself wrote a regular column, 'Cheesecake', and a short-lived comic agony column under the name Sister George. She made up imaginary problems as a peg on which to hang satirical answers:

> I am 37 years old and am having an affair with a gorgeous blond who was just 16 last week. The problem is, I think he's cheating on me. We don't go to bed as much as first, and when we do get there I have to do all the work. I'm not happy. And it was the same with my last three affairs, who were respectively aged 17, 15 and 13. —Frustrated Chicken Hunter
>
> Dear FCH, Your problem besets many. Youth has many advantages but lacks experience. It is silly to expect complete physical and mental satisfaction with a sixteen-year-old; and the law as it stands is against you too. Why not aim for a few pullets in their twenties, or, better still, a hen in your own age group?[147]

This is hardly viciously satirical, rather a quite wise and pertinent comment on the endemic obsession with youth in gay culture. Today to mention affairs aged 15 and 13 so light-heartedly would be unthinkable, but it was not this that caused a storm. In the following issue appeared this Editorial written by Gini in response to the negative feedback she received:

> SISTER GEORGE IS DEAD! A friend's brutal reply to Sister George last month: 'I have taken your advice and happily now killed myself,' signed FCH'. In view of his and several others' respected opinions, Sister George, reluctantly, is withdrawn.[148]

The readership's puzzling over-reaction seems to indicate that there were many sensitive 'chicken hunters' among them who took the original piece personally.

Women were never more than 25 per cent of the membership, in London as elsewhere, but those who were members were dynamic, articulate women who punched well above their weight in terms of their contributions. The CHE groups they operated in were by and large supportive; however elsewhere there were groups which were *de facto* men only, and wished that they were men only *de jure* as well. Most of the misogyny is more covert than overt, with the faux-courtly passive-aggressive use of 'Ladies',* and its terror of 'Women's Lib':

> For some strange reason Women's Lib first appealed for my inferior support. I can't think why. The bra-burning bit turned me off … because I thought bras were only worn these days by transvestites anyway. Then I couldn't quite see what they were so steamed up about.[149]

The women, both in the Letters Page and in their articles, spent a large part of their energy explaining to an assumed male readership what they were doing and how it felt. Gillian Love Taylor picked up on the power of words, and in passing started the debate on the word 'Queer', which would be reclaimed in the later 1980s by activists, in much the same way the word 'Nigger' was reclaimed by Black activists: 'If gay people continue even jokingly to use this, we are internalising our oppression and describing ourselves as different from heterosexuals in a prejudicial way.' She also picked up on 'Ladies':

> In another article Alexon Massey frequently refers to some people as 'ladies'. Surely there are men and women, and distinctions such as ladies and gentlemen are false and chauvinistic. As often as not 'ladies' is used as

* The same assumptions can't be made about the use of the term 'girls', which was common through most of the 1970s on both male and female lips. Many lesbians, at least within CHE, would have referred to themselves as 'gay girls', and 'gay women' would have been the height of progressive feminism.

> a put-down for women. Likewise, over 18 adults are men and women, not as sometimes 'girls' or 'boys'. Why don't we give each other the benefit of being fully adult and fully human?[150]

Gini Stevens herself appealed to the men to put themselves in the women's place:

> I should like to know how a shy gay male would react to being faced with a room full of females? I can tell you that your first impulse at being the only woman there is to run. Gradually you grow used to being about as unobtrusive as Marlene Dietrich entertaining the troops. …
>
> Everyone is fantastically friendly, but such attentions can be daunting to those unaccustomed to them, and women are not always prepared to be as outspoken as men! …
>
> My advice is, if you *want* more women in your group, tread softly at first, don't overwhelm them with questions when you don't know them. Be friendly without being over-effusive. And don't get me wrong, BUT talks on 'cottages' or men's VD (illustrated in glorious colour!) are riveting topics for us as menstruation would be for you We can only inform others by overcoming the ignorance among ourselves.[151]

Beyond that, there were genuine discussions of women's issues, and a sense of women talking to other women:

> Many women have been pushed into the Women's Liberation Movement out of dissatisfaction with groups like CHE. For literally hundreds of years … women have been active in pressure groups of all kinds. … And almost without exception, although generally few in number, women have done the dirty work. We have arranged speakers, taken minutes, done the books, made the coffee and sandwiches, turned up in rotten weather, … but women have never determined policy, been in the limelight, taken credit for what we have done. … We women also feel guilty about concentrating on our own oppression. After all, we are taught that our womanliness consists in 'giving ourselves', caring for others, putting ourselves last. …
>
> While women are still expending their emotional and physical energies for overridingly male organisations, they are not using their energies for themselves and other women. … The sisters in CHE are working for a change in society's attitudes towards them. But public attitudes towards lesbians will never change unless the status and importance of the whole class of women changes. The attitudes of CHE's men to women seem little different from those of men at large, but space prevents my mentioning every instance of *Lunch* writers insulting and denigrating women. …
>
> We cannot demand respect from others when we do not yet feel it for ourselves. To do this we need our own organisations where *we* decide, where we refuse to play a subordinate part, where we are free to develop our potential as women.[152]

And there was extensive coverage of CHE women's conferences.* Nevertheless Gini still got flak for not enough women's articles, accused of ghettoising women into the 'Cheesecake' column. Liz Stanley, CHE's women's officer, wrote:

> As one of the 'girls' in CHE, I resent being allocated to the girls' corner, cheesecake or not; I resent being allocated to any corner because of my sex. I resent being patronised because I'm a woman. We spend a lot of time discussing how to attract more women into CHE; a beginning would be to stop trying to emulate the liberal-minded *Guardian* with its infamous women's page.

Gini's response was characteristically wry:

> The idea [of the 'Cheesecake' column] was to lend light relief to a magazine initially put out by a heavily male-orientated CHE; to be a sour, spicy, racy, bitchy incognito corner preferably drawn from the females' angle. … I'm sorry if you gathered that women are only relegated to that spot. There are few women/girls I haven't asked to submit articles to *Lunch*. Those that have have insisted on hiding their identity. … What more can I do? Use thumbscrews?[153]

She must, however, have been doing something right, because by the time she left in June 1973, there were more women subscribers than men.

In *Lunch* there were discussions of all the CHE concerns of the day, some of which shone a light into the lives of homosexuals whose predicaments at that time were never talked about elsewhere, and which subsequently became major topics of discussion and concern. For example, the issue of alcoholism among lesbians and gay men is still alive and well in 2014, with gay men three times more likely to become alcoholics than their straight counterparts. Only in the twenty-first century did dedicated support groups start to appear; Alcoholics Anonymous only took up the issue of alcohol abuse by lesbians and gay men in 2013. But in 1971 a reader wrote to *Lunch*:

> As a recovered alcoholic I naturally have spent a great deal too much time in pubs and drinking clubs and it was usually my experience to find gay bars a good deal less friendly and relaxed than were those which catered for a 'normal' clientele. Whereas in the 'normal' pub it was fairly easy to engage one's neighbour in conversation, in a gay bar I always ran the risk of a cold-shouldering snub or a hurting put-down. It was, therefore, my practice in these places to drink myself into such a condition that I could approach anyone and still feel inured to any resulting rebuff which might come my way.

---

* These are covered in detail in Volume Two, in the chapter 'Cases, causes and crises'.

> I do not, of course, blame my alcoholism on the frigid cliquish atmosphere of so many gay bars; I feel simply that my disease may have made me more acutely and self-destructively sensitive to something which has been the experience of many homosexuals who don't happen to look like the Apollo Belvedere. …
>
> Speaking personally I should find it a relief to be in a place where I did not feel obliged to buy a drink to justify my presence, but I also feel that as many means as possible of opening doors between gay people should be provided there, whether they wish at any given moment to have a sexual partner or simply a sympathetic listener.[154]

There was also talk of setting up a CHE Housing Co-operative, to combat discrimination by landlords and mortgage companies.* Attempts were made to start an Accommodation Bureau – 'Enthusiastic and energetic helpers will be needed to check on the existence and suitability etc. of accommodation' – and appeals went out for flats and houses, so that homosexuals could form gay or lesbian households and bypass the risk of bigoted eviction. It never took off, partly because of the administration involved and partly because too many offers came with sexual strings attached.†

Another member floated the idea of a gay Employment Agency; the idea of homosexuals going out of their way to employ other homosexuals was raised in the debates on the 1967 Sexual Offences Act as a possible consequence of the legalisation of homosexuality. This spectre of a 'gay mafia' seemed about to be realised.

The issue of gay marriage was discussed, as it was in the national *Bulletins*. For those in favour, the Netherlands provided the inspiration:

> There had been a marvellous reception for two Rotterdam gay boys who 'married' in 1967 – giving rise to a splash story in the *News of the World* (a few days before the Sexual Offences Act became law in Britain) with the screaming headline: COULD IT HAPPEN HERE? Just after the 'wedding ceremony' the two boys told me how wonderful everybody had been at the time of the 'marriage' and how neighbours had joined in like one happy family at the reception.[155]

During the debates in 2013 about the pros and cons of same-sex civil

* The first UK gay housing co-op, Stonewall Housing (no connection to the Stonewall lobbying group), was set up in 1983. It was named Stonewall (after the Stonewall riots in New York in June 1969) when the Charity Commissioners rejected the first name, Queer Street, on the grounds that it was offensive to homosexuals. In 2014 it provides supported housing for forty young LGBT people, as well as offering housing advice and campaigning.

† It was left to London's Gay Switchboard, which started in 1974, to run the first free accommodation helpline; this was one of its most popular services for many years.

marriage, many of those LGBT people supporting it, while never wanting it for themselves, saw it as a vital symbol of equality. 'A. H. W.' made this same point in a letter of 1973:

> Such feelings [of fear, guilt and self-hatred] cannot be given up until the causes are eliminated. The homosexual will always be a persecuted third-rate citizen until the following changes in our living pattern have been made:
>
> Legal marriages between those of the same sex come into being which rank *pari passu* with marriages between those of the opposite sex.
>
> Discrimination and fun-poking at homosexuals to be rebuked or even punished in a similar manner as racial discrimination is.[156]

The parallel demand, for legal protection against discrimination, was seen as more practicable than legalising gay relationships, and CHE-prompted attempts were made to tag it on to the Sex Discrimination Act of 1975. However in the twenty-first century legal recognition of same-sex relationships in the form of Civil Partnerships was to pip anti-discrimination measures to the legislative post by two years.

There were plenty, however, who wanted nothing to do with the trappings of Heterosexism and the Family, even when, as members of a reformist rather than revolutionary organisation, they thought marriage fine for the majority. One such was Julian Greensleeves:

> Equality with … is not the same as imitation of. … Whereas heterosexual marriage is a natural consequence of society, its homosexual counterpart strikes me as artificial and superfluous. When there is a union between two people of the same sex, where concern for the well-being of vulnerable offspring is irrelevant, the permanence of that union is not a prerequisite but an option. Homosexual marriage has no tradition and, when people want to initiate it, I wonder why. My impression is that a prop is wanted; they feel the need to shore up what otherwise might collapse, given the pressures which beset such a relationship. Marriage, instead of being merely consequent upon the union, becomes an end in itself. …
>
> Cannot the goals of those advocating such marriage [social recognition, joint mortgages etc.] be achieved without the foisting of a connubial charivari on the rest of us?[157]

No poll was ever taken of the CHE membership's approval of gay marriage, but it is probably fair to generalise that those on the 'right wing' were in favour, and those on the 'left wing' were against. There were similar left/right divisions over whether or not to offer legal and other support for men who cottaged:

> At the moment, what does the public know of us? They know – and see – that a lot of disgraceful things go on in their public conveniences. They

> have only to look at their walls. … And one must admit that the goings on in these places give us a bad name. It is time we were known for more than the sex angle we are known for now. …
>
> The average Gay person does not need such places. I am sure there is a great deal more for us than meeting complete strangers for a five-minute fling and then never meeting each other again. …
>
> The public will never accept us while we have a total disregard for their feelings. After all, it is us who are doing the asking and demanding. One feels that demonstrating and holding grand Balls in Kensington Town Hall will not free us either – in fact will only get us laughed at. One feels that being Gay must be dealt with in a manner the public will accept. … How much better to meet someone and settle down instead of going from one to the other, as if sex were our most important need. One true man is all I'd want.[158]

On the other side, there were those who even advocated setting up a CHE sauna. Peter Norman described a visit to one such in Amsterdam,* couched in comedic terms of guarded disapproval:

> Some couples relished an audience, and encouraged all comers to join in; others petulantly snapped the curtain shut against prying eyes … on the floor above, the scene was repeated with the addition of a large very dark room for public gropes, mainly patronised by those who looked their best in the dark … here every participant was offering himself as a sex object not a person. No polite conversation here with the old, the ugly and the shy. What could be more male-dominated? More of a ghetto? More sexist? … I wonder how many people don't make it, and I wonder whether actually watching others having it off makes their frustration far greater than an ordinary failure after an evening's drinking. And how many people become addicts – always believing that next time will be the one?[159]

However, 'T. R.' from Blackburn advocated saunas in much the same way as early AIDS organisations, particularly in America, urged health authorities to work through the bathhouses rather than close them down:

> I want CHE to have an interest in a sauna. I want to get people out of cottages, out of the commercial clubs and pubs. It will be a sexist ghetto, but it will be better than trolling on Wimbledon Common or having sex in the front seat of a car. Does everything have to be meaningful? Can't we have sex for mutual pleasure, and if afterwards a friendship develops, all well and good. Casual sex is here to stay and I for one would rather have it openly in an Amsterdam sauna than furtively in a London cottage.[160]

---

* He did not need to go so far; there were saunas in London in the early 1970s, as well as Turkish baths, which attracted homosexual men.

These arguments and issues show the extent to which CHE collectively subscribed to the 'assimilation' movement of Western reformist gay organisations of the post-war period, but also a significant dissent within the organisation insisting that homosexuals were not just heterosexuals whose sexual interests pointed in a different direction.

The magazine had regular injections of humour as well, some of it gently poking fun at CHE itself. Even by 1972 the organisation had a reputation for top-heavy bureaucracy:

> Not everyone appreciates the organisation that goes on behind the scenes of any great national campaign. We asked one of the 3,261 vice-presidents of the Be-Nice-To-Norms Committee to let us see a sample of the 94-page minutes of the executive committee. …
>
> Present: All those who hadn't fallen out with each other since the last meeting.
>
> Apologies for absence: inc. Michael and Tony's friend Baroness P., Michael and Tony, Ivor and *his* friend Ricky, ANTONY GREY (who hadn't been invited). …
>
> The Chairman's Resignation: It was formally agreed that the Chairman had not resigned; he had only fallen asleep. …
>
> The General Secretary asked to go to the lavatory: As everyone seemed anxious to follow him the meeting was formally declared closed, after 13 hours 23 minutes .05 seconds discussion. (Thank you, Lenny. Lovely timekeeping as usual.)[161]

These arguments and topics, even the humour, would have been of general interest to a readership beyond CHE. Since the magazine found itself on sale in bookshops and newspaper kiosks within six months of starting, it needed a wider appeal. However it never completely shed its other brief of being the in-house CHE journal. Its coverage of CHE events could be idiosyncratic, personal and vivid. Sometimes it is the only record which survives of key events. Rodney Slatford was at the first CHE visit to Speakers' Corner on 25 June 1972:

> CHE was obviously going strong somewhere, because long before I reached our pitch I recognised a blue leaflet tucked under the arm of a dog-collared clergyman. A coloured lady who squeezed past me looked at my badge, then at my face, wrinkled her nose in disapproval, and walked off. She must have been one of the few not deeply struck by the sincerity with which Vivian Waldron was quietly putting our case to a mostly amused, but seldom hostile, public. There he was, on his kitchen steps, quite openly telling everybody how he viewed his own sexuality, and the enjoyment he got from being homosexual. He had accepted his condition, which was quite incurable (No, of course it's not a disease) and was all the happier for doing so. Congratulations to him for being the perfect

> advertisement for male homosexuals; let's hope that he will give us a repeat performance.
>
> It was the girls' turn next. Jackie Forster mounted the steps and spoke clearly and impressively about the plight of lesbians. She told us all what a lesbian was (WE knew, but I suspect many of THEM didn't). It was good to hear the feminine angle. … I doubt whether anyone could have put the ladies' point over better. 'Don't worry that we will run off with your husbands, dears. We're just not interested!!'
>
> Don Hendry was next, who explained that he had brought up five children on his own and that he was also gay. No, he wouldn't want his kids to be homosexual, although the choice wasn't his.
>
> Gini Stevens brought out the point that we were a larger minority than black people in this country and not just interested in sex, despite our label, before persistent heckling made her abandon the stand.[162]

49. Jackie Forster at Speakers' Corner

While some of the speakers' remarks are very much of their time and smack of self-oppression, nothing can detract from the sheer guts of those taking part. The level of hatred shown to speakers could be terrifying, like the venom shown by the woman who said that if you became a homosexual you were a whore, and couldn't enter the Kingdom of Heaven; then spat in the face of Vivian Waldron.

But the speakers learned, too. Big, big boards to advertise who they were; thousands of cheap throwaway leaflets; repeating the same message every fifteen minutes because the crowd is constantly changing. One thing however it took a long time to learn; CHE had an almost mystical belief in liberalism, and in allowing a platform to opponents who would never have reciprocated the courtesy:

> Please, may we never allow one of the opposition onto the box. We are there to promote *our* cause – not to be told by some rather off man that he is 'wearing a chastity belt, back and front, in case we get him, and that he'd chop 'em off.'[163]

But there were aspects of this navel-gazing which would never have appealed to the outside reader. At best, such pieces were a matter of indifference, such as the extended notes on each of the new members of the national EC elected in May 1972. At worst it was washing the filthiest of dirty linen in public, as when Roger Baker lambasted the LCC so strongly that scorch marks seem to appear on the paper:

> At one or two meetings I have met young Derek Brookfield who is looking for office premises. But not only is he doing that single-handed, he is also, it seems, having to visit each group to persuade them to offer money for the project. And no doubt if as and when Derek has, single-handed, got the money and the office, it will be Derek who has to ensure that it is adequately staffed and run. Frankly, I find this appalling. We have seen it happen before; an eager guy comes to help, everything is put on him, then he meets indifference and goes away. So much for the Management Committee's wonderful move towards 'organising people to give effect to the strong wishes … for a London office.'
>
> Then the LMC* has taken four hours, eleven people and lots of sandwiches to 'make the provisional appointment of a new membership secretary'. Gosh.
>
> And then, 'a revision of the methods used for inducting new members into London CHE.' This is a massive joke. The immediate results of this dynamic move was that at my last new members' meeting four people turned up who had been before. And I am still getting calls from people who attended meetings here weeks, months ago and have not yet heard from anyone. … The LMC is irrelevant, inefficient and incompetent.[164]

Gini was never one to allow the dictates of Public Relations to get in the way of lively copy.

The physical quality of *Lunch* improved over the years. From a nasty thick sawdust-like cover it moved to semi-gloss by Issue 9. Proper typesetting improved the appearance from Issue 15. It grew from 14 pages to 40 at its peak. Photographs, which originally looked like poor photocopies, became

* London Management Committee.

both clear and pleasurable, and the layout became more professional. However, by June 1973 *Lunch* was in crisis. With Gini gone and no obvious successor, it was now losing money, after having broken even or better for more than a year. It was losing readership, and even identity, to the new *Gay News*, now firmly established at the end of its first year as *the* national gay magazine. What was *Lunch* for, when *Gay News* did so much of what it did, but better?

There was a three-month hiatus, after which it re-emerged as a much glossier, more arts-oriented, and more intellectual magazine, with less CHE content and scant female writing. It failed to find its market, and folded with more losses, paid for from the London Building Fund, and by long-suffering London local groups. Ironically, the editor for the last issues was David Seligman, a former member of GLF and one of the founders of the very *Gay News* which killed *Lunch* off. By 1974, *Gay News* would itself become the 'house journal' of CHE.*

The original pan-London meeting had spawned three major projects. Of these FRIEND was by far the most successful, as a counselling organisation which brought support to thousands of lesbians and gay men over the next forty years, with a kind of individual personal attention which was impossible to provide in an ordinary CHE group.† Many more people benefited from referral to sympathetic specialist help, where before it would have been pot luck whether or not they ran across a homophobic doctor, social worker or priest. Moreover, the training which lesbian and gay volunteers got within FRIEND gave some a taste for this kind of work, and as a result far more open lesbians and gay men entered the caring professions as therapists of one kind or another. FRIEND also greatly increased the sensitivity of other, non-gay, support organisations towards LGBT issues, through their own outreach training programmes.

Though the London club project ran into the ground from a combination of house price inflation, lack of finance and lack of specialist skills, it did at least start what became a London institution and a fixture in the LGBT calendar, the Winter Fairs (later Winter Pride), which lasted twenty years.

Lunch was a key magazine in the history of gay publishing, and the one which, over the 30 months of its existence, staked out most of the territory which subsequent lesbian and gay magazines also cultivated. It took the political seriousness of the in-house CHE *Bulletin* and married it to the more popular formats and interests of the 'fluffy' *Jeremy*. Perhaps most importantly,

---

* Seligman subsequently edited a short-lived magazine called *After Lunch*.

† By 2014 most of the regional Friend groups had disappeared, but London Friend was still flourishing with its own premises in King's Cross, which also served as CHE's London address.

it became the platform on which the arguments were played out about gay identity and gay values, about what being homosexual meant and how it could be expressed. *Gay News* benefited greatly from it, and, through *Gay News*, most subsequent journals up to *The Pink Paper*, as well as a host of regional magazines.

However, not content with its *grands projets*, London CHE was at the same time throwing up more local groups across the city, and a mushrooming series of specialist groups – social, cultural and political – of such variety and prolixity that by mid-1973 any gay or lesbian Londoner could have filled every night of their week twice over with companionable homo activity. This remarkable explosion of energy and talent, and the creation of a self-consciously homosexual culture, is the subject of the next chapter.

Notes to Chapter Five

1 Jeremy Seabrook, 'An evening in the Royal Oak', from *A lasting relationship*, 122.

2 Peter Norman, interviewed by the author, 25 February 2014.

3 Ibid.

4 D. R. G. Neaumann-Cooke, 'Minutes of first meeting of Group A discussion group', 2 March 1965. HCA/ NORMAN/1.

5 D. R. G. Neaumann-Cooke, 'Homosexual lifestyles'. Undated [1965]. HCA/NORMAN /1.

6 D. R. G. Neaumann-Cooke, 'Letter to Group A members', undated [1965]. HCA/NORMAN /1.

7 Ibid.

8 Peter Norman, interviewed by the author, 25 February 2014.

9 Paul Temperton to Allan Horsfall, 'Latest news on local groups', 15 July 1970. HCA/CHE/5/1/73.

10 Roger Baker to Paul Temperton, 'George Mortimer', 5 September 1970. HCA/CHE/5/3/21.

11 George Mortimer to Allan Horsfall, 'NCSS', 26 July1970. HCA/CHE/ 5/1/73.

12 Roger Baker to Paul Temperton, 'London report', 1 September 1970. HCA/CHE/5/3/21.

13 Alan Wakeman, interviewed by the author, 15 April 2014.

14 Roger Baker to Paul Temperton, 'Local groups report', 29 August 1970. HCA/CHE/5/3/21.

15 Roger Baker to Paul Temperton, 'Report on Kingsway Group', 22 October 1970. HCA/CHE/5/3/21.

16 David Forsyth, Leaflet about the Paintbox Club, 19 October 1970. HCA/CHE/Norman/5.

17 John D. Stamford, 'Viewpoint – the homosexual revolution', *Spartacus*, 13 (July 1970), 5.

18 J. Marley and N. Myers, 'A boom time for the male order game', *Brighton Evening Argus,* 14 December 1970, 4.

19 Ibid.

20 Paul Temperton, CHE *Bulletin*, Jan/ Feb 1971, HCA/CHE/4/1, 4.

21 Editor's Letter, *Spartacus*, 14 (August 1970), 4.

22 Roger Baker, 'CHE', *Spartacus*, 19 (January 1971), 35–36.

23 David Seligman, 'A gay life – we interview Roger Baker', *After Lunch*, 1/2 (Winter 1976), 18–19.

24 Ibid.

[25] Ibid.

[26] Ibid.

[27] Baker, *Drag*, 27.

[28] Ibid, 29.

[29] David Seligman, 'A gay life – we interview Roger Baker', *After Lunch*, 1/2 (Winter 1976), 18–19.

[30] Andrew Lumsden, interviewed by the author, 10 April 2014.

[31] Michael Moor, interviewed by the author, 9 September 2012.

[32] 'Yes, there may be many like him, but is Jeremy really so gay?' *Daily Mirror*, 8 August 1969, 11.

[33] Ibid.

[34] Michael Moor, interviewed by the author, 9 September 2012.

[35] George Mortimer, 'London groups', CHE *Bulletin*, August 1970. HCA/CHE/Norman/1, 1.

[36] Michael Moor, interviewed by the author, 9 September 2012.

[37] Roger Baker to Paul Temperton, 'George Mortimer', 5 September 1970. HCA/CHE/5/3.

[38] Roger Baker to Paul Temperton, 'Meeting of London convenors, 24 November 1970. HCA/CHE/5/3/24.

[39] Roger Baker, 'Progress report', *Lunch* 1 (September 1971).

[40] Brian Sewell, interviewed by the author, 20 September 2012.

[41] Ibid.

[42] Brian Sewell, *Outsider II*, 47.

[43] Roger Baker to Allan Horsfall, 'London Groups progress report', 7 January 1971. HCA/CHE/5/3.

[44] Paul Temperton, interviewed by the author, 28 March 2011.

[45] Peter Norman, interviewed by the author, 25 February 2014.

[46] Ibid.

[47] Robin Bloxsidge, interviewed by the author, 27 August 2012.

[48] Glenys Parry, interviewed by the author, 27 August 2012.

[49] Tony Ryde, interviewed by the author, 5 December 2012.

[50] Ibid.

[51] 'Group News', *Lunch*, 1 (September 1971), 11.

[52] 'London CHE', *Lunch*, 10 (July 1972), 24.

[53] Jackie Forster, interviewed by Margot Farnham, May 1990. NSA/C456/87/05.

[54] Roger Baker, 'London Report', CHE *Bulletin*, November 1970. HCA/CHE/4/1/5, 3.

[55] Brian Sewell, interviewed by the author, 20 September 2012.

[56] David Hyde, 'Ring the changes', *Lunch*, 6 (March 1972), 11.

[57] Ibid.

[58] Ibid.

[59] Roger Baker to Paul Temperton, 'London developments', 20 November 1970. HCA/CHE/5/3.

[60] 'Homosexuals are not to be frowned upon', *Waltham Forest Guardian and Gazette*, 4 December 1970, 7.

[61] Tony Ryde to Paul Temperton, 'About Waltham Forest', 15 June 1971. HCA/CHE/5/3.

[62] Paul Temperton to Tony Ryde, 'About Waltham Forest CHE', 21 June 1971. HCA/CHE/5/60/7.

[63] Mike Winter to Michael De-la-Noy, 'Group plans', 10 May 1971. HCA/CHE/2/1/20.

[64] Mike Winter, 'Walthamstow CHE group constitution', ratified 17 May 1971. HCA/CHE/2/1/20.

[65] Paul Temperton, 'Briefing to EC', 23 October 1971. HCA/CHE/2/1/20.

[66] Paul Temperton to Terry Johnson, 'Mike Winter', 15 October 1971. HCA/CHE/5/55/107.

[67] Tony Ryde, Minutes of meeting, 2 April 1971. HCA/CHE/Williams/26.

[68] Peter Norman, 'Notes on public speaking for local groups talk', 1972. HCA/CHE/Norman/8.

[69] Tony Ryde, Minutes of meeting, 2 April 1971. HCA/CHE/Williams/26.

[70] Ibid.

[71] Peter Robins, interviewed by the author, 20 September 2012.

[72] Tony Ryde, interviewed by the author, 2 September 2012.

[73] Ibid.

[74] Michael Launder, 'Report to the CHE Malvern Conference'. HCA/CHE/2/17/71.

[75] Ibid.

[76] Michael Launder to Michael De-la-Noy, 'Proposed Task Force', 11 June 1971. HCA/AT/7/84.

[77] H. Robertson, 'Newsdesk: FRIEND', *Lunch* 3 (November 1971) 16-17.

[78] Ibid.

[79] Ibid.

[80] Michael Launder, 'Report on FRIEND to the EC', 17 May 1972. HCA/CHE/2/1/67.

[81] H. Robertson, 'Friend in the dark', *Lunch*, 7 (April 1972), 24-25.

[82] H. Robertson and Michael Butler, 'Hints on befriending', *Lunch*, 9 (June 1972), 15.

[83] Michael Launder, 'Report to the CHE Malvern Conference'. HCA/CHE/2/17/71.

[84] Alan Swerdlow, interviewed by the author, 10 September 2012.

[85] Sue Wise, interviewed by the author, 17 August 2012.

[86] Liz Stanley, interviewed by the author, 17 August 2012.

[87] Michael Launder, 'Friend – at work', *Lunch* 16 (January 1973), 10–12

[88] Ibid.

[89] Bernard Greaves, interviewed by the author, 18 September 2012.

[90] Michael Launder, Report to the EC, 17 May 1972. HCA/CHE/2/1/13.

[91] NFHO, 'Report on conference on befriending, 2–3 September 1972'. HCA/AT/14/104, 2.

[92] Manchester FRIEND, 'Guidelines to befrienders', undated. HCA/CHE/7/125.

[93] Ibid.

[94] Tony Ryde, Report to EC meeting, 6 February 1973. HCA/CHE/Norman/11.

[95] Ibid.

[96] Ibid.

[97] David Kerr, 'Letter from Albany Society to CHE EC', 29 May 1973, quoted in Ted Clapham, 'Report to EC of 10 June 1973'. HCA/CHE/2/2/74.

[98] Tony Ryde, interviewed by the author, 5 December 2012.

[99] Peter Robins, interviewed by the author, 20 September 2012.

[100] Roger Baker, 'The Winter Fair', *Lunch*, 4 (December 1971), 13–14.

[101] William Blackledge, 'Memo 1 to group convenors', September 1971. HCA/Williams/26.

[102] William Blackledge to London group convenors, 'What do members want?', 11 February 1972. HCA/Williams/26.

[103] Peter Robins, interviewed by the author, 20 September 2012.

[104] 'CHE shows the way', *Gay News*, 11, undated [1972].

[105] 'Alan', 'All the fun of the fair,' *Lunch*, 15 (December 1972), 18-19.

[106] Ralph Norton, 'Fragment found in Great James Street', *Lunch*, 15 (December 1972), 19.

[107] Brian Sewell, 'Our need for roots: the question of club premises', *Lunch*, 1 (September 1971), 5–6.

[108] Brian Sewell, Peter Robins and Michael Moor, 'People not Paper', 1971. HCA/CHE/7/101.

109 David Smith to Teck Ong, 'London Centre fundraising', 14 September 1971. HCA/Williams/26.

110 Tony Ryde, 'Report on Centre finances for the EC', 4 December 1971. HCA/CHE/Norman/8.

111 Michael Steed, 'Report to EC meeting', 15 January 1972. HCA/CHE/2/1/46.

112 CHE EC minutes, 15 January 1972. HCA/CHE/2/1/26.

113 Michael Moor, Newsdesk: Our Own Place', *Lunch,* 10 (June 1972), 18.

114 LCC, 'Report to EC Meeting', 25 November 1972. HCA/CHE/2/1/110.

115 Ibid.

116 Ibid

117 Brian Sewell, interviewed by the author, 20 September 2012.

118 Report from the Club Working Party, discussed at London Monday Group AGM, 25 March 1974. HCA/CHE/Norman/10.

119 Tony Ryde, interviewed by the author, 5 December 2012.

120 Derek Brookfield, 'Premises, premises!', *Lunch*, 11 (August 1972), 27.

121 Group One, Minutes of meeting, 6 August 1971. HCA/Williams/26.

122 Michael Steed, CHELIC Briefing Paper for EC, 14 October 1972. HCA/CHE/3/1/19.

123 'CHELIC: A meeting place', *Lunch*, 19 (April 1973), 30.

124 'Scrubbers Party', *LMG Newsletter*, January 1973. HCA/CHE/7/91.

125 Peter Norman, interviewed by the author, 25 February 2014.

126 Michael Yelland to Paul Temperton, 'London members', 7 August 1972. HCA/CHE/60/39.

127 Paul Temperton to Martin George, 'London members', 31 July 1972. HCA/CHE/59/36.

128 Peter Robins, interviewed by the author, 20 September 2012.

129 *Kensington CHE Newsletter*, December 1973. HCA/CHE/Norman/10.

130 Ed Smith to Ian Buist, 'Visit to CHELIC etc.', 23 January 1973. HCA/EPHEMERA/1233/8.

131 Peter Norman to Audrey Barry, 'Access to CHELIC', undated [late 1973?]. HCA/CHE/Norman/10.

132 Joe Taylor to Volunteers, undated [September 1973 ?]. HCA/CHE/NORMAN/11.

133 T. Williams to Martin George, 'Levy for CHELIC', 1 May 1974. HCA/CHE/5/60/69.

134 Barrie Kenyon, 'Treasurer's Report to LCC', 7 April 1976. HCA/CHE/7/100.

135 Brian Sewell, interviewed by the author, 20 September 2012.

136 Tony Ryde, 'Minutes of pan-London Meeting', 2 April 1971. HCA/CHE/WILLIAMS/26.

137 David Hyde, 'CHE and *Lunch*', *Lunch*, 4 (December 1971), 24.

138 David Smith, 'Intolerable form of censorship', *Lunch*, 7 (April 1972), 33.

139 Leeds GLF, *Broadsheet* 4, February 1972. HCA/CHE/NORMAN 6.

140 George Melly, 'George Melly', *Lunch*, 8 (May 1972), 6–11.

141 Quentin Crisp, 'Brazen homosexual', *Lunch*, 10 (July 1972), 10–15.

142 David Hockney, 'Profile', *Lunch*, 12, (September 1972), 4–8.

143 Jimmy Savile, '*Speakeasy* with Jimmy Savile', *Lunch*, 17 (February 1973), 4-7.

144 'B. M. M.', 'A homosexual woman's story', *Lunch*, 18 (March 1973), 18–20.

145 Ibid.

146 Ibid.

147 'Sister George', 'Sister George replies', *Lunch*, 12 (September 1972), 20.

[148] Gini Stevens, 'Editorial', *Lunch*, 13 (October 1972), 3.

[149] Alexon Massey, 'The right crate for a clockwork orange', *Lunch*, 13 (October 1972), 20.

[150] Gillian Love Taylor, 'Commenting on October *Lunch*…', *Lunch*, 16 (January 1973), 25–26.

[151] 'Cheesecake', 'Why so few women in CHE?', *Lunch*, 2 (October 1971) [but says September on inside front contents page], 7.

[152] S. Philips, 'Letter of solidarity to my sisters in CHE', *Lunch*, 8 (May 1972) 12–13.

[153] Liz Stanley and Gini Stevens, Letters, *Lunch*, 12 (September 1972), 25.

[154] H. Robertson, Letters to the Editor, *Lunch*, 1 (September 1971), 6.

[155] Griffith Vaughan Williams, 'That wonderful Dutch acceptance', *Lunch*, 11 (August 1972), 9.

[156] 'A. H. W.', 'Homosexuals need to wear badges', *Lunch*, 20 (May 1973), 24.

[157] Julian Greensleeves, 'What's the point of single-sex marriages?' *Lunch*, 16 (January 1973), 26.

[158] D. Rampton, 'Look to ourselves', *Lunch*, 2 (October 1971), 9.

[159] Peter Norman, 'Innocent in the sauna', *Lunch*, 14 (November 1972), 16–17.

[160] 'TR', 'Come out of the clouds, Peter!', *Lunch*, 15 (December 1972), 37.

[161] Michael De-la-Noy, 'It is agreed I sign…' *Lunch*, 22 (October 1973), 31.

[162] Rodney Slatford, 'Speakers' Corner', *Lunch*, 11 (August 1972), 16–17.

[163] Ibid.

[164] Roger Baker, 'Letter on the Centre,' *Lunch*, 12 (September 1972), 28.

Chapter Six: Special Interests

Contents

The London factor

London is very big, and very rich. As such it generates one fifth of the UK's GDP with one seventh of the population. It sucks in capital and talent, those seeking high culture and those pursuing personal freedom. It offers anonymity and escape. No wonder, then, that so many homosexuals have gravitated to London to become the people they know themselves to be. They have also in the last century found a pre-existent subculture to become part of. There are no accurate figures for the relative population density of homosexuals in different parts of the country, but it is generally agreed that the greatest lavender concentration is in the capital.

This gives lesbian and gay Londoners the opportunity for the luxury of separatism. In a town which is only large enough to support one gay bar, you are likely to find in that bar both lesbians and gay men, young people and old, and a whole variety of sexualities and sexual interests. In London, and to a lesser extent in other large cities such as Manchester, there have been historically sufficient homosexuals of a shared taste to support a leather bar (Princess of Prussia, Coleherne), a 'chicken' bar (Father Redcap), an 'elephant's graveyard' (City of Quebec), a clone bar (King's Arms), a drag bar (Vauxhall Tavern), and clubs and bars for women (Royal Oak, the Gateways).

It also makes it more possible to have arguments and fallings-out without dire consequence. In that small-town bar, where there is a quarrel or a major and bitter break-up of a relationship, someone is going to find themselves out in the cold, unless the transaction is handled with grace. If the same thing happens in a large city, there is always another group to go to, or to found; if a relationship sunders, plenty more fish in the sea. Whatever the belief, argument, principle or row, you are likely to find others who will agree with you, support you, or follow you. Within the history of CHE, there are fallings-out in groups in a variety of places, large and small; but never so bitter, so fractious and so frequent as in London.

Equally, in the sociable alternative to the commercial scene, when there is a sufficient number of people with another shared interest apart from their sexuality, it becomes possible to set up groups to cater to that interest. The effect of this is twofold. Firstly, for those who take part it expands ideas of what 'being homosexual' means, not by the either/or, lust/love binaries associated with the word 'homophile', but by adding layers of activity and relationships on top of the emotional/sexual affects associated with defining as homosexual. Secondly, where the activity involves the creative arts (writing/performing etc.) there are the beginnings of a self-consciously gay culture. Those identified as homosexual are reaching to an audience which is also identified as homosexual, in a virtuous circle which allows shared terms of reference, exploration of shared dilemmas, the humour of recognised circumstance, common cause. This affirmation contributes to, and reinforces, a sense of community, in the way that Yiddish theatre reinforced New York Jewish communities, or blues bound together black communities in the Southern States. Music hall songs did much the same for working class audiences in Britain in the late nineteenth and early twentieth centuries.

This chapter explores the ways in which CHE members in London created that diversity of special interests, allowing several types of social relationships, and also, through performance, a particular kind of affirmative gay culture. At the same time new members continued to pour in throughout 1971–72, so that by the beginning of 1973 there were twelve numbered CHE groups, as well as several geographically based ones.

London Group 6

Little is known of Group 6, since it produced no newsletter The first formal meeting was on 19 May 1971 at the Coach and Horses off Oxford Street. The first chairman, Ken Glazier, was previously a member of London Group 2, and was known as a 'national loyalist', and an opponent of any form of London separatism. He was also a stickler for formality and working to the constitutional letter, developing a fine feud with Brian Sewell over what he saw as Sewell's participation in 'a monster that was getting out of control'. Sewell in turn labelled him one of the 'couch potatoes'; those who would stick 'on a point of order, Mr Chairman', and find umpteen reasons why anything shouldn't be done.

The group itself was active enough to organise a coach trip to Brighton for all the London groups in September that year. Despite Sewell's strictures, Glazier was sufficiently respected to be nominated as a candidate for the National Executive in the first elections, although he did not, in the end, choose to stand. He was one of the instigators of the London-wide Political Action Group, founded to combat what was generally seen as the political apathy of most London groups; clearly Sewell's opinion was a partial one. He remained involved in the group as chairman for the next five years, someone who was most comfortable within a smaller, more secure and more familiar ambit.* The Group changed its name to Marylebone CHE† in January 1973, and continued an equally even, uneventful, and blameless life under its new name.

* In 1974 Ken founded The [Gay] Transport Group, still flourishing in 2014. He also wrote a number of books about London buses.

† Later it became Marylebone and Paddington CHE, known as MaryPad. In 2014 it was the last surviving local CHE group (others have continued under other names).

London Group 7 (Croydon)

London Group 7 started formally at almost exactly the same time as London Group 6, although it had grown informally over the previous nine months. Groups 1 to 7 were founder members of the LCC, according to the constitution the committee adopted on 7 June. It also started the trend to localisation by becoming the first group within the capital to identify itself with a geographical area. That this happened was largely down to a high-class and very well-known Greek hairdresser and psychic, Andy V;* Andy, who was bisexual and had a salon in Covent Garden, was taken by a friend to a meeting of the Kingsway Group† in the summer of 1970. It was a large meeting, nearly a hundred people, and he went back twice. The group drew members from all over London, and among them were a couple of people from Croydon. They started talking about what a dump Croydon was from the gay point of view, with but a few bleak toilets, which were subject to police raids. From this conversation, Andy decided to start hosting tea-parties at weekends in his large semi-basement flat in South Norwood. These continued for several months, and grew by word of mouth. As word got around, so did Andy's telephone number. He started getting large numbers of calls from people wanting sex, and so changed his phone number and gave up on the gatherings.

By this time a group had cohered. Among the people in it were several who were already CHE members and, in addition to coming to Norwood, went to one of the groups already meeting in the West End. Among these was Wallace Grevatt, a Modern History lecturer in his thirties. He came into CHE as a gay man who had the experience behind him to be confident of his sexuality: 'At his minor public school he thought every boy was homosexual; at Bangor University he discovered some students were not.'[1]

He and his boyfriend Malcolm Martindale (Group Secretary) were both prominent in local Liberal Party politics, and friends of Michael Steed. Wallace had a slight trace of a Welsh accent and wore a rather obvious wig. At one time he had wanted to get into the BBC, and continued to maintain contacts there as an unofficial historian of broadcasting. He was an outdoor type, but also an inveterate collector. It didn't take much to get him to show off his complete collection of old copies of *Radio Times*, and in later years he was to write a history‡ of *Children's Hour*.§ He lived in Reigate; though hardly near

---

* To this day he remains in the closet.

† Andy's memory of the details is hazy, but the Kingsway Group was the only group it could have been on this timeline and in this area.

‡ *BBC Children's Hour*, ed. Trevor Hill, Book Guild 1988.

§ BBC Radio's young people's service which broadcast seven days a week, 5–6 p.m., from 1922 to 1964.

Croydon, it was only half an hour by train, and it was a lot easier to get to Croydon than to Kingsway.

By September 1971 the group was calling itself the Croydon Group and producing its first local group newsletter – the first, indeed, in the country. Its first meetings were at the house of a member, Rex Ingram, but by June 1971 it was meeting at the Cherry Orchard, a large mock-Tudor 1930s roadhouse five minutes' walk from East Croydon station. From the start it seems to have been quite a serious group. Grevatt, with his understanding of a conventional political party, made sure they took rather dry and formal proposals about constitutions and structures seriously.

The early newsletters radiate tremendous energy:

> All sorts of plans and ideas are under way in Croydon CHE! It is all tremendously exciting. It's great to hear from so many in the group and over the phone how they share the committee's enthusiasm. …
>
> Be Gay with CHE and Enjoy Each Day, it's Great to be Gay![2]

This almost breathless eagerness is characteristic of Wallace throughout his six years in CHE, and one of his great gifts was to rope large numbers of people in for projects, and to inspire them. Sometimes it was patronising, sounding like a scoutmaster whipping his reluctant patrols along a cross-country run; sometimes, when trying to persuade people into something he knew they really didn't want to do, it sounded desperate. But within the Croydon group, it worked. They were active in the campaign against David Reuben's book, *Everything You Wanted to Know About Sex, but were Afraid to Ask.** Wallace and the group also organised crash pads for sixty people for the first CHE National Council† to be held in London, in December 1971.

Like many groups, they found problems with getting advertisements into local papers ('We do not accept ads of this nature' – *Surrey Mirror* Group). The *Croydon Advertiser* likewise turned them down. Wallace took these refusals up in energetic correspondence with the papers' editors, but got no change out of them. But there was hope:

> A Catford member has told us about another group he belongs to, a group of 50/50 homo and hetero.‡ I will try to get a link-up. I understand from him that the *South London Press* will carry an ad. Could we therefore include the paper in the new attempt, please? … We realise that there is so much

* For more on this campaign, see Volume Two.

† For more about CHE structure and National Councils, see Volume Two.

‡ This is Rev. Tony Cross's Integroup, an assimilationist organisation of people of varied sexualities. The first Integroup was in Catford in 1970, the second in Golders Green in 1972.

> that can be done – so many in our area that need to be contacted – we want an all-out recruitment drive.[3]

The need was demonstrated by letters from people who wrote in to the newsletter. Wallace quoted one such in a letter to National Office:

> I know you'll understand when I say I hope you can realise how important a piece of paper like this is to someone to whom the dates it contains are the only landmarks in an immediate future that is like an uncharted minefield.[4]

This sense, that there were numberless isolated homosexuals 'out there' who would benefit from CHE, if only some way could be found to tell them about it, was common to nearly all local groups, but especially those frustrated by rejection from local newspapers or councils. Croydon CHE came up with a radical idea. They would put leaflets through letter boxes, much as canvassers at Election Time did. Rather than go out on a limb, Wallace Grevatt ran the idea past National Office:

> Our object is to divide the Croydon area into districts and circulate the houses and flats systematically street by street. ... We would also like to know that our proposed scheme will not in any way offend the law, especially as we will not be using envelopes for distribution.[5]

And he sent a copy of their proposed leaflet for clearance. Paul Temperton and Allan Horsfall heard the alarm bells, although they were careful not to stifle group initiative explicitly:

> We are a little concerned about the plan because the distribution of literature to households which have not asked for it is a new departure for CHE and one which might cause some hostile reaction from un-sympathetic recipients of our literature. Although such people have no legal redress against us, they could make rather a lot of fuss about it, and you may consider that this might be counterproductive. Our advice therefore would be that you should only go ahead with this plan in the knowledge that you may have to cope with a certain amount of hostility.[6]

Not to put too fine a point on it, Paul and Allan were shitting themselves. Any hostility was far more likely to come their way than Wallace's, and 'a certain amount' was magnificent understatement. The warning, though, was sufficient; Wallace decided the group was not strong enough to cope with hostility and existing members would run a mile. The plan was officially 'postponed', unofficially dropped. In some ways this was characteristic of Wallace, who, behind his façade of confidence and bonhomie, was a man beset with doubts about whether he was doing the right thing and needed constant reassurance and support from 'people in authority'.

At the beginning of 1972, the group had another problem, this time with The Cherry Orchard. For the first meeting of the New Year, John Eden was the first to arrive, to set out the room, and he knocked as usual on the side door.* He was told in no uncertain terms that the group was no longer welcome. Hastily they decided to reconvene at a nearby member's flat. John stood guard at the pub to redirect people, and over thirty members squeezed into Tony Naylor's living room. The evening was saved, and almost immediately they moved to The Greyhound, a large rather beaten-up music venue† not far from the Fairfield Halls. For formal meetings they used the local Unitarian church hall.

In one way getting chucked out of 'The Cherry Orchard' was their own fault. They had never told the landlord what the group was – Wallace's uncertainty again:

> In passing let me stress that if no other lesson is to be learned from this murky tale, it is always best to inform the proprietor exactly who you represent rather than vaguely mutter about it's being a group meeting to discuss current affairs. At the time we thought it propitious to conceal our true identity; during the whole eight months period the management never asked us to divulge any further information. …
>
> Members will recall negotiating invariably past a bloody great Alsatian which roamed the corridors, and often the heating facilities were Spartan; in fact it was usually the licensee's wife who made sure we had some warmth. … At the December meeting several of us observed policemen snooping around the building, and a late arrival actually saw two constables listening in outside the door of our meeting room.[7]

Some groups were happily ensconced at the same venue for years. The London Monday Group stayed at the Chepstow Arms in Notting Hill for over fifteen years. Others such as Croydon and Wandsworth were plagued with venue difficulties. It is significant how meekly they put up with these. When GLF members were refused service at the Champion in September 1971, the response was a sit-in which led to five arrests. Croydon CHE by contrast wrote letters of protest to the licensee and the directors of Charrington's, and got a very bland brush-off from Mr A. R. Baxter to the effect that it was up to the licensee to decide who he served; though there was talk of taking it further, they had no idea how to do so. It wasn't until 1975, at the Annual Conference in Sheffield, that enough members were sufficiently confident to stage a sit-in at a local pub which refused delegates service.

---

* Pubs did not have all-day opening until 1988, and closed in the afternoon before then.

† Among the many groups and soloists who played live there on the way to fame and fortune were David Bowie, Status Quo, Roxy Music, Deep Purple and, when it became a punk venue later, The Jam.

Peter Katin

Among very early members of the group were two who were to become extremely prominent in CHE. The pianist Peter Katin had been born and raised locally, and now lived in South Croydon. He had been the first British musician to undertake a solo tour in the USSR after the war; an acclaimed favourite at the Proms, he was one of the best-known pianists in the country, with a particular reputation for Chopin and Rachmaninov. Although he was bisexual, he lived with his wife and two children in a house which also had a large music studio attached.

He was no stranger to homosexual campaigning. He had long been concerned about police entrapment. He had been a supporter of the HLRS, corresponded with Antony Grey, and gave a benefit recital for the Society at the Wigmore Hall in 1966. This was an extremely brave thing to do, because although Katin never came out formally, there would have been an assumption on the part of many of his audience that he must have been homosexual if he supported this cause.

There was some unpleasant flak when he later gave a recital for the CHE Music Group* at St John's, Smith Square. A woman went to the concert, and only after she got there discovered whose benefit it was in aid of. She wrote to Katin, ℅ the Arts Council, with a covering letter saying that the Arts Council shouldn't be funding St John's if the venue was going to put on filth such as Chopin for homosexuals. The Arts Council wrote back to say they could see nothing wrong with the recital, and she didn't have to go to the thing if she didn't want to.

Doris Locke's point was that it had not been advertised as a benefit concert; Katin replied that the poster said it was promoted by the CHE Music Group and he also made jocular reference to the proximity of her address to his, in South Croydon. So far, so civilised; but she did not let go. Her letter to Katin is venomous:

> I certainly did not notice the words CHE Music Group in the newspaper advertisement of your recital but even if I had, I could hardly have imagined such a clumsy method of trying to force recognition of homosexuals on to unsuspecting members of a concert audience. The CHE leaflet is staggering in its aggressive impudence and quite sickening, but none of the belligerent demands for recognition from these people can transform them into decent beings or make them acceptable to those who enjoy a normal life. … I can see that your feelings would be completely insensitive to those of a lady finding herself through no fault of her own in a gathering largely composed of your CHE upholders. I am not distressed

---

* See page 487.

> over the proximity of our addresses as you suggest, as it could have been so much worse – you might have lived next door.[8]

Once the gloves were off, Katin had no option but to reply in kind, within the limits of his essentially reserved nature:

> I gave very careful thought to the aims of CHE before deciding whether or not to give it my support, and it is not for you to write objectionably vulgar letters to me because you do not, from sheer ignorance, agree with my decision. You do not even have any statistics to substantiate your claim that the audience *was* largely composed of CHE upholders. You were under no obligation to read the leaflet which attempted to tell you about CHE itself, any more than you are under an obligation to read leaflets which give you information about the Samaritans, the Marriage Guidance Council, the Disabled Living Foundation, the Communist Party, British Airways or St John's itself. If you did not like what you read you could simply have discarded it from your mind, but you chose to take the monumentally idiotic step of announcing a boycott of my concert appearances – your loss, of course.[9]

Katin was one of the people who joined CHE during the time of Esquire Clubs, which he supported, and became an early member of the Correspondence Club, though he did not stay long:

> A kind of mailing list was sent out of everybody's name and address, and [we were asked] if we wanted to be included, so the people would get in touch with us. … And I got, oh, loads of letters, some of them very silly. … I gave that up actually, because I got a number of letters, all saying, 'Are you *the* Peter Katin?' And I thought, 'Oh dear, this is going to be boring.'[10]

But when he found out there was a local CHE group starting virtually down the road from him, he joined it. He gave his first recital for group members and friends in December 1971, in his studio, a light and airy extension with two pianos, and room for about seventy people.

His wife Eva was, as she has always been, entirely supportive. At the time she was a volunteer for the Marriage Guidance Council, and later joined the Samaritans, where she staffed the phone line until well into her eighties.

> She was absolutely marvellous. She really was. She was very amused at first, and I said, well, this is very serious, and I set her down and sort of explained it all to her. She was always being set upon to go and give talks, and this that and the other, and I told her about this and she said, I don't think I'd be any good at giving a talk. What do you want to do? I said, well, I could give recitals, And she was very, very helpful, she was marvellous … when there were parties, Eva sort of disappeared. She'd go to the theatre or come back much later on, sort of appear at about two o'clock in the morning. She was very easy-going about it.[11]

So, it seems, were his children. At the time of his first concert, his younger son, Andrew, was about 13:

> I told him a little bit about what it was going to be about, it'd be a party. Cos it was. An hour's recital and drinks afterwards. Caution was thrown to the wind, people all brought loads of bottles and things like that, I said [to Andrew] they are homosexuals – most of them are. I thought I'd just make it as brief as possible. … A lot of the people who used to come to these things were airline pilots. British Airways, and so on. I found that he was kidnapping them, not for that reason either. He'd put them all in the breakfast room, bring out some books and ask them questions about aircraft. And they couldn't even get a drink![12]

These recitals were strictly limited to CHE members; on the one occasion he yielded to pressure to open it to the general public, it was a disaster:

> It was like any other gay party, of a rather less desirable kind, where people had screaming rows. … And I said no, this is not why I organised this. I don't know where the silver's going to go. They really weren't very nice.[13]

Over the next five years there would be half a dozen recitals in South Croydon, as well as performances for other local groups,* benefits for National CHE, and talks. Katin was to prove a popular guest speaker with local groups, talking about music and his life as a touring pianist – never about homosexuality. What made him popular was that he always stayed to mingle with the group afterwards. In person Peter is an unassertive, almost diffident man of impeccable manners, and there was no question of the 'star' appearing *de haut en bas*. He went to talk to Tyneside CHE in 1973:

> Peter talked about some of his experiences early in his career as well as his more recent life, and it was something of a surprise (though perhaps it shouldn't have been) to learn about some of the problems he'd had along the way to his present standing as a concert pianist of international repute. … The drinking and socialising continued until closing time and Peter stayed with us until the end.[14]

Rose Robertson and Parents' Enquiry

The other Croydon member who would prove important to the wider gay movement was Rose Robertson. A heterosexual grandmother in her late 50s, she was at first sight an unlikely member. She was small, square-jawed, with her long hair up in a tight bun, and working as a secretary. She came to CHE

---

* In 1974 Tunbridge Wells District Council banned a Katin concert for local CHE groups in the Assembly Rooms. The incident will be covered more fully in Volume Two.

via the Integroup branch in Catford, where she lived. However, appearances were deceptive. As a teenager she had twice run away from an unloving home to join touring troupes of actors. In 1941 she was recruited to the Special Operations Executive (SOE) which had been set up to work on spying and sabotage in occupied Europe, as well as supporting local resistance movements. It was a very tough and dangerous occupation, and one which Rose could never talk about in later life without experiencing intense anxiety and agitation. She was parachuted into France,* where she acted as a go-between twixt the Resistance and Allied Intelligence in London. She was stopped and interrogated by German troops several times, that bun of hair concealing a miniature SOE pistol for dire emergency. She had hairsbreadth escapes. She told Glenys Parry about one of them, in a late-night 'girls-together' conversation:

> We were talking about premonitions and she said she really believed … it had saved her life once. … It was one of these *in vino veritas* stories. … She'd been parachuted into France and she was due to meet the Resistance at this café in this small provincial town. And it was quiet, it was mid-evening, eight o'clock, nine o'clock, and she arrived at this place, and as she walked towards the café door, she could sort of feel the hairs on the back of her neck prickle. There was just something about it that didn't feel right. She couldn't put a finger on what it was because the street was quiet … the café seemed normal, people were inside. It wasn't a very clement night, it was raining. Anyway, there was just something about it felt, sixth sense, felt wrong. So she held back and waited, and waited, and after about an hour the door of this café burst open and Gestapo came out with these people and bundled them into a van, and she realised they'd been waiting for her, and that it had been a sort of Gestapo trap, really.
>
> So then, she had this awful problem of getting back to England, because her situation was that she couldn't use her normal way back, so she had to lie low. So she hid in some pipes. Ceramic pipes. Then she made her way back and got on a boat. She got back to London. But then, she was debriefed. Because they assumed you'd been turned, so if you didn't come back and you'd been missing for more than forty-eight hours after your assignation, you'd been captured and tortured and turned. And so it was assumed that you were going to be a double agent, as it were. So your debriefing in London was rigorous. And lasted day and night, for three days. But she convinced them it wasn't a story.[15]

Her network had been betrayed, and most of her fellow-agents were captured and killed. Nevertheless, she was sent back to France several times.

---

* It is not clear how she acquired the fluent French and in-depth knowledge of France which were seen as an essential qualification for the work.

There were two experiences which led her in the direction of gay rights. During the war she was billeted on two Resistance members, whom she walked in on while they were having sex. After an awkward few days in which nothing was said, she finally worked up the bottle to ask them about it. The story they told of family rejection chimed in with her own teenage experience which led to her running away from home. Perhaps even more crucially, she was letting rooms in Catford in the 1960s, and among her lodgers were two young men she realised were lovers. They told much the same story as the Frenchmen.

These experiences focused her particularly on parent/child relationships, and she came into CHE wanting to do something about parental rejection of lesbian and gay children. However, CHE itself was convoluted in its attitudes to teenagers, as has been discussed. Croydon CHE itself did not admit under-21s, while Rose was convinced from talking to her gay lodgers and their friends that support was needed much, much earlier. After a few months, with the Croydon Group membership standing at over fifty and rising, a new group split from it, Lewisham/Catford CHE, with Rose as 'chairman' from January 1972. Some months after this, she resigned to concentrate on Parents' Enquiry, the support group for parents of lesbian and gay children, which she was to run from her home as an independent organisation for the next thirty years. Parents' Enquiry was to be a favourite cause for CHE groups to fundraise for, and Rose herself was a regular speaker at CHE conferences and groups for many years.

As Croydon was establishing itself, London Groups 8 to 13 also started. Homosexuals from all over the Home Counties were gravitating to Central London. Members came from as far afield as Guildford, Chelmsford, Northampton, Tonbridge and even Brighton. This created a kind of two-way traffic: as some members went back to their home towns invigorated to start groups in their own area, existing groups on the periphery of London – Chilterns, Windsor, Reading – struggled to retain members lured into the Big City.

London Group 8

The LCC welcomed London Group 8 to the Committee as a new group in July 1971. It met briefly in the Spartan Club,* but was driven out by the noise of the club proper at the other end of the room. They reverted to the Two Brewers in Monmouth Street and subsequently moved to the London Information Centre. The Secretary was Vivian Waldron, a tall distinguished

* In Tachbrook Street, Victoria.

man with a shock of white hair, a retired Civil Servant from the Ministry of National Insurance.* He was a restless man, of great energy, and for a long time sublimated this into hobbies – acting, walking, gardening, part-time picture dealing. He'd been through seven different schools as a child, thanks to a father who was a peripatetic Methodist minister. He was a committed Trade Unionist who taught himself a law degree in his spare time. Sexually he was a late developer. He told TV presenter Mavis Nicholson:

> I had absolutely no one to talk to until I was in my mid-twenties. … I hadn't even heard the word [homosexual] until I read a book when I was about twenty-two and I said to myself, 'Ah! That's me.' Until that time I hadn't realised there was anybody else who had the same sort of strong feelings that I had. …
>
> People talk about going through a homosexual phase. I went through a heterosexual phase, between the ages of about six and ten. I remember being madly in love with a girl called Olive, but after that age I ceased to be physically interested in girls, but I've always liked girls.[16]

One consequence of his late development was a desire to make up sexually for lost time. He had two lodgers in his quite large flat. Brian Sewell remembers:

> Vivian shared a splendid flat with two other people, and – and someone would fork out a fiver for a guardsman, and then if the guardsman was feeling generous he would see to more than one of them. And then eventually there was a guardsman who stayed, and became a rather saintly bloke because he looked after them all, saw them all off to their graves. And nobody in the rest of the block could have thought anything of it.[17]

Certainly looking at his activities for the early 1970s, there is a sense of a man in a hurry, making up for lost time. In his group he organised long country walks, five in the summer of 1972. He was the first organiser of the Speakers' Corner group, arranging a practice session with pretend hecklers at the Two Brewers. In *Lunch* he issued an appeal for people to come along to Hyde Park on 26 June 1972, with their kitchen stepladders. After that the group appeared every Sunday, and some weekday evenings as well.

It was Waldron who initiated CHE's first employment campaign. In 1971 the Industrial Relations Act introduced the idea that dismissal from a job had to be 'fair'. For some time there was optimism that this might prevent dismissal on the grounds of homosexuality, as being homosexual was irrelevant to the ability to perform the task.† As 'Moonlighter', a barrister member of

* Later amalgamated with the Ministry of Pensions, and superseded in 1968 by the Department of Health and Social Security.

† This hope was to be proved false at the end of the decade, when an Industrial Tribunal ruled in the case of John Saunders [*Saunders v. Scottish National Camps Association Ltd*

CHE, wrote in *Lunch*:

50. Vivian Waldron at Speakers' Corner

> If one takes the case of the homosexual in the light of the present law, the mere fact that a person is homosexual will not entitle him to be dismissed. Of course a homosexual may behave in a certain way which would enable his dismissal to be justified under the heading of conduct, or in an indirect way it might affect his capacity for any job. However, I should have thought it very questionable whether the reason often advocated for not employing a homosexual in any work involving an element of security, the fact that he is liable to pressures in the form of some sort of blackmail, would constitute a valid reason for dismissing such an employee.[18]

Group 8 seized on this. They wrote to the EC suggesting it should conduct a survey of employers, to ask about their attitudes to the employment of gay staff. The EC said, 'Do it yourself.' The Group came up with a hundred suitable employers, and drafted the letter to go to them. The list was whittled down to the fifty who employed the most people. The Group sent the letter, but with scant response. What replies there were, were bland, but evasive.

Waldron became chair of Group 8 in 1973, and later of the LCC. He appeared regularly on the increasing number of radio slots which opened up in 1972–73; he joined London Friend almost as soon as it started, and became the national co-ordinator after Michael Launder dropped out. Only ill-health forced him to slow down by 1976.

[1981] IRLR 277 (SCOT)] that even if employers were not entitled to be prejudiced themselves, they were entitled to take the prejudices of others into account when dismissing an employee.

London Groups 9–13

Group 9 was chaired by Peter Robins, a man of great wit and some acerbity. His problem was that he was working at the BBC:

> I had been working on various BBC programmes, in radio, and I had recently suffered a dreadful financial setback, as a result of a relationship going wrong, and at that time I had been promoted to becoming a duty editor on the *Today* programme. And that meant night work, so I thought, 'Heavens above! I'm not meeting anybody when I go along the embankment, the local park, the Putney towpath or whatever. What am I to do?' And then I saw this advertisement. So I admit there was a certain selfishness. However, I was very conscious right from the beginning that I'd had an easy ride, as a person, as opposed to the lad or lass in some factory bench in Slough or something. So I was glad to answer the advertisement, and … the next thing was an invitation from Roger Baker. …
>
> And I said, 'It's got to be a Monday or Tuesday.' He said, 'We've got Thursday and Friday groups.' I said, 'You see, I'm working all night.' 'Right, I'll make a note of your name.' And bless him, within a fortnight he was on the phone, saying, 'This thing is just ballooning all over the place, and yes, I'm going to form a Tuesday group. Will you come along?' And I did, and there was about 20 people there, and a lot of discussion and chats, and he just turned to me and said, 'will you just steer it?'[19]

Peter lasted less than a year as chairman, moving on to chair Group 11 when a change in his BBC rotas upset his social arrangements. Group 9 did not last long after he left, and was reported as having collapsed by July 1972. Most of its surviving members transferred to London 10.

London 10 was set up in August 1971 by Suzy Wesselkamper. Suzy and Tom Wesselkamper were married, expatriate Americans. They were Catholics, and Tom had been a bishop in West Africa, where Suzy had been a nun. Their meeting and falling in love had been the trigger for both to leave the church in order to get married. When they came to London they got involved in social work projects with young homeless people in the Bloomsbury area. They charmingly took out an advert in *Lunch* 8:

CHE'S YOUNGEST MEMBER – MADE IN ENGLAND
DANIEL GEORGE WESSELKAMPER
February 26th 1972
9 Pounds 4 Ounces (4.2 Kilograms)
Copyright: Tom and Suzy Wesselkamper[20]

Tom was secretary of Group 3, a fine public speaker. According to *Lunch*: 'Tom Wesselkemper made a speech. … The best bit of the evening. He's terrific. Suzy says he's a ham. Made all his points and shut everyone up.'[21]

Suzy was the first female chair of a London group, and everyone regarded this as a great step forward. For the first time there seemed to be a possibility of a group with a 50/50 male/female membership. However, she did not last. John Saxby, a civil servant, was chairman by October 1972, and would remain so for several years. His partner, Peter Norman, gives a vivid picture of him in this period. He was extremely popular and well-known throughout London, mainly because of his prominent role in organising the Winter Fairs.

51. Peter Norman and John Saxby

> They worshipped him there [at Group 10]. It was amazing. Cult of personality. But he did have this knack of getting on with everybody, making everybody feel welcome, part of the crowd. I never had any of that, but he did, and they all looked up to him. There were some fairly high-powered people in it. David Starkey,* Robin Lustig.† I went to some of their meetings, but once again I found that I was at somebody else's party. … I found that wherever we went together, he was him, and I was a sort of adjunct. People would come up to me sometimes and say, 'Hello Peter – how's John?' I thought, 'What about How am I?' They all knew one another, and I didn't know them. … John spent an awful lot of time on things to do with CHE. … The main thing he did was put on the Winter Fair, and he worked on that from July every year.[22]

Group 10 was an active group socially and politically. Very much on the 'integration' wing of CHE, they proposed a leaflet specifically aimed at getting

---

* Dr David Starkey, historian and TV presenter with a particular interest in the Tudors. His series *Monarchy* charted the various styles of kingship practised by the English/British Monarchy since Saxon times. It ran for four series, 2004–2006. Later he became Chairman of the Conservative Group for Homosexual Equality. He declined to be interviewed for this book.

† Robin Lustig was Home Affairs Editor of *The Observer* at this time. Later he because a distinguished presenter on the BBC World Service, and on Radio 4 (*The World Tonight*).

heterosexuals to join the organisation, something which was part of the stated aims of the organisation, but to which only lip service was paid, at best. Yet John himself was a radical, and it was at his suggestion that members of GLF and of 'Women's Lib' came to talk to the group.

London 10 members were great letter-writers. Their first campaign was geared towards GPs, and with it came a discussion which happened in all London-wide groups contemplating action. Where to focus it? Since there were about 30,000 doctors in London, some sort of narrowing down was inevitable. The group decided to concentrate on the City of Westminster, home of about a thousand of them. The letters went out in June, using a directory of doctors from the local library. It was followed quickly by another letter, this time to clergy. They lobbied a hundred MPs in London and the Home Counties in September 1972. It is doubtful whether the MPs' correspondence achieved anything or got many replies: there was no election coming up, there was no legislation to ask them to support, and only a small number of the members' letters would have come from an MP's own constituents. However, it was a kind of muscle-flexing in the political arena. In all, Group 10 sent out over two thousand letters. The postage alone was over £60 (£740).

Groups 11 was formed in autumn 1971, Group 12 in early 1972. Group 12's chairman, Geoffrey Baggott, had previously lived in Wolverhampton, where he was secretary of the CHE group, and he was immediately collared to chair a new group when he moved to London because of work. He became not only chair of Group 12, but subsequently 'Admin Officer' of Haringey CHE, sat on the LCC and got himself onto the Working Party which looked at the structure of the national organisation in the wake of rows in 1972.* He allied himself with Group 1's Griffith Vaughan Williams, who floated the idea of fielding CHE candidates in the 1973 local council elections. 'Bad idea,' said Treasurer Michael Steed, but the two took some dissuading. There was something aggressive and confrontational about the style of both of them, and Baggott certainly had a flair for letters of protest and motions of censure.

Group 13, the last of the numbered groups, opened in February 1972. It met the second and fourth Fridays of the month in the Coachmakers' Arms; its chairman was Richard Nicholas. Its one newsletter, a handwritten sheet for September 1972, shows them going on a group theatre outing to the Noël Coward revue, *Cowardy Custard*, in November, and perhaps more improvingly, to Rosa von Praunheim and Martin Dannegger's film, *It is not the homosexual who is perverse, but the society in which he lives*, screened at the National Film Theatre in 1973, with CHE members taking part in an NFT discussion

---

* This is covered in Volume Two.

afterwards. The German activist Rosa von Praunheim was a controversial figure because of his refusal to deal in pure propaganda. Much of the film, as of his others, is a dialogue with the gay community about what it means to live a good homosexual life. *It's not the homosexual...* contains a fierce critique of the queer obsession with youth and beauty, and with the limited horizons of most gay men, who want only a conformist bourgeois marriage as their happy ending. In short, the film mirrors much of the ideological discussion current in London CHE at the time.

London Women's Group

One non-geographic London group was formed in conjunction with the numbered groups – the London Women's Group, recognised officially at the National Council of December 1971. The convenor was Jo Batchelor, but *Lunch* editor Gini Stevens was also a member. The idea of a Women's Group was not without opposition from within the male membership, and Jo reported she was criticised heavily in her own mixed group when she announced its start. However, it was only open to women who were members of mixed groups, thus sidestepping arguments about separatism.* The Women's Group had its own inductions, which were arranged by Batchelor, and within a few months there were some thirty members, who belonged to six other (mixed) groups as well. This seems to indicate that seven London CHE groups were in practice men-only. The group had significant links with the lesbian organisations Kenric, Sappho, Arena 3 and the women in GLF. It was primarily a social group, in the first instance meeting in private houses every six weeks or so. It moved to the Museum Tavern, home of the Bloomsbury Group, in April 1972. At about the same time it hosted a party for 150 women, mainly CHE members, including a group invited down from Oxford CHE.

When the London Information Centre opened later the same year, the Women's Group moved there, meeting on the fourth Wednesday of the month before going on to a club. Members were coming from as far away as Sussex, Essex and Kent. 'We see our function as primarily a recruiting one,' wrote Jo. But they were also in the business of building the women's presence within other CHE groups. There was some argument about what to do with young women who joined, whether to encourage them to join the Student Group. The students wanted to induct the new young women members immediately, directly from the London Organiser, but since all their officers were male, Jo was insistent that they needed a female contact first, and:

* See Volume Two.

> I then place them in a group. So far no women have wanted to join the students group. … All the young ones are in other groups. We hope to send them along in groups to student meetings, to encourage them to join.[23]

The importance of going to things in groups, of not being the only woman walking into a roomful of men, was very clear to both Jo and Gini, who wrote about it in *Lunch*. However, the limits of the group's awareness of sexual politics can be seen in a protest made by Janet Shenderey, the group representative at the National Council of September 1972. She reported that the group objected to the word 'lesbian' in a new national leaflet, and it was left to a man, local groups organiser Peter Norman, to explain that 'The word lesbians [is included] because the public tends to think of homosexuals only as being men.'[24] This also reveals a certain ideological distance between the ordinary London women members and the women on the National Executive who had a hand in devising and approving the leaflet in question. Liz Stanley and Glenys Parry had strong connections with both the Women's Movement and GLF, and the use of the word 'lesbian' as self-description would have seemed entirely natural to them.

There was something cosy, but also rather in-bred, about all these numbered groups. With people easily able to go to meetings of groups other than their own, at the same venue; with convenors such as Peter Robins transferring to other groups; and with social networks extending throughout all the groups through parties, joint activities and larger meetings, it was very easy for everybody to know – or know of – everybody else. Friendships could be volatile – best chums one day, not on speaking terms the next. It was a period of camp nicknames, more or less affectionate – the Couch Parties, Dolly Carrycot, the Laundress, the Codfish. Manchester in turn had its nicknames for Londoners – the Fruit Bat (Griffith Vaughan Williams), Rita Bobbins (Peter Robins).

In particular, the coach trips going out of London were bonding experiences, if only because outside the safer cultural confines of central London, things could go wrong. You were far more likely to encounter homophobia, but you would also have the experience of confronting it in a large group. Tony Ryde remembers one such occasion:

> There was a member of the group [Group 4] who lived in Woking, and we took a coach trip down to a party that he was throwing, and we parked the coach in a nearby pub. And the pub publican was having an affair with my sister. I said to the coach driver, 'I'm sure you'll be alright parking in this pub because I know the publican.' It was only three houses from where the party was. But the publican was not amused when he came out – he was drunk actually. There was a tremendous row, where he stormed up to the

> coach as we were all getting on to go off home to London, and he was potentially going to be extremely abusive.[25]

The enemy was not always external. With groups combining to go on trips, bringing along friends and friends of friends to fill up coaches, there was always the chance that someone unsavoury might join the party without anyone knowing. Complete strangers could come along for the ride, everyone assuming that they had come with someone else. Brian Sewell and Peter Robins remember:

> BRIAN: There was a summer do … somewhere out towards Guildford or Dorking. … There was some old monster with tarot cards. And he liked dressing in drag. He used to borrow his housekeeper's drag. Very old cape, from another generation. I left early because I hate tarot! I remember feeling very ill-at-ease about this superstitious business. Distinctly creepy.
>
> PETER: But there was a coach. And Roger, rather unwisely I thought, collected all of the subs towards the cost of the coach on the way out. And when we got back to the coach there was an ashen-faced Roger Baker saying that the money's been pinched from his inside pocket. And I think it had. I don't think he was playing silly buggers. So we all had to put our hands in our pockets and find another fiver, or a ten bob note, whatever it was. We never did find who lifted it.[26]

Despite the levity of Peter's account, there was a clear sense of shock, even betrayal. This was meant to be safe space, among friends, people who were all supposedly on the same side, in the same boat. It was always a hard lesson to learn, that homosexuals could be as unreliable, even treacherous, as anyone else.

'People not Paper'

There was a crisis at the top. The LCC Chairman was about to have a nervous breakdown. Earlier in 1971, the LCC had hastily set up its constitution so that the Chairman was also the London organiser, with responsibility for recruitment and induction, liaison with the National Office, and a press spokesman. This trio of roles was gruelling by any standards. Tony Ryde as first Chairman was also co-opted onto the EC in Manchester, where he found himself further stretched with other portfolios such as the National Federation of Homophile Organisations.* He was the kind of person who would always volunteer to fill a gap where no one else could be found to do the job, whether it was soothing suspicious Advertising Managers on the *Evening Standard* or making a banner

* NFHO – see Volume Two.

to take on the first Gay Pride March. Others, knowing that he could be relied on to fill the gaps, let him get on with it, and so the situation spiralled. And all this CHE work was in addition to his full-time job at BP. Paul Temperton was extremely anxious for him: 'Where the hell do you find 40 hours a week for CHE work? That's nearly six hours a day! For chrissake ease off or you'll burn yourself out.'[27]

No wonder he found himself on the verge of a nervous breakdown.

Tony was given a three-month sabbatical, and in his place came an administrative triumvirate of Brian Sewell, Peter Robins and Michael Moor. That it took three people to replace Tony was a measure of how much he was taking on himself. New members were joining at such a rate that the load of inducting them was split between five people: Roger Baker came back to meet and greet the referrals from London members – the 'word-of-mouths' – the rest being handled by Brian Sewell, Tom Wesselkemper and two others. Roger reported to Paul that:

> The set-up now seems to be that Peter Robins (who is excellent), Brian Sewell and Michael Moor run the organisation with Tony Ryde drifting about in a flowered hat to open bazaars, and me as Recruiting Officer. Sorry to keep altering the structure but it is necessary as things grow and get more ramified, and we all now seem to be pointing roughly in the same direction – apart from Brian, who is still absolutely hung up over the age-of-consent thing.[28]

As Baker indicates, some things had to change if London CHE and its groups were to keep up with the numbers joining, and provide what they needed. The structural alterations were proposed in a document entitled 'People Not Paper'. It was put out in the name of the triumvirate, but stylistically has Brian Sewell's fingerprints all over it. It opens:

> We are not unaware of the irony whereby, having called our interim report PEOPLE NOT PAPER, we have now offered the longest document you have so far been asked to consider in the London Committee. Nevertheless we ask you to bear with us for there has not been – until now – an opportunity in this young organisation for a group of people to discuss, argue, suggest and recommend anything more than the very immediate future.
>
> You will easily find gaps. You will no doubt disagree in detail. … [But] if you throw this out, we are back where we started, not in disarray, but with a newborn organisation seemingly unwilling to accept that its first steps should be directed in this or that or any direction. Let us make a start.[29]

In short, if CHE cannot be everything to everybody, it must decide on the something it can be to somebody, or it will end up being nothing to anybody.

'People Not Paper' proposes two possible models for CHE: (A) the campaigning:

> That CHE should be and remain a ginger group meeting with some frequency to discuss tactics for recruiting new members who will educate the public in the matter of inequalities; press influential bodies (political and social) to reform our laws, and organise, from time to time, fund raising functions to that end.[30]

and (B) the social:

> That CHE should consider primarily its existing membership and, having offered them initial confidence and companionship through stable membership, should build on equalities such as we have (the right to operate social clubs in relevant areas), develop a counselling service and look towards homes for the elderly as well as sports, cultural and holiday facilities.[31]

While 'People not Paper' recognises that the two are not mutually exclusive, it is clear that the hearts of the writers lie in pursuing the second. To follow the first is to risk a flat lining membership as the 'social' members leave in droves, with only a rump of activists remaining.

At the same time, the writers acknowledge that to prioritise social projects is to have a different emphasis from the national organisation. If social projects are developed, this will take them beyond something merely social, to create a complete Friendly Society offering support and co-operative enterprises almost literally from the cradle to the grave. Their proposed solution to the tug in different directions is to rewrite the national constitution:

> There may be a case, however, for pressing the National Executive to write into the constitution the need for CHE to consider people as a whole, not just as manifesto and march fodder. … Only by offering them the visible challenge of such projects as a Club, a Sports Centre and a Holiday Guest House, which finally depend on their own efforts, can we hope to hold anyone other than the most devoted campaigners who, if one is realistic, can never be expected to count for more than one in ten of any movement.[32]

The dilemma, the conflict dissected in 'People not Paper', is the one which bedevilled CHE throughout its fifteen to twenty years of active life, but behind the dilemma was also the dismal fact that CHE could never muster enough skills, enthusiasm or sheer numbers of people to achieve more than a fraction of its ambitions in any direction. In their own personal enthusiasm for the social projects, Brian, Peter and Michael wildly overestimated the available capacity for any project.

The proposed restructuring of London CHE is aimed at diverting people into working on the social projects, but also at ensuring that nobody was ever again put into Tony Ryde's wildly overworked position:

> It should be obvious that no single man has the time to tackle the vast amount of work and the various tasks that span the administration of the Greater London area. … Therefore, a new, hopefully well-defined structure for administration has been carefully designed and discussed, to ensure that no one person shall be asked to undertake an impossible amount of work and to preserve a group small enough to be workable.[33]

In practice, the structure was elaborate, and, for all the talk of avoiding bureaucracy, bureaucratic.

The chairman had the most important role, and Brian et al. were very conscious of the importance of having a 'name' and 'reputation' as both figurehead and spokesman. This led to a certain snobbery:

> The chairman is the titular and political head and will hopefully come from the highest possible echelons of society. He must be representative of London CHE, bringing suitable confidence to the grass roots, by virtue of personality and reputation in the capital. The need for such a man, and indeed as many as possible as honorary officers, is obvious.[34]

It was one of the London criticisms of Manchester that there was nobody charismatic who could be called on to speak with authority and flair for the membership. Allan Horsfall was almost perversely and deliberately uncharismatic, Paul Temperton a self-effacing, self-confessed backroom boy. Only Ike Cowen (and later, Glenys Parry) had anything like the combination of qualities needed. However Ike, in addition to being the CHE legal officer, had a full-time job as a lecturer at Keele University, ran groups in Nottingham, and acted as secretary to the Association of Law Lecturers. He was reluctant to take on more.

But if there was a shortage of leadership qualities in Manchester, it was by no means clear who had them, or who was of sufficient reputation, in the capital. Who would be prepared to put in the time and put their reputation on the line?* 'People not Paper' offered no suggestions, and it does not seem to have been seriously discussed.

The chairman would have three deputy chairmen, one of whom would be responsible for all the working parties on the Club, Friend, social activities, etc. This deputy would report for all of them to the LCC: 'The function of a working party is we feel to work and to be seen to be working, not to have time to be writing monthly reports and attending monthly committee meetings.'[35]

* As Peter Norman noted, the qualities they were looking for in this 'impressiveness' role really attached to the numerous Vice-Presidents whom CHE was then recruiting.

A second deputy would look after the standard range of officers – treasurer, secretary, fundraiser etc. One of these would be the press officer, which Roger Baker was waiting in the wings to take over. He had already been banging on about the need for a national press officer.

The third deputy would be responsible for local groups, and under her/him would be five convenors for different parts of London (North, South, East, West, Central), plus, significantly, one for women.

> We are seriously perturbed that in an organisation such as our own which has Equality in its title as well as in its listed aims, so little has yet been done in London for women. To argue that little has been asked for is irrelevant. If the girls can't be offered shopping facilities they will shop elsewhere. We must offer them help.[36]

The automatic equation of 'girls' and shopping is somewhat dubious, but the concern for gender equality is genuine, the suggestions are practical.

'People not Paper' urged the immediate appointment of a women's convenor, with a voice on the LCC. Women would be offered a 'dual citizenship system' – membership of any London Group and of the first women's group. 'Once established, we feel others would follow.' London accepted the need for a part of the service to be dedicated to encouraging women's membership and fostering women's groups long before the rest of the organisation caught up.

Most importantly, the triumvirate reorganised local groups. These would cease to meet in Central London and would have local roots in boroughs:

> We would ask you to bear in mind the essential identities that may well be observed in different parts of London. It is possible for example that a group based on Richmond would be more social in character, a Hampstead group is likely to contain more intellectuals and a Leyton group would need a vigorous and action-minded chairman. We have suggested elsewhere that more affluent members from Central London might be encouraged to travel out as ginger groups to the suburbs.[37]

New groups on a geographical basis started to appear from March 1972. Wandsworth (Wandsworth-Richmond), Crouch End (later called Haringey), East London (also called Ilford), Ealing, Enfield, Highbury & Islington (also called North London), Kensington, Kilburn, Lewisham, Stepney (an offshoot of London 11), and Streatham all appeared in this year.* Existing groups started changing their names at the beginning of 1973. Croydon already had its local identity, for historical reasons.

---

* Of these, Wandsworth, Highbury & Islington, and Kensington are all treated in later volumes.

Peter Naughton and Enfield CHE

Enfield CHE was founded by Peter Naughton, who was co-opted onto the National Executive in late 1972 as a financial whizz-kid and fundraiser. He was a bluff, bearded, barrel-chested man, with a facetious style, and the antithesis of any homosexual stereotype. Behind the almost school-boyish sense of humour lay a keen managerial brain. He was to bring his commercial analytical skills to bear on CHE from 1973 onwards, as part of a new generation with an increasingly professional approach to running the organisation.

His coming-out and entry into CHE at the comparatively late age of 30 intersects with several other strands of the story:

> I was working in Liverpool at the time, and I had a girlfriend, and I was trying desperately to be straight, and we all went to the office Christmas party, had a jolly good time, and then we all went back to our families for Christmas. And come the New Year, she came to me and said, 'I've proposed to the boy next door who was my childhood sweetheart and he said yes, so we're getting married.' So I was very unceremoniously dumped. And, I thought, 'Well, I probably really am, as we used to call it in those days, queer, so I'd better start doing something about it.'[38]

And so he entered 1971 with a new vision of himself and his sexuality. There was only one problem – finding out anything about gay life and where he could meet any others like himself.

> I had great difficulty actually finding out anything. There used to be a magazine called *Spartacus*. ... I found their address from somewhere, ... and actually paid a visit down to Brighton. I didn't meet the man himself, but whoever ran the office. So he gave me lots of information, and some addresses, one of which was CHE. So I wrote off and was told that there was actually a group just starting in Liverpool, meeting in the Methodist church,* so I went along, very small group, big church, but very amiable, and welcoming. One of the members of the group took me home and I had my first gay sexual encounter.[39]

The experience was enough to bind him into CHE. He got invited to more meetings, and then, in June 1972, to a National Council in Bristol. Always the extrovert and willing to say what he thought, he impressed Allan Horsfall enough to be co-opted in November onto the Executive, initially as a fundraiser. Then:

---

* There is no record of meetings at a church, Methodist or otherwise, in the early days of Liverpool CHE. The group did however meet briefly in the Friends' Meeting House.

> To my complete amazement there was a vacancy for a vice chair,* so I started going to meetings as vice chair, not knowing what was going on. Not long into all of this, Allan became unwell, and had to stand down. So, all of a sudden, I was chairing meetings. … I didn't know anything about it, I'd been Out for a matter of months, or maybe a year by then, but I was out of my depth, and Michael Steed said, 'Why don't we swap jobs? I'll become chair and you become treasurer. I said yes, yes, thank you, thank you. So that's how I became treasurer.[40]

The story shows yet again the somewhat haphazard way in which CHE involved people, acquiring board members and a skills base almost at random.

In 1972, work took Peter to London, and a house in Enfield. He came armed with letters of introduction to the A & B Club in Rupert Court, and the Rockingham.†

> The leader of the Liverpool group at that stage‡ said, '[Gasp!] You're going to London? I'd better give you some addresses.' 'Addresses?' 'You'll need some letters of introduction to get in to places in London.' … So I arrived down here, armed with these letters, and went [to the A & B Club], with my little letter of introduction, the back steps on Rupert Court, knocked on the door, the door opened. I said, 'I have a letter from Robin.' 'Oh, you have a letter!' The door opened – 'Come in, you're very welcome.' It's just so amazing – isn't it? – that you needed a letter of introduction? 'He's a bona fide queer, you can let him in! He's not a spy from the police or something like that.'[41]

The story of CHE illustrates, among other things, the high degree of social and physical mobility among lesbians and gay men, and the way in which that was harnessed in the development of new groups, and the spread of ideas. It seemed inevitable, with Peter's level of energy and organisational abilities, that he should found a local group where there was none, in the area where he lived:

> That was hard work, but it was that grassroots kind of work that, looking back on it, you can say, at one level it was shambolic, but at the other it was impressive, that we've suddenly found all these people that are almost entirely living in the closet. But all of a sudden, they're coming to a meeting with other gay guys, and talking about things that they probably never talked to anybody about before. That was happening all over the country, and you begin to see that, in terms of getting the ordinary, run-of-the-mill,

---

* Following Tony Ryde's resignation in March 1973. The other changes Peter refers to occurred outside the time frame of this volume.

† Not to be confused with Reg Kilduff's club in Manchester.

‡ Robin Bloxsidge.

> seriously employed, managerial-type gay guys to [come out] it was CHE that did that. And it seems to me, that's been the bedrock, of the whole gay rights movement since then. … And I can't think we'd be where we are today if that hadn't have happened.[42]

It was a small group. Just twelve at the first meeting, of whom ten joined up. Peter compensated by doing a lot of outreach, organising joint activities with larger, longer-established groups. There were exchange visits with South Herts and Cambridge CHE groups. There was a joint party with London Central at the Spartan Club, a coach trip to Brighton with Highbury & Islington and Wandsworth & Richmond. It was enough to build up the group to a healthy number by the time Peter handed over as convenor after a year to Peter Bodger. Although Naughton originally provided in the local group's constitution for both a social secretary and a campaigns secretary, to 'ensure that the proper weight was given to both sides of the group's interests from the very beginning', in practice, the group remained primarily social. It lasted approximately ten years.

Other London groups

By contrast, Ealing CHE was more political. Founded in March 1972, one of its first actions was to distribute a questionnaire to all the candidates in the Uxbridge by-election of December that year, canvassing their views on aspects of gay rights. Intriguingly, an early *Gay News* makes a veiled reference to a 'West London group' holding orgies and giving blue movie shows on Good Friday. Since Ealing CHE was the only group truly in West London, it must be the prime candidate for this enterprising activity.

The Group lasted barely a year. In June 1973 Peter Norman noted in his Local Groups Report to the EC:

> This was never a very successful group and has now been wound up; members have been given info on other groups in London and encouraged to join them. I am concerned that the London Co-ordinating Committee took no action to help the group when it was obviously in trouble, and intend to ask the LCC whether they see it as their responsibility (as I had assumed) to set up and help local groups in London.[43]

Started in April 1972, Ilford CHE was another group founded out of an unease at the bourgeois nature of the existing groups. George Jordan was in London Group 1, but wrote to *Lunch*:

> I was at the meeting at the Coachmakers' Arms on Fri 4 February when the BBC were in attendance. The meeting went off well and when the television people left we had an informal discussion. The point was made

> that nearly all CHE members were middle class, very few working class, and those who were, didn't come to CHE meetings. I am a maintenance engineer, which makes me as much a working man as anyone. I know quite a few working class men in my area (Ilford) who are homosexuals, but when I approach them about becoming members of CHE they decline. Some say they might join us, but do not want to be known as a member of a group.
>
> I should like to form a group in or around Ilford, making myself the convenor if required, if I could get enough people interested. ... I think it's about time the working man's thoughts were made known in CHE.[44]

The first meeting was at Wanstead Quakers, where George had to reassure the Secretary that Friends' Meeting Houses were playing host to CHE groups all over the country. It was a group where many people had not knowingly talked socially to another homosexual ever before. East London CHE (as it later became) was one of the few to have an all-women committee: Mary Cooke as chairman,* Suzanne Gould secretary and Carol Garrard treasurer. Carol became the second chairman when Mary resigned. In consequence of this high female visibility, about half the membership was female, and about a third of the people at any meeting would be women. An early talk was about 'The Gay Woman's Attitude'. When they were invited to the Gaysoc at Queen Mary's College, they sent two lesbians to give the talk. Their newsletter advertised the London Women's Group regularly.

They continued to meet at the Friends' Meeting House in Leytonstone, but grew so fast that they had to move into a bigger room. Even so they were on occasion sitting three deep, and so uncomfortable that they adjourned quickly to a local pub. The group alternated formal meetings with pub gatherings at The Angel, a large mock-Tudor pub in Stratford, and coffee evenings at Roy and Keith's (The Lavender Girls).

Kilburn CHE held its first meeting in May 1972, its chair being Alan Louis. Louis supplied photographs to *Lunch* and also ran a disco which he used for CHE on many occasions. He worked the dances at the first national conference in Morecambe in 1973, and many subsequent conferences. He joined the CHE Executive in the 1990s, and remained active in the organisation until his death in 2010.

Stepney CHE, starting in November 1972, was chaired by Michael Harth, a writer and pianist in his mid-forties. Harth was the paper boy delivering *Lunch* monthly to outlets round London in his little red van. His day job was as a masseur, something which was only partly about the money because Harth was a compulsive cottager and cruiser, what would now be labelled a sex addict:

---

* They still used the word 'chairman', even when the officer in question was a woman.

> I was quite bored with the fact that the sex was so dull. None of them wanted to be screwed. It was all hand jobs. Nothing could be more boring. The scene has changed a lot in that area, and that is a mark of how far we've come. Because these guys had no sexual self-confidence whatever. They didn't even have sexual expectations. It was quite sad really.[45]

Later he would run the escort agency MEN. His politics, inasmuch as he had politics, were not so much right-wing as virulently anti-left-wing. He was fiercely opposed to CHE campaigning in any political way, although not to the educational function of the organisation:

> We … deplore very strongly the tendency to imagine that campaigning means political activity. Whilst we agree that a certain amount of this is of some value at the present time, we consider that the greatest need now is for education of the general public (and, we fear, many gays themselves) through the Arts, journalism etc. Thus a number of our members are actively engaged in such important fields as the Drama, Music and Writers' Groups. Above all we encourage our members to enjoy themselves, since it is in this personal sphere that the worst effects of our social oppression make themselves felt.[46]

He became known to *Lunch* readers as the hammer of those lefties who trailed the connections between gay rights and socialism in their own letters to the paper. These he laid into with fine invective, opening on one occasion:

> Of all the perversions, political activism appears to me to be the most vile, based as it almost invariably is on some form of power-seeking, an activity which necessarily implies someone over whom power is sought; compared to this, even the most trivialising kind of sexual encounter is a miracle of warmth and human feeling, for at least the participants are pleasure-oriented.[47]

This outburst brought Harth an admirer from a surprising source. The composer Sorabji, at this time aged eighty, was an avid reader of the magazine, and wrote him a personal letter, ℅ the Editor, inviting him to visit. Kaikhosru Shapurji Sorabji, as he called himself,* came from a wealthy Parsee family in Mumbai, and had an anguished relationship with his own sexuality. He had consulted Havelock Ellis about it, and Ellis gave him some sort of reassurance, in return for which Sorabji dedicated his Seventh Piano Concerto to him. However, his equilibrium was shattered by a blackmail incident, and he retired, bruised, to seclusion in a four-bedroom house called 'The Eye'

* Real name Leon Dudley Sorabji.

which he built himself in Corfe Castle.* Here he composed mainly piano music of great length and fiendish complexity† – and read *Lunch*. When Harth received his letter, he accepted the invitation, and the next time he was visiting his parents in Bournemouth, drove over on his French motorised bicycle to see him:

> He had a notice on his gate, 'No Hawkers, No Sailors, No Sisters of Mercy.' Something like that. Very idiosyncratic. He was quite a character. … We had very similar ideas. I'm basically an elitist. I think the most important thing in the world is quality, because there's basically not that much of it. And we should spend more effort on quality and less on the ordinary. He was of similar thinking. And he gave me a book by a guy called René Guénon‡ called *The Reign of Quantity*, which is the same sort of idea.[48]

Harth started the group in reaction to what he found in Group 11:

> We all decided we'd do a trip to Hampton Court, and they wanted somebody to organise it, so I said I would. So I duly went along, … and out of all the 25 or so who said they were coming, only one other turned up. I'm afraid it was typical. … I founded [Stepney CHE] because something wasn't right, I wasn't very happy about something. I'm not sure what it was. I probably thought [Group 11] was too piss-elegant, too middle class. I'm middle class myself, but I have the standard middle class taste for rough trade. … So you could say I'm a bit schizo.[49]

However, if Michael Harth was hoping to get trade through the group, he was doomed to disappointment. Stepney CHE mainly held coffee evenings. As a group it all revolved around Michael, who had numerous other interests, and when he left to concentrate on writing and the writers' group, the Stepney group folded. It was 'derecognised', in the CHE jargon, in March 1975.

Streatham CHE's big campaign was literary. It started when someone came across this paragraph:

> It must be an awful experience for parents to find that their sons and daughters are abnormal in any way. To discover that their loved ones are homosexual is, perhaps, the most upsetting experience of all. Normal people look upon homosexuals in a variety of ways. Some feel sorry for them, others feel loathing and disgust, and very few feel comfortable in the presence of a known homosexual.[50]

---

* Corfe Castle is a village in Dorset, and gave rise to the *canard* that Sorabji lived in a castle, which he did nothing to discredit as it enhanced his reputation for remoteness and eccentricity.

† His *Opus Clavicembalisticum* lasts four hours.

‡ A French mystical philosopher heavily influenced by both Hinduism and Islam.

This was from *Science and Living*, a textbook which was being used in schools Year 6, as part of Social Studies. Incensed, the group initiated a campaign to record and to combat prejudiced material. They started a register of all homophobic material published since 1967, with a view to getting publishers and authors to correct factual inaccuracy, and libraries to withdraw the offending books from circulation. It was the kind of campaign calculated to appeal to both male and female members, and Streatham's membership was at least 30 per cent women. The campaign grew over time until Streatham CHE was one of the authorities other groups referred to when compiling bibliographies or creating libraries themselves. Their list was divided into several sections: medical, including psychiatric; popular scientific (e.g. Blue Penguins); reference works (including encyclopaedias) and counselling guides; novels. When the list was circulated, there was a preface explaining that it was important work because there were so few books to redress the general prejudiced balance: ' "Experts" still talk about arrested development, dominant mothers and passive fathers, being "made" or seduced into becoming gay, about cures and controls.'[51] Sue Bradley, the campaign co-ordinator, appealed for donations of books, suggestions and asked for practical advice in tackling publishers.

Crouch End group, an offshoot of Highbury & Islington CHE, found itself involved in a political fracas right from the start, simply trying to find somewhere to meet. The first organiser was Derek Brookfield, moving on first from London Monday Group and them from Highbury. Having been turned down by a variety of venues, he decided to turn rejection to the group's advantage by going public in the pages of the *Hornsey Journal*:

> A newly formed Crouch End group cannot find a place to meet because, they feel, of local prejudice. They are the 30 or ... 40 members of the Crouch End group of the Campaign for Homosexual Equality, which includes a Haringey Borough Council official, schoolteachers, two local clergymen and one doctor, three college lecturers and two or three students, several Civil Servants, and a salesman. Not all members of this group are homosexual but those who are not agree that homosexuals should have equality with heterosexuals. ... Now the prospect of extinction faces the group – unless they can find a meeting place.[52]

A full-page article in the *Hornsey Journal* features a large photograph of Brookfield, in his early 30s, in a black polo neck sweater and thick pebble glasses. He sports thick, wild black hair, rather long, and looks considerably more radical than most convenors. Clearly he got on rather well with the reporter, Kay Collier, because the *Journal* story involved her ringing up the people who turned him down and confronting them with their own prejudice.* Harold

---

* The strap to the article is 'Kay Collier uncovers what seems to be local prejudice'.

Sumpton of the Quakers said, 'We don't wish to be associated with any group campaigning for a sectional purpose: we feel it would lead to misunderstanding.' This despite hiring out to the Campaign for Nuclear Disarmament. Six churches turned them down, although one did so indirectly by wanting an astronomical hire fee. The Anglican vicar, Rev. Brooke K. Lunn of St Luke's, told Kay:

> They wanted to use our church hall, but I didn't approve of it at all. Theirs is a propaganda body – their name tells us that. Their aim is to get society to treat the homosexual as being as normal as anyone else, and I don't agree with it. This is not in accordance with Christian teaching, which regards homosexuality as a deviation from the norm. ... The organisation concerned is not aimed at helping homosexuals to adjust to the rest of society.[53]

The Mountview Theatre Club pleaded that they were rehearsing all the time. Kay also tackled the pubs, who said that the group would not be welcome, or they only catered for wedding parties. But the greatest space in the story was reserved for the Council, which Brookfield claimed had offered them a room in a school three months earlier, but had then gone back on the offer. Mrs Sheila Berkery Smith, the Chairman of the Haringey Education Committee, told the *Journal*:

> I am not against their having a meeting place, but what they asked for specifically was to meet on school premises, less appropriate, in my opinion for such meetings than council premises. School premises are cheaper, but we do not allow the use of these for various kinds of functions; for instance, where alcohol is involved, because there is caretaker resistance. In the case of this particular group there might be teacher and parent objection.[54]

Teachers, she said, were concerned about leaflets which might be picked up by pupils in the mornings after such meetings; 'It may well be that I am being over-protective, but if all this group wants is somewhere to meet, I will try to find them somewhere other than school premises.'[55]

The article concluded with an appeal for suggestions, and asked anyone with bright ideas to contact Brookfield; it gave his home address and phone number, which was still extraordinarily brave at a this time.

The story could, and did, run and run. A few weeks later, the topic came up in a full council meeting:

> Education chairman and council leader Cllr Mrs Sheila Berkery Smith was rebuked at last week's meeting of Haringey Council for denying a meeting place in one of Haringey's schools for the Campaign for Homosexual Equality.

> Cllr Geoffrey Pollard … felt that the refusal amounted to a belief that letting school premises would mean a danger to children, but this was a misguided one, born out of prejudice.
>
> Cllr Chris Hannington felt that the negative answer given to the organisation was a form of moral censorship which should have had a wider involvement of members. The Campaign for Homosexual Equality was not going to make any use of school premises which would 'leave any evil lurking under the desks for the children to find in the morning'.[56]

Mrs Berkery Smith repeated the defence she used to the *Hornsey Journal*: 'Of course *I'm* not prejudiced, but there are others (teachers/caretakers/parents) who might object (though I haven't actually asked them)'. This might be termed the Bigot's Human Shield, and was deployed equally in turning down CHE conferences in later years. In this case, the most important group whose opinion was ignored was that of the pupils themselves, and there was evidence that they were far more tolerant than those who claimed to be protecting them. A couple of weeks before this row, the Headmaster of a large local comprehensive school, Charles Loades, had called off a talk to be given to senior pupils by members of GLF. The pupils wrote to the *Hornsey Journal* in protest:

> 'We all feel very strongly about this that we should be treated in this childlike manner.' They claimed most of the staff were in favour of the talk; half the fifth form had already been given a similar talk. They felt this week's talk had been called off because a parent was concerned.[57]

By the time the council came to discuss the matter, it was really a non-story. Mrs Berkery Smith was as good as her word, and found the group a meeting place in a local library. There had also been a palace coup within the group. Brookfield, like many who lead from the front, was a man impatient of committees. Peter Norman reported to the EC in Feb 1973:

> There is dissatisfaction with the acting chairman, and the LMC have been urging him to call regular meetings and form a committee. … Various London members are taking up the dispute, but meanwhile the group is not functioning.[58]

By May, Brookfield had been booted out, and a committee elected. Fred Olliphant, the new Chair, wrote to the *Hornsey Journal* to thank the paper for its support during a time of crisis. He wrote % the CHELIC office.

Some of the numbered groups mutated into local groups – Group 10 became the London Monday Group, named for the day it met; Group 6 took the name Marylebone, subsequently adding '& Paddington'; Groups 1, 2 and 3 combined and mutated into London West End, or CHEWEG, retaining the chairman of Group 1, Griffith Vaughan Williams. Group 4, which had another female chair, in the person of radio producer Babs Todd, took the name Bloomsbury Group, with a nice sense of historical continuity. Mainly because of Babs and her partner Jackie Forster, who also ran the magazine and social group, Sappho, Bloomsbury had a 50/50 male/female membership. Groups 11, 12, and 13 also merged to form Central London Group. Others such as Groups 5 and 9, bled of members by the new local groups, simply folded.

Most of the groups carried on the traditional mixture of social and discussion groups, but some stood out because of particular interests and projects. Streatham and especially London Monday became prominent through the range of well-known speakers they attracted. Lewisham, through the involvement of Rose Robertson, developed a close working relationship with Parents' Enquiry, and in 1977 wrote and produced their own 45-minute film *David is Homosexual.** The West End group became particularly active in campaigning around issues affecting older gay men. Of the numbered groups, only Group 8 soldiered on, remaining as such until 1976, when it changed its name to Piccadilly Group.

More on 'People not Paper'

'People not Paper' is a remarkable read today, for two reasons. Firstly, it is the only occasion on which anyone put any thought into the long-term development of CHE as a significant 'social service' for homosexuals, with all that that might imply. Here is the first consideration of older gays, which would become a major theme of CHE work through the report that the West End Group produced in 1974, and through the 'older gays' portfolio on the National Executive which existed into the 1980s. 'PNP' is almost breath-taking in its ambition:

> If we accept long term planning of the social service of CHE as important we shall have within a few years a number of pensioners on our books. Help for elderly members is no less important than for those who are below the present age of consent or those who are in emotional distress or those who have been in prison. ... It is not too early to decide how far Task Force is to extend its activities. Whatever is decided we must soon put out delicate feelers in the matter of visiting those who would be members except that they are on pension and feel that they would not happily fit in at a general group meeting. Certainly visiting the elderly in small groups might be started relatively soon. Once our own Club is established there is no reason to suppose that we couldn't consider the

* No copies of *David is Homosexual* appear to have survived.

> sponsoring and running – we are all perforce self-reliant – of an Old People's Home.[59]

It is equally pioneering in its mention of disabled gays, albeit not maybe in terms we would want to use now: 'We must start to make delicate overtures to societies for the Blind. The Deaf must not be forgotten. Have we considered those disabled by War, Accidents and Polio?'*[60]

To this end it proposed setting up more working groups, and in so doing raised one issue which was to haunt CHE for the next ten years – paedophilia:

> NEW COMMITTEES OF ENQUIRY
> CHE and Pornography
> 'Do we shut the door on the Pederast?'
> Old People
> The disabled
> CHE sports centre
> Holiday schemes.[61]

If in the light of subsequent developments this seems almost a *folie de grandeur*, there was at the time reason to be optimistic. Members were joining at an astonishing rate:

> We have now reached a point where the Greater London area has an enrolled membership of approaching 500 served by ten London groups (one of them nominally though not predominantly 'local' already – Croydon) and by the time this document is being considered it is likely that there will be another hundred members. … We can say that during the period September 1970 and September 1971 membership in London grew from something around 100 to 500 – a growth rate of 400%. It may continue at this pace. If we are relatively conservative in our estimate it would seem feasible to suggest that by September 1972 London CHE could have over 1500 members.[62]

What money could not be raised, what plans not achieved, by 1,500 sets of eyes, arms, brains? There were other dreams too. Peter Robins recalled:

> I lived very near the War Museum at the time, and I had quite a nice large sitting room, and I had people round on Sunday evenings and all the rest of it, and Tony Ryde was there, and begged a lift from Brian [Sewell] to go somewhere or other – one of the railway stations, I suspect. Brian gave

* Poliomyelitis was a paralysing, sometimes fatal, disease now eliminated in the UK. There were a few hundred cases a year in the early twentieth century, but after World War Two it suddenly grew to epidemic proportions, with 8,000 British cases in 1948. For ten years there were several thousand cases a year, until the Salk and Sabin vaccines started to reduce the incidence of new cases in the 1960s. At the time of writing 'People not paper', the majority of polio sufferers were in their late teens and early twenties.

> him a lift, and I'd never seen Brian white-faced before, but he came back, and he said, 'That man Tony Ryde! We drove past the Shell building, and he said to me, 'Oh, that's where I work until CHE can afford to pay me full time'. Brian was furious. I thought, 'God, what have we come to?'[63]

It was not so hard to understand, that a man who was working forty hours a week in his spare time for something he believed in passionately should dream that one day he would be paid for doing it. If Manchester could have Paul Temperton, why shouldn't London have Tony Ryde?

'People not Paper' was to come up for consideration at the second London mass meeting, held at Conway Hall in October 1971. Brian Sewell, desperate to push it forward, and conscious that ordinary members were impatient for action, sent out an agenda which raised eyebrows and hackles:

> We do not want an atmosphere of acrimony and reproach, but all members must be encouraged to criticise (as helpfully as possible) and it may be that some heads will have to fall. …
>
> We are very concerned that while a few members now put a great deal of time and energy into CHE's affairs, grass roots seem to be getting very little out of it, and some 50% of members do not renew their subscriptions.[64]

It was quite reasonable to suggest that if people were not doing what they had said they'd do, perhaps somebody else would be able to do it instead. However, talk of 'heads rolling' made some both fearful and antagonistic. Paul Temperton came down from Manchester and was on the receiving end of Brian's tongue. Chairman of the Student Group Colin Darracott saw it all as a storm in a teacup. He wrote to Peter Norman in the wake of the Holborn meeting:

> Poor Paul gets a lot of buffeting but seems to hold up so well. I'm sure I would be a lot less pleasant a person if I had to face the wrath of the Sewells, Staffords, Darracotts and such like. … It wastes so much time and energy which could be devoted to other things.
>
> I am also glad that you weren't too put off by London's obstreperousness. Brian Sewell has an unfortunately cutting manner of speech, but he is nevertheless concerned about the whole, nationally as well as just our cabbage patch. He is still Manchester's arch-critic, but he is not anti. I only wish I could be more involved nationally, but by living in London one has a lot of effort cut out just to see that people here behave, which they don't.[65]

David Hyde, editor of *Lunch*, commiserated as well:

> I'm told you had to put up with one of Brian Sewell's sessions a few days ago. A lot of people are getting rather anxious about the way he is going

> about things down here. I for one am intending to let him have a taste of his own medicine some time, possibly at the October meeting.[66]

To which Paul, the mildest of men, could only reply that Brian had been 'unnecessarily unpleasant'. Others objected to Brian's hustling too:

> I'm afraid I cannot agree to circulate the 'agenda' for the Conway Hall meeting in the form in which it has been sent. It seems to me to be a propaganda sheet representing the views of the rump membership of Group 3. … Its tone is such as to invite acrimony and recrimination whatever exhortations may be made to the contrary, and I fail to see how this can help to hold CHE together. … The IE [Interim Executive] is exceeding its remit in bypassing the London Committee to present recommendations direct to the membership at an open meeting where … they will be quite unprepared for adequate consideration of proposals and will be able only to produce a half-baked response. Unless this item is withdrawn from the agenda I shall feel unable to recommend my members to attend the meeting. … In the IE the London Committee appears to have created a monster which is getting out of control. … I shall seek through the proper channels to bring it under control before irreparable damage is done to London CHE.'[67]

So wrote Ken Glazier, the Chairman of Group 1, always one for the 'proper channels', to Brian. The tone suggests a deep personal animosity beyond the ostensible subject, and it is true that Sewell was a figure who aroused strong reactions. Tall and strikingly handsome, with a shock of curly hair, he stood out literally and metaphorically from the ruck. His distinctive speech, with its drawled, fractured vowels and clipped consonants, was usually taken as a mark of aristocracy, although his personal background was far more complex than that. To Michael Moor:

> He appeared to be from a different social milieu to the one that I was familiar with. To me, middle-class, this was definitely on a higher plane! … *Brideshead Revisited* comes to mind. It's a lightweight linen jacket and curly hair. No teddy bear. But probably a striped sweater.[68]

Though Tony Ryde found him 'extraordinarily committed and sensible', his manner particularly intimidated people from outside the capital, to whom he was the epitome of urban sophistication. People such as Robin Bloxsidge:

> He was a very dominant person, and his views were always very stridently and forcefully expressed, a typical sort of waspish humour, which was actually really very amusing – if you weren't on the end of it. I was rather overwhelmed by these more worldly people.[69]

Others such as Tony Ryde found Peter Robins the difficult one:

> I can remember going down to his house in South London, and storming on his door because he was refusing to co-operate on something, we couldn't get in touch with him, he wasn't answering the phone, sort of done a UDI,* and I'm sure that for a period he was completely uncontactable. And the only way we could get to him was to go down one evening, a group of us, and bang on his door. And he got frightfully upset because we woke his mother up.[70]

Brian Sewell certainly remembers feeling beleaguered, having a sense of wading through treacle in order to get anything done. Against this inertia were pitted himself, Peter and a select few:

> Everything that Peter and I and others who were with us came up with somehow got a drag anchor attached to it by everybody else. … And whenever there was a committee of any kind, there were people who would say, 'Oh please, through the Chair, through the Chair.' So we weren't allowed to have a discussion direct, … Manchester's only contribution was to act as a brake. … Manchester as far as I remember never agreed to anything. Peter was absolutely fundamental to the common sense of whatever it was we did. … It was Peter's practical wisdom that prevented CHE from making a total prat of itself from time to time.[71]

Second Mass Meeting

At the October mass meeting, Brian and Peter found themselves, slightly to their discomfort, on the large stage at one end of the room, alongside Tony Ryde and Glenys Parry. Roger Baker, the working class Nottingham boy, was a bit scathing about people being on the platform by virtue of having the 'right' accent and the 'right' background, although Peter Norman insists, 'It wasn't that at all, it was, "What do you want to see done?" '

Nevertheless Roger's egalitarian view is quite clear in the anonymous article he wrote for *Lunch* immediately after the meeting. It's in the form of a dialogue between two slightly dim, not very politically-minded but well-meaning queens:

> — We all sat down on …
> — We? Who are We?
> — The common members. We all sat in the audience and they –
> — They? Who are they?
> — Our leaders. They all sat up on the platform in a row. It really did you good to sit there looking up to them. And such lovely voices some of

---

* Unilateral Declaration of Independence: the phrase came into common use when Rhodesia (now Zimbabwe) declared independence on 11 November 1965.

> them have, ever so public school. SO comforting to know that the right sort of people are in charge, don't you think? ... It gives such a good impression.[72]

Ironically, Brian never saw himself in that leadership role. But for the moment, they were there, under the spotlight, defending 'People not Paper' from the likes of Ken Glazier and David Hyde. Glazier had been right in his refusal to circulate the agenda to this extent: Brian couldn't expect a mass meeting of three hundred people to discuss a 22-page report which they'd only just seen. It was referred back to the LCC, where most of its provisions were argued out of court.

Shortly after the meeting, the 'Commonwealth Triumvirate' was over and there was a 'restoration of the monarchy' (Peter Robins' words). Sewell disappeared off to the States, Moor took a break, and Robins returned 'to the small country pleasures of Group 9'. Tony Ryde was back in the saddle as chairman, with his own agenda for fundraising for a national centre, as we have seen.

> — Then we had reports from the working parties.
> — And have they done much?
> — Not really.
> — Not very encouraging, was it?
> — No. But it's lovely to hear them talk.[73]

Among the groups which hadn't done very much were two new ones which interested individuals set up without any kind of mandate: a Legal Working Party, chaired by Griffith Vaughan Williams, and one on pornography. In the four months of its existence, the only action the Legal Working Party had undertaken was to try to set up a meeting with Tony Smythe, General Secretary of the National Council for Civil Liberties, and it had failed even to do that.

> — Then we heard that another group is going to be set up too, to do a survey on pornography for Lord Longford.
> — What on earth for?
> — That's what someone asked.
> — And what was the answer?
> — No-one was allowed to give one.[74]

Pornography Working Party

The CHE Pornography Working Party was set up in response to Lord Longford's self-appointed Commission on Pornography, which started work in the summer of 1971. Earlier that year he had, as a fervent Roman Catholic, come under the influence of the Nationwide Festival of Light movement,* and Mary Whitehouse in particular. He was persuaded to spearhead the Commission of Inquiry into Pornography after Whitehouse's intervention had led to the prosecution of *The Little Red School Book*.† In addition, *Oh! Calcutta!*‡ had pushed the boundaries of what was acceptable on stage, after the abolition in 1968 of the Lord Chamberlain's role as the official theatre censor. A Festival of Light Rally in Trafalgar Square attracted 50,000 people. Longford initiated a debate in the House of Lords on pornography, and then started gathering together 'a few friends' to form a self-appointed commission.

GLF made a much-publicised intervention to subvert a Festival of Light rally at Westminster Central Hall; CHE at least toyed with the idea of taking Longford at his word when he invited submissions to his Commission from all interested parties. Or rather, a few members did. Roger Baker, an enthusiastic porn user as Brian Sewell discovered at his induction, smelt a rat before the Commission even got going. Pornography was a favourite discussion topic at local groups, many of the discussions being led by Baker.

Baker picked up on the Commission's potential for making mischief, and in particular on the way in which it could swing public opinion on pornography, resulting in more repressive censorship. Baker was prophetic in this, because, in the wake of the Report, Indecent Displays Bills were brought

---

* This was founded in late 1970 by two Evangelical missionaries, Peter and Janet Hill, newly returned from India, who were shocked by the 'permissive society' they found. They established a series of local committees and recruited a number of well-known supporters who also lent their names to Lord Longford's Committee on Pornography. Over 70 Festival of Light rallies were held around Britain, and a chain of some 300 beacons was lit, often with local authority participation. Over 100,000 people took part in this first flurry of activity.

† *The Little Red Book for Students*, to give it its full title, was written by two Danish school teachers, and published in an English language version in 1971. It was aimed at young people in their teens, and encouraged them to question authority and adults ('paper tigers'). Out of its 208 pages, 30 discussed drugs and alcohol in a non-judgemental way, and a further 20 covered sex, including homosexuality. Largely as a result of Whitehouse's campaign, it was prosecuted for obscenity in July 1971, and the publishers fined £50. Belated seizures however meant that 17,000 copies were already in circulation. A slightly revised version was published shortly afterwards, and the prosecution substantially increased sales. The case was appealed up to the European Court of Human Rights in 1976 (*Handyside v. United Kingdom*). The court rejected the appeal.

‡ *Oh Calcutta!*, a musical revue curated by Kenneth Tynan with material by, among others, Samuel Beckett, Edna O'Brien, Sam Shepard and John Lennon, opened on Broadway in 1970 and in London in 1971. Unlike the discreet nudity of *Hair*, here the cast were naked and in full lights for extended sections of the show, including complete sketches and dance numbers. It ran on Broadway for over 6,000 performances and in London for nearly 4,000. It illustrated dramatically the shift in taste which had occurred in the previous three years.

forward as Private Members' Bills on an almost yearly basis until one was finally passed in 1981. CHE was to keep a wary eye on all these, in case more restrictive definitions of obscenity and other illiberal provisions were smuggled in.

However Roger was the first to sniff the possibility of legislation, even before Longford reported, and to point to a rational response to the issue, which would advocate curtailing the public display of offensive images, but keep the right to choose to view them in private intact:

> More recently we have Lord Longford who has recruited that well-known expert on pornography, Cliff Richard, and many others to help him look into the armpits of society and have a good sniff. We know that in a year they will emerge, picking the hairs off their suits and screaming for deodorants. So would most of us. And there's no reason to sneer at Lord Longford for setting up his commission. After all, many campaigns that ultimately affected our laws were the result of private enterprise by sympathetic persons. …
>
> Totally opposed to censorship in any form, I am opposed to tasteless and sometimes embarrassing displays outside cinemas, bookshops and strip clubs. If I feel like pushing 525 new pennies over a counter for a set of sexy stills of well-hung studs in amazing unthought-of-before positions, well, that's my business; however I should hate to see the aforesaid studs well hung outside my friendly local porn shop in the crowded village street.[75]

Baker's suggestion of a pre-emptive strike made sense, given Longford's agenda. Longford's committee was a strange beast, the 52-strong 'final list of members' a hotchpotch of celebs and shrinks, clerics, headmasters and journalists. Alongside Cliff Richard and Jimmy Savile were 'Mrs Sara Binney, housewife' and 'Martin Hughes, student'. Perhaps those with the most media clout were Malcolm Muggeridge and Peregrine Worsthorne, deputy editor of the *Sunday Telegraph*. Novelists Kingsley Amis and Elizabeth Jane Howard lent their names. Clerics included Methodist Lord Soper, Trevor Huddleston (Bishop of Stepney) and the Archbishop of York (Donald Coggan, later Archbishop of Canterbury).* Soper was to distance himself from the final report, and it is not clear how much active involvement with the Commission any of these concerned worthies had had individually. Soper claimed that he had had none when challenged by Peter Norman:

> I discovered there were several references to homosexuality which were extremely disparaging in the Longford Report, and so I raised this at the EC, and drafted a letter for the Chairman to send to him [Soper], saying,

* One person notable by her absence was Whitehouse herself.

'What do you think you were doing?' And he wrote back saying, 'Ah yes, I see what you mean. Perhaps we could discuss it sometime if you're ever around this way.' … Which I did. … I felt some trepidation, but he was perfectly nice. It turned out he had been ill all the time that the Longford Report was being written, and he hadn't been at a single meeting, and didn't know what was in it. And so he [Soper] stood up in the House of Lords, to his great credit, I thought, when it came to a discussion of the Pornography Report, and said that he dissociated himself from these disparaging references to homosexual people, and Lord Longford stood up and said he regretted that they had been in the report and they shouldn't have been, so I thought, 'Yes!'[76]

Paul Temperton seized on this exchange in the Lords,[77] and wrote to Longford demanding a retraction of these disparaging sections in the second edition. There was no reply. Trevor Huddleston also came to dissociate himself from the Festival of Light and the Longford Report, after discussions with a GLF awareness group.

When Longford originally invited submissions, it was the idea of Colin Darracott* to respond. Darracott was a recent Oxford graduate of complex sexuality with an interest in porn. For about six months he acted as bright and energetic secretary and gofer to Brian's various working parties. Sewell's memories were very positive:

Colin came down from Oxford full of enthusiasm for CHE. And he had a summer in which he could be useful. He was sharing with a couple of other recent graduates [in Ealing]. I found out where he was and one Saturday morning we met for coffee. He was very useful, very bright. If you wanted something printed, he'd get it printed. He was a 'Do' kind of person.[78]

Colin was living in the Strand Palace Hotel; Shell Oil had recruited him as a trainee manager and housed all trainees on a floor there, where they could become immersed in the corporate culture. Here he lived, breathed and socialised Shell, twenty-four hours a day. While housed in Oil Purdah, he had the bright idea of writing to Longford, and was much surprised to get a phone call almost immediately from his office, offering a meeting. Longford had been an academic, but was a gullible and extraordinarily naïve man for all his personal kindness and academic brilliance. He had already been lampooned by the press, while visiting strip clubs in Denmark. When he was asked what he thought of these joints, he was quoted as saying he hadn't expected the audience participation. Colin took along Brian Sewell and Peter Robins to see

---

* Colin was to become involved in local Lib. Dem. politics and ended up serving on Bath and North East Somerset Council.

Longford. According to Sewell:

> He was quite impossibly mad. No, not mad, but stupid. 'Tell me, is it correct that all the porn shops in Soho are run by homosexuals?' We looked at one another, and said, 'Really? Why?' 'Well, it stands to reason. You couldn't have them run by heterosexuals because any man could go in there and find it was being run by his neighbour across the road. What would he think then?' ... Right at the beginning of this discussion we had with the good Lord, he said, 'Do you mind if my secretary stays in the room and pours the coffee?' 'Why?' 'Well, she's a woman.'[79]

Evidently Longford did not feel safe in a room alone with three gay men, and needed the protection of a female. The CHE delegates were also rather miffed to learn that he had never heard of CHE, although he knew of the Gay Liberation Front.

Brian went away having made an offer to try and organise a nation-wide survey of gay men's attitudes to pornography. Group 1 agreed by a vote of 30 to 2 to devise a quite detailed and lengthy questionnaire, the results of which would go to Longford: But then the idea hit a rock. To print, distribute, and collect the questionnaires, to analyse and forward them, would cost £50 – more than the London group would pay. Would Longford pay? Was the deadline for replying flexible? Longford's office was silent for some time. Eventually word came, there was no money, no flexibility and all responses had to be in by Christmas 1971.

Meanwhile, there were many members who wouldn't touch the Longford Commission with a bargepole:

> Longford retains enough political acumen to know how to use CHE, and not let it use him. Accordingly, his movement will use CHE's evidence, such as it is, to strengthen his case. That case cannot conceivably do CHE any good at all. Why they should then spend time, energy and even money on furthering the work of the commission is an utter mystery; no dedicated saboteur of CHE could have thought of a better way to weaken it.
>
> —John Cowell, Gp. 4.

> For society as a whole homosexuality is in some obscure way bound up with pornography: deviation is considered ipso facto pornographic. It is this prejudice we must fight and ... you cannot attempt to break down a prejudice by tacitly agreeing with it. —Charles Murdoch[80]

Since it was to be a nation-wide survey, the project went forward for consideration to the EC. It too steered a wide berth of the Commission. Brian was out on a limb. Reluctantly he admitted defeat and wrote to Lord Longford. He was frank:

> I still think that this was a sane thing to do,* and you underlined its sanity when you told us that you thought that most Soho pornographers must be homosexual because they dislike having women in their shops – pornography is essentially a man's interest, and you were potty to imagine that your pretty young researchers would get an accurate impression of the market, though they may well have got you the answers you think you want. It was a mistake to assume that CHE could be swept along on the tide of our enthusiasm. I am still convinced you would be wrong to neglect the views of responsible homosexuals, but it would be wiser and quicker for you to interview a selection of men like our various chairmen whose views are representative of the groups they head; they will range from perfectly reasonable but total opposition to your enquiry, to an equally reasonable willingness to answer you.
>
> It is my duty to CHE to avoid waste of time and money on a survey that you cannot use because we cannot complete it until next spring.[81]

In the event, the only person connected to CHE who gave evidence to Longford was his friend, fallen Tory MP Ian Harvey, whom Longford had encouraged to write his autobiography.† However, he might have saved himself the bother, in that this was an enquiry which had made up its mind as to its conclusions before it entered the arena. Thus the survey, by Maurice Yaffe of the Institute of Psychiatry, of the scientific evidence of the effects of pornography on the consumer, which the Longford Commission itself requested and published,[82] concludes that 'in the present state of knowledge it is not possible to draw any useful conclusions which might be applied to this problem and related issues'[83] but the rest of the report insists, on no evidential basis, that pornography is 'addictive', responsible for venereal disease, illegitimacy, relationship breakdown and promiscuity and should therefore be banned.

A draft Bill attached to the Report, to amend the Obscene Publications and Theatres Acts, expands the definition of 'obscenity', brings broadcasting and film under the scope of the Obscene Publications Act and removes the defence of 'public good'. The display of 'indecent' materials is subject to very heavy fines (no definition of 'indecency') and so is acting or modelling in them.

---

* i.e. to consult homosexuals. Sewell is naïvely suggesting that since Longford's views on homosexuality were so dotty, the views of genuine homosexuals might have tempered them.

† Other homosexuals wrote to the Commission sad, lonely and self-hating letters, which only confirmed its belief in the connection between porn and inadequacy. Colin Darracott and Peter Robins are also listed in the Longford Report (p. 440) as being among those who gave evidence, but there is no evidence of their involvement beyond the afternoon tea described here, and neither is quoted.

> It is quite untrue to say … that there is no evidence that pornography does harm. There is plenty of evidence that it sometimes does harm, that it can therefore do harm. … There is no alibi here for inaction. No great social reform has ever waited for statistical information or irrefutable proof.[84]

However, the Longford Commission was in the future for our two fictitious queens at Conway Hall in October 1971, where they broke for tea:

> — Then there was an interval, but it didn't last long.
> — Why ever not?
> — The Chairman wanted to get on with the meeting.
> — So you all had to sit down and shut up again.
> — 'Fraid so. …
> — Glenys … and everyone else said how nice it was to see all our faces.
> — Were the people from Manchester there too?
> — Well, there was a lot of talk about laying the Manchester Ghost. Which we did. By that stage I was glad to lay anything.
> — So it all ended happily?
> — I think so.
> — And you all got together and had a really good talk.
> — Not exactly. We had to be out of the hall very quickly and it was closing time.
> — So what did you do?
> — I went home alone.[85]

Among the visitors, rather reluctantly, was Peter Norman, who saw a crucial – indeed, the central – aspect of CHE's policy at stake:

> The reality of it was, as we saw it in Manchester, there was a body of people in London, including Brian [Sewell], who didn't support the view that the age of consent should be reduced to 16, and of course we felt that they were completely wrong about that, because it was absolutely opposed to the very name of the organisation. And it felt from our point of view that the EC were being summoned to account for themselves by these uppity Londoners who were trying to dismantle the organisation that we were trying to build up. Allan Horsfall … would not go to this meeting to be pilloried by these people. But I was Vice Chairman at the time, so I had to go.
>
> I don't think I'd ever spoken to such a big group of people before. Two hundred people. And I had to defend this policy which I agreed with, though I could see some good reasons for querying … whether it was wise to make it a central plank of the campaign at that time. … But I went along and said my piece, and Brian Sewell seemed to be mollified, he didn't make such a fuss as it seemed he would do. He said to me, 'You see, I don't have horns.' [86]

For all his nerves, Peter's contribution seems to have impressed at least one person mightily. At a party later that evening at Roger Baker's, he met the convenor of London 10, John Saxby. Saxby was a curly-haired, bearded, outgoing man and very sexy. He took Peter back to his flat in South Kensington, and that was that. Love at first sight:

> I remember I asked Robin what I should do about this, and he said, 'Well, you're not getting any younger, you're 29. You might not get a better offer!' So that's how that meeting changed my life.[87]

It took five months for Peter to organise a move to London, during which time they snatched weekends together, and even official CHE letters from LMG Chairman to national local groups organiser were signed off with a dozen kisses ('just a sample'). After a 'coming-together party' – the nearest available marker for a partnership commitment – they subsequently lived together for twelve years. As the *Lunch* article said, it all ended happily. For two at least.

Other Mass Meetings

There were more mass meetings at roughly six-monthly intervals, either at the Conway Hall or at the Holborn Assembly Rooms. They could be highly charged. Brian Sewell recalled one in particular:

> I remember one at the Conway Hall which was really quite explosive and dramatic, and I thought a great step was about to be taken. And of course it never was. And the great step was, there were a number of elderly men there, who said, 'What we want more than anything else in the world is an old people's home that is exclusively for faggots. Because we can't think of anything worse than being stuck in the average old people's home, with everybody desperately heterosexual, and little old ladies of 93 are going to make passes, and that's not what we want. And somehow or other that burgeoned immediately, because people were standing up and saying, 'Yes, you can buy a decent house for whatever – ten thousand pounds or something –
>
> 'Well, where's the money coming from?' said the Roger Bakers of this world. Whereupon somebody put his hand in his pocket and threw a handful of change at the platform. And all sorts of other people were doing that, so money was flying all over the place. … I think they counted it and it was three hundred and something pounds. … I thought, 'God, this is exciting! This is going to happen!' And it never did.'[88]

The needs of elderly gay men were to be championed by the West End Group, which produced a report on 'the plight of the aged homosexual' in 1974.*

---

* See Volume Three.

The meeting of June 1972, this time in the Holborn Assembly Rooms, was less stormy than its predecessors, according to Roger Baker, writing in the new *Gay News*. By now there was more concern with presentation. The stage was festooned in flowers donated by a local gay florist. The chair for the day was Gavin Clare, Chairman of Group 2 after Angus Forsyth. But the subjects remained much the same, most crucially the Club. By now the building fund stood at £449.96. The two hundred members present were told that the Manchester initiatives under Esquire Clubs were now a dead duck. Roger Baker wrote: 'It looks as though it is up to London CHE to do it, being bigger and therefore richer (though not necessarily wiser) than the provincial groups.'[89]

52. Invitation to mass meeting, June 1972

So did the members want a COC-type club or merely a permanent office space? To teacher David Bell, a club would be 'the one thing CHE is known for the world over'. Some doubted the wisdom of competing with commercial gay clubs, others thought the project would succumb to the 'church hall syndrome' and no-one would come. There were endless reasons not to do anything. However:

> the temperature rose just before half time when one guy, obviously cheesed off with the debating, stood up and threw a 50p piece on the floor and bullied everyone to do the same. His idea was action now and to hell with the chat. His enthusiasm was infectious as that little episode added an instant £70.86 to the building fund.[90]

The man was Donald Hendry, unknown save for this intervention. His 'marvellous fairground eloquence' raised the money in less than ten minutes. What Roger described has marked similarities to Brian's account, so much so that the question must be whether they are talking about the same event. However, Brian's account of the older gay men's contribution, which tallies with other developments within CHE, must leave at least the doubt that throwing money on the stage was not a one-off, might even have been a regular ritual to appease the gods of apathy.

This meeting gave the go-ahead to the London Office, as opposed to the Club, if only for the sake of getting something off the ground rather than nothing:

> After coffee the chairman suggested we should begin with unlicensed premises, providing an information centre, meeting place, office and telephone number, like the GLF Switchboard. Brian Sewell and Peter Robins were in favour, while David Bell, his sights set on the COC's Amsterdam building, opposed starting in such a modest way. After discussion, a large majority voted in favour of looking for unlicensed premises at the earliest possible moment.[91]

This is the first mass meeting at which Jackie Forster makes an appearance. She is wearing 'a gorgeous plumade'. One of the reasons she worked so effectively with men, saying harsh truths but retaining a store of affection and goodwill, was her very highly developed sense of 'Camp'. 'Do you spend any time at all thinking about lesbians?' she asked, almost rhetorically. 'Equality must mean more girls in CHE.' And why isn't anyone doing more about campaigning? Why has there been no reaction to the verdict in the *International Times* case? There has, reassured Tony Ryde. We are in touch with MPs. … 'Have you written to yours?' he demanded of the members present.

Special interest groups (SIGs)

One of the more significant developments which the July 1972 meeting brought to the fore was the emergence of special interest groups (SIGs). This marks a progress in the development of gay identity and of gay space.

The first stage of finding identity is the discussion of self, the defining issues for homosexuals, and the rudiments of an awareness of demands and rights.

The second stage, developing more confidence, turns the attention of the individual member from the internal to the external, to talks about members' interests and other subjects unrelated to gay identity, but within the confines of the already-created gay space in the familiar room visited fortnightly or monthly.

The third stage is taking 'gay space' out into a non-gay environment, the group creating a bubble in which it is safe to 'act gay' and be oneself, even if the wider surroundings are not so supportive. The creation of SIGs is an aspect of this last, in which lesbians and gay men can 'be gay' or 'act gay' while sharing other activities, as well as in non-gay external space.

Part of the creation of gay identity occurs in the formation of friendship networks among lesbians and gay men unrelated to the search for sexual partners or life partners. One of the necessary skills to acquire in pursuance of a gay identity is the ability to relate in non-sexual ways, and the ability simply to communicate with each other as an exercise in sociability. SIGs through the imposition of a shared purpose provide the framework for that to happen. Further, these activities often include an element of public performance, using the word in the widest sense:

> We heard that gramophone enthusiasts, poetry-lovers, drama-buffs, car rally maniacs, musical souls, sporting types were now being catered for by a series of groups set up to pursue these hobbies. There was to be a choir as well, and a sports club. And a dining club.[92]

Paul Temperton in the Manchester office was well aware that convenors ran out of ideas for discussion, or interesting people to invite to speak. They were all too conscious of the possibility of boredom setting in, once the basic ground – the 'crash course in homosexuality' – had been covered. As usual, Paul sought the solution from within the ranks of the membership. He invited members to volunteer to go to other groups to talk about their pet subjects, and circulated a directory of members prepared to do so, their subjects, and what facilities or props they would need. The list showed a strong interest in the occult, and tarot in particular. Roger Bradshaw ('I am a practising white witch') offered to talk on 'Ritual Witchcraft Today' within a hundred mile radius of Blackburn, and to take along an exhibition of tools used by witches. Alternatively, he could talk about field sports. Ceramics, canals, drag (Roger Baker), Alaska all had their expert speakers. But the most versatile speaker was Michael Harth, who offered:

> Basis of character-reading in modern astrology (have D.F.Astrol.S.); home wine and liqueur making; Liszt, the man and his music; Liszt and the

> invention of the symphonic poem. London and outskirts. (Need a record player and pref. a piano).[93]

It was a logical extension of social activities for people to band together for particular purposes. However, although many SIGs were social, others formed the beginning of action groups to effect change in attitudes towards homosexuality in particular areas of work, forerunners of the LGBT groups within trades unions, professions or political parties. By March 1973 the following were in full swing:

Camping	Music	Political action
Cycling	Drama	Athletics
Gardening	Revue and Cabaret	Film Unit
German	Poetry	Eurogroup
Hill Walking	Gay writers	Canal cruising

Other groups were being mooted:

Languages	Wine making	Chess
Librarians	Women's group	Yoga
Mountaineering	Rambling	Swimming
Photography	Football	Table Tennis
Rock Climbing	Hour Glass group*	Badminton
Social Workers	Jewish Liaison group	Bridge
Teachers	Art & Sculpture	
Walking	Railway Society (CHEmin-de-fer)	

These groups largely went their own way and did not produce newsletters, nor did they advertise extensively. Their activities can mainly be glimpsed by passing references. However, some are better documented than others, and some led to serious political developments, as well as to other projects.

Vivian Waldron's walking group, for example, created in London Group 8, gradually took in more people until it became London-wide. It started exchanging visits with other walking groups (Oldham, Manchester, Liverpool, Oxford, Chilterns, Birmingham) and in 1976, led by Birmingham CHE, they all joined into the national Gay Outdoor Club, which, in 2014, still had about 1,600 members. It also covers several of the other outdoor activities listed above, including climbing, cycling, canoeing, indoor sports and caving. Waldron himself was adamant about the value of these groups:

> Of course we are out to change public opinion … but we are also out to change homosexuals. And they are changing here and now and it is greatly

* A lunching group for workers with an hour to spare, which met on Wednesdays in Billy's Baked Potato in Holborn.

> to the credit of people running poetry reading circles, music clubs, drama groups and motoring clubs … that these changes are taking place in the life of the individual. And it is from these now liberated homosexuals that the campaigners and leaders of the future are likely to come.
>
> The second reason we need interest groups is because if we are to have a drive to increase membership we must have something to offer newly-joined members apart from formal group meetings, the occasional dance and campaigning. A third reason is that they are so enjoyable. Some of us are in danger … of becoming official homosexuals. We spend our spare time reading homosexual literature, attending meetings of homosexuals, organising other homosexuals, until there is little about our lives to recommend them to the critical homosexual or anyone else.[94]

Today SIGs would be likely to be found in forums on the internet, which are capable of attracting a number of like-minded people to the narrowest, most specialised concern. In CHE SIGs grew over the period 1973–75, during which time, as Michael Steed put it:

> there were members to form all sorts of groups, and there was a tendency to form a group for anything – Chris Bowden-Smith had a gay Girobank users' group, which was an officially registered affinity group for the Girobank.* So in a way it was part of the collective development of self-consciousness coming out. If there was any bit of civil society where you could have an organisation, and you knew somebody else who was gay you formed a gay group. And within CHE if you met somebody else who liked doing something in common, you formed a group.[95]

So not only were SIGs part of the growth of self-consciousness and confidence on the part of members, they were part of the move to visibility, the registration of a gay presence and a gay interest in all aspects of civil society.

CHE Music Group

The music group was one of the first to get off the ground, in the wake of a Peter Katin recital at his home. It was also the source of a fierce, if petty, spat, which illustrates the classic tendency in small organisations for would-be big fish to be protective of their domains. A few members of Katin's audience floated the idea of regular music appreciation, and on the back of this Alistair

* National Girobank was launched by the Labour government in 1968 as a move to extend banking to a wider section of the population; it operated through Post Office branches, and pioneered the use of transfers between accounts instead of cheques. It was privatised in 1990, and absorbed into the Alliance and Leicester Building Society and subsequently Santander Bank.

Nicholl advertised in *Lunch* and circulated a questionnaire about musical tastes. This stressed the purely musical nature of the group. It would organise recitals by members and guests in people's homes; it would arrange record evenings and concert trips; it would put people in touch with each other with similar musical interests, such as organ music or collecting 78s. It was all very serious and high-minded.

He got twenty-three replies. However, in the meantime, Bill Dalziel of Group 12 had got together his own music group, based on personal friends but also attracting members of the West End groups purely by word of mouth. Both Nicholl and Dalziel got in touch with Paul Temperton, asking for publicity, and claiming to be *the* music group. Naturally Paul told them to talk to each other. Dalziel wrote to Nicholl, and got a curt brush-off:

> Not sure who gave you my name and address but it was without my agreement. You have spelt my name incorrectly. … There really is no point in writing to me further on this matter. Am sorry but am not able to spend the time on correspondence nor I'm afraid on attending meetings not connected with this project.[96]

Nicholl was spitting at the impertinence of Dalziel in starting what he thought was a 'rival', and rather trivial, group, and miffed that no senior CHE figure had discouraged him:

> It doesn't sound from his didactic written note to me that this will much affect the Music Club project, which is intended for those with serious musical interests. Nor does it seem so far that he would be an appropriate person to help run the London Music Club. It may be that his circle will cater for those who want a further Group type of activity (all chat and meetings!)[97]

Nicholl was a martinet obsessed with doing things 'correctly' (i.e. his way) in what would be a group entirely run by him, handing down 'culture'. However, by August 1972 he was standing down, and handing on his baton. His explanation of the new arrangements to Paul Temperton was an unwitting giveaway as to why such a snobbish and abrasive person was the last man you would want running a social group. He was handing over, he said:

> to three excellent CHE members, all professional men of great enthusiasm, who see the importance of the project in its aim to provide properly organised get-togethers in small groups of CHE people who have a fairly serious interest in music for its own sake. A number of those who replied are professional and semi-professional musicians, and several others are already involved in the … organisation of amateur musical activities. Many are clearly busy people and would not be prepared to attend aimless meetings. Since there is nothing that needs discussing at the moment it is

> not considered useful to hold a general meeting at this time; many would not or could not turn up and it would be a waste of time.[98]

Professional men or not (they were respectively a departmental head at a Comprehensive School, a university administrator and an architectural historian), they seem not to have taken the group any further. Those who signed up must have deserted for the much more open-armed Dalziel. CHE members did not like being organised for their own good. Dalziel's publicity was much more effective, offering as it did not only music but support and companionship:

> I could keep every Saturday evening free for the specific purpose of receiving guests for record recitals. This may help solve the problem of members who live in furnished rooms, who are unable for any reason to enjoy classical music in such surroundings, or for those living at home whose families dislike classical music. Also for the visitor to London who wishes to contact CHE members at weekends and likes music, but doesn't know where to go.
>
> I am also willing to receive members during the week or Sunday, provided I'm at home. Visitors during the week may not wish to listen to music, but may just need company, someone to talk to about anything they wish.[99]

Dalziel was in some ways a rather precious upper-class queen moving in rarefied social circles, but he was kind and he was inclusive. Also, he was shy, and not one for the pubs or the cottages. One of the reasons he opened his house in this way was no doubt in the hope of attracting people to his house, and hopefully his bedroom, whom he would otherwise have been too timorous to approach. In contrast to Nicholl, he got a hundred replies, although only one from a woman. Nevertheless he was off, organising a wide range of events. 'Mr and Mrs Peter Katin' became Honorary Presidents. Rodney Slatford, a talented double bass player with one of the London orchestras, took over organising live concerts. Michael Harth, a self-taught pianist with a passion for Liszt, was Slatford's second-in-command, helping to organise the concerts. He remembers:

> Bill basically was a sweet old thing, but really his idea of the group was playing gramophone records to each other, which I wasn't very interested in and Rodney thought was ridiculous. So Rodney organised some proper concerts. We hired Leighton House.* £100 it cost us in those days – it was £1,500 when I last looked. And we got a professional pianist to play, a

* Leighton House, the elaborate Moorish-influenced home of gay painter Frederick Leighton in Holland Park, was the venue for many CHE recitals through the 1970s, organised by Kensington CHE among others.

> young guy just coming up. I think he got a tenner. This is what it was like in those days. And Rodney's boyfriend [David Watkins] was a harpist, so I know we put on an event with this guy and two of his friends. In drag. … It was a live event and that was what Rodney was into. At some time [Rodney] did a bit of announcing on the BBC. … I heard much later that Bill got murdered in the street. It was difficult to imagine because he was the most inoffensive creature. Very sad.[100]

The musical soirée at Leighton House was the first of what became almost monthly events. The 'surprise Ladies' Harp Trio' at the first one played Grétry's *Danse des Femmes*, and a specially commissioned suite for solo harp, played by David Watkins:

> A three-movement suite specially composed for David was of a light-weight nature, technically demanding and even contained a short nocturnal parody. … He excelled in making his pianissimos successfully inaudible on occasion. … Altogether a splendid evening, tinged with an extra-ordinary yet subtle erotic element.[101]

This project converted into a subscription series in April 1973, which allowed for rather better musicians.

Others who appeared over the next few months were Simon Lindley, who was to become the organist at Leeds Town Hall and Leeds Minster for forty years.* Graham Johnson, one of the foremost accompanists in Britain today, with complete recordings of lieder by Schubert and Schumann under his belt, accompanied tenor Stuart Hackett in autumn 1973. It was followed, in something of a coup, by the soon-to-be Master of the Queen's Music, Malcolm Williamson, 'talking and presenting, with audience participation, his now famous opera, *Genesis*.'† One gay couple in the group had a hobby of collecting musical instruments, so several evenings were held at their house in Feltham, where members could experiment on their phonofiddle and other oddities in the collection. In November they started a classical music disco.

They also had speakers on musical subjects. The gay jazz bass player and composer Graham Collier came to talk about the history of jazz, while Bernard Sanders-Crawley, general manager of 'a famous concert hall', spilled the beans about backstage goings-on, including:

> the soprano who, making her debut on the concert platform, suddenly developed an attack of nerves five minutes before her appearance and

---

* Among his compositions was an 'Ave Maria' which has been performed and recorded frequently, and is featured on the Katherine Jenkins album, *Sacred Arias*.

† Properly speaking *Genesis* is a 'cassation', a mini-opera with lots of audience participation. Williamson wrote ten of these mainly for children, to teach them how operas were 'made'.

> locked herself in the loo. He also referred to the idiosyncrasy of a famous concert pianist who would go straight to the gents to ensure that he would find a fresh, unwrapped roll of toilet paper. He insisted that no hand but his own came into contact with the paper once it left the factory.[102]

The Music Group continued until the 1980s, when it was promoting gay cabaret performers such as Mark Bunyan and Alan Pope alongside more traditional classical fare. It later renamed itself 'the Allegro Music Group' and was still in existence in 2014, putting on record evenings and going to concerts.

CHE Players

Homosexual society and performance have always gone hand in hand. In the gay poems of Meleager's *Greek Anthology*, romance is theatrically hopeless, theatrically ecstatic. The molly houses of the eighteenth century had their elaborate dressing, dancing, courtship and marriage rituals. The two most famous homosexuals of the mid nineteenth century, Boulton and Park, performed both onstage and off, and at their trial treated the court like an audience; they were frequently applauded. In modern times, one of the most active and inventive GLF groups was the Street Theatre Group, which in turn spawned Bloolips; but it is notable that street theatre is directed towards a general (presumed heterosexual) audience – a guerrilla action of confrontation, agitprop. When GLF tried to start a more conventional drama group and put on plays, it folded very quickly. However, in some respects street theatre was only a symbolic extension and expression of the whole political ethos and tactics of GLF, which were at all levels theatrically subversive – the fifteen foot cucumber for Pan Books, the djellaba in court to confound notions of what is or is not drag. Lesbians abseiling and invading newsrooms – camp, subversive, theatrical.

CHE's theatre is more conventional, but nonetheless exercises all the binding and affirmative, or satiric and questioning, powers of community art, in which one part of a community reflects or interrogates another part. There has been much debate across the decades about what exactly gay theatre is. At its purest, where LGBT people speak to other LGBT people, unmediated by the need to consider or explain to a non-gay audience, it is communication within a community, 'by, with and for…' It is also entertaining the troops.

Theatre had always had a strong following among CHE members. Visits to West End shows were a regular feature of social programmes, and many local groups all over the country mounted their own Christmas pantos, or organised play readings. The Croydon Group's 1971 Christmas dinner, for example, featured Michael Launder's impersonations and Wallace Grevatt doing 'royal pronouncements'.

The CHE Drama Group got off the mark in early 1972. As in so many other things, Roger Baker was a leading force. He was clearly a performer *manqué*; his after-dinner speech at Croydon's 1971 Christmas dinner was more in the way of a cabaret. By February 1972 'some CHE members' were mounting an 'entertainment' as part of a Victorian evening at Fulham Town Hall. The bill lists:

Miss Liz Evans	Songstress
Mr Gavin Clare	Crooner
The Hon. Madam Fred	Purley [*sic*] Queen
Mr Roger Baker	Monologuist Extraordinary
Mr Tony Crabbe	Magician
Mr James Horne	The Galloping Major

The circumstances of the performance were not propitious. The entertainment went ahead during a power cut. There was no heating and no stage lighting. The hall, which was 1930s rather than 1890s, was bare and only half full.

> So there was your cosy Olde Tyme atmosphere gone for a burton right away. … Most of us sat there defiant. Let them performers just try. Bless 'em, they did, and with one or two painful exceptions actually forced us to clap, sing and enjoy it in spite of ourselves. …
>
> Halfway through we became aware that the indomitable Norman Burroughs and his disciples had got the sausages and mash cleverly at the ready, A queue quickly formed in a ladylike manner and the whole thing went off like orange clockwork; each sausage hot and delicately browned with creamy white mashed spuds restored to some semblance of warmth and life. The audience returned to the battle strengthened in their determination to respond to absolutely nothing.
>
> Gavin Clare's act was good by any standards, his campery funny and delicate and his one sentimental song gentle and sweet without the saccharine. The genuine 90s touch of a conjurer on the bill would have fallen flat in less capable hands than Anthony Crabbe's. Urbane and apparently unaware of the uproar and general bad manners at the back of the hall, he performed some very clever tricks.[103]

Joe Wiebkin of Group 11 performed Noël Coward monologues, and a couple of old melodramatic songs sung straight 'which I suppose is easy if you are Joe Wiebkin and can look both dishy and distinguished simultaneously.'[104] Roger Baker himself was a little the worse for wear:

> Unfortunately the bangers, or beer, or both had done their deadly work and the actor's nightmare, amnesia, set in. We all sweated it out with him until, like many another splendid old trouper (Eddie Cantor, Sophie Tucker, Barbra Streisand) he quickly recovered and soon had us all eating out of his hand, or somewhere, again.[105]

James Solario performed operatic arias and brought the house down with his version of 'Bless this House'. The review concludes, 'It is an interesting thought that for CHE's first show we were able to uncover (only metaphorically, unfortunately) such jewels. How many more must the casket contain? And what about CHE's girls?'[106]

No later productions were to get such detailed reviews. But this was enthusiasm enough to kick-start a 'proper' Theatre Group. In August 1972 *Lunch* announced:

> The CHE Players has been formed and is already affiliated to the British Drama League. So far envisaged are regular play-readings and a one-act play to be performed in the Conway Hall on the evening of our second Winter Fair (Nov 4th). A section is interested in the revue and musical comedy side of the theatre and plan a revue in the near future.[107]

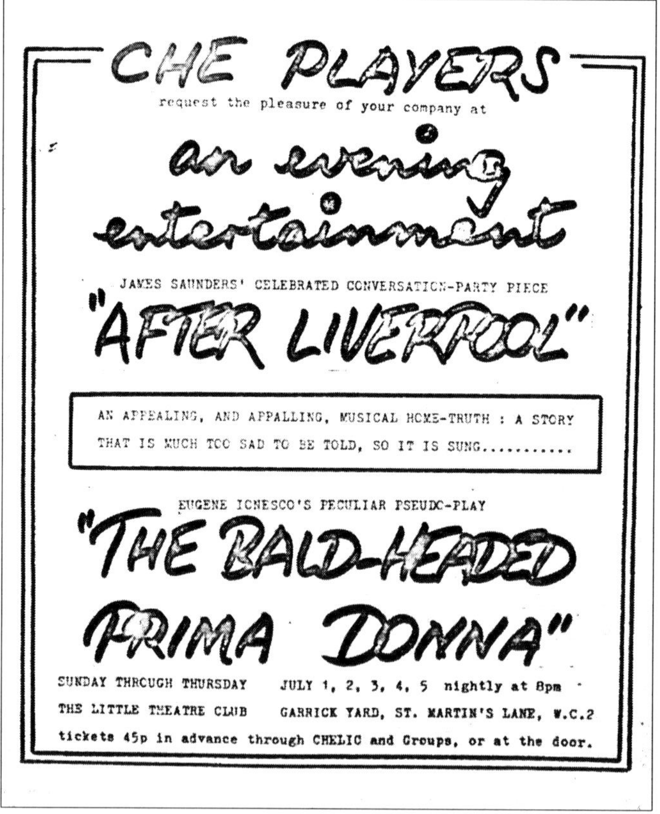

53. CHE Players flyer

Home-made revue and cabaret continued to form entertainment at major CHE events for the next three years, including the Annual Conferences at

Morecambe in 1973 and Malvern in 1974. In early 1973 the revue group had a four-day run of a revue at the Rehearsal Club, in aid of FRIEND. Hot on the heels of this the following article appeared in *Lunch*:

> I was just gazing indigently at my reflection, when this complete stranger approached me and asked, 'Do you fancy doing a striptease?'
>
> Taken aback by his boldness, I responded feebly, 'It would depend on the temperature.' … Could we discuss remuneration?'
>
> 'Lucre!' he moaned in tones of deep derision, 'Did you not apprehend that this was to be a charitable enterprise? … It's for CHE. … 'The CHE Players, not content with producing an original play by one of their members, are also planning a Gay Revue.'
>
> 'You don't get me in gold lamé,' I interrupted hastily. 'Or sequins.'
>
> 'You're barking up the wrong holly bush. The idea behind the show is to look at various aspects of gay life as it really is, and to avoid the usual caricatures. All the songs and sketches will be original material.'
>
> 'You mean no drag?'
>
> 'No drag.'
>
> 'No camp?'
>
> 'No camp.'
>
> 'No naked orgies?'
>
> 'Perhaps we could discuss that at my place,' he agreed, nonchalantly pausing at the next chemist's shop.[108]

There is no record of this revue taking place in 1973, but the description of the content, and the aspiration to 'real' representation of gay life, without caricature, is significant, and not only as a corrective to the media distortion which was a constant complaint of CHE members and other LGBT people from the 1970s onwards. People were desperate for validation, and one of the most vivid, immediate forms of validation is to see oneself on stage.

When Gay Sweatshop came to devise its own first touring show, *Mr X*, in 1975, it was a series of sketches of what gay life was 'really' like, threaded together on the coming-out process of Mr Average Gay, 'Mr X'. Since it was co-written by Roger Baker and Drew Griffiths, and Roger was so involved in the CHE theatre and revue groups, it seems likely that both the philosophy and material of *Mr X* originated in this CHE project.

The contact for the group was Babs Todd. Her partner Jackie Forster, who had featured in several feature films in the 1950s while having a parallel career as one of the first female TV correspondents, was a regular CHE Players performer, though memories of her appearances are vague. Peter Robins recalls her appearing in a sketch after the second Winter Fair: 'I remember Jackie Forster in dungarees wielding a large spanner … in one of the plays which were put on by the women.'[109]

The second Winter Fair featured both the Revue and Theatre Groups, with sketches halfway through the disco and elsewhere a triple bill of two one-acters by N. F. Simpson, *Gladys Otherwise* and *One Blast and Have Done*, coupled with Harold Pinter's sketch *Trouble in the Works*. Jackie most probably appeared in the Pinter, playing the foreman, Wills, registering the workers' protest at the factory output. Only she in the group would have had the skills to get her mouth round Pinter's tongue-twisting dialogue:

> WILLS: They hate and detest your lovely parallel male stud couplings, and the straight flange pump connectors, and back nuts, and front nuts, *and* the bronze draw-off cock without handwheel and the bronze draw-off cock with handwheel! …
> FIBBS: What do they want to make in its place?
> WILLS: Trouble.[110]

Her half-purring, half-booming contralto would have milked every *double entendre* for what it was worth, and one can imagine the relish with which 'trouble-making' Forster would have said the word, 'Trouble'.

The group met weekly at the Museum Tavern, opposite the British Museum, the meeting place also of Babs Todd's Bloomsbury Group. They had a regular diet of play-readings, but they also rehearsed there for more polished public performances.

In June 1973 the CHE Players, as they were now called, took over the Little Theatre Club, off St. Martin's Lane, for a week's run of a double bill, James Saunders' *After Liverpool*, 'an appealing, and appalling, musical home-truth: a story too sad to be told, so it is sung', coupled with Ionesco's 'peculiar pseudo-play', *The Bald Prima Donna*. The club was in an attic, with the entrance up a fire escape. Admission was 45p, and nearly every CHE group in London got up a coach party in support, so it sold out.

The theatre itself pioneered one-hour lunchtime and late night plays, and one of the plays it presented was Ed Berman's *Sagittarius*. It is not entirely fanciful to suggest that the Little Theatre Club gave Berman the idea for lunchtime seasons at the Almost Free Theatre, which he had opened in 1971; nor that the CHE Players convinced him that there was a thirsty gay market for plays presented by an avowedly gay company at lunchtime.

In August the Players were auditioning for their first, home-written, piece of gay theatre. The genre of gay theatre, plays with lesbian and gay themes written and performed by artistes who were openly homosexual and aimed at gay audiences, was to become a flourishing one with Gay Sweatshop, Bradford's General Will theatre company, and One in Ten in Birmingham in the 1970s; in the 1980s there was an explosion of other LGBT companies all over the country, including Consenting Adults in Public, Outcast, and later Homo Promos. The tradition is somewhat diluted with the movement of gay themes and issues into the mainstream and the dissolution of the tight gay communities of the past. But Homo Promos still continues, and the tradition is particularly lively in the many LGBT Youth Companies, which use drama to explore sexual identity, and to deal with issues such as homophobic bullying, in a dialogue with their heterosexual peers.

The CHE play was called *Hello Mother! Hello Father!*, and was written by one of the group under the pseudonym Butch Black. It was a coming out comedy with a happy ending. The blurb ran:

> Dave and John share a flat in London, and are surprised by the unexpected arrival of their parents. The boys try to hide from their parents the evidence of their gay life, resulting in a series of hilarious scenes. But the moment of truth comes separately for each parent and each reacts differently. The ending is, for the first time in this genre, a happy one.[111]

It had been planned for autumn 1973 at the Portcullis Theatre, Westminster, following a public reading in January. But the general manager, Mr Howsden, was not amused. *Gay News* reported:

> Mr Howsden … said that he would not permit a scene 'bordering on nudity' in his theatre. The author … says the scene to which Mr Howsden was referring was a moment when an Irish labourer in the play appears for about a minute in his underpants.
>
> 'Apparently this was too much … although the character could quite easily have appeared in pyjamas instead. I offered Mr Howsden a copy of the script so he could read the play and suggest any alterations he thought might be advisable, but he said he was "not going to be an arbiter of public morals" and slammed the phone down on me twice. He didn't say whether or not he objected to the homosexual theme of the play.'[112]

As publicity, this was a gift. 'The play they tried to ban!' 'This is undoubtedly the play that everyone in the gay world will be talking about.' It claimed to be the first gay play in London since *Boys in the Band* in 1969.

They were able to fanfare that their 'much-bruited production is ON!' when they found an alternative home at the Mercury Theatre, Notting Hill Gate. The Mercury was part of the Ballet Rambert headquarters and as well as hosting dance, it had a history of 'poetic drama' – the small space hosted the London premiere of T. S. Eliot's *Murder in the Cathedral* in 1935 and later Genet's *The Maids*.* But the production was not to be. It was cancelled when some of the actors walked out on it, for reasons which are not clear. The group never recovered.

At almost exactly the same time, a group of gay actors was meeting at Roger Baker's flat to discuss the formation of the Gay Theatre Caucus (or

* Rambert stopped presenting ballets there in 1965, although the ballet school retained it until the late 1980s.

Screaming Theatre Caucus – they couldn't quite decide on a name). Their manifesto:

> We believe that a gay theatre group is necessary in order to put across ideas that clearly cannot be presented through established means. Conventional theatre and television continue to project stereotyped images of gay people and treat homosexuality as a pathetic deviation or as a grotesque joke.
>
> GTC's object is to discover and present all kinds of plays and entertainments which have gay themes, which are politically motivated, which explore the roots of gay oppression and which are designed to work some change in their audiences.[113]

They would be full-time, and professional, and they had the offer of a theatre. American director Ed Berman and his Interaction Group offered the Almost Free Theatre, in Rupert Street in Soho, for a nine-week season of five lunchtime plays. The CHE Players simply couldn't compete.

Art and writing

There were other creative groups. The Art Group held an exhibition at the 1972 Winter Fair – photos, drawings, sketches, paintings in watercolours and oils, sculpture and pottery. They repeated the exercise in 1973. Between times they held life drawing classes and photographic sessions, where sexual temperatures were raised sometimes by handsome young models (the group collectively warned off those coming along for the wrong reasons, and cautioned against inappropriate behaviour). It operated out of the London Information Centre from 1973 onwards. This group maintained an independent life as it floated away from CHE, and continued to exhibit until the mid-1980s.

The Poetry Group was known as the Company of Nine. When they approached the landlord of the *Lamb and Flag* in Covent Garden, he asked them the name of the group making the booking. A failure of nerve led them to avoid the name CHE, and because nine poets turned up for the first meeting, they made up the name, 'Company of Nine', on the spot. The name stuck. The group met on the last Friday of every month in the upstairs room of the pub. At first it was more of a poetry-lovers' than a poets' gathering, where people would read out their favourite verse for each other. Their first meeting was on 28 July 1972, a few days after the death of the Poet Laureate, Cecil Day-Lewis. Twenty people, poets and friends, gathered for a kind of election hustings for the new Laureate. Each candidate was supported by readings from her/his work. Peter Robins and teacher David Bell, who was to play a large part in the Education Campaign* were among the founder

* See Volume Two.

members. Marie Clifton, secretary of the new Kensington Group, was the sole woman present. They all discussed the respective merits of Betjeman, Spender, Roy Fuller, William Plomer, Philip Larkin, Ted Hughes and Laurie Lee. Clearly the group was untainted with misogyny, because the 'winner' was the only woman poet on offer, Kathleen Raine, with her poem 'Shells':

> Reaching out arm-deep into bright water
> I gathered on white sand under waves
> Shells, drifted up on beaches where I alone
> Inhabit a finite world of years and days.[114]

From then on Company of Nine read the works of both members and others at themed evenings. 'The Feminine Muse' (Feb 1973) was a programme of women poets devised by Christine Bailey and presented jointly with Kensington CHE.

The Company of Nine evolved into more of a writers' support group, offering constructive criticism of work in progress. In late 1972 it published a small volume of poems, *Speaking Out*. Despite the title, with its suggestion of openness, it was strikingly closeted. Most contributors were identified by their initials – only the names of John Dawson and the lone lesbian poet Niki Delany were public.

There was remarkably little by way of a political or social dimension in what were essentially laments or celebrations of love lost, unattainable or won. In this, as in its poetic diction, it differed little from the Uranian 'ladslove' poetry of the 1890s:

> Catch the vision of him moving
> With the grace that you remember
> From the days you were his friend and
> Lover too
>
> Recall the laughter in his smile
> As he spoke to you so softly
> Of things you both had planned, and
> Both would do.
>
> Remember those hours of sleeping
> With his head upon your shoulder
> When you would touch him, but gently
> Lest he wake.[115]

Delany alone has an element of awareness of contemporary surroundings:

> Dawn by the sea, and we lie still entangled
> Limbs intertwined

Her hair spread by golden seaweed
On the rough pillow
Her eyes still closed against the early light.
The bed is narrow
And the shadowy room
Hides cracks in the ceiling, smutty curtains
And torn wallpaper with a pattern
of magenta flowers.
Outside is the shuffle of feet going past
to the toilet
And then silence again.[116]

Peter Robins was beginning at this time to discover a talent as a writer, mainly of sexy, funny short stories that would be published as *Undo Your Raincoats and Laugh* (1977). He also wrote occasional verse with a satirical theme. The poem *A Plain Man's Guide*, a defiant response to the aging process, has the hallmark of his cheerful hedonism, and is signed 'PR' in the anthology. It ends:

I'd never pin-up looks, I said
so never wept their loss
I learned at length that wit can win
and honesty outweighs charm.
Though blood and hair are thinner now
I seldom sleep alone.

It will be so when heavier snow
leathers my stubbled chin,
when the March gale trips my leg, I said,
and I dance with a bone-shaped stick.
Until all movement and desire
are stilled, I'll share my bed.[117]

The whole volume concludes with a tiny, elegant, bleak, envoi by the editor, which underlines the essential loneliness, not of the homosexual, but of all people:

There is a touch of sadness in the air
And the grief of parting;
The loneliness and dark despair –
The long night starting.[118]

The Company of Nine, like some other SIGs, grew away from CHE, and mutated into the Oscars. They started the Oscars Press, and published several volumes. The group started to give public readings of its work, under the name of the Performing Oscars. The very fact of performance affected the style of poetry, which became more declamatory and demotic. The

Performing Oscars appeared on the stage of the Cabaret Tent at Gay Pride for several years in the late 1980s and early 1990s.

Closely allied to the Company of Nine, the Gay Writers' Group formed in August 1972, and in March 1973 *Lunch* reported that it was:

> now meeting regularly once a month, and is functioning mainly as a writers' workshop where members discuss each other's work. This is not as ghastly an experience as it may sound, and has already proved of value to at least some of us. … We are also hoping to sponsor a collection of short stories. Anyone is welcome to submit their work, but all stories must have some gay relevance.[119]

The group contact and driving spirit was Michael Harth, the convenor of Stepney CHE and combative correspondent to *Lunch*. He co-founded it with Peter Robins, and an early member was Laurence Collinson, whom Harth had met at an orgy in Windsor. Harth and Robins took a revue, *Lit. Bits*, to the Edinburgh Fringe two years running, which featured a number of Harth's witty songs. This group also mutated, in 1978, into the Gay Author's Workshop (GAW), with non-CHE members now in the majority, although an energetic East London lesbian couple, Elsa Beckett and Kathryn Bell, were also officers in the Ilford-based East London CHE. The advent of digital publishing and e-books in the new century kick-started a surge in self-publishing activity, making the process of getting books into print both easier and more affordable.

As a result the GAW imprint, Paradise Press, had at the start of 2014 some thirty books on its list, mainly fiction, with another five in the immediate pipeline. Michael Harth, Elsa Beckett and Kathryn Bell remain organising members; one of the more recent recruits is Donald West, the psychiatrist/criminologist whose Penguin Special *Homosexuality* was so influential and controversial in the 1950s and 1960s. In 2012 he formally 'came out', at the age of 88, in his autobiography, *Gay Life, Straight Work*, published by Paradise.

Michael Harth was – is – a live wire, a restless man who has to be doing. In the 1970s he also ran the CHE winemaking group out of his East London home. ('There will be a full demonstration of how to make a red table wine. No expert knowledge is required to join this circle.')[120] This is one of several CHE groups we can only glimpse. Another was the FineFare Group, a cookery club. On 28 February 1973 it held a Soup and Risotto evening:

> with an instruction and discussion on the preparation of soups in general, basic stock, etc. … The meeting is intended as the forerunner of a planned meal, and subsequent meetings will be devoted to the preparation of the entrée, main course and desserts.[121]

… and the rest

CHE had a film unit as well, of a kind. Once again Roger Baker was the *éminence grise*, and he wasn't thinking small. He wanted it to be:

> Capable of producing its own gay-oriented movies from start to finish. … They could include educational, informational, documentary and campaign subjects, experimental, abstract and narrative films, material aimed directly towards the television stations, and possibly films designed for theatrical release. There will be a need for writers, directors, actors, production and camera crews, designers, sound freaks, carpenters, electricians, editors, lab technicians, still photographers, accountants, 'show biz' and copyright lawyers etc., etc. And without suggesting any sort of rip-off, anyone with access to stock, equipment and facilities will be doubly welcome; financial angels trebly so.[122]

Its first project, completed in April 1973, was a two-minute gay 'commercial', *Party Piece*, produced by Roy Fowler and directed by Bruce Wishart:

> This week, on practically no budget, it swung into action with a lot of amateur enthusiasm and a little professional assistance. This is a pilot project in the form of a two minute colour gay commercial. … Not surprisingly it has both a nude scene with a boy resembling a sort of butch Leonard Whiting* and a brief fantasy leather sequence. … It took nine hours to shoot in a borrowed flat in NW3.[123]

It was shown in late-night gay-themed double bills at the Scala Cinema in Kings Cross and the Electric in Notting Hill for two or three years.† The makers hoped that it would act as a calling card to attract finance for larger projects. They talked of being self-sufficient 'eventually', but admitted in the meantime that they would need subsidy for the first two or three films.

Even more importantly, they needed access to film processing facilities, which were cripplingly expensive at this time, as indeed was the whole film-making process before cheap digital technology turned everyone into a potential Hitchcock.

The money for the film unit was not forthcoming, but in 1977 *Nighthawks*, by Paul Hallam and Ron Peck, became the first authentic home-made gay community feature film. Several people connected with the CHE Film Unit were involved in production and fundraising.

---

* Leonard Whiting is an actor, best known then – and now – for playing Romeo in Zeffirelli's 1968 film version of *Romeo and Juliet*. He also played Dr Frankenstein in the Christopher Isherwood-scripted film version of Mary Shelley's novel, *Frankenstein: The True Story* (1973).

† It hasn't been possible to trace a copy of this.

In April 1973 Vivian Toland started to set up the CHE Eurogroup – 'for language enthusiasts'. They started with a French-speaking circle and a German-speaking circle. These were held monthly in members' houses, and nothing but French or German was allowed during the course of the evening. There was hope of Spanish and Italian circles as well, but there don't seem to have been sufficient Spanish or Italian speakers to make these viable. These circles mainly reflected a casual interest in holiday destinations, but language skills were to become more useful over the next few years, as more and more links were forged internationally. CHE regularly swapped magazines and bulletins with European LGBT organisations, and the language skills to translate them resided in London rather than Manchester. This gave London CHE a more internationalist outlook than the rest of the national organisation.

The sports groups were also ahead of their time. William Blackledge, the pan-London fundraiser and social organiser, took it on himself to organise athletics teams. He was, no doubt, looking forward to the money-making possibilities of a Sports Day, scheduled with a Garden Party for May 1972. This did not happen, though there were garden parties a-plenty. It was not until the emergence of gym culture in the early 1980s, and the Gay Games quasi-Olympic movement,* that athletics really caught on as an interest of homosexuals. Specifically, running took off as a group activity, and London Front Runners, which started in 1998, now has over 300 members.

Similarly CHE football teams were intended for a season opening in September 1972; it seems that Blackledge imagined a league of competing teams representing the different London groups, but there was little take-up. LGBT sports were far more advanced in the United States. Only when Norman Redman, convenor of Littlehampton CHE and the first openly gay referee in the Football League, got together a team, Gaystars XI, to play against heterosexuals in 1978 did a gay football team appear, although it did not last long. Lesbian footballers in women's teams became comparatively common from the 1970s onward, and there were several informal lesbian teams kicking the ball around in parks on weekends, on a private and unacknowledged basis. In general, sports participation by openly LGBT people did not become common until the twenty-first century.

The teachers' and social workers' groups were initially intended as support groups for lesbian and gay professionals, who were thought to be particularly vulnerable in their employment because of their contact with young people; the teachers' group benefited from the involvement of David Bell, a teacher at an East London comprehensive in his early twenties who had come out at his

* The first Gay Games were held in San Francisco in 1982.

school, and was instrumental in wringing from his employer, the Inner London Education Authority (ILEA), a pledge that they would not discriminate against teachers if they happened to be lesbian or gay:

> The education authority I work for in London has said most definitely that it regards the employment of heterosexual and homosexual teachers in the same way. I think it's very natural to be what I am, and I don't see that my job makes any difference.[124]

Also in the group was teacher Paul Patrick, another openly gay teacher at an ILEA comprehensive school, who later became a member of the support service, Icebreakers. It soon became clear that support for teachers was only part of what was needed. While teachers like John Warburton, sacked in 1975, were the focus of campaigns for reinstatement, the group realised that there were other areas crying out for action, in supporting LGBT students and pupils, and in providing positive role models for young gay people within the school curriculum, and not just in sex education. In this, the group, formally christened the Gay Teachers Group in 1974, found itself one of the primary ambassadors for CHE's Education Campaign, the organisation's first national campaign, in 1973–76.* Like other action groups within particular professions, political parties or Trade Unions, a small nucleus within CHE provided the initial impetus, and gradually attracted others from outside CHE who wanted to be part of the particular group and its campaigns. Slowly each group became self-sustaining, until it became completely separate. The Gay Teachers Group turned into Schools Out, which created the now-national LGBT History Month (February), as a way of presenting a solid and coherent mass of positive educational materials on LGBT history, identity and culture.

Political Action Group

The more general All-London Political Action Group, which Tony Ryde was instrumental in starting at the beginning of 1972, was the first of several attempts to free up those who wanted to concentrate on campaigning from the comparative drudgery of running local groups. This was first flagged up as a problem in *Lunch* in January of that year:

> Having called ourselves the Campaign for Homosexual Equality, it seems ironic that we should have allowed ourselves an indulgent relapse, in London at least, into a 'social club' organisation. … Many find their campaigning zeal frustrated by reluctant group committees who remain unaware, or discourage the proselytizing ambitions shown by many

* Covered in 'Cases, Causes and Crises', Volume Two.

members, who then find other organisations in which their talents are made more welcome.

We have been bustling along for 18 months with very few items of evidence that we are a 'campaigning' group.[125]

As in many voluntary organisations, and as 'People Not Paper' acknowledged, the activists constituted perhaps a tenth of the membership, and as 'can-do' people, they tended to be asked to take on anything that needed doing. Often they said yes, simply because nobody else would do it. Not only were they overloaded, within London there was no way for them to communicate with each other or to act on campaigns in concert. The LCC's interests and energies lay elsewhere. Since one of the gripes of Manchester was that London didn't do any campaigning, the EC welcomed this development 'most heartily'. Others who equated political activism with street fighting were more dismissive: 'There is a political action group in the offing. Would anyone who wants to wave a banner or start a revolution, please contact Ken Glazier.'[126]

The Political Action Group (PAG) met in CHELIC fortnightly as soon as the Centre was open. Its administrator was Centre Manager Derek Brookfield: 'In addition to its activities as an unstructured campaigning group, PAG is now responsible for mounting the Speakers' Corner exercise. More speakers, leaflets and supporters would be much appreciated.'[127]

One of its main activities after its formation was in connection with the ramifications of the Court of Appeal judgement on the *International Times* case. The Campaign Group contacted London MPs to alert them to a possible campaign to change the conspiracy laws, and took part in the meeting at the House of Commons which was called in the wake of the Court of Appeal judgement.*

Apart from this, the Political Action Group compiled a London-wide list of sympathetic doctors, social workers, lawyers and priests; these initially came from within the membership, but gradually spread out through word of mouth and advertising. Such a list was necessary because as long as they were not rooted in geographical areas, local groups in London found it hard to know where to start looking for gay-friendly professional specialists. Solicitors in particular were severely hampered by the legal restrictions placed on their advertising; even if they were sympathetic, they could be struck off for saying so publicly. By 1974 the list covered most of London, and was made available to FRIEND, London Gay Switchboard and CHELIC itself.

For another project, the group placed an advert in *Gay News*:

CHE Political Action Group are trying to establish a Legal Aid Fund for Homosexuals. The most economic effective and secure way of doing this

* See Volume Two.

> is by creating a charitable trust. In order to ensure that the trust is securely established and free from the interference of the Charity Commissioners, it is essential that an expertly drawn up trust deed is used as the governing instrument. We have no solicitors or barristers in the group and would welcome the assistance and advice of anyone with the requisite experience.[128]

It seems that, because of the *IT* appeal verdict, no amount of expertise could get around the fact that any support organisation, however worthy, purely for homosexuals was by that very fact barred from charitable status. The Legal Aid Fund never got off the ground as such, and indeed with prosecutions for 'gay crimes' rising following the passing of the 1967 Act, and with importuning cases now going mainly before magistrates instead of judges and therefore not qualifying for Legal Aid, it is likely that demand for help would have far outstripped supply. The idea, however, remained on the agenda whenever the needs of gay men were discussed, and homophobic police actions were regularly reported in *Gay News* throughout the 1970s. GLAD (Gay Legal Advice) was founded in 1977 with several of the solicitors and barristers from the Political Action Group list involved. It offered both legal advice and an extremely thorough guide to dealing with police and courts. It ran a nightly telephone advice line from 7 to 11 p.m. With GLC funding, GALOP (Gay London Police Monitoring Group) also started in 1982, to educate LGBT people about their rights under the law and to keep tabs on police behaviour. Several of its volunteers were lawyers, and again, some came from the ranks of CHE.

Six months after the PAG's inception, co-ordinator Derek Brookfield was frankly disappointed:

> Probably it is our conspicuous lack of dynamic action that has led some members to fall away – who wants yet another talking shop? The actual achievements of P.A.G. are: a) two leafleting sessions at gay bars; b) regular platforms at Speakers' Corner; c) the printing of a new display postcard for newsagents' noticeboards; d) the participation of two of our members in the Radio London 'Platform', and (indirectly) the setting up of CHELIC. That we have not achieved more stems largely from lack of members; we are still only 1% of London CHE.[129]

Much energy would be taken up in co-ordinating the London responses to the CHE questionnaire sent to local candidates in the 1973 GLC elections. There was also a hare started for that same election campaign by the then Chairman of Group 1, Griffith Vaughan Williams, who suggested that CHE should field a candidate. The suggestion had a strategic purpose, in that GLC and Parliamentary boundaries were the same. This could make a GLC election campaign a dummy run for a candidate in the general election, finding out how many homosexuals, of whom there were many thousands migrating to the capital and fleeing narrow-minded provincialism, would vote for 'their man/woman'. There was an additional advantage, in that candidates for the GLC did not need to put up a deposit, as would be required in a general election. If the GLC election showed there was some support for a gay candidate, it would be worth a punt to field a candidate at the general election and risk losing £500.

That the suggestion should come from Vaughan Williams is no surprise. He was nothing if not a drama queen, and an election had all the confrontational theatricality he could wish for, as well as thrusting him into the limelight as election agent. Moreover he was right that fielding a candidate would generate more London publicity than CHE had ever achieved so far. Even talking about standing got into the papers; at least it got into the *Brentford and Chiswick Times*:

> If organisations such as CHE – which is understood to be thinking of linking up with other minority bodies – enter the field at the GLC election and are tempted to try their luck locally at Parliamentary level, Mr Michael Barnes could find his 513-vote majority coming under pressure.[130]

There might indeed have been some sense in fielding a rainbow candidate as the paper suggests, but at this point CHE's links with other liberal/left or minority organisations apart from NCCL were tenuous to non-existent. Michael Steed as a leading election expert stamped on the idea very firmly: 'A CHE candidate, or even a slightly broader gay rights candidate, would be likely to do very badly and expose CHE's weakness.'[131] Better by far to work within existing political parties, and draw in CHE supporters to work for mainstream candidates. It would further the cause of integration, and earn you the right to press the candidates you worked for about support for gay rights. This might have been sound advice, but it might also not have been entirely disinterested, coming from a senior figure in the Liberal Party and several times parliamentary candidate.

However, Griff, being a man who never let an argument go, held on to the idea of fielding a parliamentary candidate. In 1977 the Westminster Group would put up Peter Mitchell on a Gay Rights ticket in a parliamentary by-election, with Griff as election agent.*

'Sex and Religion'

There were more mass meetings to bring the London membership together later in 1972 and through 1973. Some of these were more in the nature of

---

* See Volume Three.

panel discussions. When the Reverend Troy Perry, founder of the Metropolitan Community Church in America, visited London in September 1972, CHE organised a 'Congress' around the theme 'Sex and Religion'. With Perry on the platform was Rev. Dr Norman Pittenger, a chain-smoking cleric with the wild hair of a Michael Foot, whose theological writings, and especially the 1970 book, *Time for Consent*, were among the earliest arguing within the Church of England for a full acceptance of loving homosexual relationships. Michael Harth was at the meeting:

> It was disturbed by the Radical Fairies. They just made some sort of silly demo and I was muttering under my breath, 'Piss off.' Pittenger was interesting, but Perry was just like a stage turn. He … was a superb raconteur, and he had us all in fits. He had so much personality. … I admired Pittenger, and I thought he talked good sense and there was some meat to it. But Perry could have made a fortune on the stage. I was deeply impressed with Pittenger – there's not many people who've had that effect on me.[132]

The debate was chaired by Rev. Denis Nadin, a former volunteer in the CHE office in Manchester, recently elected onto the National Executive. Religious belief and observation, and membership of religious organisations, was and remains important for a significant number of lesbians and gay men, many of whom preferred, and prefer, to brave the stigmatisation and argue for LGBT rights within established churches, rather than to join specifically 'gay churches' such as Perry's MCC, or to reject Christianity altogether. The 'integration v. separation' debate which already raged over other aspects of gay life was equally transferrable to the churches. Nadin was to conduct non-denominational religious services at CHE conferences until he left the Executive in 1975. Thereafter the Gay (later Lesbian and Gay) Christian Movement under Rev. Richard Kirker would fulfil the same function. LGCM was based for many years at St Botolph's Church in Aldgate, where the vicar was Rev. Malcolm Johnson,* who founded the early gay social group, St Katherine's. Johnson was forced to evict LGCM from St Botolph's when the Bishop of London threatened to sue him in 1988.†

Troy Perry's visit to the UK was a trigger for an enormous amount of publicity in the mainstream press. Alan Whicker's programme, *The Lord is my Shepherd and He Knows I'm Gay*, went out on ITV a year later, in October 1973. It featured the first 'gay kiss' on British TV, in the context of a Californian 'gay marriage', and had a huge impact. Perry was the engaging and articulate

---

* Johnson has been openly gay within the church, and lived with the same partner for almost fifty years. They formed a civil partnership in 2006.

† LGCM's Central London group, 3F, was still meeting at St Botolph's in 2014.

pastor who performed the ceremony, and became an immediate celeb. in his own right. For the first time, legalising, or at least regularising, gay relationships was on the mainstream agenda, and could be talked of, in some quarters at least, without raising ridicule. It is entirely likely, given the very long lead-in times involved in television programme planning, that the first contact between Whicker's producer and Perry was made during this first UK visit to talk to CHE.

Media and publicity

CHE itself was getting better at publicity. In December 1970 Roger Baker had appeared on the BBC2 flagship discussion programme *Late Night Line-Up*, alongside John Breslin, an extremely handsome actor nicknamed Dorian Gray, who appeared in a number of popular TV series of the 1960s, from *Dixon of Dock Green* to *Doctor Who*. His other distinction was that he dubbed the voice of Steve Reeves in a series of Italian beefcake movies. Breslin had come out publicly as gay in a personal article, 'Enter an Honest Man', in *Spartacus* in early 1970, with a follow-up interview in *The People*:

> John Breslin, who will be seen in Wednesday's episode of *The Doctors*, plans a campaign to bring a new understanding of homosexuality to Britain. And he hopes that, by speaking out, other more celebrated names in entertainment will come forward. 'The only way we can change things,' he says, 'is by famous actors openly confessing they are homosexual, names that mean a lot to families who sit at home every night watching television.' Breslin believes that if one manly-looking woman's idol would come forward, the public attitude would change. 'Every night you watch television you see at least one homosexual,' he says. 'I can scarcely recall a successful comedy series that didn't include one. And many of the great screen lovers – the rugged handsome types – are homosexual.'[133]

In giving the interview and appearing on the programme, Breslin was one of the first actors to come out voluntarily. To any reader of *The People* seeing the article, there would have been a frisson of recognition, in that he was featured quite heavily in the *Doctor Who* serial, 'Spearhead from Space'* which had finished a fortnight previously. Breslin did not persuade other actors to follow him in coming out, and does not seem to have continued in this vein of activism. He was an obvious candidate for a CHE figurehead; Allan Horsfall wrote to him at the BBC, and he attended an EC meeting in March 1970. However, he was based at the time in Scotland, and so became a member of the newly-formed SMG. He doesn't seem to have taken a greatly active part.

---

* The first series to feature Jon Pertwee as the Third Doctor, and the first in colour.

In 1972 he was sighted visiting Croydon CHE to hear George Melly giving a talk, and later returned to the group to give his own talk.

It is hard to say whether his career suffered as a result of his decision to come out, since he was at best a supporting actor, and continued to appear in small parts in TV series and soaps right up to *Doctors* in 2006. Nonetheless, his unique and brave decision should be acknowledged.

Roger Baker's appearance with Breslin was a one-off. BBC TV was not to devote another programme to the subject of homosexuality for another 18 months, when two episodes of *A Question of Conscience* tackled the issue. In the meantime, the Speakers' Group, and subsequently the Political Action Group, prepared people for public speaking and media appearances, and there was a dedicated group equipped to be interviewed, and to field questions from the general public. Tony Ryde, Vivian Waldron, Gini Stevens, Roger Baker and his partner Gavin Clare, Jackie Forster and, later, David Bell were the star performers.

Between 1971 and 1973 CHE's impacts on the national press were neither as spectacular nor as frequent as those of GLF, but in London it did start to develop a regular presence on local radio, and in the summer of 1972 hit the national airwaves on Radio 1. The first Director General of the BBC, Lord Reith, had summarised the Corporation's remit as being to 'educate, inform, entertain', an ethos which hangs around still in the BBC's mission statement. So there was a certain head-scratching among the BBC executives as to how to fulfil the Reithian remit on a station geared up to pop music. The most successful attempt to combine the two was Jimmy Savile's *Speakeasy*, a pioneering blend of social platform for minority groups, idiosyncratic interviewing by the DJ host, record requests and straightforward pop-picking. The Savile programme was broadcast every Sunday, a two-hour show split into *Savile's Travels*, a youth vox pop recorded around the country, and, from 3 p m., *Speakeasy*. The subject of *Speakeasy* was never flagged up in advance; the only information given in the *Radio Times* was where the show was coming from. In May and June 1972 Savile did two shows on the subject of homosexuality, the first one featuring CHE and GLF members and the second only CHE. Gini Stevens tackled Savile about the exclusion of GLF when she interviewed him for *Lunch*:

> SAVILE: We ventilated the militant aspect when we invited the GLF on the first programme. …
>
> Q: In fact the GLF were cut out of the first programme.
>
> SAVILE: Some of them were, but they were there sufficiently to sell their case. What they were doing – and what so many people do who tend to get a little passionate – is to destroy their own case. … What I care about is that if I'm going to be bothered to talk to anybody on a

programme, I want them to be able to put their case in the best possible light, or there's no point.[134]

Lunch
Number 17/25p
February 1973
Speakeasy with Jimmy Savile/Britain's no1 homosexual/Maureen Duffy poems

54. Cover of *Lunch*, issue 17, with Jimmy Savile

GLF, or at least certain members of it, did not mix well with other groups on joint media platforms, and on Radio 1, as on Harlech TV's *Now It's Your Say* at roughly the same period, they tended to dominate and shout down other groups. After experiencing this once, producers would decide that on the whole GLF did more harm than good – an opinion shared by many homosexuals – and would not invite them back; this is why CHE had the second *Speakeasy* to itself. With an audience of millions, it was the biggest platform CHE had had to date – or indeed would have later – and particularly reached younger listeners. When they managed to get a word in edgeways over the verbose host, the CHE speakers acquitted themselves well. Doug Pollard, the *Gay News* reviewer, spent most of his feature bemoaning the difficulty he had had getting an invitation, but admitted:

> What the programme did do was to reach a number of people who have never met another gay person in their lives before … and now find they

> are not alone. In the couple of weeks following the programme, the Albany Trust alone had over a hundred letters of this kind. And it must have given courage to many others. It will have helped to ease the tensions in homes such as mine, in which I live with my parents. … It will have helped the painful process of dispelling all the history of prejudice and censure. Above all it stated loud and clear … that gayness is about love.[135]

BBC Radio London started in 1970 in the second wave of local radio development. The first commercial radio stations designed to compete with the BBC were licensed in 1972, and nineteen were launched in 1973. As with many new enterprises, there was a fluidity and freedom resulting from the fact that nobody quite knew what 'community radio' meant, who it was for and who might appear on it. Many stations were desperate for content, not having had time to set up sufficient contacts and news feeds to fill the many hours of factual and magazine programmes. Find out where the staff of the radio station drink, advised Roger Baker. Go along, make friends, buy a few rounds. Get to know the phone-in programmes, call in often; put out a press release on anything with the slightest gay relevance.

On 30 August 1972 CHE took over a Radio London programme, *Platform*, which was a 110-minute evening phone-in that also had a studio audience. It was billed in the *Radio Times* as a CHE programme:

> 8.10 p.m. – 10.00 p.m.: Radio London hands over its microphone to a group with something important to say.* This week: The Campaign for Homosexual Equality.[136]

It was discussed in *Gay News* as a CHE programme as well. However, it is an indication both of the liberalism of CHE and its growing confidence that other organisations were represented too. CHE's own *Bulletin* was more even-handed:

> It was CHE's evening and no mistake, but others were there too – people from GLF, Challenge,† *Gay News* and the NFHO. All were able to contribute when they wanted to, and what emerged in the studio and came over the air, was the sense that all these gay people had the same interests, and even where they differed on individual points, appreciated each other's view. CHE itself came over as a pretty dynamic organisation, aware of real issues and unafraid to speak out. [137]

---

* *Platform* was originally billed as for groups 'trying to change society', but evidently this was too inflammatory for 'Auntie' BBC when it came to a group of homosexuals.

† Challenge was a breakaway group from CHE founded by David Forsyth from Group 1, which claimed 120–150 members in West London. Their declared aim was to improve acceptance of homosexuals by volunteering for worthy non-gay causes e.g. working with old people, or disabled children.

Of course speakers brought their own supporters to pack the studio. The programme was so besieged with callers that Radio London extended it for an extra hour. Doug Pollard, reviewing the programme in *Gay News* from a GLF perspective, noted that the women panellists didn't say very much. There was only one woman caller, and that one planted.

> It dealt with education, adoption by gay couples, marriage and mortgage, parents, schools, young gays, old gays, women, relationships, cottaging, political and social groups, with little of the formality or prudishness that is often their hallmark. Whilst one may not necessarily agree with some of what was said, it is the first time that such a statement has been broadcast in this country, and the opportunity was fully grasped.[138]

The next issue of *Gay News* summarised the programme in more detail. The programme opened with a CHE-scripted feature in which statements expressing conventional prejudice (in working class accents) were interspersed with cold calm facts (middle class).

> It requested the right to be as respectable, as conformist and as dull as the rest of suburbia. Put on your pinny, Lavinia, you're going to be a real housewife. If CHE has its way.[139]

Some parts of the phone-in were carefully scripted, or at least prepared. Callers, supporters and friends who were organised to phone the programme were briefed with questions and positive comments. This is not uncommon for any pressure group going on the air in this way. It allowed the speakers to lay out CHE's stall on a whole range of issues. Someone asked about attitudes to cottaging:

> We do sympathise, we don't approve; the police say that they only act when a member of the public complains – we would like that member of the public to make his complaint in court to the magistrate; we would like to see and hear less of police soliciting such offences; we would like offenders to be put in touch with us by the courts.[140]

A speaker mentioned setting up a 'bust fund' for accused men to fight such cases, the project of the Political Action Group. But there wasn't entire unanimity, and the issue of adoption by gay men showed one crack in the image of solidarity.

> [Male panellists said that] a gay couple should be allowed to bring up children (after all, even if the child did turn out to be gay, as was suggested by a listener, that was no worse than being straight). Here even the studio panel and the audience disagreed – several of the women thought that a child needed a mother, but had no use for a father.[141]

The programme gave out the new London Information Centre phone number, and Derek Brookfield organised a team of volunteers to take calls after the show, in a room where the paint was still wet on the walls. They worked till two in the morning. The programme was taped, and CHE copied it, to be able to offer it for broadcasting on other local BBC stations. It's not clear if any other stations took this offer up, but it was a canny move, given the need for cheap programming of social relevance. Among all the serious discussion, the programme also featured 'A Gay Song' as performed by the group Everyone Involved. This was written by Alan Wakeman of GLF, who founded the group, with music by Michael Klein:

Listen to me sister
And hear me brother too
This song contains a message
And it might apply to you
There's a little bit of gay
In everyone today
So why not let it out
That's what we say?

Gay is natural
Gay is good
Gay is wonderful
Gay people should
All come together
And fight for our rights.[142]

This song is from the 1972 Album, *Either/Or*, of which 1,000 copies were pressed, and distributed with the instruction that it should be given away free.

After the Radio London broadcast, and for several years afterwards, London CHE became the media's only port of call for comment by homosexuals on lesbian and gay stories and issues in the news. In November 1972 Roger Baker was on a Radio 1 breakfast show talking about the new CHE education campaign. Broadcasting became more commonplace, less noted as an event.

It took rather longer to crack commercial radio. Outside London this was much more flexible. But LBC, London's word-based station, was not particularly sensitive to minority issues or participation, preferring to ape mainstream BBC Radio 4. Towards the end of 1973 Jamie Gardner and two other members of the CHE Youth Group went on air to talk about the youth perspective. Off air they discussed with the producers the possibility of a regular gay programme on the station. Although Jamie reported that they were 'interested', no such animal materialised until LWT took the initiative with the pioneering TV series *Gay Life* in 1980.

A Question of Conscience

However, it was TV which potentially offered the greatest audience, although getting on TV also occasioned the most heart-searching and the most practical problems for CHE in this period. BBC2 proposed a six-part Further Education (Open University) series for early 1972 called *A Question of Conscience*. The producer was John Eidinow, and the presenter, whose project it was, was Robert McKenzie, the wielder of the swingometer at election time and himself gay. Like many deeply closeted homosexuals he was rapacious when the opportunity arose. He was not a man to be trapped in the back of a taxi with, as Tony Ryde found out:

> I can remember simply coming out of the BBC studios … and Robert saying, 'Do you want a taxi, a lift back?' And I said, 'No, I can quite easily get the tube across London, and of course he says, 'No, no, no, you must come in the taxi'. I said, ' Well, ok, thank you very much', and as soon as I got in the taxi it was hands on the knee, which completely floored me, in my innocence, 'cause I didn't know Robert McKenzie was gay.[143]

The series examined the burning social issues of the day where Parliament had recently changed the law. It was historical, in that the reformers talked about the process of law change, what it involved, how it had happened, and sociological, in looking at how the changes had worked for the people affected. There were to be programmes on the abolition of capital punishment, abortion, the end of censorship – and two on homosexuality.

The first programme interviewed the participants in the ten-year struggle to get the Wolfenden Report implemented – a fascinating study in itself, including an astonishing claim by the then Home Secretary Rab Butler that in 1958 the Government had wanted to implement Wolfenden, but felt it had to be a Private Member's Bill and couldn't find an MP to introduce it. Wolfenden himself is there, bald, grey, cautious and schoolmasterly, also making an astonishing admission: that the only reason his Committee didn't support a lower age of consent was pure expediency. He thought that 21 was achievable, and he didn't want to go down in history as a failure, having tried for something unattainable, such as 18 or 16.

The first programme, *Consenting Party*, went out on 26 April, and the week after there was *A Taste of Freedom*, a programme largely devoted to CHE. Allan Horsfall, Glenys Parry, Tony Ryde and Rose Robertson were all interviewed. There were excerpts from a Peter Katin recital at his Croydon studio. Film showed a local group meeting addressed by Antony Grey, and a Roger Baker induction meeting transplanted to Tom and Suzy Wesselkemper's place because the Baker apartment was far too cramped and squalid for the cameras. Apart from the interviews, everything was to some extent fake.

The basic problem was finding enough people who were prepared to be seen on film. Most CHE members were still far too closeted to expose themselves in this way. The problem was most acute nationally. All the activities filmed were based in London, but initially the BBC wanted to film a National Council in action. This would have been something of a coup for CHE, showing over a hundred open homosexuals seriously engaged in campaigning on a large scale. Initially, eagerly, the EC said yes, but then had second thoughts. It was not something they could commit local group representatives to without consulting them. What if everyone voted with their feet in front of the cameras, leaving nothing but shots of empty rows?

The March 1972 meeting was to be held in Liverpool, in rooms provided by the Anglican cathedral. On 19 January Paul Temperton sent out a very long and detailed letter designed to reassure anyone coming to the Council:

> BBC2 are producing a series of programmes looking at how various social issues have passed through a legislative process. In relation to the 1967 Sexual Offences Act this means studying how the subject came up in the first place, how in the Parliamentary Process the original intentions of the Bill's proponents were modified, and how the final legislation was worked out. CHE of course fits into the last part, and the BBC intend to devote a programme to looking, through CHE, at the extent to which the position of homosexuals in society has been affected. …
>
> This presents CHE with by far the most challenging opportunity we have yet had, or are likely to have in the near future, to put across to the public, and to the thousands of gay people who have never heard of us, what we believe and are trying to achieve. …
>
> The EC has decided that this would be advantageous to the programme (and CHE) but is conscious that it may be impractical if a majority of delegates/observers do not wish to be filmed. … Unless 50% of those attending are willing to be filmed, it will reluctantly have to inform the BBC that they cannot cover the meeting. Your co-operation in making this project feasible is therefore urgently needed.[144]

With his letter went a tear-off sticker to ask how many were coming, and how many were prepared to be filmed. Only thirty people answered 'Yes'. The National Council was not filmed.

Other parts of the programme had to be set up specially. The 'group meeting' was fixed for 4 February at the *Coachmaker's Arms*; the only problem was that it was the night of a meeting of Group 1, and nobody involved in making the programme bothered to tell the group. Chairman David Smith wrote an embarrassed letter to members:

> This week I discover that the BBC had been invited to film at the same place on the same date. I was obliged to compromise, and the situation is now this: Antony Grey (Albany Trust) will talk on Law reform at 7.30 p.m.

> If there is time Glenys will, presumably, talk on (something like) Radical Reform. I cannot be clear about details except that it will be an open meeting (i.e. members from other Groups will be attending) and BBC2 will be in action for part of the evening. I hope to see you there, but if you are shy of cameras you are warned not to attend. I am sorry this has occurred. The landlord, apparently, double booked the room.[145]

He also had to write to Glenys Parry, who had been booked to speak to the Group, but, absurdly, not to appear on the programme:

> I have only just heard – by accident, incidentally! – about the TV bit. … The current situation is now this. Antony Grey is speaking (and being televised) at 7.30 p.m. on Law Reform. This will not take all evening, presumably, and there is no reason – as far as time is concerned – why you should not talk as well. This is not very flattering to you and I shall understand if you want to cry off, but I hope we shall be able to see you and proceed with the programme as far as we are able under the altered circumstances. One of the problems is that because of the cameras I have no idea how many of my group will turn up. Again, as this is now being treated as an open meeting, it is possible that there will be *more* people there; the trouble is that we are dealing with unknowns. Quite simply, I do not know what is going to happen.[146]

Glenys did come down to London for the meeting, and as a result was included as an interviewee at the last minute. Filming in a small upstairs pub room made it difficult to exclude from shot people who did not want to be filmed, and in any case what was needed was a packed and visible house. The programme makers needed people to come to the pub who were comfortable about being seen on television, and everyone else to stay away. Hence the invitation to all London groups. The BBC just about managed to fill the place.

The 'induction' meeting was similarly staged; Roger Baker explained the purpose of CHE to people who already knew it intimately, but dutifully asked naïve questions for the cameras.

When it came to the piano recital, there were serious problems finding *anyone* in Croydon prepared to be on film. Eventually Tony Ryde, Michael Launder and Michael's mother Margaret took the train down from London Bridge, and, with one other, made up the four who sat in the front row. The cameras kept in tight on them, ignoring the other nineteen packed rows where nobody wanted to be seen on telly.

> There must have been 60 or 70 people crammed into two rooms, one of which was occupied by Peter Katin, 2 pianos and a rather fidgety BBC camera team. On arrival guests were given the choice – to sit in the front four rows and be recognisable on camera – or move to the back. Predictably there was a scramble to remain incognito. … Sweating under

> boiling arc lights that bathed the audience in such radiance that specks of dandruff dazzled like snowflakes.[147]

Katin's delicate Chopin battled bravely against the whirring of cameras, and the distracting whispering of director and cameramen. During the Barcarolle Op. 60 one of the massive lights began to flicker on and off, then went out.

> At the same time the rubber plug adaptor started smoking and within seconds caught fire. One or two panicky women rushed for the door, while valiant Tony Ryde fought the flames with suede shoes and rolled up *Guardian*, and Michael Launder visualised next day's local headlines '50 fried faggots up in smoke!' The camera team seemed utterly unmoved by such activity. Peter Katin, with great equanimity, returned to where he'd left off, in dense acrid smoke, which his wife did her best to dispel with a scented aerosol spray. Miraculously their newly-laid carpets were unharmed. The electrician mended the fault and once more we reverted to mock sunshine and Chopin. [148]

When the programme was finally finished and edited, Tony Ryde was faced with one major step in his personal coming out process. Despite his position in CHE, his family did not know he was gay. He was interviewed for the *Radio Times*, with a photo, as one of the week's 'Radio Times People'. The circulation of the *Radio Times* in the early 1970s was over eight million, so Tony was coming out with a vengeance when he said:

> 'The whole time I was at university I denied that it could be true. As little as four years ago, after meeting a girl I developed a real affection for, I remember walking down the street thinking, Hooray! I'm Heterosexual! Next morning though the feeling had gone completely and, eventually, I had to admit I was homosexual.'
>
> Not everyone who knows Tony knows the truth. He doesn't, he says, make an issue of it. 'But if I'm talking to a colleague at work, and he's talking about his wife and his new baby, then I'll mention that I've lived with my boyfriend Michael for four years and that we're very happy.'[149]

He was already known to be gay at work, but he braced himself for recognition elsewhere. He rang his father, who knew he was gay, to tell him about the programme, and the possibility that his parents' neighbours and friends would see the article, or the programme, and tackle them about it. His worst fear was that his grandmother would see it. In the event, if she did see it, she said nothing.

The programme went out at 7.05 p.m. on 3 May 1972, a Wednesday. It was on BBC2, so its likely audience was between 500,000 and a million people. One of those who saw it was Ian Buist, a very senior Civil Servant who was to be extremely important in drafting CHE's Sexual Offences Bill in

1974–75. Ian's local group was Wandsworth–Richmond.* He continued to be politically active into his seventies and eighties, and even had a hand, working with Stonewall, in drafting the Civil Partnership legislation of 2003–04.

A Taste of Freedom was not the only television broadcast to feature CHE. On 31 May 1973, Vivian Waldron and David Bell appeared on Mavis Nicholson's *Good Afternoon* show.† This was again reviewed in *Gay News*. While Mavis was herself highly liberal, she cast herself as representative of the 'average' (assumed prejudiced and ignorant) audience:

> I've got three sons, and I think because of the various taboos and prejudices that I would have felt ashamed, previously, if one of my sons was a homosexual, because I have been led to believe that it was possibly my fault, that I was a domineering bossy mother or the father was weak.[150]

David Bell, the youngster, was very positive, rejecting all unnecessary talk of 'causes' and emphasising his acceptance by employer, pupils at his school, and his family. Vivian, however, the product of an earlier age, was honest enough to admit regrets when Mavis asked if either of them would have preferred to have been heterosexual ('It would have been easier, wouldn't it?'). Vivian replied:

> I would rather like to have been a parent. … When I've borrowed other people's children, perhaps to take them out for a walk, it has pleased me that other people should think I was the father. There are certain advantages in being homosexual, as well as disadvantages. On balance though, I think I and probably most homosexuals, if they were given the opportunity of starting all over again, would opt for heterosexuality. It is simpler.[151]

The desire for children is not uncommon among gay men, and in the twenty-first century is one of a number of lifestyle choices available to gay men which would have seemed impossible forty years before. However, in voicing this yearning Vivian became branded with contempt in some gay circles as 'the man who would rather have been straight'. In an era when the projection of positive images was a moral imperative for all lesbians and gay men, his view was quite unacceptable. However, the label ignores Waldron's work, week after week, advocating gay rights in front of hostile crowds at Speakers' Corner, and also as a member, and later organiser, of FRIEND.

---

* See Volume Two.

† *Good Afternoon* was broadcast by Thames Television 1972-1988. As the 'women's pages' of newspapers in the 1960s had been in the forefront of liberal treatment of homosexuality and advocating implementing Wolfenden, the broadcasting equivalent (*Women's Hour* on Radio Four, daytime TV with its largely female audience) was similarly sympathetic.

Taking Stock

By the middle of 1973 London CHE had nearly a thousand members and climbing, some twenty local groups, at least fifteen SIGs, and its own office and meeting place in the heart of the West End. Its large-scale social events such as dances and Winter Fairs were hugely successful. It had seen the rise and fall of what many saw as an upstart rival, the more radical GLF, of which more in Volume Two. It had founded the most influential and important LGBT advice and support organisation, FRIEND, which was in the process of rolling out a national network. It had published a significant monthly magazine for two years. Hardly less significant was Rose Robertson's Parents' Enquiry. The majority of the most dynamic and skilled CHE members were in London, and there was still the possibility of a proper COC-style gay club. CHE was becoming increasingly skilled in campaigning, and confident in its handling of the media. Though a few commercial clubs were just beginning to open and become more visible, London CHE at the end of 1973 was socially and politically the only game in town. Londoners could ask with some smugness, would the rest of the country ever catch up?

Nationally, CHE had also come a long way. In terms of creating 'a space to breathe', by 1973 over 3,500 people could fill their lungs in over 70 local groups. Those who could not get to meetings could derive comfort and support, develop self-esteem and ideas about rights and liberation, from *Bulletins* and *Lunch*. There were social and sociable spaces from Newcastle to the South-West, from Swansea to Canterbury. The leap, from Allan Horsfall ploughing a solitary furrow in 1958, was huge, and most of that growth had happened within the previous three years. It had happened as a result of the talents and perseverance of a few individuals who also luckily happened to catch the tide of the times, and to provide a convincing answer to the question, 'What do homosexuals want?' Well, a significant number of homosexuals at least.

In this time, the organisation had seized on the first essential for gay and lesbian awareness, the space in which to find oneself, to meet others, to develop thoughts and feelings. If Esquire Clubs had come to fruition, this would have been a physical space; a headquarters or other secure building, in which to express those thoughts and feelings, along with the moral and political ideas and ideologies they gave rise to. CHE clubs did not materialise, but space was still needed, a space where, by swapping stories and experiences, ordinary lesbians and gay men might create both a community and a common set of values and aspirations which could be pursued through collective action. The discovery of the need to be fulfilled, the need for 'space to breathe' was user-led, in that it was expressed by those who came to meetings of the North Western Committee, and by those whom Allan

Horsfall and Harold Pollard and others talked to in the Rockingham and other Manchester bars, and by those who came forward in response to adverts.

Although CHE was unable to establish clubs, the idea that there was a substitute, that where a group of LGBT people were gathered was in itself the kind of gay space in which these things could happen, was CHE's big discovery. Collectively, we could create our own gay space anywhere. The grateful response of thousands was evidence enough of the need.

This volume has concentrated on the creation of gay space, in all its manifestations, from the earnest discussion of 'What Makes Us This Way' to the fancy dress party, the car rally, or the advice line. As a result of the efforts to set up local CHE groups, thousands of people were meeting each other, arguing, laughing, having sex, offering support and advice, in different towns all over the country.

What this did not create, however, was a coherent movement, a national campaign, a coherent ideology which could be put forward by any and all CHE members, at local or national level. Although, broadly speaking, CHE members shared a sexual orientation, it by no means followed that they would share a political and moral outlook.

While Paul Temperton and Martin Stafford were working at the grass roots level, assiduously sending out the mailings, logging the new members, collecting subs, giving guidelines to convenors and acting as sounding boards and shoulders to cry on, a parallel development was taking place on the EC and among CHE strategists, to create a democratic LBGT movement, the only democratic national organisation which the UK has ever known. And beyond that, to create the platform on which that organisation could campaign, the demands on which it could agree. Before 1967, 'Equality' had a very particular meaning – it was something which gay men wanted under the law when they sought or had sex. Post-1967, it was by no means immediately clear what Equality was, and what its implications were. Only by the ongoing experience of in-Equality, and raising the awareness of in-Equality among homosexuals, many of whom continued to protest that they were not oppressed, in defiance of the evidence, would it become clear what needed to be eliminated, what promoted. As the shape of Equality became clearer, it also became clearer what was needed to achieve it; the most effective campaign strategies, the skills which needed to be developed, the communications systems and activist networks.

Volume Two will cover the process which turned CHE from a higgledy-piggledy network of individual and individualistic local groups to a bona fide national pressure group, with a degree of coherence tempered by significant dissent. National CHE grew into an awareness of itself at its first national conference, in Morecambe in 1973. This was the moment CHE itself came of age.

Notes to Chapter Six

[1] CHE 'Information sheet about EC candidates', 1973. HCA/CHE/7/84.

[2] Wallace Grevatt, 'Newsletter introduction', Croydon CHE newsletter, October 1971. CHE/HCA/5/57/83.

[3] Wallace Grevatt to Paul Temperton, 'Group advertising', 8 September 1971. HCA/CHE/5/55/70.

[4] Ibid.

[5] Wallace Grevatt to Paul Temperton, 'Door-to-door campaign', 15 June 1972. HCA/CHE/5/55/82.

[6] Paul Temperton to Wallace Grevatt, 'Door-to-door leaflets', 1972. HCA/CHE/5/55/83

[7] Wallace Grevatt, 'Everybody's welcome at a Charrington pub', *Lunch*, 6 (March 1972), 15.

[8] Doris Locke to Peter Katin, 'Letter of protest', 24 May 1974. HCA/CHE/7/16.

[9] Peter Katin to Doris Locke, 'Reply', 16 July 1974. HCA/CHE/7/16.

[10] Peter Katin, interviewed by the author, 19 November 2012.

[11] Ibid.

[12] Ibid.

[13] Ibid.

[14] Tyneside CHE *Newsletter*, June 1973. HCA/CHE/7/152.

[15] Glenys Parry, interviewed by the author, 27 August 2012.

[16] Vivian Waldron, speaking on Mavis Nicholson's *Good afternoon*, Thames Television, 31 May 1973. E. Brown Transcript. HCA/CHE/5/66.

[17] Brian Sewell, interviewed by the author, 20 September 2012.

[18] 'Moonlighter', 'Legal corner', *Lunch*, 15 (December 1972), 28.

[19] Peter Robins, interviewed by the author, 20 September 2012.

[20] Tom and Suzy Wesselkamper, Advertisement, *Lunch*, 7 (April 1972), 12.

[21] 'Did you get to the mass meeting Group 3 put on at Conway Hall?', *Lunch*, 2 (October 1971), 7–9.

[22] Peter Norman, interviewed by the author, 26 February 2014.

[23] Jo Batchelor to Paul Temperton, 'Arrangements for London women', undated [1972]. HCA/CHE/5/57/1.

[24] NC minutes, 16 September 1972. HCA/CHE/3/1/20

[25] Tony Ryde, interviewed by the author, 5 December 2012.

[26] Peter Robins and Brian Sewell, interviewed by the author, 20 September 2012.

[27] Paul Temperton to Tony Ryde, 'Material for August 1971 *Bulletin*', 14 July 1971. HCA/CHE/5/3/21.

[28] Roger Baker to Paul Temperton, 'London update', 18 August 1971. HCA/CHE/5/3/31.

[29] Brian Sewell, Peter Robins and Michael Moor, 'People not paper', 1971. HCA/CHE/7/101.

[30] Ibid.

[31] Ibid.

[32] Ibid.

[33] Ibid.

[34] Ibid.

[35] Ibid.

[36] Ibid.

[37] Ibid.

[38] Peter Naughton, interviewed by the author, 30 August 2012.

[39] Ibid.

[40] Ibid.

[41] Ibid.

[42] Ibid.

[43] Peter Norman, Local groups report to EC, 10 June 1973. HCA/CHE/2/1.

[44] George Jordan, 'Letter to *Lunch*' *Lunch*, 6 (March 1972), 29.

[45] Michael Harth, interviewed by the author, 30 May 2014.

[46] Michael Harth, 'Stepney application for recognition to National Council', April 1973. HCA/CHE/7/1/74.

[47] Michael Harth, 'Re homosexuals and socialism', *Lunch*, 13, October 1972, 12–13.

[48] Michael Harth, interviewed by the author, 30 May 2014.

[49] Ibid.

[50] *Science and living* (BBC publication, 1971), quoted in Streatham CHE newsletter, HCA/CHE/7/111.

[51] Ibid.

[52] Kay Collier, 'All he (and his group) wants … is a room somewhere', *Hornsey Journal*, 23 February 1973, 24.

[53] Ibid.

[54] Ibid.

[55] Ibid.

[56] 'Council topics: Homosexual meetings: Row over council move', *Hornsey Journal*, 23 March 1973, 6.

[57] 'Gay Lib talk to pupils called off', *Hornsey Journal*, 9 February 1973, 1.

[58] Peter Norman, Report to EC meeting, 10 February 1973. HCA/CHE/2/2.

[59] Brian Sewell, Peter Robins and Michael Moor, 'People not Paper', 1971. HCA/CHE/7/101.

[60] Ibid.

[61] Ibid.

[62] Ibid.

[63] Peter Robins, interviewed by the author, 20 September 2012.

[64] Brian Sewell, 'Mass meeting agenda', Undated [1971]. HCA/Williams/26.

[65] Colin Darracott to Peter Norman, 'Conway Hall reaction', undated [1971]. HCA/CHE/NORMAN/8.

[66] David Hyde to Paul Temperton, 'London reorganisation', 12 September 1971. HCA/CHE/5/31.

[67] Ken Glazier to Brian Sewell, 'Conway Hall mass meeting', 15 September 1971. HCA/WILLIAMS/26.

[68] Michael Moor, interviewed by the author, 8 September 2012.

[69] Robin Bloxsidge, interviewed by the author, 27 August 2012.

[70] Tony Ryde, interviewed by the author, 5 December 2012.

[71] Brian Sewell, interviewed by the author, 20 September 2012.

[72] Roger Baker, 'Did you get to the mass meeting Group 3 put on at Conway Hall?' *Lunch*, 2 (October 1971), 7–9.

[73] Ibid.

[74] Ibid.

[75] Roger Baker, 'Strong reaction to permissive society setting in', *Lunch*, 1 (September 1971), 3–4.

[76] Peter Norman, interviewed by the author, 25 February 2014.

[77] HL Deb 29 November 1972, vol. 336 col. 1291.

[78] Brian Sewell, interviewed by the author, 20 September 2012.

[79] Peter Robins, interviewed by the author, 20 September 2012.

[80] Charles Murdoch, 'Dear Sir, …', *Lunch*, 2 (November 1971), 12–13; John Cowell, Ibid., 14.

[81] Brian Sewell to Lord Longford, 'CHE participation in Longford Commission', 24 November 1971. HCA/CHE/4/1/31.

[82] Longford Commission, *Longford Report*, 460–508.

[83] Ibid., 498.

[84] Ibid., 413.

[85] 'Did you get to the mass meeting Group 3 put on at Conway Hall?', *Lunch*, 2 (October 1971), 7–9.

[86] Peter Norman, interviewed by the author, 25 February 2014.

[87] Ibid.

[88] Brian Sewell, interviewed by the author, 20 September 2012.

[89] Roger Baker, 'Platform wreathed with flowers', *Gay News*, 3, undated, [1972]. 3.

[90] Ibid.

[91] 'R. Symonds-Yat', 'Darlings, you were marvellous' *Lunch*, 11 (August 1972), 23.

[92] Ibid.

[93] 'Inter-group speakers' list', 30 April 1972. HCA/CHE/NORMAN/3.

[94] Vivian Waldron, 'A personal view', *Lunch*, 20 (May 1973), 18–19.

[95] Michael Steed, interviewed by the author, 25 November 2013.

[96] Alistair Nicholl to Bill Dalzeil, 'Music Group', 26 July 1972. HCA/CHE/5/60/65.

[97] Alistair Nicholl to Paul Temperton, 'Music Group', 29 July 1972. HCA/CHE/5/111/10.

[98] Alistair Nicholl to Paul Temperton, 'Future arrangements for Music Group', 22 August 1972. HCA/CHE/5/60/67.

[99] Bill Dalziel, 'Record Recitals Group', *Lunch*, 11 (August 1972), 24–25.

[100] Michael Harth, interviewed by the author, 30 May 2014.

[101] A. Vincent-Jones, 'A happy trio at musical soiree'. *Lunch*, 19 (April 1973), 19.

[102] C. Waston, 'CHE Music Group', *Lunch*, 17 (February 1973), 28.

[103] R. Simpson, 'Gay 90's music hall', *Lunch*, 7 (April 1972), 21–22.

[104] Ibid.

[105] Ibid.

[106] Ibid.

[107] 'Choose your group now', *Lunch*, 11 (August 1972), 24.

[108] 'Our cruising correspondent', 'Advertisement – no drag', *Lunch*, 18 (March 1973), 23.

[109] Peter Robins, interviewed by the author, 20 September 2012.

[110] Pinter, *Trouble in the works*, in *Plays 2*, 227.

[111] J. Bilton to Group Chairmen, 'CHE Players flyer', 12 November 1973. HCA/CHE/7/113.

[112] 'Newsettes: Gay play banned', *Gay News* 35, 1–28 November 1973, 24.

[113] Gay Sweatshop Manifesto, 1974. RHA/GS/1/1/1/1.

[114] Kathleen Raine, 'Shells', in *Selected Poems*, 49.

[115] 'AFB', 'A song for Mike', in *Speaking Out*, 1972, 3 HCA/WILLIAMS/26.

[116] Niki Delany, 'Dawn by the sea', in *Speaking Out*, 1972, 10. HCA/WILLIAMS/26.

[117] 'P. R.', 'A plain man's guide', in *Speaking Out*, 1972, 11. HCA/WILLIAMS/26.

[118] John Dawson, Untitled. in *Speaking Out*, 1972, 30. HCA/WILLIAMS /26.

[119] 'Writers' group', *Lunch*, 18 (March 1973), 28. HCA/WILLIAMS /26.

[120] 'CHE Wine Making', *Lunch*, 17 (February 1973), 28.

[121] Ibid.

[122] Roger Baker, 'Gay film unit forming', *Lunch*, 14 (November 1972), 29.

[123] D. Hart, 'First gay commercial', *Lunch*, 19 (April 1973), 29.

[124] David Bell, speaking on Mavis Nicholson's *Good afternoon*, Thames Television, 31 May 1973. E. Brown Transcript. HCA/CHE/5/66.

[125] Gini Stevens, Editorial, *Lunch*, 5 (January 1972), 3.

[126] David Smith, Group 1 monthly members' letter, 21 January 1972. HCA/WILLIAMS/26.

[127] Derek Brookfield to all LCC members, 'LCC news', 16 October 1972. HCA/CHE/5/60/26.

[128] 'Political action group', Advertisement, *Gay News*, 9, undated [1972]. 15.

[129] Derek Brookfield, 'LPAG report on 1972', 11 January 1973. HCA/CHE/NORMAN/4.

[130] 'GLC election could be test for bigger fight', *Brentford and Chiswick Times*, 26 October 1972, 4.

[131] Michael Steed, 'A gay vote?', *Lunch*, 15 (December 1972), 35.

[132] Michael Harth, interviewed by the author, 30 May 2014.

[133] Arthur Helliwell (Your Man of the People), 'A Plea from the heart', *The People*, 15 February 1970, 6.

[134] Gini Stevens, '*Speakeasy* with Jimmy Savile'. *Lunch*, 17 (February 1973), 4–6.

[135] Doug Pollard, 'Over there, Mr Roving Mike'. *Gay News*, 1, undated [1972], 4.

[136] *Radio Times*, 26 August – 1 September 1972, 63.

[137] CHE *Bulletin*, October 1972. HCA/CHE/4/1/52.

[138] Doug Pollard, 'Radio CHE', *Gay News*, 7, undated [1972], 3.

[139] Doug Pollard, 'CHEdio London', *Gay News*, 8, undated [1972], 5.

[140] Ibid.

[141] Ibid.

[142] Alan Wakeman, 'A Gay Song', from the album *Either/or* by Everyone Involved. Featured on *Strong Love: Songs of Gay Liberation 1972-1981*, Chapter Music CH070.

[143] Tony Ryde, interviewed by the author, 5 December 2012.

[144] Paul Temperton to local groups, 'National Council arrangements', 19 January 1971. HCA/CHE/3/1/3.

[145] David Smith to Group 1 members, 'Change to group arrangements', 27 January 1972. HCA/WILLIAMS/26.

[146] David Smith to Glenys Parry, 'Apologies', 26 January 1972, HCA/WILLIAMS/26.

[147] G. Shaw, 'At home with Peter Katin', *Lunch*, 5 (January 1972), 14.

[148] Ibid.

[149] 'Admitting the truth', *Radio Times*, 27 April 1972, 4.

[150] Mavis Nicholson, speaking on *Good afternoon*, Thames Television, 31 May 1973. E. Brown Transcript. HCA/CHE/5/66.

[151] Ibid.

Appendix A: Timeline of events

This timeline covers key events up to mid-1973. Some of these events are dealt with in Volume Two. An expanded version will appear on the website at www.amiable-warriors.uk/timeline.shtml.

1945

CHE, HLRS	Other Gay events (UK and World)	In the News...	The Arts
	First LGBT Ex-Forces Association is formed in New York.	25 April: 50 nations meet in San Francisco to hammer out the United Nations Charter. The UN officially comes in to existence on 24 October.	Evelyn Waugh's *Brideshead Revisited* is published.
	Portugal decriminalises homosexuality.	8 May: Official end of European conflict of World War 2; full enormity of concentration camps gradually emerges, including treatment of homosexual internees.	
	20 March: Death of Lord Alfred Douglas; in later life he had found Catholicism and denounced his lover Oscar Wilde as evil.		

1946

CHE, HLRS	Other Gay events (UK and World)	In the News...	The Arts
Allan Horsfall starts two years national service with the RAF, in Germany.	COC is founded in Amsterdam. It adopts 'homophile' as its preferred alternative to the word 'homosexual'. 'Homophile' had been coined in 1924 in Germany.	29 September: BBC Third Programme starts. Amid accusations of elitism and being boring ('just two dons talking to each other') it creates the space for more adventurous drama programming, and fostered the early careers of many gay writers.	
	Alec Guinness fined 10 guineas for cottaging in Liverpool. He gives his name in court as Herbert Pocket, the character he has recently played in *Great Expectations*. This, and being caught outside London, means he escapes the media attention attendant on Sir John Gielgud's trial seven years later.		
	28 August: Sir George Mowbray, president of Reading University Council, is fined £20 for importuning men in Piccadilly Circus underground station. It does not seem to have affected his career. John Wolfenden was Vice-Chancellor of the University from 1950 and will have known him.		

1947

CHE, HLRS	Other Gay events (UK and World)	In the News…	The Arts
	COC opens its first club, in Amsterdam. It invites the police to the opening night party.	1 January: The US Supreme Court rules that movie studios could not practice 'vertical integration' and have to sell off their cinemas to conform to antitrust legislation. This allows exhibitors to book foreign films, which do not have to conform to the Hays Code. As a result, films like *Victim* and *The Leather Boys* get US distribution.	30 May: *Three Blind Mice* is the BBC's and Agatha Christie's 80th birthday present to Dowager Queen Mary, who asked them for a radio thriller. QM's fondness for gay men is also catered for in the character of Christopher Wren, who likes Sergeant Trotter *very* much and gives upright Giles the willies. Female perversion is barely hinted in 'gruff, mannish' ex-magistrate Mrs Boyle. Christie recycles the material into *The Mousetrap*, which celebrates 25,000 performances in 2012, and is the longest-running play ever.
		24 November: US House of Representatives overwhelmingly approves citations for Contempt of Congress against the 'Hollywood Ten', who refused to co-operate with the House Committee on Un-American Activities. The ten are blacklisted by the major Hollywood studios the next day. The road to McCarthyism is clear.	3 December: Tennessee Williams' *A Streetcar Named Desire* opens on Broadway. It comes to London 1949. The 1951 film removes any reference to the homosexuality of Blanche's husband. Brando in the film does for the white T-shirt what Clark Gable did for the vest in *It Happened One Night* in 1934.

1948

CHE, HLRS	Other Gay events (UK and World)	In the News…	The Arts
Allan Horsfall leaves the RAF and joins his local RAF association. At the local RAFA club in Nelson he meets his life partner, Harold Pollard, 20 years his senior.	Det Danske Forbundet av 1948 is founded in Denmark.	10 December: Publication of the United Nations Universal Declaration of Human Rights.	10 January: Gore Vidal publishes *The City and the Pillar*, at some risk to his literary career. His characters are strikingly butch, in contrast to the prevailing sissylit. The protagonist Jim Willard is an athlete who, at the end of the book (in its revised version) rapes his boyhood sweetheart. But he walks away from his defiance of social convention unpunished, even stronger. There are extended pictures of gay life in the forces during WW2. The book causes so much outrage that papers refuse to review Vidal's subsequent work for many years, forcing him to publish under pseudonyms such as Edgar Box.
Antony Grey starts work in Leeds as a junior reporter on the *Yorkshire Post*. After a short time he joins the Iron and Steel Federation, where he becomes a PR officer. He remains there for 13 years.	*Vice Versa*, first American lesbian magazine, is published in Los Angeles.	Publication of Kinsey Report on *Sexual Behaviour in the Human Male*. *Sexual Behaviour in the Human Female* follows in 1953, but with hardly the same impact.	
		Poland introduces equal age of consent of 15 for homosexual and heterosexual sex.	

1949

CHE, HLRS	Other Gay events (UK and World)	In the News...	The Arts
Robert Reid, having lost his employment as a teacher because of his pre-war sex offence conviction, scrapes a living as a writer of school textbooks. Publishes *Notes on Practical Chemistry: A concise general science.*	Danish gay activists publish *Vennen,* a magazine for gay men. Initially for members of Det Danske Forbundet, it is on the newsstands by 1951. It folds in 1974.	1 February: Clothes rationing ends in Britain. After the war you were allowed 24 points a year, and a suit cost 26–28 points, a pair of shoes 9. Homosexuals who like to look nice now celebrate.	
Ike Cowen, later CHE's legal officer, leaves the RAF to start training as a barrister.			

1950

CHE, HLRS	Other Gay events (UK and World)	In the News...	The Arts
25 March: two lads (a fireman, 24, and a textile worker, 22) keep a suicide pact in Brontë country; one shoots the other in the head with a rabbit gun, then turns it on himself. His wife is eight months pregnant. The neighbours say they were both nice quiet lads. The case upsets Allan Horsfall very much.	RFSL is founded in Sweden.	East Germany reverts to the 'milder', pre-Nazi, form of Paragraph 175 regulating male homosexual acts.	Radio play by Dr Jacob Bronowski, *The Face of Violence*, is an apocalyptically urgent post-nuclear piece, about the need to come to grips with man's limitless appetite for destruction. Homosexuals appear on the sidelines as irremediable addicts of excess and triviality. Not a great advert, but the first mention of the subject by the BBC.
	International Committee for Sexual Equality (ICSE) is initiated by COC.	190 US Government employees are dismissed on grounds of their homosexuality.	Jean Genet makes his only film. *Un Chant d'Amour*, an erotic silent film about the relationship between an older and younger convict and the power play with the
	4 June: George Ives, founder of the Order of Chaeronea and friend of Wilde, Carpenter, Nicholson and Havelock Ellis, dies, and with him, the Order. This was a kind of gay mafia for self-help, but never campaigned publicly.	9 February: Senator Joseph McCarthy kicks off his witch-hunt against communists and homosexuals in the US, with a speech in West Virginia to a Republican Women's Club. The Red Scare and The Lavender Menace send government into persecution mode.	
	11 November: Mattachine Society is founded in San Francisco; the same year, California doubles the state		

	penalty for sodomy to 20 years.		prison guard, is banned for many years; it receives its premiere in a cut version at the Cinémathèque Française in 1954, but is not seen in the UK until 1971. Hull's Metropolitan District Council refused it a screening as recently as 1989.

1951

CHE, HLRS	Other Gay events (UK and World)	In the News…	The Arts
Jacqueline Mackenzie (later Jackie Forster) makes her TV acting debut in *The Triumphant.*	Publication of *The Homosexual in America: A subjective approach* by D. W. Cory.	Guy Burgess and Donald Maclean flee to Russia, following a tip-off from Kim Philby that British Counter-Intelligence has its eyes on them. Burgess – radio producer and most undiplomatic diplomat – leaked details about the Marshall Plan throughout the 1940s. A flamboyant queer, he triggers a first wave of 'lavender menace' exposés in the UK.	André Gide dies.
	California Supreme Court rules that having a homosexual clientele is not enough reason to deny a bar a liquor licence. The Black Cat in San Francisco, whose licence had been suspended in 1948, is back in business.	Greece decriminalises nearly all homosexual sex acts. The now-equal age of consent is 15.	
	12 May: first International Congress for Sexual Equality opens in Amsterdam, with representatives from six countries. The Congress sends a letter to the UN demanding equal rights for the homosexual minority.	Brian Hobson, aged 18, sucks a young man off on the back seat of a coach going to the Festival of Britain. He gets a taste for it, as he tells a Leeds court three years later, 'without any sense of shame or remorse'. In Leeds he	

		is one of 17 men in the dock and admits to sex with six of them. He is sent to prison for five years in December 1954.	

1952

CHE, HLRS	Other Gay events (UK and World)	In the News…	The Arts
	Publication of *Society and the Homosexual* by 'Gordon Westwood' (Michael Schofield).	World-wide publicity for Christine Jorgensen's gender reassignment in an operation in Copenhagen. Contrary to belief at the time, it is not the first operation of its kind.	*Spring Fire* by Vin Packer published. The genre of lesbian pulp fiction is created.
	'Vice rings' start to appear in the papers increasingly frequently: 26 October – thirteen men in Dorking: 'It started about ten years ago during the war.' 23 November – fifteen men in Kingston, Surrey: 'I cannot send you to Borstal – it is highly likely you would corrupt others there.'	20 February: The UK scraps compulsory ID cards, which were introduced as an emergency wartime measure. As a result men like John Gielgud who are brought summarily before magistrates on cottaging charges can more easily give a false name to the court.	Angus Wilson publishes his first novel, *Hemlock and After*. Bernard is given money to start a writers' colony, and struggles to do so while coming to terns with his homosexuality. His next door neighbour, Mrs Curry, procures boys for paedophiles. The decayed middle-class ambience will become typical of his writing. Written in less than a month.
	18 May: Start of a *Sunday Pictorial* exposé of 'Evil Men'. This runs for four weeks, a sensational series about the spread of the gay subculture, and the way it corrupts the young.		The lavender menace comes to Ambridge as Lady Hylberow tries to lure Christine Archer away to view Coptic churches in Ethiopia. She is disillusioned when she discovers Christine plays the field: 'Her main interest would seem to be with "boyfriends" as she calls them.'

1953

CHE, HLRS	Other Gay events (UK and World)	In the News…	The Arts
2 November: Robert Reid writes to the Letters Page of the *Daily Telegraph,* calling on Britain to adopt the Code Napoléon as regards homosexuality. All the subsequent correspondents agree with him, except for a letter from psychiatrist Clifford Allen, who believes in cure.	Det Norske Forbundet av 1948 founded in Norway.	10 January: McCarthy is appointed chairman of the Senate Permanent sub-committee on investigations, acquiring far greater power to question, bully and persecute left-wing and allegedly homosexual opponents.	Rodney Garland's *The Heart in Exile* is published. A gay psychiatrist tries to find out what has happened to his friend, who disappeared. A plea for 'tolerance' and a realistic picture of the gay subculture masqureading as a thriller. Having a central character who is gay and a psychiatrist gives the book added authority
	Publication of report on the 'Problem of Homosexuality' by the Church of England Moral Welfare Council. It favours decriminalisation and an age of consent of 21.	3 September: European Convention on Human Rights (ECHR) comes into force in all Council of Europe states, and it becomes a condition of Council membership to sign the Convention at the earliest possible moment. Sir David Maxwell Fyfe was chair of the drafting committee. From his reaction to the recommendations of the Wolfenden Committee, he clearly never imagined that the provisions of the ECHR could apply to homosexuals.	8 June: The new Queen, Elizabeth II, attends the premiere of Benjamin Britten's latest opera *Gloriana*, with his very public partner Peter Piers playing the romantic male lead. The opera, with its less than hagiographic portrait of the needy, vain Elizabeth I, goes down like a lead balloon.
	January: In Los Angeles, the first issue appears of *ONE*, the magazine of the Mattachine Society and the first gay magazine to achieve wide distribution among homosexuals in the United States.	11 October: Rupert Croft-Cooke is sent to prison for nine months for having sex with two men he picked up in Oxford Street. His book, *The Verdict of You All,* comes out at the same time as Wildeblood's account of his similar experiences, but has nothing like the same impact, being snob-	7 September: Hidden away on the Third Programme, the most positive representation of an older lesbian until the 80s. Henry Read's *The Private Life of Hilda Tablet* is based loosely on Ethel Smyth, but Hilda is an avant-garde composer, the inventor of *musique concrète renforcée.* 'Throw your voice at
	28 April: President Eisenhower signs Executive Order 10450, making homosexuality grounds for investigation and dismissal of US federal employees.		
	4 November: 83-year-old Lord Samuel, Liberal leader in the House of Lords, uses his reply to the Queen's speech proroguing Parliament to warn that 'there are pockets of immorality in our great cities which are a grave blot on our civilisation … we find that the vices of Sodom and Gomorrah, of the		

	Cities of the Plain, appear to be rife among us. If they spread, then retribution will be found.' This apocalyptic prophecy starts the ball rolling towards the Wolfenden Committee.	bish, cowardly and evasive. Croft-Cooke fled to Morocco. The fate of his poor servant, an Indian called Joseph arrested with him, has been quite forgotten, and Croft-Cooke shows no subsequent interest in, or loyalty to, him.	the note, but for God's sake, miss it!' Hilda is a force of nature, randy, unapologetic and separatist feminist *avant le jour,* with a monstrous ego which she inflicts on her 'companion', Elsa Strauss. The occasional series continues through the 1950s.
		21 October: Sir John Gielgud is arrested. He gives his details as 'Arthur Gielgud, clerk', but a stringer in court spots him, and extensive publicity results. No lasting damage to his career, though there are calls for his knighthood to be taken back. On 11 Jan, Labour MP William J Field had been convicted of the same thing and fined £15 purely on the evidence of one policeman that he had smiled at another man. Two appeals fail, and he loses his seat.	

1954

CHE, HLRS	Other Gay events (UK and World)	In the News...	The Arts
Twelve young men aged 18–21 are convicted of being part of a 'sex ring' operating at an open borstal near Monmouth. It poses a dilemma of where to send them to serve their sentence, because the punishment would normally be – Borstal. This is a case often quoted by campaigners endeavouring to change the law, and arguing that the age of consent should be at least as low as 18.	Danish activists launch the IHWO, International Homosexual World Organisation. Despite its grand title, it is mainly a publisher of an international contact magazine and a distributor of nudie photographs. It folds in 1971.	2 February: The British Medical Association suggests that there is a link between smoking and lung cancer. Sixty years later, lesbians and gay men still have substantially higher rates of smoking than heterosexuals.	January: *Calamity Jane* is released in the UK, and *Secret Love* becomes a lesbian and gay anthem after it tops the charts for nine weeks in April–May. The tune is based on a theme from the first movement of Schubert's piano Sonata D664. Doris Day's performance as the girl who just doesn't 'get' femininity strikes a chord with many a lesbian. If gay men were Friends of Dorothy, gay women were now Friends of Doris.
	André Baudry founds Arcadie in Paris.	28 April: In an adjournment debate of the House of Commons, MP Desmond Donnelly demands a Royal Commission into the law relating to, and the medical treatment of, homosexuality. He is seconded by Sir Robert Boothby. The Under Secretary at the Home Office, Sir Hugh Lucas-Tooth, announces a Departmental Committee of Enquiry into homosexuality and prostitution. Clearly it has all been decided in advance, and the debate is a bit of a charade.	22 August: In *Love and Miss Figgis* (BBC *Sunday Night Theatre*) classics mistress Miss Figgis persuades her star pupil to give up thoughts of marrying her electrician boyfriend in order to go to the University of Oxford. The feminist Miss Figgis is described as a 'child of Sappho', and quotes the Greek poet extensively.
	The first publicly available guide to gay bars appears, in America.	17 September: seventeen men are found guilty in another so-called 'vice ring'. Within an hour of being sentenced to one year's imprisonment, one of them commits suicide in the cell, using sodium cyanide. He is a former Lt Colonel and holder of the MC,	October: *Films and Filming* magazine is founded by Philip Dosse, one of a stable including *Dance and Dancing, Plays and Players* etc. These are intended by the publisher to reach out to
	25 March: Lord Montagu (12 months), Peter Wildeblood (18 months) and Michael Pitt-Rivers (18 months) are sentenced to prison for gross indecency.		
	7 June: Mathematician Alan Turing commits suicide with a poisoned apple; he had been offered the choice of two years' imprisonment or chemical castration following a gay sex conviction.		

		and had a wife and child.	a homosexual 'community' which barely exists at the time. It is not long before they run gay personal ads.
		19 October: David Maxwell Fyfe (now Lord Kilmuir) transferred from Home Secretary to Lord Chancellor. He is succeeded by Gwilym Lloyd George.	18 October: The first commercially viable transistor radio, the Regency TR-1, goes into production in the US. The 'trannie' becomes the most popular communication device in history and sells billions of copies over the next 25 years. Many a CHE group on a picnic would have 'trannies' – in both senses of the word.
			12 December: Peter Cushing and André Morell strike a particular chord with homosexuals watching *Nineteen-Eighty-Four* on TV. For them the portrait of a society where you had to watch every look, every word and every gesture is not something set in the future.

1955

CHE, HLRS	Other Gay events (UK and World)	In the News...	The Arts
Peter Wildeblood publishes *Against the Law* and circulates it to the members of the Wolfenden Committee.	Daughters of Bilitis, the first US Lesbian organisation, founded in Los Angeles.	19 January: First commercial Scrabble sets go on sale. Many a games evening organised by local CHE groups features furiously competitive games of Scrabble and Monopoly.	First edition of *Homosexuality* by D. J. West.
The Wolfenden Committee starts taking evidence from, among others, three openly gay men:	Prosecutions and mass arrests of gay men in Denmark following the seizure of publications thought to be 'a com-	1 December: In the	1 June: Premiere of Billy Wilder's *The Seven Year Itch*, with its iconic image of Marilyn Monroe standing over a New York Subway grating with her white dress blowing above her

Wildeblood, Charles Winter, director of the Fitzwilliam Museum in Cambridge, and Patrick Trevor-Roper, the Queen's optician.	mercial speculation with a sensual interest.' The campaigning organisation Det Norske Forbundet av 1948 repudiates its founders, who were involved.	wake of desegregation of interstate buses and trains, Rosa Parkes refuses to give up her seat to a white passenger when ordered to, and is arrested. The subsequent Montgomery Bus Boycott inaugurates the Martin Luther King/ Ralph Abernathy Civil Rights movement. Many young gay people become involved, and their experience of activism here feeds into later gay activist campaigns.	knees.
Antony Grey comes out to his parents, a decision he later deeply regretted for causing a lot of stress to his father who was, unbeknownst to Antony, dying.	André Baudry is prosecuted and fined for publishing in *Arcadie* magazine material thought to be a 'danger to youth'.		29 July: *This is Your Life* premieres on BBC TV, with Eamonn Andrews. The much-parodied show is remarkable for the way it air-brushes the lives of the famous, including homosexual and bisexual guests. It moves to Thames TV in 1969.
			22 September: First franchises set up by the Independent Television Authority start broadcasting. The first advert is for Gibbs SR toothpaste. As a spoiler, the BBC kill off Grace Archer the same night. Over the next 15 years independent television proves more daring in its handling of homosexual themes in both documentary and fictional strands.
			27 October: Release of *Rebel without a Cause*, which confirms James Dean's iconic status after his Oscar-nominated performance in *East of Eden.* Dean dies before the film is released. Though far too old to play a teenager, Dean graphically conveys his disturbance, and his combination of vulnerability and slightly ethereal beauty gives him huge appeal to both sexes. Everything which has

			come to light about his sexuality since has only confirmed his magnetic appeal. And his mystery. Pint-sized co-star Sal Mineo plays Plato, clearly but wordlessly in love with the troubled Jim, and is Oscar-nominated aged 16 for his performance. Mineo bravely comes out as gay in the late 1960s, and directs *Fortune and Men's Eyes* on Broadway. He is robbed and stabbed to death in 1976.

1956

CHE, HLRS	Other Gay events (UK and World)	In the News...	The Arts
29 October: Israel invades Sinai Peninsular with British and French support. PM Anthony Eden is accused of misleading Parliament. Disgust with Eden prompts Allan Horsfall to join the Labour Party and become involved with politics. He is not the only one to do so, and subsequently becomes involved in the fight for gay rights.	Arcadie in Paris organises the first club showing of Genet's film, *Un Chant d'Amour*, taking a considerable legal risk. There is no come-back.	13 March: Parliament passes the Clean Air Act, in response to the Great Smog of 1952, in which an estimated 12,000 people died. Though a great advance in terms of health and environment, it gradually destroyed one cloak under which gay men could surreptitiously contact each other for sex.	Granada TV's *Youth Wants to Know*, a current affairs programme for teenagers, discusses homosexuality.
	20 May: twenty men appear in court in Evesham, aged 17 to 81. The court decides that two men in their 30s were the ring-leaders, driving around and picking up men to have sex in their cars, or inviting them back to parties where the youngsters dressed up in drag. These two get 6 and 4 years respectively. The case against the 81-year-old is dropped, but not before he'd been named in the local	14 April: First demonstration of 2-Quad Videotape, which revolutionises the creation of TV programmes. This gives the BBC the ability to wipe hundreds of hours of historically	James Baldwin publishes *Giovanni's Room,* a complex tangle of hetero, homo and bisexual relationships which also explores themes of alienation which the writer felt suspended between two cultures. This is reflected in the central relationship between the American writer, David, and the eponymous Italian waiter. Though there is a great deal of tenderness between the two, there is exploitation between

	papers.	significant programmes in an act of cultural vandalism unparalleled since the melting down of silent film stock for its silver and camphor content. Indirectly it led to the domestic video, and the thriving home porn industry of the 1970s and 80s.	young and old, the tale ends in murder and execution, and the book never quite gets over the feeling that to be homosexual is to be less than a man.
	26 June: 'They all say that this deadly, winking, sniggering, snuggling, chromium plated, scent-impregnated, luminous, quivering, giggling, fruit-flavoured, mincing, ice-covered heap of mother-love has had the biggest reception and impact on London since Charlie Chaplin.' These words trigger Liberace's libel action against William Connor (Cassandra) which comes to court three years later, and results in damages of £8,000. The case hinges on whether Connor knew that 'fruit' is US slang for homosexual.		

1957

CHE, HLRS	Other Gay events (UK and World)	In the News…	The Arts
TV Mirror makes Jacqueline Mackenzie its cover girl. The photo will return to haunt Jackie Forster.	April: Arcadie launches the CLESPALA Club in Rue Béranger in Paris.	14 January: R. A. Butler becomes new PM Harold MacMillan's Home Secretary.	Granada TV Documentary feature *Homosexuality and the Law* coincides with the publication of the Wolfenden Report.
Antony Grey called to the bar at the Middle Temple.	4 September: Wolfenden Report appears, recommends decriminalisation of gay male sex between consenting adults (21+) in private.	6 July: Elvis Presley makes his third and last appearance on the *Ed Sullivan Show*. Following complaints about the lewdness of his wiggle during his first two appearances, he is filmed only from the waist up.	Tom of Finland, the artist of exaggerated homoerotic masculinity, first published in *Physique Pictorial* in Los Angeles.
		4 December: Lord Longford introduces	15 May: In Emlyn Williams' *Accolade*, an MP is exposed as someone who attends orgies. The bisexual Williams intended this

		a debate in the House of Lords to 'take note' of the Wolfenden Report. No vote.	as a metaphor for homosexuality. Much talk of wrestling with 'strange forces' in his nature.

1958

CHE, HLRS	Other Gay events (UK and World)	In the News...	The Arts
HLRS commissions Peter Wildeblood to write the first campaigning pamphlet, *Homosexuals and the Law.*	13 January: The US Supreme Court rules that *ONE* magazine is not obscene. It is the first time the Supreme Court has ruled on any gay issue.	The world is introduced to Bri-Nylon, named after the company which is to manufacture it, the ICI-owned British Nylon Spinners. The drip-dry shirt has arrived.	*Trouble for Two* is a weekly sitcom written by and starring Jacqueline Mackenzie and others. Two showbiz women live together, and employ an effete cleaner called Humphrey. Twenty years ahead of its time in terms of gender portrayal, the show mixed quick-fire 'bachelor girl' dialogue, kooky clowning (women wrestling!), bursting into song and jokey references *à clef* which would have been libellous, except that to sue would be to out oneself. Nancy Spain made a guest appearance in one episode. Taken off after seven episodes, alas.
3 January: Dr R. D. Reid's letter in the *Spectator* calls for support for families etc. affected by cottaging cases.		1 January: The European Economic Community (EEC) comes into effect following the Treaty of Rome of the previous May. The EEC will be transformed into the EU in 1993 after the Maastricht Treaty.	
10 January: A. E. Dyson's letter in the *Spectator* calls for a campaign group to urge implementation of Wolfenden.			
7 March: Thirty-three people, including former Prime Minister Clement Attlee, three famous novelists and one bishop, sign a letter to *The Times,* calling on the Government to implement Wolfenden		4–7 April: First march demanding unilateral nuclear disarmament goes from London to Aldermaston. It is organised by the Direct Action Committee but supported by the newly formed Campaign for Nuclear Disarmament. The march becomes an annual event in the early 1960s and at its height attracts 200,000 people. Its strategy of attracting large numbers of high-profile support-	John Stephens opens his first boutique in Carnaby Street.
10 April: Allan Horsfall is unexpectedly elected to Nelson Borough Council, which goes 100% Labour. Shortly afterwards he goes to meet Peter Wildeblood for moral support.			Brendan Behan's *Borstal Boy* published: A semi-autobiographical study of an enclosed adolescent male community in wartime, the centre of the book is the love

8 May: Inaugural meeting of the Homosexual Law Reform Society. The Secretary is Rev. A. Hallidie Smith. There is an initial gift of £250, and two gay men donate part of their house in Liverpool Road as an office. The office moves to 32 Shaftesbury Avenue in September.		ers serves as a model for the HLRS Honorary Committee and for CHE's extensive list of Honorary Vice-Presidents. Several prominent CHE activists come from a previous involvement in CND.	relationship between Brendan and Charlie, who is gay. Behan is as explicit as he dares, and clearly has a physical relationship with Charlie, although not gay himself. Also a book about growing up and finding that life isn't as simple as the propaganda might suggest.
29 May: The HLRS sets up the Albany Trust, to 'improve the psychological health of men' by research and data collection. It is so named because the founding meeting is at the flat of J. B. Priestley and Jacquetta Hawkes in the Albany, Piccadilly.		30 April: The Life Peerages Act gets royal assent, meaning women can sit in the House of Lords for the first time. Baroness Wootton is the first to be appointed. She will be a great support for the Earl of Arran piloting his Sexual Offences Bill through Parliament in 1965–66, and in general the influx of Life Peers meant a gradual loosening of the hidebound conservatism of a purely aristocratic peerage.	Iconic girls' comic *Bunty* first appears. Most girls in the 1960s look forward to their weekly 'fix' of the Four Marys and Lorna Drake – except the lesbians who didn't want to be ballet dancers. Reviled in some quarters for its sexist stereotyping and its crude class assumptions, *Bunty* still manages to respond to the times as gradually the young female characters become more self-reliant and have more interesting things to do.
20 July: Horsfall's first campaigning letter to *Reynolds News*.		26 November: Home Secretary R. A. Butler introduces a debate in the House of Commons to 'take note of' the Wolfenden Report. Agreed without a vote.	4 May: Birth of US artist/gay activist Keith Haring. By the 1990s, a Haring print was a fixture in many a gay flat, with its jolly cartoon outlines orchestrated like the Mr Men in an orgy.
29 September – 3 October: Horsfall tries informally at the Labour Party to get MPs to adopt Wolfenden. He is told there is no chance of it becoming party policy.		5 December: STD calls initiated in the UK when the queen speaks from Bristol directly to the Lord Provost in Edinburgh. The STD system cuts out the need for an intervening telephone operator. Long distance calls becomes	16 October: First broadcast of *Blue Peter*, triggering nearly sixty years of gossip and speculation about the presenters' sexu-

		private, and much easier. National CHE campaigners, especially those without their own telephones, benefit greatly.	ality. In 1962 Valerie Singleton, the object of much gossip in the LGBT community, had provided the narrative voiceover for the skinflick *Nudes of the World*.
		10 December: Ian Harvey MP fined £5 for breaking park regulations, when caught having sex with a guardsman. He insists on resigning, despite apparently having no pressure applied to do so. Later he becomes an active Vice-President of CHE.	

1959

CHE, HLRS	Other Gay events (UK and World)	In the News…	The Arts
10 January: The HLRS starts advertising for supporters in the *New Statesman* and *Spectator*.	H. Montgomery Hyde is deselected by his Northern Ireland constituency party because of his advocacy of homosexual law reform, and amid general criticism of his record as a constituency MP.	7 January: The USA cynically ditches its puppet dictator Battista and recognises the new Cuban government led by Fidel Castro. After years as something of a louche holiday paradise for richer homosexual men, Cuba becomes a place of persecution, and Castro's attitudes to homosexuality and treatment of gay men become a sticking point for many who admire him in other respects.	BBC current affairs show *In The News* features an episode on 'The Homosexual Condition'. Talking heads panel includes C. R. Hewitt (founder member and later Chairman of the HLRS under his nom de plume of C. H. Rolph) and 'a former homosexual'.
	7 January: A judge demands that the police investigate the British Friendship Society, a pen pal club in which people with similar tastes are invited to write to each other. 'One doesn't run a club like this without knowing the kind of use it is going to be put to. … A man with perverted tendencies easily gets contact with other men.' A vicar is	21 January: The European Court of Human Rights is established as a result of Article 19 of the European Convention. The Court becomes the	Bisexual Colin McInnes publishes *Absolute Beginners*. A celebration of the new vibrant coffee bar culture, the novel features large numbers of young Afro-Caribbeans, homosexuals, unapologetic rent boys, and drug addicts. The jazzy poetic dialogue casts a

	charged with having obscene photos, including one of himself 'in what appears to be a silk female garment'. He has never met any of his serviceman contacts, there was no sex, and yet he loses his living.	last place of redress after an individual's quest for justice has exhausted all national channels. As such, it gives verdicts in some cases such as Jeff Dudgeon's which significantly extend LGBT rights from the 1980s onwards.	golden glow over some less savoury situations.
	13 January: Thirteen men appear before Mr Justice Elwes in Kendal in Cumbria. Unusually, Elwes rules that the process of arrest and trial and the attendant publicity is punishment enough. He also points out that they are only on trial because they have been honest with the police, and if they hadn't pleaded guilty the police could have done nothing – an incentive for future victims not to co-operate with the police. Elwes also expresses the hope that nobody will be dismissed from their job, or lose their pension rights.	29 July: Obscene Publications Act comes into law. Previously obscenity has been regulated by common law, a case of 1868 which has allowed no defence on public interest grounds. Roy Jenkins's new law allows a defence of public good, and also innocent distribution – 'I didn't know what it was.' It also allows JPs to issue warrants for the police to seize and destroy material. The new act is used in high profile cases of the 1960s – the *Lady Chatterley* trial at the beginning and the *Oz Schoolkids Issue* at the end of the decade.	March: The belated release of *The King and I* in the UK gives homosexuals another 'Secret Love' anthem with the song 'We Kiss In A Shadow': 'Alone with our secret forever we sigh/For one smiling day to be free…' Cliff Richard records the song in 1961. 'Somewhere' from *West Side Story* will fulfil a similar function, though the lyrics aren't so directly pertinent.
	May: The Donut Riots. First recorded incident where homosexuals fight back against the police, at Cooper's Bar in LA. This, like the Stonewall Bar, is a popular hangout of drag queens and hustlers. When the LAPD arrests three people, the other customers	16 September: Xerox unveils its new plain paper copier. Cost and size mean that it will be a long time before it supersedes the duplicator, and gay activists can't say goodbye to inky fingers and seething frustration until the 1980s.	14 May: Billy Wilder's *Some Like It Hot*. Tony Curtis and Jack Lemon don drag to escape gangsters. Much anthologised last lines: Jerry: 'We can't get married at all.' – Osgood: 'Why not?' – Jerry: [normal voice] 'I'm a man!' – Osgood: [shrugs] 'Well, nobody's perfect!'
		8 October: General	24 November: *South*, an ITV Armchair Theatre, shows Peter Wyngarde as an exiled Polish officer in the Deep South, disintegrating as he realises the depth of his feeling for a young man. Very discreet, highly melodramatic, but blessed with a bravura leading performance, and brave for its day.

	start pelting them with doughnuts and coffee cups. While the police are calling up reinforcements and arresting more people, the original three escape. One is the author John Rechy.	Election – Conservatives under Harold MacMillan increase majority to 100.	Peter Marshall thunders in the *Daily Sketch*, 'There are some indecencies in life that are best left covered up.'
	19 August: George Butler hangs himself while awaiting trial for gross indecency. He has been refused bail and as a result been in prison for two months. He is 17.	17 November: First duty-free shops open at British airports. Getting your duty frees became an inescapable routine for the newly affluent Brits taking foreign holidays from the 1960s onwards.	30 November: The TV series *Probation Officer* features the first clear TV representation of a gay male couple.
	23 October: nine men come up before the judge in Sale, Cheshire. One of them, a night watchman, is Albert Goldstraw. In 1936 he was involved in the previous Sale witch hunt and got seven years' imprisonment, with two years' hard labour. This time he gets five years. Progress?		

1960

CHE, HLRS	Other Gay events (UK and World)	In the News…	The Arts
31 March: Hallidie Smith resigns as HLRS general secretary. Replaced by Mr and Mrs Newell.	19 July: National Assembly of France passes the Mirguet Amendment, which pronounces homosexuality, along with prostitution and alcoholism, 'a social scourge'.	29 June: MPs defeat Kenneth Robinson's proposal that the government should implement Wolfenden at the earliest opportunity. Vote 213–99 against.	Oscar Wilde year. Peter Finch in *The Trials of Oscar Wilde* slugs it out at the box office with Robert Morley in *Oscar Wilde*. Better than either was Micheál Mac Liammóir as Wilde in the *On Trial* BBC TV series (5 August). Unlike the movies, the aptly named Peter
May: C. H. Rolph prepares draft Sexual Offences Bill for any MP willing to sponsor it. Dusty responses from Lords who are shown it – whether for general, technical	November: Responding to the Mirguet Amendment, the	31 December: Conscription of 18-year-olds into the Armed Services (National Service) officially	

or other practical reasons is unclear.	French government doubles the penalties for public decency offences involving homosexuals (Article 330.2).	ends; last serving men discharged 13 May 1963.	Lambda's script allows Wilde his male prostitutes, who are rather jolly.
12 May: The HLRS organises its first and only large-scale public meeting at Caxton Hall in Westminster, and over 1,000 people attend. A motion to urge implementation of the Wolfenden Report is allegedly passed by 1000 votes to 3.			4 March: Hammer Films' *Never Take Sweets From a Stranger* breaks taboos in British films in its treatment of hetero-sexual child sexual abuse, with the usually cuddly Felix Aylmer as the (un-speaking) abuser. It bombs at the box office, because of the discomfort of audi-ences with the subject and the uneasy mix of courtroom and horror genres. It has never been shown on British TV.
July: Allan Horsfall asks for permission to start a Manchester branch of the HLRS. Co-Secretary Venetia Newell refuses permission: 'We always seem to get … crackpots and shifty types.'			22 March: Joan Henry's *Look on Tempests* opens at the Comedy Theatre. It examines the effects on his family when a man is accused of gross indecency. It is the first play to treat homosexuality on the West End stage after the Lord Chamberlain lifted his ban on the subject the year before. Gladys Cooper stars. Joan Henry is married to the film director J. Lee Thompson, who is best remembered for *Cape Fear* and *The Guns of Navarone*.

1961

CHE, HLRS	Other Gay events (UK and World)	In the News...	The Arts
14 January: First issue of Albany Trust's *Man and Society*. Exclusively about homosexuals, but with the promise of other subjects in future issues.	7 November: José Sarria becomes the first openly gay person in the world to run for public office on a platform of gay rights. He gets 6,000 votes, enough to plant the idea that there is a 'gay vote' to be wooed.	28 May: Peter Benensen's article 'The Forgotten Prisoners' appears in *The Observer*, leading to the formation of Amnesty International six weeks later. The article is about two students being sentenced to seven years for raising a glass to freedom in Dr Salazar's Portugal. CHE and other LGBT campaigners will spend many years trying to get Amnesty International to accept homosexuals as prisoners of conscience, which it finally does in September 1991.	11 May: Harold Pinter's *The Collection* on Rediffusion. A gay couple's relationship is threatened when one of them may (or may not) have had sex with a woman. Her husband is drawn into seduction/power games too. Rarely has sexual tension been so creepy.
March: The HLRS gets in touch with J. Arthur Rank to get permission to screen an advert about the Society's work before showings of *Boy Barrett* (the first title of the film *Victim*). Turned down, but the Society gets permission to leaflet in cinemas showing the film.		15 June: Start of the erection of the Anti-Fascist Protection Barrier, or the Berlin Wall as it was popularly known. From now on gay rights in East Germany would advance faster than in the West.	31 August: *Victim* released. The film stars Dirk Bogarde as a bisexual barrister who is blackmailed by a former (male) lover. It will initially be banned in the US.
June: After over a year of effort, Allan Horsfall finally gets his local Labour Party to debate whether to adopt Wolfenden as official party policy. Motion defeated 13–6.		16 June: dancer Rudolph Nureyev defects to the West while performing in Paris.	14 September: A gala Leicester Square opening for *A Taste of Honey*: 17-year-old Jo meets black sailor Jimmy and gets pregnant by him. She befriends a gay textile designer. Jeff, whom she invites to move in with her, and they resolve to look after the baby together, maybe even get married: 'You need someone to love you while you're looking for someone to love.' The dream is shattered when Jo's mother moves in with them. Blessed with a blistering performance from Dora Bryan as the mother, and one of great
5 July: The Danish magazine *Eos* and other foreign publications ask the Albany Trust for permission to reproduce articles from *Man and Society*. The committee agrees that it could only do the Society harm to be associated with these organisations, and withholds its		4 December: Women's control over their own fertility takes a step forward with the availability of birth	

permission.		control pills on the NHS, thanks to health minister Enoch Powell. This new freedom from consequence for women contributed significantly to the relaxation of moral codes encapsulated in the word 'swinging'.	sensitivity and integrity by Murray Melvin as Jeff, *A Taste of Honey* was the first film to posit that what every straight girl needs more than anything is a gay best friend.
			19 December: *The Children's Hour* was William Wyler's second crack at a movie version of Lilian Hellman's play of a subconsciously lesbian idyll destroyed by a vengeful and malicious pupil. Despite a more open climate, Wyler fought shy of allowing the teacher couple to show their affection. And the queer still dies.

1962

CHE, HLRS	Other Gay events (UK and World)	In the News…	The Arts
March: second HLRS delegation to see Home Secretary Butler, who tells them nothing can be done until after a general election. (The first delegation was in May 1959, shortly after the society's formation.)	1962: Czechoslovakia and Hungary decriminalise homosexuality.	1 January: Illinois becomes the first US state to repeal its sodomy laws.	Journalist Michael Davidson publishes his frank memoir, sex and all, *The World, the Flesh and Myself*. 'This is the life story of a lover of boys.'
22 October: The HLRS agrees to appoint Edgar Wright as new Secretary, but he also insists that he should do it under his pen name of Antony Grey, for fear of embarrassing	9 March: Leo Abse is refused permission to introduce his private members bill, the first Sexual Offences Bill to try to incorporate Wolfenden's recommendations.	14 October: John Vassall is sentenced to 18 years imprisonment after he'd been named as a Soviet spy by two defectors the year previously. He was set up at a party organised by the KGB, who got him very drunk and then photographed him in compromising positions with various men. He was only a junior clerk but still	The first complete authentic text of *De Profundis*, Oscar Wilde's long love-hate letter to Bosie, is finally published. Wilde's executor, Robbie Ross, donated the manuscript to the British Museum library in 1905, on condition that no-one should see it until

his family. This is a six-month trial appointment for 1.5 days a week, at a salary of £500 p.a.		provided information which helped the USSR to modernise its fleet. The KGB may have sacrificed him to protect a more senior spy. The case is soon forgotten in the bigger scandal of Profumo and Christine Keeler, but the connection between homosexuality and treachery is revived for the first time since 1951. Reformers criticising the watering down of Wolfenden in Parliament pointed out that Vassall would have still been 'illegal' after the passage of the 1967 Act.	1960, thus preventing Lord Alfred Douglas from seeing it.
			6 June: In Otto Preminger's *Advise and Consent*, a Senator (Don Murray) is blackmailed over his homosexuality by Charles Laughton in order to secure a nomination for Secretary of State. Threatened with exposure, he commits suicide. The theme resurfaces in Gore Vidal's *The Best Man* two years later, when a presidential candidate is similarly 'compromised'. No suicide this time.
		14–28 October: The day that Vassall is sentenced, the Cuban missile crisis begins when an American U-2 spy plane takes photos of Russian missiles on Cuban soil. There is a ten-day stand-off, during which time most of the world goes about its business believing that the world will end at any moment. The crisis is resolved by a deal between Khrushchev and Kennedy that the Russians will get their missiles out of Cuba if the Americans get their missiles out of Turkey. These two withdrawals are staggered so that it doesn't look like Americans have 'given in to blackmail', and the US denies any deal.	11 September: TV version of Graham Greene's *Stamboul Train*, scripted by John Hopkins, has a boozy muckraking lesbian journalist as its central character, hot on the heels of an East European spy ring. Her girlfriend, Janet, eventually gives up on her obsessive if drunken devotion, and marries a businessman.
			20 November: *The L-Shaped Room* shows an unmarried pregnant Frenchwoman moving into an anonymous boarding house in order to have the baby or to abort it. The house becomes a surrogate family, and among the members is Mavis, an old Variety

			trouper who laments the loss of her female friend, and Johnny, who has to listen to the man he loves having sex with the heroine in the room next door – the first black gay character in British cinema. Individually depressing but collectively uplifting about the possibility of renewal and acceptance in these squalid surroundings.
			10 December: Gay men viewing *Lawrence of Arabia* permit themselves a certain *frisson* at the scene between the Bey (José Ferrer) and Lawrence (Peter O'Toole); the portrayal of Lawrence's sado-masochism is subtle enough for the film to slip into the 'A' certification (PG now) while being entirely credible. And O'Toole *is* beautiful.

1963

CHE, HLRS	Other Gay events (UK and World)	In the News...	The Arts
26 June: A witch hunt in Bolton sees ten men in the dock for gross indecency, five of whom work at the local hospital. Allan Horsfall's anguished and angry letter triggers a correspondence which puts him in touch with many who will become part of NWHLRC next year.	13 January: *The Observer* runs a prominent feature about COC clubs for homosexuals in Amsterdam.	BBC Pronunciation Department sends round a memo about how to pronounce 'homosexual'. A short 'o' please, as in the Greek for 'same', not a long 'o' as in the Latin for 'man'.	*City of Night* is published – John Rechy's erotic novel of cruising in San Francisco.
	22 January: The jury stops the trial of Lawrence Summers, a 16-year-old cellarman, up for the manslaughter of the Labour MP	5 June: Secretary of State for War John Profumo resigns amid increasing rumours of	*Meeting Point*, the BBC's Sunday God slot, devotes its whole 30 minutes to *Towards a Quaker view of sex*. The programme echoes the book in using the word

26 October: The HLRS Committee accepts Antony Grey's idea for regional committees, and gives him permission to discuss it with a group of supporters in Manchester.	and former Party Chairman George Brinham. They decide, after the judge has directed them that a homosexual advance 'is about as clear a case of provocation as it is possible to have', that there is no case to answer. Summers gets a hero's welcome when he returns to his native Matlock, and sells his story for a lot of money to the *News of the World.* The Labour Party keeps quiet.	a security scandal involving his sharing of Christine Keeler's favours with Russian intelligence officer Yevgeny Ivanov.	'affection' a lot. There are numerous complaints.
October: The HLRS starts to publish *Spectrum,* a bi-monthly magazine with in-depth articles on aspects of homosexuality and counselling, with news of parliamentary campaigns and quotes from the press. The first issue has an article by journalist James Cameron on security risks: 'With sane and humane legislation, queers would be no more vulnerable than teetotallers.' The magazine runs to 30 issues, and folds for lack of cash in 1970.	11 October: Death of hugely influential artist, poet and film-maker Jean Cocteau.	28 August: James Baldwin is excluded from the Civil Rights March on Washington on the grounds that he would be too inflammatory. His well-known homosexuality is seen as a provocation.	18 March: The *Sunday Mirror* TV Critic complains about young Tim going to see his doctor (Dr Bennett on *24-Hour Call*) because he is worried about being homosexual. 'If this gets around doctors will be pestered to help with anything from a leaking tap to parking the car.'

1964

CHE, HLRS	Other Gay events (UK and World)	In the News...	The Arts
January: The Albany Trust starts its occasional series of Winter Talks. CHE Vice-President Angus Wilson gives one that autumn on 'Literature and Sexual Freedom.'	The lesbian and gay picket arrives with two actions in New York: against a psychiatrist who insists homosexuality is a mental illness, and against the local draft board over the confidentiality of gay conscripts' records.	January: Mary Whitehouse launches the 'Clean Up TV' campaign, which morphs in 1965 into the National Viewers' and Listeners' Association, and is currently called MediaWatch-UK.	Jane Rule's popular lesbian romance *Desert of the Heart* is published.
2 March: Allan Horsfall gives a talk to a church group in Ashton-under-Lyme. Parishioners guard the doors to keep the youth club and boy	The BBC proves cowardly: *Panorama* scraps an item on gay	20 April: BBC-2 starts broadcasting. This allows for greater representation of homosexual characters	Publication of Christopher Isherwood's *A Single Man.* This simple, eloquent account of a day in the life of a middle-aged professor getting over the loss of his long-term partner set new standards of realism and emotional depth

scouts out. The vicar is so apologetic he joins the NWHLRC six months later.	clubs in Amsterdam, featuring interviews with cheerful, well-adjusted homosexuals.	and themes in drama and documentary, and also has a knock-on effect on the output of BBC-1.	in its treatment of gay male characters. A very Buddhist novel too.
4 June: Allan Horsfall goes to a Manchester discussion group set up by Stanley Rowe and others; minutes record it as the first meeting of the Manchester branch of the HLRS. 2 September: Albany Trust is turned down for a lease because the landlords don't want them dealing with clients on the premises. The pressure on the tiny Shaftesbury Avenue office remains. 7 October: First formal meeting of the NWHLRC at Church House, Deansgate, Manchester. December: NWHLRC publishes its first leaflet *Something You Should Know About.* 10,000 copies initially, plus reprints. The contact address is given as 3 Robert Street, Atherton – Horsfall's home address. There is no adverse reaction.	April: *Arena 3* is started by Esmé Langley and Diana Chapman. First a social group, then additionally a magazine and support service. At first, married women have to produce signed permission from their husbands to subscribe. July: Two Tory backbenchers report to their Chief Whip that Lord Boothby and Labour MP Tom Driberg have been seen importuning young men at a dog track. Driberg's rampant passion for giving blow jobs was somehow never made public, thanks to his unscrupulous leverage using his position as a journalist and keeper of some dark Labour Party secrets (e.g. he allegedly serviced Aneurin Bevan in Bevan's office at Westminster). 22 October: Bryan Magee TV documentary on male homosexuals for *This Week*, following programmes about abortion, suicide and drug addiction. Among the shocking highlights are shots of men kissing and dancing	12 May: Twelve young men burn their draft cards in New York. It is the first such public protest in an anti-war movement which will snowball over the next eight years. 15 October: General election. Labour majority of 4 under Harold Wilson. Sir Frank Soskice appointed Home Secretary. 9 November: Parliament votes to suspend the death penalty for all offences except treason, spying, piracy and arson in a royal dockyard. This is regarded as ushering in a period of social liberalism. The suspension is regularly renewed until the death penalty is finally abolished completely in 1998.	8 March: *The Leather Boys* is a classic study of unrequited love between gay/straight best mates, set in the contemporary biking world. Straight boy Reggie loses interest in sex with Dot (Rita Tushingham) when biker Pete comes into his life. When Pete takes him to a gay bar, he realises what's going on, and rejects his friend. Reggie is last seen walking away from the camera with the word 'Dodgy' on the back of his leather jacket. Maybe there is still hope…? 6 May: Joe Orton's *Entertaining Mr Sloane* premieres at the New Arts Theatre. It is put on thanks to the sponsorship of Terence Rattigan, who invests £3,000 in West End transfer. The cheerful comedy of bisexual competition for sexual favours is broadcast on ITV on 15 July 1968, and filmed two years later. 3 June: An episode of *Z Cars* is introduced in the *Radio Times* as follows: 'A man attempts to blackmail Frank Wood. Wood has only to go to the police… Given

	together in Amsterdam, and a happy gay couple – two shop assistants who (disgusting!) met each other in church. Six members of the HLRS appear. Magee records over 200 interviews, and reworks the material into the book *One in Twenty* (1966). This is translated into eight languages and sells prodigiously over the next ten years.		normal circumstances, Wood's course of action is plain, but Wood is a homosexual, a man outside the law and unable to go to the police without incriminating himself.' *Somebody …. Help* is scripted by John Hopkins. 23 November: *House of Glass* is set in an army detention centre. Noel Currer-Briggs, whose brother directed it, thought it worth writing to Antony Grey to alert Albany Trust supporters to the interest of this ATV production. Features a pre-Compo Bill Owen, and Leonard Rossiter.

1965

CHE, HLRS	Other Gay events (UK and World)	In the News...	The Arts
March: Albany Trust discussion groups start as a means of involving the mainly gay supporters who volunteer in the office. The syllabus is controlled by Antony Grey, but they turn into social groups. Organised by George Mortimer. 7 July: Billy Ray (28) sentenced to two years and John Clarkson (19) to six months Borstal for gross indecency. The trial shocks Ray Gosling into accepting the	March: Bryan Magee TV documentary on female homosexuals for *This Week* features parents delighted their daughters have found happiness, and a couple of open school teachers. Nobody is filmed in shadow, unlike in the male equivalent. The *Daily Express* runs a panicky campaign: 'You still have time to stop this filth entering your room.' Or you could just switch off … 17 April: Franklin Kameny and the	8 March: 4,000 US troops are sent to Vietnam, the first combat troops to be drawn into the war. 18 May: The Government announces the introduction of the first blood alcohol limit for drivers, triggering an outcry about infringement of civil liberties. 6 August: At the last moment the BBC pulls the broadcast of Peter Watkins' *The War Game*, a savagely satirical view of the official British reac-	*The Killing of Sister George* opens at the Bristol Old Vic, with Beryl Reid as George and Eileen Atkins as Childie. The author, married to a lesbian, intends it as a farce, but it becomes an 'issue' play because there is so little lesbian material around. Beryl Reid wins a Tony for her portrayal of George on Broadway in 1966. The film version runs into censorship arguments over the seduction scene (not in the play) and only

need for law reform – he joins NWHLRC.	Mattachine Society of Washington stage the first of the annual pickets of the White House in aid of civil rights for homosexuals. The day after, they picket the United Nations.	tion in the event of nuclear attack. The film goes on to win a Best Documentary Oscar in 1966.	achieves a limited release in cinemas. Even today the sex scene is usually left out when the film is shown on TV.
	28 October: House of Lords passes the Earl of Arran's Sexual Offences Bill by 116 to 46.	28 September: Fidel Castro says that any Cuban who wants to emigrate to the US is free to do so. The subsequent exodus leads to the creation of a vibrant but reactionary Latino gay community in Florida.	January: The BBC's first successful TV soap, *Compact*, acquires its first effeminate character, Eliot, played by Maurice Browning, (who also made a camp villain in *The Avengers*). Completely bald, pouting, temperamental, his favourite novel is *Little Women* and he carries a small velvet cushion. He pours a healthy dose of vinegar over the heterosexual preoccupations of a thinly-disguised *Women's Own*. The BBC scraps *Compact* before Eliot can embed himself.
		6 December: Passing of the first UK Race Relations Act. This is revealed to be woefully inadequate over the next few years, and is strengthened by two further acts in 1968 and 1976. However, it recognises the problem, and the role of legislation in tackling it.	18/25 January: Two-part story in the series *Hit and Run*. Lying, self-denying queer breaks down in the dock and admits he killed a pedestrian and pins blame on the friend who rejected his advances, as an act of revenge.
		23 December: Roy Jenkins replaces Sir Frank Soskice as Home Secretary.	10 March: BBC Wednesday Play *Horror of Darkness*, starring Glenda Jackson, Nicol Williamson and Alfred Lynch. Edgy Pinteresque dialogue when Lynch's

			old college chum Nicolson turns up to reclaim his love. Cop-out ending with death of the queer. Lynch plays many gay characters in the 1960s, and, in addition to his life partner Jimmy Culliford, has flings with Nureyev and US gay playwright Doric Wilson.
			25 March: 'Hello, I'm Julian, and this is my friend Sandy.' As Hugh Paddick intones those immortal words, Julian and Sandy mince into the national consciousness on *Round the Horne*, where they hold court for four years. They give comfort to many a young queen over his Sunday lunch, while his parents have no idea what they are talking about.
			25 March: *Conscience on a Rack*, an episode of *The Human Jungle*, stories from 'a psychiatrist's casebook'. Teacher Flora Robson is discovered to be sending blackmail notes to herself out of guilt and fear that she may have 'corrupted' a younger girl.

1966

CHE, HLRS	Other Gay events (UK and World)	In the News...	The Arts
18 July: Ivan Geffen chairs a meeting of supporters in Birmingham, but a proposed West Midlands group doesn't take off.	Beaumont Society is founded to provide support for cross-dressers, transvestites and transsexuals.	The first widely available credit card, Barclaycard, is launched. The other banks launch Access cards in 1972. In 2014 debt owed on UK credit cards is £57 billion; there are 90 million debit and 58 million credit cards in circulation.	Maureen Duffy publishes *The Microcosm*, a gynocentric novel with lashings of lesbianism and a sharp portrait of The Gateways.
End of August: Allan Horsfall has to leave a conference early because of an anxiety attack. 'The truth is that I haven't had a holiday for four years, and it is beginning to show.'		11 February: Humphry Berkeley's Sexual Offences Bill receives its second reading in the House of Commons. Bill lost when General Election called.	29 January: In *Honeymoon Postponed,* an episode of *Armchair Theatre*, two honeymooners have to move in with their parents. Dad is in permanent mourning for the death of his 'best mate'. Son can't consummate the marriage, leading to the suggestion he may be homosexual. The family greet the possibility with remarkable understanding. But he isn't. Transferred to film as *The Family Way* (1966).
11 November: 150 people attend a public meeting organised by NWHLRC at the Houldsworth Hall in Manchester. Speakers are Alan Fitch MP, the Dean of Manchester, Allan Horsfall and Antony Grey. Humphry Berkeley is grounded at London Airport and pulls out at the last moment. Hardly any press coverage apart from a small paragraph in *The Guardian.*		31 March: General Election. Labour is returned with increased majority of 96. Previously their majority had been whittled down to one. Humphry Berkeley loses his seat.	25 March: Dusty Springfield's most commercially successful single, *You don't have to say you love me*, is released by Phillips. Originally an Italian hit for Pino Donaggio *(Io che non vivo),* its tremulous emotional masochism ows a certain debt to Jacques Brel's *Ne Me Quitte Pas*, and Springfield so identified with it, it took her 47 takes to get the recording right.
		16 June: The Earl of Arran's reintroduced Sexual Offences Bill passes in the House of Lords by 78 to 60 votes, less than two months after being tabled.	
		7 July: Leo Abse given leave to introduce his Sexual Offences Bill in the House of Commons, by 244 to 100 votes.	
		November: An all-	

		male jury finds Hubert Selby's *Last Exit to Brooklyn* obscene after the judge excuses women from service on the grounds that they 'might be embarrassed to read a book which deals with homosexuality, prostitution, drug taking and sexual perversion.' Originally, Wimbledon MP and Leo Abse opponent, Sir Cyril Black, had brought a private prosecution at Marlborough Magistrates Court, which found the publishers guilty despite an array of defence witnesses including Professor Frank Kermode, who compared the novel to Dickens. The defiant publishers publicly state they will continue to publish it everywhere outside the court's jurisdiction (Soho), thus provoking the Old Bailey trial. An appeal led by John Mortimer in 1968 gets the original verdict reversed.	14 April: Noel Coward's only explicitly homosexual-themed play, *A Song at Twilight*, opened at the Queen's Theatre. A writer is castigated for his dishonesty in not coming out. 11 May: *The Connoisseur,* a rare excursion for BBC1, is set in a public school where a cynical housemaster ('a connoisseur of antiques … and boys') turns a blind eye to dark doings in the dorm, possibly including rape and prostitution, in order to stay in with his best cricketers, including pretty Ian Ogilvy. An allegory of political corruption and a prototype of *If…*

1967

CHE, HLRS	Other Gay events (UK and World)	In the News...	The Arts
NWHLRC publishes new leaflet, *After the Act*, mainly drafted by Martin Stafford. Initial print run of 10,000.	April 27: Valerie Solanas self-publishes the Society for Cutting Up Men (SCUM) Manifesto, price $1 for women, $2 for men. The Society never existed; Solanas was a Dadaist guerrilla.	Norman Pittenger's *A Time for Consent: A Christian's Approach to Homosexuality* goes beyond any previous Christian writing to argue for acceptance of gay relationships according to exactly the same moral standards and criteria as heterosexual relations. Pittenger's extreme fluency as a writer and his insistence on the importance of human love led to his nickname, 'the Barbara Cartland of theology'.	David Hockney paints *A Bigger Splash*, one of a series of Californian paintings reflecting a new, calmer sybaritic lifestyle.
15 June: NWHLRC committee calls for a network of clubs for homosexuals similar to those in the Netherlands. 'Not more social workers, but more social facilities.' Martin Stafford is at his first meeting here.	27 July: Sexual Offences Act passed, partially decriminalising male homosexual acts, over a year after being introduced.	18 January: Jeremy Thorpe becomes leader of the Liberal Party.	In *Mrs Dale's Diary* (trendily renamed *The Dales*), the doyenne of radio soaps, Mrs Dale (Jessie Matthews) discovers her brother-in-law is homosexual. It makes a change from worrying about Jim. The first sympathetic portrayal of a homosexual as a leading character in a soap, but an odd choice of character to 'out', given his long history of uncomplicated heterosexuality in the programme.
3 August: NWHLRC meeting passes a resolution condemning the use of aversion therapy as a cure for homosexuality, although supporting the right of people to choose it if they so wish.	27 November: Craig Rodwell opens the Oscar Wilde Memorial Bookshop in New York.	27 June: The first ATM (cash machine) is introduced at Barclays Bank in Enfield.	15 February: First TV appearance of proto-Python Graham Chapman, on *At Last the 1948 Show*. Chapman is almost the only 'theatrical' to come out in the early 1970s, and features with his lover David Sherlock on the cover of an early *Gay News*. Chapman is one of the major funders of the magazine.
September/October: Reg Kilduff offers to hand over the Rockingham Club in Manchester to the NWHLRC for its first gay social club.		30 September: Roy Jenkins is replaced as Home Secretary by James Callaghan. Jenkins has been in office for less than two years, but has overseen the passage of both the Sexual Offences Act and the Abortion Act. Callaghan is never known for his commitment to civil liberties or gay rights.	5/14 June: *Man Alive* runs two gay programmes, one on men and one on women,
11 October: Prof. A. J. Ayer resigns as President of the HLRS. Replaced by Rev. John Robinson, Bishop of Woolwich. Financial crisis means severe cutback in staff.			
23 October: The			

NWHLRC starts advertising in local papers around Manchester			to coincide with the passing of the Sexual Offences Act. The male programme shows mostly scared lonely men with backs to camera, but 'a married woman with two children, and… what seemed a very happy, very settled couple of women'. The lesbian programme features shots of the Gateways Club.
			6 September: A week after the SOA comes into force, a hotel manager wants to throw out a middle-aged man (George Cole) and his young USAF lover. C. P. Taylor's *Friends* twists the knife of class consciousness and convention; the manager retreats when he discovers they are both officers. And fathers.

1968

CHE, HLRS	Other Gay events (UK and World)	In the News…	The Arts
February: Esquire Clubs set up as a private limited liability club in which all profits must go back into the club. Reg Kilduff, director of the Rockingham, Ray Gosling, Colin Harvey, Allan Horsfall and Harold Pollard are directors.	Troy Perry founds the Metropolitan Community Church in Los Angeles.	The Post Office introduces a split tier system of First Class and Second Class stamps.	Art model Quentin Crisp publishes his memoirs, *The Naked Civil Servant.* It sells only 3,500 copies until the TV version is broadcast in 1975.
6 May: The NWHLRC sends in valuers to the Rockingham. Independent valuation agreed. Two weeks later Kilduff announces he wants £7,000, and doesn't accept the independent valuation. Committee says this is exorbitant, and relations break down.	8 January: John Holland is interviewed in the *Wolverhampton Express and Star* about his plans for MANDFHAB (Male and Female Homosexual Association of Britain), including an advice line and raising money for a gay centre. He is overwhelmed by the response, and has a breakdown, causing the project to fold by the end of the year.	January: five secretaries in Surbiton offer to work an extra half hour a day for no pay, triggering the 'I'm Backing Britain', campaign, later rolled into Robert Maxwell's 'Buy British' campaign. This rather loses credibility when it emerges that the campaign T-shirts were made in Portugal.	Allan Ginsberg, always a challenging poet where his homosexuality is at issue, publishes *Please, Master*, a delirious sado-masochistic love poem to Neal Cassady. Still one of the most sexually explicit poems ever written. In 1982 he bemuses punters in 'Heaven' nightclub by reading it, anonymously, for an Amateur Talent Night. He comes second.
14 May: The HLRS rejects the idea of supporting clubs for homosexuals, and insists that Antony Grey resign as an Honorary Vice President of Esquire clubs. He was recruited, along with senior Samaritans and the NCCL secretary Tony Smythe, back in January.	9 March: Peter Spencer falls out with John Holland over the issue of admitting under-21s, and starts MAF-MAN in Nottingham, which keeps to over-21s and turns down bisexuals. This morphs into Nottingham CHE.	1 January: The Motion Pictures Association of America formally abandons the Hays Production Code and replaces it with a four-category rating system similar to Britain's. The code has been increasingly ignored by independent producers (as opposed to studios) in the 1950s and 60s, and the absence of an MPAA certificate, which has no legal value, does nothing to harm the box office of movies like *Some Like it Hot.*	17 June: US Release of *The Queen*, a ciné vérité documentary about a drag beauty contest in New York. Grade A bitching and much conversation about sexual identity and avoiding the draft. Criticised for its stereotyping and praised for its honesty in equal measure. A must for a CHE group cinema trip in the early 1970s.
28 June: Future General Secretary Paul Temperton attends his first NWHLRC meeting. He meets Martin Stafford. They start a	12 March: Homosexuals Anonymous starts meeting in Coventry Council for Social Service, having been driven from the Cathedral by lurid publicity in the local press about 'The first gay club in England'. It lasts about a year, as the more extrovert homosexuals take	22 March: Danny	28 August: BBC Wednesday Play features Simon Gray's

relationship and become responsible for the development of local CHE groups (in 1970) and for office management.	over and drive out the shy.	Cohn-Bendit leads students to occupy the administrative buildings at the University of Nanterre, triggering *les événements* leading up to the May student uprising in Paris. On 13 May a million people take to the Paris streets. Cohn-Bendit is also involved in radical sexual politics, which has since led to others accusing him of support for paedophilia.	*Spoiled.* Maths tutor has a 'moment of weakness' with a boy he's cramming in both senses of the word. Very indirect – 'It was the kind of thing we talked about once.' Mary Whitehouse approved because it did not 'normalise or justify deviation… but showed it for the tragedy it is.'
July: Albany Trust Wychcroft conference leads to the 'SK' social events at St Katherine's, Limehouse.	24 March: Sensational article in *The People* about the gay goings-on at the Hope and Anchor, Leeds.	26 July: Theatres Act abolishes the role of the Lord Chamberlain as theatre censor.	September: Bryan Forbes' *Deadfall* released, with Michael Caine. A hysterical farrago of bisexuality. Eric Portman plays an older gay man who betrays his lover to the Nazis then screws the man's wife. He incestuously marries the resulting daughter rather than explain …
September: Publicity for Esquire Clubs on Radio 4, following Gosling article in *New Society.* Earl of Arran condemns them in his column in the *Evening Standard.* Antony Grey, in a letter of reply to Ray Gosling, says the time is not ripe for clubs for homosexuals.	April: A series of police visits to the Flamingo Club in Wolverhampton result in pensioner George Smith being prosecuted for running a disorderly house. The court (and the press) is shocked at the idea of men dancing together. Smith's customers rally round him with remarkable solidarity.	5 October: Police baton-charge civil rights demonstrators in Derry, triggering the last and most bitter phase of 'the troubles'.	6 September: Pasolini's *Teorema* released: gorgeous angel Terence Stamp appears to a bourgeois family and shags each member in turn, plus the maid. Each character makes confession, and is transformed by the sex. A Catholic/Marxist/Jungian vision which so confused the Church that it gave Pasolini a special award at the Venice Film Festival, then withdrew it.
	1 July: East Germany adopts Paragraph 151 to replace Paragraph 175. It provides for sentences of up to three years for over-18s having lesbian or gay sex with under-18s. Bulgaria also legalises homosexuality this year.	7 December: Douglas Englebert demonstrates the first electronic mouse and the first hypertext system; six months previously Intel had gone into the business of manufacturing semiconductors.	27 September: *Hair* opens in London at the Shaftesbury Theatre, having waited for the
	August: First edition of *Jeremy*, a lifestyle and fashion magazine for gay men.		

			Theatres Act 1968 to abolish stage censorship. It will run for five years, until forced to close when the roof of the theatre collapses. Its tasteful nudity and cheerful praise of 'Sodomy' in the eponymous song make it notorious.
			19 December: Premiere of Lindsay Anderson's liberating, visionary *If…* Bobby Phillips of the incomparable forelock watches bewitched as prefect Wallace works out in the gym. A few scenes later they are seen asleep in each other's arms, having in the meantime presumably developed a passionate relationship. The homosexuals are on the side of the revolutionaries, as pretty Bobby mows down teachers and dignitaries with a submachine gun.

1969

CHE, HLRS	Other Gay events (UK and World)	In the News…	The Arts
1 April: NWHLRC is officially renamed the Committee for Homosexual Equality (CHE).	International activists' gathering in Denmark organised by IHWO.	2 January: Australian media mogul Rupert Murdoch buys Britain's biggest-selling newspaper, the *News of the World*.	John Schlesinger's *Midnight Cowboy* is widely seen as a portrait of a repressed gay relationship between the cowboy Joe (Jon Voigt) and Ratso (Dustin Hoffman), despite the stream of anti-gay abuse from both characters' mouths. Voigt's pretty boy looks and dazzling performance help to make this an iconic film, a cult among gay men of the time, and the only X-rated film to win an Oscar to date.
	West Germany decriminalises homosexuality; Dutch parliament votes to lower the homosexual age of consent to 16, while retaining penalties against gay sex between those over 21 and those under 21.	24 January: The LSE closes in response to large student demonstrations. Two days later LSE students occupy University of London Union to protest at the closure. Unrest spreads to other campuses, most notably Hornsey College of Art, which operates a democratic student-chosen and run syllabus for a couple of months. This is known as the Hornsey Project and becomes a model for libertarian educationalists.	In *The Gay Deceivers* two young men set up home together in order to avoid the military draft. The first film to be officially turned down by the BBC on the grounds that it was offensive to gay people.
	January: The Elmwood Association starts in Belfast following a visit by Antony Grey – the first gay organisation in Northern Ireland.	14 May: Canada introduces an equal age of consent at 14, eighteen months after the legislation was enacted. PM Pierre Trudeau tells the press, 'There's no place for the state in the bedrooms of the nation.' The age of consent is raised to 16 in 2008. The age of consent for anal sex remains higher, at 18.	August/September: *Staircase* is not the camp comedy it is marketed as, but a study of emotional dependency, a kind of queer *Steptoe and Son*; the couple in question Harry (Richard Burton) and Charles (Rex Harrison) are barbers and long-time lovers. Their relationship is threatened by Charles's impending
	28–30 June: Stonewall riots in New York.	25 June: West Germany modifies Paragraph 175 to	
	August: Colin Harvey, one of the founders of CHE, launches, with Ian Dunn, the Scottish Minorities Group, in Glasgow.		

		legalise homosexual acts for over-21s.	court case for importuning a policeman. Burton plays a blinder, deeply committed, very touching, but Harrison seems determined to distance himself and emphasise his heterosexuality by a truly appalling attempt to swish. It's also saved by dialogue which elevates bitching to poetry. Infinitely better than *Vicious*.
		20 July: Neil Armstrong and Buzz Aldrin become the first men to land on the moon. They collect about 21 kg of material and stay for about two hours. In a major, and high risk, propaganda exercise, the whole thing is broadcast live on TV worldwide, In Britain, the audience is nearly 30,000,000 – almost as many as for Di's funeral, which is a lot shorter.	

1970

CHE, HLRS	Other Gay events (UK and World)	In the News...	The Arts
CHE publishes its third leaflet, *Homosexuality Today*. This goes much beyond law reform towards a general demand for equality socially as well.	February: The Kingsway Group starts discussion meetings in Holborn. Up to 100 people attend talks. By August it has amalgamated with CHE.	1 January: Family Reform Act 1969 comes into force, effectively making the age of majority 18 for nearly everything – but not for gay sex, despite a few efforts by the Committee for Homosexual Equality to get an amendment to that effect during the passage of the bill through Parliament.	Gay Lib comes to crime writing when Joseph Hansen introduces gay private eye Dave Brandstetter in *Fadeout.*
February: First CHE local groups in West Midlands, Bristol, Manchester and Sheffield	1 May: Lavender Menace founded in New York by, among others, Rita Mae Brown and Karla Jay	16 January: Police raid the London Art Gallery and confiscate eight out of the fourteen exhibits in John Lennon's London Bag exhibition. They are a record of his wedding to Yoko Ono and contain 'erotic lithographs'.	*Maurice*, E. M. Forster's gay novel inspired by a visit to Edward Carpenter, is published. After he finished the first draft in 1914, Forster spent much of his life tinkering with it, but thought it unpublishable because he insisted on a happy ending for the gay characters. By the time it appears, the zeitgeist has moved on and it seems old-fashioned.
March: The CHE *Bulletin* enthuses about the idea of local groups, since a Club is proving so difficult to start: 'The scope for local groups is vast. It is on strong local groups that a national executive can best be based.'	13 October: First meeting of Gay Liberation Front, in the basement of the London School of Economics.	22 January: The first jumbo jet lands at Heathrow. The era of mass international travel and the global village has arrived; the world is shrinking rapidly.	17 March: *The Boys in the Band* makes it to the big screen after over 1,000 performances on Broadway. A movie which divides gay opinion still, it is hampered by the very theatrical setting and the US cliché of using games as a dramatic device (cf. *Who's Afraid of Virginia Woolf?*). On the one hand it is praised for its recognisable portraits of homosexuals at the time, complete with camp defences masking zilch self-esteem – 'We all know gays like that.'
19 March: The HLRS agrees to reconstitute itself as the Sexual Law Reform Society, with a view to preparing a report to the Criminal Law Revision Committee, currently surveying the whole field of law relating to sexuality.	27 November: GLF organises first UK demonstration by homosexuals, in Highbury Fields.	18 June: General Election. Conservative majority of 31 under Edward Heath on a 72% turnout. First election where 18-year-olds can vote.	
25 April: Harold Pollard stands down as CHE Chairman, replaced by Allan Horsfall. Paul Temperton officially replaces Allan as General Secretary. Unofficially he has	1 December: GLF produces first edition of its magazine, *Come Together.*	26 – 30 August: An estimated 700,000 attend the Isle of Wight Festival, the biggest ever pop	
	22 December: Over 1,000 people turn up for GLF ball at Kensington Town Hall, many turned away.		

been doing the Secretary's work for a year previously. The same meeting also agrees to start a Correspondence Club, a pen-pal scheme for isolated members, despite misgivings about possible police interference.

9 May: Allan Horsfall has a heart attack. Work increasingly devolves on Paul Temperton and Martin Stafford.

June: George Mortimer appointed London Organiser. He is replaced by Roger Baker in September.

10–11 July: Conference on Social Needs of the Homosexual in York, leading to the formation of the National Federation of Homophile Organisations (NFHO), a kind of umbrella group chaired by Antony Grey. The occasion also serves to bring key figures into CHE including Ike Cowen from Nottingham (Legal Officer) and Alan Swerdlow (Liverpool CHE and FRIEND).

11 September: Swinton Planning Committee rejects an application for planning permission to open a club in the

event in the world, with more people even than Woodstock. Acts include The Doors, Chicago, Jimi Hendrix, Joni Mitchell, Miles Davis, Procul Harem and The Who. Tiny Tim's rendition of 'There'll Always Be an England' is a camp classic. The descent of six times more hippies than the entire population of the island leads to a special act of parliament in 1971, prohibiting more than 5,000 people gathering on the island without a licence. The yachters and retirees will be left in peace for the next 30 years.

19 September: Jimi Hendrix dies of asphyxiation in the Samarkand Hotel in Notting Hill, having taken 18 times the recommended dose of a sleeping tablet. He is 27.

19 September: Margaret Court wins the tennis Grand Slam (US, Australian and French Opens, plus Wimbledon). For this she gets a bonus of $10,000, where a man in the same position could earn up to $1 million. The differential so infuriates Billie Jean King that she sets up the Women's Tennis

On the other hand, don't we deserve more positive representation? Either way, a milestone and a yardstick for the 1970s.

6 June: Quentin Crisp's TV debut in a *World in Action* feature. The first glimpse of the famous tiny squalid Soho flat.

12 June: The Kinks release 'Lola', the story of a confused flirtation between the singer and a possible TV/TS person. The song is characterised by a gentle humour at the expense of the singer and affection for the eponymous subject. It gets into trouble with the BBC over product placement – the reference to Coca-Cola, which is replaced by 'cherry cola' in the TOTP performance.

3 August: Much-delayed release of Cammell's and Roeg's *Performance*, starring Mick Jagger and James Fox. Dazzlingly filmed mindfuck between a gangster on the run and a reclusive rock star. Some voyeuristic lesbianism, but the homoerotic element between the guys is undermined by the fact that, in spite of the lippy and swish, they are never seen in bed together.

town centre. The councillors think it is too near a youth club and there is a danger of corruption

Fifteen CHE groups are formed by October, including four in London. Membership exceeds 600.

2 October: Antony Grey resigns from the SLRS. Joseph Rowntree Trust turns down an application from the Society for three years' funding.

24 October: First national meeting of all CHE group organisers is held in Birmingham.

4 December: London organiser Roger Baker appears on a *Late Night Line-up* special about homosexuality with Joan Bakewell, John Breslin, Anthony Storr and Michael De-la-Noy. Breslin is an actor who came out as gay in February; Storr is a psychiatrist and presumed straight; De-la-Noy (real name Walker) has replaced Antony Grey as director of the Albany Trust, having been sacked as the Archbishop of Canterbury's press secretary.

18 December: Burnley Corporation gives Planning

Association to get some leverage for the campaign for equality. Court becomes a Pentecostal minister in her native Australia, and most recently has been a prominent campaigner against same-sex marriage.

19 October: BP discovers a large oil field in the North Sea, and announces that it is big enough to start drilling.

10 November: *IT* (*International Times*) found guilty of conspiracy to corrupt public morals and outrage public decency. Publishers given £1,500 fine and two-year suspended prison sentences.

25 November: Novelist Yukio Mishima's *seppuku* suicide makes disturbing international news, in which his fascism and his homosexuality are intertwined.

6 August: Ian McKellen and James Laurenson have the first onscreen gay kiss, in BBC2's televising of the Prospect Theatre Co's production of Marlowe's *Edward II*. Bette Bourne, later founder of Bloolips and Neil Bartlett regular, has a small part. He joins GLF a few months later.

1 October: *Last Train Through Harecastle Tunnel.*, by Peter Terson. Railway enthusiast Alan aches for his son (Richard O'Sullivan) to be a real man like him, despite his obviously being a queen and spending most of his spare time trolling the toilets and cruising the streets.

4 October: 13-part BBC TV version of Sartre's *Road to Freedom*. Daniel Massey plays the main (tortured) homosexual character. The first TV play to show – discreetly – male homosexual sex (with a rent boy).

10 October: First of 69 episodes of LWT's *Upstairs Downstairs*, a historic precursor to the much inferior *Downton Abbey*. The first series goes out at 10.15 p.m., which allows it to explore 'adult content'. Originally a very feminist

Permission for a social club on Hammerton Street in the city centre. This is in an old Co-op building			conception by actors Jean Marsh and Dame Eileen Atkins, the central relationship is between Miss Elizabeth and her maid Rose (Marsh). Elizabeth has a homosexual husband. Rose shares a room and often a bed with an under maid played by Pauline Collins. The first episode is written by Fay Weldon, the second, *The Mistress and the Maids*, by CHE vice-president Maureen Duffy, although she asks for her name to be taken off the credits. For Episode 5 (*A suitable marriage* – 7 Nov), in which homosexuality features strongly, Jean Marsh tries in vain to explain to the producer why it's a bad idea to call a gay German visitor Baron von Rimmer.
			2 December: Michael Tippett's *Knot Garden* premieres at Covent Garden. The opera features a mixed-race gay couple.
			10 December: ITV play *Roll on Four O'clock*, written by Colin Welland, depicts homophobic bullying in a school. One teacher reassures the young pansy: 'As you get older you'll find other boys and men… you'll learn to live with it.'

1971

January – March: A postal strike means that there are no postal deliveries for 47 days. CHE subscriptions are reduced to a trickle for this period, and new members only come via word of mouth. A temporary cash flow crisis results.

Annual inflation rises to 8.6%, house prices rise by 11.8%. By the end of 1973 they have almost doubled, putting dreams of buying any gay centres into the realms of fantasy.

5 March: CHE adopts a constitution, effective from 1 April. Includes an elected National Executive Committee, and quarterly meetings of all group reps. Name changes to Campaign for Homosexual Equality.

1 April: Paul Temperton becomes full-time paid General Secretary at a salary of £20 per week, plus luncheon vouchers.

2 April: 120 London members turn up for the first pan-London meeting. At this meeting the magazine *Lunch* is agreed, and

Dennis Altman publishes *Homosexual Oppression and Liberation*, a seminal work for queer theorists.

Love & Abbott publish *Sappho was a Right-on Woman.*

4 February: first GLF street theatre demonstration outside Bow Street Magistrates' Court.

10 March: FHAR, the French equivalent of GLF, manifests itself in disruption of a radio programme on which Arcadie is appearing.

28 August: GLF youth group organises march from Hyde Park to Trafalgar Square to protest about age of consent.

September: Members of CHE and GLF hold a joint fringe meeting at the Liberal Party Conference in Scarborough, organised by the CHE Vice Chair, Michael Steed, a prominent Liberal. At the meeting Bernard Greaves draws attention to the local police's habit of spying on toilets and entrapment; as a result the Liberals vote to boycott Scarborough in future.

David Hockney finishes his painting, *Mr and Mrs Clark and Percy,* the only painting by a living artist to get into the top ten paintings in Britain, as voted by *Today* listeners in 2005. It is a wedding present for designer Ossie Clark, whose best man is Hockney. Clark is bisexual and continues having affairs after marriage. Percy is a white cat; in medieval and renaissance art, the cat symbolises infidelity.

Finland and Austria decriminalise male homosexuality.

1 January: Divorce Reform Act comes into force. This introduces the concept of 'no fault' divorces, and reduces the period of marriage necessary before divorce to two years. This year for the first time the number of divorces tops 100,000, a threefold increase on ten years previously.

3 January: BBC Open University begins. Ostensibly making programmes for OU students to tie in with OU courses, this broadcasting strand is

14 January: W. Stephen Gilbert's *Circle Line* hits the screens as a BBC1 Play for Today after a nervous delay of a year. In it a sexually experimental second-year university student goes to bed with an eager 14-year-old. A cheerful justification of the therapeutic benefits of casual sex, and guaranteed to *épater la Whitehouse.* The NVLA lists it in its top ten horrors of the year. 'How long can the BBC get away with this?' thunders the *Sunday Post.* The BBC takes fright and wipes the tape within three months of broadcast.

29 March: A man and a woman sit plunged in grief in *The Waiting Room* of a hospital in the play by John Bowen. He has lost his lover in a road accident, she her husband. Slowly they realise that this is the same man. Unsentimental study of loss, and the way supposed mutual friends melt away, embarrassed by tragedy.

1 May: Visconti's much-misunderstood *Death in Venice* premieres in London.

the Task Force set up which will in time become FRIEND. It also agrees to try to set up a London Club.

10 May: CHE takes possession of its new offices at 28 Kennedy Street in central Manchester. A gaggle of volunteers get out the paint brushes immediately.

26 May: Licensee Ken Pilling gives an interview on Radio Blackburn in which he announces the club for Burnley will become a reality. The story is picked up by local and national radio, and Granada TV.

11 June: A local Christian coalition in Burnley forms a 'Stop The Club' Committee. The local Co-op takes fright at the ensuing publicity and withdraws the offer of a lease.

19 June: First national GLF think-in in Leeds. CHE attends and the two organisations agree to work together where possible.

30 July: 200–300 people turn out at Burnley Public Library to hear the arguments for a club at a public meeting. This is extremely rowdy, but CHE is

9 September: Massive GLF disruption of Festival of Light rally at Central Hall, Westminster

October: Leeds GLF produces the first edition of the Leeds *Broadsheet*, the main communication between GLF and CHE groups over the next two years.

30 October: NFHO formally comes into existence. The 15 month delay is caused by rows over the perceived authoritarianism of the organisation, and the difficulty of setting membership fees for such a variety of groups. CHE don't trust the ambitions of Antony Grey and is always suspicious that NFHO is trying to become *the* national organisation.

1 November: First edition of *Body Politic,* Canadian gay paper/magazine of high intellectual content and fearless journalism. Twice prosecuted for obscenity, it is very influential on other publications, including *Gay News.* It folds in 1987.

responsible for some of the key gay documentaries of the 1970s. These also have a life of many years as teaching aids.

15 February: UK adopts decimal currency.

1 April: *Little Red Schoolbook* published and immediately seized. It is successfully prosecuted for obscenity, and appeals to the Lords and the European Court of Human Rights both fail. However, the government, unusually, lets publisher Richard Handyside bring out a version with a mutually agreed (censored) text.

8 October: Pan Books publish paperback version of David Reuben's *Everything You Wanted to Know About Sex but Were Afraid to Ask.*

28 October: House of Commons votes in favour of Britain joining the European Community.

Dismissed by some as tawdry, the film yearns after ideal, unachievable beauty as Visconti photographs Tadzio (Bjorn Andressen) as if he were Michaelangelo's David.

2 July: After a number of personnel changes, *Queen* performs its first live gig with its classic line-up. Farrokh Bulsara has just changed his name to Freddie Mercury, and is joined on stage by Brian May, Roger Taylor and John Deacon.

Panorama runs 18-minute feature on GLF. 24 September: GLF members appear on Thames TV's *Today* programme.

17 December: David Bowie releases 'Queen Bitch' as part of the album *Hunky Dory*. The first of Bowie's genderfuck bisexual offerings, heavily influenced by Lou Reid and the Velvet Underground. A swirling ambiguity of pronouns makes it slightly unclear exactly who the singer's so jealous of, but the use of 'cruising', 'swishy' and the title itself pushes it firmly to the effeminate male side. 'She's so swishy in her satin and tat. … My God! I could do better than that.'

supported by 15–20 members of GLF, and a mass 'coming-out' shows that about half the audience is homosexual. CHE is elated by the success of the meeting as a PR and consciousness-raising exercise.			
September: First edition of the London magazine *Lunch*, with David Hyde as editor.			
4 September: The first National Council is held in Birmingham. The NCs, where each local group is allowed one vote on motions of national policy, will be held around the country every 3 months. They will also be places for swapping ideas and experiences, and for partying.			
20 November: first CHE Winter Fair at Conway Hall.			
4 December: London Women's Group is recognised at National Council. This is mainly a social/induction group to ease new members into joining mixed groups, and also to provide a social space to meet with London GLF women and others, away from men. Women are expected to have membership of a mixed group as well as the women's group.			

1972

CHE, HLRS	Other Gay events (UK and World)	In the News…	The Arts
January: CHE hosts its first youth conference, in Manchester. Both CHE and GLF members take part.	Radical gay organisation FUORI founded in Italy	Sweden allows transsexuals legally to change sex, and offers free hormone therapy.	*Under the Age* has a queenie bartender, Suzie, presiding over a group of young toughs, all of whom are drinking under age and some having sex under age as well. A conversation piece by gay playwright E. A. Whitehead, and directed by Alan Clarke, best known for *Scum* but ever a sympathetic portrayer of dispossessed youth. In a pioneering move, BBC2 stages a studio discussion immediately afterwards, in which GLF's John Chesterman attacks the negative characterisation of a gay bar. This rather misses the point, that young people will respect those who respect them, especially people who are themselves oppressed.
February: CHE Elections are held by postal ballot, having been postponed from the previous summer. The first semi-elected EC includes Robin Bloxsidge, who becomes responsible for discrimination, Bernard Greaves, responsible for political action, and Liz Stanley, the women's officer.	Norway decriminalises male homosexuality, with the abolition of S213 of its penal code. Age of consent 16.	Lancaster team captain Luke Fitzgerald clearly seen on *University Challenge* wearing a gay badge. The producer tries to cut it out with very close-cropped filming – but to no effect.	*Escape from the Shadows*, Robin Maugham's candid autobiography, describes his struggle to free himself from his bullying father, his cynical and manipulative queer uncle Somerset Maugham, and from the guilt occasioned by his homosexual feelings.
February: The EC backs an education campaign, supporting the idea of approaching head teachers for permission to give talks to senior schoolchildren, and to distribute leaflets to the kids outside the school anyway if permission is refused. They backtrack on this a month later, in response to uproar at the NC, and insist it would only be done through official channels.	March: NCCL/GLF questionnaire on harassment distributed to all CHE members with the March *Bulletin*. NCCL wants to write a report for law-makers based on the responses, but there are not enough; the level of self-esteem is such that most people aren't even aware of oppression. The report is never written. The NCCL 'bust card' *Your Rights on Arrest* goes out at the same time.	4 January: First hand-held scientific calculator comes onto the market, at a cost of £200.	Gay anthems start to
April: A row about producing separate advertising posters and leaflets for women, giving a female contact in London. The EC	5 May: FRIEND starts advertising its regular telephone service staffed by volunteers operating Monday to Friday, 7.30–9.30 pm. Prior to this there are only informal counselling arrangements, and all calls are answered by Michael Launder or Michael Butler from the Samaritans.	22 January: Britain, Ireland, Norway and Denmark sign a Treaty of Accession to join the EEC, to come into force on 1 January 1973. Norwegian voters repudiated the treaty before then, so Norway never joins.	
	June: first edition of *Gay News* appears.	30 January: Bloody Sunday in Derry, when 14 unarmed civil rights demonstrators are shot by British soldiers. Internment without trial has been introduced the previous year, with hundreds being imprisoned in Long Kesh and twenty killed in the ensuing riots. Bloody Sunday is	

wants all recruitment to go through the national office, but the women insist that CHE will never recruit women unless they are put in touch with a woman in the first instance. They win, after many prominent CHE women members threaten to resign.

May/June: CHE takes part in two episodes of Jimmy Saville's *Speakeasy*, the first with GLF and the second on its own. This is the largest audience CHE has achieved to date, and the phones at the London Office, staffed by volunteers, don't stop ringing afterwards for twelve hours, despite having two extra lines put in for the occasion.

June: CHE membership stands at 1,750

1 July: Carnival Parade from Trafalgar Square to Hyde Park. First Gay Pride March designated as such. Several CHE groups attend.

17 August: Weymouth Council votes to refuse facilities to CHE for a conference in 1973. One Alderman calls it 'a disgusting idea. Just how low can we get in this town to raise money?' As a result, Morecambe beckons.

The initial predominance of former members of GLF gives it a slightly critical stance towards CHE, but CHE's Glenys Parry is Northern Correspondent, and with the decline of GLF *Gay News* becomes more supportive. Early editions are undated.

Autumn: CHE fringe meetings at both Liberal and Labour Party conferences.

followed by IRA retaliation on 21 July (Bloody Friday – nine killed) and 31July (Bloody Monday – nine killed).

14 June: *IT* loses appeal against conviction on conspiracy charges. The Law Lords judgement rules that decriminalising acts does not make them fully lawful.

22 August: John Wojtowicz and Sal Naturale hold several Chase Manhattan Bank employees to ransom in New York. Wojtowicz is trying to raise money for his boyfriend's sex change operation. The events are fictionalised in the film *Dog Day Afternoon.*

1 September: School leaving age raised from 15 to 16.

appear: Madeline Davies' *Stonewall Nation*, produced by the Mattachine Society; Alan Wakeman's *A Gay Song*, recorded with Everyone Allowed and distributed free; Eric Presland's *We Were In There*, premiered improbably at an Oxford May Ball.

January: David Bowie outs himself as bisexual in an interview with Melody Maker; *John, I'm Only Dancing*, in which the singer reassures his boyfriend that he has no sexual interest in the girl he's with, follows in September. Despite the subject matter, the single has ample airplay and reaches No.12 in the UK charts. However, TOTP ban the video, featurong Lindsay Kemp's androgynous mime troupe.

5 February: David Hockney becomes the first openly gay castaway on *Desert Island Discs*. His chosen book for the island is a work of pornography – Floyd Carter's *Route 69*.

13 February: Film version of *Cabaret* released in the US; in it, bisexuality is seen as rather fun.

17 March: John

6 September: Having agreed a deal for the 1973 Conference, Morecambe Council rats on it, claiming that the hall where it is to be held is a fire hazard. Since the Fire Brigades Union will have its own conference there a month after CHE's, this is clearly a lie. But CHE gets round this lack of co-operation by hiring the pier privately, ensuring a conference can take place, even if it costs more.			Waters' *Pink Flamingos* is released in the US. Refused a certificate in the UK, it became a cult thanks to club screenings, and causes 20 years' controversy as to whether Divine actually ate dog poo for the movie – Waters says he did in his memoir *Shock Value* (1982)
22 September: Open meeting on the church and homosexuality at Holborn Assembly Rooms. Speakers are Rev. Norman Pittenger and, from America, Rev. Troy Perry.			8 September: Pilot episode of *Are You Being Served?,* part of BBC Comedy Playhouse. In the pilot Mr Humphreys is a minor character and not at all effete. Writers David Croft and Jeremy Lloyd ask him to camp it up, in the face of stiff opposition from within the BBC.
September: Liverpool CHE organises a successful teach-in for local social workers, doctors, probation officers etc., in Liverpool's Anglican Cathedral. Cathedral authorities defy protests from churchgoers and editorials in the press.			26 October: *A Life is Forever.* Bleak prison drama in which a young gay prisoner, McCallister, pursues his heterosexual cellmate, looking for love and protection. The straight man beats him up, but later punches another man who's abusing the boy. It seems McCallister has found his protection. Praised at the time for its realism and Tony Meyer's cute bum.
15 December: CHE members and GLF activists disrupt a BMA seminar on homosexuality, and follow it up in early 1973 with a pamphlet addressed to doctors. 5,000 copies distributed.			

1973

CHE, HLRS	Other Gay events (UK and World)	In the News...	The Arts
LBC's *Call-In* features Jackie Forster and Denis Lemon fielding calls from a woman with a gay son and Brent of Fulham asking 'What do you do in bed?' CHE, FRIEND and Parents' Enquiry contribute 'planted' calls.	COC organises an international rights seminar in Amsterdam. Six countries attend.	West Germany reduces homosexual age of consent from 21 to 18. It remains 14 for heterosexuals.	Lou Reid's *Walk on the Wild Side* reaches No 10 in UK singles chart, in a bowdlerised version which omits lines about oral sex. The version from the LP is popular at gay discos, and *Goodnight Ladies*, also from the album *Transformer*, often closes proceedings.
Members of Liverpool CHE take part in The World In Action's *Joe*, the first programme to deal with the full horrors of aversion therapy. Joe has electrodes tied to his legs while being shown a picture of a naked man with a moustache riding a horse. The CHE condemnation is rather undermined by the fact that no-one talking has personal experience of the practice. *Gay News* calls the programme 'nothing less than a free advert for aversion therapy'.	Icebreakers founded, an offshoot of the GLF counter-psychiatry group. Early members include Nettie Pollard, and Peter Norman and Roger Baker from CHE.	22 January: The US Supreme Court judgement in the case of *Roe v. Wade* overturns the right of US states to outlaw abortion.	Rita Mae Brown publishes *Rubyfruit Jungle*. What might have been seen as just another coming-of-age lesbian novel is made unique by its savage sense of humour and its Southern setting. In its day its explicitness was remarkable.
13 January: First national FRIEND conference.	19 July: CHE disaffiliates from NFHO, following the example of SMG. If Grey ever had any Napoleonic ambitions, which he denies, they are now as dust.	8 March: Provisional IRA plants bombs in the Old Bailey and Whitehall. In September there are further bombs in King's Cross and Euston stations, and in Oxford Street and Sloane Square. Suddenly the activities of the Angry Brigade seem very small beer.	Francis Bacon paints the Black Triptych, reflecting his grief at the suicide of his partner George Dyer.
27 January: 120 women attend CHE's first women's conference.	15 December: The American Psychiatric Association removes homosexuality from its second Diagnostic and Statistical Manual of Mental Disorders (DSM-II). This is first reflected in the seventh printing of the manual the following year. This follows a campaign led by Frank Kameny and American GLF. At the 1971 APA Conference Kameny seizes the microphone and yells, 'Psychiatry is the enemy incarnate, psychiatry has waged a relentless	3 April: First hand-held mobile phone call made by Motorola inventor Martin Cooper. The phone weighs about 2 kg.	6 March: Granada's *World in Action* broadcasts *Conversations with a gay Liberal.*
March: First national employment campaign, with a		12 April: Labour takes control of the Greater London Council. Illtyd Harrington becomes chairman of Policy and Resources. Harrington is gay, and becomes the focus for new attempts to obtain funding for lesbian and gay causes, including a Gay Centre.	26 March: Death of Noël Coward.
			13 July: Fassbinder scripts and produces *Tenderness of the Wolves*, about a homosexual rapist and murderer who drinks the blood

questionnaire to major employers in the private and public sector. Replies are slow in coming, and bland and evasive.	war of extinction against us.'	20 September: Tennis champion Billy Jean King beats Bobby Riggs in a 'Battle of the Sexes' circus which the world's Number One female player takes on mainly in order to stop the disreputable antics of a loudmouth hustler bringing the game into disrepute. Rampant speculation that she is a lesbian is confirmed during a 'palimony' suit in 1980, making King the first tennis player to come out.	of his boy-victims, strips their flesh for dinner parties with his cannibal friends, and boils the bones for soup. Makes *Cruising* look like *Love Story*. Later claimed as a satire on the predatory commercial gay scene. Come now, The Fridge was never like *this*.
6–8 April: First CHE National Conference in Morecambe.		17 October: OPEC starts an oil embargo against countries which supported Israel in the Yom Kippur war, triggering an oil crisis. Over a year the price of crude oil rises from $3 to $12 a barrel. The UK escapes direct sanctions because Edward Heath refuses to allow US planes to use British airfields to fly arms to Israel, and the Government embargoes sales of arms and supplies to either side. However, it can't escape the price increases caused by the ubiquitous use of petroleum products in manufacture, and transport costs. The small hatchback car becomes popular.	29 September: Death of W. H. Auden.
31 May: CHE members appear on Mavis Nicholson's *Good Afternoon* programme on Thames Television.			8 October: LBC starts broadcasting in London.
June: CHE has over 3,000 members and 70 local groups.			30 October: Armchair Theatre's *Golden Road* sees Cass and Jim take in a lodger, Anna, and Cass and Anna end up sleeping together. Jim walks out, taking their daughter with him. It's clear that the only way Cass is going to see her daughter again is by stopping seeing Anna. The play ends on a shot of Anna standing at the front door, locked out of the house. Heartbreaking. Nowadays this would be a great campaigning tool for lesbians, but this was pre-video recorders for most people.
July: Paul Temperton resigns, intending to leave in September. Allan Horsfall resigns as Chairman, but is persuaded to stay on until a new General Secretary is found. He subsequently becomes President for Life. Martin Stafford, now feeling totally isolated within the organisation, also resigns.			

Appendix B: Local CHE Groups (to April 1973)

The 'Recognised' column gives the date when the group was officially recognised e.g. by a National Council.

Groups in Volume One are in **bold**; groups in Volume Two are in *italic*; groups in both volumes are in ***bold italic***.

Name	Start date	Recog-nised	Other information
Kingsway Group	**Feb 70**		**Not officially CHE until Aug 1970, when combined with London 1.**
Nottingham	*Feb 70*	*Dec 71*	*Folded in Winter 1970–71; re-formed Sept 71.*
West Midlands	**Mar 70**		**Split into Wolverhampton CHE and Birmingham CHE.**
Bristol	***Apr 70***	***Dec 71***	
Oxford University	**May 70**	**Dec 71**	**Amalgamated with Town Group Autumn 1974.**
Sheffield University Homophile Society	*Jun 70*		*Started Gay Action Group winter 1970. Folded early 1971.*
Birmingham	**Aug 70**	**Sep 71**	**Offshoot of West Midlands CHE.**
Wolverhampton	**Aug 70**	**Dec 71**	**Offshoot of West Midlands CHE.**
London 1	**Aug 70**	**Sep 71**	**Included Kingsway Group members.**
London 2	**Sep 70**	**Sep 71**	
Gay Cambridge	*Sep 70*	*Dec 71*	*Mixed group: Cambridge CHE within it.*
Liverpool	**Sep 70**	**Sep 71**	
North East Lancs	Oct 70		
London 3	**Oct 70**	**Sep 71**	
London 4	**Oct 70**	**Sep 71**	**Renamed Bloomsbury**
Chilterns	**Nov 70**	**Sep 71**	
Teesside	*Nov 70*	*Sep 71*	*Also called Darlington CHE.*
Waltham Forest	**Dec 70**		**Folded by October 1971.**
Manchester Homophile Society	*Jan 71*	*Sep 71*	*Student Group at Man. Uni founded by Martin Stafford. Became Manchester Young CHE Mar 1972.*

London 5	**Jan 71**	**Sep 71**	**Became London Student Group.**
London 6	**Feb 71**	**Sep 71**	**Became Marylebone, later Marylebone and Paddington (MaryPad).**
London 7	**Mar 71**	**Sep 71**	**Renamed Croydon.**
Leeds	*Mar 71*	*Sep 71*	
Windsor	Apr 71	Sep 71	
Belfast	*May 71*	*Dec 71*	*Amalgamated with GLF to form Belfast Gay Liberation Society May 1973.*
London 8	**Jun 71**	**Sep 71**	**Renamed Piccadilly.**
Oxford Town	*Jun 71*	*Dec 71*	*Amalgamated with University autumn 1974.*
South Essex	*Jul 71*	*Dec 71*	
Manchester	Jul 71	Sep 71	
London 9	**Aug 71**	**Sep 71**	**Merged with London Monday Nov 1972.**
London 10	**Aug 71**	**Dec 71**	**Became London Monday Nov 1972.**
Trans-Pennine	Sep 71	Dec 71	
London Student Group	**Sep 71**		**Name change from London 5. Mainly UCL students; became CHE Youth Group Mar 1972.**
Croydon	**Sep 71**		**Name change from London 7.**
Cardiff	*Sep 71*	*Jun 72*	
Teesside 2	*Sep 71*	*Sep 72*	*Splinter group from Teesside 1.*
South Herts	**Sep 71**	**Dec 71**	
London 11	**Oct 71**	**Dec 71**	**Became part of London Central Feb 1973.**
Bristol 2	*Oct 71*	*Dec 71*	*Breakaway from Bristol CHE.*
Harrow Gay Unity	*Oct 71*		*Originally GLF, broke away July 1972 to become Harrow Gay Unity. Joined CHE 1974.*
Sheffield	*Oct 71*	*Dec 71*	*Mixed town and student group; split into social and action groups, 1972.*
East Kent	*Oct 71*	*Dec 71*	
London Women's Group	***Oct 71***	***Dec 71***	
Reading Students	*Oct 71*	*Dec 71*	*Opened to GLF people and others, changed name to Reading Gay Alliance Aug 1972.*
South West Hants	Oct 71	Dec 71	Or South Hants. Changed name to Southampton/ Bournemouth, then just Bournemouth
University of York	Nov 71		Combined with Town Group June 1972.
Wirral	Nov 71	Dec 71	Offshoot of Liverpool.
Bristol Youth Group	Nov 71	Jun 72	
Bath Gay Awareness	*Nov 71*	*Sep 72*	*Mixed group of CHE and non-CHE.*
Huddersfield	Nov 71		From Trans-Pennine CHE.
Leicester	*Nov 71*	*Sep 72*	*Originally Leicester Gay Awareness and independent.*

Liverpool Student Group	Jan 72	Mar 72	Spin-off from Liverpool; existing CHE members at Univ. of Liverpool.
London 12	**Feb 72**	**Mar 72**	**Became part of London Central Feb 1973.**
Marylebone	Feb 72		From London 6.
Lewisham	*Feb 72*	*Mar 72*	
Northampton	Feb 72	Jun 72	Also called Northants-Beds.
Norwich	Feb 72	Mar 72	
London Youth Group	**Mar 72**		**Name change from London Student Group.**
Liverpool Youth Group	Mar 72		Spin-off from Liverpool CHE because of age policy; re-amalgamated Feb 1973 when Liverpool lowered age limit to 16.
Ealing	**Mar 72**	**Jun 72**	**Also called Ealing & Acton. Wound up June 1973.**
London 13	**Apr 72**	**Jun 72**	**Became part of London Central Feb 1973.**
Ilford	**Apr 72**		**Became East London CHE.**
South West Wales	Apr 72	Jun 72	Spin-off from Bristol CHE.
Kensington	*Apr 72*	*Jun 72*	*Also known as 'The Good Companions'.*
Preston	*Apr 72*	*Jun 73*	
Swansea	May 72		Initially a student group.
Bradford	*May 72*	*Sep 72*	*Offshoot of Leeds CHE.*
Brighton	*May 72*	*Nov 72*	
Hampstead & Kilburn	**May 72**	**Sep 72**	**Also known as Hampstead CHE, or Kilburn CHE.**
Kent Youth Group	*May 72*	*Sep 72*	*Spin-off from East Kent group because of their age restrictions.*
Highbury & Islington	*May 72*	*Jun 72*	*Also 'North London CHE' or simply 'Islington CHE'.*
Stoke-on-Trent	May 72	Sep 72	
York	Jun 72	Sep 72	
Wolverhampton Women's Group	Jun 72		
Tunbridge Wells	*Jun 72*	*Sep 72*	Probably the group referred to as 'West Kent' in the May 1972 *Broadsheet.*
Barking	Jun 72		Spin off from South Essex. Folded by November.
Guildford	Jun 72	Jun 72	Largely from members of London groups; changed name to Surrey CHE Feb 1973.
Portsmouth	Jun 72	Nov 72	Formed from South West Hants CHE.
Tyneside	*Jul 72*	*Sep 72*	
East Lancs	Jul 72		Split from Trans-Pennine. Also called Blackburn & Burnley.
Crouch End	**Aug 72**		**Became Haringey CHE**

Halifax & Humberside	Aug 72		Splinter from Trans-Pennine.
Shropshire	*Aug 72*	*Nov 72*	
Wolverhampton Workers Group	*Sep 72*	*Nov 72*	*Subgroup of Wolverhampton; renamed Black Country CHE April 1973.*
Richmond & Putney	*Sep 72*	*Nov 72*	*Also known as Wandsworth & Richmond.*
Lancaster	Autumn 72		Self-styled. Not recognised.
Manchester Women's Group	*Oct 72*		*Not official CHE group, but members encouraged to join CHE, and extensively reported in Bulletin etc.*
Bolton	Oct 72	Nov 72	
Colchester	Oct 72		Withdrew request for recognition Nov 72: wanted to become GLF group.
South Durham/ North Yorkshire	Jul 72		From Teesside 2.
Harrogate	Oct 72		
Southampton	*Nov 72*	*Apr 73*	*Members of Portsmouth and Bournemouth; initially called Integroup.*
East London	**Nov 72**	**Nov 72**	**From Ilford CHE.**
Enfield	**Nov 72**	**Nov 72**	
Stepney	**Nov 72**	**Apr 73**	**Wound up Mar 1975.**
Blackpool	*Nov 72*		*Offshoot of Liverpool CHE.*
Streatham	Jan 73	Apr 73	
Cambridge Women's Group	Jan 73		
Central London	Feb 73		Formed from London 11–13.
Newport, Gwent	*Feb 73*	*Jun 73*	*From Cardiff CHE.*
New Brighton	Early 1973		Offshoot of Liverpool.
Surrey CHE	*Feb 73*		*Name change from Guildford CHE; also known as Woking CHE.*
Sheffield Students	Feb 73		Breakaway from main Sheffield CHE.
London West End	*Feb 73*		*Amalgamation of Groups 1–3.*
Guernsey	**Feb 73**		
Haringey	Feb 73	Apr 73	From Crouch End CHE.
Basildon	Mar 73		Went dormant quickly; re-founded 1978.
Doncaster	Mar 73	Apr 73	

Bibliography

Journals consulted at Hall-Carpenter archives

The Advocate, HCA/ JOURNALS/74.

After Lunch, HCA/ JOURNALS/63G.

Arena 3, HCA/ JOURNALS/63E.

Gay News, HCA/ JOURNALS/294.

Lunch, HCA/ JOURNALS/45.

Spartacus, HCA/JOURNALS/438.

Books

ALDRICH, Robert (ed.) *Gay life and culture – a world history* (London: Thames and Hudson, 2006).

—— and WOTHERSPOON, Garry, *Who's who in contemporary lesbian and gay history* (London: Thames and Hudson, 2006).

ALLEN, Clifford, *Homosexuality – its nature causation and treatment* (London: Staples, 1958).

ALPERT, Harriet (ed.) *We are everywhere* (California: Crossing Press, 1988).

ALTMAN, Dennis, *Homosexual oppression and liberation* (New York: Avon Books, 1971).

ANNAN, Noel, *Our age: Portrait of a generation* (London: Weidenfeld and Nicholson, 1990).

AYOUB, Philip and PATERNOTTE, David (eds), *LGBT activity: The making of Europe – a rainbow Europe* (Basingstoke: Palgrave Macmillan, 2014).

BAILEY, Derrick Sherwin, *Homosexuality and the Western Christian tradition* (London: Longmans Green & Co, 1955).

—— (ed.) *Sexual offenders and social punishment* (London, CIB, 1956).

BAKER, Roger, *Drag* (London: Triton Books, 1968).

BELL, Barbara, *Just take your frock off* (Brighton, UK: Ourstory Books, 1999).

BERG, Charles (ed.), *Homosexuality: A subjective and objective investigation* (Allen and Unwin, 1958).

BERGLER, Edmund, *Homosexuality: Disease or way of life?* (New York: Hill and Wang, 1956).

BERMAN, Ed (ed.), *Homosexual acts* (London: InterAction Inprint, 1975).

BOGARDE, Dirk, *Snakes and ladders* (London: Chatto and Windus, 1978).

BOOTHBY, Robert, *Recollections of a rebel* (London: Hutchinson, 1978).

BOSWELL, John, *Christianity, social tolerance and homosexuality* (Chicago: University of Chicago Press, 1981).

BRASIUS, Mark and PHELAN, Shane, *We are everywhere* (New York: Routledge, 1997)

BRITISH MEDICAL ASSOCIATION: Special Committee of the BMA, *Homosexuality and prostitution: Memorandum of evidence to the Departmental Committee* (London: BMA, 1955).

BROME, Victor, *J. B. Priestley* (London: Hamish Hamilton, 1988).

BUTLER, Judith, *Gender crimes* (New York: Routledge, 1999 edition).

CANT, Bob. and HEMMINGS, Susan (eds), *Radical records* (London and New York: Routledge, 1988).

CARPENTER, Edward, *The intermediate sex* (London: Allan and Unwin, 1908).

CHALFONT, Baron (Arthur Gwynne Jones), *Montgomery of Alamein* (London: Atheneum, 1976).

CHESSER, Eustace, *Live and let live* (London: Heinemann, 1958).

CHURCH INFORMATION BOARD, *The problem of homosexuality* (London: Church of England Moral Welfare Council, 1953).

CLANCY, George, *Gay New York* (New York: Basic Books, 1994).

COCKS, Harry, *Classified: The secret history of the personal column* (London: Random House, 2009).

COLLINS, Marcus (ed.), *The Permissive society and its enemies: Sixties British culture* (London: Rivers Oram Press, 2007).

COLLINSON, Laurence, *Cupid's crescent* (London: Grandma Press, 1973).

COLLIS, Rose, *Portraits to the wall* (London: Cassell, 1994).

—— *Coral Browne* (London: Oberon, 2007).

COOK, Matt, *London and the culture of homosexuality 1885–1914* (Cambridge: Cambridge University Press, 2003).

COOKE, Bill, *The blasphemy depot: 100 years of the Rationalist Press Association* (London: RPA, 2003).

COOTE, Stephen (ed.), *Penguin book of homosexual verse* (London: Allen Lane, 1986, second edition).

CORY, Donald Webster [Edward Sagarin], *The homosexual in America – a subjective approach* (New York: Greenberg, 1951).

—— 'Changing Attitudes towards Homosexuals', *ONE – The Homosexual Magazine*, September 1952.

—— *The homosexual outlook* (London: Peter Neville, 1953).

—— *Homosexuality: A cross-cultural approach* (New York: Julian Press, 1956).

COWARD, Noël, *The lyrics of Noël Coward* (London: Mandarin Paperbacks, 1995).

CROFT-COOKE, Rupert, *The life for me* (London: Macmillan and Co, 1952).

—— *The verdict of you all* (London: Secker and Warburg, 1955).

DALEY, Harry, *This small cloud* (London: Weidenfeld and Nicholson, 1986).

DAVENPORT-HINES, Richard, *Sex, death and punishment* (London: Fontana, 1990).

DAVID, Hugh, *On Queer Street: Social history 1895–1995* (London: Harper Collins, 1997).

DAVIDSON, Michael, *The world, the flesh and myself* (London: Arthur Barker, 1962).

DE SALES, St Francis, *Philothea, or introduction to the devout life* (New York: Joseph F. Wagner, 1924).

D'EMILIO, John, *Sexual politics, sexual communities* (Chicago: University of Chicago Press, 1983).

—— *Making trouble* (New York: Routledge, 1992).

DENT, Alan, *Mrs Patrick Campbell* (London: Museum Press, 1961).

DYSON, A. E., *Freedom in love* (London: SPCK, 1974).

EDER, Franz X, HALL, Lesley And HEKMA, Gert (eds), *Sexual cultures in Europe: National histories* (Manchester: Manchester University Press, 1999).

ELLIS, Albert, 'Are homosexuals necessarily neurotic?', *ONE – The Homosexual Magazine*, April 1955.

ELLIS, Havelock, and SYMONDS, John Addington, *Studies in the psychology of sex, Vol. 1: Sexual inversion* (London: Wilson and Macmillan, 1897).

FAULKS, Sebastian, *The fatal Englishman* (London: Hutchinson, 1996).

FERENCZI, Sandor, *Contributions to psycho-analysis* (London: Stanley Phillips, 1916).

FORD, Charles Henri and TYLER, Parker, *The young and evil* (Paris: Obelisk Press, 1933).

FORD, Clellan S. and BEACH, Frank A., *Patterns of sexual behaviour* (London, Eyre and Spottiswoode, 1952).

FREEMAN, Edward A. *The reign of William Rufus and the accession of Henry the First* (Oxford: Clarendon Press, 1882).

FRIEDMAN, S. and SARAH, E., *On the problem of men: two feminist conferences* (London: The Women's Press, 1982).

FROST, Brian (ed.), *The tactics of pressure: A critical review of six British pressure groups* (London: Galliard, 1975).

GARLAND, Rodney, *The heart in exile* (London: W. H. Allen, 1953).

—— *The troubled midnight* (London: W. H. Allen, 1954).

GELLERT, Roger, *Quaint honour* (London: Secker and Warburg, 1958).

GLOVER, Edward, *The roots of crime* (London: Imago, 1962).

GOSLING, Ray, *Sum total* (UK: Pomona Press, 2004 reprint).

GRAHN, *Another mother tongue: Gay words, gay worlds* (Boston: Beacon Press, 1984).

GREY, Antony [Anthony Edgar Gartside Wright], *Quest for justice: Towards homosexual emancipation* (London: Sinclair-Stevenson, 1992).

—— *Speaking of Sex: The limits of language* (London: Cassell, 1993).

—— *Speaking out: Writings on sex, law, politics and society 1954-95* (London: Cassell, 1997).

HALPERIN, David M., *How to do the history of homosexuality* (Chicago, University of Chicago Press, 2002).

HAMILTON, Nigel, *Montgomery: D-Day commander* (Dulles, VA: Potomac Books, 2007).

HANSCOMBE, G. E. and LUMSDEN, Andrew, *Title fight: The battle for Gay News* (London: Brilliance Books, 1983).

HANSEN, S. and JENSEN, J., *The little red book for students* (London: Stage 1 Publishers: 1971).

HARVEY, Ian, *To fall like Lucifer* (London: Sidgwick and Jackson, 1971).

HAUSER, Richard, *The homosexual society* (London: Mayflower-Dell, 1965).

HAWKES, Jacquetta, *A quest of love* (London: Chatto & Windus, 1980).

HENRY, George W., 'Pastoral counselling for homosexuals', *Pastoral Psychology*, November 1951.

HERON, Alastair (ed.), *Towards a Quaker view of sex* (London: Friends' Home Service Committee, 1963).

HIGGINS, Patrick, *A queer reader* (London: Fourth Estate, 1993).

—— *Heterosexual dictatorship* (London: Fourth Estate, 1996).

HODGES, Andrew and HUTTER, David, *With downcast gays* (Toronto: Pink Triangle Press, 1977 edition).

HOMFRAY, Mike, *Provincial queens* (Berne, Switzerland: Peter Lang, 2007).

HOMOSEXUAL LAW REFORM SOCIETY, *Homosexuals and the law* (London: HLRS, 1958).

HONORE, Tony, *Sex law* (London: Duckworth, 1978).

HORSFALL, Allan, 'Battling for Wolfenden', in CANT, R. and HEMMING, S. (eds), *Radical Records: Thirty years of lesbian and gay history* (London: Routledge, 1988).

HOULBROOK, Matt, *Queer London: Perils and pleasures in the sexual metropolis, 1918–1957* (Chicago: University of Chicago Press, 2006).

HOWES, Keith, *Broadcasting it* (London: Cassell, 1993).

—— *Outspoken: Gay News interviews 1976–83* (London: Cassell, 1995).

HOWES, Robert, *Gay West: Civil society, community and LGBT history in Bristol and Bath 1970 to 2010* (Bristol: SilverWood Books, 2011).

HUNTER, John Francis, *The gay insider* (New York: Stonehill Publishing, 1972).

HUREWITZ, Daniel, *Bohemian Los Angeles* (Berkeley: University of California, 2007).

HYDE, H. Montgomery, *The other love* (London: Heinemann, 1970).

JACKSON, Julian, *Living in Arcadia: Homosexuality, politics and morality in France from the liberation to AIDS* (Chicago: University of Chicago Press, 2009).

JAMES, Robert Rhodes, *Bob Boothby, a portrait* (London: Hodder and Stoughton, 1991).

JEFFERY-POULTER, Stephen: see POULTER, Stephen.

JENNINGS, Rebecca, *Tomboys and bachelor girls* (Manchester: Manchester University Press, 2007).

JOAD, C. E. M., *The book of Joad – An aggressive autobiography* (London: Faber and Faber, 1935).

JOHNSON, David K., *The lavender scare* (Chicago: University of Chicago Press, 2004).

KAMENY, Franklin E., 'Gay is good' in WEITGE, Ralph W. (ed.), *The same sex* (Philadelphia: Pilgrim, 1969).

LANGLEY, Noel, *The loner* (London: Triton, 1967).

LAURITSON, John and THORSTAT, David, *Early homosexual rights movement* (New York: Times Change Press, 1974).

LEVAY, Simon, *Gay, straight and the reason why* (Oxford: Oxford University Press, 2012).

LINDOP, A. B. N. E., *Details of Jeremy Stratton* (London: William Heinemann, 1955).

LOFSTROM, Jan, *Scandinavian homosexualities* (New York: Haworth Press, 1998).

LONGFORD COMMISSION, *Pornography: The Longford Report* (London: Coronet Books, 1972).

LUCAS, Ian, *Impertinent decorum: Gay theatrical manoevres* (London: Cassell, 1994).

LUMSDEN, Andrew, *Souvenirs of Sirmione* (London: One Roof Press, 2010).

MACKENZIE, Compton, *Thin ice* (London: Chatto and Windus, 1956).

MAGEE, Bryan Edgar, *One in twenty: A study of homosexuality in men and women* (London: Secker and Warburg, 1966).

MARCUSE, Herbert, *Eros and civilisation* (London: Routledge and Kegan Paul, 1956).

MARLOWE, Kenneth, *Mr Madam: Confessions of a male madam* (New York: Luxor Press, 1965).

MARSHALL, Arthur, *Life's rich pageant* (London: Hamish Hamilton, 1983).

MARTIN, Kenneth, *Aubade* (London: Chapman and Hall, 1957).

MCKEAN, Samuel H. (ed.) *Encyclopedia of psychology* (Brussels: Prathes, 1928).

MEEKER, Martin, 'Behind the mask of respectability', *Journal of the History of Sexuality*, 10/1 (2001), 78–116.

—— *Contacts desired: Gay and lesbian communications and community* (Chicago: University of Chicago Press, 2006).

MERRICK, Jeffrey and SIBALIS, Michael (eds), *Homosexuality in French history and culture* (New York: Harrington Press, 2001).

MIDDLETON, Warren (ed.), *The betrayal of youth* (London: CL Publications, 1986).

MILL, John Stuart, *On liberty* (London: Longman, Green, 1859).

MILLER, Neil, *Out of the past* (London: Vintage, 1995).

NELSON, Michael, *A room in Chelsea Square* (London: GMP, 1986 reprint).

NICHOLS, Beverley, *Father figure* (London: Heinemann, 1972).

NAERSSEN, A. X. VAN (ed.), *Gay life in Dutch society* (New York: Hartington Park Press, 1987).

O'GRADY, Paul, *At my mother's knee… and other low joints* (London: Transworld Publishers, 2008).

—— *The devil rides out* (London: Transworld Publishers, 2010).

ORWELL, George [Eric Arthur Blair], *The road to Wigan Pier* (London: Victor Gollancz, 1937).

PEDLER, Garth, *A prep school in Somerset* (Oxford: Gresham Books, 2007).

PINTER, Harold, *Plays 2* (London: Faber & Faber, 1991).

PLOSCOW, Morris, *Homosexuality, sodomy and crimes against nature* (New York: Prentice-Hall, 1951).

PLUMMER, Ken (ed.), *Modern homosexuality: Fragments of lesbian and gay experiences* (London: Routledge, 1992).

PLUMMER, Douglas, *Queer people* (London: W. H. Allen, 1963).

POULTER, Stephen, *Parliament, homosexuality and public opinion* (BA Hons thesis, University of Southampton, unpublished, 1980).

—— (as JEFFREY-POULTER, Stephen), *Queers, peers and Commons* (London: Routledge, 1991).

PRAUNHEIM, Rosa VON, *Army of lovers* (London: Gay Men's Press, 1980).

PRISON MEDICAL SERVICE (PMS), *Report of an enquiry by Roger Page into medical services of HMPS* (London: Prison Medical Reform Council [PMRC], 1943).

RAINE, Kathleen, *Selected poems* (Great Barrington, MA: Lindisfarne Press, 1980).

REES, J. T. and USILL, H. V., *They stand apart* (London: William Heinemann, 1955).

REID, Robert. D., *The case of the homosexual* (Chislehurst: Prison Medical Reform Council, 1944).

REUBEN, David, *Everything you always wanted to know about sex* (London: W. H. Allen, 1969).

RICH, Adrienne, *Compulsory heterosexuality and lesbian existence* (London: Onlywoman Press, 1981).

RICHARDS, Peter G., *Parliament and conscience* (London: Allen and Unwin, 1970).

RICHMOND, Len and NOGUERA, Gary, *The gay liberation book* (San Francisco: Ramparts Press, 1973).

ROBERTS, Aymer, *Forbidden freedom* (London: Linden Press, 1960).

ROBINS, Peter, *Undo your raincoats and laugh* (Brentford: Red Robin Publications, 1977).

ROBINSON, J. A. T., *The place of law in the field of sex* (London: Sexual Law Reform Society, 1972).

ROLPH, C. H., *The trial of Lady Chatterley* (London: Penguin Books, 1961).

RUEDA, Enrique,*The homosexual network* (Old Greenwich, CT: Devin Adair, 1982).

RUPP, Leila J., *Sapphistries: A global history of love between women* (New York: NY University Press, 2009).

RUSSO, Vito, *The celluloid closet: Homosexuality in the movies* (New York: Harper and Row, 1987).

SAGARIN, Edward: see CORY, Donald Webster.

SCHOFIELD, Michael: see WESTWOOD, Gordon.

SEABROOK, Jeremy, *A lasting relationship: Homosexuals and society* (London: Allen Lane, 1976).

SEWELL, Brian, *Outsider I* (London: Quartet Books, 2011).

—— *Outsider II* (London: Quartet Books, 2012).

SHAW, G. B., *Imprisonment* (Chislehurst: Prison Medical Reform Council, 1944).

SOCARIDES, Charles W., *The overt homosexual* (London and New York: Macmillan, 1958; London and New York: Grune and Stratton, 1968).

STEKEL, Wilhelm, MD, *Homosexual neurosis* (New York: Emerson Books, 1950).

STEWART, William, *Cassell's queer companion* (London: Cassell 1995).

TELLIER, André, *Twilight men* (London: T Werner Laurie – privately printed, 1933).

TIMMONS, Stuart, *The trouble with Harry Hay* (Boston: Alyson Press, 1990).

TSANG, Daniel (ed), *The age taboo: Gay male sexuality, power and consent* (London: GMP, 1981).

UPCHURCH, Charles, *Before Wilde: Sex between men in Britain's age of reform* (Berkeley, CA: University of California Press, 2009).

VICKERS, Emma, *Queen and country: Same sex desire in the British Armed Forces 1939-1945* (Manchester: Manchester University Press, 2014).

WALTON, Tony (ed.), *Out of the shadows: A history of the pioneering London gay groups and organisations, 1967–2000* (London: Bona Street Press, 2010).

WEEKS, Jeffrey, *Coming out* (London: Quartet Books, 1977).

WEST, D. J., *Homosexuality* (London: Duckworth, 1955).

WESTWOOD, Gordon [Michael Schofield], *Society and the homosexual* (London: Victor Gollancz, 1952).

—— *A minority* (London: Longmans, Green, 1960).

WILDEBLOOD, Peter, *Against the law* (London: Weidenfeld and Nicholson, 1955).

—— *A way of life* (London: Weidenfeld and Nicholson, 1956).

WOLFENDEN, John, *Turning points* (London: Bodley Head, 1976).

WRIGHT, Edgar: see GREY, Antony

Index

Index to main text, compiled by W. Stephen Gilbert.

fn refers to a footnote, *ill* to an illustration within the text

H

I

J

K

O

P

Q

Y

Some comments on this book

From Charles Upchurch, Associate Professor of History, Florida State University

In *Amiable Warriors*, Peter Scott-Presland draws much-needed attention to the work of Allan Horsfall, the Campaign for Homosexual Equality, and the grassroots organizational efforts that took place across Britain in the postwar decades. Thoroughly researched and engagingly written, this is an important work that deserves a wide audience.

From Jeffrey Weeks, Research Professor, Arts and Human Sciences, South Bank University

I enormously enjoyed it. Reading it was a bit like being immersed in a great Victorian novel, with intense detail and vivid character sketches, and a gently unrolling plot. I genuinely found it quite gripping, even though I knew many of the cast and the general outline very well. The author's grasp of detail is astonishing, and his energy in both doing the research and in developing the narrative is very impressive. And entirely convincing. Although I lived through much of this, and have done a lot of research myself since, I learnt quite a lot of new things, especially about the enormous energy of grass roots initiatives. … It's a very important achievement, and a major contribution to LGBT history. I am looking forward to the future volumes. …

This landmark book remembers a crucial but partly forgotten history, of the Campaign for Homosexual Equality, the largest grassroots LGBT organisation we have ever seen in Britain.

In fine detail, with wit and compassion, Peter Scott-Presland documents the ways in which key individuals, working at first in intense isolation, bit by bit created the spaces which allowed dozens, then hundreds, and ultimately thousands of LGBT people to find their voices, create their identities, and to build the future. If we seek their monument, look around us.

From Peter Tatchell, human rights campaigner

If you want to understand how we won LGBTI law reform in the UK, read this history of the pioneering Campaign for Homosexual Equality – and remember with pride the CHE campaigners who trailblazed the equal rights we now enjoy.

From Ken Plummer, Emeritus Professor of Sociology, University of Essex

Amiable Warriors is a magnificent achievement. Peter Scott-Presland has given us a wonderful gift that future generations can cherish. In this richly documented, meticulously crafted and beautifully written study we are shown the earliest days of struggles to bring about a more human world. I look forward to more volumes to come. …

From Jeff Evans, Director of Academic Affairs, Schools Out / LGBT History Month

Spanning the years before and after the 1967 Sexual Offences Act, *Amiable Warriors* provides a remarkable and seminal contribution to our understanding of the beginnings of the British grass-roots Human/Gay Rights campaign. The origins of many campaigns and organisations that today are respected and 'mainstream' are revealed in Peter Scott-Presland's History of CHE. He tells the extraordinary story of pioneering endeavour using extensive oral and written testimony from those directly involved; it is an impeccably researched piece of work. It is however, not an uncritical reading of those heady early years, it is grounded in the practical realities faced by those pioneers of the first popular democratic 'homosexual' reform movement. We wait eagerly for Volume Two.

From Dr Matt Cook, Senior Lecturer in History & Gender Studies, Birkbeck, London University

Through exhaustive research and by taking local and individual lives seriously, Scott Presland captures the extraordinary reach, range and impact of the CHE. He deftly connects the growth and shifting fortunes of the organisation to social and cultural change since the sixties and rightly insists on its significance in the daily lives and politics of thousands of lesbians and gay men in Britain. Engaging and rich in detail, *Amiable Warriors* is both a great read and a fantastic resource.

From Dr Emma Vickers, Senior Lecturer in History Humanities and Social Science, Liverpool John Moores University

It's a richly textured and exceptionally useful book that makes an important contribution to the history of LGBT activism in Britain. I've been slowly reading Volume One and I even used some of it for my teaching last week. It's rather marvellous!